No man could ask for finer
family and friends.

This book is dedicated to
Doug and Macie.

Contents at a Glance

1	Local Database in a Client-Server World	. . . .	1
2	Windows into Your Data	. . . .	17
3	Text Files	. . . .	57
4	Using Binary Files	. . . .	91
5	A New String Class	. . . .	123
6	Using Database Files	. . . .	175
7	A LayoutManager for Database Applications	. . . . .	231
8	The MenuPanel for User Control	. . . .	273
9	The JDB Front-End Code	. . . .	323
10	Application Initialization Data	. . . .	381
11	Designing Object and Relational Databases	. . . . . .	413
12	The All-Purpose Data-Entry Form	. . . .	435
13	Components of the DEForm	. . . .	471
14	Combining the ScrollWin with the DEForm	. . . . . .	505
15	Creating New DBFs	. . . .	563
16	The JDBnew Class	. . . .	603

17   Variable-Length Storage 643
18   B-Trees and Other Pyramids 697
19   Building B-Trees 717
20   The Indexable Interface and NDX Class 753
21   Index-Based Scrolling 805
22   Object Databases, Very Fast 835
     Index 899

Table of Contents

Acknowledgments xix
Introduction xxi

1   Local Database in a Client-Server World   1
The Plan of this Book   3
Going on Tour   6
    Using the Foo Class   6
    Understanding the Foo Class   6
Consistent Java File Structure   6
    Overall Structure   7
    Class Structure   7
    Data Structure   7
    Method Structure   9
    A Class Template   12
    Exceptions   15
Summary   15

2   Windows into Your Data   17
Interfaces Are Incredible   18
    The Problem   20
    The Interface Solution   21

Interfaces Are Squirrels, Not Shrubs 21
The Scrollable Interface 22
    Items Zero Through Last Impose No Limits 23
    Strings Are Not the Scroller's Problem 23
    There's One More Thing 23
    The Complete Listing 23
The ImScrollable Class 24
The ScrollWin Class 27
    Using the ScrollWin Class 28
    Understanding the ScrollWin Class 30
    The Complete ScrollWin Listing 41
Summary 56

3   Text Files 57
The TxtFile Class 59
    Using the TxtFile Class 60
    Understanding the TxtFile Class 62
    The Complete TxtFile Listing 70
The PointerList Class 77
    Using the PointerList Class 78
    Understanding the PointerList Class 79
    The Complete PointerList Listing 82
The TextViewer Mainline 85
    Understanding the TextViewer Class 85
    The Complete TextViewer Listing 88
    Your Project 90
Summary 90

4   Using Binary Files 91
The BinFile Class 93
    Using the BinFile Class 94
    Understanding BinFile's Data Members 96
    Understanding BinFile's File I/O 96
    Understanding the Other BinFile Methods 101
    The Full BinFile Listing 105
The FDlib Class 111
    Understanding the FDlib Methods 111
    The Full FDlib Listing 114
The FileViewer Class 115
    Understanding the FileViewer 117
    The Full FileViewer Listing 118
    Your Project 120
Summary 120

|||||| 5   A New String Class   123

Evaluating the MRString Class 124

The Advantages of MRStrings 124

The Disadvantages of MRStrings 125

Using MRStrings Effectively 125

Constructing MRStrings 126

Using the MRString Constructors 127

Understanding the MRString Constructors 127

MRString Public Methods 130

Using the MRString Public Methods 130

Understanding the MRString Public Methods 137

MRString Static Methods 147

Using the Static Boolean Functions 147

Using the Other Static Functions 149

MRString Private Methods 149

The Full MRString Listing 152

Your Project 172

Summary 173

|||||| 6   Using Database Files   175

The Database File 176

A Fast History of the DBF 177

The DBF Structure 178

The FileViewer Mainline 182

Understanding the FileViewer 183

The Complete FileViewer Listing 185

The MsgBox Class 187

Using the MsgBox Class 188

Understanding the MsgBox Class 189

The Full MsgBox Listing 191

The DBF Class 195

Using the DBF Class 195

Understanding the DBF Class 198

The Full DBF Listing 214

Summary 230

|||||| 7   A LayoutManager for Database Applications   231

Using the CenterLayout 232

The Origin of the CenterLayout 232

Using the CenterLayout 233

The Complete Center.java Listing 235

Understanding the CenterLayout LayoutManager 237

Understanding the CenterLayout Code 238

The Full CenterLayout.java Listing 242
Using the ChoicesLayout 248
Understanding Choices.java 250
The Full Choices.java Listing 251
Understanding the ChoicesLayout LayoutManager 253
Choices Layout Theory 253
Understanding the ChoicesLayout Code 257
The Full ChoicesLayout.java Listing 264
Summary 271

8 The McnuPanel for User Control 273
Using the MenuPanel—the User's View 274
Using the MenuPanel—the Programmer's View 276
Creating the Menu 276
Handling the Menu Events 277
The Full MenuSample.java Listing 278
Understanding the MenuPanel 281
Understanding the MenuPanel Code 282
The Full MenuPanel.java Listing 288
Understanding the MenuLib 301
Understanding the PromptPanel 304
Understanding the RRectPromptPainter 306
Understanding the RRectPromptPainter Code 307
The Full RRectPromptPainter.java Listing 311
Understanding the PromptPainter 315
Summary 320

9 The JDB Front-End Code 323
Running the Java DataBase System 324
Intermission 330
Understanding JDBlib.java 330
Understanding JDBmenus.java 333
Understanding the JDBmenus Code 334
The Full JDBmenus.java Listing 336
Understanding JDB.java 339
The JDB.java Data Members 340
The JDB.java Public Methods 342
The JDB.java Private Methods 347
The Full JDB.java Listing 350
The Other JDB Menus 363
The Full JDBopts.java Listing 363
The Full JDBmenopts.java Listing 366
The Full JDBcolors.java Listing 371

The Full JDBshapes.java Listing 376

Summary 379

||||||| 10   Application Initialization Data 381

Using JDBini 383

Users Using JDB.INI 383

Programmers Using JDBini.java 384

Understanding JDBini 385

Understanding JDBini's Common Elements 385

Understanding JDBini's File Writing 387

Understanding JDBini's File Reading 393

The Full JDBini.java Listing 402

Summary 411

||||||| 11   Designing Object and Relational Databases 413

Beginning with Objects and Events 414

Objects 415

Events 415

Processes and Other Classes 416

Characteristics 417

Beware of Paperwork 417

Relationships 418

Detail Tables 419

Repeating Characteristics 420

Characteristic Histories 423

Method Summary 424

Step 1. Objects 425

Step 2. Events 425

Step 3. Characteristics 425

Step 4. Relationships 425

Step 5. Repeating Characteristics 426

Step 6. Characteristic Histories 426

Real Design Rules 426

Normalization 427

First-Normal Form 427

Second-Normal Form 427

Third-Normal Form 429

Boyce-Codd Normal Form 429

More Normal Forms 431

Redundant Data 432

Totals 432

Current Values 433

Summary 433

||||| 12 The All-Purpose Data-Entry Form 435
        Looking at JDB 436
            Running JDB 436
            The DEForm's Design 441
        A JDB Warning and a Blinker 443
            This Is a New JDB.java 443
            The Blinker 443
        The DEForm Class 445
            Using the DEForm Class 445
            Understanding the DEForm Class 446
            The Full DEForm.java Listing 453
        Summary 469

||||| 13 Components of the DEForm 471
        The DEButtonPanel Class 472
            Laying Out the DEButtonPanel 472
            The Full DEButtonPanel Listing 473
        The MRLabel Class 475
            Understanding the MRLabel Class 475
            The Full MRLabel.java Listing 476
        The DELayout LayoutManager 480
            Using the DELayout 480
            Understanding the DELayout 481
            The Full DELayout.java Listing 484
        The DEPanel Class 491
            Using the DEPanel Class 492
            Understanding the DEPanel Class 492
            The Full DEPanel.java Listing 494
        The DEField and MRTextField Classes 499
        Summary 503

||||| 14 Combining the ScrollWin with the DEForm 505
        The Editable Interface 506
            The Editable Methods 506
            The Full Editable.java Listing 507
        The DataBoss Class 508
            Understanding the DataBoss 509
            The Full DataBoss.java Listing 515
        The JDBboss Menu 522
        The New DBF Class 527
            Designing Deep or Flat Class Families 527
            Understanding the New DBF Class 528
            The Full DBF Listing 529

The New ScrollWin Class 546
Summary 560

15   Creating New DBFs **563**
Using JDB 564
The Mysterious .DBS 565
Creating a DBF 566
Creating a Phone List Table 568
The JDBclose Menu Class 571
Understanding the JDBclose Method 573
The Full JDBclose.java Listing 574
The New JDB Mainline 577
The New Data 577
The New Public Close Methods 578
The New and Revised Private Methods 581
The Full JDB.java Listing 585
Summary 602

16   The JDBnew Class **603**
JDBnew's Data 604
The Public Methods 605
The Public, Nonstatic Methods 605
The Public, Static Methods 609
The Private Methods 614
The create_stru_file( ) Method 615
The Error-Reporting Routines 617
The full_stru_name( ) Method 617
The little_end2( ) Method 618
The Error-Checking Methods 618
The Field-Buffer Methods 619
The DBF-Writing Methods 620
The Full JDBnew.java Listing 625
Summary 640

17   Variable-Length Storage **643**
The dBASE Memo Field 645
Using the HeapFile 645
Opening and Closing HeapFiles 646
Managing HeapFile Storage 646
Reading and Writing HeapFile Data 648
Storing HeapFile Pointers 648
Understanding the HeapFile 649
The HeapFile in Theory 649

The HeapFile's Data Members 652
The HeapFile's Public Methods 653
The HeapFile's Private Methods 662
The HeapFile's Private Class 675
The Full HeapFile.java Listing 676
Summary 695

18   **B-Trees and Other Pyramids** 697
Binary Searching 698
The Binary Search Algorithm 699
The Binary Search Speed 699
Binary Trees 700
Using an Index File 700
Using a Binary Tree 701
Building Binary Trees 703
B-Trees 705
B-Trees Are Pyramids, Not Trees 705
The B-Tree's Nodes 707
Searching the B-Tree 708
Inserting into the B-Tree 708
Deleting from the B-Tree 712
Summary 715

19   **Building B-Trees** 717
Implementing B-Trees 718
Typical Indexes 718
Node Sizes and Tree Heights 720
Node Construction 722
Tree Construction 723
Efficient File I/O 724
Linear and Binary Searches 725
Generating Random Strings 725
Faking the Locate( ) Method 726
A Real, Linear Locate( ) 727
Changing to a Binary Locate( ) 727
Benefits and Costs 728
The Test Program 729
Understanding the Btree_node Class 735
The Btree_node's Data Members 735
The Btree_node's Public Methods 736
The Btree_node's Private Method 742
Btree_node.java's Full Listing 744
Summary 751

‖‖‖ **20**	**The Indexable Interface and NDX Class**	. . . .	**753**
	A Mainline NDX User	. . . .	754
	Indexable	. . . .	756
	The fakeNDX Class	. . . .	757
	The NDX Class	. . . .	761
	Using the NDX Class	. . . .	761
	Understanding the NDX Class	. . . .	763
	The Full NDX.java Listing	. . . .	783
	The New BinFile Class	. . . .	797
	Summary	. . . .	803
‖‖‖ **21**	**Index-Based Scrolling**	. . . .	**805**
	Abandoning Physical Order	. . . .	806
	The Indexable RandNames Class	. . . .	807
	The ScrollNDX Mainline	. . . .	810
	ScrollableX	. . . .	811
	The ScrollWinX Class	. . . .	812
	Using the ScrollWinX Class	. . . .	813
	Understanding the ScrollWinX Class	. . . .	813
	The Full ScrollWinX.java Listing	. . . .	819
	Summary	. . . .	834
‖‖‖ **22**	**Object Databases, Very Fast**	. . . .	**835**
	Tables Are Object Tools	. . . .	836
	Storing Data Is Storing Objects	. . . .	836
	DBFs Store Data Members	. . . .	837
	Use, Don't Abuse, HeapFile Storage	. . . .	838
	BinFileXO	. . . .	838
	Disk I/O by the Block	. . . .	839
	Using the BinFileXO	. . . .	839
	Understanding the BinFileXO Class	. . . .	841
	The Full BinFileXO Listing	. . . .	847
	Btree_node	. . . .	852
	Understanding the Btree_node Class	. . . .	853
	The Full Btree_node.java Listing	. . . .	856
	Understanding the NDX Class	. . . .	867
	The Disk-Buffering Strategy	. . . .	867
	Understanding the NDX Class' Code	. . . .	868
	The Full NDX Class Listing	. . . .	876
	Summary	. . . .	897
	Index	. . . .	**899**

Acknowledgments

These are the people, in chronological order, who were involved in the creation of this book:

The author decided on the topic and wrote a proposal, which he sent to

Matt Wagner, the author's agent at Waterside Productions, who was enthusiastic about the concept and presented it to

Wendy Rinaldi, senior acquisitions editor at Osborne/McGraw-Hill, who signed the book and assigned it to

Joe O'Neil, technical editor, without whom more of the author's mistakes would still be in the book, and

Janet Walden, senior project editor at Osborne/McGraw-Hill, who engaged and supervised (among others)

Jan Jue, copy editor, who fixed most of the author's writing (and who knew that "writeable" was misspelled, but also was smart enough to leave it that way since it's a variable name).

Finally, Amanda Rinehart, without whom the author could not have run all the tests that made the NDX class perform like a thoroughbred.

Thanks to all, and thanks also to the production crew who made bits into books; especially the anonymous artist(s) who did those fun icons.

Introduction

I was interviewing software industry gurus for an article on "The Future of Programming Languages" back in the fall of 1995, when Java was being born. Sun had announced it as a small language useful for writing Web-based applets. My article spotlighted four trends; Java was one of them and I was pleased with having discovered this relatively unknown language that some industry insiders said was going to be important.

Magazines have long lead times. After I submitted my article, Netscape announced support for Java, then the other industry players lined up behind it and finally Microsoft licensed it. It made the cover article in *Business Week*. Between Thanksgiving and Christmas it was the talk of the industry.

My article appeared after New Year's Day. By then, predicting that Java would be hot was like predicting darkness after sunset. But I wasn't about to give up.

Having predicted the future, I decided to join the future. I got the JDK and started to teach myself Java. After all, I'd written C and then C++ for years. At the time I was busy writing a book for C++ beginners, which made me keenly aware of the amount of baggage that language had accumulated over the years. Playing with Java was more fun!

I began to see that Sun had been lying low. What they really had was a vastly improved language derived from C++. It was a brilliant marketing ploy to position it as a Web language, but the fact was that this was a tremendous, general-purpose application programming language.

By late summer 1996, when editor Michael Sprague (then at MIS Press) called and asked if I could do a book on Visual J++, I was a Java old-timer. That is, I was a few months ahead of all but the pioneers. Of course, no one else could boast much more experience than I had, so I went ahead with the Java book. It was a good chance to begin full-time work on Java.

It wasn't long before I decided that Java was exactly what C++ needed. The 80/20 rule tells you that 20 percent of a language holds 80 percent of the useful features. Java threw out 80 percent of C++ and kept the best 20 percent. Then Java added some useful new features, like built-in support for threads and interfaces. Finally, it invented a universal GUI. Writing to the AWT is a piece of cake compared to writing for Windows. It's clean and simple, especially if you compare it to MFC.

But I missed my database capabilities. I've got a personal time-management system (my latest version is written in Visual Basic) that I depend on to keep organized and to keep my projects on track. I wanted to build a better one and I wanted to use Java. But I needed the ability to open multiple data tables and to access those tables in multiple sort orders.

Well, if you want something badly enough, you'll just do it yourself. Which is why this book was born. I thought that if I needed something, then other Java programmers would feel the same way. The fact that you're reading this proves that there was at least a little truth in that assumption.

Writing the software, and then this book, has kept me away from rewriting that time-management system, but it's a project I'm going back to immediately. (Yes, I'm writing this introduction after the rest of the book has been typeset.)

The hardest decision we faced was the version question. JDK 1.1 is about to be replaced by the first release of JDK 1.2 (which may be known as JDK 2.0 before it gets out of beta). But I stuck with JDK 1.0 code for this book, for several reasons.

First, our tools didn't support JDK 1.1. Visual J++ and Visual Cafe, the two leading Java IDEs when I started this book, were both 1.0 tools. Borland's J Builder and Sybase's PowerJ, which both look good, weren't available then. The 1.1 version of Visual Cafe has only just been released. Microsoft promises an updated, vastly improved J++, but wages an escalating war with Sun while we wait.

More important, lots of Java programmers are still working on applets for the Web. Most applet programmers are still sticking with 1.0, because Netscape's Navaigator 3 and Microsoft's Internet Explorer 3 are still the dominant Web browsers. Until they are substantially replaced by the 4.*x* versions that you need to run 1.1 applets, JDK 1.0 applets will dominate.

That decision did come back to bite me, as you'll see when you meet the sad story of the death of my masked data-entry field class. Otherwise, though, I think it was the right one. JDK 1.0 code will work in the later versions of Java (almost). The reverse is not true.

You, of course, can use 1.1 and later Java versions too, although you'll have to do some minor revisions.

That brings up the question of what you can do with this software. If you own this book, you are licensed to use it almost anyway you like. There are just a couple of things you can't do. First, the publisher and I are in the business of providing instructional materials for programmers. If you want to compete with us in that endeavor, you have to write your own code. Second, I consult with and program for software companies. Code for resale in software products must be licensed from me.

Otherwise, it's pretty much an open question whether you are paying for a software license and getting a free book, or buying a book and getting the software thrown in free. We want you to use it, to build great applications, to become a hero.

I hope you get a lot out of this book, and put these classes to good use in your applications. While you turn to Chapter 1, I'm going to turn to that time-management application. Good luck, and happy Java programming!

Chapter 1

Local Database in a Client-Server World

W elcome to *Java Database Development*! This book is for Java programmers who want to add local database capabilities to their Java applications. As I write this, you can't write to disk if you're running in the sandbox, so you can't use these classes in applets. Sun Microsystems says this will change Real Soon Now, so you may be able to use these classes in applets by the time you get this book. I hope so. On the other hand, Java's biggest future is in applications.

The classes in this book give you the tools you need to add database capabilities to your applications. They're vendor independent and they're pure Java. (It's up to you to get your applications certified "100% Pure Java" if you want. These classes shouldn't be a source of trouble for certification.) They're not only written in pure Java, they are very careful about possible platform dependencies, such as in filename conventions.

These classes are a lot like the rest of Java. At first you'll need to learn all the underlying concepts. That's the hard part. Once you understand, you'll find that it's no trouble at all to use these classes.

I'll elaborate a little. If you're like me, you found the Runnable interface and the whole thread thing complex at first. It didn't help that the documentation provided all the details but no overview.

Eventually, working with all the details, I finally got it. Interfaces made sense. The Runnable interface couldn't be simpler. The Thread is simple to create and use.

In this book, I'll try to start with the overview, before we get to the details. While the rest of Java may think it's fun to make you figure everything out yourself, I don't go along. I like things explained clearly. That way the easy concepts will be easy and the complex things will be as simple as possible.

The opening paragraphs of each chapter will tell you about the chapter, so you'll know where you're going. Each chapter ends with a short "Summary" section that recaps where we've been.

Since this is the first chapter, it will start with an overview of the whole book. The last section of the last chapter is a recap of the whole book.

TOUR

Tour guides like this explain how to use the book most efficiently. They'll tell you to skip some things if you don't need all the details. They'll tell you to pay close attention to items that will become critically important in the near future.

After the book overview, I'll explain our unique Tour guides. Sometimes you'll be happy to use a class as is, letting its inner workings be a black box. Other times (such as when you've decided that you want to make some tweaks inside the black box) you'll want all the details. The Tour guides tell you where to focus, depending on your needs.

Next I'll go over my Java source file structure with you. It's embodied in a template that I use as the starting point for all my files. I'm fairly rigorous about structuring all my files the same way. I doubt you'll like it at first. I'll bet that a third of the way into this book, though, you'll be darned glad I did it this way. You'll be able to look at any of my source files, and you'll know instantly where everything is.

We'll start with the overview of the whole book.

The Plan of this Book

TOUR

Are you in a furious hurry? Did you get this book because you need the (pick one) class and you can't wait to start using it? Scan this section or find the class in the index, turn to it, and dive in.

Reading the information that follows on my file structures will, however, make it a lot easier for you to handle the source code. It's highly recommended. (We're all in a hurry, after all.)

Applications need databases. Client-server applications tie into back-end databases. In Java you access server databases with JDBC. I've yet to see a client-server application that didn't benefit from client-side local databases, however.

For example, let's talk about a shared contact base the marketing people use. It would be handier for everyone if there were also a local, unshared contact list. Nobody but you needs your mother-in-law's phone number, after all.

Then there's that powerful group-scheduling software the development team is using. It's going to get more use if each developer also has private scheduling capability. (Fred is breaking down his piece of the project into pieces so small they concern just Fred; Sally is mapping out her training schedule for an upcoming half marathon. The team should be spared these details.)

If you're accustomed to using databases, you know that they're a much better tool than simply writing file I/O as the application demands it. This book will give you lots of classes that meet your local database needs.

This is what we'll cover, chapter-by-chapter:

Chapter 1: Local Database in a Client-Server World   This chapter introduces the subject, provides an overview of the book, and introduces the structure of all the source files you'll meet in the rest of the book.

Chapter 2: Windows into Your Data   The ScrollWin class provides a generic scrolling window capability that we'll use for text files, binary files, DBF files, and more.

Chapter 3: Text Files   Here we put the ScrollWin to use to create a text file viewer. It only takes four lines of code.

Chapter 4: Using Binary Files   The BinFile class is the base that TxtFile extended. It handles the bottom-level details of opening and closing disk files. We'll also provide a hex and ASCII dump format. This will be handy when the time comes to look at the internals of DBF and index files.

Chapter 5: A New String Class   The MRString is like Java's String, but has far more capability. If you create your own XXString, you'll have a class that always has exactly the features you need.

Chapter 6: Using DataBase Files   The DBF class extends the BinFile with enough intelligence to read and write the header, footer, and data records of a PC-standard DBF file. UNIX programmers will be happy that they can finally read these PC files, in spite of the presence of little-endian data.

Chapter 7: A LayoutManager for Database Applications   For fun, and as a base for the JDB application, we'll do layout managers. One will be the base for the whole JDB application.

Chapter 8: The MenuPanel for User Control   JDB's menus are all built on these MenuPanel objects.

Chapter 9: The JDB Front-End Code   The Java DataBase (JDB) application edits any DBF file. We'll use a special version of the DBF to create, store, and edit the structure data that defines your relational tables. JDB has a customizable front end, which leads us to Chapter 10.

Chapter 10: Application Initialization Data   Applications that can be customized by the user should remember the user's preferences. In this chapter, we'll use the StreamTokenizer to make reading INI files simple.

Chapter 11: Designing Object and Relational Databases   If you think you know something about database design, don't miss this chapter. My methods are radically simpler than traditional ones, but are provably sound.

Chapter 12: The All-Purpose Data-Entry Form   JDB grows an instant data-entry form for any DBF. It reads the structure information, uses the field names to label data-entry fields, and lays the fields out in a usable manner. Its not an end-user tool, but as programmer, you get an instant data-editing tool without writing a line of code.

Chapter 13: Components of the DEForm   This chapter explains the supporting classes needed to provide instant data-entry forms.

Chapter 14: Combining the ScrollWin with the DEForm   Combining a scrolling window with a data-entry form provides a powerful combination. You scroll through a list of names, for example, and the full record—name, address, telephone, and so on—appears in a separate data-entry window. Keeping the two coordinated is the job of the DataBoss class.

Chapter 15: Creating New DBFs   It's not enough to be able to look into existing DBF files. You have to be able to define and create new ones, too. The DBS (DataBase

Structure) file meets this need. JDB can create a DBS from scratch, or from the structure of an existing DBF. And it can create new DBFs from the data definitions in the DBS file.

Chapter 16: The JDBnew Class   Chapter 15 provides the overview. Chapter 16 explains the internals. If you like bits, bytes, and hex dumps, this chapter's for you.

Chapter 17: Variable-Length Storage   The HeapFile uses a disk file to create a data heap. Just ask for as many bytes as you like, and the HeapFile will return a pointer to them, as long as your disk's not full. Store the pointer and you'll still have the storage tomorrow. You can use it and say that it works by magic. Or you can dive into the details of its circular-first-fit allocation strategy and continuous garbage collection.

Chapter 18: B-Trees and Other Pyramids   B-trees are the magic by which a single database can appear sorted in several orders, simultaneously. They also let you find one record among thousands in submillisecond time. This chapter explains why they're needed and how they work. Do tough algorithms put you off? This one's explained with children's building blocks.

Chapter 19: Building B-Trees   Chapter 18 explains the theory. Chapter 19 explains how to translate the theory into practice. I explain my improvement to the classic B-tree that provides a big speed gain.

Chapter 20: The Indexable Interface and NDX Class   The NDX neatly encapsulates a B-tree index file. It's incredibly simple to use. Its code isn't trivial, though. (This chapter's code doesn't have the speed optimizations. Those come in Chapter 22.)

Chapter 21: Index-Based Scrolling   So far we've scrolled through our data in physical file order. Here we break free and use index order. (For example, you can show your contact list alphabetically by name; by name within country; or any way you like.)

Chapter 22: Object Databases, Very Fast   I provide some advice here on using the classes you've already seen to handle objects, as well as relational data. Then we look at the BinFileXO (binary file, extended for objects), which combines stream I/O simplicity with random-access speed. We look at replacing stream I/O with our own custom, high-speed code. Finally, we replace most I/O with data buffering. The bottom line: our indexes compete well with ones written in C++.

Going on Tour

Maybe you understand these Tour guides already. If you're confident you do, skip this section.

I provide the *Tour guides* to let you know what you can skip. I always provide something special to reward the diligent reader who doesn't skip sections, even though the Tour guides have suggested a shortcut.

The people who skipped this section won't know, for example, that Chapter 11 (on database design) can be read whenever you like. You'll need to know about my primary keys before some of the indexing material in Chapter 18 makes sense. Anytime before then would be fine. Right now would be fine! The material there's worth the price of this book.

With the exception of this chapter, Chapter 11, and Chapter 18, all the others are best read with your computer turned on and the chapter's code loaded into your favorite Java tool. I hope that you learn a lot from reading my words. I *know* that you'll learn a lot from trying small modifications to make each class better suit your needs.

Even though I try to reward the diligent, you won't want to read everything straight through. You can use any of my classes as a black box. There are sections like these:

Using the Foo Class

The "Using" sections tell you what you need to know to use the class as a black box. Often, that will be enough.

Understanding the Foo Class

The "Understanding" sections explain all the data and methods in each class, skipping only the trivial routines (such as paramString( ) methods). A careful read here will set you up when you decide to customize or improve on my work.

Consistent Java File Structure

Unless you're the one in the furious hurry, don't skip this section. It may seem strange at first, but after a few chapters, you'll start to swear by, not at, my organization.

I used to group routines in a file by category, putting bunches of routines—those related to one use—together. Eventually, I decided that this technique became increasingly less helpful as the size of my projects increased. For big projects, where you need all the help you can get, it just didn't work at all.

I could never find the routine I needed. Today I adopt a single structure for all my Java files. It's never ideal for any one file, but since it's always the same, I can always find what I want. If you're doing applications, try this technique (unless you already use it, in which case you know what I mean). For simple applets you can get by with almost any (dis)organization. For larger jobs, though, consistency pays.

Overall Structure

If you write for publication, a consistent file organization also means that your readers know what to expect. You'll be able to find things in my classes quickly. Dependably. This makes anyone's code more useful to the next person who has to read it. Overall, my code looks like this:

1. Header
2. Public class
3. Private class(es), if needed
4. Footer

Class Structure

Each class is structured the same way:

1. Declaration
2. Data members
3. Public methods
4. Private methods

In general, I always work downward from least to most protective. Public members come before protected ones. Protected ones come before private ones. If I were ever to find need for protected methods, for example, they'd come between the public and private ones. (I seldom find need for them.)

Data Structure

Object instance variables come before classwide static ones. This means that you'll start by looking at the more important variables, and you can ignore the class statics (often, final static constants) if you're not actually writing code. If you're writing code, you'll probably find it easiest to pull the final static constants out. Listing 1-1 (EventList.txt on disk) shows what I've done with the Event class final statics.

Listing 1-1:
Final static
event
wallpaper

```
// EventList.txt -- java.Event class constants
// Copyright 1997, Martin L. Rinehart

---------- private static final int -----------
WINDOW_EVENT = 200    KEY_EVENT   = 400
MOUSE_EVENT = 500    SCROLL_EVENT = 600
LIST_EVENT  = 700    MISC_EVENT   = 1000
```

```
----------- public static final int -----------
SHIFT_MASK = 1 << 0   WINDOW_DESTROY   = 201
CTRL_MASK  = 1 << 1   WINDOW_EXPOSE    = 202
META_MASK  = 1 << 2   WINDOW_ICONIFY   = 203
ALT_MASK   = 1 << 3   WINDOW_DEICONIFY = 204
                      WINDOW_MOVED     = 205
HOME = 1000
END  = 1001   KEY_PRESS           = 401
PGUP = 1002   KEY_RELEASE         = 402
PGDN = 1003   KEY_ACTION          = 403
UP   = 1004   KEY_ACTION_RELEASE  = 404
DOWN = 1005
LEFT = 1006   MOUSE_DOWN = 501
RIGHT = 1007  MOUSE_UP   = 502
              MOUSE_MOVE = 503
F1   = 1008   MOUSE_ENTER = 504
F2   = 1009   MOUSE_EXIT  = 505
F3   = 1010   MOUSE_DRAG  = 506
F4   = 1011
F5   = 1012   SCROLL_LINE_UP    = 601
F6   = 1013   SCROLL_LINE_DOWN  = 602
F7   = 1014   SCROLL_PAGE_UP    = 603
F8   = 1015   SCROLL_PAGE_DOWN  = 604
F9   = 1016   SCROLL_ABSOLUTE   = 605
F10  = 1017
F11  = 1018   ACTION_EVENT = 1001
F12  = 1019   LOAD_FILE  = 1002
              SAVE_FILE  = 1003
LIST_SELECT   = 701   GOT_FOCUS  = 1004
LIST_DESELECT = 702   LOST_FOCUS = 1005

// end of EventList.txt
```

When I'm working on event-handling code, I open this file and drop it in a corner of the screen where at least a little will peek through. It's wallpaper until you need to know, for example, the difference between a 401 and a 403.

Within the data and method groupings, members with the same protection are grouped in increasing protection order: public, protected, and last, private. Presumably you'll be most interested in public variables. Private ones you can ignore unless you want to completely understand the code (perhaps to rewrite portions to meet your own requirements).

Method Structure

I organize my methods this way:

1. Main (optional)
2. Constructor(s)
3. Public data access (getXxx, isXxx, and setXxx)
4. Other public methods
5. Private methods

Main

I include a main( ) in many .class files. It will usually be commented out, but will be available for testing the class as a stand-alone. I use this comment scheme:

```
/* add a '/' to the front of this line to uncomment main()
   public static void main( String[] args ) {

     // code here

   }
   // */
```

As just written, the whole routine is commented out within the /* ... */ multiline comment characters. Adding a single slash in front of the "/*" turns the top line into a single-line comment. The tokenizer reads "//* ..." as a single-line comment, so the multiline comment doesn't get started.

The trailing "// */" is also a single-line comment, unless a multiline comment is open. (If a multiline comment is open, the tokenizer looks for the closing "*/", ignoring all intervening characters, including "//" characters.) If you have syntax highlighting turned on, you can see by the color change what happens when you add and remove the extra "/" character in the indicated spot.

With that explained, I promise to avoid all other temptations to write "clever" Java code.

Constructors

In a nontrivial class, I provide multiple constructors so that any parameter with a reasonable default can be omitted, this way:

```
// constructors:

  foo() {
    this( "Default String" );
  }

  foo( String s )
    this( s, default_int );
  }
```

```
foo( String s, int i ) {

   // code here uses String and int
}
```

If multiple constructors exist with equal numbers of parameters, I pick an order that appeals to me.

Public Data-Access Methods

The 1.1 release of the JDK regularizes most data-access methods. The value of foo is returned by getFoo( ), unless foo is boolean, in which case you ask isFoo( ). It will be set by setFoo( ). Show( ) and hide( ), for one example, are superseded by setVisible( ), which takes a single boolean argument.

I've used the same trio for my public data access, as well. The order is

1. getWhatever( )   3. setWhatever( )
2. isWhatever( )

Within these groups, the order is alphabetical. I sort the underscore character as if it were a space (it sorts first) in all the data and method groups.

Other Public Methods

I use three groups for other public methods:

1. Class-specific public methods   3. Event-handling methods
2. Overriding but not event-handling
   methods

These groups are easiest to understand in reverse order. The *event-handling* methods include handleEvent( ), keyDown( ), and so on. They override the defaults in the Component class. (That includes anything derived from Frame, Window, Dialog, Panel, Container, and many more.) Since this code is based on the JDK 1.0 model, classes not derived from a Component omit this section.

The second section includes *overriding* methods that do *not* handle events. I very often write a paint( ) method here. I'm also fond of resize( ) and frequently will have a show( ), too. If your mental model includes paint( ) among the event-handling functions, you'll have to remember that my mental model doesn't. (The paint( ) method does respond to events, but you won't find it if you go back to Listing 1-1.)

All other public methods are part of the first group, which is often empty. Sometimes, though, it's where the real work gets done.

Within these groups, the methods are in alphabetical order.

Private Methods

The private methods come last. They are in alphabetical order. If alphabetical order separates logical companions, I'll often change otherwise sensible names. Consider this:

```
// Private methods:

   ... lots here

   private whatever hide_thingie()

   ... more here

   private whatever show_thingie()

   ...
```

This has the possibly undesirable effect of widely separating these methods. A little work on the names often cures this problem:

```
// Private methods:

   ... lots here

   private whatever thingie_hide()
   private whatever thingie_show()

   ... more here
```

If you use VCafe, you know that searches are directional. The alphabetic arrangement always tells you which way to search. The search in VJ++ is circular—cursor to end, then start to cursor—so the order isn't as important. Both products would benefit from adding the other's algorithm as an option.

It would be very nice if our products' text editors would let you select a method from a list, rather than forcing you to use text searching to find what you want. Visual Basic does this nicely. VCafe copies Visual Basic's approach, but does it so badly that it's just a waste of screen real estate. VJ++ doesn't even try.

VCafe implements the concept beautifully in the class browser, which proves they could do it in the text editor if they set their minds to it. The class browser's great, and you can edit in it, but it takes too much screen real estate away from editing.

Until they get this right, searching for the last character of the return type, a space, and then the name of the function usually will hop right to the function. To locate foo( ), which returns void, look for "d foo". This will almost never stop at any of the calls to foo( ).

A Class Template

I start each class by editing a file called template.java. I immediately rename it and then change all the occurrences of "template" to the new name. This gives me a well-organized start (not to mention, some useful reminders).

Now that you know how my classes are organized, the template file shown in Listing 1-2 will be meaningful.

Listing 1-2:
My class
template

```
// template.java -- comment here
// Copyright 1997, Martin L. Rinehart

/*
     Starting point for new .java files
*/

import java.awt.*;

class template extends Object {

// -------------------- data members --------------------

// there are no public data members

// there are no protected data members

// there are no static data members
     // there are no public static data members
     // there are no private static data members
     // there are no final static data members
```

```
// ------------------- public methods -------------------

    /*
        public static void main( String[] args ) {

            ( new template() ).show();
        }
    // */

// constructor:

    template() {
    }

// there are no data access getXxx() methods
// there are no data access isXxx() methods
// there are no data access setXxx() methods

// there are no public, class-specific methods

// public, non-event overriding method:

    public String paramString() {

        return "template";
    }

// public, event-handling method:

    public boolean handleEvent( Event e ) {

        if ( e.id == Event.WINDOW_DESTROY ) {
            // hide(); or System.exit( 0 );
            return true;
        }

        return super.handleEvent( e );
    }

    /*
    public boolean gotFocus( Event e, Object o )
```

```
         public boolean keyDown( Event e, int k )
         public boolean keyUp ( Event e, int k )

         public boolean lostFocus( Event e, Object o )

         public boolean mouseDown ( Event e, int x, int y )
         public boolean mouseDrag ( Event e, int x, int y )
         public boolean mouseEnter( Event e, int x, int y )
         public boolean mouseExit ( Event e, int x, int y )
         public boolean mouseMove ( Event e, int x, int y )
         public boolean mouseUp  ( Event e, int x, int y )
         */

// ------------------- private methods -------------------
// there are no private methods

} // end of template class

// there are no private classes in template.java

/*
     Extended documentation for template.java not required
*/

// end of template.java
```

Do you remember all the parameters to all the event-handling methods? I don't. But my template never forgets.

I try to remember to delete ridiculous lines. For example, if there are no static data members, this is stupid:

```
// there are no static data members
     // there are no public static data members
     // there are no private static data members
     // there are no final static data members
```

You can delete the three subcategories if the first line applies. When you add a static, however, you'll delete the words "there are no" from the category line and one of the subcategories, so that it all makes sense.

Similarly, the comment near the end that says "Extended documentation ... not required" is dumb, but readable, if you forget to remove it. Some well-chosen words of explanation are in order, in most cases.

Bear in mind that if you are not accompanying your code with a book, such as this one, you'd better use more in-file comments than I've used in this code.

Exceptions

There are ways in which my organization is incomplete. There are times when this much organization is overkill. A well-designed system lets you make intelligent exceptions.

Missing Pieces

I've already mentioned that my organization, and its reflection in my template, is incomplete. There are no protected functions, for example. You'd just fill them in between the public and private ones, adding an appropriate heading.

There's no organization within the private class area. For a major private class, I copy the appropriate part of the template.

Simple Things

Sometimes, simplicity is its own reward. If a private class only has a few members, for example, I'll just add them, without using the template.

I hope that I never write an interface so complex that it will benefit from this template. My interfaces are all so simple that just listing the members in alphabetical order is simpler and more readable.

Summary

The "Summary" sections give you a chance to review the contents of each chapter. They're designed not so much for reading as for a checklist that you'll use to think about each point.

TOUR

We began by looking at each chapter in this book. The book begins with a simple progression from text file to binary file to DBF (data table) file. Then it gets into the JDB application, which is a programmers' tool for editing data in DBFs. It also lets you define and create DBFs. Then the book goes on to more advanced topics, such as storing variable-length data and providing B-tree indexes.

We looked briefly at the Tour guides that tell you which sections to read carefully and which you can skip. I pointed out that in the skippable sections, the diligent reader will always find something special.

Finally, we looked at the file structure I'll be using for all the classes in this book. Within each class I put the data members first, the methods second. Within those categories I organize by descending order of protection: public, protected, and private. Within subsections, I put everything in alphabetical order. Once you get used to this organization, you'll be able to find whatever you need in any of my code files.

Are you ready to dive into database programming? I'm up for it, but we're not quite ready. You can't see the contents of disk files. Before we start on databases, let's create a tool that we can use to look at them.

Chapter 2

Windows into Your Data

As I explained in Chapter 1, you can't program what you can't see. We're going to start by programming a general-purpose scroller. We'll use it as a window into text files beginning in Chapter 3. We'll add a view of generic binary files in Chapter 4. By Chapter 6, the same scroller will be looking into database files, too.

This scroller scrolls anything. At one time, I didn't think you could write a scroller that would be completely general purpose. I tried and failed in the good old days (before object-oriented programming). I thought objects would help, but I tried again and failed with an object-oriented approach. I wasn't going to try again, but with Java's interfaces, my first attempt at a specific-purpose scroller produced a totally general-purpose one.

We'll look at interfaces before we begin, because the rest of the book will feature code built on interfaces. I'll try to show you a new way of looking at them that suggests what they can do. Interfaces are squirrels, not shrubs. (Yes, I *will* explain that statement!)

Then we'll go on to the Scrollable interface, which provides the magic that lets you drop almost anything you like into our general-purpose scroll window. It's only got three functions and one of them is trivial.

The ImScrollable class, which we'll look at next, builds an object whose only purpose is to implement the Scrollable interface. This lets us pop up a scroll window and see the ScrollWin object in action.

Finally, we'll dive into the ScrollWin class itself. You'll see that this is a very simple scroll window, but it meets our needs. While we're looking at it, I'll make some suggestions for writing a better one. Before we get started, let's look at some ScrollWin objects in action.

Figure 2-1 shows a ScrollWin object looking at a text file. The text happens to be ScrollWin.java. We'll use a ScrollWin to build a text file viewer in Chapter 3.

Figure 2-2 shows a ScrollWin object looking into a generic binary file. In this case, the file is BinFile.class. (Look closely at the hex dump. The signature of a Java class is in the first four bytes. In hex they're CAFEBABE. "Sun" rhymes with "fun.") We'll extend our text file viewer to binary in Chapter 4.

Figure 2-3 shows another ScrollWin looking into a sample database file. In Chapter 6 you'll see that this is a binary file with a defined structure. Adding three simple functions lets our DBF (database file) object scroll in a ScrollWin.

You'll see when we get to our mainline here that there's really no limit to what the ScrollWin can let you scroll through. Here we won't even bother with a file.

Before we start scrolling, let me explain why interfaces are like squirrels, not shrubs.

Interfaces Are Incredible

The Sun JDK documentation suggested that interfaces were some sort of poor person's substitute for multiple inheritance. Lots of us repeated that misinformation. (See my

ScrollWin.java

```
// ScrollWin.java -- a generic scrolling Window
// Copyright 1997, Martin L. Rinehart

// this code is completely documented in:
// _Java Database Development_, Martin Rinehart,
// Osborne/McGraw-Hill, 1997

/*
□This window will scroll anything that implements
□the Scrollable interface.

□It will synchronize with a data databoss if an object
□that implements databoss is provided.
*/

import java.awt.*;

class ScrollWin extends Frame {
```

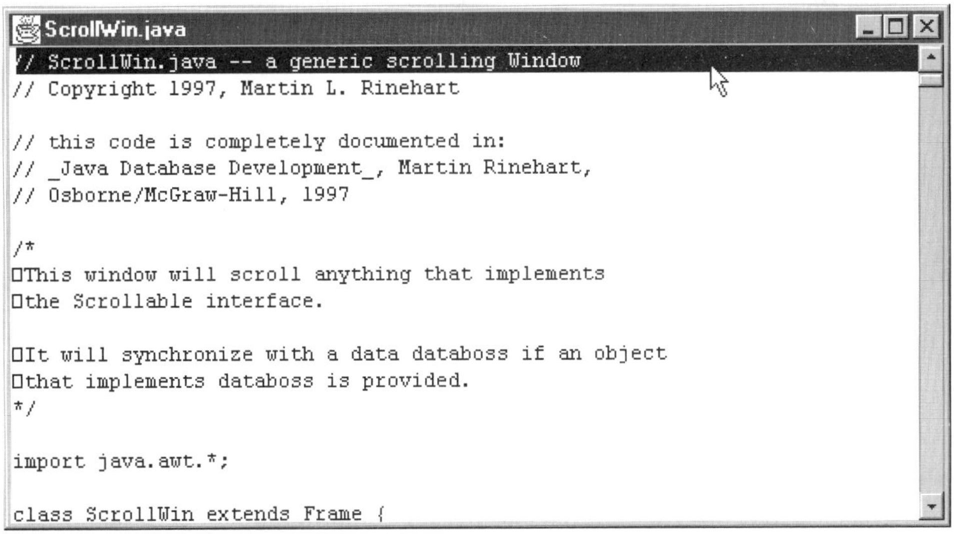

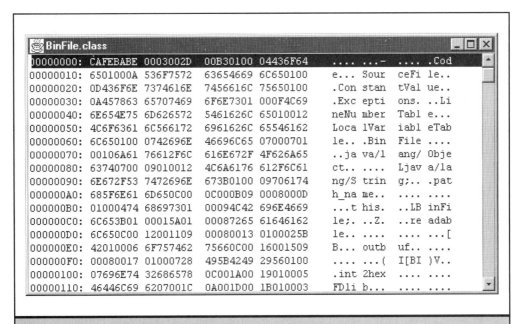

Figure 2-1. *A ScrollWin looks at a text file*

BinFile.class

```
00000000: CAFEBABE 0003002D  00B30100 04436F64   .... ...-  .... .Cod
00000010: 6501000A 536F7572  63654669 6C650100   e... Sour  ceFi le..
00000020: 0D436F6E 7374616E  7456616C 75650100   .Con stan  tVal ue..
00000030: 0A457863 65707469  6F6E7301 000F4C69   .Exc epti  ons. ..Li
00000040: 6E654E75 6D626572  5461626C 65010012   neNu mber  Tabl e...
00000050: 4C6F6361 6C566172  6961626C 65546162   Loca lVar  iabl eTab
00000060: 6C650100 0742696E  46696C65 07000701   le.. .Bin  File ....
00000070: 00106A61 76612F6C  616E672F 4F626A65   ..ja va/l  ang/ Obje
00000080: 63740700 09010012  4C6A6176 612F6C61   ct.. ....  Ljav a/la
00000090: 6E672F53 7472696E  673B0100 09706174   ng/S trin  g;.. .pat
000000A0: 685F6E61 6D650C00  0C000B09 0008000D   h_na me..  .... ....
000000B0: 01000474 68697301  00094C42 696E4669   ...t his.  ..LB inFi
000000C0: 6C653B01 00015A01  00087265 61646162   le;. ..Z.  ..re adab
000000D0: 6C650C00 12001109  00080013 0100025B   le.. ....  .... ...[
000000E0: 42010006 6F757462  75660C00 16001509   B... outb  uf.. ....
000000F0: 00080017 01000728  495B4249 29560100   .... ...(  I[BI )V..
00000100: 07696E74 32686578  0C001A00 19010005   .int 2hex  .... ....
00000110: 46446C69 6207001C  0A001D00 1B010003   FDli b...  .... ....
```

Figure 2-2. *A ScrollWin looks into a generic binary file*

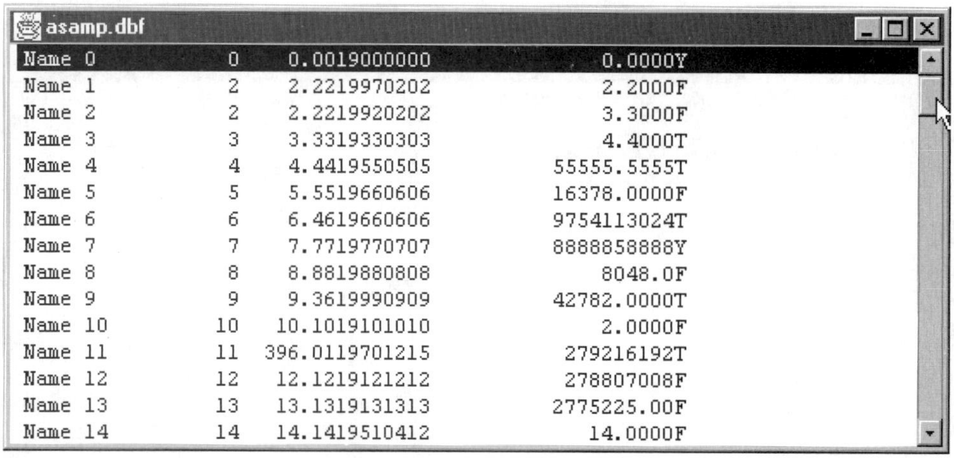

```
asamp.dbf                                                        _ □ ✕
Name 0           0    0.0019000000              0.0000Y
Name 1           2    2.2219970202              2.2000F
Name 2           2    2.2219920202              3.3000F
Name 3           3    3.3319330303              4.4000T
Name 4           4    4.4419550505          55555.5555T
Name 5           5    5.5519660606          16378.0000F
Name 6           6    6.4619660606          9754113024T
Name 7           7    7.7719770707          8888858888Y
Name 8           8    8.8819880808             8048.0F
Name 9           9    9.3619990909          42782.0000T
Name 10         10   10.1019101010              2.0000F
Name 11         11  396.0119701215          279216192T
Name 12         12   12.1219121212           278807008F
Name 13         13   13.1319131313          2775225.00F
Name 14         14   14.1419510412             14.0000F
```

Figure 2-3.   *A ScrollWin looks into a DBF file*

book, *Java Programming with Visual J++* , MIS Press, 1996, for a typical example of this stupidity.)

As I wrote more Java, I found repeatedly that I was able to solve formerly complex problems with simple interfaces. The solutions were simple. Before interfaces, I'd thought the problems were unsolvable. Scrolling windows are a perfect example.

The Problem

Every programming tool seems to provide some sort of scrolling window. I use them for a while and then they fail me. Array-based scrollers fail when you need to look at lists too large to reasonably fit in RAM. So you switch to a file-based scrolling window.

Then you find that the scroller will only show the data in the file in its physical order. You, of course, need to show it in some other order. You could re-sort the file, but then you won't be able to use your scroller as the user adds new data (unless the user always adds aardvarks, then beavers, cheetahs, and so on).

Finally, when you think you've got the included scroller working for you, you decide that you really need to add first-letter sensitivity. You want the scroller to automatically hop to the first entry starting with "S" when the user presses "S". Then you want it to hop to "Sm" when the user continues with an "m". The included scroller either has no first-letter capability, or it has only a single letter. (On the "m", it hops to entries starting with "m"—good luck finding "Smith".)

So I always find that I need to toss the included scrollers and write my own. Always! Your built-in scroller has multiindex and multiletter sensitivity? Good. Now I want to integrate it with a record-view panel that scrolls in response to scroller movements. I also want the scroller to move in response to record-view keystrokes or button clicks. Can the built-in scroller become a partner with your data entry work? I didn't think so.

I've always found, though, that no single scroller would work for the variety of things you need to scroll. Those combo and list boxes hold many short lists that should be in RAM-based arrays. Handling these is dramatically different from handling large data files.

Writing one scroller always seemed like a necessary evil. My holy grail was always the single scroller that handled all my scrolling needs. I never figured out a way to do that.

The Interface Solution

I revisited the issue for my database work in Java. I thought that scrolling was a behavior that many types of things could exhibit. That suggested a quality that I named *Scrollable.*

As you'll see when we get to the Scrollable interface, you don't need too much to make something Scrollable. I realized as I was designing the Scrollable interface that I'd be able to write a general-purpose scroller to handle anything that was Scrollable, and that it wouldn't be too much trouble to make things Scrollable.

There was nothing in the interface that cared whether the Scrollable class was in RAM or on disk. For that matter, it could be anywhere in cyberspace. The scroller wouldn't know or care.

The simplicity of this convinced me that here was something new, and that its description as a substitute for multiple inheritance was grossly misleading.

Interfaces Are Squirrels, Not Shrubs

Once I had decided that my original understanding of interfaces was wrong, finding the truth wasn't hard. I started with trees and shrubs.

Trees (the ones outdoors, not in your computer) grow from a single stem. Shrubs, as both botanists and gardeners will tell you, have multiple stems. In a single-inheritance system, such as Java, classes have a single stem. In a multiple-inheritance system, such as C++, classes can have multiple stems.

The official definition of interfaces suggested that they could help us get shrub-like behavior from our tree-like classes. The value of multiple inheritance has been debated in the C++ universe for years. Java settled on trees.

Shrubs are generally smaller than trees, too. That suggests a conclusion about the engineering of these things that is also applicable to the computer-based structures. If you want big, strong structures, maybe one stem is the right number of stems.

Interfaces are useful things that you can attach to your big, strong structures. I'd been adding interfaces to rather complex classes for some time without giving it too much thought. They didn't function like additional stems.

They functioned like squirrels. Have you ever watched squirrels in the forest? They're scared when they're on the ground. They're happy up in the trees. They hop from tree to tree, using the branches as their trails. You might call their paths highways. Gathering fallen nuts brings them down, occasionally, but they prefer to follow their own highways, free from dangerous predators.

Interfaces allow our objects to work together up in their branches. You can build a complex structure and later add an interface that you never anticipated. A well-designed interface won't disrupt the basic functioning. For example, if I'm having trouble debugging a complex structure, I often give it a quick Scrollable interface. Then I can look at it in a ScrollWin, like the five-minute job I showed at the start of this chapter.

It's no accident that many of our most commonly used interfaces end with "able." The Thread's Runnable interface is a perfect example. Scrollable is another example. These interfaces are behaviors that the class claims it is *able* to do. It makes this promise to something that can take advantage of this ability.

The squirrel analogy stresses the essential point that these interfaces do not have anything to do with our singly inherited tree trunks. They work way up in the branches. For example, my scrolling window does not implement Runnable. If you find that you want to launch these windows on separate threads, you can add the Runnable interface without even bothering to study the existing code.

I consider this a fundamental extension of the object-oriented technology. All my code now depends on interfaces just as much as my C++ code depended on inheritance. The multiple inheritance I used in C++ (I avoided it whenever possible) is, in truth, a crude substitute for interfaces.

With that introduction, we're ready to dive into the code.

The Scrollable Interface

This is our first code section. This is the first box that explains the shortcuts you can take to get exactly what you need out of each section.
TOUR
Unlike almost all the others, there's no shortcut. On the other hand, the code's so short that you don't need one.

When I first designed the Scrollable interface, I could think of only two things that an object would need to do so that a general-purpose scroller could handle it:

- Tell the scroller how many items it held
- Return a string describing each item it held

To simplify the design, I assumed that each Scrollable thing would have item 0, item 1, and so on. Then it would only need to tell the scroller what number the last item had.

Items Zero Through Last Impose No Limits

My first design had the Scrollable object report both a starting and an ending number. This made the design of the scroller more complex, and it didn't make the scroller/Scrollable combination more powerful.

The Scrollable object may, in fact, only be telling the scroller about a very small subset of its contents. For example, a sales detail file could contain hundreds of thousands of entries pertaining to tens of thousands of individual sales. A single sale might include three widgets, two doohickeys, and one left-handed fribble.

The Scrollable object could tell the scroller that it had items 0 through 2. The first item in a sale is three widgets. It would tell the scroller that the last object in a three-item sale was number two. The fact that hundreds of thousands of other entries exist in the file wouldn't be known by, or be relevant to, the scroller. The scroller would know that it had items 0, 1, and 2 to handle.

Strings Are Not the Scroller's Problem

The Scrollable object reports a string to the scroller. The contents of this string aren't relevant to the scroller. It assumes that the string contains information that will be useful to a user who is scrolling through the contents of the Scrollable. If the Scrollable is reporting random text, that doesn't concern the scroller.

There's One More Thing

My first Scrollable interface had getFirst( ), getLast( ), and getString( ) functions. I quickly realized that getFirst( ) wasn't necessary. The Scrollable could return data about any item it held as item zero. But in practice, there was one more item that was needed.

Some things can be scrolled nicely by use of proportional fonts. For example, the user can scroll through a list of customer names. These will be more readable in a proportional font.

On the other hand, a proportional font is disastrous in other applications. I first wrote my binary file without the ability to tell the scroller that a monospaced font was required. I was expecting results neatly lined up in columns. I got unreadable, useless results.

So the final addition was a function, useMonospace( ), that the scroller calls to see if the Scrollable needs its returned strings displayed in monospace for applications that require nice columns of data.

The Complete Listing

Listing 2-1 shows the Scrollable interface. You can see that making any object that collects individual pieces Scrollable is almost trivially simple.

Your getLast( ) just returns a number. Remember that this is the number of the last item. If you have ten items, your getLast( ) returns 9.

The getString( ) function can be elaborate or simple. When we scroll data files, for example, I just copy the record buffer (byte array) into a String.

Finally, the useMonospace( ) routine is a one-liner, returning true or false.

Listing 2-1:
Scrollable—a
very simple
interface

```
// Scrollable.java -- the interface the scroller uses
// Copyright 1997, Martin L. Rinehart

// this code is completely documented in:
// _Java Database Development_, Martin Rinehart,
// Osborne/McGraw-Hill, 1997

interface Scrollable {

// Scrollable has three public methods:

    // return the last item number
    public int getLast();

    // return a string representing scrollable[index]
    // index is from zero through getLast()
    public String getString(int index);

    // true if the output requires a monospaced font
    public boolean useMonospace();
}

// end of Scrollable.java
```

The ScrollWin creates a window into your Scrollable object. If an object is Scrollable, the ScrollWin can scroll it. The next class shows this clearly.

The ImScrollable Class

TOUR

This class is trivial and very short. But it clearly demonstrates the ScrollWin and the related Scrollable interface. Don't skip it!

I've written a class called ImScrollable. As the name suggests, it can be scrolled with a ScrollWin object. Its getLast( ) method returns 100. Its getString( ) method returns "Line 0" for the first line, "Line 1" for the next, and so on, through "Line 100." Its useMonospace( ) function returns false. That's all that's needed to create something you can look at in a ScrollWin.

The mainline creates a new ImScrollable and launches it in a ScrollWin with an appropriate title. Then it tells the ScrollWin to end the application when its close button is clicked. A call to show( ) the ScrollWin completes the mainline. This is the whole mainline:

```
ImScrollable is = new ImScrollable();

ScrollWin sw = new ScrollWin( is,
    "I'm Scrollable!" );
sw.setEndApp( true );
sw.show();
```

If you think that's simple, take a look at the getString( ) method:

```
public String getString( int index ) {

    return new String( "Line " + index );
}
```

Listing 2-2 shows the complete file.

Listing 2-2:
ImScrollable.
java

```
// ImScrollable.java
// Copyright 1997, Martin L. Rinehart

// this code is completely documented in:
// _Java Database Development_, Martin Rinehart,
// Osborne/McGraw-Hill, 1997

/*
    A class that implements Scrollable, for testing
    the ScrollWin class.
*/

import java.awt.*;

class ImScrollable implements Scrollable {

// -------------------- data members --------------------
// there are no data members
```

```
// ------------------- public methods -------------------

    //*
        public static void main( String[] args ) {

            ImScrollable is = new ImScrollable();

            ScrollWin sw = new ScrollWin( is,
                "I'm Scrollable!" );
            sw.setEndApp( true );
            sw.show();
        }
    // */

// public, class-specific methods:

    public int getLast() {

        return 100;
    }

    public String getString( int index ) {

        return new String( "Line " + index );
    }

    public boolean useMonospace() {

        return false; // true's better!
    }

// ------------------- private methods -------------------
// there are no private methods

} // end of ImScrollable class

// end of ImScrollable.java
```

Figure 2-4 shows the ScrollWin looking at the end of an ImScrollable object.

Ready for your first project? If you haven't already done so, load the full project from the book's disk and run it. Then convince yourself that the ScrollWin really is scrolling ImScrollable by changing ImScrollable's getString( ) method. Replacing "i"

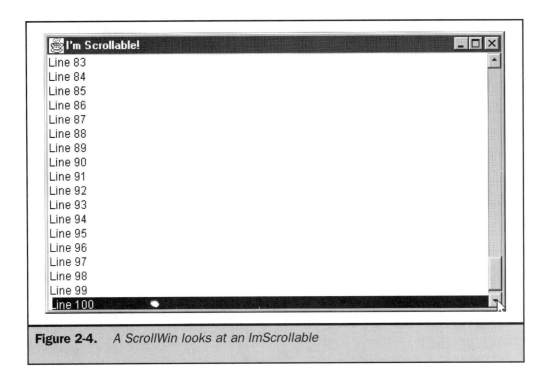

Figure 2-4.   *A ScrollWin looks at an ImScrollable*

with "10 * i" will do the trick. (Of course, if you like standing on your head, replacing "i" with "100 - i" would be more interesting.)

Now that you've seen ImScrollable work, let's go on to find out how the ScrollWin class works.

The ScrollWin Class

To use scrolling windows in your own code, read the introductory remarks and the section "Using the ScrollWin Class." Skip the "Understanding" section until you are ready to write your own, much better, scroller.

TOUR

The ScrollWin class creates a generic scrolling window that will let you or your users scroll through anything that implements Scrollable. That's the good news.

The bad news is that this book is about databases, not about user interfaces. This is user interface code. I knew that we'd want to look at all of our data, so I spent enough time on this tool to make it work. And not a minute more.

This does all its scrolling by simply repainting the entire page. For page-up and page-down operations, this is fine. For scrolling up or down by a single line, it's pathetic. This should be done by moving the contents of the window up or down, and then repainting just the new line.

A well-written scroller would call the Scrollable for 100 lines if the Scrollable had 100 items and you held down the DOWN ARROW scrolling from the top to the bottom. With this version, in a 20-line window it would display items 0 through 19 initially. Then it will request strings 1 through 20 to move down a line. Then items 2 through 21, and so on. This will request about 1,600 items to scroll down our 100-line Scrollable.

The vertical scroll bar used here does not report drags correctly. As you drag the elevator car, nothing happens. When you release the car, the file is correctly positioned. This bug has been corrected in JDK 1.1. With 1.1, your file will move along very nicely as you drag the car.

In both Visual Cafe and Visual J++, the reports from clicks on the PageUp area of the scroll bar sometimes work. Other times, this area sends single-line up events. Other times it even sends single-line and page-down events. Again, JDK 1.1 corrects this.

In Visual J++, keystroke events are not reported until you click inside the scroll window. After a click, the action keys become operable. Visual Cafe does not have this problem.

In JDK 1.1, the vertical scroll bar is given focus, which causes half of it to blink annoyingly. This may not be a bug; it may be a six-legged feature.

Don't let the rather extensive bug report scare you. Most of our other user interface components will have a better report. There won't be any bug reports for the database code, because I found bugs there completely unacceptable. This book isn't about user interface code.

If missing optimal operation by an order of magnitude or more doesn't bother you, and you can put up with the bugs, the good news is applicable. This class makes scrolling through *anything* a piece of cake.

Using the ScrollWin Class

Using this class is extremely simple. You need something that is Scrollable, such as a TxtFile. Assuming you have a file A.TXT available, and assuming that A.TXT really is a text file, this will create a Scrollable and let the user scroll through it:

```
// build a scrollable
    TxtFile t = new TxtFile( "A.TXT" );
```

```
// launch it in a scroll window
    ScrollWin sw = new ScrollWin( t );
    sw.show();
```

There are few complications beyond this.

The Constructors

There are two constructors. Both require a Scrollable. If you aren't being totally simplistic, adding a String will put a title of your choice in the scroll window's title bar. Without the title, you get a fairly foolish "Scroll Window" by default.

These are the constructors:

```
ScrollWin( Scrollable s )
```

```
ScrollWin( Scrollable s, String title )
```

Termination

What happens when the user clicks the window-closing button? In our TextViewer, this scroll window *is* the application, so the application terminates. In most cases you will have a scroll window that is part of a larger application, so you won't be very happy if your scroll window does a System.exit( ).

If you want the application to terminate when the close button is pressed, use setEndApp( ), this way:

```
setEndApp( true );
```

The default behavior is to hide the scroll window but not to terminate the application. If you don't want the close button to work at all, turn it off, this way:

```
setRefuseClose( true );
```

Both EndApp and RefuseClose default to false. I have no idea what will happen if you set them both true. (You could look at how handleEvent( ) treats Event.WINDOW_DESTROY to find out, but don't. That's undocumented behavior that might be changed.)

Other Publics

You can call any of the public functions inherited from Frame and the classes Frame extends. The resize( ) and setTitle( ) functions are two you might want to use.

There are three public data members. These allow you to set the DataBoss and the termination control variables. (Whether you call setEndApp( ) or assign directly to end_app is a matter of taste.)

We'll meet the DataBoss when we start to use a ScrollWin and a data entry panel simultaneously. In this version of ScrollWin, there's a private DataBoss class that turns this feature off. (Without the stub, you'll need an actual DataBoss class. My DataBoss itself needs lots of other classes. The stub eliminates all this.)

The other public functions aren't relevant until we start using the DataBoss. They provide functions that let the scroller scroll in response to commands from another object. These aren't necessary for most purposes.

Understanding the ScrollWin Class

We'll look at the data members briefly, and then we'll take a detailed look at the methods.

ScrollWin's Data Members

Here we'll review the data members in the order they're shown in the file: public, protected, private, and static.

SCROLLWIN'S PUBLIC DATA MEMBERS   The public data members are

- DataBoss DataBoss
- boolean end_app
- boolean refuse_close

The DataBoss is used when you need to coordinate the scroll window with another window that can also provide data navigation. This is invaluable for database work, as we'll see later. For now, it's an unnecessary complication.

The booleans end_app and refuse_close can be set directly, or via setEndApp( ) and setRefuseClose( ) functions. If end_app is true, clicking the close button terminates the application. This is needed for simple applications, such as our TextViewer.

The refuse_close variable has the opposite meaning. It turns the close button's effect to null. The normal effect of the close button is to hide the scroll window. Setting both end_app and refuse_close to true is a programming error.

SCROLLWIN'S PROTECTED DATA MEMBERS   The paint logic precalculates the ints client_height and client_width. These are in pixels. The int client_rows is the number of rows of text available. The resize( ) logic changes the size the user sets to

the nearest integral number of rows. It uses the leading and font_height (in pixels) to calculate this.

The ints old_height and old_width record the size of the window after a resizing operation. They're checked prior to painting to see if the window's been resized.

The int hilite_row keeps the number of the currently highlighted window row. Zero is the top visible row. The int last_top_row holds the number of the last data item that can be used as a top row, keeping the window full. The int s_last is the number returned by the Scrollable's getLast( ) function. If s_last is 99, for example, last_top_row in a 20-line window will be 80. The int top_row will vary from zero through last_top_row, depending on which Scrollable item is at row zero in the display.

In addition to these variables, the protected data members include the scroll window's font, Scrollable object, and vertical scroll bar.

SCROLLWIN'S PRIVATE DATA MEMBERS   Painting is done on a private class object. The class is scroll_canvas and the object is called canvas.

The boolean font_set is set true when the work of setting the font is done. (This includes getting the font's height and adjusting the vertical size to fit an integral number of rows, including appropriate leading between rows.)

The initialize boolean is set true by the constructor, which triggers calculation of row height. The paint_working boolean is set true when resize( ) is called by the paint routine. After the user resizes the window, the painter will resize recursively when it adjusts the window to accommodate an integral number of rows. The resize flag limits the potential recursion.

SCROLLWIN'S STATIC DATA MEMBERS   Four final static members are used to describe the navigation commands from an external (DataBoss) object. They are

- go_home
- go_prev
- go_next
- go_end

ScrollWin's Code

We'll cover the public methods—constructors, data access, and other publics—first. Then we'll look at the private methods.

SCROLLWIN CONSTRUCTORS   The basic constructor takes a single parameter, the Scrollable object. It calls the Frame constructor, stores the Scrollable in scroll_object, and uses the Scrollable's getLast( ) to set s_last.

It uses the default BorderLayout layout manager. It puts the scroll_canvas into the center and puts a scroll bar in the east area. (The other areas are unused.)

Finally, the constructor does some initialization:

```
        hilite_row = 0;
        initialize = true;

        DataBoss = null;

          resize( 500, 300 );
```

The second constructor takes an additional parameter, a String for the Frame's title bar. It uses the first constructor and then calls setTitle( ) with the new title.

SCROLLWIN DATA ACCESS METHODS   With just this one exception, I'll not comment on trivial access routines, like this:

```
    public void setEndApp( boolean b ) {

        end_app = b;
    }
```

I assume that you'll be looking at the code and that you'll not need any help understanding the getWhatever( ), isWhatever( ), and setWhatever( ) routines.

I will, however, mention any unusual features. Here, for example, the setWhatever( ) routines do not have complementary get( ) or is( ) routines. I don't think this is generally a good idea. On the other hand, I've had no use for the get( ) and is( ) routines, so including them would simply waste bytes in the executable. Wasting executable bytes is always a bad idea.

SCROLLWIN'S OTHER PUBLIC METHODS   The other public methods begin with navigate( ), which is used by the DataBoss to forward commands from an alternate object capable of navigating a Scrollable data set. It's just a switch built with the final static navigation constants, like this:

```
    switch ( where ) {
        case go_home:
            home();
            break;

        case go_prev:
            up();
            break;

      . . .
```

The resetLast( ) method is called by the DataBoss when an attached data entry window says that it has performed an append operation. It calls the scroll_object for a new getLast( ) and then does an end( ) operation (as if the END key had been pressed).

The paint( ) method is straightforward, except in its use of the paint_working boolean. The resize( ) method needs to know if it is being called by a user-driven resizing operation or by the paint( ) method.

The problem is that paint( ) may call for a resize( ). The resize( ) operation itself will trigger a call to paint( ). I always worry about recursion in a resize/paint combination. In this case, the recursion would be strictly finite, stopping as soon as the height were adjusted to an integral number of rows. I always use these recursion preventers, even when there's no possibility of the recursion being infinite. This is the general scheme:

```
if ( im_working ) return; // no recursion

im_working = true;

    do_work_here();
    resize();        // or whatever

im_working = false;
```

I always include a paramString( ), which the JDK machinery will use to construct an appropriate toString( ) result. If your code never needs to be debugged, these are a waste of bytes. The bytes you waste here will help you get any system up and running more quickly. And they'll help the programmers who use your objects get their systems up and running more quickly.

The handleEvent( ) routine handles Event.WINDOW_DESTROY appropriately, respecting the refuse_close and end_app booleans. It also coordinates with an end-user menu that the DataBoss controls. This menu lets the user show and hide the scroll and data-editing windows. We'll cover this later.

The handleEvent( ) method also calls the private navigation methods in response to elevator clicks, this way:

```
if ( e.id == Event.SCROLL_LINE_UP ) {
    up();
    return true;
}
```

```
if ( e.id == Event.SCROLL_LINE_DOWN ) {
    down();
    return true;
}
```

The Event.SCROLL_ABSOLUTE is issued in response to dragging the elevator car. In version 1.0, it's sent once at the end of a drag operation. In version 1.1 it's sent during the drag so that the window contents move smoothly during the scroll. This logic does the job badly in 1.0 and well in 1.1:

```
if ( e.id == Event.SCROLL_ABSOLUTE ) {
    int v = vscroll.getValue();
    top_row = v <= last_top_row ?
        v : last_top_row;
    repaint();
    return true;
}
```

For the scroll bar to correctly set the size of the elevator car, you have to tell it that, for example, there are 100 lines in a 100-line file. But you want to scroll the top row only down to line 80 if the window shows 20 lines. That's what the conditional that sets top_row is up to.

SCROLLWIN PRIVATE METHODS   The first private method is calc_row_height( ), which does a lot of work setting the font, and then has three simple lines that actually calculate row height. The basic complication is that you don't know about the availability of fonts on the user's computer. Arial, for example, is universally available on Windows computers (3.x, 9x, and NT) but it's not known elsewhere.

I specify "Courier" for a basic monospace font and "Helvetica," the most common sans-serif font, for a basic proportional font. (In Windows it will map to MS Sans Serif or Arial.) You'll see in the code that I've chosen Font.PLAIN over using the font style that was already set, but I've left the alternative available if you want to use it.

After setting the font, the routine gets the necessary font. (You specify 13-point Helvetica; a user's machine actually sets 12-point MS Sans Serif as the best available approximation.) This is the code:

```
private void calc_row_height( Graphics g ) {

    String font_name;
    font_name = scroll_object.useMonospace() ?
```

```
            "Courier" : "Helvetica";

        Font f = g.getFont();
        g.setFont( new Font(font_name,
            /* f.getStyle() */ Font.PLAIN, f.getSize() ) );
        s_font = g.getFont();

        font_height = s_font.getSize();
        leading = ( font_height + 3 ) / 5;
        row_height = font_height + leading;
    }
```

The down( ) routine is called in response to a DOWN ARROW keypress or a click on the down arrow of the scroll bar. If the highlight bar is not at the bottom of the window, it moves down. If it's at the bottom row, the file scrolls by one bar. At least that's the general theory.

In practice you have to remember that the window might not be filled with data. The number of rows in the window may be larger than the total number of elements in the Scrollable. And there's a special case created when the user drags the bottom of the window down to a larger size and the end row was already showing. In that case, there will be additional empty space available.

The first check says, "move the hilite_row down, if it's not at the bottom":

```
        if ( hilite_row < client_rows - 1 ) {
            hilite_row++;
```

The next check says, "but double-check that you didn't just drop past the end of the items in the Scrollable":

```
        if ( (hilite_row + top_row) > s_last )
            hilite_row--;
```

Finally, if the highlight row was at the bottom, one more check increments top_row—which will change from displaying lines 10 through 20, for example, to 11 through 21—but only if this doesn't exceed the maximum:

```
        if ( top_row < last_top_row ) {
            top_row++;
```

The other navigation routines are similar collections of detailed checks. I know of no way to get this part of a scroller's code to work correctly the first time. When you decide to do your own (and I highly recommend that you do), write a small window that continuously displays all the relevant variables (top_row, last_top_row, hilite_row, and so on) as you scroll.

This is the end( ) routine, called by an END keypress and by the DataBoss after a go_end navigation or an append operation:

```
private void end() {

    if ( (top_row < last_top_row) ||
        (hilite_row < ( s_last - last_top_row )) ) {
        top_row = last_top_row;
        hilite_row = s_last - last_top_row;
        repaint();
    }

}
```

The go_to( ) routine navigates to a specific record. (For "record" you should substitute an item label appropriate to what you're scrolling.) It moves just the highlight bar when the selected record is already showing.

The handle_keypress( ) routine handles the defined action keys in a switch, like this:

```
switch (e.key) {

    case Event.UP:
        up();
        return true;

    case Event.DOWN:
        down();
        return true;

    . . .
```

The home( ), pgdn( ), and pgup( ) routines also navigate. See the remarks earlier pertaining to the end( ) routine when you're ready to build your own scroller.

The next-to-last private routine is resize( ), which starts by computing the size, in pixels, of the scrolling space (client area) in the scroll window:

```
client_height = size().height - insets().top -
    insets().bottom;
```

To understand the next calculation, you have to know the layout of the window. I originally put leading above the first row of text and below the last. It didn't look good. The layout I settled on is simply a row of text followed by the leading pixels. A row of leading seems to look better at the bottom, although it's not strictly necessary.

This is the arrangement I settled on:

```
// client area is laid out:
//    text
//   [ leading
//    text ] . . .
//    leading
```

The first calculation finds the number of client rows. It forces the window to expand to accommodate at least one row:

```
// round to integral # of rows:
if ( client_height < row_height)
    client_rows = 1;
else
    client_rows = client_height / row_height;
```

Once you know the number of rows, you can calculate the client area height and then resize to accommodate an integral number of rows:

```
client_height = row_height * client_rows;

resize( size().width, client_height +
    insets().top + insets().bottom );
```

This settled size is then recorded. These values will be checked the next time paint( ) is called to see if this sizing process needs to be repeated. After recording old_height and old_width, the appropriate last_top_row is set:

```
last_top_row = s_last - client_rows + 1;
if ( last_top_row < 0 ) last_top_row = 0;
```

That conditional is true when, for example, you have three items to display in four or more rows. The vertical scroller is displayed when there is actual scrolling to be done (that is, the number of items exceeds the number of rows in the window):

```
if ( last_top_row > 0 ) vscroll.show();
else vscroll.hide();
```

Finally, the width is set, allowing for insets( ) and for the scroll bar, if it is showing:

```
client_width = size().width - insets().left -
    insets().right -
    ( vscroll.isVisible() ?
        vscroll.size().width : 0 );
```

The up( ) navigation routine is the last private method. Again, refer to the comments under end( ) when you are ready to replace this scroller with a better one.

The ScrollWin's Private Classes

There are two private classes here. The first is the scroll_canvas, which extends the Canvas object. For the scroller I've built, this is an unnecessary complication. However, for a smarter scroller, one that scrolled single lines with bitblt operations and that highlighted with XOR painting, you'll probably want a Canvas.

There are no data members except for one final static constant that's currently unused. The constructor records a reference to the parent ScrollWin object. The heavy lifting is done by the paint( ) method.

THE scroll_canvas's paint( ) METHOD   The first check is for an empty set. This reports "<empty file>" when there are no items in the Scrollable:

```
if ( parent.s_last == -1 ) {

    paint_empty_line( g );
    return;
}
```

Next it sets the Graphics context's font and sets the vertical scroller:

```
g.setFont( parent.s_font );
if ( parent.vscroll.isShowing() ) set_vscroll();
```

The main job is to loop over the items from top_row through the last item in the Scrollable, or to the last row that fits in the window, whichever is less. The int max is the last item in the Scrollable that will be displayed. This is the calculation:

```
int max = parent.client_rows + parent.top_row - 1;
max = max > parent.s_last ?
    parent.s_last : max;
```

This might display a full page of data, or it might display less. (Don't forget that exception where the user drags down the bottom of a page that was already showing the last row.) This is the calculation of the number of rows showing and whether that completely fills the window:

```
int rows_showing =
    parent.s_last - parent.top_row + 1;
boolean filled =
    rows_showing == parent.client_rows;
```

Next there is a strange check that's needed when, for example, an edit process may have deleted rows. It ensures that the hilight row doesn't come in the empty space between the end of the items in the Scrollable and the bottom of the window.

```
if ( (!filled) && (parent.hilite_row >
    ( parent.client_rows - 1 )) )
        if ( parent.client_rows > 0 )
            parent.hilite_row =
                parent.client_rows - 1;
```

Next we set up the for loop. The int print_pos is initialized to the font's height. (When you Graphics.drawString( ), the y position is the font's baseline. By starting at the font's full height—including its descent—we actually leave some leading above the first line.) This is the setup:

```
int print_pos = parent.font_height;
int print_row = 0;
```

Finally, after all that trouble, we're ready to do the real work of displaying lines:

```
for ( int i = parent.top_row; i <= max; i++ ) {

    paint_line( g, i, print_pos,
        print_row == parent.hilite_row );

    print_pos += parent.row_height;
    print_row++;
```

THE scroll_canvas's OTHER METHODS The public handleEvent( ) and private handle_click( ) methods work together to give events over the Canvas the same treatment that the parent ScrollWin gives them.

The paint_empty_line( ) method is called when the Scrollable has no contents. The string "<empty file>" works quite nicely if you're working with databases. You might prefer something more general. This is the code:

```
private void paint_empty_line( Graphics g ) {

    g.drawString( "<empty file>", 1,
        parent.font_height );
}
```

The paint_line( ) routine is the one that does the heavy lifting in the scroll_canvas class. It draws a black string on a white background, except for the highlighted line, which it draws in white on black. If there is an associated DataBoss object, it tells that object to set the record shown in the highlighted line via

```
if ( parent.DataBoss != null )
    parent.DataBoss.setRecord( recno );
```

After adjusting the colors for normal or highlighted use, it writes the text

```
g.drawString( parent.scroll_object.
    getString(recno), 1, print_pos );
```

The set_vscroll( ) routine sets up the vertical scroller. If the last_top_row is zero, it doesn't bother, since the scroll bar is hidden.

The what_row( ) routine is currently unused.

THE DATABOSS PRIVATE CLASS   In the scroll window there are lines of code like this:

```
if ( DataBoss != null )
    DataBoss.scroll_click();
```

The DataBoss is a DataBoss class object. The DataBoss class, in turn, uses objects of several other classes. If your application is like our TextViewer, simply making these classes available (moving copies into the working directory or including their directory as an input source) would add about 25K to the size of the executable.

By keeping the classes elsewhere, this compiles correctly and saves wasted space:

```
class DataBoss {

    void scroll_click() {}
    void setRecord( int i ) {}
}
```

Of course, you'll have to remember that you've disabled the DataBoss feature when you do this. Using a DataBoss-less ScrollWin for our TextViewer and using inheritance to add the DataBoss features to a more sophisticated ScrollWin is the correct approach. Remind me to do that if I write a book about user interface code.

The Complete ScrollWin Listing

Listing 2-3 shows the full ScrollWin.java file.

Listing 2-3:
ScrollWin.java

```
// ScrollWin.java -- a generic scrolling Window
// Copyright 1997, Martin L. Rinehart

// this code is completely documented in:
// _Java Database Development_, Martin Rinehart,
// Osborne/McGraw-Hill, 1997

/*

    This window will scroll anything that implements
    the Scrollable interface.

    It will synchronize with a data DataBoss if an object
    that implements DataBoss is provided.
*/
```

```java
 import java.awt.*;

class ScrollWin extends Frame {

// -------------------- data members --------------------

// public data members:

    public DataBoss DataBoss;

    public boolean end_app;

     public boolean refuse_close;

// protected data members:

    protected int client_height;
    protected int client_rows;
    protected int client_width;

    protected int font_height;

    protected int hilite_row;

    protected int last_top_row;
    protected int leading;

    protected int old_height;
    protected int old_width;

    protected int row_height;

    protected Font s_font;
    protected int s_last;
    protected Scrollable scroll_object;

    protected int top_row;

    protected Scrollbar vscroll;

// private data members:
```

```
    private scroll_canvas canvas;

    private boolean font_set = true;

    private boolean initialize;

    private boolean paint_working;

// static data members

    // there are no public static data members
    // there are no private static data members

    // final static data members:

    final static int go_home = -4;
    final static int go_prev = -3;
    final static int go_next = -2;
    final static int go_end  = -1;

// -------------------- public methods --------------------

// constructors:

    ScrollWin( Scrollable s ) {

        super( "Scroll Window" );

        scroll_object = s;
        s_last = s.getLast();

        vscroll = new Scrollbar(); // defaults to vertical
        vscroll.setBackground( Color.lightGray );
        add( "East", vscroll );

        canvas = new scroll_canvas( this );
        add( "Center", canvas );
```

```
            hilite_row = 0;
            initialize = true;

        DataBoss = null;

            resize( 500, 300 );
    }

    ScrollWin( Scrollable s, String title ) {
        this( s );
        setTitle( title );
    }

// there are no data access getXxx() methods
// there are no data access isXxx() methods

// data access setXxx() methods:

    public void setEndApp( boolean b ) {

        end_app = b;
    }

    public void setRefuseClose( boolean b ) {

        refuse_close = b;
    }

    public void setDataBoss ( DataBoss d ) {

        DataBoss = d;
    }

// public, class-specific method:

    public void navigate( int where ) {

        switch ( where ) {
            case go_home:
                home();
```

```
                break;

            case go_prev:
                up();
                break;

            case go_next:
                down();
                break;

            case go_end:
                end();
                break;

            default:
                go_to( where );
        }
    }

    public void resetLast() {

        s_last = scroll_object.getLast();
          end();
    }

// public, non-event overriding methods:

    public void paint( Graphics g ) {

        if ( initialize )  {
            calc_row_height( g );
            initialize = false;
        }

        if ( paint_working ) return;
        paint_working = true;

        if ( (size().width != old_width) ||

            (size().height != old_height) ) {
```

```
                resize();
        }
        canvas.repaint();
        paint_working = false;
    }

    public String paramString() {

            return "wid: " + client_width +
                " hgt: " + client_height +
                " rows: " + client_rows;
    }

    public void repaint() {

            super.repaint();
    }

// public, event-handling method:

    public boolean handleEvent( Event e ) {

        if ( e.id == Event.WINDOW_DESTROY ) {

            if ( DataBoss != null ) {

                DataBoss.scroll_click();
                return true;
            }

            if ( refuse_close )
                return true;

            else if ( end_app )
                System.exit( 0 );

            else
                hide();

            return true;
        }
```

```
        if ( e.id == Event.KEY_ACTION )
            if ( handle_keypress(e) )
                return true;

        if ( e.id == Event.SCROLL_LINE_UP ) {
            up();
            return true;
        }

        if ( e.id == Event.SCROLL_LINE_DOWN ) {
            down();
            return true;
        }

        if ( e.id == Event.SCROLL_PAGE_UP ) {
            pgup();
            return true;
        }

        if ( e.id == Event.SCROLL_PAGE_DOWN ) {
            pgdn();
            return true;
        }

        if ( e.id == Event.SCROLL_ABSOLUTE ) {
            int v = vscroll.getValue();
            top_row = v <= last_top_row ?
                v : last_top_row;
            repaint();
            return true;
        }

        return super.handleEvent( e );
    }

// ------------------- private methods -------------------

// private methods:

    private void calc_row_height( Graphics g ) {
```

```
        String font_name;
        font_name = scroll_object.useMonospace() ?
            "Courier" : "Helvetica";

        Font f = g.getFont();
        g.setFont( new Font(font_name,
            /* f.getStyle() */ Font.PLAIN, f.getSize() ) );
        s_font = g.getFont();

        font_height = s_font.getSize();
        leading = ( font_height + 3 ) / 5;
        row_height = font_height + leading;
    }

    private void down() {

        if ( hilite_row < client_rows - 1 ) {
            hilite_row++;
            if ( (hilite_row + top_row) > s_last )
                hilite_row--;
            repaint();
            return;
        }

        if ( top_row < last_top_row ) {
            top_row++;
            repaint();
        }
    }

    private void end() {

        if ( (top_row < last_top_row) ||
            (hilite_row < ( s_last - last_top_row )) ) {
            top_row = last_top_row;
            hilite_row = s_last - last_top_row;
            repaint();
        }
    }

    private void go_to( int recno ) {
```

```
        // if recno is visible, don't move page
        if ( (recno >= top_row) &&
            (( recno - top_row ) <= client_rows) ) {
            hilite_row = recno - top_row;
        }

        repaint();
    }

private boolean handle_keypress( Event e ) {

    switch (e.key) {

        case Event.UP:
            up();
            return true;

        case Event.DOWN:
            down();
            return true;

        case Event.PGUP:
            pgup();
            return true;

        case Event.PGDN:
            pgdn();
            return true;

        case Event.HOME:
            home();
            return true;

        case Event.END:
            end();
            return true;
    }
    return false;
}

private void home() {
```

```
        if ( (top_row > 0) || (hilite_row > 0) ) {
            top_row = 0;
            hilite_row = 0;
            repaint();
        }
    }

    private void pgdn() {

        if ( top_row < last_top_row ) {
            top_row += client_rows;
            top_row = top_row > last_top_row ?
                last_top_row : top_row;
            repaint();
            return;
        }
        int last_row = s_last - last_top_row;

        if ( hilite_row < last_row ) {
            hilite_row = last_row;
            repaint();
        }
    }

    private void pgup() {

        if ( top_row > 0 ) {
            top_row -= client_rows;
            top_row = top_row < 0 ? 0 : top_row;
            repaint();
            return;
        }

        if ( hilite_row > 0 ) {
            hilite_row = 0;
            repaint();
        }
    }

    private void resize() {
```

```
        client_height = size().height - insets().top -
            insets().bottom;

// client area is laid out:
//    text
//  [ leading
//    text ] . . .
//    leading

        // round to integral # of rows:
        if ( client_height < row_height)
            client_rows = 1;
        else
            client_rows = client_height / row_height;

        client_height = row_height * client_rows;

        resize( size().width, client_height +
            insets().top + insets().bottom );

        old_width = size().width;
        old_height = size().height;

        last_top_row = s_last - client_rows + 1;
        if ( last_top_row < 0 ) last_top_row = 0;

        if ( last_top_row > 0 ) vscroll.show();
        else vscroll.hide();

        client_width = size().width - insets().left -
            insets().right -
            ( vscroll.isVisible() ?
                vscroll.size().width : 0 );
    }

    private void up() {

        if ( hilite_row > 0 ) {
            hilite_row--;
            repaint();
            return;
```

```
            }

        if ( top_row > 0  ) {
            top_row--;
            repaint();
        }
    }

} // end of ScrollWin class

// private class in ScrollWin.java:

class scroll_canvas extends Canvas {

// there are no public data members

// protected data member:

    protected ScrollWin parent;

// final static data member:

    final static int paint_delay = 1000;

// constructor:

    scroll_canvas( ScrollWin sw ) {
        parent = sw;
    }

// public, non-event overriding method:

    public void paint( Graphics g ) {

        if ( parent.s_last == -1 ) {

            paint_empty_line( g );
            return;
        }

        g.setFont( parent.s_font );
```

```
            if ( parent.vscroll.isShowing() ) set_vscroll();

            int max = parent.client_rows + parent.top_row - 1;
            max = max > parent.s_last ?
                parent.s_last : max;

            int rows_showing =
                parent.s_last - parent.top_row + 1;
            boolean filled =
                rows_showing == parent.client_rows;

            if ( (!filled) && (parent.hilite_row >
                ( parent.client_rows - 1 )) )
                    if ( parent.client_rows > 0 )
                        parent.hilite_row =
                            parent.client_rows - 1;

            int print_pos = parent.font_height;
            int print_row = 0;
            for ( int i = parent.top_row; i <= max; i++ ) {

                paint_line( g, i, print_pos,
                    print_row == parent.hilite_row );

                print_pos += parent.row_height;
                print_row++;
            }
        }
    }

// public, event-handling method:

    public boolean handleEvent( Event e ) {

        if ( e.id == Event.MOUSE_DOWN ) {
            handle_click( e );
            return true;
        }

          if ( (parent.DataBoss != null) &&
                (e.id == Event.WINDOW_DESTROY) ) {
```

```
                    parent.DataBoss.scroll_click();
                    return true;
             }
         return super.handleEvent( e );
    }

// private methods:

    private void handle_click( Event e ) {

        parent.hilite_row = what_row( e.y );

        if ( (parent.top_row + parent.hilite_row) >
            parent.s_last )
            parent.hilite_row = parent.s_last -
                parent.top_row;

        repaint();
    }

     private void paint_empty_line( Graphics g ) {

         g.drawString( "<empty file>", 1,

             parent.font_height );
     }

    private void paint_line( Graphics g, int recno,
        int print_pos, boolean hilite ) {

        if ( hilite ) {

            if ( parent.DataBoss != null )
                parent.DataBoss.setRecord( recno );

            g.setColor( Color.black );
            g.fillRect(
                parent.insets().left,
                print_pos + parent.leading -
                    parent.row_height,
                parent.client_width,
```

```
                parent.row_height );
            g.setColor( Color.white );
        }
        else {
            g.setColor( Color.black );
        }

        g.drawString( parent.scroll_object.
            getString(recno), 1, print_pos );
    }

    private void set_vscroll() {

        if ( parent.last_top_row >  0 )
            parent.vscroll.setValues(
                (parent.s_last * parent.top_row) /
                    parent.last_top_row,
                parent.client_rows,
                0,
                parent.s_last );
    }

    private int what_row( int y ) {

        while ( parent.row_height == 0 )
            Thread.yield();

        return ( y + 1 ) / parent.row_height;
    }

} // end of scroll_canvas

class DataBoss {

    void scroll_click() {}
    void setRecord( int i ) {}
}

// end of ScrollWin.java
```

Summary

We began by thinking about interfaces in general. In spite of what Sun's documentation says, I'm convinced that interfaces are a fundamental addition to object technology. They let you add capabilities to classes without needing to think about the class's complexities. Unlike inheritance, which goes down to the lowest level (the tree's trunk), interfaces can be attached at a very high level (up in the branches). The general-purpose scroller that we looked at here was a project that I couldn't make work before I saw interfaces.

We put the theory into practice with a Scrollable interface. You saw that this is a simple, three-method interface. Still, it's enough to get the job done, which is all you ever want an interface to do.

The ImScrollable class consisted of a four-line mainline and three one-line methods implementing the Scrollable interface. It's enough to launch a ScrollWin that you can run.

Then we dove into the ScrollWin class, which was not as trivial. The ScrollWin object can scroll anything that implements ImScrollable. You saw pictures of it handling text files, binary files, and database files. If you ran this chapter's projects, you saw an example that wasn't file based.

If you examined the code, you found that the ScrollWin here is one that could be greatly improved. If the user scrolls a page at a time, it's not bad. But if the user scrolls a line at a time, it's about an order of magnitude less efficient than it could be.

Chapter 3

Text Files

In Chapter 2 we looked at ScrollWin and the Scrollable interface. With these tools, we'll be ready to look at local files of any description. In this chapter, we'll begin with the basic text file.

I just built a TextViewer application. It's perfect for showing READ.ME files. The user picks a file from a standard file-opening dialog box. Then, courtesy of a ScrollWin object, the expected vertical scroll bar and navigations keystrokes are available for viewing the file. It took about five minutes!

I wouldn't have said that if it weren't true. Sorry to say, it's not quite the whole truth.

It took another half hour to add some reasonable behaviors when the file-open dialog box was canceled, when the file existed but couldn't be opened, and when the file that was picked didn't turn out to be a text file. Then it took another three-quarters of an hour to resolve the irritating differences between Visual Cafe and Visual J++. Murphy's Law has *not* been repealed.

OK, enough honesty. Back to hype mode. With well-designed classes, you just flow from object to object and everything happens beautifully. The FileDialog takes care of picking a file from the directories. You open a TxtFile object by passing the constructor the name the user chooses. Then you pass the TxtFile to the constructor of the ScrollWin along with a window title. You're doing very complex stuff, but the code's dead simple.

Here's the code of the TextViewer, with all the annoying error details left out:

```
FileDialog fd = new FileDialog( new Frame(),
    "Open Text File" );
fd.show();

TxtFile tf = new TxtFile( fd.getFile() );

ScrollWin sw = new ScrollWin( tf, fd.getFile() );
sw.show();
```

That's the five-minute program version. It works! The magic is that the TxtFile implements the Scrollable interface.

Figure 3-1 shows the original text file in which I'm writing this chapter. You can see these words, just as they look on my screen.

Next we'll take a close look at the TxtFile class that makes this simple programming possible. Then we'll take a look at the PointerList class that TxtFile depends on for support. Finally, we'll look at the real TextViewer mainline, with all the annoying details put back in place.

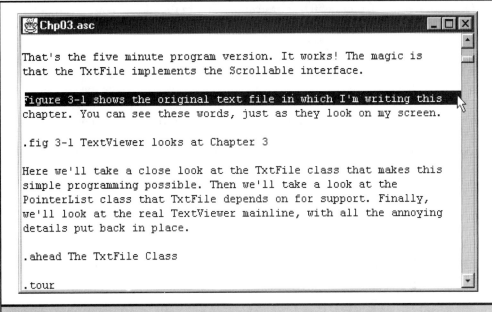

Figure 3-1.   *TextViewer looks at Chapter 3*

The TxtFile Class

To become a TxtFile user, just read up to "Understanding the TxtFile Class." Pay close attention to the overall remarks made in the following paragraphs, however.

The package java.io does *not* include a good mechanism for handling plain text files—files of printable characters organized in strings of varying lengths, separated by end-of-line characters. In my TxtFile class I've provided one very simple way of handling these files.

I read the entire file into RAM in one big byte array. This is highly efficient, but is obviously inapplicable for very large files. It's also important to note that byte arrays don't support chars. This works for common PC, Mac, and UNIX files, such as source code files. It will not handle Unicode character files.

The big array method works, for example, with even the largest chapters in this book (listings included). It will work for almost every Java source file ever written. (You've got to say "almost" because somewhere there's a total nut who's built a ridiculous counter example.) If you like, you can use the JDB tool to open every source file in this book simultaneously. Unless you've got a very small computer, you'll have no problem.

On the other hand, there will be applications where the file sizes are so large that this RAM-based approach will be inapplicable. (For database files, I wouldn't think of trying to read the entire file into RAM. That would limit you to just small files. Databases tend to get large quickly.)

Along with reading the files into RAM, the TxtFile prepares arrays of integers in objects I call *PointerLists*. These are really just integer arrays that have the convenient trait of growing as you add to them, not bothering you about setting dimensions in advance. Access to any line of the text file is achieved by creating a string from a range of bytes. The range is set by use of fast calls to these PointerLists. You'll see that this runs very quickly. Most operations appear to be instantaneous. This is a good class to show to your non-Java friends when they ask, "Isn't Java slow?"

TxtFile reads the file in one big gulp. It then breaks the file into individual lines, which is a system-dependent process. TxtFile uses linefeeds, carriage returns, and carriage return/linefeed pairs as delimiters. This handles text files on UNIX systems, Macintoshes, and on PCs using DOS, Windows, or OS/2. It would fail on a system that used some other newline character. Using java.io's one-byte-at-a-time stream handling would avoid this potential problem, but it would cost a lot in efficiency.

One word of warning before we start: we're not beginning at the beginning. The TxtFile extends the BinFile class, which we'll cover in the next chapter. That class hides the essentially uninteresting mechanics of opening and closing the file, for example.

The BinFile is made Scrollable by code that simply reads it 16 bytes at a time. But then there's the necessity for producing a nice hex display of those frequently unprintable bytes, accompanied by a nice printable display of the printable ones. It gets quite involved with issues that are necessary if you want to look at binary files, but that aren't relevant for looking at text. So for now, when you see the BinFile, consider it a black box. We'll open it up and lay it bare in the next chapter.

One final word of warning: This TxtFile makes any sort of file reading simple. It's not suitable for read/write applications, such as a text editor. It uses pointers into a byte array. For text editing, you'd want to use pointers into a linked list. When you get to that part of the logic, you'll see that the array structure is a part that you could replace with linked lists (or whatever fits the application) without disturbing the rest of the class.

Using the TxtFile Class

Using the TxtFile couldn't be much simpler. You pass the name of the file you want in the constructor. Then you ask it to getString(i), where i is the line you want. That returns a String holding the specified line of the file. The first line is zero and the getLast( ) function returns the number of the last line.

This would be trivial if it weren't for the number of things that can go wrong whenever you open a file. The file might not exist. The file might be locked by another process. The file might not be a text file.

To handle all the possibilities, the object has a public variable, readable. The readable variable is only set true if everything is acceptable. On any error, readable is false. Another public, the String message, holds a message that you can display to the user. The message will say, "File not found," or whatever is appropriate.

At present, java.io has no concept of file locking. If it can't read a file, it will throw an IOException. You can't, as yet, recognize that there is a temporary record lock placed by another user, for example. For our purposes, however, unlocked, single-user access is just fine. For files on a server, you should use JDBC to connect to a multiuser database.

Using the TxtFile Constructors

There are two constructors:

```
TxtFile( String pathname )
```

```
TxtFile( String pathname, String access )
```

The pathname contains the system-dependent disk, directory, and name information. If you use the FileDialog to select a file, your code will not be system dependent. If you hard-code the pathname, you will probably cause problems on at least some platforms.

The access string can be either "r" for read-only access or "rw" for read-write access. Anything else is an error. Read-only access is the default used by the simpler constructor.

Using TxtFile's Data Access Methods

The two primary access tools are the ones defined by the Scrollable interface:

- int getLast( )
- String getString(int index)

The lines of the file (actually, of the RAM-based copy of the file) are numbered zero through getLast( ). The getString( ) method returns a String for any line. It does not include the end-of-line terminators.

A maximum width is initially set by the TxtFile to the full length of the file. It's theoretically possible to read a 100K file as a single String 100K long. The ScrollWin, for example, only displays as much of the String as fits in its width. It would show this absurd case as one line. It makes no provision for horizontal scrolling.

To work with this sort of restriction, you can set the maximum width to a lesser value. You might set it to the width of the scroller, for example. The TxtFile will divide an otherwise unbroken line into pieces each as long as the maximum, up to the remainder piece. With an 80-column maximum, for example, a 170-byte input line would become two lines of 80 bytes each, followed by a 10-byte stub. If that 170-byte line were line 0 in the file, it would be returned as Strings 0, 1, and 2. The next line of the file would be (or start at) String 3.

This is controlled by

- void setMaxWidth(int new_maximum)
- int getMaxWidth( )

The getMaxWidth( ) does not refer to the length of the longest line. It simply returns the value set by setMaxWidth( ).

Using TxtFile's Other Public Methods

The useMonospace( ) method, required by the Scrollable interface, returns false. There is also a paramString( ) method.

Although the method is private, you may also wish to look at the test_for_text( ) method, to see how TxtFile distinguishes text from other files, even though the rest of the "Understanding" section isn't relevant to your immediate needs.

Understanding the TxtFile Class

Here we'll cover the data members and then the code. You'll see that the big array used here works for read access, but wouldn't be convenient for a text editor, for example. In fact, the TxtFile has no provision for writing its data back to disk.

You could easily use the TxtFile, however, to read and split a text file, and then copy its contents to a linked list structure appropriate for a text editor. Or you could discard the whole file-read mechanism and replace it with your own. It's not a lot of code.

Let's get started on the data.

TxtFile's Data Members

The TxtFile has five protected data members and three final static constants.

TXTFILE'S PROTECTED DATA MEMBERS   The byte array, file_bytes, contains a byte-for-byte copy of the disk file.

The int last_string_num contains the number that will be reported by the getLast( ) method.

Two PointerList objects, line_begins and line_sizes, contain lists of integers. They would be arrays, but there is no convenient way to dimension an array before you have done the work of dividing the file into individual strings. Element i of line_begins is the starting location of string i in file_bytes. The ith element of line_sizes contains the number of bytes that start at that location.

Finally, the int max_width holds the value (if any) you set for the longest allowable line width.

TXTFILE'S FINAL STATIC DATA MEMBERS   For convenience, a value K is set to 1024. That makes the other final statics more readable:

```
final static int test_size = 2*K;
final static int max_file_length = 128*K;
```

The test_size is used by the test_for_text( ) function. That function will report that the file is text if the first test_size bytes are acceptable.

The max_file_length is used to refuse to open larger files. My value is quite conservative.

TxtFile's Methods

We'll cover the constructors first. Then we'll get to the data access methods. There are no other interesting public methods. (I consider paramString( ) to be well worth the trouble of writing it. But that doesn't make it *interesting*.) Finally, of course, we'll look at the private methods.

TXTFILE'S CONSTRUCTORS   The first constructor lets you omit the access string when read-only access is acceptable. The way this class is written, that should always be the case.

```
TxtFile( String pathname ) {

    this( pathname, "r" ); // default to read-only
}
```

The second constructor accepts pathname and access strings. It passes both of these to the BinFile constructor, this way:

```
TxtFile ( String pathname, String access ) {

    super( pathname, access );
```

The BinFile takes care of opening the file. If it encounters any problems, it sets readable to false and places a String (which is ignored here) in the public message variable. TxtFile just surrenders if there is any problem:

```
if ( ! readable ) // could not open
    return;
```

Next it checks to see if the file is within the class's size range and exits appropriately if not:

```
if ( file_length > max_file_length ) {

    message = "file too big";
    readable = false;
    return;
}
```

Then it tests to see if the file is a text file and again returns with an appropriate message if not:

```
if ( ! test_for_text() ) { // includes unprintables?

    message = "Not a text file";
    readable = false;

    return;
}
```

If the file is small enough and tests acceptably for text, the whole file is read in at once. Again, an exit is taken with an appropriate message if there is any problem:

```
if ( ! read_whole_file() ) {

    message = "Failure during whole file read";
    readable = false;

    return;
}
```

The next line effectively eliminates the max_width test that would otherwise divide long lines into more manageable pieces. The object that creates the TxtFile has to call setMaxWidth( ) if it has a better idea.

```
max_width = file_length;
```

Finally, the big character array is divided into individual strings. It's not physically separated; the appropriate pointer lists are established that let TxtFile instantly respond to the request for a particular String.

```
        divide_into_lines();
```

TXTFILE'S DATA ACCESS METHODS   The getLast( ) member of the Scrollable interface actually fibs when there are no strings. You'll see why when you look at the getString( ) method.

```
public int getLast() {

    if ( file_length == 0 )
        return 0;

    return line_begins.length() - 1;

}
```

The getString( ) method does the real work. It returns the empty file message or returns a String built from file_bytes starting at line_begins[index], and using line_sizes[index] bytes. Since line_begins and line_sizes are PointerList objects, you can't really use subscript notation, although that's the idea. This is the method:

```
public String getString( int index ) {

    if ( file_length == 0 )
        return " <empty file>";

    return new String( file_bytes, 0,
        line_begins.getPointer(index),
        line_sizes.getPointer(index) );
}
```

Did I say earlier that useMonospace( ) returns false? For general text file use, perhaps it should. But in all my testing, the only text files I had handy were source code, which is better handled in monospace. I'm afraid that this temporary setting forgot to change itself back to false:

```
public boolean useMonospace() {

    return true;
}
```

TXTFILE'S PRIVATE METHODS   The getString( ) method is quick and simple. That's because it depends on divide_into_lines( ) hard work in getting the PointerLists prepared. The divide_into_lines( ) method starts by creating the lists:

```
line_begins = new PointerList();
line_sizes = new PointerList();
```

Next it sets some initial values. The int i is the index into the file_bytes array. The in_line boolean is true when the process is somewhere inside a line (started, but not yet at an EOL). The int size is incremented as each byte is processed.

```
int i = 0;
boolean in_line = false;
int size = 0;
```

The basic algorithm is

```
loop:
    starting a new line?
        add the current location to line_begins

    march down the array, incrementing size until
    you come to the first EOL
        add the size to line_sizes
        set the flag to begin a new line

    goto loop
```

Now let's add some details. As this pseudocode shows, there are two EOL characters (CR and LF), the CR/LF pair, and the max_width approximation of an EOL to think about:

```
while ( i < file_bytes.length ) {

    if ( !in_line )
        initialize things
        in_line = true
```

```
        if ( file_bytes[i] == 13 ) {
         process as an EOL

         if CR is followed by LF, skip the LF

        }
        else if ( file_bytes[i] == 10 ) {
         process as an EOL
        }
        else if ( size == max_width ) {
         process as an EOL
        }
    else { // grow the current string
            size++;
            i++;
        }
  }
```

Once you understand these principles, you should be able to make sense of the full code:

```
      while ( i < file_bytes.length ) {

        if ( !in_line ) {

            size = 0;
            line_begins.add(i);
            in_line = true;
        }

        if ( file_bytes[i] == 13 ) {

            line_sizes.add( size );
            in_line = false;
            i++;

            // skip over LF in CR/LF pair
            if ( i < file_bytes.length )
                if ( file_bytes[i] == 10 )
                    i++;
```

```
      }
      else if ( file_bytes[i] == 10 ) {

            line_sizes.add( size );
            in_line = false;
            i++;
      }
      else if ( size == max_width ) {

            line_sizes.add( size );
            line_begins.add( i );
            size = 1;
            i++;
      }
      else {

            size++;
            i++;

      }

}
```

Let's complete the algorithm with the final thought. After we've come to the end of the file, we've probably left our machinery thinking that it's in the middle of a line. You have to add the final size to the line_sizes PointerList:

```
if ( in_line )
      line_sizes.add( size );
```

All my life I've dealt with neat buffering schemes that handled files one buffer-full at a time. I started on yet another one, but then asked myself if this were still necessary. Skipping the error handling, this is all you need to do:

```
file_bytes = new byte[file_length];

raf.seek( 0 );
raf.read( file_bytes );
```

That's about as simple as it gets, no? Even with all the nitty-gritty details, this routine's still close to trivial:

```
        private boolean read_whole_file() {

// this is the BIG GULP method

            file_bytes = new byte[file_length];

            try {

                raf.seek( 0 );
                int bytes_read = raf.read( file_bytes );
                if ( bytes_read < file_length ) throw new
                        IOException();
            }
            catch ( IOException ioe ) {

                message = "file read error";
                readable = false;
                return false;

            }

            return true;
        }
```

The final private method is test_for_text( ), which will return true when it's
satisfied that the file really is a text file. It creates a new byte array test_size bytes long
and reads test_size bytes into that array. (It has to allow for files that are shorter than
test_size, too.)

```
        int test_size = file_length > this.test_size ?
            this.test_size : file_length;

        file_bytes = new byte[test_size];

        try {

            raf.seek( 0 );
            int bytes_read = raf.read( file_bytes );
            if ( bytes_read < test_size )
                throw new IOException();
        }
```

```
catch ( IOException ioe ) {

    message = "file read error";
    readable = false;
    return false;
}
```

Then it tests each byte in the array. It passes any byte from space (32) on up. (This passes some suspicious characters, such as 127 and all the bytes with the high bit set. I use them all in code.) It also passes newlines, returns, and tabs. If it finds anything else, the file flunks the test. (You might find this too severe. Some applications might pass one or two bad characters, for example.) This is the test code:

```
for ( int i = 0 ; i < test_size ; i++ ) {

    if ( file_bytes[i] > 31 )
        continue;

    if ( file_bytes[i] == (byte) '\n' )
        continue;

    if ( file_bytes[i] == (byte) '\r' )
        continue;

    if ( file_bytes[i] == (byte) '\t' )
        continue;

    return false;
}

return true;
```

The Complete TxtFile Listing

Listing 3-1 shows the complete TxtFile.java file.

Listing 3-1:
TxtFile.java

```
// TxtFile.java -- Text File class
// Copyright 1997, Martin L. Rinehart

// this code is completely documented in:
```

```
// _Java Database Development_, Martin Rinehart,
// Osborne/McGraw-Hill, 1997

/*
    handle plain text files (e.g., Java source)
*/

import java.io.*;

class TxtFile extends BinFile implements Scrollable {

// -------------------- data members --------------------

// there are no public data members

// protected data members:

    byte[] file_bytes;

    int last_string_num;

    PointerList line_begins;
    PointerList line_sizes;

    int max_width;

// static data members

    // there are no public static data members
    // there are no private static data members

    // final static data member:

    final static int K = 1024;

    final static int test_size = 2*K;
    final static int max_file_length = 128*K;

// -------------------- public methods --------------------

// constructors:
```

```java
TxtFile( String pathname ) {

    this( pathname, "r" ); // default to read-only
}

TxtFile ( String pathname, String access ) {

    super( pathname, access );

    if ( ! readable ) // could not open
        return;

    if ( file_length > max_file_length ) {
        message = "file too big";
        readable = false;
        return;
    }

    if ( ! test_for_text() ) { // includes unprintables?

        message = "Not a text file";
        readable = false;

        return;
    }

    if ( ! read_whole_file() ) {

        message = "Failure during whole file read";
        readable = false;

        return;
    }

    max_width = file_length;

    divide_into_lines();
}

// data access getXxx() methods:
```

```
    public int getLast() {

        if ( file_length == 0 )
            return 0;

        return line_begins.length() - 1;

    }

    public int getMaxWidth() {

        return max_width;
    }

    public String getString( int index ) {

        if ( file_length == 0 )
            return " <empty file>";

        return new String( file_bytes, 0,
            line_begins.getPointer(index),
            line_sizes.getPointer(index) );
    }
// there are no data access isXxx() methods

// data access setXxx() methods

    public void setMaxWidth( int mw ) {

        max_width = mw;
    }

// public, class-specific method:

    public boolean useMonospace() {

        return true;
    }
```

```
// public, non-event overriding method:

    public String paramString() {

        return "File " + path_name +
            ", file_length " + file_length;
    }

// there are no public, event-handling method:

// ------------------ private methods ------------------

// private methods:

    private void divide_into_lines() {

        /*
                entire file is in byte[] file_bytes

                this divides it into lines terminated by
                returns, by linefeeds or by return/linefeed
                pairs.

                note that this is system-dependent but as
                coded it will work in most cases in Unix, Mac
                and PC files
        */

        line_begins = new PointerList();
        line_sizes = new PointerList();

        int i = 0;
        boolean in_line = false;
        int size = 0;

        while ( i < file_bytes.length ) {

            if ( !in_line ) {

                size = 0;
                line_begins.add(i);
```

```
            in_line = true;
        }

        if ( file_bytes[i] == 13 ) {

            line_sizes.add( size );
            in_line = false;
            i++;

            // skip over LF in CR/LF pair
            if ( i < file_bytes.length )
                if ( file_bytes[i] == 10 )
                    i++;

        }
        else if ( file_bytes[i] == 10 ) {

            line_sizes.add( size );
            in_line = false;
            i++;
        }
        else if ( size == max_width ) {

            line_sizes.add( size );
            line_begins.add( i );
            size = 1;
            i++;
        }
        else {

            size++;
            i++;
        }
    }

    if ( in_line )
        line_sizes.add( size );
}

private boolean read_whole_file() {
```

```java
// this is the BIG GULP method

    file_bytes = new byte[file_length];

    try {

        raf.seek( 0 );
        int bytes_read = raf.read( file_bytes );
        if ( bytes_read < file_length ) throw new
            IOException();
    }
    catch ( IOException ioe ) {

        message = "file read error";
        readable = false;
        return false;
    }

    return true;
}

private boolean test_for_text() {

    int test_size = file_length > this.test_size ?
        this.test_size : file_length;

    file_bytes = new byte[test_size];

    try {

        raf.seek( 0 );
        int bytes_read = raf.read( file_bytes );
        if ( bytes_read < test_size )
            throw new IOException();
    }
    catch ( IOException ioe ) {

        message = "file read error";
        readable = false;
        return false;
    }
```

```
        for ( int i = 0 ; i < test_size ; i++ ) {

            if ( file_bytes[i] > 31 )
                continue;

            if ( file_bytes[i] == (byte) '\n' )
                continue;

            if ( file_bytes[i] == (byte) '\r' )
                continue;

            if ( file_bytes[i] == (byte) '\t' )
                continue;

            return false;
        }

        return true;
    }

} // end of TxtFile class

// there are no private classes in TxtFile.java

// end of TxtFile.java
```

The PointerList Class

 PointerList is an internal support class. For the fastest tour, skip it entirely. On the other hand, it's a nice bit of Java that you might want to use or copy whenever you need an array but can't predict the size you'll need.

The worst single thing about the PointerList class is probably its name. It acquired its name from its first intended use as a supporting actor for the TxtFile class. That class was originally to have string begin and end pointers. Before it was done, the end pointers had turned into sizes, not pointers.

The PointerList class was just as useful for sizes as it was for pointers. Anyway, a C purist would call those pointers array indexes, not pointers at all. (Of course, I'd fire back that even C's pointers are offsets from segment registers in an Intel chip, so these array indexes are every bit as valid as pointers as C's pointers.)

At any rate, this class provides an array-like list of integers without the requirement for preallocating space for the array. It's most useful in applications—such as dividing a text file into individual lines—where you can't reasonably predict the size array you'll need in advance.

Using the PointerList Class

The PointerList class has simple constructors. It's got simple data access and class-specific public methods, too. It's easy to use and adequately efficient for heavy use.

Using PointerList Constructors

You create a PointerList with one of these constructors:

- PointerList( )
- PointerList(int starting_size)

The default starting size is 256. If you thought your PointerList was going to be very small, you might want to force it to a very small initial size. On the other hand, you might know that you were going to need a lot, so you could start it at a larger initial size.

Bear in mind that the array used internally grows by 50 percent every time it runs out of space. This means that it grows faster (and less often) as it gets larger.

Using PointerList Data Access Methods

The getPointer( ) and setPointer( ) functions provide access to the data in the list, this way:

```
// pl is a PointerList

pl.getPointer(i)     // roughly: pl[i]
pl.setPointer(i, n) // roughly: pl[i] = n
```

Using PointerList's Other Public Methods

The key to using a PointerList effectively is to fill it via the add( ) method. That's done with statements like this:

```
pl.add( new_int );
```

The length( ) method returns the PointerList's number of active elements. As with an array, if length( ) is n, the last element is n – 1. An element you add( ) is located at the value of pl.length( ) immediately before the add( ), this way:

```
int where = pl.length();

pl.add( new_int );

// pl.getPointer( where ) returns new_int
```

This class's usefulness is largely due to its simplicity. (My hero is the person who designed the Runnable interface. One method, no parameters! That's elegant. I keep that design in mind as a noble goal.)

Understanding the PointerList Class

The PointerList is a short, simple class. Its data is just two instance variables and one final static. The methods aren't quite that simple, but they come close.

PointerList Data Members

The PointerList has two protected data members: an integer array (pointers) and an int (length). If you don't override the default by adding an integer argument to the constructor, the pointers array is initialized to a final static, start_size, which I set to 256.

PointerList Public Members

The PointerList constructors are a very tidy, what-you-see-is-what-you-get pair:

```
PointerList() {

    this( start_size );
}

PointerList( int starting_size ) {

    pointers = new int[starting_size];
    length = 0;
}
```

The data access members are completely straightforward, except for the Exception thrown here:

```
public int getPointer( int index ) {

    // if the index is too large but still within the
    // allocated array space, Java won't throw an
    // exception

    if ( index >= length )
        throw new ArrayIndexOutOfBoundsException();

    return pointers[index];
}
```

Like a bad array access, any invalid index into the PointerList will be greeted by an ArrayIndexOutOfBoundsException. The one that Java would not catch is the case when the specified member exists in the pointers array, but hasn't actually been given a value yet—which is where getPointer( ) has to step in and throw its own exception.

The other interesting public method is add( ). It uses a try/catch pair to take advantage of Java's exception handling. It's pointless to check array bounds in Java. The run time will do that for you. Catching imposes no run-time cost when the exception isn't thrown. This is how to make Java work for you here:

```
public void add( int new_ptr ) {

    try {

    // just add it, most of the time
        pointers[length] = new_ptr;
        length++;
    }

    catch ( ArrayIndexOutOfBoundsException x ) {

    // grow by 50%
        int[] new_pointers = new int[
            ( pointers.length * 3 ) / 2];

        System.arraycopy( pointers, 0,
            new_pointers, 0, length );

        pointers = new_pointers;
```

```
                    // then add it
                        pointers[length] = new_ptr;
                        length++;
                }
        }
```

System.arraycopy( )

On an Intel chip, you can do the following:

```
    ES = dest_array;

    dest_index = 0;
    DS = source_array;

    source_index = 0;


    count = number_of_elements_to_move;
    while ( count > 0 ) {
        ES[dest_index] = DS[source_index];

        dest_index++;

        source_index++;
        count--;

    }
```

In Intel assembler, all those values go into registers and the while loop is exactly one instruction! The copy proceeds at about one value per clock cycle. (It was only 5 clocks per value on the original 8086.)

When you use arraycopy( ), you let the implementors take advantage of platform-specific capabilities, such as a 100MHz Pentium that lets you move about 100,000 integers in a millisecond. If you haven't begun using arraycopy( ) whenever it fits, today would be a good day to start.

There are no private methods or classes in PointerList.

The Complete PointerList Listing

So you can see all this *in situ*, Listing 3-2 is the complete class.

Listing 3-2:
PointerList.
java

```java
// PointerList.java -- growable array of integer pointers
// Copyright 1997, Martin L. Rinehart

// this code is completely documented in:
// _Java Database Development_, Martin Rinehart,
// Osborne/McGraw-Hill, 1997

/*
    Maintains an array of integers. Expands the array as
    needed.

    The add() method never throws an exception. It expands
    the array as needed.

    The getPointer() and setPointer() methods will throw
    an exception if the index is negative or too large.
*/

import java.io.*;

class PointerList {

// -------------------- data members --------------------

// there are no public data members

// protected data members:

    int length;

    int[] pointers;

// static data members

    // there are no public static data members
    // there are no private static data members
```

```
    // final static data member:

    final static int start_size = 256;

// -------------------- public methods --------------------

// constructors:

    PointerList() {

        this( start_size );
    }

    PointerList( int starting_size ) {

        pointers = new int[starting_size];
        length = 0;
    }

// data access getXxx() method:

    public int getPointer( int index ) {
        // if the index is too large but still within the
        // allocated array space, Java won't throw an
        // exception

        if ( index >= length )
            throw new ArrayIndexOutOfBoundsException();

        return pointers[index];
    }

// there are no data access isXxx() methods

// data access setXxx() method:

    public void setPointer( int index, int value ) {

        // if the index is too large but still within the
        // allocated array space, Java won't throw an
        // exception
```

```
            if ( index >= length ) throw new
                ArrayIndexOutOfBoundsException();

            pointers[index] = value;
    }

// public, class-specific methods:

    public void add( int new_ptr ) {

        try {

        // just add it, most of the time
            pointers[length] = new_ptr;
            length++;
        }

        catch ( ArrayIndexOutOfBoundsException x ) {

        // grow by 50%
            int[] new_pointers = new int[
                ( pointers.length * 3 ) / 2];
             System.arraycopy( pointers, 0,
                new_pointers, 0, length );

            pointers = new_pointers;

        // then add it
            pointers[length] = new_ptr;
            length++;
        }
    }

    public int length() {

        return length;
    }

// public, non-event overriding method:
```

```
    public String paramString() {

        return "length " + length;
    }

// there are no public, event-handling methods:

// ------------------ private methods ------------------
// there are no private methods

} // end of PointerList class

// there are no private classes in PointerList.java

// end of PointerList.java
```

The TextViewer Mainline

To use the TextViewer, just run it as an application. This short section documents main( ), which is the only member (data or code) of the TextViewer class.

TOUR

Understanding the TextViewer Class

I pointed out at the beginning of this chapter that the TextViewer is about 10 percent direct work and 90 percent error-handling code. Here we'll look at the full details. It won't take long.

It begins by creating and showing a FileDialog:

```
        FileDialog fd = new FileDialog( new Frame(),
            "Open Text File" );
        fd.show();
```

The user will pick a file, and it will be available through getFile( ), right? Well, mostly right. Figure 3-2 shows the user clicking the Cancel button in a FileDialog.

If the user cancels the dialog box without picking a file, the getFile( ) function returns null. In this application, that's the end of the program:

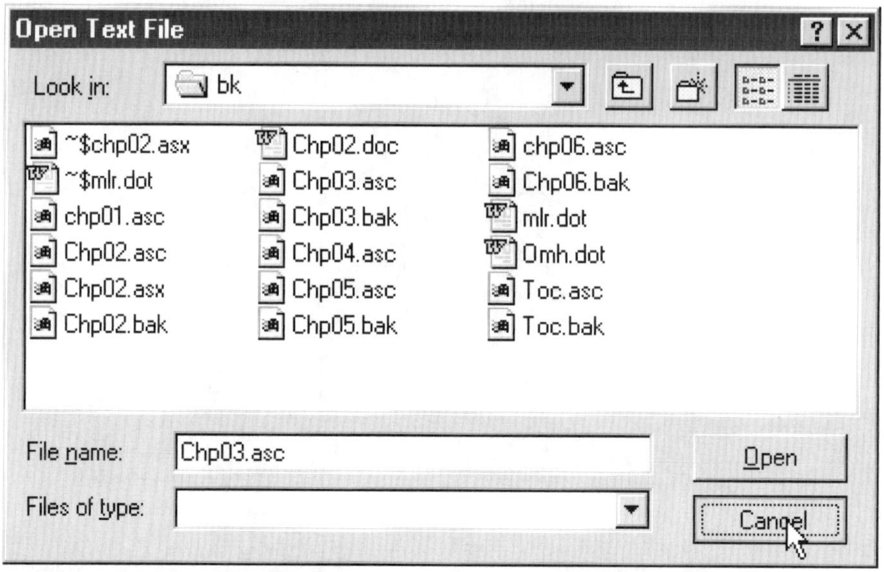

Figure 3-2. *FileDialog getting a Cancel, not a choice*

```
// exit if user cancels
if ( fd.getFile() == null )
    System.exit( 0 );
```

The next job is to use the filename to create a new TxtFile object. If successful, you'll have a new TxtFile in RAM from which you can then getString(i) to retrieve any line. This is all you need to do when you're successful:

```
TxtFile tf = new TxtFile( fd.getFile() );
```

Unfortunately, there are lots of reasons why the process might fail. This code suggests the most likely cause of error and holds the Java window open so that the user can see the error message:

```
if ( ! tf.readable ) {

    System.out.println(
        fd.getFile() + " is not a text file" );
```

```
System.out.println(
    "    press any key to continue" );

try{

    System.in.read();
    System.exit( 1 );
}
catch ( IOException ioe ) {;}
}
```

The "press any key..." message and the try/catch pause are completely unnecessary in Visual Cafe. You see the message in the Messages window. In Visual J++, on the other hand, the message is written to the DOS Java window, which closes when the application terminates. You won't see it at all without the pause.

More unfortunately, the pause logic doesn't really work in Visual Cafe. The Messages window will ask you to press any key, but you can't provide the keystroke to the application through that window.

On the other hand, the pause logic is correct when you run TextViewer outside of the Visual Cafe environment. Inside Visual Cafe, you can click the application end button, in lieu of pressing a key.

Finally, after all the possible errors have been handled, we're ready to launch a new ScrollWin, which lets us scroll through the text file. Here's that logic:

```
ScrollWin sw = new ScrollWin( tf, fd.getFile() );

sw.setEndApp( true );
sw.show();
```

Figure 3-3 shows the TextViewer looking at this bit of this chapter's original source file on my computer.

If it weren't for error handling, this would be the world's simplest program. Or at least it would be close.

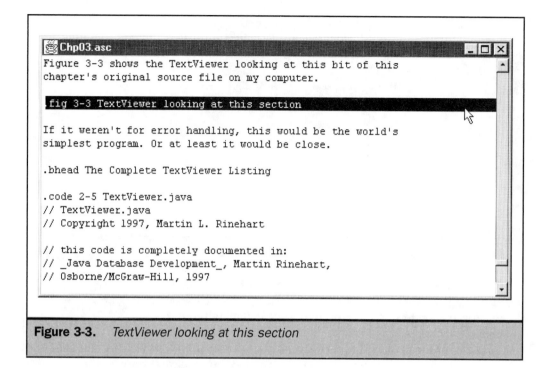

Figure 3-3. *TextViewer looking at this section*

The Complete TextViewer Listing

In case your library copy doesn't have the disk, Listing 3-3 shows the full TextViewer class.

Listing 3-3:
TextViewer.
java

```java
// TextViewer.java
// Copyright 1997, Martin L. Rinehart

// this code is completely documented in:
// _Java Database Development_, Martin Rinehart,
// Osborne/McGraw-Hill, 1997

import java.awt.*;
import java.io.*;

class TextViewer extends Frame {

    // -------------------- data members --------------------
```

```
// there are no data members

// -------------------- public methods --------------------

// main:
    public static void main( String[] args ) {

        FileDialog fd = new FileDialog( new Frame(),
            "Open Text File" );
        fd.show();

        // exit if user cancels
        if ( fd.getFile() == null )
            System.exit( 0 );

        TxtFile tf = new TxtFile( fd.getFile() );

        if ( ! tf.readable ) {

            System.out.println(
                fd.getFile() + " is not a text file" );
            System.out.println(
                "   press any key to continue" );

            try{

                System.in.read();
                System.exit( 1 );
            }
            catch ( IOException ioe ) {;}
        }


        // TxtFile implements Scrollable
        ScrollWin sw = new ScrollWin( tf, fd.getFile() );

        sw.setEndApp( true );
        sw.show();
    }
```

```
// there are no other methods
}

// end of TextViewer.java
```

Your Project

Displaying messages in the Java window (on a PC, it's a DOS window) isn't good practice. There's a MsgBox class coming up that pops up a message in a box, centered in the screen. This TextViewer will benefit from a MsgBox.

Your project, if you want to accept, is to scan forward to find the MsgBox, read its "Using" section, and then come back and use one here. (Hint: you'll find it in Chapter 6.)

Summary

I started this chapter by showing you how quick and easy it was to build a TextViewer application using our ScrollWin and TxtFile objects. I confessed, however, that the annoying details of error-handling code turned a five-minute job into over an hour's work. Of course, programming a TextViewer in an hour isn't too bad, is it?

After the introduction, we dove into the TxtFile class. It extends the BinFile, which we've left for the next chapter. The TxtFile is simple to use. You open one by passing the name as returned by the FileDialog object.

The actual name and path to a file are system dependent. If you use the FileDialog, the system dependencies are isolated and treated correctly on each platform, so your code is not system dependent.

The same calls that the Scrollable interface specifies will work for any other text file reader's purpose: getLast( ) and getString(i), where i is the line number you want to retrieve. This class works well for any application that needs to read text files.

In looking at the internals, you saw that the TxtFile works by reading the entire file into a byte array in RAM and then creating a list of pointers (integers actually) that make looking up a single line an almost instantaneous process. Its internal structure is as small and fast as possible for reading. You'll need to replace it with a linked list structure for read/write applications, such as text editing.

The PointerList class keeps a list of integers (which could be used as pointers into an array, as the TxtFile shows) that function like an array. Unlike an array, you don't have to dimension it in advance. You just add( ) as many integers as you like and access them through functions, not through subscripting.

Finally, we looked at the TextViewer mainline with all the annoying details in place. Although it's not quite as simple as the five-line version I showed at the outset, it's still a good example of using classes to encapsulate the details and letting your main program be simple.

Chapter 4

Using Binary Files

In the last chapter we used the BinFile object as a handy way of avoiding the actual trouble of dealing with Java's RandomAccessFile class. That class is the one that covers the details of each operating system's binary file I/O. In this chapter, we'll dive in at Java's lowest level. And—since binary files could be, for example, large database files—we'll read the pieces we need instead of reading the whole file in one big gulp.

By reading the file directly from disk, as needed, we get almost unlimited file size capacity. Actually, since our Scrollable interface uses an integer index in the getString( ) method, we're only able to scroll through 2Gb records. That's about three orders of magnitude past the top size I'd recommend for client database work. (A good DBMS costs a lot more than this book. But if you're dealing with multimillion-record databases, that's probably money well spent.)

We're going to have a FileViewer application as one output from this chapter's code. The FileViewer will attempt to open a file as a text file and display it as Chapter 3's TextViewer did. If the file is not a text file, it will display a hex and ASCII dump of the contents of the file.

Before we get to the FileViewer, we'll look at the BinFile class. We'll look closely at using it, and then for those whose requirements go deeper, we'll dive into all the details.

The BinFile uses supporting routines in the FDlib class. This provides very low-level code converting—for example, an integer to 8 hexadecimal digits.

Why this low-level code? You'll see in Chapter 5 that the ability to view a binary file is critical to understanding a "foreign" (that means, foreign to us—someone else designed it) data file structure. For example, Figure 4-1 shows our FileViewer peering into the details of the header of a DBF file, whose structure we'll look at in Chapter 6.

Should I throw in some enthusiastic remarks about just how easy it was to build the FileViewer? OK, I'll skip them. It would have been dead simple (the BinFile implements Scrollable, so a ScrollWin's all you need) except for all the annoying little details.

Is that what programming's coming to? Objects do the main job and we're left to deal with the annoying little details (ALD)? Maybe one of you brilliant young Edisons-to-be will invent a new paradigm that skips the ALD. *ALD-free* programming. That'll be a fantastic paradigm.

While we're waiting for ALD-free coding, let's get back to work, starting with the BinFile itself.

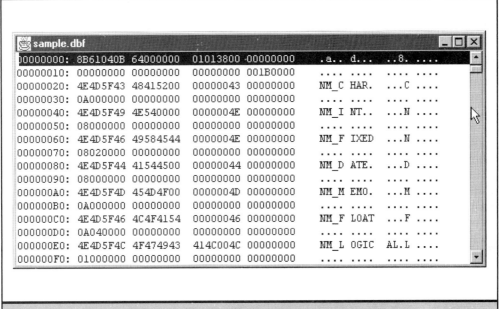

Figure 4-1.   *FileViewer examines a DBF file*

The BinFile Class

TOUR

In Chapter 3 we covered the use of the BinFile very briefly. Here the "Using" section expands on that base. If you are content to leave the output (conversions from bytes input to printable hex output) as a black box, read through "Understanding BinFile's File I/O." That will show you how to use binary files when you need to access specific binary file formats other than the DBF form we'll be using for our database work.

The section "Understanding the Other BinFile Methods" will show you how the bytes are converted to hex output, among other details. Some of you will find that familiar. If you've never actually converted bits to output (lots of you have always used supplied functions) you'll find this interesting.

The BinFile class is built on an included (not extended) RandomAccessFile. Where possible, it removes the lowest-level use of those files. Everything you do with a RandomAccessFile can throw an IOException. Compare these two code fragments:

```
// BinFile:

   BinFile bf = new BinFile( pathname );
   if ( !bf.isReadable() )

      . . .


// RandomAccessFile:

   RandomAccessFile raf;
   try {

      raf = new RandomAccessFile( pathname );
   }
   catch ( IOException ioe ) {


      . . .

   }
```

The BinFile's code is a lot more readable, although both do the same thing. BinFile's close( ) method eliminates the error handling entirely.

The BinFile does not provide cover for the read( ) and write( ) methods of the RandomAccessFile. The reason for this omission is that I couldn't think of any cover that simplified their use. As you saw with the TxtFile, the simple way to handle a particular file type is to extend the BinFile class and write whatever read and write functions you need. You'll see another example of this in Chapter 6 when we get to reading and writing database files.

Let's begin with a closer look at the public methods of the BinFile class.

Using the BinFile Class

The BinFile provides two handy constructors, several data access methods, and a very simple close( ). The constructors provide the open( ) functionality. That's where we'll begin.

Using BinFile's Constructors

You can open a new BinFile with one of these:

- BinFile(String pathname)
- BinFile(String pathname, String access)

These are identical to the constructors for the TxtFile, except that they'll open any file at all. (As you saw in the last chapter, the TxtFile is opened internally as a BinFile.) The pathname parameter provides the platform-specific location and name of a file. If you use the FileDialog's getFile( ) method, you'll have a platform-independent method of opening a file.

The access string can be either "r" for read, or "rw" for read and write. If you omit this parameter, "r" is the default.

Using BinFile's Data Access Methods

The data access methods are

- String getFileName( )
- int getLast( )
- String getMessage( )
- String getString(int index)
- boolean isReadable( )
- boolean isWriteable( )

The pathname string that is passed to the constructor is recorded as a data member of the BinFile object. The getFileName( ) method returns this string.

The getLast( ) public returns the highest index that you can provide to the getString( ) function. The getString( ) returns a group of 16 bytes printed in hex and as printable characters for the bytes that *are* printable characters. Calling getString(0) returns bytes 0 through 15, calling getString(1) returns bytes 16 through 31, and so on. Calling getString(getLast( )) returns a final group, probably less than a full 16 bytes.

The getMessage( ) function returns the message that is set on opening the file. You can use this to show the user the cause for a file not being readable.

The isReadable( ) and isWriteable( ) methods return the information they promise. If the file is not opened for "rw" access, isWriteable( ) will return false. My personal dumb mistake is to forget this, use just the pathname in the constructor, and then wonder why the file isn't writeable. I've done that so often that I'm tempted to change the default access to "rw". I've resisted that temptation. If you can't resist, don't blame me when you start seeing weird results when you inadvertently get multiple copies of the same file open for writing. Remember, Java doesn't understand file or record locking.

Using BinFile's Other Public Methods

The close( ) method closes the BinFile. Internally it uses a try and catch, which catches IOExceptions. The only file-closing problem I've seen in 30 years of programming is when I've tried to close a file that I didn't open. If your code doesn't immediately check isReadable( ) (or isWriteable( )) after calling the constructor, you could have a problem here. But I don't care, because you'll have worse problems before you get to close( ).

> Occasionally Visual J++ will have trouble opening a file for read access if it is open already. (For example, using FileViewer to view one of its own .class files can trigger this bug.) It opens an empty scroll window, shows nothing, and responds to nothing. Pressing CTRL-ALT-DEL will cure this problem.
>
> Opening a file multiple times for read access is theoretically not a problem. Funny things happen when theories meet Murphy's Law. Visual Cafe doesn't seem to have this problem.

The final public method is useMonospace( ), which returns true. I suggest that you change this return to false for at least one run. It's amusing, if not really useful.

Understanding BinFile's Data Members

The int bytes_read is used after a low-level read. The read( ) method of the RandomAccessFile returns the number of bytes it read, which may be different from the number of bytes you expected, signaling a file-read problem. It may also be short because you've reached the end of the file.

The int file_length records the length of the file, in bytes. The String path_name records the pathname value given to the constructor.

The int file_rows is specific to the Scrollable interface. For scrolling we'll be returning Strings, formatting the file as a series of 16-byte records. A 32-byte file will have two rows; a 33-byte file will have three rows. The int last_row is returned by getLast( ). It will be zero for files up to 16 bytes long, one for files up to 32 bytes, and so on.

The byte arrays inbuf and outbuf are used, respectively, to read the file and to format output for the getString( ) method.

The RandomAccessFile raf is the actual file object provided by the java.io package. The booleans readable and writeable record its status.

The final static int len_outbuf is a constant for the length of the byte array used to build the getString output.

Understanding BinFile's File I/O

This section discusses the methods that do the BinFile's file handling. It's separated from the coverage of the other methods because some of you will be interested in the file I/O but won't care about the other problems the BinFile addresses.

Of course, real code generally doesn't divide itself into categories that are completely neat. This is no exception. We'll meet some other details as we look at these functions. Code's like that.

We'll cover file opening, reading, and closing.

Opening the RandomAccessFile

Opening is done in the constructor. There are two constructors; the first just adds read-only access if you don't specify access:

```
BinFile( String pathname ) {
    this( pathname, "r" ); // default to read-only
}
```

The two-parameter constructor does the real work. It starts by saving the pathname you provide and by setting readable and writeable to false:

```
BinFile( String pathname, String access ) {

    path_name = pathname;
    readable = writeable = false;
```

Then it checks for a valid access code. Given a valid code, it calls the bin_open method to do the actual file opening. (We'll jump ahead to cover that private method next.) If the file is opened successfully, it creates the necessary input and output buffers:

```
if ( access.equals("r") || access.equals("rw") ) {

    if ( bin_open(access) ) {

        message = "OK";
        readable = true;
        writeable = access.equals("rw");

        inbuf = new byte[16];
        outbuf = new byte[len_outbuf];
    }
    else {
        message = "Could not open " + path_name;
    }

}
else {

    message = "Access '" + access + "' not valid";
}
```

If you ever see the "Access not valid" message, you've made a programming mistake. Now let's take a look at the bin_open( ) method.

Just as our BinFile constructor does the file opening, the RandomAccessFile's constructor does the lowest-level opening. It throws an IOException if it can't open the file. (We don't distinguish among the reasons: file doesn't exist, file locked by another process, access permission refused, or whatever.)

There are two nonobvious parts to this function. First, the RandomAccessFile's length( ) method returns a long. I don't want to deal with files that are 2Gb or larger (remember, we're programming client databases here, not data warehouses). That's why this function returns false if file_rows is too large.

You C programmers will recognize this line as dividing by 16, rounding up:

```
file_rows = (file_length+15) >> 4;
```

Remember that in Java the shift is arithmetic: if the high bit is set, the high bits are filled with ones. (The >>> operator fills the high bits with zeros, regardless of the original high bit.)

The other note is that almost anything you do with a RandomAccessFile can throw an IOException. That includes the call to raf.length( ), which is why there are two nested try and catch blocks.

With those remarks, this should all make sense:

```
    private boolean bin_open(String access) {

    // returns true on success

        try {
            raf = new RandomAccessFile( path_name, access );
            try {
                file_length = (int) raf.length();
                file_rows = (file_length+15) >> 4;
                if ( file_rows > 0x80000000L )
                    return false;

                // note: rows are 0 thru last_row
                last_row = ( (int) file_rows ) - 1;
                return true;
            }
            catch ( IOException ioe ) {
                return false;
            }
        }
        catch ( IOException ioe ) {
```

```
        return false;
    }
}
```

Reading the RandomAccessFile

There are several read( ) methods defined for the RandomAccessFile class. I find the byte array read the most useful:

```
// raf is an open RandomAccessFile

byte[] inbuf = new byte[100];

raf.read( inbuf ); // tries to read 100 bytes
```

It attempts to fill your buffer with bytes from the file. The file is initially opened at location zero. A file pointer is maintained that advances after a read to point to the next (unread) byte. You can use the seek( ) method to explicitly position this pointer.

You DOS programmers who are used to having seeks that work relative to the file's beginning, current, or end positions will need to adjust your thinking. Java seeks only from the beginning of the file, so you'll need to do a little extra coding if you want the other capabilities.

If you have never used direct access to random files, bear in mind that the seek( ) method simply tells the operating system where to start the read. It doesn't seek in the sense that a call in an indexed file to find the first person named "Smith" will trigger a seek.

The seek term was chosen originally because the operating system has to translate our file location into an actual physical disk location. For our purposes, the file is a set of contiguous bytes starting at byte zero and ending at length – 1. The operating system will deal with such problems as fragmented files, physical sector boundaries, and so on.

Again, for those who don't have direct bit-flipping experience, this multiplies by 16:

```
int file_loc = index << 4; // 16 bytes at a time

    // same as:

int file_loc = index * 16;
```

Some compilers are smart enough to generate shifts whenever you multiply by a power of two. Some aren't.

The reading is done in the getString( ) method. It computes the location (16 times the index), seek( )s to that location, and then reads inbuf, which is a byte array 16 bytes long. A catch block handles the possible errors.

Reading less than a full buffer is *not* an error that triggers an IOException. As this code shows, it's what you expect to happen at the end of the file.

The work of preparing the output string (which we'll cover in the next section) is done by the prepare_outbuf( ) routine. That routine is smart enough to work with a bytes_read number that's less than 16. This is the code:

```
public String getString( int index ) {

    // a string representing scrollable[index]
    // index is from zero through getLast()

    int file_loc = index << 4; // 16 bytes at a time
    try {
        raf.seek( file_loc );
        bytes_read = raf.read( inbuf );
    }
    catch (IOException ioe) {
        bytes_read = 0;
        message = "File read error";
    }

    prepare_outbuf( index );

    return new String(outbuf, 0);
}
```

Closing the RandomAccessFile

Even the RandomAccessFile's close( ) method can throw an IOException. As I mentioned earlier, this generally means that you're trying to close a file that you didn't open. I ignore that possibility.

```
public void close() {

    if ( raf != null ) {
        try { raf.close(); }
```

```
            catch( IOException ioe ) {}
    }
}
```

Understanding the Other BinFile Methods

The other methods include a number of uninteresting public methods and the private methods that prepare output from the input. We'll start with the one public method that deserves comment.

Understanding the Other Public BinFile Methods

Most of the other public methods are straightforward data access ones that simply return the appropriate protected data member. The getLast( ) method has an additional wrinkle. It attempts to do something reasonable even if you've called it for a file that isn't readable:

```
public int getLast() {

    // returns last item #
    return readable ? last_row : -1;
}
```

Understanding the Other Private BinFile Methods

To understand these private methods, take another look at the output line returned by getString( ). Figure 4-2 shows an example. On the left, the line starts with a location. It continues in the center with a hex dump of the 16 bytes it's reporting. On the right it finishes with an ASCII dump of the printable characters.

Before we go on, I'll take a look ahead. Wayne Ratliff invented the DBF file format working on an 8-bit microcomputer that featured a very primitive program, DEBUG.COM, which could dump data in this format. The format he chose for the DBF file dumps very nicely in this format, which is certainly not a coincidence.

Take a look at the sample database file shown in Figure 4-2. The header shows data about each field in the file. The first two lines are general data. These are followed by two lines for each field, beginning with the field's name. The field's type (C for character, numerics would be N, and so on) is also apparent.

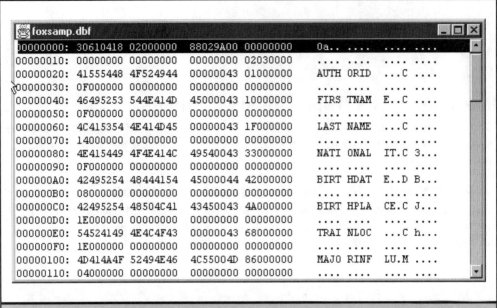

Figure 4-2.   *FileViewer looking at a DBF header*

If you have a PC, you'll find a program called DEBUG.COM or DEBUG.EXE somewhere in your directories. If you do, try this command sequence (stripped of the comments):

```
debug <DOSfilename> // load file in debugger
d                   // dump a screenful
d                   // dump another
q                   // quit DEBUG.
```

Of course, being able to click on a vertical scroll bar is, certainly, somewhat more convenient. Now let's return to the code.

To take these methods in logical order, prepare_outbuf( ) is the controller. It calls prep_loc( ) to write the location part of the output line, prep_hex( ) to prepare the hex dump, and prep_asc( ) for the ASCII dump. We'll take these functions in alphabetical order, as they appear in the file, so that someone using this section for reference won't be totally frustrated.

PREPARING THE ASCII DUMP   The library function byte2asc( ) returns the input byte if it represents a printable character. Otherwise, it returns a period indicating an unprintable character. (No one ever thought of a way to distinguish the real period from one that is a placeholder for an unprintable.)

This starts writing at position 50 in the output buffer. It writes the characters in groups of four, separated by spaces. It inserts an extra space between the second and third group of four. This is the code:

```
private void prep_asc() {

    int outloc = 50;

    for ( byte i = 0; i < bytes_read; i++ ) {
        outbuf[outloc] = FDlib.byte2asc( inbuf[i] );
        outloc++;

        if ( (i==3) || (i==11) ) {
            outbuf[outloc++] = (byte) ' ';
        }
        else if ( i == 7 ) {
            outbuf[outloc++] = (byte) ' ';
            outbuf[outloc++] = (byte) ' ';
        }
    }
}
```

PREPARING THE HEX DUMP   The hard work in preparing the hex dump is done by the library routine byte2hex( ). That takes an input byte and writes it as two hex digits. It places the output into a byte array starting at a location, both of which are passed as parameters.

This routine separates its output into 8-digit (4-byte) strings by inserting spaces. It adds an additional space between the second and third groups. This is the code:

```
private void prep_hex() {

    int outloc = 10;

    for ( byte i = 0; i < bytes_read; i++ ) {
        FDlib.byte2hex( inbuf[i], outbuf, outloc );
        outloc += 2;

        if ( (i == 3) || (i == 11) ) {
            outbuf[outloc++] = (byte) ' ';
```

```
        }
        else if ( i == 7 ) {
            outbuf[outloc++] = (byte) ' ';
            outbuf[outloc++] = (byte) ' ';
        }
    }
}
```

PREPARING THE LOCATION　　The location is shown as a hex location, which works well since we're showing groups of 0x10 bytes at a time. The hard work is done by the library routine int2hex( ). That routine accepts an input integer and writes it as 8 hex digits into a byte array at an output location specified in the calling arguments.

After the hex location is written, a colon and space are appended. This is the code:

```
private void prep_loc(int loc) {

    FDlib.int2hex( (loc<<4), outbuf, 0 );
    outbuf[8] = (byte) ':';
    outbuf[9] = (byte) ' ';
}
```

Is that cast to byte really necessary? Visual J++ insists that you include it. Visual Cafe is more open-minded about it. Reading the language specification, I get the idea that Visual J++ is right.

Of course, that could mean that the specification needs work. I don't see why the compiler needs me to explain that a space (numeric 32) needs a cast to fit into a byte. After all, 32 fits nicely in a byte, with two bits to spare.

This invites mistakes. For constant assignments, I'd have the compiler do them without a cast when the value fits, and generate an error when it doesn't. The cast is an annoyance when the value fits and will bury a mistake if the values don't fit.

PREPARING THE OUTPUT BUFFER　　The prepare_outbuf( ) routine is the controller that creates a full output buffer after the input buffer is read. It starts by clearing the output buffer to spaces. Then it creates the location, hex dump, and ASCII dump by calling the appropriate routines.

```
        private void prepare_outbuf(int loc) {

// outbuf gets location, then hex, then ascii

            for ( int i = 0; i < len_outbuf; i++ )
                outbuf[i] = (byte) ' ';

            prep_loc(loc);
            prep_hex();
            prep_asc();
        }
```

The Full BinFile Listing

Listing 4-1 shows the full BinFile.java file.

Listing 4-1:
BinFile.java

```
// BinFile.java -- Binary File class
// Copyright 1997, Martin L. Rinehart

// this code is completely documented in:
// _Java Database Development_, Martin Rinehart,
// Osborne/McGraw-Hill, 1997

/*
    handle any file as a binary, random access file
*/

import java.io.*;

class BinFile implements Scrollable {

// -------------------- data members --------------------

// there are no public data members

// protected data members:

    protected int bytes_read;

    protected int file_length;
    protected String path_name;
```

```
    protected int file_rows;

    protected byte[] inbuf;
    protected int last_row;

    protected String message;

    protected byte[] outbuf;

    protected RandomAccessFile raf;
    protected boolean readable;

     protected boolean writeable;

// static data members

    // there are no public static data members
    // there are no private static data members

    // final static data member:

    final static int len_outbuf = 82;

// ------------------- public methods -------------------

// constructors:

    BinFile( String pathname ) {
        this( pathname, "r" ); // default to read-only
    }

    BinFile( String pathname, String access ) {

        path_name = pathname;
        readable = writeable = false;

        if ( access.equals("r") || access.equals("rw") ) {

            if ( bin_open(access) ) {
```

```java
            message = "OK";
            readable = true;
            writeable = access.equals("rw");

            inbuf = new byte[16];
            outbuf = new byte[len_outbuf];
        }
        else {
            message = "Could not open " + path_name;
        }

    }
    else {

        message = "Access '" + access + "' not valid";
    }
}

// data access getXxx() methods:

    public String getFileName() {

        return path_name;
    }

    public int getLast() {

        // returns last item #
        return readable ? last_row : -1;
    }

    public String getMessage() {

        return message;
    }

    public String getString( int index ) {

        // a string representing scrollable[index]
        // index is from zero through getLast()
```

```java
        int file_loc = index << 4; // 16 bytes at a time
        try {
            raf.seek( file_loc );
            bytes_read = raf.read( inbuf );
        }
        catch (IOException ioe) {
            bytes_read = 0;
            message = "File read error";
        }

        prepare_outbuf( index );

        return new String(outbuf, 0);
    }

// data access isXxx() methods:

    public boolean isReadable() {

        return readable;
    }

    public boolean isWriteable() {

        return writeable;
    }

// there are no data access setXxx() methods

// public, class-specific methods:

    public void close() {

        if ( raf != null ) {
            try { raf.close(); }
            catch( IOException ioe ) {}
        }
    }

    public boolean useMonospace() {
```

```
            return true;
    }

// public, non-event overriding method:

    public String paramString() {

            return path_name + " read: " + readable
            + " write: " + writeable;
    }

// there are no public, event-handling methods

// ------------------ private methods ------------------

// private methods:

    private boolean bin_open(String access) {

    // returns true on success

        try {
            raf = new RandomAccessFile( path_name, access );
            try {
                file_length = (int) raf.length();
                file_rows = (file_length+15) >> 4;
                if ( file_rows > 0x80000000L )
                    return false;

                // note: rows are 0 thru last_row
                last_row = ( (int) file_rows ) - 1;
                return true;
            }
            catch ( IOException ioe ) {
                return false;
            }
        }
        catch ( IOException ioe ) {
            return false;
        }
    }
```

```java
private void prep_asc() {

    int outloc = 50;

    for ( byte i = 0; i < bytes_read; i++ ) {
        outbuf[outloc] = FDlib.byte2asc( inbuf[i] );
        outloc++;

        if ( (i==3) || (i==11) ) {
            outbuf[outloc++] = (byte) ' ';
        }
        else if ( i == 7 ) {
            outbuf[outloc++] = (byte) ' ';
            outbuf[outloc++] = (byte) ' ';
        }
    }
}

private void prep_hex() {

    int outloc = 10;

    for ( byte i = 0; i < bytes_read; i++ ) {
        FDlib.byte2hex( inbuf[i], outbuf, outloc );
        outloc += 2;

        if ( (i == 3) || (i == 11) ) {
            outbuf[outloc++] = (byte) ' ';
        }
        else if ( i == 7 ) {
            outbuf[outloc++] = (byte) ' ';
            outbuf[outloc++] = (byte) ' ';
        }
    }
}

private void prep_loc(int loc) {

    FDlib.int2hex( (loc<<4), outbuf, 0 );
    outbuf[8] = (byte) ':';
```

```
            outbuf[9] = (byte) ' ';
    }

    private void prepare_outbuf(int loc) {

// outbuf gets location, then hex, then ascii

        for ( int i = 0; i < len_outbuf; i++ )
            outbuf[i] = (byte) ' ';

        prep_loc(loc);
        prep_hex();
        prep_asc();
    }

} // end of BinFile class

// there are no private classes in BinFile.java

// end of BinFile.java
```

The FDlib Class

TOUR

This class can be safely ignored. On the other hand, if you've never done conversions, you'll see here how it's done.

The FDlib class is only a class because Java insists that we structure it that way. It's really just the library routines used in the file-dump process. BinFile can't live without these routines.

Understanding the FDlib Methods

There are four public functions in this class. The first three convert to hexadecimal and the last converts to ASCII.

The byte2hex( ) function underlies int2hex( ). In turn, the nibble2hexdigit( ) function underlies byte2hex. We'll look at these from the top level on down.

Converting an Integer to Hexadecimal

The int parameter, i, will be converted to eight hex digits in the output array out[ ], starting at index outloc in the output array.

It works from left to right, converting one byte at a time into two hex digits. To get the leftmost byte, the integer is shifted 24 bits to the right and then cast as a byte. The byte cast tells Java to drop all but the least-significant eight bits. The result is written to two bytes starting at out[outloc] by the byte2hex( ) function. Then the outloc is increased by two.

This pattern is repeated, except that each shift is for eight bits less than the previous shift, for the next three pairs of digits. This is the method:

```java
public static void int2hex( int i, byte[] out,
    int outloc) {

    byte2hex( (byte) (i>>24), out, outloc );
    outloc += 2;
    byte2hex( (byte) (i>>16), out, outloc );
    outloc += 2;
    byte2hex( (byte) (i>>8), out, outloc );
    outloc += 2;
    byte2hex( (byte) i, out, outloc );
}
```

Converting a Byte to Hexadecimal

The four-bit-wide halves of a byte are called *nibbles*. The byte2hex( ) function writes the left nibble to out[outloc], and the right nibble to out[outloc+1]. The actual conversion from nibble to hex digit is done by the nibble2hexdigit( ) function, which we'll cover next.

As in the int2hex process, the bits are shifted to move the left nibble into the right-side position to access the high bits. (It's traditional—if technically incorrect—to refer to the left and right nibbles. More accurately, refer to the "more-significant" and "less-significant" nibbles. After all, the ">>" operator shifts right, not toward less-significant bits, doesn't it?)

This is the function:

```java
public static void byte2hex( byte b, byte[] out,
    int outloc ) {

    out[outloc++] = nibble2hexdigit( (byte) (b >> 4) );
    out[outloc]   = nibble2hexdigit( (byte) b );
}
```

Converting a Nibble to a Hex Digit

The first step is to mask off the left digits. That leaves the byte with a value between 0 and 15. Values less than ten are returned by adding "0". This is independent of the actual value of "0"—it works for ASCII and any other output table, provided only that the digits in the table are in order.

The digits "A" through "F" are created, when the byte exceeds nine, by subtracting 10 from the byte and then adding "A". Again, this is independent of the output table, provided that the table has the capital letters in sequence, beginning with "A".

Remember that Java does all its arithmetic by promoting the smaller types to integer and then doing integer math. That's why you need to cast byte expressions back to byte if you want bytes.

This is the code:

```java
public static byte nibble2hexdigit( byte b ) {

    b &= 0x0F;

    if ( b < 10 )
        return (byte) ('0' + b);

    return (byte) ('A' + b - 10);
}
```

Converting a Byte to ASCII

This function doesn't really do a conversion. It just masks the unprintable values by replacing them with periods. The printable byte values are left unchanged.

This is the function:

```java
public static byte byte2asc( byte b ) {

    if ( (b < 32) || (b > 127) )
        return (byte) '.';

    else return b;
}
```

Note that this version treats bytes above 127 as unprintable. In our TxtFile we treated high-bit bytes as text. Again, this is a subjective matter. My opinion here is based on the likelihood that these bytes in a binary file represent code, binary numbers, or other nontext data.

The Full FDlib Listing

Listing 4-2 shows the full FDlib.java file.

Listing 4-2:
FDlib.java

```java
// FDlib.java -- Library routines for File Dump utility
// Copyright 1997, Martin L. Rinehart


// this code is completely documented in:
// _Java Database Development_, Martin Rinehart,
// Osborne/McGraw-Hill, 1997

/*
    Conversions to hexadecimal and ASCII
*/

public class FDlib {

// FDlib has four public, static methods:

    public static void int2hex( int i, byte[] out,
        int outloc) {

        byte2hex( (byte) (i>>24), out, outloc );
        outloc += 2;
        byte2hex( (byte) (i>>16), out, outloc );
        outloc += 2;
        byte2hex( (byte) (i>>8), out, outloc );
        outloc += 2;
        byte2hex( (byte) i, out, outloc );
    }

    public static void byte2hex( byte b, byte[] out,
        int outloc ) {

        out[outloc++] = nibble2hexdigit( (byte) (b >> 4) );
        out[outloc]   = nibble2hexdigit( (byte) b );
    }
```

```
public static byte nibble2hexdigit( byte b ) {

    b &= 0x0F;

    if ( b < 10 ) return (byte) ('0' + b);
    return (byte) ('A' + b - 10);
}

public static byte byte2asc( byte b ) {

    if ( (b < 32) || (b > 127) )
        return (byte) '.';
    else
        return b;
    }
}

// end of FDlib.java
```

The FileViewer Class

The FileViewer is a superset of the TextViewer. Since it's not significantly larger, you can use it to supersede the TextViewer in your toolkit. It works just like the TextViewer if you use it to open a text file. Instead of sending an error message, however, it opens nontext files as binary files that it shows in our combined hex and ASCII dump format.

There's no "Using" section here since this is an application mainline. Everyone should at least skim the "Understanding" section since it shows you how to handle the ALD (annoying little details) that exists for TxtFile and BinFile objects.

Figure 4-3 shows FileViewer looking at its own source in FileViewer.java, and Figure 4-4 shows the very different result I got when I opened FileViewer.class.

Once again, you can see Sun's CAFEBABE signature when you look at the hex dump of a class file. It's part of the Java Virtual Machine specification. (Need a short break? Make up some good puns based on CAFEBABE. Extra credit for full limericks.)

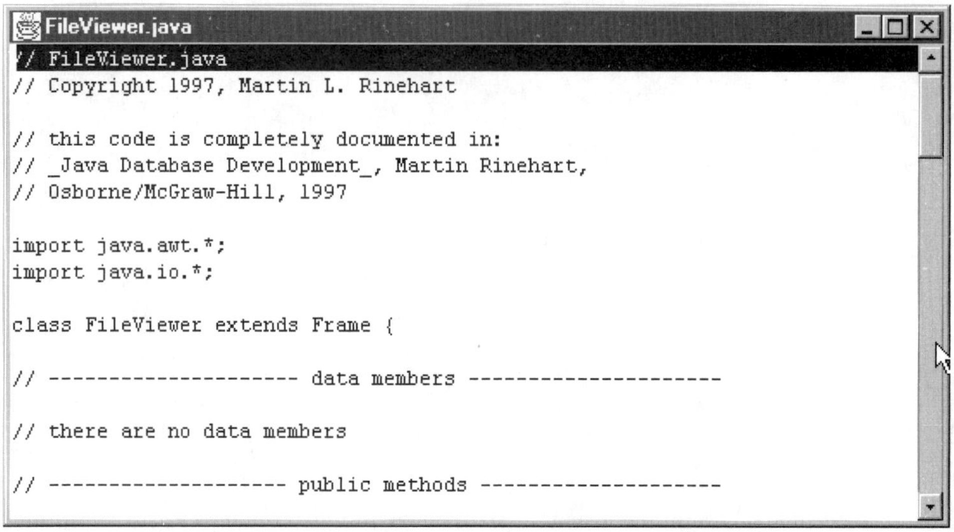

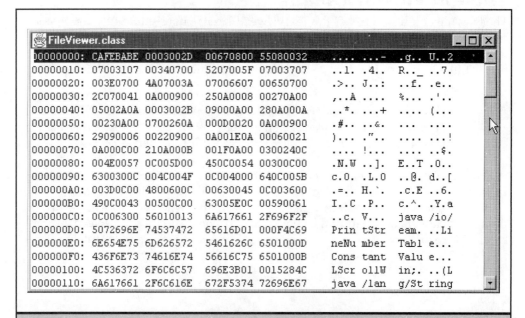

Figure 4-3. FileViewer reading FileViewer.java source code

Figure 4-4. FileViewer reading FileViewer.java executable code

Understanding the FileViewer

Like the TextViewer, the FileViewer has nothing but a main( ) routine. Also like the TextViewer, it begins by launching a FileDialog and exiting immediately if the user cancels out:

```
FileDialog fd = new FileDialog( new Frame(),
    "Open File" );
fd.show();

// exit if user cancels
if ( fd.getFile() == null )
    System.exit( 0 );
```

Next the FileViewer continues by attempting to open the file as a text file. If the TxtFile object is not readable, then it makes another try, this time opening it as a binary file. Only if this fails (file locked by another or access permission denied, perhaps) it gives up and issues an error message:

```
TxtFile tf = new TxtFile( fd.getFile() );

BinFile bf = null;
if ( ! tf.readable ) {

    bf = new BinFile( fd.getFile() );

    if ( ! bf.readable ) {

      System.out.println(
          "   press any key to continue" );

      try{

          System.in.read();
          System.exit( 1 );
        }
      catch ( IOException ioe ) {;}
    }
}
```

With the file successfully opened, it creates a ScrollWin and launches the file in the ScrollWin. This is the code:

```
ScrollWin sw;

 // TxtFile and BinFile implement Scrollable
 if ( tf.readable ) {

     sw = new ScrollWin( tf, fd.getFile() );
 }
 else
     sw = new ScrollWin( bf, fd.getFile() );

 sw.setEndApp( true );
 sw.resize( 550, 300 );
 sw.show();
```

Do you like the way that two types of objects are used in the calls to the ScrollWin constructor? While the TxtFile extends the BinFile, it's not inheritance that makes this possible. This is possible because they are both Scrollable.

Of course, if a BinFile is Scrollable, anything that extends it is also Scrollable, since it has the necessary methods. But the TxtFile has its own implementation of the Scrollable interface. (You really wouldn't like your text files dumped in hex would you? That wouldn't be right for most uses.)

The Full FileViewer Listing

Listing 4-3 shows the full FileViewer.java file.

Listing 4-3:
FileViewer.java

```
// FileViewer.java
// Copyright 1997, Martin L. Rinehart

// this code is completely documented in:
// _Java Database Development_, Martin Rinehart,
// Osborne/McGraw-Hill, 1997

import java.awt.*;
import java.io.*;

class FileViewer extends Frame {

    // -------------------- data members --------------------
```

```java
// there are no data members

// -------------------- public methods --------------------

// main:
    public static void main( String[] args ) {

        FileDialog fd = new FileDialog( new Frame(),
            "Open File" );
        fd.show();

        // exit if user cancels
        if ( fd.getFile() == null )
            System.exit( 0 );

        TxtFile tf = new TxtFile( fd.getFile() );

        BinFile bf = null;
        if ( ! tf.readable ) {

            bf = new BinFile( fd.getFile() );

            if ( ! bf.readable ) {

                System.out.println(
                    "   press any key to continue" );

                try{

                    System.in.read();
                    System.exit( 1 );
                }
                catch ( IOException ioe ) {;}
            }
        }

        ScrollWin sw;

        // TxtFile and BinFile implement Scrollable
        if ( tf.readable ) {
```

```
                        sw = new ScrollWin( tf, fd.getFile() );
                }
                else
                    sw = new ScrollWin( bf, fd.getFile() );

                sw.setEndApp( true );
                sw.resize( 550, 300 );
                 sw.show();
            }

    // there are no other methods
    }

    // end of FileViewer.java
```

Your Project

If you got the MsgBox to replace the error message in Chapter 3's project, you can repeat that here. (That's just a few lines of code to copy.)

The real project here is to make an alternate BinFile dumper that is useful for tracing down text constants in executables, for example. I'd like it to print 80-byte lines with the printables displayed and the nonprintables replaced by periods. (Hint: Extend BinFile and override getLast( ) and getString( ). Not counting comments and whitespace, this shouldn't run more than a couple of dozen lines.)

When you get it working, throw out your old TextViewer and make a copy of FileViewer that you call TextViewer. Then change the new TextViewer so that it uses your text-oriented binary file reader.

Summary

In this chapter we've taken the BinFile from a black box that we used to build TxtFile and put it in a clear box, where we can see and understand the inner workings.

We started by taking a look at using the BinFile. You'd already done this in Chapter 3, when we used a BinFile to build the TxtFile. The general use of the BinFile is to extend it, let it provide file-opening and -closing services, and then write class-specific read and write routines.

We saw when we looked at the BinFile's use of the underlying RandomAccessFile object, that all input and output, even requesting an open file's length, can throw an IOException, so you have to embed it in try and catch blocks. Otherwise, the file I/O operations are what you would expect.

The other BinFile methods support the Scrollable interface and the construction of the dump format. The latter job takes more code than the former.

The FDlib class provides low-level library methods for preparing the file-dump format. These include conversions of integers, bytes, and nibbles to hexadecimal digits, as well as converting bytes to ASCII.

Finally, we took a look at the FileViewer application. As with the TextViewer before it, once the classes it needed were available, building a TextViewer was just a matter of building with those classes and then handling all the annoying little details (ALD).

We've been working steadily toward the DBF class, which handles the database file binary format. To get prepared, we've gone through text files and now binary files. In Chapter 5, we're going to need to take a break to look at my personal version of the String class, the MRString. You'll see that this functions as an extended version of String, which is a final class that can't be extended.

Chapter 5

A New String Class

In Chapter 3 we used text files. In Chapter 4 we met the generic binary file. Next on our list is the database file, which we'll discuss in Chapter 6. The DBF class (from "database file" and the PC file format with the DBF extension) makes heavy use of *MRString* objects, which we'll cover here.

What's an MRString? It's my own version of the String class. It does almost everything the String class does, and it adds a great deal. For example, the String doesn't have functions for inserting, deleting, and replacing characters. MRStrings do this and more.

In fact, MRStrings are at their best when I come across something they don't do. I recently found a need for making the first, and only the first, character of a string uppercase. I had toUpper( ) and toLower( ) methods. Now I've got toUlower( ).

Java's Strings certainly have their advantages, but when you meet something they don't do, you've got another annoying little detail to code. MRStrings don't have ALDs. Their functionality grows to meet their requirements.

You'll see when we get to DBFs that the MRString objects become as common as String objects. I've been writing code for too long to want to use something just because I wrote it. I use MRStrings because they more than pay their way.

However, like everything else in code, MRStrings are a compromise. I don't use them all the time and I hope you won't, either. We'll start by looking at their strengths and weaknesses.

Evaluating the MRString Class

I think MRStrings are great. They have every capability I need. I define *need* this way: if I want a function badly enough to code and test it, then I need it. By that definition, MRStrings have every function I need.

Of course, nothing is without a price. Drop an MRString into an applet and you've just spent over 10K in the executable. Using a String is a lot cheaper. Let's look more closely at the advantages and disadvantages before we get on to the code.

The Advantages of MRStrings

Let's consider some of the things you can do with MRStrings that you can't do with Strings, starting with creating them. You can make an MRString from a single byte. You can make an MRString from another MRString, specifying the width. (That can be padded to a longer size, and it can be truncated to a shorter size.) You can build an MRString from another MRString, specifying starting and ending locations, too.

You can delete characters in an MRString—either a single character or any number of characters. Similarly, you can insert one or more characters into an MRString, at either end or in the middle.

You can get the last character, or you can get the location of the last nonblank character. Speaking of nonblanks, you can pad an MRString to any length, on the left or on the right.

The nextWord( ) and prevWord( ) methods return the location of the start of the next word to the right or left of a selected point. These are invaluable when you're doing any text editing.

Additionally, the MRString class sports a selection of class statics that can be applied to Strings and chars. These include isAlpha( ), isDigit( ), isLower( ), isUpper( ), and so on. For example, asking if a String isDigits( ) tells you if a String can be interpreted as a positive integer.

More important than any of these functions is the one I'm going to find necessary tomorrow. Whatever it is, the MRString will have that capability. It will have it tomorrow. It's already got everything I need today.

The Disadvantages of MRStrings

I really should have mentioned performance in the section on the advantages of MRStrings, but I'll bet many of you were expecting to see it here. The MRString uses System.arraycopy( ) for all of the heavy lifting. I doubt you'll find the MRString to be much slower than the native String.

There are some disadvantages, though. First, the MRString class adds over 10K to the executable. This is a small price in an application, but should be seriously considered for applet programming. There's nothing in the MRString class that you can't do with Strings and a little programming.

There are also disadvantages inherent in the String class's very privileged position in the Java language. The equal operator and the plus (concatenation) operator accept String objects. Consider these pairs:

```
String foo = "contents of foo";
MRString foo = new MRString( "contents of foo" );

foo = foo + "!";            // String
foo = foo.concat( "!" );    // MRString
```

The Java syntax that treats Strings as a special class certainly helps make them more convenient. These conveniences aren't available to any other class.

Finally, some people think the name MRString isn't well chosen. Mickey Rooney, Mary Roberts, and I don't agree. On the other hand, if you prefer FFStrings, Fred Friendly, we won't argue with your choice. That's the reason text editors can search and replace.

Using MRStrings Effectively

I didn't build MRStrings because I disagreed with the design choices Sun's Java team made. I agree with them wholeheartedly. Small is good.

If you want to see a language that includes every function that anyone ever thought might be useful, consider Visual Basic. It's about ten times the size of Java. It costs 3MB to launch a "Hello, world!" window. (I should add that Visual Basic is still my product of choice when I want to write a Windows-specific application.)

The U. S. government got tired of systems written in different languages, so they designed Ada. It does absolutely everything the government (millions of employees!) needs to do. To ensure its widespread adoption, Washington made its use mandatory on all government projects. In spite of that multibillion-dollar backing, Ada still didn't catch on. Small is good.

If you are programming an applet, think carefully before you take an MRString approach. If you are programming an application, you'll probably find the MRString approach almost universally appealing.

Just be sure to take one simple precaution. Start by commenting out every method in the class. Then uncomment methods as you find you need them. The result will be a class with no waste.

Constructing MRStrings

TOUR

We're going to dive into the MRString class in depth here. If you can't wait to get on to the DBF class in the next chapter, go to the source listing and study the methods. They are listed in a long comment at the top of the MRString.java file. For any that you don't understand, refer back to this documentation.

A word of warning: Many MRString methods work in the original position. If you call foo.toUpper( ), the contents of foo will be converted to uppercase. It's easy to hide this effect if you use these methods on the right side of an assignment statement. Always read the code (most methods are very short) before using an MRString method.

Normally, we begin by looking at a class's data members. We'll dispose of that right now. MRStrings have a char array called chars and an integer length called length. Nothing else. The only point to note is that chars.length may exceed the value of length. When you truncate an MRString on the right, for example, the value of length is reset, without changing the char array. The value of chars.length tells you how much room you have. The length value tells you how much is in use.

Now let's go on to the code.

In each of the code sections, starting here with constructors, we'll begin with a section on using the methods, and then we'll look at the code in an "Understanding" section. Decide for yourself whether the "Understanding" is useful for your immediate requirements. You may find it more helpful to postpone the detailed look at the code until you have an immediate need for a particular method.

You will find that much of the code is very short and easy to understand.

Using the MRString Constructors

MRStrings have a richer set of constructors than the String class. These are your choices:

- MRString(byte b)
- MRString(byte[ ] b)
- MRString(char c)
- MRString(int width)
- MRString(String s)
- MRString(MRString m)
- MRString(MRString m, int width)
- MRString(MRString m, int from, int to)

The last three constructors build an MRString starting with another MRString. The first of these simply copies the MRString.

The next-to-last constructor uses the width argument to create an MRString that is not necessarily the same size as the MRString passed to the constructor. It could be truncated (the right is chopped off) or expanded (the right is zero-filled).

The final constructor lets you build an MRString from a substring of another MRString. All the MRString methods that have from and to arguments are like String methods with from and to arguments. The from argument is the starting location and to is one past the end location. If you haven't found this out for yourself yet, I'll applaud the Java design decision on this one. It's strange, but it works beautifully.

Understanding the MRString Constructors

The MRString constructors all create the array chars and assign the length. Most of them also fill the chars array with initial data.

Constructing an MRString from a Byte

This constructor takes a single byte and uses it to form a one-char MRString. (Pop quiz for Javameisters: Can you create a String from a byte? Try it.)

```
MRString( byte b ) {

    chars = new char[1];
    length = 1;
    chars[0] = (char) b;
}
```

Constructing an MRString from an Array of Bytes

This constructor cannot take advantage of the System.arraycopy( ) method. Remember that the char is a two-byte unicode char.

```
MRString( byte[] b ) {

    chars = new char[b.length];
    length = b.length;

    for ( int i = 0 ; i < length ; i++ )
        chars[i] = (char) b[i];
}
```

Constructing an MRString from a Char

This constructor also creates a one-character-long MRString.

```
MRString( char c ) {

    chars = new char[1];
    chars[0] = c;
    length = 1;
}
```

Constructing an MRString from an Integer

In this constructor, the int specifies the width of the MRString. Bear in mind that Java will initialize all the chars to zero.

```
MRString( int i ) {
    chars = new char[i];
    length = I;
}
```

Constructing an MRString from a String

This constructor initializes a new MRString with the contents of a String object. It uses the String's getChars( ) function, which we presume is as well coded as the System.arraycopy( ) method (or is, in fact, built on that method).

Note that a null reference is converted to a null string. These are, of course, very different.

```
MRString( String s ) {

    if ( s == null )
        s = "";

    chars = new char[s.length()];
    s.getChars( 0, s.length(), chars, 0 );
    length = s.length();
}
```

Constructing an MRString from an MRString

This is functionally equivalent to building an MRString from a String. I didn't include this constructor when I first wrote the class. It became apparent in practice that this was, in fact, a very useful tool.

```
MRString( MRString m ) {

    if ( m == null )
        m = new MRString( "" );

    chars = new char[m.length];
    length = m.length;

    System.arraycopy( m.chars, 0, chars, 0,
        length );
}
```

Constructing an MRString from an MRString and a Width

Note that this constructor also treats a null reference as a null string. If you study the conditional in the System.arraycopy( ) argument, you see how this will either truncate or expand the MRString.

```
MRString( MRString m, int width ) {

    chars = new char[width];
    length = width;

    if ( m != null )
        System.arraycopy( m.chars, 0, chars, 0,
```

```
                          width < m.length ? width : m.length );
    }
```

Constructing an MRString from an MRString and a Range

This constructor lets you make a new MRString from a substring. The substring( )
method uses this constructor. In turn, this constructor is a customer for the MRString
constructor that takes a single int argument.

```
    MRString( MRString m, int from, int to ) {

        // from "from" to, but not including, "to"

        if ( m == null )
            m = new MRString( to - 1 );

        length = to - from;
        chars = new char[length];

        System.arraycopy( m.chars, from, chars, 0, length );
    }
```

MRString Public Methods

In most classes we'll start with the data access methods. There is only one in
MRString, getChars( ). As you probably guessed, it returns the array of chars. To be
consistent with the String class, the length value is returned by length( ), not
getLength( ).

There are too many class-specific public methods for me to remember, even though
I wrote them all. For easy reference, I've listed them in a comment at the top
of the file.

This section will introduce and explain each of the methods.

Using the MRString Public Methods

We'll take these in alphabetical order, with comments directing you to related
functions when necessary.

MRString charAt

There is one charAt( ) method:

```
    public MRString charAt( int loc )
```

It returns the char at the specified location.

MRString concat

There are eight or ten concat functions, including these:

```
public MRString concat( MRString m )
public MRString concat( String s )
public MRString concat( Object o )
public MRString concat( byte b )
public MRString concat( int i )
public MRString concat( long l )
public MRString concat( boolean b )
public MRString concat( double d )
```

Like the String concatenation operation, these convert the argument to a readable form and add it as additional characters to the MRString. Objects are converted using their toString( ) methods.

The two additional forms not listed here exist in fact, but not in code: short and float. If you use a short, it will be promoted to int and the int form will be called. Similarly, a float will promote to double.

MRString copy

This method returns a copy of the MRString:

```
public MRString copy()
```

This is not an exact copy. The length of the new MRString will equal the length of its chars array. This might not be true for the source MRString.

MRString delete

The delete( ) methods let you delete a single character or a group of characters:

```
public MRString delete( int where )
public MRString delete( int where, int how_long )
```

boolean endsWith

These two methods return true if the MRString's right side matches the value of the argument:

```
public boolean endsWith( String s );
public boolean endsWith( MRString m );
```

int indexOf

The indexOf( ) methods parallel the String's methods of the same name:

```
public int indexOf( int ch )
public int indexOf( int ch, int fromIndex )
```

They return the location of the first occurrence of the int ch, cast to char. The first form searches from zero while the second searches from the specified location. Negative one is returned if ch is not found.

MRString insert

These insert( ) methods are available:

```
public MRString insert( MRString m, int where )
public MRString insert( char c, int where )
public MRString insert( int i, int where )
public MRString insert( String s, int where )
```

In each case, the value of the where argument can range from 0 through the length of the string. If it is equal to length, a concatenation is performed. Otherwise, the other argument is converted to a string form and inserted into chars.

int intValue

If the MRString contains all digits, intValue( ) returns its value interpreted as a decimal integer. This is the form:

```
public int intValue()
```

You should call and get a true value from isDigits( ) before you use intValue( ). Strings that are not all digits will return the intValue through the first nondigit. Strings that don't start with a digit will return 0.

Leading and trailing whitespace is trimmed before the evaluation.

char lastChar

This method returns the single char at the end of the MRString:

```
public char lastChar()
```

An exception is thrown if the length of the string is 0.

int lastNonblankLoc

This method returns the index of the last nonwhitespace character:

```
public int lastNonblankLoc()
```

Negative one is returned when the MRString is null or all whitespace.

MRString left

This method returns a new MRString with the specified number of characters starting from the left.

```
public MRString left( int len )
```

If len exceeds the length of the original MRString, the new MRString is zero-filled on the right.

MRString leftPadTo

This method blank-pads an MRString on the left:

```
public MRString leftPadTo( int len );
```

It pads the MRString itself. If len is less than the length of the MRString, the MRString is truncated, not padded.

A reference to itself is returned.

int length

This is the method that might be known as getLength( ):

```
public int length()
```

The name was chosen to be consistent with the String class.

int nextWord

This method returns the location of the start of the next word in an MRString:

```
public int nextWord( int from )
```

A *word* is defined as any contiguous group of nonwhitespace characters. With its companion prevWord( ), this method is used, for example, to respond appropriately to CTRL-LEFT ARROW or CTRL-RIGHT ARROW presses.

More precisely, if the from location is nonwhite, a pointer is advanced until a whitespace character is reached. Then (or starting here, if the original character was whitespace) the pointer is advanced until a nonwhite character is found. The location of that character is returned. If this algorithm does not find a character, the length of the MRString is returned.

MRString padTo

These padTo( ) methods let you pad an MRString with blanks or any character out to a specified length.

```
public MRString padTo( int width )
public MRString padTo( int width, char pad_char )
```

The padding is done on the string itself. A reference to itself is returned.

If the width is equal to the original length, the MRString is unchanged. If the width is less than the original length, the MRString is truncated on the right.

If the width is greater than the original MRString's length, new characters are added on the right, filled with the specified padding character. A blank is used if the pad_char argument is omitted.

int prevWord

The prevWord( ) function is a companion to nextWord( ). This is its form:

```
public int prevWord( int from )
```

The prevWord( ) method returns the location of a word beginning to the left of the index argument. If no word begins to the left, zero is returned.

A word is defined as any contiguous group of nonwhite characters.

This is the algorithm: A character is defined as the start of a word if it is nonwhite and it is at location zero or the character to its left is whitespace. If the from index is the start of a word, decrement it. If the from index is a whitespace character, decrement the index until a nonwhitespace character is reached. Then continue decrementing the index until a word-starting character is found.

MRString replace

These methods let you replace an individual character in an MRString:

```
public MRString replace( int where, char c )
public MRString replace( int where, int i )
```

If the second (replacement character) argument is an int, it is cast to char.

A word of warning here: No exception is thrown if the where argument is larger than length – 1 if the chars array happens to be sufficiently larger than length.

MRString right

The right( ) method lets you return an MRString formed from a specified length of the right side of an existing MRString:

```
public MRString right( int len )
```

An exception will be thrown if the len argument is larger than the length of the source MRString.

MRString substring

These substring( ) methods match the substring( ) methods of the String class:

```
public MRString substring( int from )
public MRString substring( int from, int to )
```

If the to argument is omitted, the substring starts at the from index and continues for the length of the string. If to is supplied, the substring starts at from and continues to the character preceding to.

MRString toLower

This method replaces any uppercase alphabetic characters in the MRString with equivalent lowercase characters:

```
public MRString toLower()
```

Note that the replacement is done in the MRString itself and a reference to itself is returned.

Only characters in the range "A" to "Z" are replaced. This will miss other unicode characters in some national alphabets.

MRString toUpper

This method replaces any lowercase alphabetic characters in the MRString with equivalent uppercase characters:

```
public MRString toUpper()
```

Note that the replacement is done in the MRString itself and a reference to itself is returned.

Only characters in the range "a" to "z" are replaced. This will miss other unicode characters in some national alphabets.

MRString trim

This method performs the same service, trimming leading and trailing whitespace, as the String.trim( ) method:

```
public MRString trim()
```

The trim is performed on the MRString itself. The method returns a reference to itself.

MRString trimLeft

These methods trim from the left of an MRString:

```
public MRString trimLeft()
public MRString trimLeft( int nchars )
```

The first method trims leading whitespace; the second trims the specified number of characters. If supplied, the nchars argument cannot exceed the length of the MRString.

The trim is performed on the MRString itself. The method returns a reference to itself.

MRString trimRight

These methods trim from the right of an MRString:

```
public MRString trimRight()
public MRString trimRight( int nchars )
```

The first method trims trailing whitespace; the second trims the specified number of characters. If supplied, the nchars argument cannot exceed the length of the MRString. The trim is performed on the MRString itself. The method returns a reference to itself.

Understanding the MRString Public Methods

This section will include only some of the methods, because in many cases, comments would be superfluous. Consider charAt as an example:

```
public char charAt( int loc ) {

        return chars[loc];
}
```

There's really not a lot to add, is there?

Here I'll mention just the methods that seem to profit from further explanation.

Using System.arraycopy

If you haven't started using System.arraycopy whenever possible, today would be a good day to start. The syntax is

```
System.arraycopy( source array, source start,
    dest array, dest start, length )
```

You'll see arraycopy( ) used very often here, since it's probably the best way to move data around.

MRString concat(MRString m)

This concat( ) routine is typical of those that work on the MRString itself, not on a copy. It begins by creating a new char array. Then it uses arraycopy( ) to move the chars from the original MRString starting at zero, and then another arraycopy( ) to add in the chars from the argument MRString.

This is the code:

```
public MRString concat( MRString m ) {

    int new_len = length + m.length();
    char[] mc = new char[new_len];

    System.arraycopy( chars, 0, mc, 0, length );
    System.arraycopy( m.chars, 0, mc, length,
        m.length );

    chars = mc;
    length = new_len;

    return this;
}
```

Returning a reference to itself makes it possible to chain these in expressions, such as:

```
mrs.concat( "foo" ).concat("bar");
```

(From here on the variable mrs will be used as an unspecified MRString object reference.)

MRString concat(byte b)

The standard Java display of a byte is as a hex value. That annoys me when the byte is a printable character. This is my treatment:

```
public MRString concat( byte b ) {

    if ( b > ' ' )
        return concat( "'" + b + "'" );
    else
        return concat( "0x" + b );
}
```

MRString concat(long l)

I've used existing code whenever possible to keep the size of this class down. (As you've noticed, it's not small.) This is a good example:

```
public MRString concat( long l ) {

    return concat( new Long(l) );
}
```

The concat(Object) concatenates the toString( ) of the Object. By creating a Long object, I save the trouble of converting the long value to a string since Long.toString( ) will do that for us.

MRString delete

The delete( ) methods are a good example of the use of default values to get more flexibility at very little cost in code. The first delete just calls the second with an added parameter:

```
public MRString delete( int where ) {

    return delete( where, 1 );
}

public MRString delete( int where, int how_long ) {

    if ( how_long > 0 )
        System.arraycopy( chars, where + how_long,
            chars, where, length - where - how_long );

    length = length - how_long;

    return this;
}
```

boolean endsWith(MRString m)

This routine is used in code like this:

```
// fd is a FileDialog, checked for non-null

MRString pathname = new MRString( fd.getFile() );

if ( pathname.endsWith(".DBF") )
    // open as database file
```

The opening conditional checks to see if the length of the ending is greater than the length of the MRString, in which case there definitely isn't a match.

If that didn't apply, the rest of the routine looks for m.chars[i] (the end pattern) matching chars[i] (the MRString). This is the code:

```
public boolean endsWith( MRString m ) {

    if ( m.length > length )
        return false;

    int j = length - m.length;
    for ( int i = 0 ; i < m.length ; i++ ) {

        if ( m.chars[i] != chars[j] )
            return false;

        j++;
    }
    return true;

}
```

MRString insert(MRString m, int where)

All the insert( ) methods depend on this one to do the actual work.

```
public MRString insert( MRString m, int where ) {
```

It begins by creating a new char array, long enough for the original MRString plus the insertion:

```
int new_len = length + m.length;
char[] mc = new char[new_len];
```

Then it copies the first part of the original MRString if the insertion isn't at the left end:

```
if ( where > 0 )
    System.arraycopy( chars, 0, mc, 0, where );
```

Next it copies in the insertion, being careful not to crash if the new string is null:

```
        if ( m.length > 0 )
            System.arraycopy( m.chars, 0, mc, where,
                m.length );
```

If the insertion wasn't at the end, it copies the right-hand part of the original:

```
        if ( where < length )
            System.arraycopy( chars, where, mc,
                where+m.length, length - where );
```

Finally, a little tidying up and the process is completed:

```
        chars = mc;
        length = new_len;

        return this;
    }
```

int intValue( )

The intValue( ) routine is not really an int value. It's just a positive integer value. A leading sign will cause it to return zero, as this code shows:

```
    public int intValue() {

        // assumes isDigit(this) returned true
        // (no sign!)

        MRString m = new MRString( this );
        m.trim();

        int val = 0;
        for ( int i = 0 ; i < m.length ; i++ ) {

            if ( ! isDigit(m.chars[i]) )
                break;

            val = ( 10 * val ) + ( m.chars[i] - (byte) '0' );
        }
        return val;
    }
```

MRString leftPadTo(int len)

The first check that leftPadTo makes is to see if it is padding to the existing length, in which case there's nothing to do:

```
public MRString leftPadTo( int len ) {

    if ( len == length )
        return this;
```

Next the routine checks for truncation (the length to pad to is less than the current length). It truncates on the left by copying from right to left:

```
if ( len < length ) {

    System.arraycopy( chars, length-len,
        chars, 0, len );
    length = len;
    return this;
}
```

The third case is a genuine padding on the left. This is handled by creating a new chars array, padding with blanks, and then copying the existing values:

```
// len > length
char[] new_chars = new char[len];
int offset = len - length;

for ( int i = 0 ; i < len ; i++ ) {

    if ( i < offset )
        new_chars[i] = ' ';
    else
        new_chars[i] = chars[i - offset];
}
chars = new_chars;
length = len;

return this;
}
```

int nextWord(int from)

The interesting point about nextWord( ) is the simplicity of its definition. As this code shows, a word is just contiguous nonblanks:

```
public int nextWord( int from ) {

    int ptr = from;

    while ( (ptr < chars.length) &&
        !isWhite(chars[ptr]) )
            ptr++;

    while ( (ptr < chars.length) &&
        isWhite(chars[ptr]) )
            ptr++;

    return ptr;
}
```

Try your editors (I'll bet they're all different!) to see alternatives. I'm not sure that any of the alternatives is better.

MRString padTo(int width, char pad_char)

The padTo function works like the mirror image of the leftPadTo. It starts with a quick exit when the padded size is the current size:

```
public MRString padTo( int width, char pad_char ) {

    if ( length == width )
        return this;
```

Then it truncates on the right. That's simply a matter of changing the length variable:

```
if ( length > width ) {
    length = width;
    return this;
}
```

Last, it does a bit of real work to expand chars, copy the old data, and blank-fill the rest:

```
char[] old_chars = chars;
chars = new char[width];

int old_length = length;
length = width;

System.arraycopy(
        old_chars, 0, chars, 0, old_length );

for ( int i = 0 ; i < length ; i++ )
    if ( chars[i] == 0 )
        chars[i] = pad_char;

return this;
}
```

int prevWord(int from)

The prevWord( ) method uses the same simple definition that the nextWord( ) method uses: a word is any set of contiguous nonwhite characters. The code isn't as simple as the definition, however.

It starts with a quick exit if the index is the leftmost character:

```
public int prevWord( int from ) {

    if ( from == 0 )
        return 0;
```

Then it dispenses with the current character!

```
int ptr = from - 1;
```

This works, because if the current character was the start of a word, it needs to back up into the adjoining whitespace. If it's whitespace, it will back up into either more whitespace or the end of the word to the left—either is OK. Otherwise, it will remain in the word for which it needs to find the start.

The next job is to set a flag:

```
boolean was_in_word = false;
```

Then it backs up through any whitespace to find the right end of the word to the left. (If it is already in a word, this loop doesn't execute at all.) This is that step:

```
while ( (ptr > 0) &&
    isWhite(chars[ptr]) )
        ptr--;
```

The next job is to find the left end of the current word. This is done by finding the first whitespace character to the left:

```
while( (ptr > 0) &&
    !isWhite(chars[ptr]) ) {

        ptr--;
        was_in_word = true;
}
```

Then it realizes that the whitespace was one too far, so it points to the last nonwhite. The flag is needed for the case where it backed up in whitespace at the left end of the string. If it bumped into the left boundary without finding a word, this returns zero, not one:

```
if ( was_in_word &&
    isWhite(chars[ptr]) )
        ptr++;

return ptr;
}
```

MRString trimLeft( )

The trimLeft( ) method begins by creating a pointer, and working from zero to the right, looks for a nonblank (not whitespace) character:

```
public MRString trimLeft() {

    int non_blank = 0;

    while ( (non_blank < length) &&
            (isWhite( chars[non_blank] )) )
        non_blank++;
```

If the first character is nonblank, there's nothing to do:

```
    if ( non_blank == 0 )
        return this;
```

If the whole string is blank, the process is also simple. In this case, the string is set to zero length and the job is done:

```
    if ( non_blank == length ) {

        length = 0;
        return this;
    }
```

If neither of the preceding applies, there is a bit of real work to be done. System.arraycopy( ) is used to shift the characters so that the first nonblank becomes character zero. Normally, I'd shift the characters and then set length, but in this case length's new value was useful in the shift, so I set it first.

This is the final code:

```
    int old_length = length;
    length = old_length - non_blank;

    System.arraycopy( chars, non_blank,
        chars, 0, length );

    return this;
}
```

That completes the discussion of the public methods, except for the static ones, which we'll look at next.

MRString Static Methods

The MRString class also provides a convenient place to collect code that would otherwise reside in a procedural library. (A genuine procedural library would be nice for these routines.)

The statics include these boolean functions:

- isAlpha( )
- isDigit( ) and isDigits( )
- isLower( )
- isUpper( )
- isVarName( )
- isWhite( )

They also include char and String functions for

- toLower( )
- toUlower( ) (capitalize the first character only)
- toUpper( )

We'll discuss using these functions here. There's no need to discuss the internals. Once you see what the functions do, the implementations are completely straightforward.

Using the Static Boolean Functions

The boolean functions tell you what a thing is. I've grouped them in five categories.

Alphabetic Characters

This function decides if a char is alphabetic:

```
public static boolean isAlpha( char c )
```

Actually, it decides if the char is in the range "A" to "Z" or in the range "a" to "z." Characters outside that range are not alphabetic.

This makes no attempt to consider the many characters used in different languages that use the high bit or a unicode representation.

This function works well for applications such as reading source code. It's not suited to applications such as word processing.

Decimal Digits

These functions return true if their argument is a decimal digit or string of digits:

```
public static boolean isDigit( byte b )
public static boolean isDigit( char c )
public static boolean isDigits( MRString m )
```

The isDigits( ) function returns true only if every character in the MRString is a digit.

Lowercase and Uppercase Alphabetics

These functions return true if the char is an alphabetic char in the appropriate range:

```
public static boolean isLower( char c )
public static boolean isUpper( char c )
```

Again, these use the simplest definition. The isLower( ) function returns true for characters in the range "a" through "z." The isUpper( ) function returns true for characters in the range "A" through "Z."

These definitions work for code processing, for example, but not for word processing.

Variable Names

One common definition of a variable name is that the name begins with an alphabetic character and continues with zero or more alphabetic, decimal digit, or underscore characters. This function uses that definition:

```
public static boolean isVarName( char c )
```

For many languages (including Java) this definition isn't accurate. You'll need to code language-specific versions. This one works correctly for the field names in our database files.

Whitespace

This function returns true for every ASCII character from zero through 32:

```
public static boolean isWhite( char c )
```

This returns true for space, tab, return, and linefeed characters. It also returns true for all the other control characters. I've found in many applications that this is not a practical problem.

Using the Other Static Functions

Three groups of functions manipulate the case of alphabetic characters. (See isAlpha( ), isLower( ), and isUpper( ) earlier for the rather limited definition used.) These functions convert any alphabetic character to lowercase:

```
public static char toLower( char c )
public static String toLower( String s )
```

This function converts a String's first character to uppercase (if it's alphabetic) and converts the rest to lowercase:

```
public static String toUlower( String s )
```

In data entry, the Ulower( ) form is useful for first names, but frequently fails for family names (Jacques deFrance, Otto vonGerman, and so on).

These two functions convert alphabetic characters to uppercase:

```
public static char toUpper( char c )
public static String toUpper( String s )
```

All of these functions return nonalphabetic characters unchanged.

MRString Private Methods

There are no private methods.

In the section of the source file where you'd look for private methods, there is a long main( )—public static void, of course—commented out. Also commented out are three print( ) methods that main uses. Those are close enough to private so that we can reasonably discuss the whole thing here.

To add a new MRString function, I write the code and uncomment the mainline. I add some tests to the end of the main( ) code and run this as a stand-alone program. The new test results show up in the bottom of the Java window. Figure 5-1 shows the results of the current tests in Visual Cafe.

Figure 5-2 shows the same results from Visual J++. In this instance, you can see that the DOS window has been filled and overflowed. Visual Cafe's Messages window also was filled and overflowed, but its vertical scroll bar lets you back up to find what you've missed.

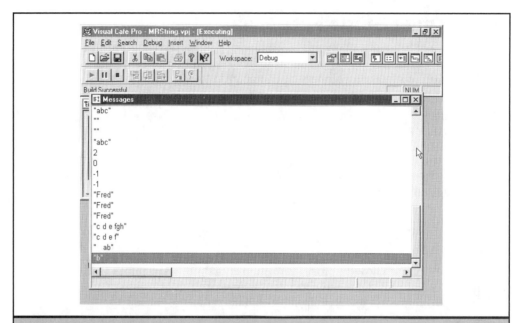

Figure 5-1. MRString test results in Visual Cafe

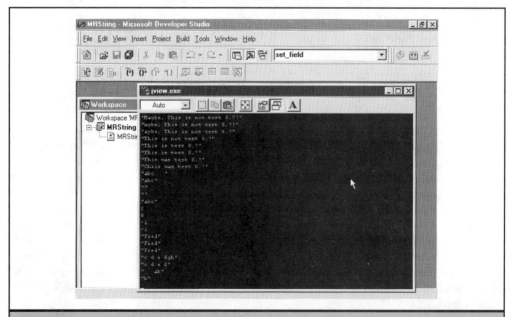

Figure 5-2. MRString test results in Visual J++

In Visual J++ the old tests scroll quickly out of sight, of course. To use this main( ) yourself, comment out most of the tests. Run with just the ones you are interested in uncommented.

Figures 5-1 and 5-2 don't show my working setups. Screen shots are taken at 640x480 resolution to print within the limits of this page's width. I normally program at 1280x1024.

If you change to a lower resolution in Visual J++, the IDE doesn't notice. You'll have lots of your favorite toolbar buttons somewhere off the right edge of the screen where you can't get to them. I lose stuff like build and execute. This is no good.

Visual Cafe wraps your toolbars to fit the available width, which is the mess you see in Figure 5-1. It may not be pretty, but it's there. Unfortunately, the wrapped mess will be your very own mess when you go back to a higher resolution. Did you have everything laid out perfectly at 1280x1024? Good! Now lay it out all over again, please.

You tell me which is worse.

In some cases I've done a good job of testing. For example, consider these lastNonblankLoc( ) tests:

```
print( new MRString( "abc" ).lastNonblankLoc() );
print( new MRString( "a  " ).lastNonblankLoc() );
print( new MRString( "   " ).lastNonblankLoc() );
print( new MRString( "" ).lastNonblankLoc() );
```

These tests check with no trailing whitespace, with trailing whitespace, with only whitespace, and for null strings. I think that's an exhaustive test. (You create an exhaustive test by looking at the code to figure out the set of different paths it could take.)

Unfortunately, the quality of these tests is not uniform. Some sets are exhaustive and some aren't. Others don't even exist. This is an area where you can definitely make improvements.

Testing

Tests should be exhaustive, not exhausting.

There is no prize for making lots of tests. These four all return different results, but they all use the same path through the code:

```
print( new MRString( "abc  " ).lastNonblankLoc() );
print( new MRString( "ab   " ).lastNonblankLoc() );
print( new MRString( "a    " ).lastNonblankLoc() );
print( new MRString( "abcd " ).lastNonblankLoc() );
```

If the first one gives a correct answer, they all will. This is not really four tests. It's one test repeated four times. You win the testing prize by testing each possible path through the function, not by repeating one path over and over.

The Full MRString Listing

Listing 5-1 shows the full MRString.java file.

Listing 5-1:
MRString.java

```
// MRString.java -- a String-like class
// Copyright 1997, Martin Rinehart

// this code is completely documented in:
// _Java Database Development_, Martin Rinehart,
// Osborne/McGraw-Hill, 1997

/*
  Constructors:
    MRString( byte b )
    MRString( byte[] b )
    MRString( char c )
    MRString( int width )
    MRString( String s )
    MRString( MRString m )
    MRString( MRString m, int width )
    MRString( MRString m, int from, int to )

  Data access:
    public char[] getChars()
```

```
Class-specific:
  public MRString charAt( int loc )
  public MRString concat( MRString m )
  public MRString concat( String s )
  public MRString concat( Object o )
  public MRString concat( byte b )
  public MRString concat( int i )
  public MRString concat( long l )
  public MRString concat( boolean b )
  public MRString concat( double d )

  public MRString copy()

  public MRString delete( int where )
  public MRString delete( int where, int how_long )

  public boolean endsWith( String s );
  public boolean endsWith( MRString m );

  public int indexOf( int ch )
  public int indexOf( int ch, int fromIndex )

  public MRString insert( MRString m, int where )
  public MRString insert( char c, int where )
  public MRString insert( int i, int where )
  public MRString insert( String s, int where )

  public int intValue()

  public char lastChar()
  public int lastNonblankLoc()

  public MRString left( int len )

  public MRString leftPadTo( int len );

  public int length()

  public int nextWord( int from )

  public MRString padTo( int width )
  public MRString padTo( int width, char pad_char )
```

```
      public int prevWord( int from )

      public MRString replace( int where, char c )
      public MRString replace( int where, int i )

      public MRString right( int len )

      public MRString substring( int from )
      public MRString substring( int from, int to )

      public MRString toLower()
      public MRString toUpper()

      public MRString trim()
      public MRString trimLeft()
      public MRString trimLeft( int nchars )
      public MRString trimRight()
      public MRString trimRight( int nchars )

    Non-event, overriding:
      public String paramString()
      public String toString()

    Class static:
      public static boolean isAlpha( char c )
      public static boolean isDigit( byte b )
      public static boolean isDigit( char c )
      public static boolean isDigits( MRString m )
      public static boolean isLower( char c )
      public static boolean isUpper( char c )
      public static boolean isVarName( char c )
      public static boolean isWhite( char c )

      public static char toLower( char c )
      public static String toLower( String s )

      public static String toUlower( String s )

      public static char toUpper( char c )
      public static String toUpper( String s )

*/
```

```java
import java.io.*;

class MRString extends Object {

// -------------------- data members --------------------

// there are no public data members

// protected data members

    protected char[] chars;
    protected int length;

// there are no static data members

// -------------------- public methods --------------------

// constructors:

    MRString( byte b ) {

        chars = new char[1];
        length = 1;
        chars[0] = (char) b;
    }

    MRString( byte[] b ) {

        chars = new char[b.length];
        length = b.length;

        for ( int i = 0 ; i < length ; i++ )
            chars[i] = (char) b[i];
    }

    MRString( char c ) {

        chars = new char[1];
        chars[0] = c;
        length = 1;
    }
```

```
MRString( int i ) {

    chars = new char[i];
    length = i;
}

MRString( String s ) {

    if ( s == null )
        s = "";

    chars = new char[s.length()];
    s.getChars( 0, s.length(), chars, 0 );
    length = s.length();
}

MRString( MRString m ) {

    if ( m == null )
        m = new MRString( "" );

    chars = new char[m.length];
    length = m.length;

    System.arraycopy( m.chars, 0, chars, 0,
        length );
}

MRString( MRString m, int width ) {

    chars = new char[width];
    length = width;

    if ( m != null )
        System.arraycopy( m.chars, 0, chars, 0,
            width < m.length ? width : m.length );
}

MRString( MRString m, int from, int to ) {

    // from "from" to, but not including, "to"
```

```
            if ( m == null )
                m = new MRString( to - 1 );

            length = to - from;
            chars = new char[length];

            System.arraycopy( m.chars, from, chars, 0, length );
        }

// data access getXxx() method:

    public char[] getChars() {

            return chars;
        }


    // to be consistent with String, length is accessed via
    // length(), not getLength()

// public, class-specific methods:

    public char charAt( int loc ) {

            return chars[loc];
        }

    public MRString concat( MRString m ) {

            int new_len = length + m.length();
            char[] mc = new char[new_len];

            System.arraycopy( chars, 0, mc, 0, length );
            System.arraycopy( m.chars, 0, mc, length,
                m.length );

            chars = mc;
            length = new_len;

            return this;
        }
```

```java
public MRString concat( String s ) {

    return concat( new MRString(s) );
}

public MRString concat( Object o ) {

    return concat( new MRString(o.toString( )) );
}

public MRString concat( byte b ) {

    if ( b > ' ' )
        return concat( "'" + b + "'" );
    else
        return concat( "0x" + b );
}

 // int also handles short
public MRString concat( int i ) {

    return concat( new Integer(i) );
}

public MRString concat( long l ) {

    return concat( new Long(l) );
}

public MRString concat( boolean b ) {

    return concat( new Boolean(b) );
}

 // double also handles float
public MRString concat( double d ) {

    return concat( new Double(d) );
}

 public MRString copy() {
```

```java
            return new MRString( this );
    }

public MRString delete( int where ) {

    return delete( where, 1 );
}

public MRString delete( int where, int how_long ) {

    if ( how_long > 0 )
        System.arraycopy( chars, where + how_long,
            chars, where, length - where - how_long );

    length = length - how_long;

    return this;
}

 public boolean endsWith( String s ) {

    return endsWith( new MRString(s) );
 }

 public boolean endsWith( MRString m ) {

    if ( m.length > length )
        return false;

    int j = length - m.length;
    for ( int i = 0 ; i < m.length ; i++ ) {

        if ( m.chars[i] != chars[j] )
            return false;

        j++;
    }
    return true;
}

 public int indexOf( int ch ) {
```

```java
            return indexOf( ch, 0 );
    }

    public int indexOf( int ch, int fromIndex ) {

        int index = -1;

        for ( int i = fromIndex ; i < length ; i++ )
            if ( chars[i] == ch ) {

                index = i;
                break;
            }

        return index;
    }

public MRString insert( MRString m, int where ) {

    int new_len = length + m.length;
    char[] mc = new char[new_len];

    if ( where > 0 )
        System.arraycopy( chars, 0, mc, 0, where );

    if ( m.length > 0 )
        System.arraycopy( m.chars, 0, mc, where,
            m.length );

    if ( where < length )
        System.arraycopy( chars, where, mc,
            where+m.length, length - where );

    chars = mc;
    length = new_len;

    return this;
}

    public MRString insert( char c, int where ) {
```

```java
        return insert( new MRString(c), where );
}

public MRString insert( int i, int where ) {

        return insert( (char) i, where );
}

public MRString insert( String s, int where ) {

        return insert( new MRString(s), where );
}

public char lastChar() {

        return chars[length-1];
}

public int intValue() {

        // assumes isDigit(this) returned true
        // (no sign!)

        MRString m = new MRString( this );
        m.trim();

        int val = 0;
        for ( int i = 0 ; i < m.length ; i++ ) {

            if ( ! isDigit(m.chars[i]) )
                break;

            val = ( 10 * val ) +
                ( m.chars[i] - (byte) '0' );
        }
        return val;
}

public int lastNonblankLoc() {

        int i;
        for ( i = length - 1 ; i >= 0 ; i-- ) {
```

```java
                if ( ! isWhite(chars[i]) )
                    return i;
        }
        return -1;
    }

    public MRString left( int len ) {

        return new MRString( this, 0, len );
    }

    public MRString leftPadTo( int len ) {

        if ( len == length )
            return this;

        if ( len < length ) {

            System.arraycopy( chars, length-len,
                chars, 0, len );
            length = len;
            return this;
        }

        // len > length
        char[] new_chars = new char[len];
        int offset = len - length;

        for ( int i = 0 ; i < len ; i++ ) {

            if ( i < offset )
                new_chars[i] = ' ';
            else
                new_chars[i] = chars[i - offset];
        }
        chars = new_chars;
        length = len;

        return this;
    }

    public int length() {
```

```
        return length;
}

public int nextWord( int from ) {

    int ptr = from;

    while ( (ptr < chars.length) &&
        !isWhite(chars[ptr]) )
            ptr++;

    while ( (ptr < chars.length) &&
        isWhite(chars[ptr]) )
            ptr++;

    return ptr;
}

public MRString padTo( int width ) {

    return padTo( width, ' ' );
}

public MRString padTo( int width, char pad_char ) {

    if ( length == width )
        return this;

    if ( length > width ) {
        length = width;
        return this;
    }

    char[] old_chars = chars;
    chars = new char[width];

    int old_length = length;
    length = width;

    System.arraycopy(
            old_chars, 0, chars, 0, old_length );
```

```java
        for ( int i = 0 ; i < length ; i++ )
            if ( chars[i] == 0 )
                chars[i] = pad_char;

        return this;
    }

public int prevWord( int from ) {

        if ( from == 0 )
            return 0;

        int ptr = from - 1;

        boolean was_in_word = false;

        while ( (ptr > 0) &&
            isWhite(chars[ptr]) )
                ptr--;

        while( (ptr > 0) &&
            !isWhite(chars[ptr]) ) {

                ptr--;
                was_in_word = true;
        }

        if ( was_in_word &&
            isWhite(chars[ptr]) )
                ptr++;

        return ptr;
    }

public MRString replace( int where, char c ) {

        chars[where] = c;
        return this;
    }

public MRString replace( int where, int i ) {
```

```
        return replace( where, (char) i );
    }

public MRString right( int len ) {

    return new MRString( this, length - len, length );
}

 public MRString substring( int from ) {

     // from "from" through end
     return new MRString( this, from, length );
 }

public MRString substring( int from, int to ) {

    // from "from" up to, but not including, "to"
    return new MRString( this, from, to );
}

 public MRString toLower() {

     for ( int i = 0 ; i < length ; i++ )
         chars[i] = toLower( chars[i] );

     return this;
 }

 public MRString toUpper() {

     for ( int i = 0 ; i < length ; i++ )
         chars[i] = toUpper( chars[i] );

     return this;
 }

 public MRString trim() {

     // trim leading and trailing blanks
     return trimLeft().trimRight();
 }
```

```java
public MRString trimLeft() {

    int non_blank = 0;

    while ( (non_blank < length) &&
        (isWhite( chars[non_blank] )) )
        non_blank++;

    if ( non_blank == 0 )
        return this;

    if ( non_blank == length ) {

        length = 0;
        return this;
    }

    int old_length = length;
    length = old_length - non_blank;

    System.arraycopy( chars, non_blank,
        chars, 0, length );

    return this;
}

public MRString trimLeft( int nchars ) {

    System.arraycopy( chars, nchars, chars, 0,
        length - nchars );

    length -= nchars;

    return this;
}

public MRString trimRight() {

    int non_blank = length;

    while ( (non_blank > 0) &&
        (isWhite( chars[non_blank-1] )) )
```

```
                    non_blank--;

            length = non_blank;

            return this;
        }

    public MRString trimRight( int nchars ) {

            length -= nchars;

            return this;
        }

// public, non-event overriding methods

    public String paramString() {

            return new String( chars, 0, length );
        }

    public String toString() {

            return paramString();
        }

// there are no public, event-handling methods

// public static methods:

    public static boolean isAlpha( char c ) {

            char x = toUpper( c );
            return ( x >= 'A' ) && ( x <= 'Z' );
        }

    public static boolean isDigit( byte b ) {

            return ( b >=  (byte) '0' ) && ( b <= (byte) '9' );
        }

    public static boolean isDigit( char c ) {
```

```
        return ( c >= '0' ) && ( c <= '9' );
}

public static boolean isDigits( MRString m ) {

    for ( int i = 0 ; i < m.length ; i++ ) {

        if ( !isDigit(m.chars[i]) )
            return false;
    }
    return true;
}

public static boolean isLower( char c ) {

    return ( c >= 'a' ) && ( c <= 'z' );
}

public static boolean isUpper( char c ) {

    return ( c >= 'A' ) && ( c <= 'Z' );
}

public static boolean isVarName( char c ) {

    return     ( isAlpha(c) ) ||
            ( isDigit(c) ) ||
            ( c == '_' );
}

public static boolean isVarName( MRString m ) {

    if ( m.length < 1 )
        return false;

    if ( ! isAlpha(m.chars[0]) )
        return false;

    if ( m.length > 1 ) {

        for ( int i = 1 ; i < m.length ; i++ ) {
```

```
                if ( ! isVarName(m.chars[i]) )
                    return false;
        }
    }
    return true;
}

public static boolean isWhite( char c ) {

    // this looks like a kludge, but I've
    // come to trust it -- MR
    return ( c <= ' ' );
}

public static char toLower( char c ) {

    if ( isUpper(c) )
        return ( char ) ( 'a' + c - 'A' );
    else
        return c;
}

public static String toLower( String s ) {

    return ( (new MRString( s )).toLower().toString() );
}

public static String toUlower( String s ) {

    /* "fred" or "FRED" or "fReD" or whatever is
        converted to:
        "Fred"
    */

    MRString m = new MRString( s );
    m.toLower();

    if ( m.length > 0 )
        m.chars[0] = toUpper( m.chars[0] );

    return m.toString();
}
```

```java
    public static char toUpper( char c ) {

        if ( isLower(c) )
            return ( char ) ( 'A' + c - 'a' );
        else
            return c;
    }

    public static String toUpper( String s ) {

        return ( (new MRString( s )).toUpper().toString() );
    }

// ------------------- private methods -------------------

//* lose this line to create a stand-alone test app
// tests:
    public static void main( String[] args ) {

    MRString m = new MRString( "test" );
    print( m ); // toString

    MRString m2 = new MRString( m );
    print( m2 );

    MRString m3 = new MRString( new MRString("") );
    print( m3 );

    MRString m4 = ( new MRString("test 4") ).copy();
    print( m4 );

    MRString m5 = new MRString( m4, 0, 4 );
    print( m5 );

    MRString m6 = new MRString( "This is a test." );
    print( m6.left(7) );
    print( m6.right(7) );
    print( m6.substring(0, 4) );
    print( m6.substring(5, 9) );
    print( m6.substring(10, m6.length( )) );
```

```
MRString m7 = new MRString( "This is " );
print( m7.concat("a test.") );
print( m7.concat(new
    java.awt.Rectangle( 1, 2, 3, 4 )) );
MRString m8 = new MRString( "This is test " );
print( m8.concat(8).concat(".") );

print( m8.insert(" not", 7) );
print( m8.insert("Maybe, ", 0) );
print( m8.insert("!", m8.length( )) );
  print( m8.insert("?", m8.length( )-1) );

print( m8.delete(0) );
print( m8.delete(m8.length( )-1) );
print( m8.delete(0, 6) );
print( m8.delete(8, 4) );

  print( m8.replace(m8.length()-1, '?') );

  m8.insert( 'w', 5 );
  print( m8.replace(6, 'a') );
  m8.insert( 'r', 2 );
  m8.replace( 0, 'C' );
  print( m8.replace(m8.length()-1, '!') );

  MRString m9 = new MRString( "   abc    " );
  print( m9.trimLeft() );
  print( m9.trimRight() );
  print( new MRString( "   " ).trimLeft() );
  print( new MRString( "   " ).trimRight() );
  print( new MRString( " abc " ).trim() );

  print( new MRString( "abc" ).lastNonblankLoc() );
  print( new MRString( "a  " ).lastNonblankLoc() );
  print( new MRString( "    " ).lastNonblankLoc() );
  print( new MRString( "" ).lastNonblankLoc() );

  print( toUlower("FRED") );
  print( toUlower("fred") );
  print( toUlower("fReD") );
```

```
        MRString m10 = new MRString( "abc d e fgh" );
        print( m10.trimLeft(2) );
        print( m10.trimRight(2) );

        MRString m11 = new MRString( "ab" );
        print( m11.leftPadTo(5) );
        print( m11.leftPadTo(1) );

        try { System.in.read(); } // pause needed for VJ++
        catch ( IOException ioe ) {}
    }

    static void print( MRString m ) {

        System.out.println( "\"" + m + "\"" );
    }

    static void print( int i ) {

        System.out.println( i );
    }

    static void print( String s ) {

        print( new MRString(s) );
    }

// end of tests */

} // end of MRString class

// there are no private classes in MRString.java

// end of MRString.java
```

Your Project

Think about the MRString methods. What isn't there that you need? What about
reversing the string? What about hash values?

No ideas? Here's one that I'll use if you write it:

```
Font bestFit( Rectangle r, Font f )
```

The bestFit( ) method returns the Font it was passed with the Font's size modified so that the MRString fills the Rectangle. (By "fill" I mean that either its length or height, whichever is more restrictive, fills the Rectangle.)

Your project is to add a new method to the MRString class, and to add the test code you need. If you write the bestFit( ) method, you'll need to make a more elaborate main( ) than I've provided.

Want extra credit? One weakness of my test procedure is there's no way of being sure tests that were once successfully passed remain successfully passed. An automated approach that lets the test routine check the results (as opposed to letting the programmer check the results) would be a worthwhile improvement.

Maybe one of you would like to organize a Web or FTP site where we can collect our methods? Let me know.

Summary

In this chapter we took a break between binary and database files. The DBF class we'll get to in Chapter 6 uses MRStrings heavily, so we looked at them here.

The MRString is my substitute for the native String class. (You can't extend String—it's final.) I add all the string-manipulation features I need to make this class do everything I want with strings.

This approach has advantages and disadvantages. The MRString, for example, has methods to insert, delete, and replace characters and substrings. You won't find these in the String class. On the other hand, adding an MRString costs 10K. That's a cheap price in an application, but is a serious cost for an applet. Also, MRStrings can't take advantage of the String's special place in Java's assignment and concatenation operators.

We spent some time looking at each of the constructors and methods of the MRString. This will serve as backup to your basic source of quick reference: the extended comment at the top of the MRString.java file.

In addition to the MRString methods, the class also supplies static methods that perform basic boolean operations such as isWhite( ), isDigit( ), and other character tests. These are also listed at the top of the source file.

Finally, we looked at the mainline test routine which lives, commented out, in the MRString.java source file. It lets you use MRString as a stand-alone application when you add new methods. This encourages exhaustive testing, which takes more thought than actual work.

Now we've finished the precursor. We're ready to go on to the database file. Chapter 6 will show you its internal format and the software I've provided that encapsulates that information in an easy-to-use class.

Chapter 6

Using Database Files

In this chapter we'll discuss the DBF class and look at a new FileViewer mainline that uses the DBF class. While the DBF is a lot more complex than the TxtFile or BinFile, using it is no more complex, you'll be glad to see. We'll also cover the MsgBox class, which lets you get a more professional user interface with no more trouble than the System.out work we've been doing.

We'll start with a close look at the DBF file. It's a way of storing a table of data that's become almost universal on PCs. Its popularity dates back to the original success of dBASE II in 1979 and 1980 (before IBM introduced the original PC). Its continued use comes from its straightforward design.

After looking at the DBF file, we'll go on to the new FileViewer mainline. You'll see that the DBF class neatly encapsulates the complexities of the DBF file. They're no more trouble to pop into a ScrollWin than TxtFiles or BinFiles were. You'll also see the MRString put to good use, as well as a MsgBox.

The MsgBox is our first class in this chapter. It lets you pop up an information dialog box with almost no coding and at very little cost in executable size. It's an idea I've adopted from Visual Basic. By throwing away every feature I didn't think was critically important, I've kept it tiny.

Finally, we'll dive into the DBF class itself. It's a large one and it includes features that are way ahead of our other work, such as being able to create a Vector of DEField (data-entry field) objects. Later you'll see how this fits together in our JDB (Java Database) application.

We'll begin with the DBF file structure.

The Database File

In relational databases, all data is stored in tables. The database files we'll use store tables. The format I've chosen is the PC's DBF format. Originally used in the first best-selling database product, dBASE, the DBF format has become a *lingua franca* of data tables. It is read by almost all PC database, spreadsheet, and word processing programs.

As we'll see, this table's format is simple and adequate for our needs. It stores a few header items in the PC's little-endian format, but we'll read the header as a byte array and then use Java to convert the appropriate bytes into numbers Java understands. It's actually more trouble than you might suppose, but the end result is that we can use the DBF without becoming platform specific.

Actually, the DBF is misnamed. It doesn't store a database. It stores a single data table. A database is made up of multiple tables and, for efficiency, additional data structures for variable-length text (or other items) and for indexes that logically sort the tables and permit rapid searching.

You can, however, use the DBF as one structure within a database, which we'll do. This lets you share data with, for example, all the popular PC productivity applications. Let's begin with a quick look at the history of this popular format.

A Fast History of the DBF

In the 1970s, NASA's Jeb Long invented a data-handling language and implemented it on a mainframe computer at the Jet Propulsion Laboratory (JPL) in Pasadena. (Rocket science has more sex appeal, but space exploration involves keeping track of lots of nuts and bolts, too.) Long's language, known as JPLDIS ("JIP-uhl-dis"—Jet Propulsion Laboratory's Display Information System) made it easy to define and implement tables. It enabled you to add, edit, and delete records in these tables. And it let you perform the basic relational operations, such as joining tables.

Another programmer at JPL, Wayne Ratliff, had an early, 8-bit microcomputer at home as a hobby. He decided to implement Long's fourth-generation language (4GL) on his microcomputer. The first application was to keep track of the office football pool.

Wayne worked in Z-80 assembler. (The Z-80 was an 8-bit microprocessor that dominated the early, hobbyist period of the development of personal computers.) He managed to code the database work and an interpreter for the 4GL, and to still provide data space within his 48K RAM space. (The early operating system, CP/M, took less than 4K of this space.)

Wayne began marketing his program to other hobbyists. He named it Vulcan. It came to the attention of Hal Lashlee and George Tate, who were running an early software distribution company out of Tate's garage. They acquired marketing rights and renamed the product dBASE II.

George partnered with a marketing professional, Hal Pawluk, in promoting the product. (Lashlee, an accountant, didn't get involved in day-to-day operations.) Through a combination of brilliant marketing and the simple fact that dBASE II was a superior product in its day, this became the leading database-management software for CP/M-based computers. They named their company Ashton-Tate.

Would they have succeeded selling "dBASE I" from "Lashlee-Tate"? They might have, because the product was better than its competitors. Certainly success came more rapidly and market dominance was more complete because of Ashton-Tate's early marketing orientation.

The introduction of the PC in 1981 and then of the PC-XT in 1983 (the latter featured a whopping 10MB hard disk, the first from a major manufacturer) helped make the personal computer a viable machine for small database work. While some companies stumbled (the inventors of the spreadsheet lost their market lead to PC-specific upstart Lotus Development; the dominant WordStar word-processing program was overtaken by WordPerfect), Ashton-Tate continued to dominate databases.

The dBASE data format was published by Ashton-Tate, which actively encouraged others to use it. Spreadsheets read DBF files (tables map nicely into spreadsheets). Word processors used the DBF format for mail-merge applications. Graphics programs read DBFs. (In the early days, graphing was a separate application, not part of every spreadsheet and word processor.) And, of course, competing database products accessed DBF-based data.

The dBASE product is still available from Borland, although that company has hinted that they may have released the last version of the product. The Xbase language is still used in Microsoft's FoxPro and CA's Clipper products. And the DBF format is still a widely used, *de facto* standard in numerous PC applications.

The DBF Structure

You don't need to know the format of a DBF file—the DBF class needs to know this format. However, you'll need to know what's in this structure in order to take advantage of it.

There's enough information in this section to rewrite the DBF class, although you'll probably never need to. What you will need to know, though, is that character fields shorter than the allotted field length are normally blank-padded, not zero-filled, and that the decimal point is actually included in the fixed-point numeric fields.

So don't skip this section, but don't give it a painstakingly slow read, either.

Let's take a look at the DBF format. If you have this chapter's files loaded into your Java database working directory, you can look at ASAMP.BIN with the FileViewer application to see the internals of this file.

You won't see the structure, you'll see the table contents if you use ASAMP.DBF. Figure 6-1 shows the improved FileViewer that we'll discuss in this chapter looking at ASAMP.DBF. This is the data in the table records of the ASAMP data table. Just as our FileViewer (in Chapter 4) looked at a file to see if it could be viewed as text (in preference to the generic hex dump for binary files), the FileViewer in this chapter attempts to open files whose names end with ".DBF" as DBF files. If the format is acceptable, it will scroll through the data records.

There is a copy of ASAMP.DBF on disk named ASAMP.BIN. The two files are identical, but FileViewer only opens files ending with ".DBF" as database files. So ASAMP.BIN will be opened as a binary file. Figure 6-2 shows the hex dump of the header of this file.

This dump is, as we noted in Chapter 4, nearly identical to the early CP/M-based debugger DEBUG.COM. (There's an updated but mostly compatible DEBUG.COM or DEBUG.EXE still on many current PCs.) It's no accident that Wayne's file format is highly compatible with this dump format.

The DBF's Overall Structure

The DBF has three components:

- Header
- Records
- Footer

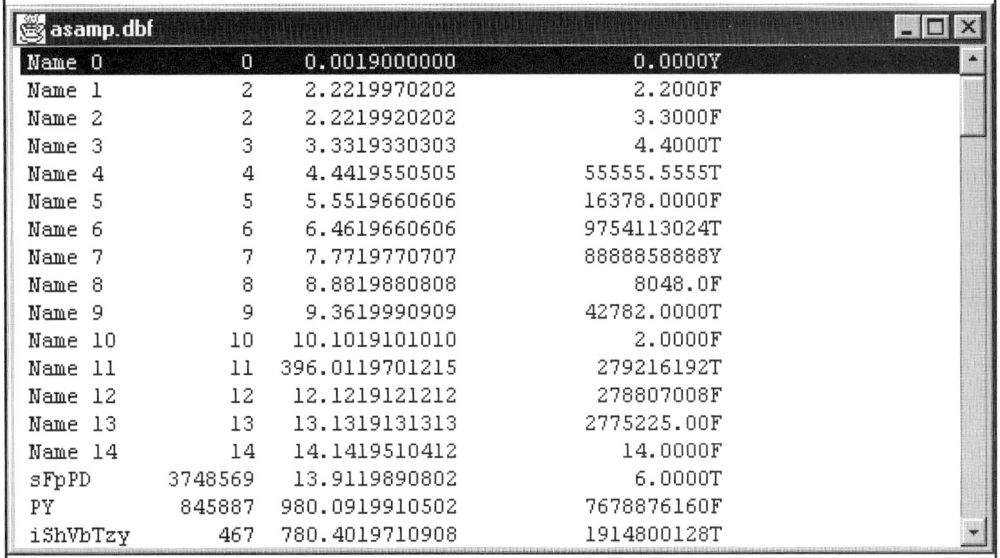

asamp.dbf

Name 0	0	0.0019000000	0.0000Y
Name 1	2	2.2219970202	2.2000F
Name 2	2	2.2219920202	3.3000F
Name 3	3	3.3319330303	4.4000T
Name 4	4	4.4419550505	55555.5555T
Name 5	5	5.5519660606	16378.0000F
Name 6	6	6.4619660606	9754113024T
Name 7	7	7.7719770707	8888858888Y
Name 8	8	8.8819880808	8048.0F
Name 9	9	9.3619990909	42782.0000T
Name 10	10	10.1019101010	2.0000F
Name 11	11	396.0119701215	279216192T
Name 12	12	12.1219121212	278807008F
Name 13	13	13.1319131313	2775225.00F
Name 14	14	14.1419510412	14.0000F
sFpPD	3748569	13.9119890802	6.0000T
PY	845887	980.0919910502	7678876160F
iShVbTzy	467	780.4019710908	1914800128T

Figure 6-1. *Looking at ASAMP.DBF*

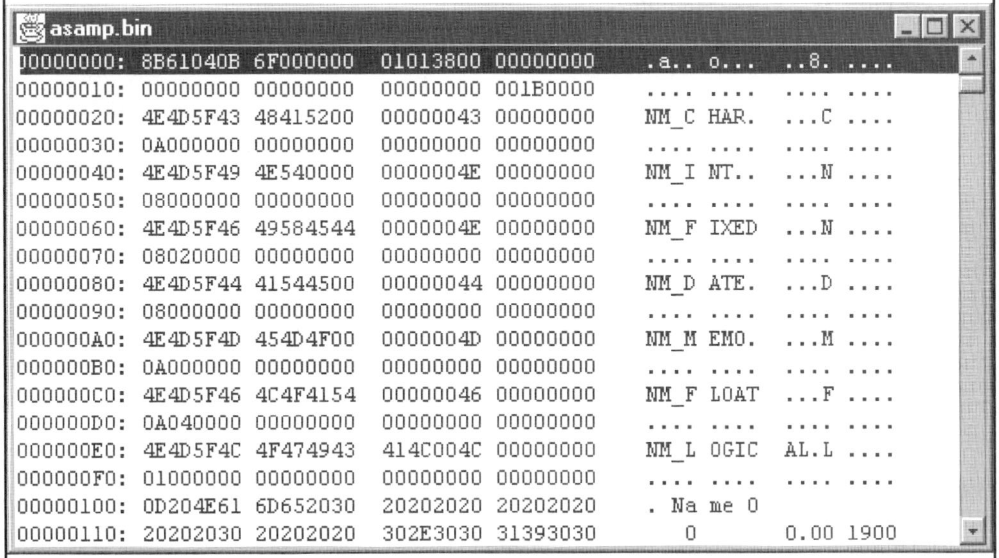

asamp.bin

```
00000000: 8B61040B 6F000000 01013800 00000000   .a.. o... ..8. ....
00000010: 00000000 00000000 00000000 001B0000   .... .... .... ....
00000020: 4E4D5F43 48415200 00000043 00000000   NM_C HAR. ...C ....
00000030: 0A000000 00000000 00000000 00000000   .... .... .... ....
00000040: 4E4D5F49 4E540000 0000004E 00000000   NM_I NT.. ...N ....
00000050: 08000000 00000000 00000000 00000000   .... .... .... ....
00000060: 4E4D5F46 49584544 0000004E 00000000   NM_F IXED ...N ....
00000070: 08020000 00000000 00000000 00000000   .... .... .... ....
00000080: 4E4D5F44 41544500 00000044 00000000   NM_D ATE. ...D ....
00000090: 08000000 00000000 00000000 00000000   .... .... .... ....
000000A0: 4E4D5F4D 454D4F00 0000004D 00000000   NM_M EMO. ...M ....
000000B0: 0A000000 00000000 00000000 00000000   .... .... .... ....
000000C0: 4E4D5F46 4C4F4154 00000046 00000000   NM_F LOAT ...F ....
000000D0: 0A040000 00000000 00000000 00000000   .... .... .... ....
000000E0: 4E4D5F4C 4F474943 414C004C 00000000   NM_L OGIC AL.L ....
000000F0: 01000000 00000000 00000000 00000000   .... .... .... ....
00000100: 0D204E61 6D652030 20202020 20202020   . Na me 0
00000110: 20202030 20202020 302E3030 31393030      0      0.00 1900
```

Figure 6-2. *Looking at ASAMP.BIN*

The header has data about the file, such as how many records it contains and how large they are. It also has data about the structure of the records, such as how many fields they have, and the name, type, and size of each field.

The records portion contains the data itself. In addition to each field in each record, there is a flag that says a record has been deleted when it's set.

The footer is two bytes including the CTRL-Z that reminds us of the early CP/M-based microcomputers.

The Header's Structure

The header also has three parts:

- Tablewide data header
- Field data records
- Footer

The tablewide data is stored in the first 32 bytes of the header. The field data is stored in 32-byte records following the header. The first field's data is in bytes 32–63; the second in 64–95, and so on. In the original dBASE format, the footer followed the last field record.

In the FoxPro DBF, which we'll also accommodate, the number of field records can exceed the actual number of fields. In the unused field records, the name is zero-filled.

The important subfields in the tablewide header are

Byte 0	ID
Bytes 1–3	Date of last update
Bytes 4–7	Number of records (all numbers are little-endian)
Bytes 8–9	Number of fields (size of header in FoxPro DBFs)
Bytes 10–11	Length of the data records

We can ignore the ID byte. It's used differently by different DBF-creating programs. The dBASE IDs and the FoxPro IDs, for example, are different.

The date of the last update is stored in YMD form. The Y value in byte 1 is the number of years since 1900. (Just as many old COBOL programs will fail in the year 2000, this format will fail in 2156. My DBF class ignores the Java treatment of bytes as signed integers, so it won't survive the year 2027 without a bit of improvement.)

The three numbers are little-endian. Java specifically requires big-endian numbers. (Most of Sun's Java design is first-class software engineering. Occasionally, though, their prejudices show. In this case, they use the byte order native to their workstations, ignoring the fact that the opposite byte order is used by the vast majority of all desktop computers.) When we get to "Understanding" this code, we'll look at the correct way to read a little-endian number. It's trickier than I thought it would be when I wrote my first (buggy) version.

Other positions in the tablewide header are used for product-specific purposes. Zero-filling them will work for our purposes.

The important subfields in the field record are

Bytes 0–9	Field's name
Byte 11	Field's type
Byte 16	Field's width
Byte 17	Number of decimal places, when applicable

The field's name is zero-terminated. Field names shorter than ten characters are zero-filled on the right. Byte 10 is always zero, which simplifies the name-handling software. The names are used in the Xbase 4GL. They are always stored in uppercase, and the 4GL was not case sensitive.

The original types were

- C for character data
- N for numbers
- D for dates
- L for logical

Many other types have been added. You should stick to these four, however, for sharing data with other programs. For building your own applications, you can add whatever types you like. Just remember that your own types won't be accessible outside your application.

Typical additions include F, for floating-point data, and M, for memo fields. A *memo* is a variable-length data field originally intended for applications such as writing short memoranda in a medical treatment database. The DBF requires fixed record length, so this field is implemented as a 10-byte pointer to an entry in a separate file that holds the actual memo text. This technique has been extended from just text to including pointers to all multimedia data types (sound, pictures, animations, and so on).

Unused positions in the field record are zero-filled.

The Record's Structure

The record data is written as consecutive, fixed-length records starting immediately after the field-record footer. There are no pad bytes between fields or records.

The record begins with a byte that is set to a space for an active record and is an asterisk if the record has been deleted. (In the 4GL, a deleted flag controlled processing. If the flag was set, which was the default, deleted records were not shown—they disappeared as if they were physically deleted.)

By flagging deleted records, there was never a need to physically remove the record. If you expected that many records would be deleted when you designed an application, the correct treatment was to write an append routine that reused the deleted record's space. If deletions were uncommon, you simply ignored them. An intermediate course used a batch utility to physically remove the deleted records periodically, such as during week- or month-end processing.

The remainder of the table record is simply the fields, as specified in the header, written to their specified lengths. There is no space between fields.

Character data is normally written with blank padding. Zeros in character data were originally an error. This proved impractical in many applications (consider sending control strings to a printer or other device), and later versions permitted embedded zero characters.

Numeric data is written, surprisingly, with an actual period character at the location of the decimal point when the decimals value is greater than zero. A 4-byte number with two decimal places is written as "1.23", for example.

Logical data was originally written as "T" or "F". Later databases allowed "Y" and "N" as synonyms for "T" and "F". Current versions also allow these letters in lowercase.

The Footers

At the end of the field-definition records, a return (0x0D) terminates the field definitions.

At the end of the file, a CTRL-Z (0x1A) terminates the file. This was the end-of-file marker in the CP/M operating system. (The operating system held the length as an integral number of file buffer units. The default buffer was 128 characters. It was up to the application to find the actual end within the last buffer.)

With that look into the internals of the DBF, we're ready to look at the software. We'll begin with the new FileViewer mainline.

The FileViewer Mainline

TOUR

The FileViewer is a consumer of the services of the classes we're using. Don't skip the FileViewer—it shows you how to use these classes.
   Sorry about the lack of choice here. Freedom will reign again with the next class.

With the introduction of the DBF class, our FileViewer becomes a fairly capable utility. It can display the contents of database files, text files, or generic binary files. Courtesy of the ScrollWin and its Scrollable interface, you can readily look at each of these types.

Understanding the FileViewer

The FileViewer in this version starts as it did before, launching a FileDialog to get a file from the user and exiting if the user cancels out of that dialog box:

```
FileDialog fd = new FileDialog( new Frame(),
    "Open File" );
fd.show();

// exit if user cancels
if ( fd.getFile() == null )
    System.exit( 0 );
```

Next it creates one each of the items it might need to look at the file:

```
DBF dbf = null;
TxtFile tf = null;
BinFile bf = null;
```

Then it begins the process of opening an appropriate object by creating an MRString from the name the FileDialog returns. This makes it very easy to attempt to open a DBF if the name ends with ".DBF". This is how it's done:

```
MRString m = new MRString( fd.getFile() );

if ( m.toUpper().endsWith(".DBF") ) {

    dbf = new DBF( fd.getFile() );
    if ( ! dbf.readable )
        dbf = null;
}
```

If the file is not a valid DBF, the FileViewer will try to open it first as text, and then, if that fails, as a generic binary file, this way:

```
if ( dbf == null ) {

    tf = new TxtFile( fd.getFile() );
```

```
if ( ! tf.readable ) {

    bf = new BinFile( fd.getFile() );
```

Since the DBF uses the MsgBox class to pop up messages, I added a MsgBox to the FileViewer. This replaces the use of the Java window for message output—it's much more professional. The MsgBox pops up an information box that waits for an OK click. It's not really modal, which is the way I like it. We'll look at the MsgBox more closely in the next section.

This is the code that handles the situation in which none of the file opening procedures worked:

```
if ( ! bf.readable ) {

    MsgBox mb = new MsgBox(
        "Could not open " + fd.getFile(),
        "No File Opened" );
    mb.show();
    while ( mb.isVisible() )
        ;

    System.exit( 1 );
}
```

Next the mainline creates a new ScrollWin object with the DBF, TxtFile, or BinFile it has opened:

```
ScrollWin sw = null;

// TxtFile, BinFile and DBF implement Scrollable
if ( dbf != null ) {

    sw = new ScrollWin( dbf, fd.getFile() );
}
else if ( tf.readable ) {

    sw = new ScrollWin( tf, fd.getFile() );
}
else if ( bf.readable )
    sw = new ScrollWin( bf, fd.getFile() );
```

Finally, the ScrollWin is prepared for use and then launched:

```
if ( sw != null ) {

    sw.setEndApp( true );
    sw.resize( 550, 300 );
     sw.show();
}
```

The Complete FileViewer Listing

Listing 6-1 shows the full FileViewer.java file. It's becoming more complex with each iteration, but I think you'll agree that even with handling all those annoying little details, it does a lot of work for very little effort in programming.

Listing 6-1:
FileViewer-
.java

```
// FileViewer.java
// Copyright 1997, Martin L. Rinehart

// this code is completely documented in:
// _Java Database Development_, Martin Rinehart,
// Osborne/McGraw-Hill, 1997

import java.awt.*;
import java.io.*;

class FileViewer extends Frame {

// -------------------- data members --------------------

// there are no data members

// -------------------- public methods --------------------

// main:
    public static void main( String[] args ) {

        FileDialog fd = new FileDialog( new Frame(),
            "Open File" );
        fd.show();

        // exit if user cancels
        if ( fd.getFile() == null )
```

```
        System.exit( 0 );

DBF dbf = null;
TxtFile tf = null;
BinFile bf = null;

MRString m = new MRString( fd.getFile() );

if ( m.toUpper().endsWith(".DBF") ) {

    dbf = new DBF( fd.getFile() );
    if ( ! dbf.readable )
        dbf = null;
}

if ( dbf == null ) {

    tf = new TxtFile( fd.getFile() );

    if ( ! tf.readable ) {

        bf = new BinFile( fd.getFile() );

        if ( ! bf.readable ) {

            MsgBox mb = new MsgBox(
                "Could not open " + fd.getFile(),
                "No File Opened" );
            mb.show();
            while ( mb.isVisible() )
                ;

            System.exit( 1 );
        }
    }
}

ScrollWin sw = null;

// TxtFile, BinFile and DBF implement Scrollable
if ( dbf != null ) {
```

```
            sw = new ScrollWin( dbf, fd.getFile() );
        }
        else if ( tf.readable ) {

            sw = new ScrollWin( tf, fd.getFile() );
        }
        else if ( bf.readable )
            sw = new ScrollWin( bf, fd.getFile() );

        if ( sw != null ) {

            sw.setEndApp( true );
            sw.resize( 550, 300 );
            sw.show();
        }
    }

// there are no other methods
}


// end of FileViewer.java
```

The MsgBox Class

TOUR

To use the MsgBox, just read the "Using" section and skip "Understanding." You won't miss anything.

    You'll want to come back to "Understanding" soon enough, I'll predict. The MsgBox spawns extended versions as quickly as any class I know. We'll meet the YNBox (display a message and get a yes or no answer) later on. You may want to add a Help button to the basic MsgBox, or perhaps a Cancel button. The "Understanding" section won't feel neglected if you leave it until just before you make one of these extensions.

    Microsoft's Visual Basic has a built-in function that launches a message box. It sports an elaborate (and RAM-consuming) array of parameter-based options. I wanted the functionality without the RAM consumption. Since 80 percent of my uses provided just a message, or a message and a window title, I limited the MsgBox to supporting just that much of the Visual Basic msgbox functionality.

These are very handy and, as you saw with the improvement to the FileViewer, they let your quick-and-dirty utilities look a lot more professional. Using them is very simple.

Using the MsgBox Class

You use one of two constructors to create a MsgBox:

```
MsgBox( String msg )
MsgBox( String msg, String title )
```

With the first form, you pass the message string. It adds the title, "Attention". With the second form, you pass the message and a title for the window.

You launch the MsgBox( ) by calling the show( ) method. The FileViewer's MsgBox code is typical:

```
MsgBox mb = new MsgBox(
    "Could not open " + fd.getFile(),
    "No File Opened" );
mb.show();
```

This creates a semi-standard information box. Its first originality is in the Java-style OK button that takes the full width of the bottom of the box, as shown here:

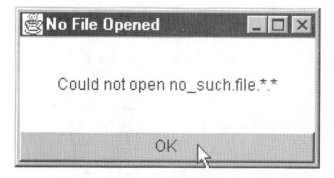

The other unusual feature of the MsgBox is that it is *not* modal. Modal information boxes are one of my pet peeves. To me, they let the software designer say, "What I have to say here is so important that I won't let you keep using your computer until you acknowledge me."

Doesn't that frost your cake? How in the world can anyone except the person at the computer judge the importance of some message? I'll reserve that sort of annoyance for messages that are absolutely critical: "Prescribing drug X with drug Y may cause cardiac arrest!" That should be modal.

Modal messages are like italics. If you get *carried away* and use them *all the time* as if your thoughts are *vitally* important, the reader just tunes them out. Use them rarely, when they're really justified, and they'll be effective.

In the case of FileViewer, the MsgBox reporting the error would flash for an instant (if you were lucky) before the application closed down, so you wouldn't be doing the job. Since this MsgBox is launched at the very end of the application's run, the addition in FileViewer is necessary to make the box visible:

```
while ( mb.isVisible() )
    ;
```

Should that bit of code use Thread.sleep( )? Go ahead and add it if you like. As written it's a rather CPU-intensive way of keeping a message visible. On the other hand, chances are excellent that the very next thing the user will do is click the OK button, which will end the message and the waste. I prefer to save RAM by omitting the extra code.

If your message box is not displayed at the end of the application's run, it will stay around until the user clicks OK or the application terminates. Even if the user leaves several boxes lying around the desktop, they all get cleaned up when the launching application terminates.

Understanding the MsgBox Class

In this section we'll look at the public parts of MsgBox and then at the private parts. It's a very simple, small class. I kept it as small as I could so I could use it whenever I wanted, without worrying about RAM-use expense.

The Public Parts of MsgBox

The MsgBox has public data and methods. The data explains itself:

```
public String message;
public String title;
```

The methods are only slightly more complex. The simpler of two constructors adds the "Attention" title. The second constructor designs and forms the message box. It uses the default BorderLayout, placing the message in the Center region and the OK button in the South, this way:

```
        resize( good_width(), 120 );

        Label lblMessage = new Label( message );
        lblMessage.setAlignment( Label.CENTER );
        add( "Center", lblMessage );

        add( "South", new OKbtn(this) );
```

It overcomes a serious bug in both Visual Cafe and VJ++ by showing and then immediately hiding itself. (If you're lucky, you won't get an annoying flicker. If you're even luckier, the vendors will have found and fixed the bug by the time you read this.)

```
    // center in screen:
        show(); hide(); // get control of position
```

The bug is that the functions that position the window on the screen (the move( ) and the reshape( ) methods) don't do anything until the window has been displayed. Regardless of your code, Windows will decide where the opening display is positioned. Once Windows has made up its mind, however, it lets you decide from there on.

This code uses the Toolkit to check the size of the physical screen and display the MsgBox in its center:

```
        Toolkit tk = getToolkit();
        Dimension d = tk.getScreenSize();

        move ( (d.width - size().width)/2,
               (d.height - size().height)/2 );
```

The other public methods are routine. The handleEvent( ) method hides and discards the message box after a click on the window-closing button.

The Private Parts of MsgBox

The good_width( ) method finds a width that's adequate to display the message and to leave a decent margin. It guesses that the user's display is using a default window font not larger than 12 points. (The Windows default is 8 points, but many users reset this to 10.) It uses the larger of the space required for the title or for the message, this way:

```
// fm is a FontMetrics object

    wid1 = 50 + fm.stringWidth( message );
    wid2 = 150 + fm.stringWidth( title );

    if ( wid1 > wid2 )
        return wid1;
    else
        return wid2;
```

In addition to the good_width( ) private method, there is a private class for the OK button. This class creates a button labeled "OK" and records a reference to its parent when you create it:

```
MsgBox parent;

OKbtn( MsgBox mb ) {

    super( "  OK  " );
    parent = mb;

}
```

Then the handleEvent( ), which is only called for a click of some sort, turns the button into another window-closing alternative, this way:

```
public boolean handleEvent( Event e ) {

    parent.postEvent( new Event(null,
        Event.WINDOW_DESTROY, null) );

    return true;
}
```

The Full MsgBox Listing

The full listing of MsgBox.java is in Listing 6-2. You can use this to create your own versions of the MsgBox class. You can even use it to create a modal message box, if you have to display information that's potentially life-saving.

Listing 6-2:
MsgBox.java

```java
// MsgBox.java -- VB-style message box for Java
// Copyright 1997, Martin L. Rinehart

// this code is completely documented in:
// _Java Database Development_, Martin Rinehart,
// Osborne/McGraw-Hill, 1997

/*
    Pop up an information box without a lot of coding.
*/

import java.awt.*;

class MsgBox extends Frame {

// -------------------- data members --------------------

// public data members:

    public String message;

    public String title;

// there are no protected data members

// there are no static data members

// -------------------- public methods --------------------

// constructors:

    MsgBox( String msg ) {
        this( msg, "Attention" );
    }

    MsgBox( String msg, String title ) {

        super( title );
        this.title = title;
        message = msg;

        resize( good_width(), 120 );
```

```
        Label lblMessage = new Label( message );
        lblMessage.setAlignment( Label.CENTER );
        add( "Center", lblMessage );

        add( "South", new OKbtn(this) );

    // center in screen:
        show(); hide(); // get control of position

        Toolkit tk = getToolkit();
        Dimension d = tk.getScreenSize();

        move ( (d.width - size().width)/2,
              (d.height - size().height)/2 );
    }

// there are no data access getXxx() methods
// there are no data access isXxx() methods
// there are no data access setXxx() methods

// there are no public, class-specific methods

// public, non-event overriding method:

    public String paramString() {

        return "msg: " + message +
            " title: " + title;
    }

// public, event-handling method:

    public boolean handleEvent( Event e ) {

        if ( e.id == Event.WINDOW_DESTROY ) {
            hide();
            dispose();
            return true;
        }
        return super.handleEvent( e );
    }
```

```
// ------------------ private methods ------------------

// private method:

    private int good_width() {

        int wid1, wid2;

        setFont( new Font("Helvetica", Font.PLAIN, 12) );
        FontMetrics fm = getFontMetrics( getFont() );

        wid1 = 50 + fm.stringWidth( message );
        wid2 = 150 + fm.stringWidth( title );

        if ( wid1 > wid2 )
            return wid1;
        else
            return wid2;
    }

} // end of MsgBox class

// private class in MsgBox.java:

class OKbtn extends Button {

    MsgBox parent;

    OKbtn( MsgBox mb ) {

        super( "  OK  " );
        parent = mb;

    }

    public boolean handleEvent( Event e ) {

        parent.postEvent( new Event(null,
            Event.WINDOW_DESTROY, null) );

        return true;
    }
```

```
} // end of OKbtn

// end of MsgBox.java
```

The DBF Class

TOUR

We'll be using DBF objects to store relational data. Later you'll see that this same structure can store objects as well. So the DBF will be our primary database tool.
You'll need to have a complete grasp of the "Using" section as we go forward. It's up to you to decide if the "Understanding" section is necessary now or can be postponed until you're ready to modify this key class.

The DBF class lets you use DBF files without any concern for its underlying format or other details. In our FileViewer use we're just displaying the getString( ) result, for which DBFs are as simple as TxtFiles.

In most database applications, we'll want the record divided into values for each field, of course. You'll see as we go through this class that there's a lot more here than we are using currently, including the ability to pass individual field values and the ability to perform the needed add, edit, and delete data functions.

You'll also see several additional classes that we'll be treating as black boxes in this chapter. (We'll get to them as we develop the additional classes used in our JDB application.)

Before we begin, I'd like to emphasize a point. While DBFs make it easy to handle many kinds of data, they're just a tool. The carpenter's toolbox doesn't build the house. Building a house takes a carpenter who knows how to use the tools. DBFs won't build database applications, either. It's time for you database carpenters to roll up your sleeves.

Using the DBF Class

You've seen that the DBF implements the Scrollable interface and can be used like the TxtFile or BinFile. However, the DBF is far more powerful than these simple types.

Its basic purpose is to store records, which are groups of individual field values. Most uses access those fields. Even most scrolling windows use those fields.

The getString( ) method returns the entire record as a String. You'll typically want your user to look at a single field (occasionally two or three fields) for scrolling uses. For example, in a set of people you would probably scroll on their last names. Your scroll window would show the last name on the left with additional identifying data to the right of the last name. (You do that, of course, by extending the DBF class and overriding the getString( ) method in the extending class.)

We'll begin our study of the DBF's public interface with the public data.

Using the DBF's Public Data

Four data items are public in the DBF class, which makes them convenient to read. These data items should never be assigned values directly. If you're in a team programming environment and there is some question about the team members, you'll probably want to make these protected data members, instead of allowing public access.

These are the public data members:

```
public String file_name;
public String message;
public boolean readable;
public boolean writeable;
```

The file_name is the name (optionally including the path) that you use in calling the constructor. The message is the String that the constructor assigns. It reports any problems or it reports success. The booleans readable and, if you want write access, writeable, are the ones you should check after calling the constructor.

Using the DBF's Public Methods

We'll begin with the DBF's constructors, which will be familiar to you since they're just like the TxtFile and BinFile constructors. Then we'll go on to the data-access and other public methods. You'll see that the Scrollable interface is the same as it is for the other file types, but the DBF supports a rich array of capabilities beyond that interface.

USING THE DBF'S CONSTRUCTORS   As with the other files, you create a new DBF by passing the name of the file (with optional path information) to the constructor. The default access is "r", for read-only. You add an additional parameter, "rw", if you want read and write access.

To avoid being platform specific, use a FileDialog to get the filename, this way:

```
// fd is a FileDialog that was shown and which
// returns a non-null value for getFile()

DBF foo = new DBF( fd.getFile() ); // read access
DBF foo = new DBF( fd.getFile(), "rw" ); // read/write
```

After calling the constructor, check readable or writeable to see if you have gained the access you want. It's an annoying little detail, but I don't know how to avoid it.

USING THE DBF'S DATA-ACCESS METHODS

The data-access getXxx( ) methods are

- Vector getDEFs( )
- Vector getFieldVals( )
- String getFileName( )
- int getLast( )
- String getName( )
- int getNumFields( )
- String getString(int index)
- Vector getValues(int recno)

The getDEFs( ) method returns a Vector of DEField objects. We'll get to the DEField later. It is a data-entry field appropriately masked to accept data valid for the field's type. This data mask, for example, gets a North American telephone number:

```
"(999) 999-9999"
```

A DEField with that mask would permit the user to enter digits at the location of the "9"s. It doesn't let the user access the other characters in the field. For now, you can ignore the getDEFs( ) method.

The getFieldVals( ) returns a Vector of MRStrings. They are the field's name, type, length, and, for numerics, number of decimal places. Calling getFieldVals(0) gets this information for the first field in the record. The last field is getNumFields( ) − 1.

The getFileName( ) and getName( ) methods both return the value of the public file_name String. (I could never remember which was correct, so I made them both correct.)

The getLast( ) and getString( ) methods are your old friends from the Scrollable interface. The getNumFields( ) method does just what it promises.

The getValues( ) method returns a Vector of Strings. The length of the Vector is the number of fields in the record, and the value of each String is the value of the corresponding field in the record.

There is one isXxx( ) method:

- boolean isDeleted( )

The isDeleted( ) method returns true if the current record (see the go( ) method) is marked deleted.

These are the setXxx( ) methods:

- void setDeleted(int recno, boolean del_status)
- void setValues(int recno, Vector vals)

The setDeleted( ) method lets you set a record's status to deleted (del_status is true) or make nondeleted a formerly deleted record (del_status is false).

The setValues( ) method is the counterpart of the getValues( ) method. The common data-entry procedure is to call getValues( ) and then let the user (using a data-entry screen) edit the data. When the user is done, the values Vector is reassembled from the data-entry screen and returned to the DBF, which updates the current record with the new values.

USING THE DBF'S OTHER PUBLIC METHODS   The other public methods include

- void close( )
- void dbf_read(String fn)
- void go(int recno)

- void replace( )
- boolean useMonospace( )

The close( ) method closes the DBF file, saving you the bother of creating try and catch blocks. The dbf_read( ) method is called by the constructor. You might want to make it a private method.

The go( ) method makes the specified record the current record. Subsequent record-specific actions, such as getValues( ), setValues( ), isDeleted( ), and setDeleted( ), are actions on this record. The go( ) method updates the record buffer with the values from the specified record. It does *not* save the current record before changing to the new record.

The replace( ) method is called by methods such as setValues( ). It pushes the current values in the record buffer into the file. You would call this if you were writing a utility that directly manipulated the record buffer. (For example, a test data generator might fill the buffer with random values appropriate to each field's type.)

The useMonospace( ) method returns true as part of the Scrollable interface. In an extending class that overrides getString( ) you might also want to override this method.

Understanding the DBF Class

This section opens up the DBF, beginning with the data members. After a quick look at the data, we'll go on to the public and private methods, and finish up with a look at the private field structure class.

Understanding the DBF's Data Members

We've already looked at the public members. To hop ahead, there are two final static members, DELETED and NOT_DELETED, which hold the byte-sized flags ' ' and '*'. The rest of the data members are protected.

A String, access, holds the "r" or "rw" that was used in opening the file.

An int, date_last_update, holds the date read from bytes 1, 2, and 3 of the file header. This int is in YYYYMMDD format.

A Vector, fields, keeps a list of field structure (fld_stru) objects. Each fld_stru object has the field's name, type, length, and decimals as specified in the DBF header.

These fields are self-explanatory:

```
int len_header;
int len_record;

int num_recs;
int num_fields;
```

As with the BinFile, a RandomAccessFile, raf, encapsulates the disk file.

The DBF uses a byte array, record_buffer, to hold the current record and an int, record_number, to keep track of the location in the file.

A Vector, values, holds the value of each field as a String. Your application normally gets data from the values Vector and sets the record by returning updated data in this Vector.

Understanding the DBF's Public Methods

In this section we'll look at the constructors first. Then we'll go on to the data-access methods, and last, we'll look at the other public methods.

UNDERSTANDING THE DBF'S CONSTRUCTORS   The job of the first constructor is simply to add the default "r" (read) access string to a call to the other constructor:

```
DBF( String pathname ) {

    this( pathname, "r" );
}
```

The second constructor starts by storing the access method:

```
DBF( String pathname, String access ) {

    this.access = access;
```

Then it creates the fields Vector and initializes readable and writeable:

```
fields = new Vector();
readable = writeable = false;
```

The hard work is done by the dbf_read( ) method, which we'll cover later in this chapter:

```
dbf_read( pathname );
```

The last step is to create and null-fill the values constructor, if the DBF is readable:

```
if ( readable ) {

    values = new Vector( num_fields );
    for ( int i = 0 ; i < num_fields ; i++ )
        values.addElement( null );
}
```

UNDERSTANDING THE DBF'S DATA-ACCESS METHODS The getDEFs( ) method creates and returns a new Vector, filled with DEField objects. (We'll get to DEFields later. They let you appropriately mask user input, providing one piece of the data validation puzzle.) As you can see, the real work here is delegated to the make_def( ) private method:

```
Vector def_vec = new Vector( num_fields );

for ( int i = 0 ; i < num_fields ; i++ )
    def_vec.addElement( make_def(i) );

return def_vec;
```

The getFieldVals( ) method returns a Vector of MRStrings holding a field's name, type, length, and number of decimal places. Looking ahead, our JDB application lets you drop a DBF's header data into a data table. That table holds one field's data in each record. The columns are name, type, length, and decimals.

The basic function of the JDB is to let you edit a DBF's data contents. When you edit this table definition data, you are revising a table definition. The JDB can construct a new DBF from the revised definition. This lets the JDB's data editor serve for both data content and data definition.

The MRStrings here are used in the data editor. The method starts by creating a Vector and fld_stru object:

```
Vector vals = new Vector();
fld_stru fs = ( fld_stru ) fields.elementAt( fno );
```

Then it creates and adjusts the MRStrings. The name, for example, is padded to the ten-character length:

```
MRString m = new MRString( fs.name );
m.padTo( 10 );
```

The length and decimals are right-justified, which is what you expect to see when you enter an integer. This is the length code:

```
m = new MRString( "" + (int)(fs.length) );
m.leftPadTo( 5 );
vals.addElement( m.toString() );
```

This is a good example of an MRString's convenient habit of being able to do exactly what we want done.

The methods getFileName( ), getLast( ), getName( ), and getNumFields( ) are all trivial. The getString( ) method uses the go( ) method to go to the appropriate record (read it into the buffer) and then returns the buffer, recast as a String:

```
go( index );
return new String( record_buffer, 0 );
```

Similarly, the getValues( ) method also relies on go( ). Additionally, it uses read_values( ), which we'll get to later in this chapter:

```
go( recno );
read_values();
return values;
```

The first byte of the record is either an asterisk (DELETED) or a space (NOT_DELETED), which makes the isDeleted( ) method simple:

```
go( recno );
return record_buffer[0] == DELETED;
```

The setDeleted( ) method first goes to and sets the flag byte in the buffer:

```
        if ( recno != record_number )
            go( recno );

        byte b = del_status ? DELETED : NOT_DELETED;

        record_buffer[0] = b;
```

Then it writes the updated record to disk:

```
        try {
            raf.seek( file_pos(record_number) );
            raf.write( b );
        }
        catch ( IOException ioe ) {;}
```

The setValues( ) begins by checking for a mistake, and showing an appropriate message, if needed:

```
        public void setValues( int recno, Vector vals ) {

        if ( !writeable ) {
            ( new MsgBox(".DBF is not writeable") ).show();
            return;
        }
```

If the DBF is writeable, it goes on to the actual updating. This also delegates the hard work to the write_fields( ) private method, which we'll get to later in this chapter:

```
        values = vals;
          go( recno );
        write_fields( recno );
```

UNDERSTANDING THE DBF'S OTHER PUBLIC METHODS   The close( ) method uses the necessary try and catch blocks, so you don't have to:

```
public void close() {

    try {
        raf.close();
    }
    catch ( IOException ioe ) {
    }
}
```

The dbf_read( ) method does the hard work for the constructors. This is one that is the real master of the DBF file's structure. It starts by opening the file or by returning a simple message if it fails:

```
try {
    raf = new RandomAccessFile( fn, access );
}

catch (IOException ioe) {
    message = "File open error";
    return;
}
```

On success, it creates and reads the file header:

```
byte[] buffer = new byte[32];

try {
    raf.read( buffer );
}

catch (IOException ioe) {
    message = "File read error";
    return;
}
```

Then it creates the vital data members for this DBF. The file_name is just saved. The date is put into an integer in YYYYMMDD format, this way:

```
date_last_update =
    (1900 + buffer[1]) * 10000 ;
date_last_update += buffer[2]*100 ;
date_last_update += buffer[3];
```

The number of records, the length of the header, the number of fields, and the length of the record are then set. The int_from4( ) and int_from2( ) methods take care of the conversion from little-endian to Java integer data. (This is platform independent. You can't, however, use stream I/O methods like readInt( ) to access this data.)

```
num_recs = int_from4 ( buffer, 4 );
len_header = int_from2 ( buffer, 8 );
num_fields = ( (len_header - 1) / 32 ) - 1;
    // num_fields will be reset
    // for FoxPro .DBFs

len_record = int_from2 ( buffer, 10 );
```

The FoxPro format uses additional, null-filled field structure records. (I don't know why. Adding a field to a DBF requires a complete rewrite of the entire data section, so allowing spares here doesn't appear to have any purpose.) You'll see the appropriate adjustment later in this chapter.

Next the record_buffer is created and filled with blanks:

```
record_buffer = new byte[len_record];
  for ( int i = 0 ; i < len_record ; i++ )
      record_buffer[i] = (byte) ' ';
```

This completes the general work. Next a for loop handles one field at a time. It begins by reading the field structure record into the same buffer that held the file header record:

```
try {
    raf.read( buffer );
}
catch (IOException ioe) {
    message = "File read error";
    return;
}
```

A return character in byte zero ends the list of fields. You have entered the unused data fields in the FoxPro format if the type byte is null. This code makes these checks and adjusts the number of fields, if necessary:

```
if ( (buffer[0] == 0xD) ||
     (buffer[11] == 0 ) ) {

    num_fields = i;
    break;
}
```

For live fields, the next step is to fill a fld_stru object with the data from the field structure record. This is fairly straightforward. We convert from the zero-padded field name to a blank-padded one here. Also, the unsigned_byte( ) function is used to convert the length byte to an integer. (This converts 0xFF to 255. A cast would make that a –1. I'll let you guess how I figured that out.) This is the code:

```
fld_stru fs = new fld_stru();

for ( byte b = 0 ; b < 10 ; b++ ) {

    if ( buffer[b] > 0 )
        fs.name[b] = buffer[b];
    else
        fs.name[b] = (byte) ' ';

}
```

```
fs.type = buffer[11];
fs.length = ( byte )
        unsigned_byte( buffer[16] );
fs.decimals = buffer[17];
```

Two decimal places are used for the number of decimals. Since this limits the value to 99, there's no need to apply the unsigned_byte( ) function for this value.

After handling the fields, the last work is to handle the readable and writeable booleans:

```
readable = num_fields > 0;
if ( access.equals("rw") )
        writeable = readable;
```

The field_string( ) method converts a field's definition into a human-readable form. It's commented out, but I've left it for future use. (You'll probably be glad it's there when you start adding your own field types.)

The go( ) method is a real workhorse. You've seen it being used five different places already. While it's heavily used, it's still simple:

```
public void go( int recno ) {

    try {
        raf.seek( file_pos(recno) );
        record_number = recno;

        raf.read( record_buffer );
    }
    catch (IOException ioe) {;}

}
```

It's up to your application to pass go( ) an argument between zero and the number of records minus one. The original catch block for this function was better-looking, but as the bug box notes, it didn't get the job done.

The java.awt doesn't specify what happens when you seek past the existing end of a RandomAccessFile. Being curious, I decided to find out.

I backed up the hard disk on an old computer and then tried to read from a spot past the end of the file, using Visual J++. It's a good thing I was backed up. The operation behaved as if it had been successfully performed. The crash came a bit later.

Visual Cafe wasn't any better. It, too, pretended to work successfully, but splattered random bits all over RAM. My opinion is that both vendors flunked this test and that it's a very serious matter.

The replace( ) method is the last public one. It does its job and it provides append functionality, too. You can reasonably write data beginning with the byte immediately following the file's last current byte. The replace( ) method supports this normal append when the record number equals the number of records.

Note that it doesn't append (or otherwise handle) if the record number is larger than the number of records. It's up to your application to present values from zero through the number of records.

In a team programming environment, you'll probably want to add some form of error checking to catch programmer mistakes. Add it here and to go( ).

This is the replace( ) code:

```
public void replace( int recno ) {

    // check for append
    if ( recno == num_recs ) {
        num_recs++;
        rewrite_numrecs();
    }

    // go ahead
    try {
        raf.seek( file_pos(recno) );
        record_number = recno;

        raf.write( record_buffer );
    }
    catch ( IOException ioe) {

        ( new MsgBox("Write failure") ).show();
        System.out.println( "Write failed: " +
```

```
                              ioe.toString() );
          }
      }
```

Understanding the DBF's Private Methods

The first private method, get_dec_init( ), returns a String set up with a default initial value for a numeric field. The default value is zero. The string is a zero followed by a decimal point (I use a period, which some of you will want to change) and more zeros. In a 6-byte-long field with two decimal places, the string returned will be "   0.00".

The get_dec_mask( ) function establishes a mask used by the data-entry field. For the six-long, two-decimal-place field mentioned earlier, the mask would be "009.99". The zero and nine characters allow entry of any digit. The zero characters may also be blank. This ensures that the user will enter characters that can reasonably be interpreted as a decimal number.

The get_init( ) method returns an initial value. That's a null string for character data, "12/31/1999" for date data (you may have a better idea), the appropriately filled string for numerics, and a "Y" value for a logical field.

The get_int_init( ) method returns the String filled with zero characters. The get_int_mask( ) function returns a string with the appropriate number of leading zeros followed by a "9" in the last position.

The get_mask( ) method returns all "x" characters for character data. This mask allows entry of anything the user types. (It's equivalent to no mask at all.) The date mask is "99/99/9999", which allows only digits in the "9" positions and doesn't permit entry in the "/" positions. The numeric types are handled by their individual functions, get_int_mask( ) and get_dec_mask( ). The mask for a logical is "L", which allows "N" or "F" for false, and "Y" or "T" for true. It accepts input in either case, but converts lowercase to uppercase.

The file_pos( ) method converts an integer record number to a long file location, corresponding to the starting byte (deleted flag) of the specified record. It depends on the record number being a valid one. This is the code:

```
    private long file_pos( int recno )
        throws IOException {

        if ( (recno < 0) || (recno >= num_recs) )
            throw( new IOException("Bad record number") );

        return ( (long) len_header ) +
            ( (long) len_record ) * recno;

    }
```

Java's insistence that all integers are signed certainly simplifies the language, but it's a pain in the posterior when you have to do something like converting input bytes into numbers. This code is more complex by far than the same job in C or assembler. To be fair, however, I should point out that it's only needed because we're dealing with a little-endian, PC-specific file format in a way that converts it to a platform-independent format.

This routine converts two bytes. It reads the first, using the unsigned_byte( ) routine (convert 0xFF to 255, not −1) into an integer. Then it shifts left. Last, it adds the second byte, again using the unsigned_byte( ) routine to handle values over 127 correctly. This is the code:

```
    private int int_from2( byte[] b, int start ) {

  // reads int from little-endian byte array buffer

        int result;
        result = unsigned_byte( b[start+1] );

        result <<=8;
        result += unsigned_byte( b[start] );

        return result;

    }
```

The routine that handles four bytes, int_from4( ), does the same job, but it has more work to do:

```
    private int int_from4( byte[] b, int start ) {

  // reads long from little-endian byte array buffer

        int result;
        result = unsigned_byte( b[start+3] );

        result <<= 8;
        result += unsigned_byte( b[start+2] );

        result <<= 8;
        result += unsigned_byte( b[start+1] );
```

```
        result <<=8;
        result += unsigned_byte( b[start] );

        return result;
    }
```

Converting an integer to a 4-byte array is a matter of masking off the bits appropriate for the particular byte, and then shifting the result into the right (least-significant) byte. Casting the result as a byte throws away the left (more-significant) three bytes of the integer. This is the code:

```
    private byte[] int_to4( int n ) {

// makes little-endian 4-byte array from int
        byte[] b = new byte[4];

        b[0] = ( byte )    (n & 0xFF);
        b[1] = ( byte ) ( (n & 0xFF00) >> 8 );
        b[2] = ( byte ) ( (n & 0xFF0000) >> 16 );
        b[3] = ( byte ) ( (n & 0xFF000000) >> 24 );

        return b;
    }
```

Ready for a pop quiz? What would happen if you didn't mask off the higher bytes in the assignment to b[0]? Specifically, what would happen if the input value were negative?

I don't know the answer, by the way. It's simple enough to get the answer by trying it out, but I didn't. I wouldn't be sure that the answer one Java gave matched the answers for every other Java, would you? Better safe than sorry. I warned you that this little-endian stuff would get tricky, didn't I?

The make_def( ) method returns a DEField. When we get to the DEField, this will make complete sense. If you've not seen that class, ignore the method.

The non_null_string( ) method returns a String matching the input argument, except that null characters are replaced with blanks.

The read_field( ) method is called by the read_values( ) method. The latter reads all the values in the record. The read_field( ) method places the value of an individual field into the values Vector. It's straightforward, copying the appropriate bytes except in the case of a date, when it does this conversion:

```
// change YYYYMMDD to MM/DD/YYYY
byte[] d = new byte[10];
d[0] = record_buffer[bufloc + 4];
d[1] = record_buffer[bufloc + 5];
d[2] = (byte) '/';
d[3] = record_buffer[bufloc + 6];
d[4] = record_buffer[bufloc + 7];
d[5] = (byte) '/';
d[6] = record_buffer[bufloc];
d[7] = record_buffer[bufloc + 1];
d[8] = record_buffer[bufloc + 2];
d[9] = record_buffer[bufloc + 3];
```

The read_values( ) method loops over the fields, reading each one in turn. For this purpose, reading means appropriately setting the values Vector based on the current contents of the file record buffer. This is the code:

```
private void read_values() {

    fld_stru fs;

    int recloc = 1; // point past deleted byte
    for ( int i = 0 ; i < num_fields ; i++ ) {

        fs = (fld_stru) fields.elementAt(i);
        read_field( i, fs, recloc );
        recloc += fs.length;
    }
}
```

The DBF file's header can be safely ignored, except that the number of records needs to be updated after each append operation. This method handles that job for the replace( ) method:

```
private void rewrite_numrecs() {

    try {
        raf.seek( 4 );
        raf.write( int_to4(num_recs) );
    }
```

```
        catch ( IOException ioe ) {;}
    }
```

The type_string( ) returns a String matching a field's type byte. If you think of a better method, please drop me a message. It certainly looks like I've done this the hard way, doesn't it?

```
    private String type_string( byte b ) {

        switch( b ) {
            case 'C': return "C";
            case 'D': return "D";
            case 'L': return "L";
            case 'N': return "N";
            case 'F': return "F";
        }
        return "U";
    }
```

Don't be too quick to decide that you've got a better way, however. Make sure that you've got a smaller executable-size cost than I do.

When you assign a smaller integer type to a larger type, the assignment is done by sign extension. This means that a byte equal to minus one becomes an integer, still equal to minus one. That is completely wrong, however, when you need a byte that represents values between 0 and 255. This method meets that need, however:

```
    private int unsigned_byte( byte b ) {

        return ( (int) b ) & 0x000000FF;
    }
```

Casting a byte as an int extends the sign of the result. (You get 0x000000XX for positive values; 0xFFFFFFXX for negative values.) That's the same as assigning a byte to an int. To get the unsigned value, you have to undo the result of the sign extension by masking off the left (more significant) three bytes. The good news is that you've just seen the last of the little-endian fiddling functions.

The write_field( ) method is the reverse of read_field( ), naturally. Like its counterpart, its basic job is to transfer bytes from the values Vector to their homes in the record buffer. Again, the exception is the date value, which is converted this way:

```
// change MM/DD/YYYY to YYYYMMDD
byte[] d = new byte[10];
s.getBytes( 0, 10, d, 0 );

record_buffer[recloc]   = d[6];
record_buffer[recloc+1] = d[7];
record_buffer[recloc+2] = d[8];
record_buffer[recloc+3] = d[9];

record_buffer[recloc+4] = d[0];
record_buffer[recloc+5] = d[1];

record_buffer[recloc+6] = d[3];
record_buffer[recloc+7] = d[4];
```

That moves the ten characters of the "MM/DD/YYYY" String into a 10-byte array. Then it picks out the eight bytes that it wants for the "YYYYMMDD" form. This is another method, by the way, where it looks fairly klutzy as written, but the only alternatives I could find were worse.

The write_fields( ) method is straightforward. It calls write_field( ) in a loop, handling all the fields. As it loops, it updates a record location, incrementing it by the length of each field it processes. And that's the last private method in this large class.

Understanding the DBF's Private Class

The fld_stru class stores the data we need about each field. It's trivial:

```
class fld_stru {

    public byte[] name;
    public byte type;
    public byte length;
    public byte decimals;

    fld_stru() {
        name = new byte[10];
    }
}
```

Leaving the integer values there as bytes makes the transfer to and from the file's header, where they're stored as bytes, simple. If I were rewriting this today, however, I'd think about changing them to ints.

The Full DBF Listing

This is the full DBF class file. We'll cover the Editable interface when we get to data entry. Ignore it for now.

Listing 6-3:
DBF.java

```java
// DBF.java -- DBF (.DBF file) class
// Copyright 1997, Martin L. Rinehart


// this code is completely documented in:
// _Java Database Development_, Martin Rinehart,
// Osborne/McGraw-Hill, 1997

/*
  Uses a .DBF file as a Java object that stores and
  retrieves records.
*/

import java.awt.*;
import java.io.*;
import java.util.*;

class DBF implements Scrollable, Editable {

// -------------------- data members --------------------

// public data members:

    public String file_name;

    public String message;

    public boolean readable;

    public boolean writeable;

// protected data members:

    protected String access; // "r" or "rw"

    protected int date_last_update;

    protected Vector fields;
```

```java
    protected int len_header;
    protected int len_record;

    protected int num_recs;
    protected int num_fields;

    protected RandomAccessFile raf;
    protected byte[] record_buffer;
    protected int record_number;

    protected byte type_byte;

    protected Vector values;

// static data members
    // there are no public static data members
    // there are no private static data members

    // final static data members:

    final static byte DELETED     = (byte) '*';
    final static byte NOT_DELETED = (byte) ' ';

// -------------------- public methods --------------------

// constructors:

    DBF( String pathname ) {

        this( pathname, "r" );
    }

    DBF( String pathname, String access ) {

        this.access = access;

        fields = new Vector();
        readable = writeable = false;
        dbf_read( pathname );

        if ( readable ) {
```

```
                    values = new Vector( num_fields );
                    for ( int i = 0 ; i < num_fields ; i++ )
                        values.addElement( null );
            }
        }

// data access getXxx() methods:

    public Vector getDEFs() {

        Vector def_vec = new Vector( num_fields );

        for ( int i = 0 ; i < num_fields ; i++ )
            def_vec.addElement( make_def(i) );

        return def_vec;
    }

    public Vector getFieldVals( int fno ) {

        Vector vals = new Vector();
        fld_stru fs = ( fld_stru ) fields.elementAt( fno );

        MRString m = new MRString( fs.name );
        m.padTo( 10 );

        vals.addElement( m.toString() );

        vals.addElement( new MRString(fs.type).toString() );

        m = new MRString( "" + (int)(fs.length) );
        m.leftPadTo( 5 );
        vals.addElement( m.toString() );

        m = new MRString( (byte)
            ( fs.decimals + ( byte ) '0') );
        m.leftPadTo( 2 );
        vals.addElement( m.toString() );

        return vals;
    }

    public String getFileName() {
```

```
            return file_name;
    }

    public int getLast() {

        // returns last item #
        return num_recs - 1;
    }

     public String getName() {

            return file_name;
     }

     public int getNumFields() {

            return num_fields;
     }

    public String getString(int index) {

        // a string representing scrollable[index]
        // index is from zero through getLast()

        go( index );
        return new String( record_buffer, 0 );
    }

    public Vector getValues( int recno ) {

        go( recno );
        read_values();
        return values;
    }

// data access isXxx() method:

    public boolean isDeleted( int recno ) {

        go( recno );
        return record_buffer[0] == DELETED;
    }
```

```java
// data access setXxx() methods:

    public void setDeleted( int recno,
        boolean del_status ) {

        if ( recno != record_number )
            go( recno );

        byte b = del_status ? DELETED : NOT_DELETED;

        record_buffer[0] = b;

        try {
            raf.seek( file_pos(record_number) );
            raf.write( b );
        }
        catch ( IOException ioe ) {;}
    }

    public void setValues( int recno, Vector vals ) {

        if ( !writeable ) {
            ( new MsgBox(".DBF is not writeable") ).show();
            return;
        }
        values = vals;
          go( recno );
        write_fields( recno );
    }

// public, class-specific methods:

    public void close() {

        try {
            raf.close();
        }
        catch ( IOException ioe ) {
        }
    }

    public void dbf_read( String fn ) {
```

```
    try {
        raf = new RandomAccessFile( fn, access );
    }

    catch (IOException ioe) {
        message = "File open error";
        return;
    }

    byte[] buffer = new byte[32];

    try {
        raf.read( buffer );
    }

    catch (IOException ioe) {
        message = "File read error";
        return;
    }

// ready to read; DBF header is in buffer[]

    file_name = fn;

    date_last_update =
        (1900 + buffer[1]) * 10000 ;
    date_last_update += buffer[2]*100 ;
    date_last_update += buffer[3];

    num_recs = int_from4( buffer, 4 );
    len_header = int_from2( buffer, 8 );
    num_fields = ( (len_header - 1) / 32 ) - 1;
        // num_fields will be reset
        // for FoxPro .DBFs

    len_record = int_from2( buffer, 10 );

    record_buffer = new byte[len_record];
      for ( int i = 0 ; i < len_record ; i++ )
          record_buffer[i] = (byte) ' ';

    for ( int i = 0 ; i < num_fields ; i++ ) {
```

```
            try {
                raf.read( buffer );
            }
            catch (IOException ioe) {
                message = "File read error";
                return;
            }

            if ( (buffer[0] == 0xD) ||
                 (buffer[11] == 0 ) ) {

                num_fields = i;
                break;
            }

            fld_stru fs = new fld_stru();

            for ( byte b = 0 ; b < 10 ; b++ ) {

                    if ( buffer[b] > 0 )
                        fs.name[b] = buffer[b];
                    else
                        fs.name[b] = (byte) ' ';
                }

            fs.type = buffer[11];
            fs.length = ( byte )
                    unsigned_byte( buffer[16] );
            fs.decimals = buffer[17];

            fields.addElement( fs );
        }

    readable = num_fields > 0;
    if ( access.equals("rw") )
            writeable = readable;
    }
/*
    public String field_string( int i ) {

        fld_stru fs = (fld_stru) fields.elementAt(i);
```

```
        return non_null_string( fs.name, 10 ) +
            " " + (char) fs.type +
            " " + fs.length +
            " " + fs.decimals;
    }
*/
    public void go( int recno ) {

        try {
            raf.seek( file_pos(recno) );
            record_number = recno;

            raf.read( record_buffer );
        }
        catch (IOException ioe) {;}
    }

    public void replace( int recno ) {

        // check for append
        if ( recno == num_recs ) {
            num_recs++;
            rewrite_numrecs();
        }

        // go ahead
        try {
            raf.seek( file_pos(recno) );
            record_number = recno;

            raf.write( record_buffer );
        }
        catch ( IOException ioe) {

            ( new MsgBox("Write failure") ).show();
            System.out.println( "Write failed: " +
                ioe.toString() );
        }
    }

    public boolean useMonospace() {
```

```
            return true;
        }

// public, non-event overriding method:

    public String paramString() {

        return file_name + " read: " + readable +
            " write " + writeable;
    }

// there are no public, event-handling methods

// ------------------- private methods -------------------

// private methods:

    private String get_dec_init( fld_stru fs ) {

        byte[] b = new byte[fs.length];

        int dpos = fs.length - fs.decimals - 1;
        if ( dpos > 0 ) {

            for ( int i = 0 ; i < dpos ; i++ )
                b[i] = (byte) '0';
        }

        if ( dpos > -1 ) b[dpos] = (byte) '.';
        if ( dpos < fs.length - 1 ) {

            for ( int i = dpos ; i < fs.length ; i++ )
                b[i] = (byte) '0';
        }
        return new String( b, 0 );
    }

    private String get_dec_mask( fld_stru fs ) {

        byte b[] = new byte[fs.length];
        int dpos = fs.length - fs.decimals - 1;
```

```
        if ( dpos > 0 ) {

            for ( int i = 0 ; i < (dpos - 1) ; i++ )
                b[i] = (byte) '0';

                b[dpos-1] = (byte) '9';
        }
        if ( dpos > -1 )
            b[dpos] = (byte) '.';

        if ( dpos < fs.length - 1 ) {

            for ( int i = dpos+1 ; i < fs.length ; i++ )
                b[i] = (byte) '9';
        }
        return new String( b, 0 );
    }

    private String get_init( fld_stru fs ) {

        switch ( fs.type ) {
            case 'C': {
                return "";
            }

            case 'D': {
                return "12/31/1999";
            }

            case 'N':
            case 'F': {
                if ( fs.decimals == 0 )
                    return get_int_init( fs );
                else
                    return get_dec_init( fs );

            }

            case 'L':
                return "Y";

            default:
```

```
                    return "";
        }
}

private String get_int_init( fld_stru fs ) {

    byte[] b = new byte[fs.length];

    for ( int i = 0 ; i < fs.length ; i++ )
        b[i] = (byte) '0';

    return new String( b, 0 );
}

private String get_int_mask( fld_stru fs ) {

    byte b[] = new byte[fs.length];

    for ( int i = 0 ; i < ( fs.length-1 ) ; i++ )
        b[i] = (byte) '0';

      b[fs.length-1] = (byte) '9';

    return new String( b, 0 );
}

private String get_mask( fld_stru fs ) {

    switch ( fs.type ) {

        case 'C': {
            return "x";
        }

        case 'D': {
            return "99/99/9999";
        }

        case 'N':
        case 'F': {
            if ( fs.decimals == 0 )
                return get_int_mask( fs );
```

```
                else
                    return get_dec_mask( fs );
            }

            case 'L':
                return "L";

            default:
                return "x";
        }
    }

    private long file_pos( int recno )
        throws IOException {

        if ( (recno < 0) || (recno >= num_recs) )
            throw( new IOException("Bad record number") );

        return ( (long) len_header ) +
            ( (long) len_record ) * recno;

    }

    private int int_from2( byte[] b, int start ) {

// reads int from little-endian byte array buffer

        int result;
        result = unsigned_byte( b[start+1] );

        result <<=8;
        result += unsigned_byte( b[start] );

        return result;

    }

    private int int_from4( byte[] b, int start ) {

// reads long from little-endian byte array buffer

        int result;
```

```
        result = unsigned_byte( b[start+3] );

        result <<= 8;
        result += unsigned_byte( b[start+2] );

        result <<= 8;
        result += unsigned_byte( b[start+1] );

        result <<=8;
        result += unsigned_byte( b[start] );

        return result;
    }

    private byte[] int_to4( int n ) {

// makes little-endian 4-byte array from int
        byte[] b = new byte[4];

        b[0] = ( byte )   (n & 0xFF);
        b[1] = ( byte ) ( (n & 0xFF00) >> 8 );
        b[2] = ( byte ) ( (n & 0xFF0000) >> 16 );
        b[3] = ( byte ) ( (n & 0xFF000000) >> 24 );

        return b;
    }

    private DEField make_def( int index ) {

        fld_stru fs = new fld_stru();
        fs = (fld_stru) fields.elementAt( index );

        String label = ( new String( fs.name, 0 ) ).trim();
        label = MRString.toUlower( label );
        String mask = get_mask( fs );

        int width = fs.type == 'D' ? 10 : fs.length;

        String init = get_init( fs );

        DEField def = new DEField(
                label, mask, width, init );
```

```
        return def;
    }

    private String non_null_string( byte[] b, int len ) {

// returns string of b[] thru last non-zero byte

        int i = 0;
        while ( i < len && b[i] > 0 ) i++;

        return new String( b, 0, 0, i );
    }

    private void read_field( int fldno,
        fld_stru fs, int bufloc ) {

        if ( fs.type == 'D' ) {

            // change YYYYMMDD to MM/DD/YYYY
            byte[] d = new byte[10];
            d[0] = record_buffer[bufloc + 4];
            d[1] = record_buffer[bufloc + 5];
            d[2] = (byte) '/';
            d[3] = record_buffer[bufloc + 6];
            d[4] = record_buffer[bufloc + 7];
            d[5] = (byte) '/';
            d[6] = record_buffer[bufloc];
            d[7] = record_buffer[bufloc + 1];
            d[8] = record_buffer[bufloc + 2];
            d[9] = record_buffer[bufloc + 3];

            values.setElementAt
                ( new String(d, 0), fldno );
        }
        else
            values.setElementAt
                ( new String(record_buffer, 0, bufloc,
                    fs.length), fldno );
    }

    private void read_values() {
```

```
        fld_stru fs;

        int recloc = 1; // point past deleted byte
        for ( int i = 0 ; i < num_fields ; i++ ) {

            fs = (fld_stru) fields.elementAt(i);
            read_field( i, fs, recloc );
            recloc += fs.length;
        }
    }

    private void rewrite_numrecs() {

        try {
            raf.seek( 4 );
            raf.write( int_to4(num_recs) );
        }
        catch ( IOException ioe ) {;}
    }

    private String type_string( byte b ) {

        switch( b ) {
            case 'C': return "C";
            case 'D': return "D";
            case 'L': return "L";
            case 'N': return "N";
            case 'F': return "F";
        }
        return "U";
    }

    private int unsigned_byte( byte b ) {

        return ( (int) b ) & 0x000000FF;
    }

    private void write_field( int fldno,
        fld_stru fs, int recloc ) {

        String s = ( String ) ( values.elementAt(fldno) );
```

```
        if ( fs.type == 'D' ) {

            // change MM/DD/YYYY to YYYYMMDD
            byte[] d = new byte[10];
            s.getBytes( 0, 10, d, 0 );

            record_buffer[recloc]   = d[6];
            record_buffer[recloc+1] = d[7];
            record_buffer[recloc+2] = d[8];
            record_buffer[recloc+3] = d[9];

            record_buffer[recloc+4] = d[0];
            record_buffer[recloc+5] = d[1];

            record_buffer[recloc+6] = d[3];
            record_buffer[recloc+7] = d[4];
        }
        else
            s.getBytes(
                    0, fs.length, record_buffer, recloc );
    }

    private void write_fields( int recno  ) {

        fld_stru fs;
        int recloc = 1;

         for ( int i = 0 ; i < num_fields ; i++ ) {

            fs = (fld_stru) fields.elementAt(i);
            write_field( i, fs, recloc );
            recloc += fs.length;
        }

        replace( recno );
    }

} // end of DBF class

// private class in DBF.java:

class fld_stru {
```

```
        public byte[] name;
        public byte type;
        public byte length;
        public byte decimals;

        fld_stru() {
            name = new byte[10];
        }
    }

// end of DBF.java
```

Summary

We began by looking at the history and structure of the DBF file. It's become widely used on PCs. It's read by most PC applications that have any ability to import data.

The structure is straightforward. A header holds information about the data. Then the data records are stored with no wasted space. A two-byte footer ends the file. The header begins with global data (number of records, record length, and so on) and then has a record for each field, including the field's name, type, and length.

We moved next to the new FileViewer mainline. It adds the DBF to the list of files that it understands. Popping a DBF into a ScrollWin is no more trouble than the other files, since the DBF class implements the Scrollable interface. The MRString method endsWith( ) makes it easy to check for files whose names end with DBF. I took advantage of this by copying the sample DBF to a file ended with a .BIN extension. FileViewer opened the DBF version as a DBF and the BIN as a BinFile. The latter form made it easy to look at the file header.

Then we went on to the MsgBox. This is an idea I borrowed from Visual Basic. My version has very few features, which keeps it tiny. The MsgBox lets you pop up an information box, providing a more professional approach than writing to the Java window.

Then we went into the DBF class. This is a large class with many features more advanced than we are now using. As we get into the JDB application, we'll put them all to good use.

If you dove into the code, you saw that handling little-endian data in a general way (not getting platform-specific code) was not simple. Java's insistence that all integer types are signed may keep the language simple, but it definitely made this job hard.

Chapter 7

A LayoutManager for
Database Applications

I love to cook. And I wash dishes, too. Chapter 6 was sort of the dishwashing of database work. You know it's necessary, but that still doesn't make it fun. Now it's time to have some fun!

In this chapter we're going to take a look at two LayoutManagers. The first, the CenterLayout, was my first try at writing a LayoutManager. Its job is to center a Panel in a Frame (or, perhaps, another Panel), leaving a border.

The second, ChoicesLayout, is one I use for all my menus. It lets the user stretch, scrunch, and generally arrange a tear-off menu to his or her liking. You can stretch out a tall, vertical menu or a wide, horizontal one. If your screen's borders are full, you can use a more square menu shape, getting a grid of choices. Best of all, you can stretch or scrunch the menu to be big and highly readable, or to be tiny, saving precious screen real estate.

If you want to see this in action, look ahead to Chapter 9 or load the JDB application and click Options | Menus and start to adjust things. The entire JDB application's user control is built from multiple ChoicesLayout-based objects.

We'll start with the CenterLayout.

Using the CenterLayout

I'm a big fan of the Frame's default BorderLayout. I had even been using a BorderLayout for Frames when I wanted to center a single Panel in the Frame, leaving a nice border. I dropped Labels with all-blank strings in the North, East, South, and West regions to get this effect. Figure 7-1 shows a centered Button.

In practice, I invariably use a Panel as the component to center. As Figure 7-1 clearly shows, however, the CenterLayout will center a Component or anything that extends java.awt.Component.

Now for a brief detour, which, I promise, will get us back on track quickly.

The Origin of the CenterLayout

I created a Visual Basic time-management application. For the main menu I used five drawings of the main parts of the application, plus the word "eXit" in a box. Each of the drawings was square. Then I hand-coded resize logic that chose a 1x6, 2x3, 3x2, or 6x1 layout, based on the shape the user chose.

The result was very nice indeed. You get to resize it to any size you like. If you use different screen resolutions, you know that what works at 640x480, for example, is unreadable at 1280x1024. That's not a problem when you can just grab a corner and drag out the size you like.

Naturally, I decided to use a similar main menu for the JDB application. I thought that if I could generalize the process of choosing the right arrangement (for example, picking a 2x3 grid or a 3x2 grid), we'd have one piece of software that handled the entire front end of the application. And it would be useful for menus, toolbars, color palettes, and all sorts of things that presented a set of choices to the user.

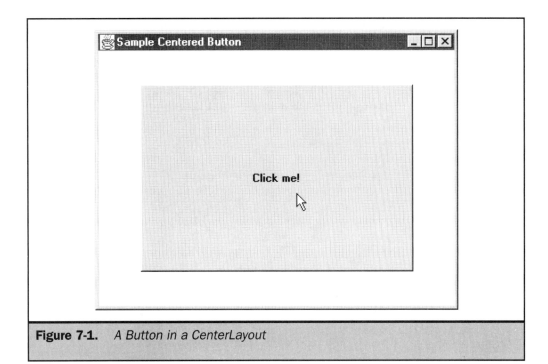

Figure 7-1. *A Button in a CenterLayout*

A pad of graph paper and a long weekend later, I had the mathematics worked out. I quickly whipped up a test program. It worked, but it was a kludge. I saw that what was really needed was a LayoutManager. I'd never programmed a LayoutManager, so I decided to start with a simple one.

The CenterLayout was born. I thought it would be useful (it is) and less complex than the ChoicesLayout (it isn't). I also thought it would teach me what I needed to know to write the ChoicesLayout (it did).

You'll see when we get into the code that the centering job is not as trivial as it appears at first sight. But it is trivially simple to use.

Using the CenterLayout

This chapter's code includes two projects, Center and Choices. The Center project, of course, is the one that uses the CenterLayout. The file Center.java shows the use of the CenterLayout. This is the code:

```
setTitle( "Sample Centered Button" );
resize( 400, 300 );

setLayout( new CenterLayout( 4 ) );

add( new thingie() );
```

The CenterLayout constructor argument (4, in this case) is the ratio of centered thing size to border size. This example uses margins that are one quarter the width of the Component you are centering. This example centers a *thingie,* a private class that is a Button reading "Click me!" as you saw in Figure 7-1.

Why use a thingie object? The thingie overrides the Component's minimumSize( ) and preferredSize( ) methods. This is the relevant part of the thingie class:

```
public Dimension minimumSize() {

    return new Dimension( 100, 20 );
}

public Dimension preferredSize() {

    return new Dimension( 300, 200 );
}
```

As the user resizes the Frame that holds the CenterLayout, the behavior between the minimum and the preferred sizes is what we've discussed. The space is apportioned between the centered component and the margins based on your specification to the CenterLayout.

The centered component is not enlarged past its preferred size. Use a large size if you don't mind near-infinite stretch. Use a smaller size if you have, for example, a graphic that won't successfully expand indefinitely.

The minimum size is the smallest that the CenterLayout allows. Below this the margins are discarded. Note that this does *not* control the size of the enclosing Frame. If the user makes its client area smaller than the Component's minimum size, the Component won't fit. It will be resized to its minimum and clipped on the right and bottom. You have to add resize( ) logic to the Frame if you need to force it to fit the whole centered component.

The rest of the thingie class sets up the button's title and closes down the application when the user clicks the button.

One final note about the mainline's code. It has this weird constructor:

```
Center( int i ) {

    // don't call this constructor!
    // VCafe will write stuff here
}
```

I generally like Visual Cafe's two-way coding ability. Sometimes, though, I don't want it to touch my constructor. Since it only works on the first constructor, the easy work-around is to put in a bogus constructor (with fake parameters) like this one. Then it can do whatever it wants, without getting into the code you really use.

TOUR

Spend a moment looking at the Center.java listing, just to convince yourself that using this LayoutManager really is simple. Then skip the entire "Understanding" section, unless you want to write your own LayoutManager classes.

If you want to implement the LayoutManager interface, read carefully my comment in the addLayoutComponent( ) method. It ends with "Ugh." That has a lot to do with the rather substantial amount of my time that was burned because the behavior I document isn't reasonable and it isn't documented by our vendors.

The Complete Center.java Listing

This is the mainline for the Center project.

Listing 7-1:
Center.java,
a mainline
for the
CenterLayout

```
// Center.java -- Sample CenterLayout use
// Copyright 1997, Martin L. Rinehart

/*
    Shows the CenterLayout LayoutManager in operation
*/

import java.awt.*;

class Center extends Frame {

// -------------------- data members --------------------

// there are no data members

// ------------------- public methods -------------------

    //*
        public static void main( String[] args ) {

            ( new Center() ).show();
        }
    // */

// constructors:

    Center( int i ) {
```

```
            // don't call this constructor!
            // VCafe will write stuff here
        }

        Center() {

            setTitle( "Sample Centered Button" );
            resize( 400, 300 );

            setLayout( new CenterLayout( 4 ) );

            add( new thingie() );
        }

// there are no data access methods

// there are no public, class-specific methods

// public, non-event overriding method:

        public String paramString() {

            return "Center";
        }

// public, event-handling method:

        public boolean handleEvent( Event e ) {

            if ( e.id == Event.WINDOW_DESTROY ) {
                System.exit( 0 );
                return true;
            }

            return super.handleEvent( e );
        }

// ------------------ private methods --------------------
// there are no private methods
```

```
} // end of Center class

// private class in Center.java:

class thingie extends Button {

    thingie() {

        super( "Click me!" );
    }

    public boolean handleEvent( Event e ) {

        System.exit( 0 );
        return true;
    }

    public Dimension minimumSize() {

        return new Dimension( 100, 20 );
    }

    public Dimension preferredSize() {

        return new Dimension( 300, 200 );
    }

} // end of class thingie

// end of Center.java
```

Understanding the
CenterLayout LayoutManager

Writing CenterLayout.java had the two effects I wanted. It created a LayoutManager that was handy for centering things, and it taught me how to write a LayoutManager. Strictly speaking, the latter topic is not the subject of this book.

I'm going to include it anyway, since it's neither difficult nor adequately documented elsewhere. Once you know how it's done, you'll write lots of your own LayoutManagers. You'll see that I do this for the CenterLayout here and for the ChoicesLayout we'll look at next. Later we'll add another custom LayoutManager for our data-entry panels, which are, speaking as strictly as before, definitely part of the subject of this book.

Understanding the CenterLayout Code

The CenterLayout class implements the LayoutManager interface. It's different from other LayoutManagers since it assumes that its parent Container has just one Component. It still will show you how to write your own LayoutManagers.

There's only one data member, margin_divisor, which is the margin size ratio you pass to the constructor. Two constructors exist. A no-parameter constructor calls the second one with the default value, ten, for the margin_divisor. The second, one-parameter constructor simply stores the value it is passed. Methods getMarginDivisor( ) and setMarginDivisor( ) perform their expected functions.

The rest of the class implements the LayoutManager interface.

The addLayoutComponent( ) Method

To quote from my comment in the listing: Ugh. This method is called by the add( ) method of a Container, but only when you use the two-parameter form—*add("South", thingie)* works; *add(thingie)* doesn't call this method. You don't need this method to access the contents of the parent Container, so I simply provide an empty method with a caustic comment.

The layoutContainer( ) Method

This method is called with a reference to the parent Container that you will lay out. You can access the Components in the parent with countComponents( ) and getComponent( ) calls.

My layout begins by getting the parent's size and insets:

```
Dimension psize = parent.size();
Insets insets = parent.insets();
```

This check ensures that you don't lay out an empty Container:

```
if ( parent.countComponents() == 0 )
    return; // nothing to lay out
```

If there is something to lay out, CenterLayout grabs the first Component. Note that it uses the name *panel*, but in fact deals with any Component, not just with Panels.

```
Component panel = parent.getComponent( 0 );
```

Next CenterLayout gets the panel's minimum and preferred sizes, and it declares variables for the computations:

```
Dimension min_size = panel.minimumSize();
Dimension pref_size = panel.preferredSize();

int hmar, vmar; // horizontal/vertical margins
int hsize, vsize; // centered Container's size
```

Then come two sections that do the actual layout. The first, which I'll cover here, does the horizontal layout. The other does the vertical layout. It's identical to the horizontal one, except that all widths become heights, left and right become top and bottom, and so on.

The first computation finds the width of the parent's client area:

```
int net_wid = psize.width - insets.left -
    insets.right;
```

Next we compute the width of the centered component, leaving one unit for each margin and the margin_divisor's number of units for the centered item, in the special case of a sub-minimal panel:

```
if ( min_size.width < 11 ) // 10 is Panel default
    min_size.width = ( net_wid * margin_divisor )
        / ( margin_divisor + 2 );
```

Then the preferred size is forced to be at least as large as the minimum:

```
if ( pref_size.width < min_size.width )
    pref_size.width = min_size.width;
```

Next the margin and component sizes are set for three distinct cases. If the width is less than the minimum, the setting is simple:

```
if ( net_wid < min_size.width ) {

    hmar = 0;
    hsize = net_wid;
}
```

The next case happens when the minimum size fits, but there isn't enough room for the specified margins:

```
else if ( (net_wid-min_size.width) <
        (( 2 * min_size.width ) / margin_divisor) ) {

    hsize = min_size.width;
    hmar = ( net_wid - hsize ) / 2;
}
```

When there's room, the regular computation is done:

```
else {

    hmar = net_wid / ( margin_divisor + 2 );
    hsize = net_wid - ( 2 * hmar );
}
```

A fourth case, when there's more than enough room for the preferred size, is handled after the fact, this way:

```
if ( hsize > pref_size.width ) {

    hsize = pref_size.width;
    hmar = ( net_wid - hsize ) / 2;
}
```

The next section of the layoutContainer( ) method does the same job for the vertical layout. Once that's done, the final step is to actually lay out the Container. Since we have just one Component to lay out, that's a simple job. The left edge is hmar units from the left insets; the width is the size we calculated. The vertical layout is similar:

```
panel.reshape( insets.left + hmar,
        insets.top + vmar, hsize, vsize );
```

The minimumLayoutSize( ) Method

When you lay out a Frame, the job's done when it's done. Bear in mind that a LayoutManager could be laying out a Panel. That Panel could, in turn, be part of another Panel, which also needs to be laid out. For this reason, you should be able to provide minimum and preferred size information.

Providing this information is complicated by the fact that you don't know what the parent Container is, or what the Component you are laying out is. So you have to write logic like this:

```
if ( parent instanceof Frame ) {

    Frame f = (Frame) parent;
    hinset = f.insets().left + f.insets().right;
    vinset = f.insets().top + f.insets().bottom;
}
```

The rest of this function behaves correctly when it is laying out a Panel. If you need to lay out other Components, you'll need to add more logic. You would use this technique:

```
Dimension psize = new Dimension( 0, 0 );

Component panel = null;
if ( parent.countComponents() > 0 )
    panel = parent.getComponent( 0 );

if ( (panel != null) &&
    (panel instanceof Container) ) {

    Container c = (Container) panel;
    LayoutManager lm = c.getLayout();

    if ( lm != null )
        psize = lm.minimumLayoutSize( c );
}

return new Dimension(
    hinset + psize.width,
    vinset + psize.height );
}
```

The preferredLayoutSize( ) Method

The preferredLayoutSize( ) method has the same use and the same problems that you just saw in the minimumLayoutSize( ) method. For a CenterLayout layout centering a

Panel, the preferred size is the size of the Panel, plus the insets of the parent Container if it's a Frame. Refer to the full listing for all the ALD.

The removeLayoutComponent( ) Method

If you don't use the addLayoutComponent( ) method, then this one couldn't be simpler:

```
public void removeLayoutComponent( Component comp ) {

}
```

Since this method is specified in the LayoutManager interface, you have to provide it. There's no law that says it has to do something, however.

The Full CenterLayout.java Listing

Listing 7-2 shows the full CenterLayout.java file.

Listing 7-2:
The
CenterLayout
Layout-
Manager

```
// CenterLayout.java -- Layout Manager with margins
// Copyright 1997, Martin L. Rinehart

// this code is completely documented in:
// _Java Database Development_, Martin Rinehart,
// Osborne/McGraw-Hill, 1997

/*
    Uses a single Component (probably a Panel) and places
    it in the Container's center, leaving margins around
    it, if possible.

    See notes at bottom for margin-sizing rules.
*/

import java.awt.*;

class CenterLayout implements LayoutManager {

// -------------------- data members --------------------

// there are no public data members

// protected data member:
```

```
    protected int margin_divisor;

// there are no static data members

// -------------------- public methods --------------------

// constructors:

    CenterLayout() {

        this( 10 ); // default margin_divisor
    }

    CenterLayout( int md ) {

        margin_divisor = md;
    }

// data access getXxx() method:

    public int getMarginDivisor() {

        return margin_divisor;
    }

// there are no data access isXxx() methods

// data access setXxx() method:

    public void setMarginDivisor( int md ) {

        margin_divisor = md;
    }

// public, class-specific methods:
    public void addLayoutComponent( String name,
        Component comp ) {

        /* This gets called by Container.add() in
           this form:

            add( "WhereverWherever", Component );
```

```
                    But it's not called by Container.add() in
                    this form:

                     add( Component );

                    Ugh.
             */
    }


    public void layoutContainer( Container parent ) {

            Dimension psize = parent.size();
            Insets insets = parent.insets();

            if ( parent.countComponents() == 0 )
                return; // nothing to lay out

            Component panel = parent.getComponent( 0 );

            Dimension min_size = panel.minimumSize();
            Dimension pref_size = panel.preferredSize();

            int hmar, vmar; // horizontal/vertical margins
            int hsize, vsize; // centered Container's size

      // compute layout horizontally
            int net_wid = psize.width - insets.left -
                insets.right;

            if ( min_size.width < 11 ) // 10 is Panel default
                min_size.width = ( net_wid * margin_divisor )
                    / ( margin_divisor + 2 );

            if ( pref_size.width < min_size.width )
                pref_size.width = min_size.width;

            if ( net_wid < min_size.width ) {

                hmar = 0;
                hsize = net_wid;
            }
            else if ( (net_wid-min_size.width) <
```

```
                    (( 2 * min_size.width ) / margin_divisor) ) {

                hsize = min_size.width;
                hmar = ( net_wid - hsize ) / 2;
        }
         else {

                hmar = net_wid / ( margin_divisor + 2 );
                hsize = net_wid - ( 2 * hmar );
            }
            if ( hsize > pref_size.width ) {

                hsize = pref_size.width;
                hmar = ( net_wid - hsize ) / 2;
            }

// compute layout vertically
        int net_hgt = psize.height - insets.top -
            insets.bottom;

        if ( min_size.height < 11 ) // 10 is Panel default

            min_size.height = ( net_hgt * margin_divisor )
                / ( margin_divisor + 2 );

        if ( pref_size.height < min_size.height )
            pref_size.height = min_size.height;

        if ( net_hgt < min_size.height ) {

            vmar = 0;
            vsize = net_hgt;
        }
        else if ( (net_hgt-min_size.height) <
            (( 2 * min_size.height ) / margin_divisor) ) {

            vsize = min_size.height;
            vmar = ( net_hgt - vsize ) / 2;
        }
         else {
```

```
            vmar = net_hgt / ( margin_divisor + 2 );
            vsize = net_hgt - ( 2 * vmar );
        }
        if ( vsize > pref_size.height ) {

            vsize = pref_size.height;
            vmar = ( net_hgt - vsize ) / 2;
        }

// layout centered Container
        panel.reshape( insets.left + hmar,
            insets.top + vmar, hsize, vsize );
    }

public Dimension minimumLayoutSize(
    Container parent ) {

    int hinset - 0;
    int vinset = 0;

    if ( parent instanceof Frame ) {

        Frame f = (Frame) parent;
        hinset = f.insets().left + f.insets().right;
        vinset = f.insets().top + f.insets().bottom;
    }

    Dimension psize = new Dimension( 0, 0 );

    Component panel = null;
    if ( parent.countComponents() > 0 )
        panel = parent.getComponent( 0 );

    if ( (panel != null) &&
        (panel instanceof Container) ) {

        Container c = (Container) panel;
        LayoutManager lm = c.getLayout();

        if ( lm != null )
            psize = lm.minimumLayoutSize( c );
    }
```

```
        return new Dimension(
            hinset + psize.width,
            vinset + psize.height );
    }

    public Dimension preferredLayoutSize(
        Container parent ) {

        int hinset, vinset;

        Frame f = (Frame) parent;
        hinset = f.insets().left + f.insets().right;
        vinset = f.insets().top + f.insets().bottom;

        Component panel = null;
        if ( parent.countComponents() > 0 )
            panel = parent.getComponent( 0 );

        Dimension psize;
        if ( panel != null )
            psize = panel.preferredSize();
        else
            psize = new Dimension( 10, 10 );

        return new Dimension(
            hinset + (( margin_divisor + 2 ) *
                psize.width) / margin_divisor,
            vinset + (( margin_divisor + 2 ) *
                psize.height) / margin_divisor );
    }

    public void removeLayoutComponent( Component comp ) {

    }

// public, non-event overriding method:

    public String paramString() {

        return "margin_divisor = " + margin_divisor;
    }
```

```
// there are no public event-handling methods

// ------------------ private methods ------------------
// there are no private methods

} // end of CenterLayout class

// there are no private classes in CenterLayout.java

/*
    The following rules are applied in both the
    vertical and horizontal dimensions:

    If the size of the Container is less than Component's
    minimum size, the Component entirely fills the
    container.

    If the Container is larger than the Component's min-
    imum size, the excess is allocated to the margin
    until the margin equals the margin divisor specified.

    If the margin divisor is 8, for instance, 1/8 the
    size of the Component is placed on both sides of the
    Component.

    Once the Component reaches its preferred size, all
    additional space is allocated to the margins.
*/

// end of CenterLayout.java
```

Using the ChoicesLayout

The ChoicesLayout has a much more sophisticated job to do. If you want to see it in action, build the Choices project and start resizing. Figures 7-2, 7-3, and 7-4 show the sample buttons in a Frame laid out by the ChoicesLayout, based on the way the user sizes the Frame.

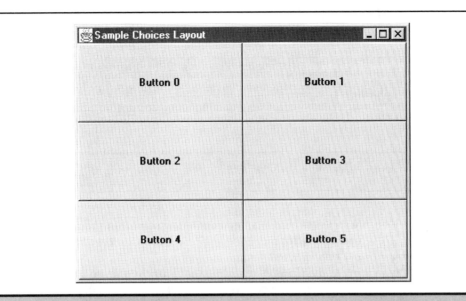

Figure 7-2.   *A grid best fits these Buttons*

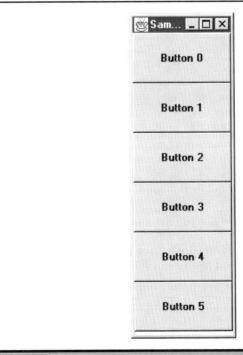

Figure 7-3.   *The same Buttons, stacked up*

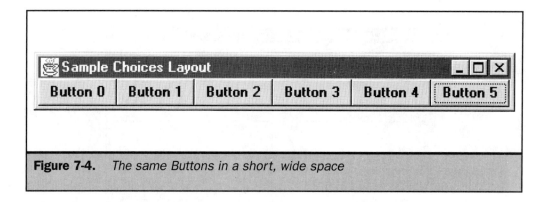

Figure 7-4. *The same Buttons in a short, wide space*

This looks a lot more sophisticated than just centering something to provide a margin, doesn't it? Actually, it *is* a lot more sophisticated, but ChoicesLayout.java is only 15 lines longer than CenterLayout.

We'll begin by looking at the Choices mainline that launched those buttons. You'll see that its only complication is getting six different labels on those buttons, which isn't really very complicated.

Understanding Choices.java

This is the constructor that does the job:

```
Choices() {

    setTitle( "Sample Choices Layout" );
    resize( 400, 300 );

    setLayout( new ChoicesLayout( 1/4.0 ) );

    for ( int i = 0 ; i <  6 ; i++ )
        add( new Button("Button " + i) );
}
```

The argument to the ChoicesLayout constructor is your target aspect ratio, height to width. Don't forget to make at least one of those numbers a double, or you'll do an integer divide and get a zero result passed to the LayoutManager, which isn't at all what you want.

You just set the ChoicesLayout, giving it a target aspect ratio. Then you add( ) whatever components you want it to lay out. Simple enough?

You can add the Components before or after you set the ChoicesLayout as your LayoutManager, too. You can even add and delete Components as you go. JDB's file-closing menu, for example, grows as you open more files.

You can check the full listing of Choices.java if you want to confirm that there really isn't any more work than you just saw.

The Full Choices.java Listing

This is the full listing for Choices.java.

Listing 7-3:
The Choices
.java Choice-
Layout
Mainline

```java
// Choices.java -- Sample ChoicesLayout use
// Copyright 1997, Martin L. Rinehart

/*
      Shows the ChoicesLayout LayoutManager in operation
*/

import java.awt.*;

class Choices extends Frame {

// -------------------- data members --------------------

// there are no data members

// ------------------- public methods -------------------

    //*
        public static void main( String[] args ) {

                ( new Choices() ).show();
        }
    // */

// constructors:
```

```
    Choices( int i ) {

        // don't call this constructor!
        // VCafe will write stuff here
    }

    Choices() {

        setTitle( "Sample Choices Layout" );
        resize( 400, 300 );

        setLayout( new ChoicesLayout( 1/4.0 ) );

        for ( int i = 0 ; i <  6 ; i++ )
            add( new Button("Button " + i) );
    }

// there are no data access methods

// there are no public, class-specific methods

// public, non-event overriding method:

    public String paramString() {

        return "Choices";
    }

// public, event-handling method:

    public boolean handleEvent( Event e ) {

        if ( e.id == Event.WINDOW_DESTROY ) {
            System.exit( 0 );
            return true;
        }

        return super.handleEvent( e );
    }

// ------------------- private methods -------------------
// there are no private methods
```

```
} // end of Choices class

// there are no private classes in Choices.java

// end of Choices.java
```

Understanding the ChoicesLayout LayoutManager

TOUR

If you like mathematics, you'll love this section. If you don't like math, pat this one on the head as if it were a friendly puppy and go on to the "Summary" at the end of this chapter.

But if you skip this section, remember this warning: ChoicesLayout does not return valid minimum or preferred sizes. You can fix this by writing these routines, but that will cost a lot for a feature that I haven't yet found necessary. Alternatively, you could extend this class with one that returns a hard-coded answer, if you find a case where this is a problem.

When I did the Visual Basic application that introduced this technology in a hard-coded way, I knew that I wanted a general-purpose version. Java, with its LayoutManager interface, seemed like the right home.

Wanting something and having it are two different things, of course. Before I could code it, I had to figure it out. I'll begin with a discussion of the mathematics of laying out an array of choices. After the theory, the implementation will make sense.

Choices Layout Theory

I know that mathematicians have studied tiling and other, similar geometric problems. Unfortunately, I haven't studied any of this math. This I had to work out from the ground up.

The general idea is to use the screen real estate that the user provides in the best possible way. The best possible way is the one that shows all the choices, shows them as close to the target aspect ratio as possible, and wastes minimal space.

Defining Reasonable Layouts

To arrange six things, the reasonable layouts are 1x6, 2x3, 3x2, and 6x1. It's obvious that a 7x1 grid wastes a space if you only have six things. Similarly, a 3x3 grid wastes three spaces and is unreasonable for six things. On the other hand, a 3x3 grid may be the best layout if you have seven things, even though it will have two empty spaces.

Assume that you want to lay out N things in R rows and C columns. This is a definition of *reasonable* that can be explained to a mere computer:

- Rule 1: (R * C) >= N
- Rule 2: (R * (C-1)) < N
- Rule 3: ((R-1) * C) < N

Rule 1 says that you have to have enough space to fit all N things. Rule 2 says that you can't have any empty columns. Similarly, Rule 3 says that you can't have any empty rows.

When we actually do the layout, we'll place the first choice at the top left and follow it with the rest of the choices, working from left to right and top to bottom. If you popped things into place at random, Rules 2 and 3 wouldn't be adequate.

Enumerating Reasonable Layouts

One strategy for choosing a layout is to enumerate all the layouts that are *reasonable* as just defined. Then you compute the aspect ratio of the choices in each layout and choose the one that is closest to your target. With some small coding efficiencies added, this is exactly what the ChoicesLayout does.

I began by listing reasonable layouts, this way:

```
N: RxC

1: 1x1
2: 1x2, 2x1
3: 1x3, 2x2, 3x1
4: 1x4, 2x2, 4x1
5: 1x5, 2x3, 3x2, 5x1
6: 1x6, 2x3, 3x2, 6x1
7: 1x7, 2x4, 3x3, 4x2, 7x1
```

Note that in each case the number of rows increments by one until it reaches a crossover point. After the crossover, the number of columns decreases by one until it reaches one. The crossover point is the ceiling of the square root of N, where the ceiling function rounds nonintegral results up to the next higher integer.

The number of reasonable arrangements is, this tells you, small. Mathematically it's not more than twice the square root of N (for example, eight possible arrangements for 16 items; 20 possible arrangements for 100 items).

This pseudocode creates the set of all possible reasonable arrangements of N things:

```
find_reasonables( int N )

    Set reasonables = new, empty set
    int crossover = ceiling( square_root(N) )

    int row, col

    for row = 1 to crossover
        reasonables.add_pair( row, counterpart(row, N) )

    for col = counterpart(crossover) - 1 downto 1
        reasonables.add_pair( counterpart(col, N), col )
```

The counterpart( ) function returns the reasonable number of rows given a number of columns, or the reasonable number of columns given the number of rows. Mathematically, that's the ceiling of N divided by the other number. If N is 6, counterpart(3, N) is 2. Actually, the counterpart(3, N) is 2 for N from 4 through 6, 3 for N from 7 through 9, and so on.

After I worked this out, the only remaining problem was how to compare two aspect ratios to decide which was a better fit.

Comparing Aspect Ratios to a Target

Given some number of things to lay out, N, and a target aspect ratio, T, you begin by enumerating the reasonable layouts. Next you grab the first reasonable layout (always 1xN) and compute the aspect ratio of laid out things, given that arrangement. Then you grab the next reasonable layout and compute its resulting component aspect ratio.

If the first one is better (closer to the target) than the second, you stop. The first one's best because the series moves continuously in the same direction. 1xN gives the highest resulting aspect ratio for the laid out parts. Nx1 gives the lowest.

If the first one is not as good as the second, you continue. Then you compare the second to the third, and so on. The question is: how do you decide which of two aspect ratios is better?

If both computed values are on the same side of your target, it's simple: choose the one closer to the target. (Target is 0.25; computed values are 0.4 and 0.3; 0.3 is better.) But what do you do when the ratios are on opposite sides of the target?

It turns out that 1.2 and 0.8 are not equally good choices if the target ratio is 1. The 0.8 ratio is 4:5. The break-even ratio on the other side of the target is 5:4, or 1.25. Your alternative, 1.2, is better than 5:4, so it's closer to 1 than 4:5.

For ratios close to 1, this probably doesn't mean much. But as your ratios get farther apart, it's vitally important. A ratio of 0.2 (1:5) is equal to a ratio of 5.0 (5:1) if 1 is your target. A ratio of 2.0 or 3.0 is a much better choice if the alternative is 0.2 and the target is 1. When comparing aspect ratios, you could say that 3.0 is closer to 1.0 than 0.2 is to 1.0. This wasn't obvious, at first.

In general two ratios, A and B, are equally good approximations of a target T when this is true:

```
Ratio Rule:

Aspect ratios A and B are equally good approximations
of target T when

    ( T / A ) = ( B / T )
```

If you really need to know why that's true, I've saved my notes. (Several pages wander around that derivation.) If you just want to prove to yourself that it's true, run a ChoicesLayout until you think it might have made a mistake. Slap a piece of graph paper over the screen and trace its arrangement. Switch to a different color pen or pencil and draw the arrangement you guessed would be better.

That's what I did. Then I did it some more. Finally I got tired of trying to outguess the computer. I'm pretty sure that the rule is correct.

Given the Ratio Rule, you can easily use it to compute the ratio on the opposite side of a target, T, that is just as good as some ratio, A:

```
EqualButOppositeA = ( T * T ) / A
```

If you can compute the equal ratio on the opposite side of T, it's easy to compare two ratios on opposite sides. You compute EqualButOppositeA and compare it with B. If B's closer to T, go with B. Otherwise, A's the better choice.

Efficient Algorithms

I've already noted that since the aspect ratios go down as the number of rows goes up, you only need to compare possibilities until you come to one that's worse. Actually, when you get to the ratios on opposite sides of the target, one of those two is the best choice. You don't need to go on to be sure that you'll be getting worse.

You'll find the one you want halfway through the set of reasonable choices, on average, so the number of tests you'll make is about the square root of N, for N things. That's not a practical problem for menus, toolbars, or palettes.

If you go back to the algorithm for enumerating the reasonable arrangements, you'll see that it's easy to put the choice logic right into that algorithm, so you don't really have to actually enumerate the set. You just start with the first two choices. If you need to go on, the second choice becomes the first and you generate the next reasonable layout and compare again.

I saw that you could be more efficient by making an intelligent choice to start looking at 1xN or Nx1. I wrote that up, but it took more code than expected to make a decent choice. Eventually I decided that the code cost outweighed the possible savings.

Finally, I'm pretty sure that there is a direct computation by which you could toss the aspect ratio of the space available, the number of items to arrange, and the target aspect ratio into a single formula that would respond with the correct number of rows (or columns). I derived such a formula, but when I implemented it, it didn't work. That means the derivation was wrong. My time for writing ChoicesLayout ran out, so I've left that as an open problem.

Understanding the ChoicesLayout Code

We'll cover the public, class-specific functions first, and then the private functions that support the layoutContainer( ) method. First, though, let's dispense with some preliminaries.

I use the term *cell* to refer to the individual items being laid out. The *container* is the thing in which the cells are laid out. Writing about cell_aspect_ratio and container_aspect_ratio helps you understand what aspect ratio is being used.

With that convention in mind, the data is self-explanatory.

Here the constructors and other public functions are simple enough not to require comment, so we can start on the interesting code.

The Public, Class-Specific Methods

There is only one serious method here: layoutContainer( ). Let's dispense with the others. The addLayoutComponent( ) method does nothing. You'll see that it contains the same comment as the CenterLayout. I'm going to give a hearty "Ugh" in all my LayoutManagers. Maybe someone will get annoyed enough to do something. Since addLayoutComponent( ) does nothing, removeLayoutComponent( ) can do the same.

Much worse, the minimumLayoutSize( ) and preferredLayoutSize( ) methods are essentially unwritten. They both return a 0x0 Dimension, which is probably bad for the minimum and certainly wrong for the preferred size. This remains unwritten because I've never needed it. Waste not, want not? (I'll certainly be flamed by some unsuspecting web programmers who get caught by this bug. They will not have bought this book, of course. No doubt they'll complain that I didn't deliver good value for their money.)

Now let's get to the layoutContainer( ) method, which is most definitely not empty. It begins by upgrading the name of the parameter to something I find more explicit:

```
public void layoutContainer( Container parent ) {

    layout_container = parent ;
```

Since layout_container is a protected data member, that also makes the reference available to the rest of the private routines.

Next a quick count and check is done, exiting if there's no work:

```
number_of_items =
    layout_container.countComponents() ;

if ( number_of_items == 0 )
    return ;
```

Then I work with that ALD, the insets:

```
int h_inset, v_inset ;
int h_origin, v_origin ;

h_inset = layout_container.insets().left +
    layout_container.insets().right ;
v_inset = layout_container.insets().top +
    layout_container.insets().bottom ;

h_origin = layout_container.insets().left ;
v_origin = layout_container.insets().top ;
container_width =
    layout_container.size().width - h_inset ;
container_height =
    layout_container.size().height - v_inset ;
```

One simple call and the whole matter of choosing an arrangement is delegated to a private method, postponing this problem:

```
calculate_cols_rows() ;
```

The calculate_cols_rows( ) method sets two data members—cols and rows—that specify how the container is divided into cells. With that decided, actually laying out the components isn't hard at all:

```
int c = 0, r = 0 ;

for ( int i = 0 ;
    i < layout_container.countComponents() ;
    i++ ) {

    layout_container.getComponent(i).reshape(
        h_origin + (c * cell_width),
        v_origin + (r * cell_height),
        cell_width, cell_height ) ;

    c++ ;
    if ( c == cols ) {
        c = 0 ;
        r++ ;
    }
}
```

Isn't life simple when you can just delegate the hard parts to subordinates? (I'll try to forget that, for me, this delegation just meant pushing the problem off for later.)

The Private Methods

We'll take these methods in alphabetical order, as they appear in the source code. The first calculates the aspect ratio of the cells—given a number of columns and rows—and the aspect ratio of the container. (You'll find some graph paper very helpful for verifying this one.) This is the whole function:

```
private double calc_ar( int cols, int rows ) {

    // cell aspect ratio = rectangle's ar
    // times cols divided by rows

    return container_aspect_ratio *
        ( (double) cols ) / rows ;
}
```

Next we get to calc_layout( ), which is the place where the number of columns and rows is chosen. It begins by dispensing with the easiest case:

```
if ( number_of_items == 1 ) {
    cols = 1 ;
    rows = 1 ;
    return ;
}
```

Then it goes on to dispense with the case of just two items. It uses the second_is_better( ) method. You pass second_is_better( ) two aspect ratios, and it returns true if the second one is a better approximation of the target. This is the two-item code:

```
double first_ar = calc_ar( 1, number_of_items ) ;
double second_ar = calc_ar( number_of_items, 1 ) ;

boolean cols_first = second_is_better
    ( first_ar, second_ar ) ;

if ( number_of_items == 2 ) {

    cols = cols_first ? 2 : 1 ;
    rows = cols_first ? 1 : 2 ;
    return ;
}
```

Past two, we use the algorithm that counts up to a crossover point and then back down. It calls the crossover point *magic,* for some reason that must have seemed sensible when I wrote it. As we discussed in the theory section, that's the ceiling of the square root of the number of items:

```
double magic = Math.ceil
    ( Math.sqrt(( double ) number_of_items) ) ;
```

Counting cols up from 2 (we've already computed first_ar for 1xN), we look for a deterioration in the quality of the fit and return when we find it:

```
for ( cols = 2 ; cols <= magic ; cols++ ) {

    rows = other_dimension( cols ) ;
    second_ar = calc_ar( cols, rows ) ;

    if ( !second_is_better(first_ar, second_ar) ) {
        cols-- ;
        rows = other_dimension( cols ) ;
        return ;
    }
    else
        first_ar = second_ar ;
}
```

If we haven't found the right layout at the crossover, we continue to count the rows back down to 1, still looking for the best layout:

```
for ( --rows ; rows > 0 ; rows-- ) {

    cols = other_dimension( rows ) ;
    second_ar = calc_ar( cols, rows ) ;
    if ( !second_is_better( first_ar, second_ar) ) {
        rows++ ;
        cols = other_dimension( rows ) ;
        return ;
    }
    else
        first_ar = second_ar ;
}
```

If the algorithm hasn't found a layout, the only possibility is that we need 1xN, which is set at the end:

```
rows = 1 ;
cols = number_of_items ;
```

The calculate_cols_rows( ) method is the one called by the public layoutContainer( ) method. It handles ALDs, so that the calc_layout( ) can concentrate on the mathematics. First, the container might be totally squashed:

```
if ( container_width == 0 ) {
    rows = number_of_items ;
    cols = 1 ;
    return ;
}

if ( container_height == 0 ) {
    rows = 1 ;
    cols = number_of_items ;
    return ;
}
```

Given that there's something to lay out, the container's aspect ratio is calculated, and then the number of rows and columns is determined:

```
container_aspect_ratio =
    ( (double) container_height ) /
    container_width ;

calc_layout() ; // figures cols and rows
```

Finally, the last job is to decide how big the individual cells will be:

```
cell_width = container_width / cols ;
cell_height = container_height / rows ;
}
```

There's a problem there that you might want to think about. The cell's size is an integral number of pixels, as is the container's size. This could leave up to four empty pixels at the left or bottom if you have five rows or columns. (Consider a container that's 204 pixels wide, with five 40-pixel-wide choices. It might be better to make the choices 41 pixels wide, letting the last cell lose a pixel.)

The next routine is an alternative to Math.ceil( ) plus a cast, as the comment suggests. You decide which is better:

```
private int ceiling( double d ) {

    int i = (int) d ;
    if ( i < d ) i++ ;

    return i ;
    // return (int) Math.ceil( d ) ; ??
}
```

Given one dimension, the other_dimension( ) method does just what its name suggests:

```
private int other_dimension( int dim1 ) {

    double d = ( (double) number_of_items ) / dim1 ;
    return ceiling( d ) ;
}
```

The last routine, second_is_better( ), compares two aspect ratios with a target. It starts by handling the case where both ratios are smaller than the target:

```
private boolean second_is_better( double ar1,
    double ar2 ) {

    if ( (ar1 < target_aspect_ratio) &&
         (ar2 < target_aspect_ratio) )
        return ar2 > ar1 ;
```

If that's not the case, it will handle the case where both are larger than the target:

```
    if ( (ar1 > target_aspect_ratio) &&
         (ar2 > target_aspect_ratio) )
        return ar2 < ar1 ;
```

In my notes I used the notation "x :=: y" as shorthand for "x is as good an approximation as y of a target T." You'll recognize the calculation of the equally good (or bad) approximation from the theory section earlier:

```
// A :=: B for target T when A  = (T^2)/B
double equal_ar = target_aspect_ratio *
    target_aspect_ratio / ar2 ;
```

Finally, given that equal_ar is the ratio on the other side of the target that is the equal of ar2, it's easy to choose the better approximation by comparing ar1 to equal_ar:

```
if ( ar1 <= target_aspect_ratio )
    return ar1 < equal_ar ;
else
    return ar1 > equal_ar ;
}
```

The Full ChoicesLayout.java Listing

This is the full listing of ChoicesLayout.java.

```
// ChoicesLayout.java -- for menus, toolboxes, etc.
// Copyright 1997, Martin L. Rinehart


// this code is completely documented in:
// _Java Database Development_, Martin Rinehart,
// Osborne/McGraw-Hill, 1997

/*
    Resize, reshape menus, palettes, etc. Good whenever
    the contents are all the same size.
*/

import java.awt.*;

class ChoicesLayout implements LayoutManager {

// -------------------- data members --------------------

// there are no public data members

// protected data members:
```

```
    // calculated:
        protected int cell_width;
          protected int cell_height ;
        protected int cols, rows ;
        protected double container_aspect_ratio ;

    // used:
          protected int container_height ;
        protected int container_width;

    protected Container layout_container ;

    protected int number_of_items ;

    protected double target_aspect_ratio ;

// there are no static data members

// -------------------- public methods --------------------

// constructor:

    ChoicesLayout( double ar ) {

        // ar == height / width
        target_aspect_ratio = ar ;
    }

// data access getXxx() method:

    public Dimension getDimensions() {

        return new Dimension( cols, rows );
    }

// there are no data access isXxx() methods
// there are no data access setXxx() methods


// public, class-specific methods:

    public void addLayoutComponent( String name,
```

```
            Component comp ) {

        /* This gets called by Container.add() in
           this form:

             add( "WhereverWherever", Component ) ;

             But it's not called by Container.add() in
             this form:

             add( Component ) ;

             Ugh.
        */
    }

    public void layoutContainer( Container parent ) {

        layout_container = parent ;
        number_of_items =
            layout_container.countComponents() ;

        if ( number_of_items == 0 )
            return ;

        int h_inset, v_inset ;
        int h_origin, v_origin ;

        h_inset = layout_container.insets().left +
            layout_container.insets().right ;
        v_inset = layout_container.insets().top +
            layout_container.insets().bottom ;

        h_origin = layout_container.insets().left ;
        v_origin = layout_container.insets().top ;

        container_width =
            layout_container.size().width - h_inset ;
        container_height =
            layout_container.size().height - v_inset ;

        calculate_cols_rows() ;
```

```
        int c = 0, r = 0 ;

        for ( int i = 0 ;
            i < layout_container.countComponents() ;
            i++ ) {

            layout_container.getComponent(i).reshape(
                h_origin + (c * cell_width),
                v_origin + (r * cell_height),
                cell_width, cell_height ) ;

            c++ ;
            if ( c == cols ) {
                c = 0 ;
                r++ ;
            }
        }
    }

    public Dimension minimumLayoutSize(
        Container parent ) {

        return new Dimension( 0, 0 ) ;
    }

    public Dimension preferredLayoutSize(
        Container parent ) {

        return new Dimension( 0, 0 ) ;
    }

    public void removeLayoutComponent( Component comp ) {

    }

// public, non-event overriding method:

    public String paramString() {

        return "ChoicesLayout";

    }
```

```java
// there are no public, event-handling methods

// ------------------ private methods ------------------

// private methods:

    private double calc_ar( int cols, int rows ) {

        // cell aspect ratio = rectangle's ar
        // times cols divided by rows

        return container_aspect_ratio *
            ( (double) cols ) / rows ;
    }

    private void calc_layout() {

        if ( number_of_items == 1 ) {
            cols = 1 ;
            rows = 1 ;
            return ;
        }

        double first_ar = calc_ar( 1, number_of_items ) ;
        double second_ar = calc_ar( number_of_items, 1 ) ;

        boolean cols_first = second_is_better
            ( first_ar, second_ar ) ;

        if ( number_of_items == 2 ) {
            cols = cols_first ? 2 : 1 ;
            rows = cols_first ? 1 : 2 ;
            return ;
        }

        double magic = Math.ceil
            ( Math.sqrt(( double ) number_of_items) ) ;

        for ( cols = 2 ; cols <= magic ; cols++ ) {

            rows = other_dimension( cols ) ;
            second_ar = calc_ar( cols, rows ) ;
```

```
        if ( !second_is_better(first_ar, second_ar) ) {
            cols-- ;
            rows = other_dimension( cols ) ;
            return ;
        }
        else
            first_ar = second_ar ;
    }

    for ( --rows ; rows > 0 ; rows-- ) {

        cols = other_dimension( rows ) ;
        second_ar = calc_ar( cols, rows ) ;
        if ( !second_is_better( first_ar, second_ar) ) {
            rows++ ;
            cols = other_dimension( rows ) ;
            return ;
        }
        else
            first_ar = second_ar ;
    }
    rows = 1 ;
    cols = number_of_items ;

    // returns from the two for loops above, too
}

private void calculate_cols_rows() {

    if ( container_width == 0 ) {
        rows = number_of_items ;
        cols = 1 ;
        return ;
    }

    if ( container_height == 0 ) {
        rows = 1 ;
        cols = number_of_items ;
        return ;
    }

    container_aspect_ratio =
```

```
            ( (double) container_height ) /
            container_width ;

    calc_layout() ; // figures cols and rows

    cell_width = container_width / cols ;

    cell_height = container_height / rows ;
}

private int ceiling( double d ) {

    int i = (int) d ;
    if ( i < d ) i++ ;

    return i ;
    // return (int) Math.ceil( d ) ; ??
}

private int other_dimension( int dim1 ) {

    double d = ( (double) number_of_items ) / dim1 ;
    return ceiling( d ) ;
}

private boolean second_is_better( double ar1,
    double ar2 ) {

    if ( (ar1 < target_aspect_ratio) &&
         (ar2 < target_aspect_ratio) )
        return ar2 > ar1 ;

    if ( (ar1 > target_aspect_ratio) &&
         (ar2 > target_aspect_ratio) )
        return ar2 < ar1 ;

    // A :=: B for target T when A  = (T^2)/B
    double equal_ar = target_aspect_ratio *
        target_aspect_ratio / ar2 ;

    if ( ar1 <= target_aspect_ratio )
        return ar1 < equal_ar ;
```

```
        else
            return ar1 > equal_ar ;
    }

} // end of ChoicesLayout class

// there are no private classes in ChoicesLayout.java

// end of ChoicesLayout.java
```

Summary

In this chapter we've looked at two new LayoutManagers, CenterLayout and ChoicesLayout. The first centers a Panel (or any other Component) in a Frame (or any other Container). It leaves a border based on a proportion you specify.

The Center.java mainline showed that using the CenterLayout is trivially simple. You set it into the Container as you do any other LayoutManager, and then you add the Panel or other Component.

Internally, the CenterLayout is not as simple as you might think. The complications come in when you consider the centered Component's minimum and preferred sizes. CenterLayout is programmed to handle too little room for even the minimum size; enough room for the minimum size but not enough for the border; enough room with the specified border; and more than enough room for the preferred size. It handles lots of ALD.

The ChoicesLayout is a treat to use on screen. It lets you resize an array of choices (menu prompts, toolbar icons, or whatever) to suit your machine and your mood. It divides the Frame that contains the choices into a grid that best approximates an aspect ratio that you specify, without wasting space.

Using the ChoicesLayout is also trivially simple. You set it as you do any LayoutManager, specifying the target aspect ratio as the only argument to its constructor. Then you add( ) the individual choice objects to the Container. It takes care of the rest.

Internally, the ChoicesLayout is typical of code that makes the computer do intuitively obvious things: it's complicated. If you like math, you probably loved the section on "Understanding the ChoicesLayout LayoutManager."

If you don't enjoy math (or were in a hurry and skipped the "Understanding" section), remember the warning: the ChoicesLayout doesn't return valid minimum or preferred size information. In my uses, this hasn't been a problem. But you may find that this is a serious flaw in some other use.

Chapter 8

The MenuPanel for User Control

I hope you enjoyed spending a little time on the user interface in the last chapter. Ready to roll up your sleeves and dive back into the database work? Our next database topic is creating and using INI files, so that all the customizations the user makes are saved between runs of the application.

But we don't have an application yet, so we can't really do this. We need to have some more fun at the user interface level. We're going to build JDB's front end with a bunch of menus, all employing the ChoicesLayout. We'll let our users (which means us, for now) drag these menus around the screen and set up their own customized JDB.

Then we'll write out an INI file that remembers how the application was left. We'll use a StreamTokenizer to read the INI when the application is started. That will let us reset the application to exactly the size, shape, and color that the user left it in, which is exactly what the user wants the application to do.

For those of you who insist on doing something unique, we'll let the user control the look of the menus, too. You'll see that this is very easy with Java's rounded rectangle. The hard work will be adjusting the font to fit the size the user chooses. But without adjusting the font size, the ability to resize a menu would be nearly meaningless.

Using the MenuPanel—the User's View

Your disk includes a project named Menu for this chapter. Figure 8-1 shows the default, just-launched form of the sample menu.

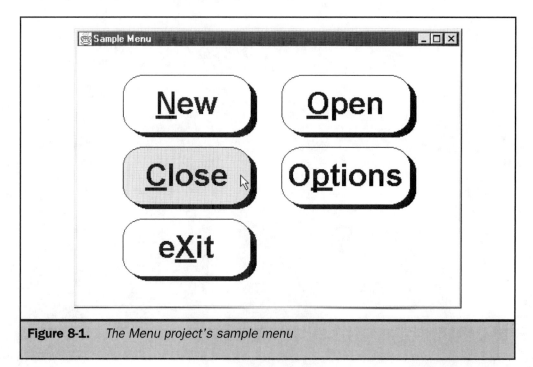

Figure 8-1. *The Menu project's sample menu*

If you're at your computer, build and run this project and give the sample menu a good workout. You'll see that the highlight follows your mouse cursor as it moves over the prompts. I like this browser-inspired behavior.

Note that you can use either the mouse or the keyboard to manipulate this menu. The underscored letters work, but only if you don't hold down the ALT key. If you're using Visual J++, note that the keyboard is inoperable until you click inside the menu. Action keys, such as the arrow keys, also work.

As you can imagine, getting the arrows to perform an intuitive action is a lot of trouble, since the arrangement of the prompts into rows and columns is variable. Worse, as noted in the bug report, this work is pretty much wasted.

You *are* remembering that Java doesn't support an underscored font option, aren't you? That underscoring is done by drawing lines, proving that you can do anything you set your mind to in Java. You could, that is, if everything in Java actually worked. As you'll gather from the bug report, that's not quite true, unfortunately.

As with the scroller, the keyboard is inoperative in Visual J++ until you've clicked in the box. That turns on keyboard events. Visual Cafe doesn't have this problem. Don't rush to replace your Visual J++ with Visual Cafe, however. When we get to the data-entry fields, you'll see that the latter has problems not shared by the former.

That wasn't good news, was it? It gets worse.

In both Visual Cafe and Visual J++, the keyboard becomes inoperative as you add more complexity to the application. In our full JDB application, there really isn't any keyboard control. All the trouble I took to underscore the selected letters is pretty much a waste.

If you're waiting for the good news, you're forgetting that this is about bugs. The rest is worse still. As I noted at the outset, this is JDK 1.0 code. JDK 1.1 changes the event model, so our event handling is all deprecated. Do you expect our vendors to spend time fixing the operation of deprecated features? I'm not sure this will ever work.

I'd prefer to charge forward and write all this in 1.1, so we could get it to work. As noted at the outset, however, that would say, "Good-bye!" to all the people who are using Netscape Navigator 3.*x* or Internet Explorer 3.*x*. That isn't an option as I write this (summer 1997).

Ugh.

Except for the bugs, this would be a brand-new but still familiar menu. Having something that looks new but doesn't take any user retraining is the best of interface results. Maybe we'll actually get those ALT key combinations back. (Use UNIX? I'm up for it, but what about the rest of the known universe?)

Have you finished fiddling with this sample menu? Changed it from vertical to horizontal to 3x2 and to 2x3? Fun, isn't it? (Once you see the ChoicesLayout technology in action, you don't want to leave it behind.)

Before we dive into the code, let me misquote Al Jolson: "You ain't seen nothin', yet." This uses default settings for the round rectangle prompts. There's a lot more fun to be had here. We'll get there. Now let's look at the code.

Using the MenuPanel—the Programmer's View

The driving mainline is MenuSample.java. (I called it just "Menu" at first, but that conflicts with the built-in Menu class.) If you think a menu as slick as this one is a lot of trouble to create, you're wrong. It's actually no trouble at all.

You can't use a menu painter, of course. Once you take a look at the code, I'm not sure you'll care. I don't.

Creating the Menu

The first thing it takes to launch a MenuPanel is a variable and a list of prompts, like this:

```
// protected data members:

    MenuPanel menu_panel;

    String[] prompts = {
        "&New",
        "&Open",
        "&Close",
        "O&ptions",
        "e&Xit"
    };
```

With those, you need a class that extends Frame to launch the menu. (I call it a *torn-off* menu.) This is the constructor that builds and presents the menu, nicely centered in the Frame:

```
    menu_panel = new MenuPanel( prompts, this );

    setLayout( new CenterLayout(10) );

    add( menu_panel );
```

The default menu behavior is to move the highlight only when the user clicks on an option. (For most uses, you'll want this old-fashioned approach.) To get the browser-like, cursor-following behavior, you need this line:

```
menu_panel.setFollowsCursor( true );
```

A little extra code that sizes the Frame and gives it a title completes this constructor. You've just seen all the trouble you'll have in using these MenuPanel-based menus. Simple, no?

Of course, that leaves the matter of actually doing something when the user clicks on an option.

Handling the Menu Events

The reason a reference to the Frame is passed to the MenuPanel constructor is to let the MenuPanel know who cares about its events. A click on a menu option is posted to the Frame so its handleEvent( ) method can take care of it.

The MenuPanel puts itself into Event.target. It returns an Integer in Event.arg. (The arg is an Object, so you have to use an Integer object, not just an int.) The intValue( ) is zero for the first menu option, one for the second, and so on. This is the relevant portion of MenuSample's handleEvent( ) method:

```
if ( (e.target == menu_panel) &&
    (e.arg != null) ) {

    int i = ( (( Integer ) e.arg).intValue() );

    if ( i == 4 )
        System.exit( 0 );

    else {

        MsgBox mb = new MsgBox( prompts[i] );
        mb.show();
    }
}
```

In most cases, you'll handle the returned value in a switch that has a block for each menu item. In this case, the first four options are handled by popping up a MsgBox that just repeats each option's prompt.

Excepting that fairly ugly line that retrieves the menu option number from Event.arg, this code is what you would do for any menu using any slick menu painter. Using the MenuPanel really couldn't be much simpler.

The Full MenuSample.java Listing

Listing 8-1 is the full MenuSample.java source file.

```java
// MenuSample.java — a sample menu
// Copyright 1997, Martin L. Rinehart

import java.awt.*;

class MenuSample extends Frame {

// ——————— data members ——————

// there are no public data members

// protected data members:

    MenuPanel menu_panel;

    String[] prompts = {
        "&New",
        "&Open",
        "&Close",
        "O&ptions",
        "e&Xit"
    };

// there are no static data members
        // there are no public static data members
        // there are no private static data members
        // there are no final static data members

// ——————— public methods ———————

    //*
        public static void main( String[] args ) {

            ( new MenuSample() ).show();
        }
```

```
        // */

// constructor:

    MenuSample( int i ) {
        // never call this constructor
        // VCafe will write stuff here
    }

    MenuSample() {

        menu_panel = new MenuPanel( prompts, this );

        setLayout( new CenterLayout(10) );

        add( menu_panel );

        setTitle( "Sample Menu" );
        resize( 500, 350 );

        menu_panel.setFollowsCursor( true );
}

// there are no data access getXxx() methods
// there are no data access isXxx() methods
// there are no data access setXxx() methods

// there are no public, class-specific methods

// public, non-event overriding method:

    public String paramString() {

        return "MenuSample";
    }

// public, event-handling method:

    public boolean handleEvent( Event e ) {

        if ( e.id == Event.WINDOW_DESTROY ) {
```

```
                System.exit( 0 );
                return true;
        }

        if ( (e.target == menu_panel) &&
             (e.arg != null) ) {

            int i = ( (( Integer ) e.arg).intValue() );

            if ( i == 4 )
                System.exit( 0 );

          else {

                MsgBox mb = new MsgBox( prompts[i] );
                mb.show();
            }
        }

        return super.handleEvent( e );
    }

    /*
    public boolean gotFocus( Event e, Object o )

    public boolean keyDown( Event e, int k )
    public boolean keyUp  ( Event e, int k )

    public boolean lostFocus( Event e, Object o )

    public boolean mouseDown ( Event e, int x, int y )
    public boolean mouseDrag ( Event e, int x, int y )
    public boolean mouseEnter( Event e, int x, int y )
    public boolean mouseExit ( Event e, int x, int y )
    public boolean mouseMove ( Event e, int x, int y )
    public boolean mouseUp   ( Event e, int x, int y )
    */


// ----------- private methods -----------
// there are no private methods
```

```
} // end of MenuSample class

// there are no private classes in MenuSample.java

// end of MenuSample.java
```

Understanding the MenuPanel

TOUR

The rest of this chapter is for you folks who want to modify the MenuPanel, or who just insist on thoroughly understanding absolutely everything. At this point everyone should fiddle with the project a bit.

Why don't you change my list of prompts to one that means something for an application you're working on. Don't forget that the option number for the eXit option is hard-coded in handleEvent( ). With that adjusted (or eliminated), rebuild the Menu project. Simple, isn't it?

Comment out the setFollowsCursor( ) line and try it that way. Got it? It's just possible that at this point you'll be happy with nothing more than a flying skim all the way to the "Summary" section. You can already use MenuPanels.

If you're here, you're hard core. My kind of people! For the rest of this chapter I'm going to be brief. This is all user interface code, so I'll not dwell on it. Of course, you can't build database applications without user interfaces, so I do think this is relevant.

We'll begin with a good look at the MenuPanel object. Before we get started, let me explain the overall structure.

The MenuPanel is the boss and does most of the work, too. The MenuPanel calls routines in MenuLib to handle the messy business of converting ampersands to underscoring the following character.

Each menu option is a MenuPanel—which extends Panel. This object's purpose is to paint the prompt in either a highlighted or normal mode. These panels, in turn, use a PromptPainter-based object to do their actual painting.

I had originally intended to have various PromptPainters available. I thought a rectangle and an oval would be nice, for examples. Then I discovered that the RoundRect draw methods handled everything from straight rectangles to ovals, with lots of choices in between, so I just use the RRectPromptPainter. (A RectPromptPainter and an OvalPromptPainter are gathering dust in some musty corner of my hard disk.)

I left the basic technology, separating the painter from the menu option panel, so that you adventurous souls would have a place to do your thing. Bitmapped images, anyone? Polygons are fun, too. Enjoy.

The RRectPromptPainter extends the PromptPainter class. The latter is a semi-abstract class. It implements all its own functions, so it's not really abstract. But it implements them in such trivial ways that you'll almost always want to extend it and override most of its methods for professional work.

Understanding the MenuPanel Code

Before we start on the code, a word on the data is in order. The longest prompt is found in the String array prompts and is stored in the variable *longest_prompt*. This is the prompt that is the key to setting the font size.

The underscored letters are stored in the byte array speed_letters. You'll see that these don't need to be unique, since the search is circular. At least it is when the bugs let a keypress event come through.

Variables that are prefixed "hi_" refer to the option in a selected or highlighted condition. The "lo_" prefix is used for nonselected options. The Color variables lo_back and lo_fore, for example, specify the color of the nonselected options.

With those notes, let's dive into the code. We'll cover constructors, nonevent public methods, public event-related methods, and last but not least, the private methods.

The MenuPanel Constructors

The first constructor is a one-liner that adds defaults to fill all the parameters for the full constructor:

```
MenuPanel( String[] prmpts, Frame f ) {

    this( prmpts, 1/3.0, new RRectPromptPainter(), f );
}
```

The full constructor begins by storing the parameter values into the appropriate data members. Then it sets up the old height and width to force a resize( ) on the first call to paint( ):

```
old_width = old_height = 0;
```

Next it sets up our good friend, the ChoicesLayout:

```
painter = pp;

layout_man =
    new ChoicesLayout( target_aspect_ratio );
setLayout( layout_man );
```

A PromptPanel is created and added for each menu option:

```
panels = new PromptPanel[num_prompts];
for ( int i = 0 ; i < num_prompts ; i++ ) {
    panels[i] = new PromptPanel(
        painter, prompts[i], i, this );
    add( panels[i] );
}
```

Then these "set_"-prefixed methods do what they promise:

```
set_longest_prompt();
set_speed_letters();
```

After setting up default colors and the default condition for the boolean, prompt_follows_cursor, the constructor finishes with calls to layout( ) and resize( ).

The MenuPanel Nonevent Public Methods

To reward you hard-core readers, the first method in this section supports dynamic menus. With add( ), you can add prompts at the end or at a specified location in the prompts array:

```
public void add( String s ) {

    add( s, prompts.length );
}

public void add( String s, int where ) {

    if ( where <= hi_prompt )
        hi_prompt++;

    if ( where <= old_hi_prompt )
        old_hi_prompt++;

    prompts = string_array_insert( prompts, s, where );
    num_prompts++;
    reset_menu();
}
```

The paint( ) method calls resize( ) when the size doesn't match the values stored in old_width or old_height. It doesn't actually do any painting. That's all taken care of by the individual menu option's PromptPainter object.

The remove( ) method provides the opposite service to add( ). It trusts your code to not call it with an invalid prompt number:

```
public void remove( int where ) {

    if ( hi_prompt == where )
        hi_prompt = old_hi_prompt = 0;
    else if ( hi_prompt == prompts.length - 1 )
        hi_prompt = old_hi_prompt =
            prompts.length - 2;

    prompts = string_array_delete( prompts, where );
    num_prompts—;
    reset_menu();
}
```

The resize( ) method is long but straightforward. Refer to the full listing for the code. Its complex jobs, such as choosing the appropriate font size, are done by calls to private methods, which we'll see shortly.

The MenuPanel Event-Related Public Methods

The event-related methods begin with keyDown( ). I'll skip that and all the keypress-related methods in this discussion since the bugs we've already noted mean that they just don't work. If you run them in an isolated menu, such as in our sample project for this chapter, you'll see that the problem isn't in this code. The problem is that the keypress events simply won't be reported in a more complex system.

The mouseDown( ) event is ignored. Mouse clicks are noted on a mouseUp( ) event. The mouseMove( ) code that gives that nice, browser-like feel is really simple:

```
public boolean mouseMove ( Event e, int x, int y ) {

    if ( prompt_follows_cursor ) {

        reset_hilite( e );
        return true;
    }
    return false;
}
```

The mouseUp( ) handler moves the highlight, handles the mouse click, and yields, so that everyone else gets a chance to do whatever may be triggered by a mouse click. You can see here that the hard work is left for private methods:

```
public boolean mouseUp    ( Event e, int x, int y ) {

    reset_hilite( e );
    handle_click( e );
    Thread.yield();
    return true;
}
```

The MenuPanel Private Methods

The end_of_row( ) method is part of the arrow key-handling technology. It's part of the complications we get because we can't assume anything about the grid of menu options. See the full listing for details.

Handling mouse clicks is done by constructing and posting an Event for the boss—the menu-containing Frame. The postEvent( ) method is the one that you call when you don't want the Event passed to Components contained by a Container. I'd explain the difference between postEvent( ) and deliverEvent( ) more thoroughly if Sun hadn't deprecated them in JDK 1.1. (While Visual J++'s documentation is generally superior to Visual Cafe's, this information is easier to get through Visual Cafe, which makes it easy to look at the Sun source.) This is the code:

```
private void handle_click( Event e ) {

    for ( int i = 0 ; i < num_prompts ; i++ ) {
        if ( e.target == panels[i] ) {
            e.arg = new Integer(i);
            e.target = this;
            boss.postEvent( e );
        }
    }
}
```

The ENTER keypress is processed like a mouse click by handle_enter( ). The handle_key_action( ) method is a big switch that makes the arrow keys do just what you expect them to do. Writing it was a challenge. I'm sorry it proved to be such an academic exercise. You might want to seriously consider removing all that code that I worked out so painstakingly. I don't have the heart.

If you throw out the keypress code, throw out the next three routines, too: handle_key_press( ), handle_speed_key( ), and matchesIgnoreCase( ).

When you get a mouse click, the target of the event is one of the PromptPanel objects. The first form of reset_hilite( ) finds the appropriate menu option and calls the next form of reset_hilite( ) with the corresponding option number:

```
private void reset_hilite( Event e ) {

    for ( int i = 0 ; i < num_prompts ; i++ ) {

        if ( e.target == panels[i] ) {

            if ( i == hi_prompt )
                return;
            else
                reset_hilite( i );
        }
    }
}
```

The second reset_hilite( ) uses an option number to actually do the work of changing the hilite:

```
private void reset_hilite( int i ) {

    old_hi_prompt = hi_prompt;
    hi_prompt = i;

    panels[old_hi_prompt].repaint();
    panels[hi_prompt].repaint();
    Thread.yield();
}
```

The reset_menu( ) routine sets up everything from scratch. This is called after an add( ) or remove( ) operation. The method finds the longest prompt again, resets the list of speed letters, and then replaces all the PromptPanels added to the MenuPanel Container. This is the code:

```
private void reset_menu() {

    set_longest_prompt();
```

```
        set_speed_letters();

        removeAll();

        panels = new PromptPanel[num_prompts];
        for ( int i = 0 ; i < num_prompts ; i++ ) {
            panels[i] = new PromptPanel(
                painter, prompts[i], i, this );
            add( panels[i] );
        }

        layout();
        resize();
    }
```

The short row_in( ) method is another one used to process arrow keys.

The set_longest_prompt( ) method is a simple one except for all the ALD. This is the method:

```
    private void set_longest_prompt() {

        longest_prompt = " ";
        int longest_width = 0;

        FontMetrics fm = getFontMetrics(
            new Font("Helvetica", Font.BOLD, 24 ) );

        for ( int i = 0 ; i < num_prompts ; i++ ) {

            int this_width = fm.stringWidth(
                MenuLib.removeAmpersand(prompts[i]) );
            if ( this_width > longest_width ) {
                longest_prompt = prompts[i];
                longest_width = this_width;
            }
        }
    }
```

The get_speed_letter( ) method retrieves the byte following the ampersand in an individual string. Note its warning:

```
private byte get_speed_letter( String s ) {

// note: this will crash if the ampersand is the
// terminal character in a prompt — which is OK when
// the prompt's hard coded. If the prompts are coming
// from a source other than code, they need to be
// checked before they get here.

    int amp_loc = s.indexOf( '&' );
    if ( amp_loc == -1 )
        return (byte) ' ';  // VJ++ requires the cast
                                    // VCafe doesn't

    return (byte) s.charAt( amp_loc + 1 );
}
```

The set_speed_letters( ) method calls the get_speed_letter( ) method for each prompt string, dropping the letter into the speed_letters array.

The start_of_row( ) method is another piece of the arrow key-handling code.

The string_array_delete( ) method performs the service it names for the remove( ) method. Similarly, the string_array_insert( ) method serves the add( ) routine, putting the new prompt into the prompts array. See the full listing for the details.

Finally, the upper( ) and wrap_to_top( ) methods also support keystroke processing.

The Full MenuPanel.java Listing

Listing 8-2 is the full MenuPanel.java source file.

Listing 8-2:
MenuPanel.
java does
Java-style
menus

```
// MenuPanel.java — stretchy, rearrangeable menu
// Copyright 1997, Martin L. Rinehart

// this code is completely documented in:
// _Java Database Development_, Martin Rinehart,
// Osborne/McGraw-Hill, 1997

/*
    You can stretch a MenuPanel wide and short, tall and
    thin or anyplace in between.
*/
```

```java
import java.awt.*;

class MenuPanel extends Panel {

// ——————————- data members ——————————-

// there are no public data members

// protected data members:

    protected Frame boss;

    protected int cols;

    protected Color hi_back;
    protected Color hi_fore;
    protected int hi_prompt;

    protected boolean im_resizing;
    protected int item_height;
    protected int item_width;

    protected ChoicesLayout layout_man;
    protected Color lo_back;
    protected Color lo_fore;
    protected String longest_prompt;

    protected int num_prompts;

    protected int old_height;
    protected int old_hi_prompt;
    protected int old_width;

    protected PromptPainter painter;
    protected PromptPanel[] panels;
    protected Font prompt_font;
    protected boolean prompt_follows_cursor;
    protected String[] prompts;

    protected double rect_aspect_ratio;
```

```
    protected int rows;

    protected byte[] speed_letters;

    protected double target_aspect_ratio;
        // desired height/width of item

// there are no static data members

// ——————— public methods ———————

// constructors:

    MenuPanel( String[] prmpts, Frame f ) {

        this( prmpts, 1/3.0, new RRectPromptPainter(), f );
    }

    MenuPanel( String[] prmpts, double ar,
        PromptPainter pp, Frame f ) {

        num_prompts = prmpts.length;
        prompts = prmpts;
        target_aspect_ratio = ar;
        boss = f;

        old_width = old_height = 0;

        painter = pp;

        layout_man =
            new ChoicesLayout( target_aspect_ratio );
        setLayout( layout_man );

        panels = new PromptPanel[num_prompts];
        for ( int i = 0 ; i < num_prompts ; i++ ) {
            panels[i] = new PromptPanel(
                painter, prompts[i], i, this );
            add( panels[i] );
        }

        set_longest_prompt();
```

```
        set_speed_letters();

        lo_fore = Color.black;
        lo_back = Color.lightGray;

        hi_fore = Color.blue;
        hi_back = Color.cyan;

        hi_prompt = 0;
        prompt_follows_cursor = false;
        layout();
        resize();
    }

// there are no data access getXxx() methods
// there are no data access isXxx() methods

// data access setXxx() methods:

    public void setFollowsCursor( boolean b ) {

        prompt_follows_cursor = b;
    }

    public void setHilight( int i ) {

        reset_hilite( i );
    }

// there are no public, class-specific methods

// public, non-event overriding methods:

    public void add( String s ) {

        add( s, prompts.length );
    }

    public void add( String s, int where ) {

        if ( where <= hi_prompt )
            hi_prompt++;
```

```
        if ( where <= old_hi_prompt )
            old_hi_prompt++;

        prompts = string_array_insert( prompts, s, where );
        num_prompts++;
        reset_menu();
    }

public void paint( Graphics g ) {

        if ( im_resizing ) return; // don't recurse

        if ( (old_width != size().width) ||
            (old_height != size().height) ) {

            resize();
        }
    }

 public String paramString() {

        return "MenuPanel";
    }

public void remove( int where ) {

        if ( hi_prompt == where )
            hi_prompt = old_hi_prompt = 0;
        else if ( hi_prompt == prompts.length - 1 )
            hi_prompt = old_hi_prompt =
                prompts.length - 2;

        prompts = string_array_delete( prompts, where );
        num_prompts--;
        reset_menu();
    }

public void resize() {

        rect_aspect_ratio =
            ( (double) size().height ) / size().width;
```

```
        old_width = size().width;
        old_height = size().height;

        if ( panels.length == 0 )
            return;

        item_width = panels[0].size().width;
        item_height = panels[0].size().height;

        Panel p = new Panel();
        p.resize( item_width, item_height );
        painter.setFont( p, longest_prompt );
        prompt_font = p.getFont();

        Dimension d = layout_man.getDimensions();
        cols = d.width;
        rows = d.height;
    }

// public, event-handling methods:

    public boolean keyDown( Event e, int k ) {

        if ( e.id == Event.KEY_ACTION ) {
           handle_key_action( e );
           return true;
         }
        else if ( e.id == Event.KEY_PRESS )
          return handle_key_press( e );

        return false;
    }

    public boolean keyUp( Event e, int k ) {

        return true;
    }

    public boolean mouseDown ( Event e, int x, int y ) {

        return true; // handle mouse in mouseUp()
    }
```

```java
        public boolean mouseMove ( Event e, int x, int y ) {

            if ( prompt_follows_cursor ) {

                reset_hilite( e );
                return true;
             }
             return false;
        }

        public boolean mouseUp    ( Event e, int x, int y ) {

            reset_hilite( e );
            handle_click( e );
            Thread.yield();
            return true;
        }

        /*
        public boolean gotFocus( Event e, Object o )

        public boolean lostFocus( Event e, Object o )

        public boolean mouseDrag ( Event e, int x, int y )
        public boolean mouseEnter( Event e, int x, int y )
        public boolean mouseExit ( Event e, int x, int y )
        */

// ----------- private methods -----------

// private methods:

        private int end_of_row( int i ) {

            int end = start_of_row( i ) + cols - 1;
            if ( end > num_prompts - 1 )
                end = num_prompts - 1;

            return end;
        }
```

```
private void handle_click( Event e ) {

    for ( int i = 0 ; i < num_prompts ; i++ ) {
        if ( e.target == panels[i] ) {
            e.arg = new Integer(i);
            e.target = this;
            boss.postEvent( e );
        }
    }
}

private void handle_enter( Event e ) {

    e.arg = new Integer( hi_prompt );
    e.target = this;
    boss.postEvent( e );
    Thread.yield();
}

private void handle_key_action( Event e ) {

    int next;
    switch ( e.key ) {

       case Event.LEFT: {

           if ( cols == 1 ) break;

           if ( hi_prompt == 0 )
               next = end_of_row( 0 );

           else if ( (hi_prompt/cols) ==
                ( ( hi_prompt-1 )/cols) )
               next = hi_prompt - 1;

           else

               next = end_of_row( hi_prompt );

           reset_hilite( next );
           break;
       }
```

```
case Event.RIGHT: {

    if ( cols == 1 ) break;

    if ( hi_prompt == num_prompts - 1 )
        next =
            start_of_row( hi_prompt );

    else if ( (hi_prompt/cols) ==
            (( hi_prompt + 1 )/cols) )
        next = hi_prompt + 1;

    else
        next = start_of_row( hi_prompt );

    reset_hilite( next );
    break;
}

case Event.UP: {

    if ( rows == 1 ) break;

    if ( hi_prompt < cols ) {

        next = hi_prompt +
            ( rows - 1 ) * cols;
        if ( next >= num_prompts )
            next -= cols;
    }
    else
        next = hi_prompt - cols;

    reset_hilite( next );
    break;
}

case Event.DOWN: {

    if ( rows == 1 ) break;
```

```
                        if ( hi_prompt > num_prompts - cols )
                            next = wrap_to_top( hi_prompt );
                        else {
                            next = hi_prompt + cols;
                            if ( next > num_prompts - 1 )
                                next = wrap_to_top( hi_prompt );
                        }

                        reset_hilite( next );
                        break;
                }
            }
        }

    private boolean handle_key_press( Event e ) {

        switch( e.key ) {

            case '\n': {
                handle_enter( e );
                return true;
            }

            default:
                return handle_speed_key( e.key );

        }
    }

    private boolean handle_speed_key( int k ) {

    // this algorithm permits duplicate spped keys

        int pno = hi_prompt - 1;
        for ( int i = 0 ; i < num_prompts ; i++ ) {
            pno++;
            if ( pno == num_prompts )
                pno = 0;
            if ( matchesIgnoreCase(
                k, speed_letters[pno]) ) {
                reset_hilite( pno );
                return true;
```

```
            }
        }
        return false;
    }

    private boolean matchesIgnoreCase( int k1, int k2 ) {

        return upper( k1 ) == upper( k2 );
    }

    private void reset_hilite( Event e ) {

        for ( int i = 0 ; i < num_prompts ; i++ ) {

            if ( e.target == panels[i] ) {

                if ( i == hi_prompt )
                    return;
                else
                    reset_hilite( i );
            }
        }
    }

    private void reset_hilite( int i ) {

        old_hi_prompt = hi_prompt;
        hi_prompt = i;

        panels[old_hi_prompt].repaint();
        panels[hi_prompt].repaint();
        Thread.yield();
    }

    private void reset_menu() {

        set_longest_prompt();
        set_speed_letters();

        removeAll();

        panels = new PromptPanel[num_prompts];
```

```
    for ( int i = 0 ; i < num_prompts ; i++ ) {
        panels[i] = new PromptPanel(
            painter, prompts[i], i, this );
        add( panels[i] );
    }

    layout();
    resize();
}

private int row_in( int i ) {

    return i / cols;
}

private void set_longest_prompt() {

    longest_prompt = "";
    int longest_width = 0;

    FontMetrics fm = getFontMetrics(
        new Font("Helvetica", Font.BOLD, 24 ) );

    for ( int i = 0 ; i < num_prompts ; i++ ) {

        int this_width = fm.stringWidth(
            MenuLib.removeAmpersand(prompts[i]) );
        if ( this_width > longest_width ) {
            longest_prompt = prompts[i];
            longest_width = this_width;
        }
    }
}

private byte get_speed_letter( String s ) {

// note: this will crash if the ampersand is the
// terminal character in a prompt — which is OK when
// the prompt's hard coded. If the prompts are coming
// from a source other than code, they need to be
// checked before they get here.
```

```
        int amp_loc = s.indexOf( '&' );
        if ( amp_loc == -1 )
            return (byte) ' ';   // VJ++ requires the cast
                                 // VCafe doesn't

        return (byte) s.charAt( amp_loc + 1 );
    }

    private void set_speed_letters() {

        speed_letters = new byte[num_prompts];
        for ( int i = 0 ; i < num_prompts ; i++ )
            speed_letters[i] =
                get_speed_letter( prompts[i] );
    }

    private int start_of_row( int i ) {

        return ( row_in(i) ) * cols;
    }

    private String[] string_array_delete(
        String[] old_strings, int where ) {

        String[] new_strings = new String[
            old_strings.length - 1];

        if ( where > 0 )
            for ( int i = 0 ; i < where ; i++ )
                new_strings[i] = old_strings[i];

        if ( where < new_strings.length )
            for ( int i = where ;
                i < new_strings.length ; i++ )
                new_strings[i] = old_strings[i+1];

        return new_strings;
    }

    private String[] string_array_insert(
        String[] old_strings, String s, int where ) {
```

```
        String[] new_strings = new String[
            old_strings.length + 1];

        if ( where > 0 )
            for ( int i = 0 ; i < where ; i++ )
                new_strings[i] = old_strings[i];

        new_strings[where] = s;

        if ( where < old_strings.length )
            for ( int i = where + 1 ;
                i < new_strings.length ; i++ )
                new_strings[i] = old_strings[i-1];

        return new_strings;
    }

    private int upper( int k ) {
        if ( (k >= 'a') && (k <= 'z') )
            return k - 'a' + 'A';
        else
            return k;
    }

    private int wrap_to_top( int i ) {

        int r = i / cols; //
        return i - r * cols;
    }

} // end of MenuPanel class

// there are no private classes in MenuPanel.java

// end of MenuPanel.java
```

Understanding the MenuLib

MenuLib has three public functions. The first, drawPrompt( ), accepts a string that may have an embedded ampersand. It draws the string, removing the ampersand (if any) and underscoring the following character. Since Java has no underscored font, the actual work of underscoring is done by filling a small rectangle, this way:

```
FontMetrics fm = c.getFontMetrics( g.getFont() );
x += fm.stringWidth( prompt.substring(0, amp_loc) );

int descent = fm.getDescent();
y += descent/4;

g.fillRect( x, y,
    fm.charWidth(prompt.charAt( amp_loc )),
    descent / 2 );
```

The other two are removeAmpersand( ) and delete_char_at( ), both of which perform the function their name promises. This code predates the MRString class. If I were doing it again today, I'd use an MRString.

Both these functions return a new String. They don't perform the job on the input String. Listing 8-3 shows the full file.

Listing 8-3:
MenuLib.java
handles
ampersand
underscoring

```
// MenuLib.java — library routines for menus
// Copyright 1997, Martin L. Rinehart

// this code is completely documented in:
// _Java Database Development_, Martin Rinehart,
// Osborne/McGraw-Hill, 1997

/*
    Handle converting "&File" to "File" with an
    underscored "F".
*/

import java.awt.*;

class MenuLib extends Object {

// ————————— data members ————————

// there are no data members

// ————————— public methods ————————

// MenuLib has three public, class-specific methods:
```

```
public static void drawPrompt( Component c,
    Graphics g, String prompt, int x, int y ) {

// drawString with "&" underscores

    int amp_loc = prompt.indexOf( '&' );

    if ( amp_loc == -1 ) {

        g.drawString( prompt, x, y );
        return;
    }

    g.drawString(
        delete_char_at(prompt, amp_loc), x, y );

    FontMetrics fm = c.getFontMetrics( g.getFont() );
    x += fm.stringWidth( prompt.substring(0, amp_loc) );

    int descent = fm.getDescent();
    y += descent/4;

    g.fillRect( x, y,
        fm.charWidth(prompt.charAt( amp_loc )),
        descent / 2 );
}

public static String removeAmpersand( String s ) {

    int amp_loc = s.indexOf( '&' );
    if ( amp_loc == -1 )
        return s;
    else
        return delete_char_at( s, amp_loc );
}

private static String delete_char_at(
    String s, int loc ) {

    if ( loc == 0 )
        return s.substring( 1, s.length() );
```

```
            else if ( loc == (s.length() - 1) )
                return s.substring( 0, s.length() - 1 );

            else
                return s.substring( 0, loc ).concat(
                    s.substring(loc+1, s.length( )) );
    }

} // end of class MenuLib

// end of MenuLib.java
```

Understanding the PromptPanel

The PromptPanel provides a Component on which we can paint, and from which we can get mouse events. The code itself is trivial, as you can see in Listing 8-4.

Listing 8-4:
PromptPanel.
java provides
components
for menu
options

```
// PromptPanel.java — carrier for menu prompts
// Copyright 1997, Martin L. Rinehart

// this code is completely documented in:
// _Java Database Development_, Martin Rinehart,
// Osborne/McGraw-Hill, 1997

/*
     These panels hold individual menu items.
*/

import java.awt.*;

class PromptPanel extends Panel {

// ------------ data members ------------

// there are no public data members

// protected data members:

    protected PromptPainter painter;
    protected MenuPanel        parent;
    protected String         prompt_text;
```

```java
    protected int who_i_am;

// there are no static data members

// ——————— public methods ———————

// constructor:

    PromptPanel( PromptPainter pp, String s,
        int who, MenuPanel par ) {

        painter = pp;
        prompt_text = s;

        who_i_am = who;
        parent = par;
    }

// there are no data access methods

// there are no public, class-specific methods

// public, non-event overriding methods:

    public void paint( Graphics g ) {

        painter.drawPrompt( this, prompt_text, g,
            parent.hi_prompt == who_i_am );
    }

     public String paramString() {

         return "prompt: " + prompt_text;
     }

// public, event-handling methods

// ——————— private methods ———————-
// there are no private methods

} // end of PromptPanel class
```

```
// there are no private classes in PromptPanel.java

// end of PromptPanel.java
```

Understanding the RRectPromptPainter

The RRectPromptPainter lets you paint widely varying menu prompts, taking advantage of the flexibility of the RoundRect drawing tool.

Other systems that provide a rounded rectangle are content to give you a rounded rectangle. Java goes much further; it lets you specify the precise amount of rounding you want in both the horizontal and vertical dimensions. The menus in Figure 8-2 are all painted by the RRectPromptPainter.

This tool lets you give the user a highly customizable front end, at very little code cost. Combining this with the flexibility that the ChoicesLayout provides probably means that no two of you will have JDB systems that look alike.

You can use this flexibility intelligently, developing a system that uses different shapes for different classes of menus. Or you can use it, as Figure 8-2 shows, just to have some fun.

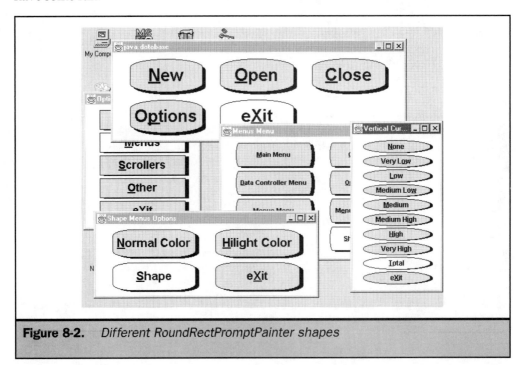

Figure 8-2. *Different RoundRectPromptPainter shapes*

Let's take a look under the hood, to see how this class works.

Understanding the RRectPromptPainter Code

The RRectPromptPainter extends the PromptPainter class. The latter is the semi-virtual class—its methods are functional but primitive. RRectPromptPainter overrides the critical methods, but lets the PromptPainter provide simple services, such as getXxx( ) and setXxx( ) methods. We'll look at the PromptPainter later in this chapter.

We'll begin exploring this class with a look at its data members.

RRectPromptPainter's Data Members

A public int, font_min_size, provides a way for you to set the minimum acceptable font size. You should probably make this value available to the user in a setup routine.

Two public doubles, hradius and vradius, control the amount of rounding in the horizontal and vertical dimensions. At a radius of 1, the curvature extends for the entire dimension. At a radius of 2, half the dimension is curved, and so on.

A final public, prompt_font, lets you set the font. This is another item that could be provided for user control in a setup routine.

The only protected data member is the int, font_size. It's the size of the font, in points.

RRectPromptPainter's Public Methods

There are two constructors. One accepts values for the horizontal and vertical curvature. The no-parameter constructor supplies default values of 3.0 and 1.5, for the horizontal and vertical radius divisors, respectively. The rest of the constructor merely stores those values and sets initial defaults, such as for colors.

The default colors for this book's code were selected to print well in black and white. You might want something a bit more colorful. See the full listing—the values you'll need to change are obvious.

The data access getXxx( ) methods are inherited from the PromptPainter. The setFont( ) method definitely isn't. (The PromptPainter just accepts the default font.)

I use Helvetica, which will become a generic, sans-serif font. In Windows you'll probably get MS Sans Serif or Arial. I also use boldface. The work here is in choosing the right size.

You call the method with a Component (in our use, the PromptPanel) and with the String to display. The String used by the MenuPanel is the longest prompt.

The method starts by choosing a size that is probably much too large:

```
font_size = c.size().height / 2;
if ( font_size < font_min_size )
    font_size = font_min_size;
```

Given an oversized font, it then steps downward, multiplying the font size by 7/8 and testing for fit by calling the fits( ) method. We'll cover the private fits( ) later in this chapter. This testing continues until the font fits or the font reaches the minimum size:

```
prompt_font = new Font(
    "Helvetica", Font.BOLD, font_size );

while ( !fits(MenuLib.removeAmpersand( s ), c) ) {

    font_size = ( 7 * font_size ) / 8;
    prompt_font = new Font( "Helvetica",
        Font.BOLD, font_size );

    if ( font_size < font_min_size ) {
        font_size = font_min_size;
        break;
    }
}
}
```

There are two drawPrompt( ) methods. The first adds the default value, false, for the hilite status:

```
public void drawPrompt(
    Panel p, String s, Graphics g ) {

    drawPrompt( p, s, g, false );
}
```

The second drawPrompt( ) does the hard work. Its job is to draw the prompt, neatly centered inside the RoundRect. It begins by establishing x and y offsets of one-tenth the Panel's width and height. These are used to center the RoundRect within the PromptPanel:

```
int x_offset = p.size().width / 10;
int y_offset = p.size().height / 10;

int rect_width =
    p.size().width - ( 2 * x_offset );
int rect_height =
    p.size().height - ( 2 * y_offset );
```

The first thing drawn is a filled RoundRect in the shadow color, slightly offset:

```
g.setColor( shadow );
g.fillRoundRect( (7*x_offset)/5,
    (7*y_offset)/4,
    rect_width, rect_height,
    (( int ) ( rect_width/hradius )),
    (( int ) ( rect_height/vradius )) );
```

Next the background color is used to paint the body of the RoundRect:

```
g.setColor( hilite ? hi_back : lo_back );

g.fillRoundRect( x_offset, y_offset,
    rect_width, rect_height,
    (( int ) ( rect_width/hradius )),
    (( int ) ( rect_height/vradius )) );
```

The shadow color is used again to draw the final RoundRect:

```
g.setColor( shadow );
g.drawRoundRect( x_offset, y_offset,
    rect_width, rect_height,
    (( int ) ( rect_width/hradius )),
    (( int ) ( rect_height/vradius )) );
```

Why the shadow color? I used black at first. That, of course, doesn't show up at all if the window is already black. Then I switched to the foreground color, which always shows up if the user has chosen a combination of colors that's readable. Then I decided to try the shadow color. (I'm not sure if that was the best choice or I just got tired of fiddling with it.)

Finally, the prompt itself is drawn, neatly centered in the RoundRect:

```
g.setFont( prompt_font );
FontMetrics fm = p.getFontMetrics( prompt_font );

int vertical_spare = p.size().height -
    fm.getAscent() - fm.getDescent();
int baseline =
    ( vertical_spare / 2 ) + fm.getAscent();
```

```
g.setColor( hilite ? hi_fore : lo_fore );

MenuLib.drawPrompt( p, g, s,
    (p.size().width - fm.stringWidth(
        MenuLib.removeAmpersand(s) ))/2,
    baseline );
```

RRectPromptPainter's Private Method

The only private method is fits( ), which reports true when the String fits inside the Component. The String will be the longest prompt, and the Component is a PromptPanel.

Actually, this method is only approximate, since precise fitting requires a detailed knowledge of the rest of the painting of the Component. This version, which works well in practice, lets the String fill three-quarters of the Component.

It starts by getting a FontMetrics object. This will be null if the Component is not on the screen:

```
FontMetrics fm = c.getFontMetrics( prompt_font );
if ( fm == null ) return true; // not on screen
```

The variable naming assumes that the prompt is a single word (which is often, but not always, the case). This code checks to see that the length of the prompt fits in three-quarters of the Component:

```
int word_length = fm.stringWidth( s );
int prompt_length = ( 3 * c.size().width ) / 4;

boolean length_ok = word_length <= prompt_length;
```

It returns false if the length is too long. If the length is adequate, it returns the value of the height check:

```
if ( !length_ok ) return false;

return fm.getAscent() <
    ( (3*c.size().height) / 4 );
```

The Full RRectPromptPainter.java Listing

Listing 8-5 is the full RRectPromptPainter.java source file.

Listing 8-5:
RRectPrompt.
java for
fancy menu
options

```java
// RRectPromptPainter.java — paints rounded rect prompts
// Copyright 1997, Martin L. Rinehart

// this code is completely documented in:
// _Java Database Development_, Martin Rinehart,
// Osborne/McGraw-Hill, 1997

/*
    Rounded rectangles vary from oval through rectangles,
    including lots of shapes in between.
*/

import java.awt.*;

class RRectPromptPainter extends PromptPainter {

// ——————- data members ——————-

// public data members:

    public int font_min_size;

    public double hradius;

    public Font prompt_font;

    public double vradius;

        // at hradius == vradius == 1 you get ovals
        // round ends: hradius = 1, vradius = 2
        // round top and bottom: h = 2, v = 1
        // rounded rectangles: h > 1, v > 1

// protected data member:

    protected int font_size;

// there are no static data members
```

```
// ————————— public methods —————————

// constructors:

    RRectPromptPainter() {

        this( 3.0, 1.5 );
    }

    RRectPromptPainter( double hrad, double vrad ) {

        font_min_size = 8;

        hi_back = Color.lightGray;
        hi_fore = Color.black;

        lo_back = Color.white;
        lo_fore = Color.black;

        shadow = Color.black;

        hradius = hrad;
        vradius = vrad;
    }

// there are no data access getXxx() methods
// there are no data access isXxx() methods

// data access setXxx() methods:

    public void setFont( Component c, String s ) {

        font_size = c.size().height / 2;
        if ( font_size < font_min_size )
            font_size = font_min_size;

        prompt_font = new Font(
            "Helvetica", Font.BOLD, font_size );

        while ( !fits(MenuLib.removeAmpersand( s ), c) ) {
```

```java
            font_size = ( 7 * font_size ) / 8;
            prompt_font = new Font( "Helvetica",
                Font.BOLD, font_size );

            if ( font_size < font_min_size ) {
                font_size = font_min_size;
                break;
            }
        }
    }

    public void setHRadius( double d ) {

        hradius = d;
    }

    public void setVRadius( double d ) {

        vradius = d;
    }

// public, class-specific methods:

    public void drawPrompt(
        Panel p, String s, Graphics g ) {

        drawPrompt( p, s, g, false );
    }

    public void drawPrompt(
        Panel p, String s, Graphics g, boolean hilite ) {

        int x_offset = p.size().width / 10;
        int y_offset = p.size().height / 10;

        int rect_width =
            p.size().width - ( 2 * x_offset );
        int rect_height =
            p.size().height - ( 2 * y_offset );

        if ( prompt_font == null )
            setFont( p, s );
```

```
        g.setColor( shadow );
        g.fillRoundRect( (7*x_offset)/5,
            (7*y_offset)/4,
            rect_width, rect_height,
            (( int ) ( rect_width/hradius )),
            (( int ) ( rect_height/vradius )) );

        g.setColor( hilite ? hi_back : lo_back );

        g.fillRoundRect( x_offset, y_offset,
            rect_width, rect_height,
            (( int ) ( rect_width/hradius )),
            (( int ) ( rect_height/vradius )) );

        g.setColor( shadow );
        g.drawRoundRect( x_offset, y_offset,
            rect_width, rect_height,
            (( int ) ( rect_width/hradius )),
            (( int ) ( rect_height/vradius )) );

        g.setFont( prompt_font );
        FontMetrics fm = p.getFontMetrics( prompt_font );

        int vertical_spare = p.size().height -
            fm.getAscent() - fm.getDescent();
        int baseline =
            ( vertical_spare / 2 ) + fm.getAscent();

        g.setColor( hilite ? hi_fore : lo_fore );

        MenuLib.drawPrompt( p, g, s,
            (p.size().width - fm.stringWidth(
                MenuLib.removeAmpersand(s) ))/2,
            baseline );
    }

// public, non-event overriding method:

    public String paramString() {

        return "hrad: " + hradius +
            " vrad: " + vradius;
```

```
        }

// there are no public, event-handling methods

// ——————— private methods ——————-

// private method:

    private boolean fits( String s, Component c ) {

        FontMetrics fm = c.getFontMetrics( prompt_font );
        if ( fm == null ) return true; // not on screen

        int word_length = fm.stringWidth( s );

        int prompt_length = ( 3 * c.size().width ) / 4;

        boolean length_ok = word_length <= prompt_length;

        if ( !length_ok ) return false;

        return fm.getAscent() <
            ( (3*c.size().height) / 4 );
    }

} // end of RRectPromptPainter class

// there are no private classes in RRectPromptPainter.java

// end of RRectPromptPainter.java
```

Understanding the PromptPainter

The one remaining class is the PromptPainter, which the RRectPainter extends. As one example of this class, consider this sophisticated logic:

```
    // set c.font to the largest size that fits
    // String s

    public void setFont( Component c, String s ) { }
```

The comments suggest the code that you ought to write for a good PromptPainter-extending class. The method does absolutely nothing, which just lets the system use the default window font size.

As another example, the data members for selectable colors are all provided, as well as the getXxx( ) and setXxx( ) methods you need to access them (which your extending class can use). But when it comes time to draw a prompt, I hope you like red for highlight and black for normal, because that's all you get.

The full listing tells the whole story.

Listing 8-6:
The generic
Prompt-
Painter.java

```java
// PromptPainter.java — trivial menu prompt painter
// Copyright 1997, Martin L. Rinehart

// this code is completely documented in:
// _Java Database Development_, Martin Rinehart,
// Osborne/McGraw-Hill, 1997

/*
    Use this as is for QD work.
    Use it as if it were abstract for polished work.

    MenuPanel uses a PromptPainter to display prompts.
    RRectPromptPainter uses this as an abstract base
    class.
*/

import java.awt.*;

class PromptPainter extends Object {

// ——————— data members ————————

// there are no public data members

// protected data members:

    protected Color hi_back;
     protected Color hi_fore;

    protected Color lo_back;
     protected Color lo_fore;

    protected Color shadow;
```

```java
// there are no static data members

// ——————— public methods ———————

// there are no constructors

// data access getXxx() methods:

    // get colors
    public Color getHiBackColor() {

        return hi_back;
    }

    public Color getHiForeColor() {

        return hi_fore;
    }

    public Color getLoBackColor() {

        return lo_back;
    }

    public Color getLoForeColor() {

        return lo_fore;
    }

    public Color getShadowColor() {

        return shadow;
    }

// there are no data access isXxx() methods

// data access setXxx() methods:

    // set c.font to the largest size that fits
    // String s

    public void setFont( Component c, String s ) { }
```

```java
// set colors
public void setHiBackColor( Color c ) {

    hi_back = c;
}

public void setHiColor( Color back, Color fore ) {

    hi_back = back;
    hi_fore = fore;
}

public void setHiColor( int back, int fore ) {

    hi_back = new Color( back );
    hi_fore = new Color( fore );
}

public void setHiForeColor( Color c ) {

    hi_fore = c;
}

public void setLoBackColor( Color c ) {

    lo_back = c;
}

public void setLoColor( Color back, Color fore ) {

    lo_back = back;
    lo_fore = fore;
}

public void setLoColor( int back, int fore ) {

    lo_back = new Color( back );
    lo_fore = new Color( fore );
}

public void setLoForeColor( Color c ) {
```

```
        lo_fore = c;
    }

    public void setShadowColor( Color c ) {

        shadow = c;
    }

// public, class-specific methods:

    // draw prompt with text s in Panel p using Graphics g

    public void drawPrompt(
        Panel p, String s, Graphics g ) {

        g.drawString( s, 5, (3 * p.size().height) / 4 );
    }

    // draw as above but hilited or not

    public void drawPrompt(
        Panel p, String s, Graphics g, boolean hi ) {

        g.setColor( hi ? Color.red : Color.black );
        drawPrompt( p, s, g );
    }

// public, non-event overriding method:

    public String paramString() {

        return "hi: " + hi_fore + " on " + hi_back +
            " lo: " + lo_fore + " on " + lo_back;
    }

// there are no public, event-handling methods

// —————— private methods ——————-
// there are no private methods

} // end of PromptPainter class
```

```
// there are no private classes in PromptPainter.java

// end of PromptPainter.java
```

Summary

We're working up to INI files, which are one universal type of local database. In this chapter we looked at the menu panel, which will provide a front end about which we can develop the INI work.

The MenuPanel makes it very simple to create a sophisticated, ChoicesLayout-enabled menu. The entire front end for the JDB system is a set of MenuPanels.

To use the MenuPanel, you create a String array that contains your menu's prompts. Then you call the MenuPanel constructor with a reference to the String array and a reference to the enclosing Frame. When you add( ) the MenuPanel to the Frame, you're done. In our sample project, I called the MenuPanel's setFollowsCursor( ) method, to get browser-like behavior.

Clicks on the menu's options are reported (with postEvent( ) calls) to the Frame. The Frame's handleEvent( ) method should look for Events with the MenuPanel as Event.target and an Integer in Event.arg that specifies the number of the clicked menu option.

After looking at the use of the MenuPanel, we looked at the code. (Well, some of us did.) The MenuPanel is the controller, and the one that does most of the work.

The MenuPanel uses PromptPanel objects for its menu prompts. The prompts are drawn on these PromptPanels. Additionally, the PromptPanel sees and reports events such as mouse clicks.

The MenuLib class holds functions that encapsulate the messy details of handling the optional ampersands in the prompt strings. As elsewhere, these are signals that the following letter is a speed key and should be underscored. Not having an underscored font characteristic, we create the underscore by drawing a tiny, filled rectangle under the appropriate letter.

The highly flexible appearance of the menu options is created by the RRectPromptPainter. Java's RoundRect draw tools let you specify separately how much curvature you want in the horizontal and vertical dimensions. This means that the RoundRect can be a plain rectangle, an oval, a traditional rounded rectangle, or a rectangle with oval ends, for some examples. The RRectPromptPainter takes care of painting the RoundRect and the option prompt String.

The plain PromptPainter class handles the same duties as the RRectPromptPainter, but in a trivial way. By inheriting from this class, the RRectPromptPainter doesn't have to include such functions as standard getXxx( ) and setXxx( ) methods.

In the next chapter we'll use the ChoicesLayout from Chapter 7 and the MenuPanel from this chapter to put together the front end for our Java DataBase application. The INI code will be in your project, so you can customize to your heart's content. Using these tools *is* a lot of fun, after all. The INI code will stay a black box until we get to Chapter 10, however. The StreamTokenizer-based reader is worth the wait.

Chapter 9

The JDB Front-End Code

In this chapter we're going to use the ChoicesLayout technology and the MenuPanels to build the front end of the Java DataBase system. This is built entirely from MenuPanels, which keeps the code size small. It's a lot of fun to customize and will make the INI work in Chapter 10 seem very worthwhile.

We'll begin by running the JDB front-end code. We'll use it to customize menu shapes and colors. You'll see that the INI technology is already in place, so your work here will be saved. Each time you run JDB, you'll start exactly where you left off, which is what most users want.

The customization is so much fun that I'll even provide a brief intermission to let you perfect your own JDB.

After the intermission, we'll get to the code, starting with JDBlib. This is a file of final, static constants that serves the same purpose as a C #include file. It will let you see all the menus and the way the menus are grouped into menu classes.

After JDBlib, we'll take a close look at just one of the menus, JDBmenus. That, of course, is the menu of menus that you pick from to customize a menu. The rest of the menus' source files will be shown at the end of the chapter—they're all short and similar to this one.

Then we'll dive into the main course, JDB itself. This provides the mainline code, supervisory services, and the main menu. You'll see that getting all these pieces to work together as a system is not a trivial job.

In this chapter, the fun comes first. As my kids tell me, "Life is uncertain. Start with dessert."

Running the Java DataBase System

The version of JDB in this chapter's project file includes only the front-end menuing system, since that's our focus. The New, Open, and Close options have been stubbed out with MsgBoxes. Although it's the subject of the next chapter, the INI reading and writing code is in this version, so you can customize your JDB and it will remember how you like it.

Let's load your version of JDB and my version. Since I'm shooting screen shots as I write this, these versions are in black and white. I'll leave it up to you to explore the colors. Screen shots also don't work well at resolutions higher than VGA. (The details get lost when the shot is reduced to fit the book's page.) Figure 9-1 shows the default face of JDB.

Figure 9-2 shows my version of JDB. You can see that mine's got a fresh, original look. The default is boring by comparison.

If you look closely, you'll see that I'm running the default over Visual J++ and my version over Visual Cafe, but that has nothing to do with the appearance of JDB. The real difference is that I've customized mine, and my preferences are stored in JDB.INI.

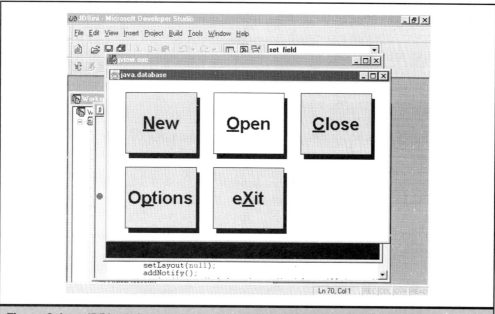

Figure 9-1. *JDB's default main menu, at 640x480*

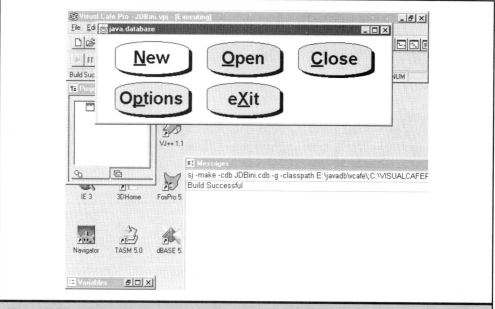

Figure 9-2. *The author's personal JDB main menu*

Portable INI Files

Windows 3.*x* used files with the INI extension to store initialization data. Windows 95 abandoned this approach in favor of a Windows-specific database known as the Registry. The Registry approach is completely Microsoft proprietary (which, I suspect, might not be incidental to Microsoft's choice of this approach).

Using a file that happens to end with the characters ".INI" is a platform-independent approach. This is an .INI extension to a DOS-based (Windows or OS/2) computer. It's just four characters to a UNIX-based OS, but it's still a valid filename. We'll use pure Java to read and write these files, so we'll be platform independent.

I've not used a file path, which means the INI file will be in the current directory. This approach has limitations, but it's portable. The alternative is to use a FileDialog to ask the user for the file's location. Hard-coding paths is a sure way to write platform-specific code, even if you do it in pure Java.

Let's make your version of JDB look better. If you haven't done it yet, load this chapter's code and open the JDB project. When you execute it, you'll get the face you saw in Figure 9-1. Click the Options choice and then click the Menus choice in the Options menu. Figure 9-3 shows the menu of menus that this pops up.

As you see, I've highlighted the Data Controller Menu choice. This is the longest prompt, so it's the one the MenuPanel has to use to select a font that fits. Since it's a long prompt, your font is small—much smaller than the other menus. How do you fix this?

You could choose a shorter prompt, but there's an easier way. Paradoxically, all you need to do is shrink the menu! Just grab the right side of the menu and move it left until your ChoicesLayout decides that a vertical layout works best. Figure 9-4 shows what happened for me when I did this.

At this point, if you dig up your Java Virtual Machine window, you'll see that it reported "JDB.INI not found" when you started your run. (At least it did if this was your first run.) Go ahead and exit now, and then choose Options | Menus again. You'll be right back where you left off, with that much-improved Menus menu.

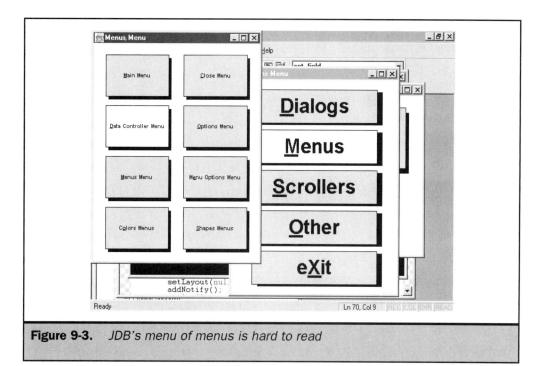

Figure 9-3. *JDB's menu of menus is hard to read*

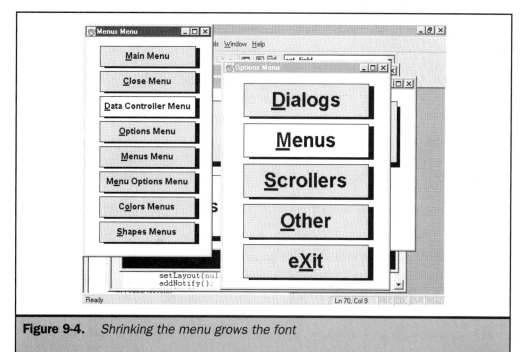

Figure 9-4. *Shrinking the menu grows the font*

Your JDB wrote JDB.INI. Mine looks like this:

```
; JDB.INI

;POSITION-DEPENDENT FILE
;   !DO NOT EDIT!

;If damaged, delete this file.

[Main_Menu]
Main_Menu = 0
Main_Menu_x = 88
Main_Menu_y = 88
Main_Menu_width = 500
Main_Menu_height = 300
Main_Menu_lo_back = -4144960
Main_Menu_lo_fore= -16777216
  . . .
```

That warning about not editing the file is fraudulent, as we'll see in Chapter 10. You can edit the values of each of these items, as long as you don't change the order. By insisting on a fixed order, we greatly reduce the amount of code it takes to read the INI.

Let's go on to edit the shape of a menu. As you choose different shapes, the shape of the selected menu is changed. The easiest way to see this is to change the shape of the shape menus. From the Menus menu pick Shape Menus. The Shape Menus Options menu will pop up. Pick Shape. This will pop up the two shape menus you see in Figure 9-5.

These menus pop up cascaded by Windows. Separate them so both are convenient, as you see in Figure 9-5. Then let the fun begin. If you leave None selected in either the horizontal or vertical dimension, the other choice is irrelevant. To see how this works, start both dimensions at Medium. Then switch one dimension a notch at a time toward Total. Got it?

Now move the other dimension one notch at a time toward Total. Figure 9-6 shows what you'll see when both dimensions are at Total.

Now I'm going to go brew a fresh cup of Java. While I'm gone, why don't you reshape all the menus to your liking? It makes more sense if you dig out the menu you are shaping so that you can see it, along with the curvature menus. Finish reading this section before you start, though.

The color menus and the shape menus are mutually exclusive, so you won't be able to see the color menus when you set the shapes. And you won't see the Close and Data Controller menus until we add the datafile capabilities to JDB, so ignore them.

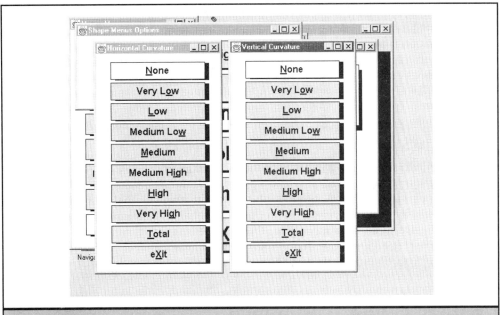

Figure 9-5. *The shape menus, nicely separated*

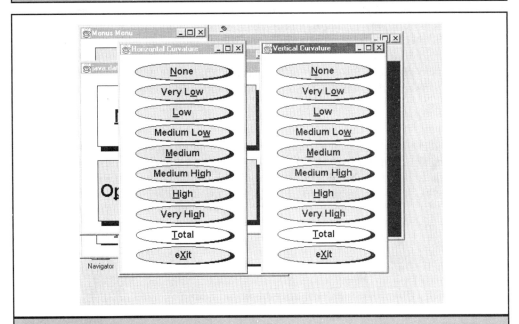

Figure 9-6. *The shape menus with Total, Total curvature*

If you get all the shapes to your liking before my coffee's ready, try setting colors. Start by setting the colors of the color menus, so you can see your work as you go. This is a fun interface, isn't it?

Setting the shape of the color menus and setting the colors of the shape menus is a nuisance, since you can't see the menus you're setting while you do the setting. Leave this step for last.

Intermission

I'm brewing Java. You're having fun playing with the JDB customization tools. (Did I waste a lot of time playing with this after I got it running? You bet I did! Between the ChoicesLayout and the RRectPromptPainter, there's no end to what you can do.)

Since I start by grinding beans, I won't be back for at least ten minutes. Have fun in the meantime. Oh, yeah. One more thing. We'll be getting into the code in the next section, so you'll need an in-depth understanding of how this works. If you're too goal-directed to just have a little fun, customize your JDB for that reason.

Understanding JDBlib.java

OK, I'm back. Are you back? Good. Now we'll dive into the code. Building these menus is just as easy as you saw in Chapter 8. Hooking them all into a coherent system is not simple, however. You've seen that the colors and shape menus are hooked to the menu you're customizing.

You may not have noticed the eXit options. Every menu that has an eXit closes all the menus it opens. Since these torn-off menus are all in their own windows, that's important. You wouldn't want to close the main menu and leave others still running. This isn't hard, but it takes some work and you can't get careless here.

TOUR

If you don't know how these pieces fit together, you'll have a hard time understanding the way the actual database pieces fit into the framework. I'd recommend that you take a look at all this. This chapter will hit the highlights. If you want to know more, you'll need to study the listings and experiment on your own.

The first code we'll look at is JDBlib.java. This is a file of constants that the rest of the code uses. You C programmers will recognize it as a #include file in a Java disguise. This is the full listing:

Listing 9-1: JDBlib.java works as a #include file

```
// JDBlib.java -- library for Java DataBase
// Copyright 1997, Martin L. Rinehart

// this code is completely documented in:
```

```
// _Java Database Development_, Martin Rinehart,
// Osborne/McGraw-Hill, 1997

// note: class members are grouped by function, not
// listed alphabetically

import java.awt.Color;

class JDBlib extends Object {

// --------------------- data members ---------------------

// this class has nothing but final static data members

    final static String[] menu_names = {
        "Main_Menu",
        "Close_Menu",
        "Data_Controller_Menu",
        "Options_Menu",
        "Menus_Menu",
        "Menu_Options_Menu",
        "Fore_Colors_Menu",
        "Back_Colors_Menu",
        "Horizontal_Shapes_Menu",
        "Vertical_Shapes_Menu"
    };

     final static String[] menu_name_prompts = {
        "&Main Menu",
        "&Close Menu",
        "&Data Controller Menu",
        "&Options Menu",
        "&Menus Menu",
        "M&enu Options Menu",
        "C&olors Menus",
        "&Shapes Menus",
    };

    final static String[] menu_options_titles = {
        "Main Menu Options",
        "Close Menu Options",
        "Data Controller Menu Options",
```

```
            "Options Menu Options",
            "Menus Menu Options",
            "Menu Options Menu Options",
            "Color Menus Options",
            "Shape Menus Options"
    };

    static final int main_menu = 0;
    static final int close_menu = 1;
    static final int data_controller_menu = 2;
    static final int options_menu = 3;
    static final int menus_menu = 4;
    static final int menu_options_menu = 5;
    static final int fore_colors_menu = 6;
    static final int back_colors_menu = 7;
    static final int horz_shapes_menu = 8;
    static final int vert_shapes_menu = 9;

    static final boolean[] is_zmenu = {
        false,  // main
        false,  // close
        true,   // data controller
        false,  // options
        false,  // menus
        false,  // menu options
        false,  // fore colors
        false,  // back colors
        false,  // horz shapes
        false   // vert shapes

        /*
            zmenu -- Zero or more in use, so special
            treatment required when setting options
        */
    };

    static final int num_menus = 10;

    static final int[][] menu_classes = {
        {0},            // main
        {1},            // close
        {2},                // data controller
```

```
        {3},                // options
        {4},                // menus
        {5},                // menu options
        {6, 7},             // colors
        {8, 9}              // shapes
    };

    static final int default_h_round = 1024; // rectangle
    static final int default_v_round = 1024;

    static final Color default_hi_fore = Color.black;
    static final Color default_hi_back = Color.white;
    static final Color default_lo_fore = Color.black;
    static final Color default_lo_back = Color.lightGray;

} // end of JDBlib class

// end of JDBlib.java
```

The string arrays include the menu names in single-word (variable name) form, prompts for the Menus menu, and titles for the Menu Options menu. (Its title varies, showing the menu you're working on.)

The final static ints enumerate the menus. The is_zmenu boolean area tells you that there could be zero or more data controller menus. The rest of the menus are permanent. They are all created at initialization time, and show( ) and hide( ) calls make them appear and disappear. The data controller menus are created, one for each opened file.

The menu_classes is an array of int arrays, all just one or two long. It's through this array that when you change shapes or colors, the JDB front end updates, for example, the main menu or both shape menus.

We'll use this library class constantly in the front end.

Understanding JDBmenus.java

Before we get to JDB, which is a large and fairly complex class, let's start with JDBmenus.java, which is the menu of menus.

The listings of the other front-end menu classes follow JDB. Except that they have different prompt lists, for example, they're substantially the same as this one.

Understanding the JDBmenus Code

The source begins with five protected data members. The JDB object reference, boss, refers to the mainline object defined in JDB.java. That includes the main menu.

The JDBmenopts, menu_options, is the Menu Options menu that will be called after you pick a menu using the JDBmenus object. This is the direct child of the Menus menu. Each menu takes responsibility for its own children, as you'll see.

The menu_panel is this object's MenuPanel. Then we get to an RRectPrompt-Painter and a String array of prompts, which will be familiar to you from Chapter 8.

These data are followed by just five methods, including a trivial paramString( ). We'll cover the other four here, starting with the constructor.

All these menus are created at startup. Popping them up and down is done by show( ) and hide( ) calls. So the constructor is called well before the menu is used. The mainline passes the first-level menu a reference to itself. Each successor level stores this reference and passes it on to its own children, if any. It's called, appropriately, boss.

```
JDBmenus( JDB dad ) {

    boss = dad;
```

The next thing is a show( ) and hide( ) pair. You'll recall that Windows does not respect your attempts to position the window before it has been shown the first time. With this pair you get annoying bits of popcorn exploding on your screen at startup, but you do get full control:

```
show(); hide(); // workaround position bug
```

After a resize( ) and setTitle( ), the prompt_painter is created, default colors are selected, and the MenuPanel is built:

```
prompt_painter = new RRectPromptPainter(
    JDBlib.default_h_round,
    JDBlib.default_v_round );
prompt_painter.setHiColor( JDBlib.default_hi_back,
    JDBlib.default_hi_fore );
prompt_painter.setLoColor( JDBlib.default_lo_back,
    JDBlib.default_lo_fore );
```

```
menu_panel = new MenuPanel( prompts,
    1/3.0, prompt_painter, this );

setLayout( new CenterLayout(32) );
add( menu_panel );

menu_panel.setFollowsCursor( false );
```

The next item is to register with the boss. This passes a reference to the MenuPanel to the boss, along with a constant from JDBlib to uniquely identify this menu.

```
boss.register( menu_panel, JDBlib.menus_menu );
```

Finally, this menu builds its subordinate menu, passing along the reference to the boss.

```
menu_options = new JDBmenopts( boss );
```

The shut_down( ) method is called by the parent menu when the time comes to exit. Each menu calls shut_down( ) in its own children and does any other necessary cleanup. Then it calls hide( )—it doesn't destroy itself. This is the code:

```
public void shut_down() {

    menu_options.shut_down();
    hide();
}
```

The handleEvent( ) method calls shut_down( ) for a WINDOW_DESTROY Event. This will hide( ) itself and its children. As a user, you see the window disappear. The other job of handleEvent( ) is to pass MenuPanel events along to the private menu_click( ) method. This is the whole routine:

```
public boolean handleEvent( Event e ) {

    if ( e.id == Event.WINDOW_DESTROY ) {
        shut_down();
        return true;
    }

    if ( e.target == menu_panel ) {
        menu_click( e );
        return true;
    }

    return true;
}
```

This routine is customized for each menu class. We'll skip the ALD and look at the heart of the routine. At this point in the method, the integer i has been retrieved from the Event. It's the index of the selected menu in the menus array. This is the code:

```
boss.setCurrentMenuClass( i );

menu_options.shut_down();
menu_options.setTitle(
    JDBlib.menu_options_titles[i] );
menu_options.show();
```

The first job is to tell the boss to set a new, current menu class. The boss uses this information to apply whatever color or shape changes to the correct menu.

Next the menu_options is shut_down( ). That's the menu that lets you pick a color or shape option. Since its shut_down( ) also closes its children, this also closes any open color or shape menu.

Then the menu_options menu is retitled for the newly selected menu class and is redisplayed. The full listing shows all the details.

The Full JDBmenus.java Listing

Listing 9-2 is the full JDBmenus.java source file.

Listing 9-2:
JDBmenus.
java prepares
the menu of
menus

```java
// JDBmenus.java --  JDB menu of menus
// Copyright 1997, Martin L. Rinehart

// this code is completely documented in:
// _Java Database Development_, Martin Rinehart,
// Osborne/McGraw-Hill, 1997

import java.awt.*;

class JDBmenus extends Frame {

// -------------------- data members --------------------

// there are no public data members

// protected data members:

    protected JDB boss;

    protected JDBmenopts menu_options;
    protected MenuPanel menu_panel;

    protected RRectPromptPainter prompt_painter;
    protected String[] prompts = JDBlib.
        menu_name_prompts;

// there are no static data members

// -------------------- public methods --------------------

// constructor:

    JDBmenus( JDB dad ) {

        boss = dad;

        show(); hide(); // workaround position bug

        resize( 300, 400 );
        setTitle( "Menus Menu" );

        prompt_painter = new RRectPromptPainter(
            JDBlib.default_h_round,
```

```
            JDBlib.default_v_round );
        prompt_painter.setHiColor( JDBlib.default_hi_back,
            JDBlib.default_hi_fore );
        prompt_painter.setLoColor( JDBlib.default_lo_back,
            JDBlib.default_lo_fore );

        menu_panel = new MenuPanel( prompts,
            1/3.0, prompt_painter, this );

        setLayout( new CenterLayout(32) );
        add( menu_panel );
        menu_panel.setFollowsCursor( false );
        boss.register( menu_panel, JDBlib.menus_menu );

        menu_options = new JDBmenopts( boss );
    }

// there are no data access methods

// public, class-specific method:

    public void shut_down() {

        menu_options.shut_down();
        hide();
    }

// public, non-event overriding method:

    public String paramString() {

        return "boss: " + boss;
    }

// public, event-handling method:

    public boolean handleEvent( Event e ) {

        if ( e.id == Event.WINDOW_DESTROY ) {
            shut_down();
            return true;
        }
```

```
            if ( e.target == menu_panel ) {
                menu_click( e );
                return true;
            }

            return true;
        }

// ------------------ private methods ------------------
// private method:

    private void menu_click( Event e ) {

        if ( e.arg == null ) return;

        int i = ( (Integer) e.arg ).intValue();

        if ( i < JDBlib.menu_classes.length ) {

            boss.setCurrentMenuClass( i );

            menu_options.shut_down();
            menu_options.setTitle(
                JDBlib.menu_options_titles[i] );
            menu_options.show();
        }
        else
            shut_down();
    }

} // end of JDBmenus class

// there are no private classes in JDBmenus.java
// end of JDBmenus.java
```

Understanding JDB.java

Are you ready for the mainline? This has all been fun to use and simple to understand, so far. As you might suspect, making the computer fun to use involves a bit of complex code. This isn't mathematically challenging, as the ChoicesLayout was, but it's definitely nontrivial code.

In this section we'll start with the data members and then work through the public and private methods. You may find that it works best for you to do a quick read and then come back to this point for a more thorough look.

The JDB.java Data Members

The data members begin with the Close menu. This is one of the child menus of JDB. It shows all the currently open files, plus an exit and a close all option.

```
protected JDBclose close_menu;
```

The next items record the current class and group of menus. Classes combine, for example, the two shape menus into a single class for setting shape and color. The current_menu_group is zero for normal color menus, one for highlight color menus, or two for shape menus.

```
protected int current_menu_class;
protected int current_menu_group;
```

Two Vectors keep track of the file-related windows and the files that you have open.

```
protected Vector file_wins;
protected Vector files;
```

A JDBini object keeps track of the INI information:

```
protected JDBini ini_file;
```

In addition to its supervisory role, JDB also incorporates the main menu. This is the String array that will be passed to its MenuPanel:

```
protected String[] main_menu_prompts = {
        "&New",
        "&Open",
        "&Close",
        "O&ptions",
        "e&Xit"
};
```

The array of MenuPanels, menu_list, is the one that will record MenuPanels as the children register them. There is also the MenuPanel that the main menu uses:

```
protected MenuPanel[] menu_list;
protected MenuPanel menu_panel;
```

A two-dimensional array of doubles keeps track of the colors, position, and shape of each menu:

```
protected double[][] menu_option_values;
```

A FileDialog will provide the platform-independent code for getting platform-specific paths:

```
protected FileDialog open_file_dialog;
```

Two more variables complete this group. One records a reference to the options menu, and the other provides the PromptPainter for the main menu:

```
protected JDBoptions option_menu;

protected RRectPromptPainter prompt_painter;
```

There is also a pair of final static arrays. The first, color_vals, records the Colors that correspond to the menu choices in the color menus:

```
protected final static Color[] color_vals = {

    Color.red, Color.green, Color.blue,
    Color.yellow, Color.cyan, Color.magenta,
    Color.orange, Color.pink, Color.white,
    Color.lightGray, Color.gray, Color.darkGray,
    Color.black
};
```

The other final static array records numeric values that underlie the choices in the curvatures menus. The first item on that menu is None, which this array approximates with a 1024 divisor. (Curvature extending for 1/1000 the length of the prompt rounds nicely to zero pixels.) At the other end, Total curvature maps to 1.0, or curvature over the whole length.

```
protected static final double[] val_table = {
    1024.0, 16.0, 12.0, 8.0,
       4.0,  3.0,  2.0, 1.5, 1.0 };
```

The JDB.java Public Methods

Now we'll get into the mainline code. We'll cover the constructors, data access methods, class-specific methods, and the handleEvent( ) method.

The JDB.java Constructors

The first constructor is a bogus one that traps the code that Visual Cafe wants to add in a method that's never called.

```
JDB( int i ) {
    // don't call this constructor
    // VCafe will write stuff here
}
```

The other constructor is the one that does the real work. It starts with the familiar overhead:

```
JDB() {

    show(); hide(); // workaround position bug

    resize ( 500, 300 );
    setTitle( "java.database" );
```

Next the MenuPanel is set up and laid out:

```
prompt_painter = new RRectPromptPainter(
    JDBlib.default_h_round,
    JDBlib.default_v_round );
prompt_painter.setHiColor( JDBlib.default_hi_back,
    JDBlib.default_hi_fore );
prompt_painter.setLoColor( JDBlib.default_lo_back,
    JDBlib.default_lo_fore );
```

```
menu_panel = new MenuPanel( main_menu_prompts,
    0.667, prompt_painter, this );
menu_panel.setFollowsCursor( true );

setLayout( new CenterLayout(32) );

add( menu_panel );
```

JDB is the object known as boss by the rest of the menus. These lines register its own menu with itself:

```
menu_list = new MenuPanel[JDBlib.num_menus];
menu_list[0] = menu_panel;
```

The Options menu is the only direct child menu. As with all the menus, JDB is responsible for its own children. The Options menu is born here:

```
option_menu = new JDBoptions( this );
```

Note that this is the menu that pops up when you click Options on the main menu. The Menu Options menu is that one that allows you to select colors or shapes for individual menus.

For the file handling, the FileDialog and Vectors are initialized:

```
open_file_dialog =
    new FileDialog( this, "Open File" );

files = new Vector();
file_wins = new Vector();
```

Another child is the Close menu, created here:

```
close_menu = new JDBclose( this );
```

Finally, the menu_option_values array is created, the JDBini is built, and the INI file is read, providing values for the array of option values:

```
menu_option_values = new double[
    JDBlib.num_menus][10];

ini_file = new JDBini( this );
JDBini.read_ini();

}
```

The JDB Public Data Access Methods

There are a number of trivial data access methods that you can see in the full listing. The nontrivial ones are called by child menus to set menu options and values. The first handles shapes and colors by calling one of two associated private methods:

```
public void setMenuOption( boolean which, Object o ) {

    // which: true == horizontal for shape
    //                 background for colors

    // o instanceof Integer for shape
    //              Color for colors

    if ( o instanceof Color )
        set_menu_color( which, (Color) o );
    else
        set_menu_shape( which,
            (( Integer ) o).intValue() );
}
```

(Did you notice that this handles at run time a decision that I could have left up to the compiler at compile time?)

The other routine is used by JDBini to set values that it reads from the INI file. It passes the values for an individual menu, and this routine assigns it to the two-dimension array:

```
public void setMenuValues( int men_num, double[] d ) {

    for ( int i = 1 ; i < 11 ; i++ )
        menu_option_values[men_num][i-1] = d[i];
}
```

The JDB Public Class-Specific Methods

The MenuPanel registration is critical in Event handling. Fortunately, it couldn't be simpler:

```
public void register( MenuPanel mp, int which_menu ) {

    menu_list[which_menu] = mp;

}
```

The next two routines set up the color menus. They are called to set the highlighted options to the currently selected values for the menu you have chosen. (If you're working on the main menu, for example, and its normal color is black on white, you want the foreground to highlight black and the background to highlight white.)

We'll cover the setupLoColorMenus( ) method here. The setupHiColorMenus( ) method is the same except for details such as the location of the values in the arrays of menu options values.

Both methods have two different setup jobs. For the zmenus they take values from the menu_option_values array. For the other menus they take the values from the individual menu. This is the start of the zmenu work:

```
Color c = new Color(
    (int) menu_option_values[menu_num][4] );
int menu_loc = find_color( c );
```

The color is picked from the appropriate slot in the values array. Then the color is translated into an associated prompt number. This value is then used to set the highlighted option for the background color menu:

```
menu_list[JDBlib.back_colors_menu].setHilight(
    menu_loc );
```

The same process is repeated to set the highlight on the foreground color menu. For the other menus, the first job is to pick out the menus MenuPanel:

```
MenuPanel mp =
    menu_list[menu_num];
```

From the MenuPanel you can get the PromptPainter. (This would work for any PromptPainter, not just the rounded rectangles we're using at present.)

```
PromptPainter pp = mp.painter;
```

From this point, the work is the same as for the zmenu. The method gets the color, looks up its menu index, and then sets the menu. It does this once for the background and again for the foreground.

Setting up the shape menus is a similar process. There is one process for the zmenus, reading values from the array, and another for the other menus, reading the values from the individual menu. This is the code the zmenu uses to set up the horizontal shape menu:

```
double rad = menu_option_values[menu_num][8];
int menu_loc = find_shape_index( rad );
menu_list[JDBlib.horz_shapes_menu].setHilight(
    menu_loc );
```

As with colors, you start by getting the appropriate value, and then you look up the index of that value in the menus prompts. You use this to set the highlight in the appropriate shape menu.

The same process is repeated for the vertical menu. For the other menus, you begin by getting the MenuPanel and then the RRectPromptPainter:

```
MenuPanel mp = menu_list[menu_num];

RRectPromptPainter rp =
    ( RRectPromptPainter ) ( mp.painter );
```

Note that this time you are dealing with values that are specific to rounded rectangles. The remainder of the setup work is similar to the zmenu setup. This is the code for the horizontal shape menu:

```
double rad = rp.hradius;
int menu_loc = find_shape_index( rad );
menu_list[JDBlib.horz_shapes_menu].setHilight(
    menu_loc );
```

The JDB Public Event-Handling Method

The handleEvent( ) method is simple. It relies on the private shut_down( ) to close the application, and on the private menu_click( ) for everything else:

```
public boolean handleEvent( Event e ) {

    if ( e.id == Event.WINDOW_DESTROY )
        shut_down();

    if ( e.target == menu_panel ) {
        menu_click( e );
        return true;
    }

    return true;
}
```

The JDB.java Private Methods

In this version, the Close option is stubbed out:

```
private void close_file() {

    MsgBox mb = new MsgBox(
        "Nothing opened, nothing closed." );
    mb.show();
}
```

A color is found by looking it up in the final static array of color values. This won't find that lovely hue someone selects by editing the INI file, however. Index zero is returned if the color isn't found:

```
private int find_color( Color c ) {

    for ( int i = 0 ; i < color_vals.length ; i++ )
        if ( c.equals(color_vals[i]) )
            return i;

    return 0;
}
```

If you hadn't noticed, the color choices in the color menus are the same as the list of Color constants in java.awt.Color.

The find_shape_index( ) works the same way, except that it's searching for a double in an array of doubles. It also defaults to zero if it can't find the entry.

The find_target_menu( ) is called to pick a menu from which to retrieve the initial setup values for color and shape. It simply returns the first menu in the current class:

```
private int find_target_menu() {

    return JDBlib.menu_classes[current_menu_class][0];
}
```

The menu_click method picks a private method to call, based on the position of the clicked option in the menu:

```
private void menu_click( Event e ) {

    if ( e.arg == null ) return;

    MsgBox mb;

    switch( (( Integer ) e.arg).intValue() ) {

        case 0:
            // new JDBnew( this );
            new_file();
            break;

        case 1:
            open_file();
            break;

        case 2:
            close_file();
            break;

        case 3:
            option_menu.show();
            break;

        case 4:
            shut_down();
    }
}
```

The new_file( ) and open_file( ) methods also stub out their actions with a MsgBox in this version.

The set_menu_color( ) takes a color value and sets it as either the background or foreground color, depending on the value of a boolean parameter. It's complicated by the fact that setting the main menu, for example, you set just the main menu's color, while setting a color for the color menus, for another example, means setting both color menus' colors.

This process starts with a controlling routine that loops over every member (in practice, one or two of them) of a menu class:

```
private void set_menu_color(
    boolean is_back, Color c ) {

    int[] mclass = JDBlib.menu_classes[
        current_menu_class];

    for ( int i = 0 ; i < mclass.length ; i++ )
        set_menu_color( mclass[i], is_back, c );
}
```

The next set_menu_color( ) method sets an individual menu, or for the zmenus, it sets the values on the values array. See the full listing for all the ALD.

The first set_menu_shape( ) is analogous to the first set_menu_color, except that it deals with a double value, not a Color object. It also loops over the one or two members of each class, calling the second set_menu_shape with a specific menu number.

The second set_menu_shape( ) is analogous to the second set_menu_color( ), too. Again, it sets the values array for zmenus. We'll look at the code that sets a non-zmenu's shape.

First, a reference to the MenuPanel is retrieved, and from that a reference to the PromptPainter:

```
MenuPanel mp = menu_list[i];
PromptPainter pp = mp.painter;
```

This is cast to the RRectPromptPainter, since these shapes are specific to that painter:

```
RRectPromptPainter rp =
    ( RRectPromptPainter ) pp;
```

Then the horizontal or vertical radius value is assigned:

```
if ( is_horizontal )
    rp.setHRadius( value );
else
    rp.setVRadius( value );
```

To complete this method, the new value is shown on screen:

```
mp.hide();
mp.show();
```

The last method, shut_down( ), writes the latest settings to the INI and then shuts down. It explicitly calls dispose( ), which would happen anyway with System.exit( ). I wouldn't put a reminder like this deep in a loop, but for this use it seemed acceptable.

```
private void shut_down() {

    JDBini.write_ini();

      if ( option_menu != null )
          option_menu.shut_down();

    dispose();
    System.exit( 0 );
}
```

The Full JDB.java Listing

This is the full listing of JDB.java used in this chapter's project files. This version omits the data-handling functions that are the core of the JDB application. We'll cover the additional methods as we get to them.

Listing 9-3:
JDB.java's
front-end
code

```
// JDB.java -- Java DataBase mainline
// Copyright 1997, Martin L. Rinehart

// this code is completely documented in:
//   Java Database Development_, Martin Rinehart,
// Osborne/McGraw-Hill, 1997
```

```java
import java.awt.*;
import java.util.Vector;

class JDB extends Frame {

// -------------------- data members --------------------

// there are no public data members

// protected data members:

    protected JDBclose close_menu;
    protected int current_menu_class;
    protected int current_menu_group;

    protected Vector file_wins;
    protected Vector files;

    protected JDBini ini_file;

    protected String[] main_menu_prompts = {
            "&New",
            "&Open",
            "&Close",
            "O&ptions",
            "e&Xit"
    };

    protected MenuPanel[] menu_list;
    protected MenuPanel menu_panel;
    protected double[][] menu_option_values;

    protected FileDialog open_file_dialog;
    protected JDBoptions option_menu;

    protected RRectPromptPainter prompt_painter;

     // static data members

     // there are no public static data members

    // protected static data members:
```

```
    protected final static Color[] color_vals = {

        Color.red, Color.green, Color.blue,
        Color.yellow, Color.cyan, Color.magenta,
        Color.orange, Color.pink, Color.white,
        Color.lightGray, Color.gray, Color.darkGray,
        Color.black
    };

    protected static final double[] val_table = {
        1024.0, 16.0, 12.0, 8.0,
           4.0,  3.0,  2.0, 1.5, 1.0 };

// -------------------- public methods --------------------

    public static void main( String[] args ) {

        ( new JDB() ).show();
    }

// constructors:

    JDB( int i ) {
        // don't call this constructor
        // VCafe will write stuff here
            //{{INIT_CONTROLS
          setLayout(null);
          addNotify();
          resize(insets().left + insets().right +
430,insets().top + insets().bottom + 270);
          setTitle("Untitled");
          //}}
          //{{INIT_MENUS
          //}}
    }

    JDB() {

        show(); hide(); // workaround position bug

        resize ( 500, 300 );
        setTitle( "java.database" );
```

```
        prompt_painter = new RRectPromptPainter(
            JDBlib.default_h_round,
            JDBlib.default_v_round );
        prompt_painter.setHiColor( JDBlib.default_hi_back,
            JDBlib.default_hi_fore );
        prompt_painter.setLoColor( JDBlib.default_lo_back,
            JDBlib.default_lo_fore );

        menu_panel = new MenuPanel( main_menu_prompts,
            0.667, prompt_painter, this );
        menu_panel.setFollowsCursor( true );

        setLayout( new CenterLayout(32) );

        add( menu_panel );

        menu_list = new MenuPanel[JDBlib.num_menus];
        menu_list[0] = menu_panel;

        option_menu = new JDBoptions( this );

        open_file_dialog =
            new FileDialog( this, "Open File" );

        files = new Vector();
        file_wins = new Vector();

        close_menu = new JDBclose( this );

        menu_option_values = new double[
            JDBlib.num_menus][10];

        ini_file = new JDBini( this );
        JDBini.read_ini();

    }

// data access getXxx() methods:

    public String getMenuName( int i ) {

        return JDBlib.menu_names[i];
```

```
        }

         public MenuPanel getMenuPanel( int i ) {

             return menu_list[i];
        }

        public double[] getMenuValues( int i ) {

             return menu_option_values[i];
        }

// there are no data access isXxx() methods

// data access setXxx() methods:

        public void setCurrentMenuClass( int i ) {

             current_menu_class = i;
        }

        public void setCurrentMenuGroup( int i ) {

             current_menu_group = i;
        }

        public void setMenuOption( boolean which, Object o ) {

             // which: true == horizontal for shape
             //                 background for colors

             // o instanceof Integer for shape
             //              Color for colors

             if ( o instanceof Color )
                 set_menu_color( which, (Color) o );
             else
                 set_menu_shape( which,
                     (( Integer ) o).intValue() );
        }

        public void setMenuValues( int men_num, double[] d ) {
```

```
        for ( int i = 1 ; i < 11 ; i++ )
            menu_option_values[men_num][i-1] = d[i];
    }

// public, class-specific methods:
    public void register( MenuPanel mp, int which_menu ) {

        menu_list[which_menu] = mp;
    }

    public void setupLoColorMenus() {

        int menu_num = find_target_menu();

        if ( JDBlib.is_zmenu[menu_num] ) {

            Color c = new Color(
                (int) menu_option_values[menu_num][4] );
            int menu_loc = find_color( c );
            menu_list[JDBlib.back_colors_menu].setHilight(
                menu_loc );

            c = new  Color (
                (int) menu_option_values[menu_num][5] );
            menu_loc = find_color( c );
            menu_list[JDBlib.fore_colors_menu].setHilight(
                menu_loc );
        }
        else {
            MenuPanel mp =
                menu_list[menu_num];

            PromptPainter pp = mp.painter;

            Color c = pp.getLoBackColor();
            int menu_loc = find_color( c );
            menu_list[JDBlib.back_colors_menu].setHilight(
                menu_loc );

            c = pp.getLoForeColor();
            menu_loc = find_color( c );
            menu_list[JDBlib.fore_colors_menu].setHilight(
```

```
                        menu_loc );
        }
    }

    public void setupHiColorMenus() {

        int menu_num = find_target_menu();

        if ( JDBlib.is_zmenu[menu_num] ) {

            Color c = new Color(
                (int) menu_option_values[menu_num][6] );
            int menu_loc = find_color( c );
            menu_list[JDBlib.back_colors_menu].setHilight(
                menu_loc );

            c = new  Color (
                (int) menu_option_values[menu_num][7] );
            menu_loc = find_color( c );
            menu_list[JDBlib.fore_colors_menu].setHilight(
                menu_loc );
        }
        else {

            MenuPanel mp =
                menu_list[menu_num];

            PromptPainter pp = mp.painter;

            Color c = pp.getHiBackColor();
            int menu_loc = find_color( c );
            menu_list[JDBlib.back_colors_menu].setHilight(
                menu_loc );

            c = pp.getHiForeColor();
            menu_loc = find_color( c );
            menu_list[JDBlib.fore_colors_menu].setHilight(
                menu_loc );
        }
    }

    public void setupShapeMenus() {
```

```
        int menu_num = find_target_menu();

        if ( JDBlib.is_zmenu[menu_num] ) {

            double rad = menu_option_values[menu_num][8];
            int menu_loc = find_shape_index( rad );
            menu_list[JDBlib.horz_shapes_menu].setHilight(
                menu_loc );

            rad = menu_option_values[menu_num][9];
            menu_loc = find_shape_index( rad );
            menu_list[JDBlib.vert_shapes_menu].setHilight(
                menu_loc );
        }
        else {

            MenuPanel mp = menu_list[menu_num];

            RRectPromptPainter rp =
                ( RRectPromptPainter ) ( mp.painter );

            double rad = rp.hradius;
            int menu_loc = find_shape_index( rad );
            menu_list[JDBlib.horz_shapes_menu].setHilight(
                menu_loc );

            rad = rp.vradius;
            menu_loc = find_shape_index( rad );
            menu_list[JDBlib.vert_shapes_menu].setHilight(
                menu_loc );
        }
    }

// public, non-event overriding method:

    public String paramString() {

        String s = "";
        for ( int i = 0 ; i < main_menu_prompts.length ;
            i++ ) {

            s = s + main_menu_prompts[i];
```

```
                    if ( i < main_menu_prompts.length - 1 )
                        s = s + ", ";
            }

            return s;
        }

// public, event-handling method:

    public boolean handleEvent( Event e ) {

        if ( e.id == Event.WINDOW_DESTROY )
            shut_down();

        if ( e.target == menu_panel ) {
            menu_click( e );
            return true;
        }

        return true;
    }

// ------------------ private methods ------------------

// private methods:

    private void close_file() {

        MsgBox mb = new MsgBox(
            "Nothing opened, nothing closed." );
        mb.show();
    }

    private int find_color( Color c ) {

        for ( int i = 0 ; i < color_vals.length ; i++ )
            if ( c.equals(color_vals[i]) )
                return i;

        return 0;
    }
```

```
private int find_shape_index( double d ) {

    for( int i = 0 ; i < val_table.length ; i++ ) {
        if ( d >= val_table[i] )
            return i;
    }
    return 0;
}

private int find_target_menu() {

    return JDBlib.menu_classes[current_menu_class][0];
}
private void menu_click( Event e ) {

    if ( e.arg == null ) return;

    MsgBox mb;

    switch( (( Integer ) e.arg).intValue() ) {

        case 0:
            // new JDBnew( this );
            new_file();
            break;

        case 1:
            open_file();
            break;

        case 2:
            close_file();
            break;

        case 3:
            option_menu.show();
            break;

        case 4:
            shut_down();
    }
}
```

```java
private void new_file() {

    MsgBox mb = new MsgBox(
        "This version doesn't create files." );
    mb.show();
}

private void open_file() {

    MsgBox mb = new MsgBox(
        "This version doesn't open files." );
    mb.show();
}

private void set_menu_color(
    boolean is_back, Color c ) {

    int[] mclass = JDBlib.menu_classes[
        current_menu_class];

    for ( int i = 0 ; i < mclass.length ; i++ )
        set_menu_color( mclass[i], is_back, c );
}

private void set_menu_color( int i,
    boolean is_back, Color c ) {

    if ( JDBlib.is_zmenu[i] ) {
        if ( current_menu_group == 0 ) { // normal color
            if ( is_back )
                menu_option_values[i][4] = c.getRGB();
            else
                menu_option_values[i][5] = c.getRGB();
        }
        else {                           // hilight color
            if ( is_back )
                menu_option_values[i][6] = c.getRGB();
            else
                menu_option_values[i][7] = c.getRGB();
        }

    }
```

```java
    else {

        MenuPanel mp = menu_list[i];
        PromptPainter pp = mp.painter;

        if ( current_menu_group == 0 ) { // normal color
            if ( is_back )
                pp.setLoBackColor( c );
            else
                pp.setLoForeColor( c );
        }
        else {                              // hilight color
            if ( is_back )
                pp.setHiBackColor( c );
            else
                pp.setHiForeColor( c );
        }

        mp.hide();
        mp.show();
        Thread.yield();
    }
}

private void set_menu_shape(
    boolean is_horizontal, int index ) {

    int[] mclass = JDBlib.menu_classes[
        current_menu_class];

    for ( int i = 0 ; i < mclass.length ; i++ )
        set_menu_shape(
            mclass[i], is_horizontal, index );
}

private void set_menu_shape(
    int i, boolean is_horizontal, int val ) {

    double value = val_table[val];

    if ( JDBlib.is_zmenu[i] ) {
```

```
                if ( is_horizontal )
                    menu_option_values[i][8] = value;
                else
                    menu_option_values[i][9] = value;
            }
            else {

                MenuPanel mp = menu_list[i];
                PromptPainter pp = mp.painter;
                RRectPromptPainter rp =
                    ( RRectPromptPainter ) pp;

                if ( is_horizontal )
                    rp.setHRadius( value );
                else
                    rp.setVRadius( value );

                mp.hide();
                mp.show();
            }
        }

    private void shut_down() {

        JDBini.write_ini();

          if ( option_menu != null )
              option_menu.shut_down();

        dispose();
        System.exit( 0 );
    }

    //{{DECLARE_CONTROLS
    //}}
    //{{DECLARE_MENUS
    //}}
} // end of JDB class

// there are no private classes in JDB.java

// end of JDB.java
```

The Other JDB Menus

The menus in this section are the Options menu (JDBopts.java), the Menu Options menu (JDBmenopts.java), the color menus (JDBcolors.java), and the shape menus (JDBshapes.java). Their full listings are given here. As you'll see, they are substantially similar to the Menus menu we covered earlier.

The Full JDBopts.java Listing

Listing 9-4 is the full JDBopts.java source file.

Listing 9-4:
JDBopts
pops up from
the main
menu

```java
// JDBoptions.java -- JDB options menu
// Copyright 1997, Martin L. Rinehart

// this code is completely documented in:
// _Java Database Development_, Martin Rinehart,
// Osborne/McGraw-Hill, 1997

import java.awt.*;

class JDBoptions extends Frame {

// -------------------- data members --------------------

// there are no public data members

// protected data members:

    protected JDB boss;

     protected JDBmenus menu_menus;
    protected MenuPanel menu_panel;

    protected RRectPromptPainter prompt_painter;
    protected String[] prompts = {
        "&Dialogs",
        "&Menus",
        "&Scrollers",
        "&Other",
        "e&Xit"
    };

// there are no static data members
```

```
// ------------------- public methods -------------------

// constructor:

    JDBoptions( JDB dad ) {

        boss = dad;

        show(); hide(); // workaround position bug

        resize( 300, 400 );
        setTitle( "Options Menu" );

        prompt_painter = new RRectPromptPainter(
            JDBlib.default_h_round,
            JDBlib.default_v_round );
        prompt_painter.setHiColor( JDBlib.default_hi_back,
            JDBlib.default_hi_fore );
        prompt_painter.setLoColor( JDBlib.default_lo_back,
            JDBlib.default_lo_fore );

        menu_panel = new MenuPanel( prompts,
            1/3.0, prompt_painter, this );

        setLayout( new CenterLayout(32) );
        add( menu_panel );
        boss.register( menu_panel, JDBlib.options_menu );

        menu_menus = new JDBmenus( boss );
    }

// there are no data access getXxx() methods
// there are no data access isXxx() methods
// there are no data access setXxx() methods

// public, class-specific method:

    public void shut_down() {

        menu_menus.shut_down();
        hide();
    }
```

```
// public, non-event overriding method:

    public String paramString() {

        return "boss: " + boss;
    }

// public, event-handling method:

    public boolean handleEvent( Event e ) {

        if ( e.id == Event.WINDOW_DESTROY ) {
            shut_down();
            return true;
        }

        if ( e.target == menu_panel ) {
            menu_click( e );
            return true;
        }

        return true;
    }

// ------------------ private methods ------------------

// private method:

    private void menu_click( Event e ) {

        if ( e.arg == null ) return;

        int i = ( (Integer) e.arg ).intValue();
        boss.setCurrentMenuClass( i );

        MsgBox mb;

        switch( i ) {

            case 0:
                mb = new MsgBox(
                    "Dialog options not yet coded.",
```

```
                    "Item Not Available" );
                mb.show();

                break;

            case 1:
                menu_menus.show();
                break;

            case 2:
                System.out.println( "Scroller Options" );
                break;

            case 3:
                System.out.println( "Other options" );
                break;

            case 4:
                shut_down();
        }

    }

} // end of JDBoptions class

// there are no private classes in JDBoptions.java

// end of JDBoptions.java
```

The Full JDBmenopts.java Listing

Listing 9-5 is the full JDBmenopts.java source file.

Listing 9-5:
JDBmenopts
lets you
choose
colors
or shapes

```
// JDBmenopts.java -- JDB menu options menu
// Copyright 1997, Martin L. Rinehart

// this code is completely documented in:
// _Java Database Development_, Martin Rinehart,
// Osborne/McGraw-Hill, 1997

import java.awt.*;
```

```
class JDBmenopts extends Frame {

// -------------------- data members --------------------

// there are no public data members

// protected data members:

    protected JDBcolors back_colors;
    protected JDB boss;

    protected JDBcolors fore_colors;

    protected JDBshapes horizontal_curve;

    protected MenuPanel menu_panel;

    protected RRectPromptPainter prompt_painter;
    protected String[] prompts = {
        "&Normal Color",
        "&Hilight Color",
        "&Shape",
        "e&Xit"
    };

     protected JDBshapes vertical_curve;

// there are no static data members

// -------------------- public methods --------------------

// constructor:

    JDBmenopts( JDB dad ) {

        boss = dad;

        show(); hide(); // workaround position bug

        resize( 400, 150 );
        prompt_painter = new RRectPromptPainter(
            JDBlib.default_h_round,
```

```
                    JDBlib.default_v_round );
        prompt_painter.setHiColor( JDBlib.default_hi_back,
            JDBlib.default_hi_fore );
        prompt_painter.setLoColor( JDBlib.default_lo_back,
            JDBlib.default_lo_fore );

        menu_panel = new MenuPanel( prompts,
            1/3.0, prompt_painter, this );

        setLayout( new CenterLayout(32) );
        add( menu_panel );
        boss.register( menu_panel,
            JDBlib.menu_options_menu );

        fore_colors = new JDBcolors( boss );
        fore_colors.menu_panel.setFollowsCursor( false );
        fore_colors.setIsBack( false );

        back_colors = new JDBcolors( boss );
        back_colors.menu_panel.setFollowsCursor( false );
        back_colors.setIsBack( true );

        boss.register( fore_colors.menu_panel,
            JDBlib.fore_colors_menu );
        boss.register( back_colors.menu_panel,
            JDBlib.back_colors_menu );

        horizontal_curve = new JDBshapes( boss );
        vertical_curve = new JDBshapes( boss );

        horizontal_curve.setTitle(
            "Horizontal Curvature" );
        horizontal_curve.setIsHorizontal( true );
        vertical_curve.setTitle(
            "Vertical Curvature" );
        vertical_curve.setIsHorizontal( false );

        boss.register( horizontal_curve.menu_panel,
            JDBlib.horz_shapes_menu );
        boss.register( vertical_curve.menu_panel,
            JDBlib.vert_shapes_menu );
    }
```

```
// there are no data access getXxx() methods
// there are no data access isXxx() methods
// there are no data access setXxx() methods

// public, class-specific method:

    public void shut_down() {

        fore_colors.shut_down();
        back_colors.shut_down();
        horizontal_curve.shut_down();
        vertical_curve.shut_down();
        hide();
    }

// public, non-event overriding method:

    public String paramString() {

        return "boss: " + boss;
    }

// public, event-handling method:

    public boolean handleEvent( Event e ) {

        if ( e.id == Event.WINDOW_DESTROY ) {
            shut_down();
            return true;
        }

        if ( e.target == menu_panel ) {
            menu_click( e );
            return true;
        }

        return true;
    }

// ------------------ private methods -------------------

// private method:
```

```
private void menu_click( Event e ) {

    if ( e.arg == null ) return;

    int i = ( (Integer) e.arg ).intValue();
    boss.setCurrentMenuGroup( i );

    switch( i ) {

        case 0:
            horizontal_curve.shut_down();
            vertical_curve.shut_down();

            boss.setupLoColorMenus();
            fore_colors.setTitle(
                "Normal Foreground" );
            fore_colors.show();
            back_colors.setTitle(
                "Normal Background" );
            back_colors.show();
            break;

        case 1:
            horizontal_curve.shut_down();
            vertical_curve.shut_down();

            boss.setupHiColorMenus();
            fore_colors.setTitle(
                "Hilight Foreground" );
            fore_colors.show();
            back_colors.setTitle(
                "Hilight Background" );
            back_colors.show();
            break;

        case 2:
            fore_colors.shut_down();
            back_colors.shut_down();

            boss.setupShapeMenus();
            horizontal_curve.show();
```

```
                    vertical_curve.show();
                    break;

            case 3:
                    shut_down();
        }

    }

} // end of JDBmenopts class

// there are no private classes in JDBmenopts.java

// end of JDBmenopts.java
```

The Full JDBcolors.java Listing

Listing 9-6 is the full JDBcolors.java source file.

Listing 9-6:
JDBcolors
selects
foreground
and
background
colors

```
// JDBcolors.java -- JDB colors menu
// Copyright 1997, Martin L. Rinehart

// this code is completely documented in:
// _Java Database Development_, Martin Rinehart,
// Osborne/McGraw-Hill, 1997

import java.awt.*;

class JDBcolors extends Frame {

// -------------------- data members --------------------

// there are no public data members

// protected data members:

    protected JDB boss ;

    protected boolean is_back ;

    protected MenuPanel menu_panel ;
```

```
    protected RRectPromptPainter prompt_painter ;
    protected String[] prompts = {
        "&Red",
        "&Green",
        "&Blue",
        "&Yellow",
        "&Cyan",
        "&Magenta",
        "&Orange",
        "&Pink",
        "&White",
        "&lightGray",
        "&Gray",
        "&darkGray",
        "Blac&k",
        "e&Xit"
    } ;

// there are no static data members

// ------------------- public methods -------------------

// constructor:

    JDBcolors( JDB dad ) {

        boss = dad ;

        show(); hide(); // workaround position bug

        resize( 500, 125 ) ;

        prompt_painter = new RRectPromptPainter(
            JDBlib.default_h_round,
            JDBlib.default_v_round ) ;
        prompt_painter.setHiColor( JDBlib.default_hi_back,
            JDBlib.default_hi_fore ) ;
        prompt_painter.setLoColor( JDBlib.default_lo_back,
            JDBlib.default_lo_fore ) ;

        menu_panel = new MenuPanel( prompts,
            1/3.0, prompt_painter, this ) ;
```

```
        setLayout( new CenterLayout(32) ) ;
        add( menu_panel ) ;
    }

// there are no data access getXxx() methods
// there are no data access isXxx() methods

// data access setXxx() method:

    public void setIsBack( boolean b ) {

        is_back = b ;
    }

// public, class-specific method:

    public void shut_down() {

        hide() ;
    }

// public, non-event overriding method:

     public String paramString() {

         return "boss: " + boss;
     }

// public, event-handling method:

    public boolean handleEvent( Event e ) {

        if ( e.id == Event.WINDOW_DESTROY ) {
            shut_down() ;
            return true ;
        }

        if ( e.target == menu_panel ) {
            menu_click( e ) ;
            return true ;
        }
```

```
        return true ;
    }

// ------------------ private methods ------------------

// private method:

    private void menu_click( Event e ) {

        if ( e.arg == null ) return ;

        switch( (( Integer ) e.arg).intValue() ) {

            case 0:
                boss.setMenuOption( is_back, Color.red ) ;
                break ;

            case 1:
                boss.setMenuOption( is_back, Color.green ) ;
                break ;

            case 2:
                boss.setMenuOption( is_back, Color.blue ) ;
                break ;

            case 3:
                boss.setMenuOption(
                    is_back, Color.yellow ) ;
                break ;

            case 4:
                boss.setMenuOption( is_back, Color.cyan ) ;
                break ;

            case 5:
                boss.setMenuOption(
                    is_back, Color.magenta ) ;
                break ;

            case 6:
                boss.setMenuOption(
                    is_back, Color.orange ) ;
```

```
                break ;

            case 7:
                boss.setMenuOption( is_back, Color.pink ) ;
                break ;

            case 8:
                boss.setMenuOption( is_back, Color.white ) ;
                break ;

            case 9:
                boss.setMenuOption(
                    is_back, Color.lightGray ) ;
                break ;

            case 10:
                boss.setMenuOption( is_back, Color.gray ) ;
                break ;

            case 11:
                boss.setMenuOption(
                    is_back, Color.darkGray ) ;
                break ;

            case 12:
                boss.setMenuOption( is_back, Color.black ) ;
                break ;

            case 13:
                shut_down() ;

        }
    }

} // end of JDBcolors class

// there are no private classes in JDBcolors.java

// end of JDBcolors.java
```

The Full JDBshapes.java Listing

Listing 9-7 is the full JDBshapes.java source file.

Listing 9-7:
JDBshapes
selects
horizontal
and vertical
curvature

```java
// JDBshapes.java -- JDB shapes menu
// Copyright 1997, Martin L. Rinehart

// this code is completely documented in:
// _Java Database Development_, Martin Rinehart,
// Osborne/McGraw-Hill, 1997

import java.awt.*;

class JDBshapes extends Frame {

// -------------------- data members --------------------

// there are no public data members

// protected data members:

    protected JDB boss;

    protected boolean is_horizontal;

    protected MenuPanel menu_panel;

    protected RRectPromptPainter prompt_painter;
    protected String[] prompts = {
        "&None",
        "Very L&ow",
        "&Low",
        "Medium Lo&w",
        "&Medium",
        "Medium H&igh",
        "&High",
        "Very Hi&gh",
        "&Total",
        "e&Xit"
    };

// there are no static data members
```

```
// ------------------- public methods -------------------

// constructor:

    JDBshapes( JDB dad ) {

        boss = dad;

        show(); hide(); // workaround position bug

        resize( 225, 400 );

        prompt_painter = new RRectPromptPainter(
            JDBlib.default_h_round,
            JDBlib.default_v_round );
        prompt_painter.setHiColor( JDBlib.default_hi_back,
            JDBlib.default_hi_fore );
        prompt_painter.setLoColor( JDBlib.default_lo_back,
            JDBlib.default_lo_fore );

        menu_panel = new MenuPanel( prompts,
            1/3.0, prompt_painter, this );

        setLayout( new CenterLayout(32) );
        add( menu_panel );
    }

// there are no data access getXxx() methods
// there are no data access isXxx() methods

// data access setXxx() method:

    public void setIsHorizontal( boolean b ) {

        is_horizontal = b;
    }

// public, class-specific method:

    public void shut_down() {

        hide();
```

```
    }

// public, non-event overriding method:

    public String paramString() {

        return "boss: " + boss;
    }

// public, event-handling method:

    public boolean handleEvent( Event e ) {

        if ( e.id == Event.WINDOW_DESTROY ) {
            shut_down();
            return true;
        }

        if ( e.target == menu_panel ) {
            menu_click( e );
            return true;
        }

        return true;
    }

// ------------------- private methods -------------------

// private method:

    private void menu_click( Event e ) {

        if ( e.arg == null ) return;

        int i = ( (Integer) e.arg ).intValue();

        if ( i < 9 )
            boss.setMenuOption( is_horizontal,
                new Integer(i) );
        else
            shut_down();
    }
```

```
} // end of JDBshapes class

// there are no private classes in JDBshapes.java

// end of JDBshapes.java
```

Summary

We began by using the included JDB front-end project. This provides most of the menus and a menu customization capability, which is, itself, just more menus. You saw that between editing the shape and color of the prompts, and using the ChoicesLayout reshaping capability, this was a powerful and fun tool for making a truly personal version of the system.

After you created your own version of JDB (is yours subtly colored, or does it look like a circus?), we got to work on the code, starting with JDBlib, a file of constant names and numbers. Putting all these in a library makes it easier to keep them consistent, and it provides a convenient reference.

After JDBlib, we looked at one of the menus, JDBmenus, the Menus menu. This was typical menu code. The other menus are listed without further discussion just before this summary. Each menu is responsible for its own children. It creates them, and via a shut_down( ) method, it hides them when they're not wanted.

Then we moved on to JDB, which contains mainline code, supervisory code, and the main menu, too. When the pieces need to interact, they turn to JDB. For example, when you select a menu to customize, JDB provides services that set the color and shape menus to reflect the current status of the menu you are customizing. It's not simple, but the effect is a system that works nicely.

In Chapter 10, we'll take the wraps off the INI handling. This will be easier than you might think. The StreamTokenizer is like a lot of Java: its concepts may be new, but once you figure out how to use it, reading the INI is as simple as possible.

Chapter 10

Application Initialization Data

In Chapter 9 you saw how flexible the front end of the JDB application is. If you followed my advice and spent some time customizing your own version, you were probably delighted that JDB had enough sense to remember exactly how you set up the application. When you restart, everything is set up exactly as you left it.

That, of course, is not magic. It's the initialization database in operation. In this case we're using an INI file that looks very much like a Windows 3.*x* INI file. This is a sample:

```
; JDB.INI

;POSITION-DEPENDENT FILE
;     !DO NOT EDIT!

;If damaged, delete this file.

[Main_Menu]
Main_Menu = 0
Main_Menu_x = 52
Main_Menu_y = 20
Main_Menu_width = 524
Main_Menu_height = 177
Main_Menu_lo_back = -4144960
Main_Menu_lo_fore= -16777216
 . . .
```

I know it's not common to call a human-readable text file a database, but it certainly is a way to store and retrieve useful information. (And I'm not sure that the color "–4144960" is all that human-readable. Are you?)

Whatever you call it, initialization data is key to doing professional applications. Users expect that they can select toolbars, menu commands, speedkeys, or whatever and have the application remember their preferences.

The magic that makes this possible for the JDB application is the JDBini class. In this chapter we'll begin with a look at the use of the JDB.INI file from a user standpoint. Then we'll review the programmer's use of JDBini, which you saw in the last chapter. (You did see it, didn't you? It took exactly four lines of code.)

We'll take a serious look at the underlying code. As you might assume from the name JDBini, this code is specific to the JDB application. You'll need to create your own XXXini class for your XXX application. Using a StreamTokenizer makes reading the data very simple, but there are some tricks you'll need to know.

We'll begin by looking at the user's point of view.

Using JDBini

The JDB.INI file starts with this cheerful greeting:

```
;  JDB.INI

;POSITION-DEPENDENT FILE
;    !DO NOT EDIT!

;If damaged, delete this file.
```

The file is position dependent, but you can go right ahead and edit it if you're careful. Just don't delete, add, or otherwise rearrange the lines. The value for Main_Menu must be zero, and it must immediately precede the value for Main_Menu_x. You can replace the value of Main_Menu_x, however.

There's no documentation that explains what Main_Menu_x's value represents. I'll bet about 99 out of 100 of you are assuming that it's the X coordinate for the main menu, though. I tried to pick self-explanatory names. (If you're the 1 out of 100, take my advice: try a day off and get a long night's sleep. Those 100-hour work weeks are starting to get to you.)

In this section we'll discuss what the user can and cannot do. Then we'll go over using JDBini from the programmer's point of view.

Users Using JDB.INI

The JDB.INI file's discouraging warnings are designed to keep the truly ignorant user at bay. The simplest way to edit JDB.INI is to run JDB, click Options, and go to work. When you change shapes, colors, and move things around, you are editing the data. Exiting the program will rewrite JDB.INI to capture your setup exactly.

Why in the world would you want to edit JDB.INI with a text editor?

Of course, if you've been around computers for a while, you realize there's always someone out there who will discover a perfectly good reason for wanting to do whatever you think should be unnecessary. In this case it was Fred.

Fred's company provides 21-inch monitors for the programmers. They work at 1280x1024 resolution, with room enough for lots of windows all at once. It's very productive. Fred's JDB is set up to appear near the lower-right corner of his screen.

But Fred is not at his screen. Fred's in seat 17A, five miles above the Earth. He's copied JDB's directory to his laptop somewhat hastily. Now his main menu is positioned with Main_Menu_x at 820, which is well past the right edge of his 640x480 laptop's screen.

Fred doesn't really want to delete the entire JDB.INI. He'd just like to bring the menus back onto the screen. Editing JDB.INI is the easy way to do this.

If Fred's an intrepid user (which he is, of course, since he's an experienced programmer), he'll ignore the warning and edit away. He'll be fine.

When we get to the data-reading software, you'll see that the first menu's signature value is zero. The next menu's signature is one. The software just tells you to delete JDB.INI if this is not the case.

So if users delete a line or two (or the file is otherwise damaged), they'll be advised to delete JDB.INI. The program won't proceed until they take that advice. Then they'll be back to the default configuration, with no serious harm done.

You'll see when we get to the code that this position-dependence saves a major amount of code.

Programmers Using JDBini.java

There's good news and then there's bad news. The good news is that you've already seen the full art of using the JDBini class in JDB.java. It's trivial.

The bad news is that it's specific to the JDB application. It's not generalized. You have to rewrite a fair amount of the code to fit each new application.

A generalized version of JDBini is certainly theoretically possible, but I'm not sure I'll want to use it even if you're kind enough to write it for me. A specific-purpose JDBini doesn't take much code. A generalized initialization approach would probably take a lot of code. (Go ahead: prove me wrong!)

You'll see in the code that the specific-purpose parts aren't overwhelmingly complex. It's just a matter of deciding what you need to store and then including everything. (JDB stores horizontal and vertical curvature data with its menus, for example. As I write this, I don't think any applications other than mine do this. That's not going to remain the case for long, I'm sure. But you'll be busy thinking of your own unique wrinkles, so this is representative of what will always be the case.)

Let's quickly review the use of JDBini in the JDB application. First, a data member is declared:

```
protected JDBini ini_file;
```

Then the object is created, and the data is read at load time:

```
ini_file = new JDBini( this );
JDBini.read_ini();
```

For JDB, the *this* argument is the JDB object. In XXXini it will be whatever object you need to track down the data you'll be saving and restoring.

After reading the data, the JDBini object is idle until it's time to close the application. Then the shut_down( ) process begins by rewriting the INI file:

```
JDBini.write_ini();
```

If you were concerned with your application's RAM footprint, you could dispose of the JDBini after the call to read_ini( ), and then create a new one before you write_ini( ).

Sometimes objects really do encapsulate complexities. This one's a good example. Don't show it to the real object enthusiasts, however. We've already heard enough hype. (Next time there's a lull in the conversation, state this proposition: static methods and all methods for one-object-only classes are really just procedural code. Be ready to argue the opposite point of view, in case everyone agrees with the proposition.)

Let's look under the hood to see how this works.

Understanding JDBini

TOUR

There's no way around this one. You need to know how this stuff works if you're going to save and restore your own applications' data. You can postpone this section until your XXX system needs its own XXXini class, though.

I chose the INI form for two reasons. First, it's a traditional way of storing customizable, application-related data. Second, and perhaps even more important, working with readable text files makes debugging relatively simple. (In your favorite IDE, you can open the INI file as if it were a source file.)

In this section, we're going to take advantage of that readable text file as we look at the code. We'll look first at the common parts of JDBini, and then we'll tour the write and read sections separately.

Understanding JDBini's Common Elements

It would be very easy to separate JDBini into two classes. The file reading is done with a StreamTokenizer. An entirely separate FileOutputStream does the file writing. You'll see that they have nothing in common. They're separate, file-based objects, and their programming couldn't be more different.

But collecting both halves of the process here is a great convenience for the calling program. Here we'll look at the data and constructor. In the next two sections we'll look at the other parts of the program.

Before we get started, don't forget that we need java.io here:

```
import java.io.*;
```

Now let's consider the data. It's all protected and static. Both reading and writing need to know who owns the data:

```
protected static JDB boss;
```

Item_num is really a global variable here. It's used in the assign( ) part of the read process:

```
protected static int item_num;
```

We need to keep track of the current menu number and have an array for its values:

```
protected static double[] men_vals = new double[11];
protected static int menu_num;
```

The last data member in this group is self-explanatory:

```
protected static byte[] output_buffer;
```

The final data member is the filename constant:

```
protected static final String file_name = "JDB.INI";
```

The other common part of the class is the constructor, which is trivial:

```
JDBini( JDB dad ) {

    boss = dad;
    output_buffer = new byte[80];

    menu_num = item_num = 0;
}
```

Understanding JDBini's File Writing

I created the template that we saw in Chapter 1 to organize these classes in a simple, consistent manner. I'm pretty sure you're getting used to it. This time, however, I'm not going to follow my own organization. We'll bypass the read_ini( ) method and start with write_ini( ).

As you study write_ini( ), you'll see exactly what is written, so you'll learn the format of the JDB.INI file. You need to know that format to understand the read_ini( ) process.

When you get to programming your own XXXini class, you'll program the write_ini( ) method first, of course. (Without it, you'd have to build a test file for your read_ini( ) method. That's a waste of time since write_ini( ) could do the job for you.)

In this section we'll look at the public write_ini( ) method and at its supporting private methods.

The Public write_ini( ) Method

The write_ini( ) method depends on write( ), which writes an empty line, and write(String), which writes a String to the output file. Both methods take a FileOutputStream argument, too. The method's first job is to create the FileOutputStream:

```
FileOutputStream ofile;

ofile = null;
try {
    ofile = new FileOutputStream( file_name );
}
catch ( IOException ioe ) {

    System.out.println( "JDB.INI open error" );
}
```

If the FileOutputStream was not successfully opened, it will be null, so the rest of the method lives inside this conditional:

```
if ( ofile != null ) {

    // write the file here
}
```

It's remotely possible that you'll have a failure writing to the file. (You could run out of disk space, for example.) The code makes a lame effort at error handling with the obligatory try and catch blocks:

```
try {

    // file written here
}
catch( IOException ioe ) {

    System.out.println(
        "Error writing to JDB.INI" );

}
```

That's it for the ALD. Now let's look at the file-writing process. It begins with a block that writes the fixed header lines. The output file looks like this:

```
; JDB.INI

;POSITION-DEPENDENT FILE
;    !DO NOT EDIT!

;If damaged, delete this file.

. . .
```

The code that writes that header is this:

```
write( ofile, "; JDB.INI" );
write( ofile );
write( ofile, ";POSITION-DEPENDENT FILE" );
write( ofile, ";    !DO NOT EDIT!" );
write( ofile );
write( ofile,
    ";If damaged, delete this file." );
write( ofile );
```

Then it does the actual writing of the block for each menu. The heavy lifting is delegated to the write_menu( ) private method:

```
int nm = JDBlib.num_menus;
for ( int i = 0; i < nm; i++ ) {
    write_menu( ofile, i );
    write( ofile );
}
```

At the end, a footer line is written and the file is closed:

```
write( ofile, " ; end of JDB.INI" );

ofile.close();
```

(Did I say "file"? That's a FileOutputStream, of course. Maybe someday we'll have an operating system where these aren't just files. Maybe.)

The Private Write-Related Methods

By using the prefix "write_" for these methods, I've grouped them at the end of the private method section, following the write( ) methods. The first of these writes an empty (whitespace) line to the stream:

```
private static void write( FileOutputStream fos )
    throws IOException{

    // writes null line
    output_buffer[0] = (byte) '\n';
    fos.write( output_buffer, 0, 1 );
}
```

If you've not used FileOutputStream, the arguments to fos.write( ) are a byte array, starting position, and length.

Adding a String parameter to write( ) writes that String to the file. If you look closely at this routine, you'll see that the first three lines are ALD. The other three do the job of converting the String to a byte array and using fos.write( ) to write it:

```
private static void write( FileOutputStream fos,
    String s ) throws IOException {

    if ( s == null ) {
        write( fos );
        return;
```

```
      }

            s.getBytes( 0, s.length(), output_buffer, 0 );
            output_buffer[s.length()] = (byte) '\n';
            fos.write( output_buffer, 0, s.length() + 1 );
      }
```

Now we'll look at write_menu( ), which is called with FileOutputStream and an integer that specifies which menu we're working on. In JDB.INI, each menu begins this way:

```
[Main_Menu]
Main_Menu = 0
```

The write_menu( ) method starts by writing those two lines with this code:

```
            String name = boss.getMenuName( menu_num );

            write( fos, "[" + name + "]" );
            write( fos, name + " = " + menu_num );
```

Then it continues to write the menu with one block of code for zmenus (zero or more) and another block for the other (show/hide) menus. Each menu continues in JDB.INI with four items that specify position and size:

```
Main_Menu_x = 52
Main_Menu_y = 20
Main_Menu_width = 524
Main_Menu_height = 177
```

These are produced by write_rect( ). The zmenus positions cannot be customized, so they are written this way:

```
            write_rect( fos,
                  new Rectangle(0, 0, 0, 0), name );
```

Next the boss is asked for an array of doubles specifying the values for this menu:

```
double[] men_vals =
    boss.getMenuValues( menu_num );
```

The rest of JDB.INI specifies the colors and curvature data this way:

```
Main_Menu_lo_back = -4144960
Main_Menu_lo_fore= -16777216
Main_Menu_hi_back = -1
Main_Menu_hi_fore= -16777216
Main_Menu_hradius = 1
Main_Menu_vradius = 2
```

(Is "–16777216" a good way of specifying black? I'd recommend that you use JDB itself, not your text editor, if you want to supply colors. Of course, if you really *must* have subtly different shades of magenta, here's your chance.)

The zmenu code that produces this result is this:

```
write( fos, name + "_lo_back = " +
    (int) men_vals[4] );
write( fos, name + "_lo_fore= " +
    (int) men_vals[5] );

write( fos, name + "_hi_back = " +
    (int) men_vals[6] );
write( fos, name + "_hi_fore= " +
    (int) men_vals[7] );

write( fos, name + "_hradius = " +
    men_vals[8] );
write( fos, name + "_vradius = " +
    men_vals[9] );
```

The other menus' values are taken from the menus themselves. The first job is to gather the necessary source references:

```
MenuPanel mp = boss.getMenuPanel( menu_num );
RRectPromptPainter rp =
    ( RRectPromptPainter )( mp.painter );
Frame f = (Frame) mp.getParent();
```

Then the position and size data is written this way:

```
write_rect( fos, f.bounds(), name );
```

The colors and curvature are written by this code:

```
write( fos, name + "_lo_back = " +
    rp.getLoBackColor().getRGB() );
write( fos, name + "_lo_fore= " +
    rp.getLoForeColor().getRGB() );

write( fos, name + "_hi_back = " +
    rp.getHiBackColor().getRGB() );
write( fos, name + "_hi_fore= " +
    rp.getHiForeColor().getRGB() );

write( fos, name + "_hradius = " + rp.hradius );
write( fos, name + "_vradius = " + rp.vradius );
```

The last private, write-related method is write_rect( ). Its job is to write these lines in JDB.INI:

```
Options_Menu_x = 3
Options_Menu_y = 109
Options_Menu_width = 211
Options_Menu_height = 238
```

The code that does that is straightforward:

```
private static void write_rect(
    FileOutputStream fos, Rectangle r, String name )
    throws IOException {

    write( fos, name + "_x = " + r.x );
    write( fos, name + "_y = " + r.y );
    write( fos, name + "_width = " + r.width );
    write( fos, name + "_height = " + r.height );
}
```

Would you prefer an uppercase "x" and "y" for the positions? This is where to make the change. Actually, you could substitute the names of your favorite vegetables if you like. The file reading ignores the names entirely, which is what we'll look at next.

Understanding JDBini's File Reading

Normally, I just use RandomAccessFile objects. But it does pay to look around in java.io every once in a while. For straight text output, you can't beat the FileOutputStream. In fact, it will work well for any case where you want to write a file starting at the beginning and continuing to the end.

You might think that its opposite number would be our reading tool of choice, but it isn't. We'll use a FileInputStream, but only to create a StreamTokenizer. It's a tool used in compilers.

Think about our JDB.INI. It's really a simple language. It does constant assignments with this syntax:

```
name = value
```

Everything else in the file can be considered a comment. You'll see that the code is a simple compiler that reads and makes appropriate assignments based on that simple syntax.

The visible structure of JDB.INI includes group header lines such as

```
[Menus_Menu]
```

The data that follows refers to the Menus menu. As you'll see, this is for our benefit. The actual reading process ignores these headers. They're just another type of comment in our trivial language.

Can you write a cogent essay on the difference between tokenizing and parsing in a compiler? If you can, skip the section on compiler technology. If you can't, the next section is for you.

An Introduction to Compiler Technology

This section won't make you an expert in compilers, but it will give you enough terminology to follow the file-reading code. As with much of Java, understanding the concepts is more complex than writing the code.

Modern compilers are written with distinct phases, such as:

- Tokenizing
- Parsing
- Code generation
- Code optimization

The *tokenizer* separates the language into component parts. If it were reading English, it would break the input into words this way:

```
// This is an input sentence.

// These are the tokens:
word "This"
word "is"
word "an"
word "input"
word "sentence"
punc "."
```

Here's a sentence in our INI language broken into tokens:

```
// Input: "Menus_Menu_x = 246"

// Tokens:
"Menus_Menu_x"
"="
"246"
EOL
```

The job of the *parser* is to take these tokens and extract their meaning in a way that the succeeding phases of the compiler can use to actually write valid output. This is an example:

```
// input: "x = (a + b) * c
// tokens: "x" "=" "(" "a" "+" "b" ")" "=" "c" EOL
```

A parser could generate an output table of operations. A four-valued table is common. The first value specifies an operation. The next two values specify the operands, and the fourth value specifies the destination of the result. We could parse our sample input to

```
// input tokens: "x" "=" "(" "a" "+" "b" ")" "=" "c" EOL

// output table:
//   Operation   Operand1      Operand2     Destination
        add          a             b           temp1
        mul        temp1           c           temp2
        store      temp2                         x
```

In operation, most tokenizers are called by the parser with a call that requests the next token. Most tokenizers handle chores such as comment skipping, presenting only valid tokens. The tokenizer is smart enough to do this:

```
    input "obj.member"
// tokens:
    obj
    .
    member

    input "1.5"
// tokens:
    1.5
```

The StreamTokenizer recognizes comments that start with "//" and comments enclosed in "/* . . . */" delimiters. It doesn't recognize our definition of a comment (any line that's not "name = value"). Any service that the tokenizer doesn't provide has to be taken over by the parser.

That introduction should be enough for you to successfully understand and use the StreamTokenizer.

The Public read_ini( ) Method

The read_ini( ) method is all ALD except for one, hardworking line:

```
                while ( parse_next_line(toker) );
```

The *toker* is the StreamTokenizer from which the parser gets tokens. The parse_next_line( ) method returns true until it gets an EOF token. With an EOF, it does any finishing work and then returns false.

Now let's look at the ALD. First, the StreamTokenizer needs a FileInputStream so it will have some data to work on. That is created this way:

```
FileInputStream ifile;

ifile = null;
try {
    ifile = new FileInputStream( file_name );
}
catch ( IOException ioe ) {

    System.out.println( "JDB.INI doesn't exist" );
    return;
}
```

Then you create the StreamTokenizer, with ifile. Three StreamTokenizer methods are called here that I'll explain individually. They customize the tokenizing to meet the requirements of different languages. This is the whole process:

```
try {

    StreamTokenizer toker = new StreamTokenizer(
        (InputStream) ifile );
    toker.commentChar( ';' );
    toker.eolIsSignificant( true );
    toker.wordChars( '_', '_' );

    int tok;

    while ( parse_next_line(toker) );
}

catch ( NullPointerException npe ) {}
```

In my JDB.INI I've prefixed comment lines with a ";" character. (We assembler programmers are all partial to that one—it's the easiest punctuation mark to type.) The StreamTokenizer can use any char for a comment character. This is for the end-of-line comments we would prefix with "//" in Java or C++. You specify comment characters to the StreamTokenizer this way:

```
toker.commentChar( ';' );
```

The eolIsSignificant( ) method specifies how you want EOLs handled. If they are significant, an EOL token will be returned at the end of a line. For languages like Java and C, EOL is not significant, so the tokenizer simply skips over EOL like any other whitespace.

The standard tokenizer recognizes a word as beginning with an alphabetic character and continuing with zero or more alphanumeric characters. Any additional characters that can be used as parts of a word have to be specified by calling the wordChars( ) method. You can call it as often as you like to add additional allowable characters. You call it with a range of characters, specifying the first and last members of the range.

All of which is to say that this call adds the underscore character as an allowable part of words:

```
toker.wordChars( '_', '_' );
```

Without that specification, "Main_Menu_x" would be returned as "Main", "_", "Menu", "_", and "x". (Would you have put the underscore into the default definition of a word? Will Java be used to write Fortran compilers?)

Now we're ready to look at the private methods that serve read_ini( ).

The Private Read-Related Methods

The call to parse_next_line( ) brings all these methods into play. We'll cover them in alphabetical order here, beginning with assign( ).

You call assign with a String and a double, like this:

```
assign( "Menus_Menu_x", 100 );
```

That would appear to assign the number 100 to "Menus_Menu_x," wouldn't it? The traditional assign( ) method would look up the name in a table of names. That table would have indexes that told you where to put the value. A hash table would probably be the best implementation.

Our assign never even looks at the String. It assigns the first value it gets to menu zero, item zero. The next assignment is to menu zero, item one. This assigns items zero through ten. At 11, the menu number is incremented and the item number is reset to zero.

The assign_menu( ) method is also called when each menu is filled. That does the actual assignment. This is the code:

```
private static void assign( String s, double d ) {

    // This position-dependent treatment of the .INI
    // makes the .INI less editable, but it saves
    // several KB by eliminating giant switches. It
    // loads faster, too.

    // The file warnings lie. You can edit the values
    // if you are careful not to add or delete items.

    men_vals[item_num++] = d;

    if ( item_num == 11 ) {
        assign_menu( men_vals );
        item_num = 0;
        menu_num++;
    }
}
```

The assign_menu( ) function is called to do the actual assignment. It begins, however, by first checking that the first of the 11 values in the values array is equal to the menu number. If it's not, the JDB.INI file is damaged. With any damage, the run is terminated with an error exit code. This may seem drastic if you don't remember that this is only called at load time. Nothing but JDB.INI is open, and no data can be lost. This is the checking code:

```
private static void assign_menu( double[] d ) {

    if ( menu_num != d[0] ) {
        System.out.println( "Damaged JDB.INI -- " +
            "delete the file and run JDB again." );

        System.out.println(
            "\n   press any key to continue..." );

        try { System.in.read(); }
        catch (IOException ioe ) {}

        System.exit( 1 );
    }
}
```

Next the boss' values array is told about the values:

```
boss.setMenuValues( menu_num, d );
```

That's all that's done for zmenus. For the rest, actual assignments are made to the Frame, MenuPanel, and RRectPromptPainters this way:

```
if ( ! JDBlib.is_zmenu[menu_num] ) {

    MenuPanel mp = boss.getMenuPanel( menu_num );
    RRectPromptPainter rp = ( RRectPromptPainter )
        mp.painter;
    Frame f = (Frame) mp.getParent();

    f.reshape( (int) d[1], (int) d[2], (int) d[3],
        (int) d[4] );
    rp.setLoBackColor( new Color (( int ) d[5]) );
    rp.setLoForeColor( new Color (( int ) d[6]) );
    rp.setHiBackColor( new Color (( int ) d[7]) );
    rp.setHiForeColor( new Color (( int ) d[8]) );

    rp.hradius = d[9];
    rp.vradius = d[10];
    }
}
```

The parser will continually call get_tok( ) when it needs the next token. The get_tok( ) method calls StreamTokenizer.nextToken( ) for the next token, with this line:

```
tok = toker.nextToken();
```

The rest of the method is ALD. On any file-read error, an EOF token is returned, which tells the parser to quit calling. This is the full method:

```
private static int get_tok(
    StreamTokenizer toker ) {

    int tok;

    try {
```

```
        tok = toker.nextToken();
    }
    catch (IOException ioe ) {
        System.out.println(
            "JDB.INI read error" );
        tok = StreamTokenizer.TT_EOF;
    }
    return tok;
}
```

Our parser is, to say the least, simplistic. But so's our language, so that's all we need. We're looking for "word", "=", and "value", followed by EOL. If we get anything else, the line's a comment, so we just fast-forward to the next EOL and start again. This is the code that looks for the word at the beginning of each line:

```
tok = get_tok( toker );

if ( tok == StreamTokenizer.TT_EOF )
    return false;
if ( tok == StreamTokenizer.TT_EOL )
    return true;
if ( tok != StreamTokenizer.TT_WORD )
    return skip_to_EOL( toker );

name = toker.sval;
```

The individual token is an int. You distinguish among the tokens by comparing them with the StreamTokenizer class constants, such as TT_EOF. If the token is a TT_WORD, the String value is available in the public StreamTokenizer.sval.

TT_EOF at the start of a line causes parse_next_line( ) to return false. An EOL at the start of the line causes it to return true but do nothing. (The line may have been null, all whitespace, or a comment.)

Anything else that's not a TT_WORD (numeric constant, operator, or other nonword character) calls skip_to_EOL( ), which does just what its name promises. It returns false if it gets an EOF before it gets an EOL.

The next step is to look for the equal sign in the next token. Operators and punctuation are returned as the value of the integer token. Again, we return false on EOF and fast-forward to EOL if we don't get the equal sign. This is the code:

```
    // get an equal sign in word 2
      tok = get_tok( toker );

      if ( tok == StreamTokenizer.TT_EOF )
         return false;
      if ( tok == StreamTokenizer.TT_EOL )
         return true;
      if ( tok != '=' )
         return skip_to_EOL( toker );
```

Finally, we want a number as the third token. There's the same ALD here. The token TT_NUMBER tells us that we've got a number.

```
    // get a number in word 3
      tok = get_tok( toker );

      if ( tok == StreamTokenizer.TT_EOF )
         return false;
      if ( tok == StreamTokenizer.TT_EOL )
         return true;
      if ( tok != StreamTokenizer.TT_NUMBER )
         return skip_to_EOL( toker );
```

At this point we've got a string, equal sign, and a number. The number for a TT_NUMBER is available in the public double, StreamTokenizer.nval, from which we grab it this way:

```
      number = toker.nval;
```

Then a call to assign( ) does the assignment:

```
      assign( name, number );
```

Finally, we ignore the rest of the line:

```
      return skip_to_EOL( toker );
```

If you think that's a lot of trouble, think about the troubles you haven't faced. Start by writing the definition of a numeric constant:

```
[optional] leading "+" or "-"
digit
[optional] more digits
[optional] decimal point
[optional] more digits
[optional] exponent
```

Convinced? If not, write the code that recognizes the optional exponent. (Don't forget that exponents can be signed. Leading zeros are common. And be prepared to handle errors.) When you get that done, you'll probably be convinced.

The other function in the read process is skip_to_EOL. Except for the EOF-related ALD, it's straightforward:

```java
private static boolean skip_to_EOL(
    StreamTokenizer toker ) {

    // returns true except at EOF

    while ( true ) {

        int tok = get_tok( toker );

        if ( tok == StreamTokenizer.TT_EOF )
            return false;
        if ( tok == StreamTokenizer.TT_EOL )
            return true;

    }

}
```

The Full JDBini.java Listing

Listing 10-1 shows the full JDBini.java file.

Listing 10-1:
JDBini.java
handles
JDB.INI

```java
// JDBini.java -- read/write JDB.INI
// Copyright 1997, Martin L. Rinehart

// this code is completely documented in:
// _Java Database Development_, Martin Rinehart,
```

```java
// Osborne/McGraw-Hill, 1997

/*
    Remembers the JDB setup between runs.
*/

import java.awt.*;
import java.io.*;

class JDBini extends Object {

// -------------------- data members --------------------

// there are no public data members
// there are no protected data members

// static data members
    // there are no public static data members

    // protected static data members:

    protected static JDB boss;

    protected static int item_num;

    protected static double[] men_vals = new double[11];
    protected static int menu_num;

    protected static byte[] output_buffer;

    // there are no private static data members
    // final static data member:

    protected static final String file_name = "JDB.INI";

// -------------------- public methods --------------------

// constructor:

    JDBini( JDB dad ) {

        boss = dad;
```

```
                output_buffer = new byte[80];

                menu_num = item_num = 0;
            }

// there are no data access methods

// public, class-specific methods:

        public static void read_ini() {

            FileInputStream ifile;

            ifile = null;
            try {
                ifile = new FileInputStream( file_name );
            }
            catch ( IOException ioe ) {

                System.out.println( "JDB.INI doesn't exist" );
                return;
            }

            try {

                StreamTokenizer toker = new StreamTokenizer(
                    (InputStream) ifile );
                toker.commentChar( ';' );
                toker.eolIsSignificant( true );
                toker.wordChars( '_', '_' );

                int tok;

                while ( parse_next_line(toker) );
            }

            catch ( NullPointerException npe ) {}
        }

        public static void write_ini() {

            FileOutputStream ofile;
```

```
        ofile = null;
        try {
            ofile = new FileOutputStream( file_name );
        }
        catch ( IOException ioe ) {

            System.out.println( "JDB.INI open error" );
        }

        if ( ofile != null ) {
            try {
                write( ofile, "; JDB.INI" );
                write( ofile );
                write( ofile, ";POSITION-DEPENDENT FILE" );
                write( ofile, ";   !DO NOT EDIT!" );
                write( ofile );
                write( ofile,
                    ";If damaged, delete this file." );
                write( ofile );

                int nm = JDBlib.num_menus;
                for ( int i = 0; i < nm; i++ ) {
                    write_menu( ofile, i );
                    write( ofile );
                }

                write( ofile, " ; end of JDB.INI" );

                ofile.close();
            }

            catch( IOException ioe ) {

                System.out.println(
                    "Error writing to JDB.INI" );
            }
        }
    }

// public, non-event overriding method:

    public String paramString() {
```

```
            return "JDB.INI, boss: " + boss;
        }

// there are no public, event-handling methods

// ------------------ private methods ------------------

// private methods:

    private static void assign( String s, double d ) {

        // This position-dependent treatment of the .INI
        // makes the .INI less editable, but it saves
        // several KB by eliminating giant switches. It
        // loads faster, too.

        // The file warnings lie. You can edit the values
        // if you are careful not to add or delete items.

        men_vals[item_num++] = d;

        if ( item_num == 11 ) {
            assign_menu( men_vals );
            item_num = 0;
            menu_num++;
        }
    }


    private static void assign_menu( double[] d ) {

        if ( menu_num != d[0] ) {
            System.out.println( "Damaged JDB.INI -- " +
                "delete the file and run JDB again." );

                System.out.println(
                    "\n   press any key to continue..." );

                try { System.in.read(); }
                catch (IOException ioe ) {}

            System.exit( 1 );
        }
```

```java
    boss.setMenuValues( menu_num, d );

    if ( ! JDBlib.is_zmenu[menu_num] ) {

        MenuPanel mp = boss.getMenuPanel( menu_num );
        RRectPromptPainter rp = ( RRectPromptPainter )
            mp.painter;
        Frame f = (Frame) mp.getParent();

        f.reshape( (int) d[1], (int) d[2], (int) d[3],
            (int) d[4] );
        rp.setLoBackColor( new Color (( int ) d[5]) );
        rp.setLoForeColor( new Color (( int ) d[6]) );
        rp.setHiBackColor( new Color (( int ) d[7]) );
        rp.setHiForeColor( new Color (( int ) d[8]) );

        rp.hradius = d[9];
        rp.vradius = d[10];
    }
}

private static int get_tok(
    StreamTokenizer toker ) {

    int tok;

    try {
        tok = toker.nextToken();
    }
    catch (IOException ioe ) {
        System.out.println(
            "JDB.INI read error" );
        tok = StreamTokenizer.TT_EOF;
    }
    return tok;
}

private static boolean parse_next_line(
    StreamTokenizer toker ) {

// calls assign() iff it gets:
//    name = number
```

```
    // just ignores everything else
    // returns true except at EOF

        int tok;
        String name;
        double number;

    // get a name in word 1
        tok = get_tok( toker );

        if ( tok == StreamTokenizer.TT_EOF )
            return false;
        if ( tok == StreamTokenizer.TT_EOL )
            return true;
        if ( tok != StreamTokenizer.TT_WORD )
            return skip_to_EOL( toker );

        name = toker.sval;

    // get an equal sign in word 2
        tok = get_tok( toker );

        if ( tok == StreamTokenizer.TT_EOF )
            return false;
        if ( tok == StreamTokenizer.TT_EOL )
            return true;
        if ( tok != '=' )
            return skip_to_EOL( toker );

    // get a number in word 3
        tok = get_tok( toker );

        if ( tok == StreamTokenizer.TT_EOF )
            return false;
        if ( tok == StreamTokenizer.TT_EOL )
            return true;
        if ( tok != StreamTokenizer.TT_NUMBER )
            return skip_to_EOL( toker );

        number = toker.nval;

        assign( name, number );
```

```java
        return skip_to_EOL( toker );
}

private static boolean skip_to_EOL(
    StreamTokenizer toker ) {

    // returns true except at EOF

    while ( true ) {

        int tok = get_tok( toker );

        if ( tok == StreamTokenizer.TT_EOF )
            return false;
        if ( tok == StreamTokenizer.TT_EOL )
            return true;
    }
}

private static void write( FileOutputStream fos )
    throws IOException{

    // writes null line
    output_buffer[0] = (byte) '\n';
    fos.write( output_buffer, 0, 1 );
}

private static void write( FileOutputStream fos,
    String s ) throws IOException {

    if ( s == null ) {
        write( fos );
        return;
    }

    s.getBytes( 0, s.length(), output_buffer, 0 );
    output_buffer[s.length()] = (byte) '\n';
    fos.write( output_buffer, 0, s.length() + 1 );
}

private static void write_menu(
    FileOutputStream fos, int menu_num )
```

```
throws IOException {

String name = boss.getMenuName( menu_num );

write( fos, "[" + name + "]" );
write( fos, name + " = " + menu_num );

if ( JDBlib.is_zmenu[menu_num] ) {

    write_rect( fos,
        new Rectangle(0, 0, 0, 0), name );

    double[] men_vals =
        boss.getMenuValues( menu_num );

    write( fos, name + "_lo_back = " +
        (int) men_vals[4] );
    write( fos, name + "_lo_fore= " +
        (int) men_vals[5] );

    write( fos, name + "_hi_back = " +
        (int) men_vals[6] );
    write( fos, name + "_hi_fore= " +
        (int) men_vals[7] );

    write( fos, name + "_hradius = " +
        men_vals[8] );
    write( fos, name + "_vradius = " +
        men_vals[9] );
}
else {

    MenuPanel mp = boss.getMenuPanel( menu_num );
    RRectPromptPainter rp =
        ( RRectPromptPainter )( mp.painter );
    Frame f = (Frame) mp.getParent();
    write_rect( fos, f.bounds(), name );

    write( fos, name + "_lo_back = " +
        rp.getLoBackColor().getRGB() );
    write( fos, name + "_lo_fore= " +
        rp.getLoForeColor().getRGB() );
```

```
                write( fos, name + "_hi_back = " +
                    rp.getHiBackColor().getRGB() );
                write( fos, name + "_hi_fore= " +
                    rp.getHiForeColor().getRGB() );

                write( fos, name + "_hradius = " + rp.hradius );
                write( fos, name + "_vradius = " + rp.vradius );
            }
        }

    private static void write_rect(
        FileOutputStream fos, Rectangle r, String name )
        throws IOException {

        write( fos, name + "_x = " + r.x );
        write( fos, name + "_y = " + r.y );
        write( fos, name + "_width = " + r.width );
        write( fos, name + "_height = " + r.height );
    }

} // end of JDBini class

// there are no private classes in JDBini.java

// end of JDBini.java
```

Summary

We started by looking at JDB.INI from the users' point of view (bearing in mind that the users include ourselves). In spite of the file's warnings, the individual data items may be edited. This lets you, for example, reposition a window.

From the programmers' point of view there is good news and bad news. First, the good news. To use JDBini, you declare a variable, call the constructor, and call read_ini( ) after your program has created the objects that will be initialized. Calling write_ini( ) at the end of the application's run completes the process. It couldn't be simpler.

The bad news is that JDBini, as the name suggests, is specific to the JDB application. Your XXX application will need an XXXini class.

Then we went on to study the program. The write_ini( ) process uses a FileOutputStream object. By writing the file in a fixed order, we let the read software be very simple.

The read_ini( ) code uses a StreamTokenizer. The latter required calls to commentChar( ) to set up an end-of-line comment, to eolIsSignificant( ) to return EOL tokens, and to wordChars( ) to add the underscore character as part of words. Once set up, the StreamTokenizer made reading the file a simple matter of parsing a trivial language.

We've now got a JDB application that is a lot of fun to customize and an INI file capability that stores and retrieves our application's setup. Now the only thing missing is the ability to actually create and use database files. We'll begin adding that capability in Chapter 12.

In Chapter 11, however, we'll take a break from coding and consider the design of databases. If you think you understand database design, you're in for a surprise.

Chapter 11

Designing Object and Relational Databases

D o you know traditional database design theory? If you do, don't skip this chapter! It presents a nontraditional method. My method is simple to follow, easy to explain or teach, and guaranteed to give you results superior to fourth-normal form. I'll bet you're skeptical right now. Read on.

If you don't know normalization theory, *fifth-normal form* is roughly equal to perfect design. The lower forms start at *first-normal form,* which simply says the data is stored in tables. Most database designers are content with third-normal form.

If you do know normalization theory, before you finish this chapter you'll probably be amazed at how simple this design business can be. You'll understand jargon like "full functional dependency," but you'll know you won't need it for designing databases.

We'll begin with the basics: objects and events. Designing a database begins with identifying objects and events. (Yes, I *do* know Chen's ER work. If you do, too, see if you don't agree that this blows it away.) When you identify objects and events, you list the characteristics of each that are important for your database's purposes.

You examine the characteristics to see what other tables you might need. *Relational* databases need separate tables for detail categories. *Object* databases can track this information in separate classes, or within the parent objects themselves.

I'll give you a simple, six-step summary of the whole procedure. When you design, you'll perform all these steps more or less simultaneously. They'll serve as a checklist after you're done.

The whole procedure is so simple that there's a section explaining classic normalization and showing how our designs compare. You'll see that our designs compare very favorably. I'll show you that your designs will be in Boyce-Codd normal form. Those who haven't met normalization before will come away from this section with a brand-new vocabulary.

Finally, I'll have a section on the intelligent use of redundant data. We'll leave theory behind and discuss how to make intelligent use of redundant data to help the users without taking unnecessary risks.

Let's begin with the basics, objects and events.

Beginning with Objects and Events

A database is a model of some useful portion of the real world. When you design a database, you have some application or applications for the data. You may want to account for past transactions or forecast future events. Whatever you have in mind, you have to design a good database if you want a good application.

Let's do the design job very badly, so you can see some of the problems you might have. We'll design the accounting system for a software distributor. For our starting design, we'll have just one table. With each sale we'll record the name and address of the customer, list the items sold (we'll have to allow enough columns for the highest number of items that might be included in a single sale), and we'll record the invoice number and any other data.

What's wrong with this database? For one, if we delete a single sale, we could lose all the information about a customer. If a customer makes a second purchase, the customer's data is entered in two places. What happens when we get a change-of-address notice from an active customer?

That customer's data is repeated in many records. Chances are excellent that the data is inconsistent. We'll get the new address recorded in one record, but not in others. There is no convenient way to ask questions such as, "How much software has X purchased?"

Our designs will be fundamentally sound because they'll be anchored in the world they model. We'll have none of these problems. You'll see that our design work doesn't even ask whether the database is object or relational until late in the process. That won't be very important for our designs.

Objects

Step 1 is to list the classes of objects we'll deal with. These are real-world objects, not software objects. The simple definition is, "If you can kick it, it's an object."

Classes of objects include customers, products, vendors, buildings, and departments. These are all things you can kick. (Just because you *can* kick something doesn't mean that you *should* kick it.)

Of course, nonkickable things are also objects. For examples, mathematical theories or musical compositions could be usefully cataloged in a database. A better definition is that an *object* is anything that is permanent, or that exists over a long time and has an independent existence—it doesn't require other objects.

Actually, I use the "kickable" definition when I design databases. It covers most practical work. Events will teach you something about what objects are not.

Events

In Java, Events are Objects, too. In our database design, they're definitely not objects. An *event* is something that happens at a point in time involving objects.

Making a sale is an event. Admitting a patient is an event. Shipping a product is an event.

In a sale, a customer is united with one or more products at a moment in time. This establishes a permanent relationship between the customer and the product(s): owner. (The customer might resell or otherwise dispose of the product later, but if that's not relevant to our system, we'll ignore it.)

Admitting a patient associates a person with a hospital at a point in time. (Presumably there will be a discharge event that later breaks the association.)

Shipping a product happens at a point in time. If our database is concerned with recognizing revenue, we might record the day the product is shipped. If our application is supposed to help us manage the loading dock, we'll record the exact minute each carton is loaded. Whatever the case, we'll have something that happened at a point in time. The event has to relate objects that are part of our system in a way that's meaningful.

The software distributor records customer information: name, address, phone, and so on. The burger joint does not know its customers. In the burger-joint system, there is no customer object. There's just a sale. The product disappears from our inventory—we don't track it beyond that point.

With no objects, we'll have no events. Any event that involves only objects that are outside our database is, by definition, not of interest. Our objects remain unchanged by that event. If you find an event that seems important but doesn't relate to your objects, ask to what objects it does relate. You've overlooked something.

Processes and Other Classes

Are there more things beyond objects and events? We'll meet more shortly, but before we go on, let's think about taxonomies in general. Here we're creating a taxonomy of the types of things about which you could record data.

The biologist divides animals into groups like mammals and reptiles. Mammals have hair, give birth to live young, and suckle their young. Reptiles have scales, lay eggs, and don't suckle their young.

Biology was stood on its ear with the discovery of the duck-billed platypus. This contrarian has hair, lays eggs, and then suckles its young. It clearly defies placement as mammal or reptile.

I'm not concerned about my taxonomy meeting its own version of the platypus. I see them all the time. Consider processes, for example.

I define a *process* as a long-duration event. No event is truly instantaneous, but for most events our databases record events at a single point in time. The product was sold on the 24th. The patient was admitted at 8:00 A.M. But suppose your business constructs homes. The process of building the home starts one day and ends many weeks later. During the process, your other objects (workers, building supplies) are brought together to create the product. A customer may be involved before the home is completed, or even before the home is started. You can kick the house, but you can't kick the process. It's a long-duration event.

If you can design well for objects and events, you can fit in processes or other platypus-like real-world phenomena. This taxonomy is a starting point. The fact that it's incomplete doesn't mean it's not useful.

Biologists, by the way, eventually accepted the platypus. They realized that their taxonomies were useful, but not necessarily complete. Mother Nature is more given to continuums than to neat classifications. Naming colors red, orange, yellow, and so on, doesn't bunch colors at those points in the spectrum. But it's still a useful taxonomy.

Characteristics

Once you've listed the classes of objects and events that your system needs to record, you list the important characteristics of each object and event. A characteristic is important if you need it for your application(s).

For a person class you'd want to know name, addresses, phone numbers, and other data. Height and weight are characteristics of people. If you're running an outpatient treatment facility, you'll record height and weight. If your gallery sells old masters, you won't record these measurements.

The first item in every list of characteristics will be an ID. When we first enter an individual object, we'll assign it a unique ID. We'll always refer to the object by that ID. We'll never reassign that ID. (Did I say "never"? Make that "NEVER.")

Our events will have an ID, a time stamp, ID(s) for the participating object(s), and any other data. This is a design for a database for a store that sells products to customers:

```
PRODUCT:              CUSTOMER:              SALE:
    product ID            customer ID            sale ID
    name                  name                   timestamp
    weight                address                customer ID
    color                 phone number(s)        products sold
    number on hand        email address
    price
```

Each product will have one record in the product table. The important characteristics will be the columns in the table. The intersection of a record (row) and column is a single field in the record.

Note how our SALE records the customer ID, not the customer data. This is called a *foreign key*. It identifies a specific customer, but it doesn't have any data about the customer. You look up data about that customer in the CUSTOMER table.

If you need to distinguish the customer ID field in the CUSTOMER table from the customer ID field in the SALE table, you call the former a *primary key*. When a primary key is used outside its home table, it becomes a foreign key.

Notice that this design handles a change-of-address notice without a hitch. Each customer's name and address are recorded in exactly one place. You edit that one record and you're done.

Beware of Paperwork

Data was collected long before computers existed. Many paper-based forms were used to record transactions. Many are still in use today. For example, there's an invoice associated with most sales.

Those papers were our predecessor model. An invoice says that Fred bought five widgets on Tuesday. The invoice isn't Fred. It didn't give Fred the widgets. It didn't take Fred's money. It simply records facts about the transaction. It's a model.

When you design a database, model the real world. Don't model someone else's model. You should be able to generate your own invoices from your system. If you need to coexist with a paperwork system, you could enter the invoice number, for example, as a characteristic of the sale.

It's dangerous to have an INVOICE table. Invoices are kickable. They're objects. The underlying reality is an event. Model reality and attach any necessary paperwork to your model. Don't model the paperwork.

Relationships

Relational databases have nothing to do with the relationships among your data items. The word "relation" is the mathematical term for a table. A *relational database* is one in which the data is stored in tables. In fact, handling real-world relationships is one of the weak points of the relational database.

There are relationships among your objects that may be important. Again, an important relationship is one that your application needs to know about. The rest are unimportant as far as your database design is concerned.

Consider your enterprise's medical benefits. If they apply to the family of the employee, you'll need to know about the family relationships between your employees. If Fred and Sally are married, you don't want to pay for Fred's wife and Sally's husband after you pay for Fred and Sally.

For each class of relationship, you'll need a table. Unless the relationships are permanent (sibling relationships are permanent, marital relationships are less permanent), your characteristics list will include an ID, the start and end dates of the relationship, IDs of the related objects, and any other information about the relationship.

Here's a sample for your health insurance:

```
FAMILY MEMBERS:
    relation ID
    start_date
    end_date
    employee ID
    related employee ID
    relationship type
```

Events are, as we noted earlier, a type of relationship. Don't repeat them here. Events usually relate one class of object (for example, customer) with another class (for example, product). The relationships we're talking about here usually relate objects in a class with other objects in the same class. (In my work, they've *always* related objects in the same class. I don't see any reason, however, to preclude cross-class relationships.)

These relationships have an inherent and unsolvable problem. One database design principle is to eliminate redundant data. (Record everything in exactly one place, and you can never have conflicting data.) Transitive relationships will complicate your life.

For you designmeisters, I don't mean the transitive relationships that third-normal form talks about, I mean the relationships that are transitive in the real world: if Sally is Sarah's sister, it's also true that Sarah is Sally's sister.

For nonredundant data storage, you would record this relationship just once. Database queries will be complicated by the fact that you often have to search two columns. But this is a minor problem.

The major problem occurs when you hire Sandra, who is sister to Sally and Sarah. The minimal amount of data is achieved by entering Sandra as sister of Sally. Then you do some fancy programming so that your software recognizes that if Sandra is sister of Sally and Sally is sister of Sarah, then Sandra is sister of Sarah.

If you get that code debugged, you'll realize that you've made a mistake. If the three women are children of the same parents, you'll reach the correct result. But once you begin to allow for death, divorce, remarriage, and so on, you'll see that only some sibling relationships are transitive. Explicitly entering all the relationships is the only way to prevent mistakes.

When you explicitly enter all the relationships, you will have entered at least some redundant data. While you are puzzling over the best compromise for your database, make sure you ask yourself this question: what happens when one of these women quits? If your application doesn't collapse, you'll be OK.

I should point out that most databases are designed to accompany applications, but databases generally end up serving multiple applications. I concentrate on the application at hand because I've learned that it's easy to specify database elements; it's difficult and expensive to collect the data.

Detail Tables

Once you have your objects, events, and necessary relationships listed along with the characteristics of each, it's time to look at the characteristics to find necessary detail tables. In a relational database, you'll need a separate table for each repeating characteristic.

For example, if your sale event can transfer multiple products to the customer (this is almost always the case), it includes one or more products, quantities, and prices. This requires a separate table in a relational database.

If you're designing for an object database, it's not necessary to create a separate class for these details. They can be stored along with the parent object. Putting the details in a separate class may shrink the parent data by an order of magnitude, however. Always consider the relational approach as a possible alternative.

Characteristics change over time. People change their hair color quite routinely. With today's contact lenses, eye color is hardly permanent. Less often, but still commonly, people change their names (perhaps taking a spouse's name after marriage).

Our tables all incorporate an ID, so changing characteristics isn't a major problem. Sometimes, however, you'll also need to create detail tables (or, for objects, array data members) to record history details.

Repeating Characteristics

Let's revisit that simple store database. It looked like this:

```
PRODUCT:            CUSTOMER:              SALE:
    product ID          customer ID            sale ID
    name                name                   timestamp
    weight              address                customer ID
    color               phone number(s)        products sold
    number on hand      email address
    price
```

There are two plural characteristics. For "phone number(s)" we can break down specific, individual fields this way:

```
CUSTOMER:
    customer ID
    name
    address
    office phone
    home phone
    mobile phone
    email address
```

For "products sold" in the sales event table, we can't do that. Novice designers may try to allow several columns for multiple instances of a single characteristic. Experienced designers reject that approach in almost every case. The right approach is to create a separate table for sale detail records. Its design might look like this:

```
SALE:               SALE_DTL:
    sale ID             sale detail ID
    timestamp           sale ID
```

```
     customer ID       product ID
                       number sold
                       price
```

Suppose Fred (remember Fred? we saw him last in seat 17A, editing JDB.INI) walks into the store and buys a widget, two doohickeys (on sale), and three thingamabobs. This is what the relevant records in the database will contain:

```
CUSTOMER:
    23, Fred,          someplace,        (999) 999-9999, ...

PRODUCT:
     14, widget,        14.2,       red, 1024, 19.95
    144, doohickey,      8.8,      blue,  127, 29.95
    145, thingamabob,   18.0,     white,    4,  3.95

SALE:
  12345, 19980201, 23

SALE_DTL:
  123456,    12345,      14,    1,     19.95
  123457,    12345,     144,    2,     24.95
  123458,    12345,     145,    3,      3.95
```

All the tables start with their ID values. Fred is customer 23, for example. (Relational databases are completely independent of column ordering. IDs are placed first by tradition. Placing them elsewhere will be no problem for the computer, but we humans will get confused.)

The PRODUCT table will probably have numeric color codes, not words like "red." And commas aren't part of the records except for data import/export operations. Otherwise these are typical tables. Of course, the many thousands of other records in these tables aren't shown here. We're looking at the handful relevant to sale 12345.

The SALE record is very simple. This is not typical of actual SALE records. Many will incorporate sales tax rates, some will need shipping data, and so on. Real databases have to reflect all the messy details of the real world. This SALE record says that the customer with ID 23 made a purchase on 2/1/98. What did he buy?

You look in the SALE_DTL table for records where the sale ID is 12345. Our example has completed this search and come up with three records. The first is for product ID 14, one unit at $19.95. This happens to be the same price that product 14 shows in the PRODUCT table. The next detail record shows two products 144 purchased for $24.95. The $29.95 price of product 144 in the PRODUCT table shows that blue doohickeys were on sale when Fred bought his.

Assembling this sale to show, for example, an invoice on the screen is very fast thanks to the magic of indexed lookups. In an earlier book I went through the time calculations for the necessary lookups to assemble a sale such as this one. I showed that if there were 10,000 customers, 100,000 sales, and 1,000,000 sale detail records, the whole lookup process still provided subsecond response. Those calculations were for a 25MHz, 80386-based machine. The moral for today: Don't worry about it. Any lookup delay gets hidden in the screen refresh process.

Use Sequential (not Random) Keys

This is a good time to mention the ID values. They are often called *keys*. The characteristics of the key are that it is a unique identifier and that it is never reassigned. The latter characteristic is redundant if you take the former seriously enough.

The simple way to generate such an ID is to assign 0 to the first record entered, 1 as the key of the next record, and so on. Initially the IDs will be the same as the record numbers. Once you delete a record, this stops being true.

A small table records the highest key assigned. The important point is that deletions never be allowed to affect the next key assigned. If your system assigned the value 100 last and then someone deletes four records at the end of the table, the highest remaining key will be 96. The next record *must* be assigned key 101.

Some DBMSes get this all wrong. They have an automatic unique ID capability, but assign random keys. They generate a random number, check it for uniqueness, and hand it out if it's not in the table. This is *completely unacceptable*.

Your customer, 12345, moved to another continent. A year or so later you've rolled the inactive customers (including 12345) onto backup media. 12345 is no longer in the database. The random, not-really-unique key mechanism gives out another 12345. Now what happens when you do an ever-to-date search of your data warehouse for customer 12345?

Right. Both customers 12345 seem to have made each other's purchases. If you start at the sales table and then look up customers based on their ID, there's no telling who you'll find. On average, you'll be right half the time. If you're trying to regenerate old invoices for 12345, your accountants (or the accountants for both customers 12345) will have unkind things to say.

Your ID value must be unique and must permanently identify exactly one record in the table. It must do that job forever. ("Forever" means from the start to the end of our system's life.)

Uniqueness applies within, not across tables. Every table I build starts with key 0. That's not a problem.

One final note on repeating characteristics. Ask yourself if the characteristic permits one or more occurrences, or if it permits zero or more occurrences. The database design will be the same, but your application software needs to know this. Occasionally you'll find some other lower limit, and you'll also find upper limits in some instances. Document these things so they get coded correctly. The design shown here will handle zero or more occurrences (which means it will certainly handle one or more) up to whatever fills your disk drive.

Characteristic Histories

In addition to these detail records for repeating characteristics, you may need detail records for characteristic histories. We said in the sample earlier that the doohickeys Fred bought at $24.95 were on sale. The PRODUCT table showed the regular price was $29.95. This is the relevant data:

```
CUSTOMER:
    23, Fred,          someplace,        (999) 999-9999, ...

PRODUCT:
     14, widget,        14.2,      red, 1024, 19.95
    144, doohickey,      8.8,     blue,  127, 29.95 <---
    145, thingamabob,   18.0,    white,    4,  3.95    |
                                                       |
SALE:                                                  |
  12345, 19980201, 23                           discount?
                                                       |
SALE_DTL:                                              |
  123456,   12345,    14,   1,    19.95                |
  123457,   12345,   144,   2,    24.95 <-----------
  123458,   12345,   145,   3,     3.95
```

Was this a sale price? Maybe the price is $29.95 today, but it was only $24.95 when Fred made his purchase. From the data given, we don't know. The $29.95 price is presented as if it were an immutable fact of life for blue doohickeys. That's probably not the truth.

When you need to maintain a historic record, you add another type of detail record. For PRODUCT prices, this design will work:

```
PRODUCT:             PROD_PRICE:
    product ID           prod_price ID
    name                 product ID
    weight               start date
```

```
color                    price
number on hand
```

These are the entries in the PROD_PRICE table for blue doohickeys:

```
PROD_PRICE:
      32,    14,    19940201,    49.95
    4279,    14,    19950201,    39.95
   14396,    14,    19960201,    34.95
   27819,    14,    19970201,    29.95
```

To find the current price of a blue doohickey, you find the last entry for product ID 14 in the PROD_PRICE table. (I assume this table is sorted by date within product ID.) Note that the start date alone is sufficient. The end date is implied by the next record's start date. If there isn't a next record, you're looking at the start date of the latest price.

When you program this, you'll find it's even simpler if you do a descending sort on the start date. That way, the first record is the current price. The first record that has a start date earlier than or equal to a target date holds the price on the target date.

Method Summary

These methods are often called "methodologies," which is too sloppy and too polysyllabic for me. In fact, even "polysyllabic" is too polysyllabic for me. A method for doing something is a method. Like biology or theology, methodology is the study of methods.

This is my method:

- List the object (kickable thing) classes.
- List the event (stuff that happens) classes.
- List each object and event's important characteristics.
- List important relationships among objects.
- Make separate tables for repeating characteristics.
- Make separate tables to record characteristic histories.

Step 1. Objects

You create one table for each class of object. Loosely, an object is anything you can kick.

Objects can be abstract things such as mathematical formulae or laws of physics. A better definition of *object* is an entity with a separate existence and a relatively long or permanent life.

In practice, focusing on kickable things lets you identify most objects.

Step 2. Events

Each class of events also gets a separate table. An event is something that happens at a point in time. Nothing useful actually gets done at a point in time, of course. But if our database works when you record a single time stamp, that's close enough to a point for our design work.

Events create a relationship among our objects at their point in time. You sell products to a customer, for example.

Events have time stamps. Objects don't. Events happen to objects. Objects exist by themselves.

(If an important event is identified in step 2 that doesn't involve any objects from step 1, you'll have at least one new class of object that should have been listed in step 1. Real design is like that.)

Step 3. Characteristics

Each object listed in step 1 and each event from step 2 is a data table. In this step you list their important characteristics. These are the fields (columns in the table). A characteristic is important if it's needed in your intended application.

Although a database should be able to serve multiple applications, you should hesitate to put in data that is not immediately useful. Collecting reliable data is never cheap.

Every table's first characteristic is an ID. For permanent uniqueness, I use integer IDs that are never reassigned after they are handed out. Deleting a record effectively deletes the ID, too.

Step 4. Relationships

An additional table is created for each important relationship. Again, a relationship is important if it's necessary for your applications.

For example, family relationships are important to avoid duplicate billing of insurance benefits.

The characteristics of a relationship table are

- An ID
- IDs of the related objects
- Other data describing the relationship

Step 5. Repeating Characteristics

Examine your characteristics for multiples or plurals. In some cases, you can break down a plural into multiple characteristics, such as phone numbers becoming home, office, and cellular. In most cases, however, a repeating characteristic requires a new detail table.

Characteristics of a repeating detail table are

- An ID
- The ID of the parent table
- Other data, possibly including other IDs

The example given was the common sales detail table. A *sale* includes one or more products sold. The *detail record* includes the ID of the product sold, the number of units, and the price.

For object databases, these details may be a separate class, or they may be included within their parent objects.

Step 6. Characteristic Histories

When you need to track the changes in a characteristic that occur over time, you need an additional table. (Again, the object designer may include this data within the parent object.)

A history table's characteristics include

- An ID
- The parent table's ID
- A start date
- The characteristic's value at the start date

Real Design Rules

These steps are idealized. Most designers write out rough lists of characteristics as soon as they identify a table. Objects suggest events and events suggest objects, so steps 1, 2, and 3 are done together.

Steps 4 and 5 are done as each table's characteristics are enumerated. Experienced designers go right to step 4, rather than listing a repeating characteristic in step 3 and then removing it in step 4. The same applies to step 5.

Steps 4 and 5 have to be repeated for the characteristics of the new tables created during steps 4 and 5. You're done when there are no more repeating characteristics and all that need histories have histories.

These steps are not useful if you attempt to let them dictate the order of the design's development. They are, however, useful as a checklist to ensure that nothing is forgotten.

I have never worked on a real-world design where the number of tables has not been far in excess of early estimates. I have not always resisted the temptation to "simplify" the design by combining tables. I have always regretted the result when I failed to resist this temptation.

The complexity of the implementation is linearly proportional to the number of tables. The complexity is geometrically proportional to the number of "simplifications" you make after you've decided your design has too many tables.

Normalization

If you know normalization, I'm going to show here that the preceding simple procedure is provably superior to a classic approach to, say, third-normal form design. If you don't know normalization, I'll teach you enough of the jargon here so you'll be able to go toe-to-toe with any classically trained database administrator.

First-Normal Form

There are five numbered normal forms, first through fifth, and there are other named intermediate normal forms. Each of the numbered normal forms is better than and inclusive of all the lower forms. A design in fourth-normal form, for example, meets all the requirements of third-normal form and adds additional desirable qualities.

If you want to become proficient with normalization, you'll need a good text and about a week. If you use my design method, your results will be consistently superior to all but the very best traditional normalization-based designs.

First-normal form specifies only that the data be stored in tables. In our first three steps we list tables, but we leave nontable data, such as repeating characteristics. Eliminating these in steps 4 and 5 puts our database design into first-normal form.

Second-Normal Form

"A database is in second-normal form if it is in first-normal form and every attribute is fully functionally dependent on the primary key."

Would you like that in English?

Let's see. An *attribute* is what we'd call the content of a field. If we had a table for books, the value in the Author field for this book would be "Rinehart." That's the author attribute for this book.

Now I'll try *primary key*. Our ID values are the primary keys in our designs. They uniquely identify a particular record. What else could we use for a unique identifier?

In the case of books, titles are almost unique. Publishers try to make them unique. For my last book, I remember seeing a book on the shelves at my local bookstore sporting my book's working title. I called my editor immediately. We changed our book's name. If I hadn't happened to be browsing that day, or if my bookstore hadn't happened to carry that title, we would have published the second book with that title, which goes to show that you can't uniquely identify a book by its title. You can, however, combine the title and publisher fields to form a unique identifier.

You might combine other attributes to try to create a key. You could, for instance, combine title and author. That combination might uniquely identify books. In normalization theory it's called a *candidate key*. The primary key is the one you select as a unique identifier. Let's choose title plus publisher, just for the sake of this discussion.

Bear with me now. I told you this was jargon rich. The "functional dependence" bit comes next.

An attribute is *functionally dependent* on a key when specification of the key specifies a single attribute value. Search your book table's title and publisher for this book, and you'll find "Rinehart" in the Author field. Always. That attribute is functionally dependent on that key. Search on just the publisher, and you'll find lots of different values in the Author field. (They publish lots of books, of course.) Author is not functionally dependent on publisher. Search on this book's title, and we fervently hope that you'll always come up with "Rinehart" in the Author field, but we can't be sure some other publisher isn't working on the same title.

Now let's add "fully" to the functional dependence concept.

An attribute is *fully functionally dependent* on a key if it is functionally dependent on the entire key, but not on any combination of key attributes less than the entire key. In our book table, "Rinehart" is uniquely determined by the combination of title and publisher. It is not uniquely determined by the publisher. We'd like to think that the title will uniquely determine "Rinehart" as the author attribute, but we're not sure. In fact, if your book table is large enough, you're sure to find an instance where one title identifies multiple author attributes, so the author is not functionally dependent on the title. Since the author attribute is functionally dependent on the full primary key—title plus publisher—but not on either part of the primary key, the author attribute is fully functionally dependent on the primary key.

All of which means that our book table is in second-normal form. Now, will you permit me to simplify things?

By assigning an *abstract key* (one not based on the data in the record) and by adopting a mechanism to ensure that these abstract keys are unique within the table, we achieve full functional dependence with no muss, no fuss, no bother. If this is the book with ID 12345 in your table, for example, its author is "Rinehart." Look up ID 12345 and you'll always get the same title, publisher, and author. Each attribute is functionally dependent on the ID.

Our IDs are a single item, not a compound of other attributes. If your key isn't compound, functional dependence is also full functional dependence. The attributes can't depend on just part of the key, because it hasn't got parts. Our ID values make all this a lot simpler, don't they?

Third-Normal Form

"A database is in third-normal form if it is in second-normal form and contains no transitive attribute dependencies."

This one's a little easier to translate, but may be harder to really understand.

If an attribute is functionally dependent on a key, you can say that the key *implies* the attribute. Our book table's ID for this book implies that the author is "Rinehart." A transitive dependency is one in which

A implies B
B implies C

transitively, A implies C

Of course, if you have precisely one key, which you do if you assign an ID as I've suggested, you'll never have transitive dependencies. Our tables are also in third-normal form.

Almost. Using my method or using traditional normalization, you can get trapped by the problem of unintended (or even unknown) dependencies. These are usually created by someone else and left around to trap unsuspecting database designers.

Suppose you've created a simple person table, which includes name, address, and phone numbers. Fred (remember Fred?) lives on the upper-east side of Manhattan. His home phone is (212) 123-4567. His ZIP code (the U. S. postal code) is 10028. His city and state are New York, NY. Have you counted the redundancies here?

The area code (the first three digits of the phone number) is 212. New York City's central borough, Manhattan, is so populous that it has its own area code: 212. The postal code 10028 identifies a small part of Manhattan. Both city and state are implied by both phone and ZIP code. The ZIP code implies the first three digits of the phone number.

This problem exists whenever your database includes portions of someone else's identification system, such as postal codes and phone numbers. You can ignore it in many applications, or you can incorporate (if they're available) the outside source's tables.

You'll find when you try to model the real world that your model probably can't avoid other people's models. The real world is a messy place.

Boyce-Codd Normal Form

Boyce-Codd normal form is a very interesting form. It has a relatively simple definition, and it is based on first-normal form, not a higher one. But it has been proven that a table (relation) in Boyce-Codd normal form is also in third-normal form.

Tables in third-normal form are not necessarily in Boyce-Codd normal form, so you can think of Boyce-Codd as 3.5-normal form. Boyce-Codd eliminates some database problems found in third-normal form designs. This is the definition:

"A relation, R, is in Boyce-Codd normal form if its key, K, implies all nonkey attributes—a, b, c, ...—and K is a superkey."

Right. That's just what you were thinking, isn't it?

No? Just in case you're not a student of this arcane area of computer science, I'll translate this into English.

Begin with this notation to describe a table (relation) R that contains fields (attributes) a, b, c, ...

```
R(a, b, c, ... )
```

This notation describes a table (relation) with a key K that implies the values of the rest of the fields (attributes):

```
R(K -> a, b, c, ... )
```

(The traditional relational literature uses all uppercase and underscores key fields. My version does the same job but avoids typesetting problems.)

The key K may itself be a concatenation of individual attributes, such as our title and publisher concatenation. For example:

```
BOOK( TITLE + PUBLISHER -> author )
```

The key is called a *superkey* if it implies all other attributes and if no portion of K less than the whole implies all other attributes. In other words, none of the components of K can be removed. Our concatenated key is a superkey because neither title nor publisher by itself will identify just one author.

In relational math, the record, or row in the table, is called a *tuple* (which rhymes with "couple"). If K is a single attribute and K implies all the fields (attributes) of the record (tuple), then K is a superkey.

If you use a unique abstract key, such as our ID values, then you can describe your relations this way:

```
R( ID -> a, b, c, ... )
```

ID is always a superkey if you define a unique ID for each record (tuple) in your table (relation). So our tables are always in Boyce-Codd normal form. Guaranteed.

I'll bet you're glad to know that. It means that you can forget about transitive dependencies and functional dependencies, including full functional dependency. You can, that is, unless you have to deal with a Traditional Database Administrator (TDA). If you have to deal with a TDA, you can launch zingers like this:

TDA: Have you removed transitive dependencies?
You: Transitive dependency? You must be stuck in third-normal form. Get with it! We're 100% in Boyce-Codd normal form.

If you're going to use an object database, you'll call our ID an object identifier, not a key. You'll see that the characteristics of an object identifier are that it must be unique within the class and it must be permanently unique. Sound familiar?

More Normal Forms

There are normal forms past Boyce-Codd, including fourth, fifth, domain-key, and projection-join normal forms. Fifth-normal form has been proven to be the end of the line. (Some observers suspect that there are additional, undiscovered avenues that will invalidate this proof and provide additional normal forms.)

Fourth-normal form designs are in Boyce-Codd normal form, but not all Boyce-Codd designs are fourth-normal form designs. Just as Boyce-Codd is better than third-normal form, fourth-normal form is better than Boyce-Codd.

Domain-key normal form is third-normal form with additional constraints. It's roughly parallel to fourth-normal form. Not all fourth-normal form designs are domain-key normal form designs. Not all domain-key normal form designs are in fourth-normal form.

Being in both domain-key normal form and fourth-normal form is better than being in just one or the other. Both imply Boyce-Codd.

Projection-join normal form is between fourth- and fifth-normal forms.

In an earlier book, I showed that my design approach yielded designs that were in both fourth-normal form and domain-key normal form. It took a whole chapter to demonstrate that, however. If you want to look it up, it's *Client-Server dBASE Programming* (Addison-Wesley, 1994). I'd suggest a trip to the library, since most of the content is about coding in dBASE IV for DOS.

In the same book I cheerfully confess that the question of whether my method actually gets to fifth-normal form is beyond my capabilities, or maybe, beyond my patience. I believe my designs are fifth-normal form, since I've never seen any of my designs show the problems that are associated with non-fifth-normal form designs.

Maybe one of you who is a real wizard with normalization could prove it, one way or another?

Redundant Data

I've just inflicted a rather heavy dose of condensed theory on you. If you didn't have a lot of fun with it, I apologize. In this section we're going to leave theory behind and get on to constructive design cheats. These are the little, practical violations of good design that can make a system really sing.

I've learned that cheating on the design by attempting to reduce the number of tables is a prescription for trouble. Don't do it.

But I've also learned that adding deliberate redundant data can be very constructive. I'll suggest two examples here. You'll find more.

Before you start adding redundant data, however, remember that you are working close to the cliff's edge. Remember these rules:

- Clearly document any redundant data.
- Clearly define the update process.
- Carefully program the recovery procedure.

Make sure that everyone involved with the data knows about the redundant data and understands that there is a possibility of inconsistency whenever there is redundancy. Storing one fact in two or more places means that the fact could be correct here and wrong there.

Database updates should be restricted to the source data. The redundant data should be strictly read-only. Edits to the source data should automatically update the redundant data.

Batch procedures should be available that re-create the redundant data from the source data. Do not assume that the online procedures for updating redundant data are adequate. (Never ignore Murphy's Law.)

With those warnings, let's begin with totals.

Totals

If you record totals in your database, you'll be storing redundant data. Actually, this isn't just a problem with totals. Any fact that is derived by the application of some formula or algorithm to the other data in your database is redundant.

On the other hand, storing totals can be very useful. You can total the individual detail items and store the total in the SALES table. That way you can see the total for a sale without accessing the detail table (which will be your largest table). Forming and answering a query such as, "What are the total sales for this customer?" is much easier.

Chances are, there are levels above the sale where additional totals can be very handy. You might total sales by product, total product sales by product categories, and so on.

If your system automatically pushes totals upward through a hierarchy, you'll have a lot of useful information available instantly. If you provide a sales total in the

PRODUCT table, for example, you can look up the product and see its sales immediately.

Program each sale to post up to PRODUCT. Don't forget returns and adjustments. Make sure that the value in PRODUCT can't be edited. Keep a batch procedure that you can run every evening that recomputes the totals from scratch, just in case.

From PRODUCT, you can continue to post changes upward into product class, storewide totals, regional totals if you have multiple stores, and so on. You can get a lot of information this way. (Information is your target output. It's what happens when you aggregate a significant amount of accurate data.)

Current Values

Remember those characteristic history tables? If prices will vary, you need a product price history table, instead of just storing the price in the PRODUCT table. You get the current price by looking into the price history table for the latest value.

You can also duplicate the current price in the PRODUCT table, so you won't need a secondary lookup to find this frequently requested item. Again, the same rules apply.

Make sure the software that updates the price history also updates the PRODUCT table's value. Ensure that the value in the PRODUCT table can't be edited. And have a batch procedure to re-create the latest prices in the PRODUCT table by reading all the history data.

Or take another approach.

Make the PRODUCT table price the source data. Let it be editable. Whenever that value is changed, post a new entry to the product price history table. The latter becomes the redundant data that is available on a read-only basis.

The batch procedure that updates the history tables will look at these tables and the PRODUCT table. It adds a record to the history table if the values are different.

It's not important that one table or the other be the source. The important point is that you decide clearly which item is source data and which item is redundant. The source data can be edited. The redundant data is read-only. Edits to the source get posted to the redundant data. Edits to the redundant data are as close to impossible as you can make them. Batch programs re-create redundant data from source data.

Summary

In this chapter I've shown you my method for designing databases. I use the same approach for relational and object databases.

Begin by identifying the classes of objects (kickable things) that are important to your system. Then identify the events (things that happen to your objects at a point in time) that are important. These are the first tables in your system.

If there are important relationships among your objects, these are described in additional tables. To avoid duplicate payments for health insurance, for example, you need to know which of your employees are related.

List the characteristics of each object, event, and relationship. These become the fields (or object data members) in each table. For the first characteristic in every table, use a unique ID value. Use integer IDs that are incremented as each record is added, and ensure that they never get deleted. Some DBMSes use random IDs that aren't dependably unique. These are unacceptable.

Then examine the characteristics for repeating (one or more, or zero or more) fields. In a relational design these require separate tables. In an object design you can make them a separate class, or keep the data as part of the parent object.

Also examine the characteristics for ones that need a history of changes. These too become separate tables in a relational design.

Keep refining your design until none of the tables has repeating characteristics and all the characteristics that need histories have associated history tables. Once that's done, your design is ready.

Next I showed that the tables in our design are automatically in Boyce-Codd normal form. In fact, they're in fourth-normal and domain-key normal forms, too. You who were new to normalization met a lot of jargon from the classic normalization approach to database design.

Finally, I suggested that you introduce some redundant data. Keeping totals, for example, simplifies many queries. Keeping the current item in the parent table eliminates a lot of looking up in history tables. This can work acceptably if you ensure that only the source data is editable. The redundant versions must be read-only, and a batch process must regularly update the redundant values from the source.

Now if only we had a tool to create data tables, we'd be able to put this knowledge to use. That, as you probably guessed, is the direction we'll be heading in Chapter 12.

Chapter 12

The All-Purpose Data-Entry Form

This chapter and the next three explain the JDB application used to edit DBF files and to edit the header from those files. By editing the header data, you can define new DBF structures. JDB uses the same editing capability for both the headers and the data. We'll cover that topic in detail in Chapter 15.

In this chapter and the next two we'll cover the ability of JDB to edit DBFs. It's elegantly simple. You choose a DBF and you get both a scroll window and a data-entry form. In Chapter 14 you'll see how those two are kept coordinated.

The data-entry form is built directly from the header data in the DBF. It's completely automatic—no programming required. You don't even need to drag objects off a tool palette and drop them on a form. The data-entry form just appears by magic, with all the fields of the DBF appropriately labeled and ready for data entry.

This chapter begins with a look at using the JDB. Then it covers some preliminaries, and finally it dives into the DEForm (Data-Entry Form) class.

In Chapter 13 we'll go into all the classes that provide objects used in building the DEForm.

Never forget that JDB's end users are ourselves, the programmers. This is not intended as an end-user tool. It's very convenient to have the data-entry form automatically created from the header of the DBF. For end-user tools, you'll want to write effective control code that ensures that only good data enters the DBF. JDB will enter anything you type. No questions asked. No help provided.

This will never compare to a nicely programmed data-entry form designed for a particular application. A "one size fits all" approach always means that no individual gets a good fit. A tool that does everything never does anything as well as a specific-purpose tool. JDB is no exception.

Let's get started.

Looking at JDB

In this section, we'll fire up the JDB system again. It's been brought up to speed when it comes to actually handling data. We'll focus on the ability to open DBFs and edit the data they contain. JDB can also create DBFs, but we'll leave that for Chapter 15.

After we look at the end-user capability, we'll look more closely at the internals of the software design.

We'll begin by running the program.

Running JDB

If you load this chapter's project file, you get to run JDB with actual database-handling capability. Here we'll focus on the overview before we narrow our focus to look at the data-entry form.

Begin by clicking the Open button, as you see in Figure 12-1.

Figure 12-1.   *Opening our first DBF*

This launches the Open File dialog. If you select any file other than a DBF or DBS (we'll cover the latter in Chapter 15), you get the same capability you saw in the FileViewer application. If you select a DBF, however, you get a whole new capability.

A word of warning: don't double-click the filename. Single-click to select a file, and then click the Open button, as you see me doing in Figure 12-2.

When you open a DBF, you get a JDBboss menu, as you see in Figure 12-3.

Double-Clicking Open Is a Problem

If you double-click a file you want to open in the Open File dialog, you'll get more than you want. The FileDialog will correctly report the file you indicated, but the dialog won't report that it handled the second click.

As a consequence, a double-click really works like a double-click on the Open File dialog, followed by an additional, unintended click on whatever happens to be hidden behind the Open File dialog box. This is often the New option of JDB's main menu, which we'll cover in Chapter 15.

This bug works identically in both Visual Cafe and Visual J++.

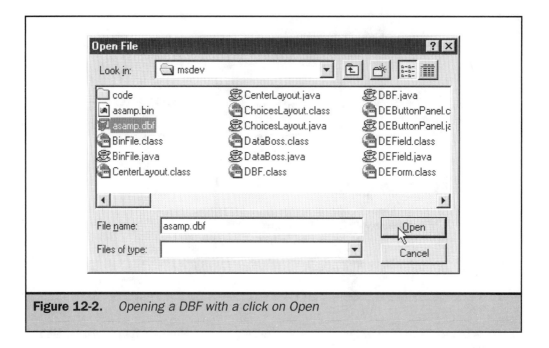

Figure 12-2. *Opening a DBF with a click on Open*

There are now two separate, cooperating control tools for the DBF's data. Our old friend the ScrollWin is still here, and a new tool, the DEForm (data-entry form) is available. If you select both Scroll and Edit on the JDBboss, and do some positioning, you'll get a setup like the one you see in Figure 12-4.

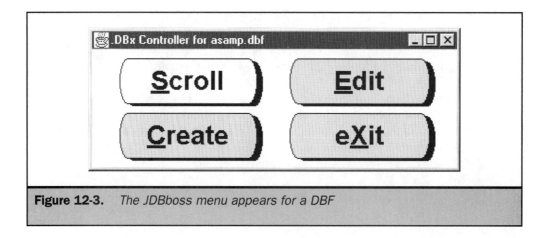

Figure 12-3. *The JDBboss menu appears for a DBF*

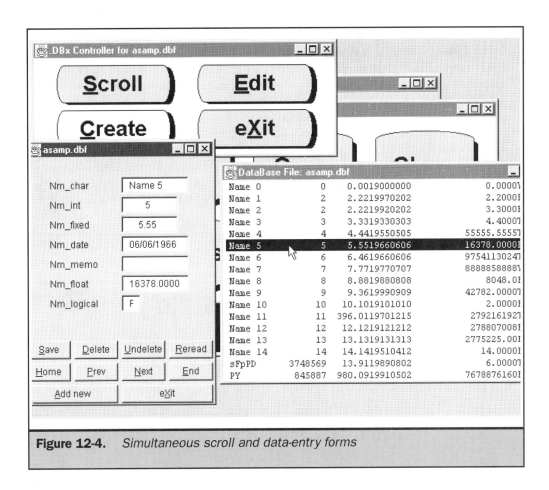

Figure 12-4.   *Simultaneous scroll and data-entry forms*

As you scroll, the data in the DEForm changes to match the selected record in the database. The DEForm also has primitive navigation capability, through its Home, Prev, Next, and End buttons. If you navigate with these buttons, you'll see the scroller reposition itself appropriately to highlight the record shown in the DEForm.

Figure 12-5 puts the spotlight on the data-entry form.

You can see, if you look carefully at Figure 12-5, that this form is resizable, like all our other tools. It's been stretched a bit over the size you saw in Figure 12-4. For your own project, make a note to improve this by expanding the font size as the user provides more screen real estate. That improvement would make this capability a valuable one.

As you edit the data, you change the contents of your TextFields, not the values in the database. When you click Save, you store the values you have entered. If you don't like what you've entered, just click Reread to restore the text fields from values in the database.

Grid and Record Views

Many commercial database products feature a choice between a spreadsheet-like grid view and an individual record view of your data. The individual record view is where you drag and drop all your favorite controls (check boxes for boolean data, a pop-up calendar for dates, and so on).

I've found that the best result is to have a scroller for navigation launched simultaneously with the individual record view. I keep my scrollers small. For example, I'll show name and postal code instead of name, address, city, state, and postal code.

Then keep the record view open, so that the user can see all the details about one selected record. It's very effective.

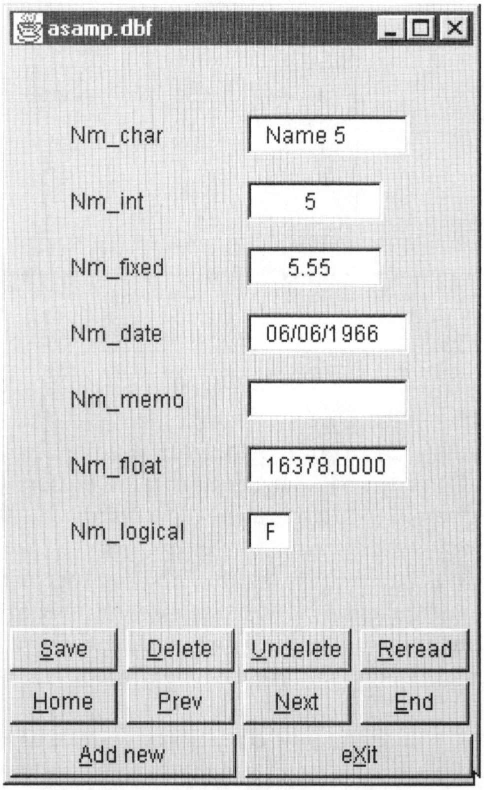

Figure 12-5.   *The data-entry form, expanded*

When you navigate, your data is automatically saved. JDB doesn't pop up a "Data changed, save it?" dialog. That sort of dialog helps beginning users, but gets in the way of experienced users. JDB is a programmers' tool, not a beginning-user program.

Don't Show This Dialog

An optimal solution might have been to provide a dialog box that pops up asking, "Data changed, save it?" with an improvement. The improvement would be the check box that reads, "Don't show this dialog in the future." That way, if you consider yourself the sort of expert who doesn't want that hand-holding dialog, you just turn it off.

Of course, that sort of optimal solution is only optimal if you assess no charge for RAM usage. JDB wouldn't be improved by the addition of a long load time.

The navigation buttons provide the simple choices that are typical of data-bound controls. I've found that the names given here (Home, Prev, Next, and End) are immediately meaningful to all classes of users. This is not true of the faddish arrows found on many controls.

With that introduction, let's look at the data-entry form's design.

The DEForm's Design

The DEForm is actually two panels:

```
 - - - - - - - - - - - - - - - - - - - - - -
|  DEForm                                    |
|   - - - - - - - - - - - - - - - - - - - -  |
|  | DEPanel                              |  |
|  |                                      |  |
|  |     (built from a Vector of DEFields)|  |
|  |                                      |  |
|  |     (uses DELayout LayoutManager)    |  |
|  |                                      |  |
|   - - - - - - - - - - - - - - - - - - - -  |
|   - - - - - - - - - - - - - - - - - - - -  |
|  |                                      |  |
|  | DEButtonPanel                        |  |
|  |                                      |  |
|   - - - - - - - - - - - - - - - - - - - -  |
|                                            |
 - - - - - - - - - - - - - - - - - - - - - -
```

The upper panel holds the data-entry fields, and the lower holds the buttons. This structure lets you extend DEPanel when you want to create a data-entry form designed for a particular application. This means that if you have a dialog-building tool, like Visual Cafe or Borland's J Builder (as I write this, Microsoft's competing Java builder is supposed to be ready in six months), you can put together any number of check boxes, radio buttons, sliders, and whatever other components you like.

The button panel reports clicks. It's up to the classes that use the DEButtonPanel to provide the services specified.

DEFields Include Labels

The DEPanel is built on a Vector of DEField objects. The DEField extends the MRTextField. Like the MRString class, MRTextField is an extended version of the TextField. Unlike MRString, MRTextField actually extends the TextField class. (As you may recall, since the String class is final, the MRString extends Object.)

The MRTextField includes a data member called "label." This is a default label that can be placed to the left of the TextField. These are written by creating MRLabel objects.

MRLabels and MRTextFields have a unique capability: they work together. If an MRLabel and an MRTextField have the same top and height values, the MRLabel's text aligns correctly with the text in the MRTextField.

Aligned Labels and TextFields

When something's sufficiently stupid, I call it a bug. Having to align a Label to different y locations than a TextField is an example where the stupidity rises to meet this standard.

Why did I have to write this myself? Isn't having the label and text misaligned just plain dumb? Why should anyone have to align these any other way?

DELayout Manages the DEPanel Layout

The layout of the DEPanel is managed by a DELayout object that implements the LayoutManager interface. As implemented, it just manages the spacing between the MRTextFields and the associated MRLabel objects.

If this book were about user interface programming, I'd be sure to include a good LayoutManager that scaled the fonts to fit the available space. This would make one data-entry form work nicely at 640x480 and then, with a simple tug on a corner, work just as well at 1280x1024. If you write one, I'd be glad to beta test it.

Before we get to the DEForm, I'll give you a word of warning and then digress. As you'll see, the digression will explain a lot that you'll meet as you look at the code in this chapter and the next two chapters.

A JDB Warning and a Blinker

Let's start with some miscellaneous notes, beginning with a warning about version incompatibilities.

This Is a New JDB.java

The JDB included here is not the one we last visited in Chapter 10. It's extended in many ways. We'll get into the specifics in Chapter 15. If you have the disk, be sure you copy the code for this chapter into your working directory. If you don't have the disk, you'll need to enter the code in this chapter and the next three to get the new JDB running.

The Blinker

I wanted to create a database-specific TextField variant. It would only let you enter numbers into numeric fields, dates into date fields, and so on. In addition, I wanted to take over the keyboard. As it stands now, a TextField in Windows gives you Windows-specific key_troke handling for keys like TAB and SHIFT-TAB.

Actually, I like most of the Windows' keystroke handling. By rewriting it in my own Java data-entry field, I'd have consistent keystroke handling across all platforms. So I set out to whip up a custom text field.

How do you write your own TextField from scratch? To begin, you need an outline. I dropped the resolution on my biggest monitor down to 640x480 and studied the way Windows drew the TextField. Then I copied the drawing using paint( ) in a Panel. It worked beautifully.

Next I needed a text-mode cursor (insertion point). I couldn't find one in the Java API, so I built my own.

There's no law that specifies any particular size for a Panel. I found that a Panel one pixel wide and a dozen pixels tall made a nice insertion point. Getting it to blink like a cursor was the next step.

Here I'll show a comment and the run( ) method from my Blinker( ) class. The rest of the class was trivial constructors and get/set methods for the two times you see here. This is the guts of the class:

```
/*

    Blinker turns a component visible and then sleeps
    for show_time milliseconds. It wakes up, hides the
    component and then sleeps for hide_time milliseconds.

    Then it wakes up and starts over.
```

```
        Blinking a cursor-sized panel (but doing nothing
        else) causes Norton Utilities CPU Utilization to
        report 0% (it's free) on a P133.
    */

    public void run() {

        while ( true ) {
            synchronized ( blinking_component ) {

                if ( blinking_component.isVisible() )
                    blinking_component.hide();
                else
                    blinking_component.show();
            }

            try {

                sleep( blinking_component.isVisible() ?
                    show_time : hide_time );
            }
            catch ( InterruptedException ie ) {

                blinking_component.show();
                yield();
            }
        }
    }
```

This worked out very nicely for an insert and overstrike mode. In insert mode the normal text cursor runs at about 500 milliseconds on and 500 milliseconds off. I went to 600 on and 400 off, just to show that my cursor was not the one Windows controls. Then I cut those values in half for a highly nervous overstrike mode.

You create a new Blinker by handing the object a reference to a component and your blink times. Almost magically, it starts to blink. Have fun with it.

This works well in both Visual Cafe and Visual J++. Unfortunately, the next step is to take over the keyboard, responding appropriately to keystrokes and command keys such as the TAB and arrow keys. Visual Cafe can't handle it. The keyboard events are not reliably reported.

Unreliable Keyboard Events

With Symantec's Visual Cafe, your code gets some keystrokes. It doesn't get others. You press a key and wait and see what happens. This is useless for data entry.

Symantec claims that the problems are in Sun Microsystems' API code. I checked that claim using the Sun JDKs (1.0 and 1.1). Symantec is correct. The Sun code is the source of the problems.

Microsoft has rewritten much of the Sun code, so the masked data-entry classes I wrote work correctly in Visual J++. (Using multiple vendors' Java tools helps you separate your own bugs from the vendors' bugs.)

Note to Symantec: I couldn't care less that you didn't write the bugs! I want them fixed.

Note to readers: I didn't want to write this section. I told Symantec that I wouldn't write it if they got the bugs fixed or provided some sort of work-around. I also said that I'd have to report the truth. Sad, isn't it?

The rest of the code for masked-field data entry is still on my machine, of course. I'm going to rework the event-handling in the JDK 1.1 paradigm and see if it works correctly. In the meantime, if you need this capability, you'll have to hunt up a Java Bean.

The DEForm Class

With the miscellaneous items covered, we can look at the data-entry form. We'll start by considering the use of the DEForm by a higher-level program, and then we'll dive into the code. While the use is trivial, the code isn't, sorry to say. On the other hand, while there's quite a bit of code, most of it is completely straightforward. Let's begin with the simple part.

Using the DEForm Class

Assume that you've created a DBF object and checked to see that it is writable. This is all you need to create a ready-to-use DEForm:

```
// dbf is a writeable DBF object

DEForm foo = ( dbf, "Window Title Goes Here" );
```

From there on, foo.show( ) is all that's needed to turn the form over to your user. Whenever people start raving about their favorite RAD tool ("You just drag and drop controls. It does all the programming for you!"), I ask why all that dragging and dropping is necessary. We just open the DBF and pass it to a DEForm. It does all the dragging and dropping for us.

This assumes that the default form is satisfactory, of course. For most applications you'll want to create a class that extends DEPanel, showing a nice face to the user. The default uses field names as labels and leaves all data verifying up to the user.

You'll see in Chapter 14 how the DataBoss is used to coordinate a ScrollWin along with the DEForm. (That one-line constructor call expands all the way to four lines. It's not too tough.)

TOUR

The next section will constantly err on the side of brevity. For many details, you'll want to refer to the full listing. I'll just highlight the main points and unencrypt the more mysterious bits of code, so you'd probably be well-advised to peruse it all.

Understanding the DEForm Class

In this section we'll look at the data, and then the public and private member functions, following the organization of the source file.

The DEForm's Data Members

The two public booleans, end_app and refuse_close, are the same here as they are in the menus. Normally, clicking the close button simply hides the window. The DEForm can be used as a simple, stand-alone application, however. For this you set end_app true. If you want the exit button ignored, set refuse_close true.

The protected boolean, appending, is set true when you are appending a new record. The protected boolean, changed, is set true when data has been changed. This is used to force storing the changed data prior to navigating from one record to another.

These four objects are noteworthy:

```
protected Editable data_store;
protected DataBoss databoss;
protected Vector defaults;
protected Label del_label;
```

The data_store is the DBF or other Editable object. Defining the data_store as an Editable object lets you use the DEForm for many things besides DBF objects. Any database accessed through JDBC will qualify if you wrap it in a class that implements Editable. (Editable, as you'll see, requires just six simple methods.)

The DataBoss object is optional. It's used when you want to coordinate a DEForm with a ScrollWin, which is the topic of Chapter 14. The Vector, defaults, contains default values to use for the fields (when appending, for example). The Label, del_label, displays the message "Deleted" at the top of the form when the record has been marked deleted.

A Vector, fields, shares a reference to the set of DEField objects with the DEPanel. Another Vector, values, is the one that comes from the Editable as you navigate and is sent to the Editable when you update values.

The int, record_number, records the number of the currently visible record.

A pair of String constants holds the label values for the del_label:

```
final static String DELETED = "Deleted";
final static String NOT_DELETED = " ";
```

Navigation constants let the DEForm communicate with the databoss:

```
final static int go_home = -4;
final static int go_prev = -3;
final static int go_next = -2;
final static int go_end  = -1;
```

Remember that clicks on the navigation buttons in the DEForm trigger movement of the highlight in any associated ScrollWin.

Finally, I've done something I don't like to do. I've established two keystroke constants. These are ones that Sun's API should provide. If you've never worked in UNIX, the value for the ENTER key will surprise you:

```
static final int ENTER = 10;
static final int TAB = 9;
```

(If you've always worked in UNIX, you wouldn't know that DOS-based systems use 13 for ENTER and 10 for linefeed.)

The DEForm's Public Methods

The public methods begin with a mainline, commented out. It tests all the possible forms of the DEField. Don't use it until you decide to bring back multiple types of DEField. Only one of these forms exists, at present.

Several constructors allow you to create a DEForm with as little as a DBF object. This is the main one:

```
DEForm( DBF dbf, String title ) {

    this( dbf.getDEFs(), title );

    setDataStore( dbf );
    record_number = -1;
      setRecord( 0 );
    appending = false;
}
```

It gets a Vector of DEFields from the DBF itself. This is used to call another constructor that does additional work. It begins by calling the Frame constructor, passing the title. After saving the reference to the fields Vector, it creates the default values Vector from the initial values of each field:

```
// record default values
    defaults = new Vector();
    for ( int i = 0 ; i < defv.size() ; i++ ) {
        DEField def =
            ( DEField ) fields.elementAt( i );
        defaults.addElement( def.getString() );
    }
```

It continues to set up sizes, properly size the Frame, and so on. Its next major job is to create the DEPanel and the DEButtonPanel that are its two main components:

```
DEPanel pFields = new DEPanel( defv );
DEButtonPanel pButtons = new DEButtonPanel();
```

It finishes by using the default BorderLayout to correctly position everything:

```
add( "North", del_label );
add( "Center", pFields );
add( "South", pButtons );
```

There are a number of setXxxx( ) methods, most of which are trivial. The interesting one is setRecord( ):

```
public void setRecord( int recno ) {

    if ( recno == record_number )
            return;

      if ( data_store == null )
            return;

    record_number = recno;
    values = data_store.getValues( recno );

    set_del();

    for ( int i = 0 ; i < values.size() ; i++ ) {

            DEField def;
            String s;

        def = (DEField) fields.elementAt(i);
        s = (String) values.elementAt(i);
        def.setString( s );
    }
}
```

The setRecord( ) method's job is to write the current record's values on the screen. This is done by picking the appropriate String value out of each String in the values Vector and assigning it to the corresponding DEField, in the fields Vector.

Note the two tests at the top. If the record number passed is the one already set, setRecord( ) does nothing. Similarly, if there is no data_store, it does nothing.

The good_height( ) and good_width( ) methods are both oversized collections of ALD. Refer to the full listing if you like.

The save_click( ) method is key. It is called when the Save button is clicked, of course. It is also called by the navigation routines if any data has been changed since the last save. It starts with a bit of ALD—handling the entry of the first record into an empty file:

```
public void save_click() {

        if ( record_number == -1 ) {
```

```
                    appending = true;
                    changed = true;
                    record_number = 0;
            }
```

Then it continues, checking the boolean, changed, which is true when we know about a change, such as via a Delete click, and calling new_values( ), which compares the current state of the TextFields to the values Vector's contents. It returns true if any are new. The reset_values( ) routine updates the values Vector from the TextFields:

```
        if ( changed || new_values() ) {
            reset_values();
```

Then there are two more jobs: updating the data_store and alerting the databoss to the changes. The databoss alerts the ScrollWin to the necessity for a refresh after any changes:

```
            if ( data_store != null )
                data_store.setValues(
                        record_number, values );
            changed = false;

            if ( databoss != null ) {

                if ( appending ) {
                    databoss.data_added();
                }
                else
                    databoss.data_changed();
            }
        }
        appending = false;
    }
```

A set_defaults( ) method uses the initial values to create default values. See the full listing for the ALD.

The paint and resize( ) methods are partners. Paint checks to see if the Frame has been resized. If it has, the resize( ) method uses good_height( ) and good_width( ) to enforce minimum sizes, taking appropriate care not to call itself recursively. Again, see the full listing for the ALD.

The handleEvent( ) method's important job is to pass button clicks to the private button_click( ) method.

The DEForm's Private Methods

The buttons each get an individual method corresponding to their titles. This is the method the Add button calls:

```
private void add_click() {

    if ( data_store == null )
        return;

    save_click();

    set_defaults();
      reset_values();
      record_number = data_store.getLast() + 1;

      changed = true;
      appending = true;
      save_click();
}
```

Bear in mind that an append operation implicitly navigates to just past the end of the existing data, so a save_click( ) is called, as it is before any navigation. The rest of the routine is self-explanatory.

The button_click( ) method is a call director. This is how it gets started:

```
private boolean button_click( Event e ) {

    Button b = (Button) e.target;
    String s = b.getLabel();

    if ( s.equals("&Save") )
        save_click();

    else if ( s.equals("&Delete") )
        delete_click();
```

The delete_click( ) and its companion, undelete_click( ), are straightforward. The end_click( ) will serve to represent all four navigation clicks:

```
private void end_click() {

    if ( data_store != null ) {

        save_click();

        if ( record_number < data_store.getLast() ) {

            setRecord( data_store.getLast() );

            if ( databoss != null )
                databoss.navigate( go_end,
                    record_number );
        }
    }
}
```

It first does a save_click( ). Then it navigates as directed, taking appropriate care not to navigate past the end of the file. Finally, it notifies the databoss, if there is one, about its operation.

The new_field( ) method is not currently used. With the DEField built on TextFields, Windows handles interfield navigation.

The new_values( ) method is the one that save_click( ) depends on to check for any changes made to the TextField's values. It's straightforward except for one nasty ALD. When you initialize an empty file, the values Vector is null at first.

```
private boolean new_values() {

    // true if any DEField doesn't match data values

    if ( values == null )
        return false; // see book!

    for ( int i = 0 ; i <= last_field ; i++ ) {

        DEField def =
            (DEField) fields.elementAt( i );

        String fld = def.getString().toString().trim();
```

```
                    String val = ( (String) values.elementAt(i) ).
                        trim();

                    if ( !fld.equals(val) )
                        return true;
            }
            return false;
        }
```

The reread_click( ) has a tricky problem. Remember that the setRecord( ) routine is programmed to do nothing when it is called to set the already set record? The reread_click( ) uses setRecord( ) by telling a little lie about where the data_store is positioned:

```
    private void reread_click() {

        // setRecord is a NOP if called for
        // current record number
        record_number++;
        setRecord( record_number - 1 );
    }
```

The reset_values( ) method updates the values Vector from the fields Vector. It has to create the values Vector when you use it on an empty file. With that one note, you'll find the code straightforward.

The other private methods are included in the full listing.

The Full DEForm.java Listing

Listing 12-1 is the full DEForm.java source file.

Listing 12-1:
DEForm.java

```
// DEForm.java -- DEPanel plus DEButtonPanel
// Copyright 1997, Martin L. Rinehart


// this code is completely documented in:
// _Java Database Development_, Martin Rinehart,
// Osborne/McGraw-Hill, 1997

/*
    This Frame holds at least one DEPanel plus a
```

```
    DEButtonPanel. It's adequate on its own as a simple
    database application. In most cases, pairing it with
    a database ScrollWin makes a more powerful, useful
    combination.
*/

import java.awt.*;
import java.util.Vector;

class DEForm extends Frame {

// -------------------- data members --------------------

// public data members:

    public boolean end_app;

     public boolean refuse_close;

// protected data members:

    protected boolean appending;

    protected boolean changed;
    protected int char_width;

    protected Editable data_store;
    protected DataBoss databoss;
    protected Vector defaults;
    protected Label del_label;

    protected int field_num;
    protected Vector fields;

    protected int last_field;

    protected int old_height;
    protected int old_width;

    protected boolean paint_working;

    protected int record_number;
```

```
        protected Vector values;

// static data members

    // there are no public static data members
    // there are no private static data members
    // final static data members:

    final static String DELETED = "Deleted";
    final static String NOT_DELETED = " ";

    final static int go_home = -4;
    final static int go_prev = -3;
    final static int go_next = -2;
    final static int go_end  = -1;

    static final int ENTER = 10;
    static final int TAB = 9;

// ------------------- public methods --------------------

/* Add a second "/" at the front of this line
    // to use this test mainline

    public static void main( String[] args ) {

        Vector defv = new Vector();
            // DEField Vector

        defv.addElement( new DEField
            ("First name: ", "Xx", 12) );
        defv.addElement( new DEField(
            "Last name: ", 20) );
        defv.addElement( new DEField(
            "Address: ", 30) );
        defv.addElement( new DEField(
            "", 30) );
        defv.addElement( new DEField(
            "City, State: ", 30) );
        defv.addElement( new DEField(
            "Phone: ", "1 (999) 999-9999") );
```

```
                DEForm def = new DEForm( defv,
                    "Comment main() out" );
            def.end_app = true;

                def.show();
        }
// */

// constructor:

    DEForm( DBF dbf ) {

        this( dbf, dbf.getFileName() );
    }

    DEForm( DBF dbf, String title ) {

        this( dbf.getDEFs(), title );

        setDataStore( dbf );
        record_number = -1;
          setRecord( 0 );
        appending = false;
    }
    DEForm( Vector defv ) {
        this( defv, "Data Entry Form" );
        appending = false;
    }

    DEForm( Vector defv, String title ) {
        super( title );
        fields = defv;

// record default values
        defaults = new Vector();
        for ( int i = 0 ; i < defv.size() ; i++ ) {
            DEField def =
                ( DEField ) fields.elementAt( i );
            defaults.addElement( def.getString() );
        }
```

```
        set_char_width();
        resize( good_width(), good_height() );

        setBackground( Color.lightGray );

        int size = fields.size();
        field_num = 0;
        last_field = size - 1;

        DEPanel pFields = new DEPanel( defv );
        DEButtonPanel pButtons = new DEButtonPanel();

        del_label = new Label( " " );

        add( "North", del_label );
        add( "Center", pFields );
        add( "South", pButtons );
    }

// there are no data access getXxx() methods
// there are no data access isXxx() methods

// data access setXxx() methods:

    public void setDataBoss( DataBoss d ) {

        databoss = d;
    }

    public void setDataStore( Editable e ) {

        data_store = e;
    }

     public void setEndApp( boolean b ) {

         end_app = b;
     }

    public void setRefuseClose( boolean b ) {

         refuse_close = b;
```

```
        }

    public void setRecord( int recno ) {

        if ( recno == record_number )
            return;

        if ( data_store == null )
            return;

        record_number = recno;
        values = data_store.getValues( recno );

        set_del();

        for ( int i = 0 ; i < values.size() ; i++ ) {

            DEField def;
            String s;

            def = (DEField) fields.elementAt(i);
            s = (String) values.elementAt(i);
            def.setString( s );
        }
    }

// public, class-specific methods:

    public int good_height() {
        return ( fields.size() + 2 ) * 26 + 104;
    }

    public int good_width() {

        int wLabels, wFields, wTotal;
        wLabels = wFields = 0;

        for ( int i = 0 ; i < fields.size() ; i++ ) {
            DEField def =
                (DEField) fields.elementAt(i);
            int lsize, fsize;
```

```
        lsize = def.getLabel().length();
        fsize = def.getString().length();

        wLabels = lsize > wLabels ? lsize : wLabels;
        wFields = fsize > wFields ? fsize : wFields;
    }

    wTotal = ( wLabels + wFields ) * char_width + 100;
    if ( wTotal < 250 ) wTotal = 250;
    return wTotal;
}

public void save_click() {

    if ( record_number == -1 ) {

        appending = true;
        changed = true;
        record_number = 0;
    }

    if ( changed || new_values() ) {
        reset_values();

        if ( data_store != null )
            data_store.setValues(
                record_number, values );
        changed = false;

        if ( databoss != null ) {

            if ( appending ) {
                databoss.data_added();
            }
            else
                databoss.data_changed();
        }
    }
    appending = false;
}

public void set_defaults() {
```

```
        DEField def;
        MRString s;

        for ( int i = 0 ; i < fields.size() ; i++ ) {

            def = ( DEField ) fields.elementAt( i );
            s = ( MRString ) defaults.elementAt( i );

            def.setString( new MRString(s) );
        }
        changed = true;
    }

// public, non-event overriding methods:

    public String paramString() {

        return "DEForm";
    }

    public void paint( Graphics g ) {

        if ( paint_working ) return;
        paint_working = true;

        if ( (size().width != old_width) ||
            (size().height != old_height) ) {

            resize();
        }
        paint_working = false;
    }

    private void resize() {

        int wid, hgt;
        boolean change;

        change = false;

        wid = size().width;
        if ( wid < good_width() ) {
```

```
            wid = good_width();
            change = true;
        }

        hgt = size().height;
        if ( hgt < good_height() ) {

            hgt = good_height();
            change = true;
        }

        if ( change )
            resize( wid, hgt );
    }

    public void show() {
        super.show();
        ( (DEField) fields.elementAt(0) ).
            requestFocus();
    }

// public, event-handling method:

    public boolean handleEvent( Event e ) {

        if ( e.target instanceof Button )
            return button_click( e );

        else if ( (e.id == Event.KEY_PRESS) &&
            (e.key == TAB) ) {
            if ( handle_tab(e) ) return true;
        }

        else if ( (e.id == Event.KEY_PRESS) &&
            (e.key == ENTER) ) {
            handle_enter( e );
            return true;
        }

        else if ( (e.id == Event.KEY_ACTION) &&
                (( e.key == Event.UP   ) ||
                 ( e.key == Event.DOWN ))
```

```
                    ) {
                handle_updown( e );
                return true;
            }

            else if ( e.id == Event.WINDOW_DESTROY ) {
                exit_click();
            }

            return super.handleEvent( e );
        }

// ----------------- private methods -------------------

// private methods:

    private void add_click() {

            if ( data_store == null )
                return;

        save_click();

        set_defaults();
          reset_values();
          record_number = data_store.getLast() + 1;

          changed = true;
          appending = true;
          save_click();
        }

    private boolean button_click( Event e ) {

        Button b = (Button) e.target;
        String s = b.getLabel();

        if ( s.equals("&Save") )
            save_click();

        else if ( s.equals("&Delete") )
            delete_click();
```

```
    else if ( s.equals("&Undelete") )
        undelete_click();

    else if ( s.equals("&Reread") )
        reread_click();

    else if ( s.equals("&Home") )
        home_click();

    else if ( s.equals("&Prev") )
        prev_click();

    else if ( s.equals("&Next") )
        next_click();

    else if ( s.equals("&End") )
        end_click();

    else if ( s.equals("&Add new") )
        add_click();

    else
        exit_click();

    return true;
}

private void delete_click() {

    if ( data_store != null )
        data_store.setDeleted( record_number, true );

    changed = true;
    set_del();

    if ( databoss != null )
        databoss.data_changed();
}

private void end_click() {

    if ( data_store != null ) {
```

```
                save_click();

                if ( record_number < data_store.getLast() ) {

                    setRecord( data_store.getLast() );

                    if ( databoss != null )
                        databoss.navigate( go_end,
                            record_number );
                }
            }
        }

    private void exit_click() {

        if ( databoss != null )
            databoss.edit_click();

          save_click();

        if ( refuse_close )
            return;

          hide();

        if ( end_app )
            System.exit( 0 );
    }

    private void handle_enter( Event e ) {

        if ( ! (e.target instanceof DEField) )
            return;

        field_num = ( (DEField) e.target ).whoami;
        new_field( field_num + 1 );
    }

    private boolean handle_tab( Event e ) {

        if ( ! (e.target instanceof DEField) )
            return false;
```

```
        field_num = ( (DEField) e.target ).whoami;

        if ( (e.modifiers & Event.SHIFT_MASK) == 0 )
            new_field( field_num + 1 );
        else
            new_field( field_num - 1 );

        return true;
    }

    private void handle_updown( Event e ) {

        if ( ! (e.target instanceof DEField) )
            return;

        field_num = ( (DEField) e.target ).whoami;
        new_field( field_num +
            (e.key == Event.DOWN ? 1 : -1) );
    }

    private void home_click() {

        if ( data_store != null ) {

            save_click();

            if ( data_store.getLast() > -1 ) {

                setRecord( 0 );

                if ( databoss != null )
                    databoss.navigate( go_home,
                        record_number );
            }
        }
    }

    private void new_field( int field_num ) {

        // wrap start to end
        if ( field_num < 0 )
            field_num = last_field;
```

```
         // wrap from end to start
    else if ( field_num > last_field )
       field_num = 0;

    ( (DEField)
      (fields.elementAt( field_num )) ).requestFocus();
}

private boolean new_values() {

    // true if any DEField doesn't match data values

    if ( values == null )
        return false; // see book!

    for ( int i = 0 ; i <= last_field ; i++ ) {

       DEField def =
            (DEField) fields.elementAt( i );

          String fld = def.getString().toString().trim();
          String val = ( (String) values.elementAt(i) ).
             trim();

          if ( !fld.equals(val) )
             return true;
    }
       return false;
 }

private void next_click() {

    if ( data_store != null ) {

       save_click();

       if ( record_number < data_store.getLast() ) {

          setRecord( record_number + 1 );

          if ( databoss != null )
```

```
                        databoss.navigate( go_next,
                              record_number );
                }

        }
}

private void prev_click() {

      if ( data_store != null ) {

            save_click();

            if ( record_number > 0 ) {

                  setRecord( record_number - 1 );

                  if ( databoss != null )
                        databoss.navigate( go_prev,
                              record_number );
            }
      }
}

private void reread_click() {

    // setRecord is a NOP if called for
    // current record number
    record_number++;
    setRecord( record_number - 1 );
}

private void reset_values() {

      // refill values Vector from screen fields

    if ( values == null ) {

            values = new Vector();
            for ( int i = 0 ; i <= last_field ; i++ )
                  values.addElement( null );
      }
```

```
        for ( int i = 0 ; i <= last_field ; i++ ) {

            DEField def =
                (DEField) fields.elementAt( i );

            values.setElementAt
                ( def.getString().toString(), i );
        }
    }

    private void set_char_width() {

        setFont( new Font("Helvetica", Font.PLAIN, 12) );

        FontMetrics fm = getFontMetrics( getFont() );
        char_width = ( fm.stringWidth( "aAbBcC. 90") )/10;

    }

    private void set_del() {

        if ( data_store != null )
            del_label.setText(
                data_store.isDeleted(record_number) ?
                DELETED : NOT_DELETED );
        else
            del_label.setText(
                del_label.getText().equals(DELETED) ?
                    NOT_DELETED : DELETED );
    }

    private void undelete_click() {

        if ( data_store != null )
            data_store.setDeleted( record_number, false );

        changed = true;
        set_del();

        if ( databoss != null )
            databoss.data_changed();
    }
```

```
    } // end of DEForm class

  // there are no private classes in DEForm.java:

  // end of DEForm.java
```

Summary

We saw that JDB has become a tool for editing data in existing DBFs. You just click Open, select a DBF, and you get a scrolling window into that DBF and a data-entry form that lets you edit the values in each field in the record. It couldn't be more convenient.

There is absolutely no control over what you enter, so it couldn't be more dangerous, either. You can type text into numeric fields and the name of your favorite vegetable into a date field. This is a programmer's tool, not an end-user tool.

I briefly discussed a project I attempted and abandoned—the data-entry text field. I showed you code for a Blinker object that can blink a text insertion-point cursor or anything else. As you go through the code you'll see lots of vestiges of this project. It's sort of like the ancient ruins in Rome—the city doesn't use them, but they're there as a reminder.

Then we went into the DEForm class. It shows a DEPanel object above a DEButtonPanel array of buttons. The DEForm can provide a simple, complete application for editing data in a table. Or it can be used in a more sophisticated application where it is combined with a scroll window that lets the user navigate in the table, while the DEForm continuously shows the full details of the record highlighted in the scroll window.

In Chapter 13, we'll go into all the classes that are used in building the DEForm. There are a lot of them, but none is too complex.

Chapter 13

Components of the DEForm

In Chapter 12 we looked at the JDB application. It creates automatic data-entry forms by reading the header of any DBF. The magic began with the DEForm class that we examined. In this chapter we'll cover the supporting classes.

We'll start with the DEButtonPanel that builds the bottom portion of the DEForm. It's very simple and shows a slick use of the supplied LayoutManagers to make a hard job simple.

Then we'll go on to take a bottom-up look at the top part of the form, beginning with the MRLabel class. This is just a Label with the bugs left out.

The MRLabel works with the DELayout LayoutManager. DELayout is a good example of a case in which a custom LayoutManager is the best choice.

Then we'll look at the DEPanel itself. It uses MRLabels down the left side and nicely aligns MRTextFields down the right.

Last, we'll look at the essentially null DEField, which extends the useful MRTextField, which is itself an extension of the TextField.

We'll get started with buttons.

The DEButtonPanel Class

Take a quick look at the constructor here and then exit. Did I mention that there really isn't anything to this class except a constructor?

Now we'll start working from the bottom up, literally. The DEForm is a combination of a DEPanel over a DEButtonPanel. Take a look at Figure 13-1 to refresh your memory.

How would you lay out those buttons? Does that look like a lot of ALD in a resize( ) method? That's what it looked like to me at first. Then I got smart.

Laying Out the DEButtonPanel

I saw a very simple, very effective trick here. There are two sizes of buttons: small and large. This suggested stacking two button grids, which is exactly what I did.

The DEButtonPanel is a stack of three items in the default BorderLayout. On top is a blank label, which adds a bit of space. In the middle is a Panel holding the small buttons in a GridLayout. On the bottom is another Panel holding the large buttons in another GridLayout.

When you look at the full listing, read the constructor closely. There's nothing else that's nontrivial in this class.

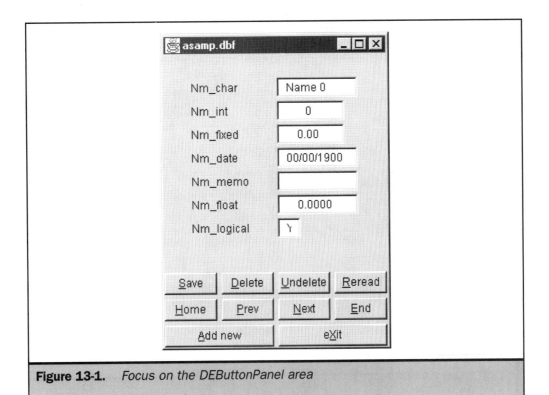

Figure 13-1. *Focus on the DEButtonPanel area*

The Full DEButtonPanel Listing

Listing 13-1 is the full DEButtonPanel.java source file.

Listing 13-1:
DEButtonPanel
.java

```
// DEButtonPanel.java -- buttons for DEForm
// Copyright 1997, Martin L. Rinehart

// this code is completely documented in:
// _Java Database Development_, Martin Rinehart,
// Osborne/McGraw-Hill, 1997

/*
    Array of buttons (Save, [Un]Delete, Prev, Next, etc.)
```

```
        for simple DB control via DEForm.
*/

import java.awt.*;

class DEButtonPanel extends Panel {

// -------------------- data members --------------------

// there are no data members

// -------------------- public methods --------------------

// constructor:

    DEButtonPanel() {

        setLayout( new BorderLayout(5, 5) );

        add( "North", new Label(" ") );

        Panel p = new Panel();
        p.setLayout( new GridLayout(2, 4, 5, 5) );
        p.add( new Button("&Save") );
        p.add( new Button("&Delete") );
        p.add( new Button("&Undelete") );
        p.add( new Button("&Reread") );
        p.add( new Button("&Home") );
        p.add( new Button("&Prev") );
        p.add( new Button("&Next") );
        p.add( new Button("&End") );

        add( "Center", p );

        Panel p2 = new Panel();
        p2.setLayout( new GridLayout(1, 2, 5, 5) );
        p2.add( new Button("&Add new") );
        p2.add( new Button("e&Xit") );

        add( "South", p2 );
    }

// there are no data access methods
```

```
// there are no public, class-specific methods

// public, non-event overriding method:

    public String paramString() {

        return bounds().toString();
    }

// there are no public, event-handling methods:

// ------------------ private methods ------------------
// there are no private methods

} // end of DEButtonPanel class

// there are no private classes in DEButtonPanel.java

// end of DEButtonPanel.java
```

The MRLabel Class

TOUR

Don't skip this one. You may decide that MRLabels will be your choice whenever you might have used a regular label.

If you've positioned a Label to the left of a TextField, I'm sure you've been annoyed to discover that the text of the label doesn't line up with the text in the TextField. In fact, maybe the word "annoyed" doesn't quite do justice to your feeling.

If you explored further, you probably discovered that a Label with its X coordinate set to zero doesn't actually start the text at zero. It indents a bit. That kind of thing really gets to me. It's as if the genius who wrote this assumed that I was too dumb to put my text where it really should be.

I got fed up. Now I'll never use another Label again. Consider the MRLabel as your chill pill for the regular Label's aggravation. It's also dead simple.

Understanding the MRLabel Class

The MRLabel is a Panel. A call to drawString( ) in the Panel's paint( ) method does the work of actually writing the label text.

I'll remind you of a couple of details here, and then let you read the code. The first detail is that a Panel's paint( ) method doesn't start the painting. Before calling your paint( ), Java clears the Panel to the background color. In the case of writing your own labels, this is exactly what you want.

The second detail to bear in mind is that the Y coordinate in a call to drawString( ) isn't the normal (top-left) corner coordinate. It's the location of the text's baseline (the bottom of most letters, excepting ones like "p" or "g" that have descenders).

The X coordinate that you provide for an MRLabel is the actual location where the MRLabel will start writing. The Y coordinate you supply is a top-left corner coordinate. The MRLabel figures out where to position the baseline of the text so that it will match the baseline of the text in a matching TextField.

The whole business of setting an appropriate X and Y location for a drawString( ) call is just ALD. Skip this one, if your labels will be left-justified. The code will show you how to use MRLabel.CENTER and MRLabel.RIGHT alignment.

The Full MRLabel.java Listing

Listing 13-2 is the full MRLabel.java source file.

Listing 13-2:
MRLabel.java

```
// MRLabel.java -- Label work-alike class
// Copyright 1997, Martin L. Rinehart

// this code is completely documented in:
// _Java Database Development_, Martin Rinehart,
// Osborne/McGraw-Hill, 1997

/*
    like Label, but:
        a) text really starts at x=0
        b) drawn foreground color on background color

    this is a Panel!
*/

import java.awt.*;

class MRLabel extends Panel {

// -------------------- data members --------------------

// there are no public data members
```

```
// protected data members

    protected String text;
    protected int alignment;

// static data members
    // there are no public static data members
    // there are no private static data members

    // final static data members

    final static int LEFT = 0;
    final static int CENTER = 1;
    final static int RIGHT = 2;

// -------------------- public methods --------------------

// constructors

    MRLabel() {

        this( "" );
    }

    MRLabel( String s ) {

        this( s, 0 );
    }

    MRLabel( String s, int align ) {

        text = s;
        alignment = align;
    }

// data access getXxx() methods

    public int getAlignment() {

        return alignment;
    }
```

```java
    public String getText() {

        return text;
    }

// there are no data access isXxx() methods

// data access setXxx() methods

    public void setAlignment( int align ) {

        // up to programmer to select LEFT, CENTER or RIGHT
        alignment = align;
    }

    public void setText( String s ) {

        text = s;
    }

// there are no public, class-specific methods

// public, non-event overriding methods

    public Dimension minimumSize() {

        FontMetrics fm = get_fm();

        return new Dimension( fm.stringWidth(text),
            fm.getHeight() );
    }

    public void paint( Graphics g ) {

        // background is automatically cleared to its color

        // Font and FontMetrics
        Font f = getFont() != null ? getFont() :
            new Font( "Helvetica", Font.BOLD, 12 );
        FontMetrics fm = getFontMetrics( f );
        g.setFont( f );
```

```
        // compute x
        int x = 0;

        if ( alignment == LEFT ) {
            // use defaults
        }
        else if ( alignment == CENTER ) {

            x = ( size().width -
                fm.stringWidth( text) ) / 2;
            if ( x < 0 ) x = 0;

        }
        else { // align == RIGHT (or any error)

            x = size().width - fm.stringWidth( text );
            if ( x < 0 ) x = 0;
        }

        // compute baseline

        int free_pixels = size().height - fm.getHeight();
        int bottom_space = free_pixels / 2;
        int baseline = size().height - bottom_space -
            fm.getDescent();

        g.setColor( getForeground() );
        g.drawString( text, x, baseline );
    }

public String paramString() {

    return text +
        ( alignment == LEFT ? " left " :
          alignment == CENTER ? " center " :
            " right " ) +
        getBackground() + " on " + getForeground();

}

public Dimension preferredSize() {
```

```
            Dimension d = minimumSize();
            d.width += 4;
            d.height += 4;

            return d;
    }

// there are no public, event-handling methods

// ------------------ private methods ------------------

    private FontMetrics get_fm() {

        Font f = getFont();

        return getFontMetrics( f != null ?
            f : new Font("Helvetica", Font.BOLD, 12) );
    }
} // end of MRLabel class

// there are no private classes in MRLabel.java

// end of MRLabel.java
```

The DELayout LayoutManager

TOUR

Read the "Using the DELayout" section. Once you know what the DELayout does, then you decide whether you want to read the "Understanding" section and the listing that follows.

Sometimes you can use the existing LayoutManagers. Our button layout was an excellent example. Sometimes you can't. If you have alternating labels and text fields, a simple GridLayout will use the left half of a Panel for the labels and the right half for the fields. That's not how you'd lay this out by hand.

Using the DELayout

Working manually with a dialog editor, like Visual Cafe's, you'd put the labels down the left side and then align the fields so they're just to the right of the longest label. This is what DELayout does.

It assumes that the Components you've added to your Panel are alternating MRLabels and TextFields. Our DEFields are an extension of MRTextFields, which are themselves extensions of TextFields, so this requirement is met by our DEPanel.

You could mix labels with something other than TextFields, too. For example, you could use null labels next to CheckBoxes. At least I think you could. I'll leave this tricky stuff up to you.

You could also use plain Labels, not MRLabels. If you don't want your labels correctly aligned with your TextFields, this is the way to go.

After you add( ) your Components to your Panel, this line is all you need:

```
setLayout( new DELayout(5, 5) );
```

The arguments are the minimum horizontal and vertical spacings between components, in pixels. If you omit them, they default to zero.

You can assign your DELayout before you add( ) components, too. It doesn't matter.

What the DELayout won't do that it should do, is adjust your font size up or down as the Panel is stretched. When you get this worked out, please send me a copy.

Understanding the DELayout

The data members are all ints or Dimensions, and they're all measured in pixels. The spacers, hspace and vspace, are the ones you pass as the optional constructor arguments. They're initialized to zeros (explicitly initialized, which is redundant, of course, as Java does this anyway).

Understanding the DELayout Public Methods

The constructor with parameters simply stores your values into hspace and vspace.

As with all the LayoutManagers I write, addLayoutComponent( ) and removeLayoutComponent( ) are empty. (I omitted the "Ugh!" comment in this one.)

As usual, the heavy lifting is done in the layoutContainer( ) method. You'll see that all the code uses names like "long_label_width" and "minimum_field_size," but the programming only looks at Components in a parent Container. You could use this reasonably to lay out a Frame. You could use it unreasonably with all sorts of Components.

The code starts by assigning various key numbers:

```
psize = parent.size();

long_label_width = longest_label_width( parent );
pref_fld_size = preferred_field_size( parent );
min_fld_size = minimum_field_size( parent );

int nflds = parent.countComponents() / 2;
```

Then it assigns some abbreviations to key values for the horizontal computation:

```
// compute horizontal layout
    int lbl_wid = long_label_width;
    int fld_wid = min_fld_size.width;
    int tot_wid = psize.width;
```

The actual horizontal spacing is the free space, divided by three (left margin, space between labels and fields, and right margin):

```
int hspace =
    ( tot_wid - lbl_wid - fld_wid ) / 3;
```

That's the simple job. The problem starts if there isn't enough space. This is the scrunch code:

```
if ( hspace < 1 ) {

    hspace = 1;
    int work_wid = tot_wid - 3;

    double ratio = ( (double) work_wid ) /
        ( lbl_wid + fld_wid );

    fld_wid = ( int ) ( ratio * fld_wid );
    lbl_wid = ( int ) ( ratio * lbl_wid );
}
```

The vertical computation is simpler:

```
// compute vertical layout
    int fld_hgt = min_fld_size.height;
    int tot_hgt = psize.height;

    int vspace = ( tot_hgt - (nflds * fld_hgt) ) /
        ( nflds + 1 );

    if ( vspace < 0 ) {
```

```
                    vspace = 0;
                    fld_hgt = tot_hgt / nflds;
        }
```

At this point we're ready to do the layout. This is done by cycling down the rows, reshaping the label and the field. The label is reshaped to fit. The field's size is not enlarged past its preferred size. This is the code:

```
// layout components
    int top = vspace;

    for ( int i = 0 ; i < nflds ; i++ ) {

        Component c;

    // Label on left
        c = parent.getComponent( i*2 );
        c.reshape( hspace, top, lbl_wid, fld_hgt );

    // TextField on right;
        c = parent.getComponent( (i*2)+1 );

        int wid = fld_wid;
        if ( wid > c.preferredSize().width )
            wid = c.preferredSize().width;
        c.reshape( hspace + lbl_wid + hspace, top,
            wid, fld_hgt );

        top += vspace + fld_hgt;
    }
```

The minimumLayoutSize( ) and preferredLayoutSize( ) methods are, as usual, more complex than you would hope. Both delegate all their hard work to private methods, however.

Understanding the DELayout Private Methods

The get_fm( ) method returns the FontMetrics object that the rest of the code uses for computing sizes. It's completely straightforward.

The longest_label_width( ) method's name explains its goal. It uses the FontMetrics object returned by get_fm( ) to compute the length of each label's text. This is the loop that does the computation:

```
for ( int i = 0 ; i < ncomps ; i += 2 ) {

    Component c = parent.getComponent(i);

    if ( c instanceof MRLabel ) {

        String s = ( (MRLabel) c ).getText();
        int l = fm.stringWidth( s );

        if ( l > longest_width )
            longest_width = l;
    }
}
```

Note that this has the bad habit of ignoring anything that's not an MRLabel. This works for DEPanels, but you might want to improve it to let your DELayout be more versatile.

The minimum_field_size( ) and preferred_field_size( ) methods are nearly identical. They both return the largest value of any of the odd-numbered Components. (The labels are 0, 2,…. and the labeled Components are 1, 3,….) This is the loop that finds the minimum field size:

```
for ( int i = 0 ; i < (ncomps / 2) ; i++ ) {

    Component c = parent.getComponent(i*2 + 1);

    Dimension m = c.minimumSize();

    if ( m.width > d.width )
        d.width = m.width;

    if ( m.height > d.height )
        d.height = m.height;
}
```

The Full DELayout.java Listing

Listing 13-3 is the full DELayout.java source file.

Listing 13-3:
DELayout.java

```
// DELayout.java -- Data Entry panel layout
// Copyright 1997, Martin L. Rinehart
```

```
// this code is completely documented in:
// _Java Database Development_, Martin Rinehart,
// Osborne/McGraw-Hill, 1997

/*
    Lays out a panel that has alternating MRLabel and
    TextField (or MRTextField, etc.) components.

    Allows left-side space for longest label. Aligns
    left-side edge of TextFields.

    Does not stretch (leaves empty space) past
    preferredSize().

    Scrunches, if needed, vertically and horizontally.
*/

import java.awt.*;

class DELayout implements LayoutManager {

// --------------------- data members ---------------------

// there are no public data members

// protected data members

    protected int hspace = 0;
        // space between components, in pixels

    protected int long_label_width;

    protected Dimension min_fld_size;

    protected Dimension pref_fld_size;
    protected Dimension psize;
        // parent container size

    protected int vspace = 0;
        // space between components, in pixels

// there are no static data members
```

```
// -------------------- public methods --------------------

// constructors

    DELayout() {
    }

    DELayout( int hspace, int vspace ) {

        this.hspace = hspace;
        this.vspace = vspace;
    }

// there are no data access methods

// public, class-specific methods

    public void addLayoutComponent( String name,
        Component comp ) {

      /* This gets called by Container.add() in
         this form:

          add( "Wherever", Component ) ;

         But it's not called by Container.add() in
         this form:

          add( Component ) ;
      */
    }

    public void layoutContainer( Container parent ) {

        psize = parent.size();

        long_label_width = longest_label_width( parent );
        pref_fld_size = preferred_field_size( parent );
        min_fld_size = minimum_field_size( parent );

        int nflds = parent.countComponents() / 2;
```

```
// compute horizontal layout
    int lbl_wid = long_label_width;
    int fld_wid = min_fld_size.width;
    int tot_wid = psize.width;

    int hspace =
        ( tot_wid - lbl_wid - fld_wid ) / 3;

    if ( hspace < 1 ) {

        hspace = 1;
        int work_wid = tot_wid - 3;

        double ratio = ( (double) work_wid ) /
            ( lbl_wid + fld_wid );

        fld_wid = ( int ) ( ratio * fld_wid );
        lbl_wid = ( int ) ( ratio * lbl_wid );
    }

// compute vertical layout
    int fld_hgt = min_fld_size.height;
    int tot_hgt = psize.height;

    int vspace = ( tot_hgt - (nflds * fld_hgt) ) /
        ( nflds + 1 );

    if ( vspace < 0 ) {

        vspace = 0;
        fld_hgt = tot_hgt / nflds;
    }

// layout components
    int top = vspace;

    for ( int i = 0 ; i < nflds ; i++ ) {

        Component c;

    // Label on left
        c = parent.getComponent( i*2 );
```

```
            c.reshape( hspace, top, lbl_wid, fld_hgt );

        // TextField on right
            c = parent.getComponent( (i*2)+1 );

            int wid = fld_wid;
            if ( wid > c.preferredSize().width )
                wid = c.preferredSize().width;
            c.reshape( hspace + lbl_wid + hspace, top,
                wid, fld_hgt );

            top += vspace + fld_hgt;
        }
    }

    public Dimension minimumLayoutSize(
        Container parent ) {

        int label_width = longest_label_width( parent );
        Dimension msize = minimum_field_size( parent );

        int wid = label_width + hspace + msize.width;

        return new Dimension( wid, msize.height );
    }

    public Dimension preferredLayoutSize(
        Container parent ) {

        int label_width = longest_label_width( parent );
        Dimension psize = preferred_field_size( parent );

        int wid = label_width + hspace + psize.width;

        return new Dimension( wid, psize.height );
    }

    public void removeLayoutComponent( Component comp ) {

        // since we never add() a component . . .
    }
```

```
// public, non-event overriding methods
    public String paramString() {

        return "hspace = " + hspace +
            " vspace = " + vspace;
    }

// there are no public, event-handling methods

// ------------------ private methods ------------------

    private FontMetrics get_fm( Container c ) {

        Font f = c.getFont();

        return c.getFontMetrics( f != null ?
            c.getFont() :
            new Font("Helvetica", Font.BOLD, 12) );
    }

    private int longest_label_width( Container parent ) {

        int ncomps = parent.countComponents();

        if ( ncomps < 2 )
            return 0;

        FontMetrics fm = get_fm( parent );

        int longest_width = 0;

        for ( int i = 0 ; i < ncomps ; i += 2 ) {

            Component c = parent.getComponent(i);

            if ( c instanceof MRLabel ) {

                String s = ( (MRLabel) c ).getText();
                int l = fm.stringWidth( s );

                if ( l > longest_width )
                    longest_width = l;
```

```
              }
          }
          return longest_width;
      }

      private Dimension minimum_field_size(
          Container parent ) {

          Dimension d = new Dimension( 0, 0 );
          int ncomps = parent.countComponents();

          if ( ncomps < 2 )
              return d;

          for ( int i = 0 ; i < (ncomps / 2) ; i++ ) {

              Component c = parent.getComponent(i*2 + 1);

              Dimension m = c.minimumSize();

              if ( m.width > d.width )
                  d.width = m.width;

              if ( m.height > d.height )
                  d.height = m.height;
          }
          return d;
      }

      private Dimension preferred_field_size(
          Container parent ) {

          Dimension d = new Dimension( 0, 0 );
          int ncomps = parent.countComponents();

          if ( ncomps < 2 )
              return d;

          for ( int i = 0 ; i < (ncomps / 2) ; i++ ) {

              Component c = parent.getComponent(i);
```

```
            Dimension p = c.preferredSize();

            if ( p.width > d.width )
                d.width = p.width;

            if ( p.height > d.height )
                d.height = p.height;
        }
        return d;
    }

} // end of DELayout class

// there are no private classes in DELayout.java

/*

    DELayout lays out the DEPanel. The components of a
    DEPanel are alternating MRLabels and MRTextFields.

    DELayout puts the label 0 to the left of field 1;
    label 2 to the left of field 3, etc.

    Note: given equal "y" locations, the text in an
    MRLabel aligns with the text in an MRTextField. This
    simplifies DELayout's job.

*/

// end of DELayout.java
```

The DEPanel Class

The DEPanel is one of two things. In our all-purpose tool, it's a way to edit the data in absolutely any DBF file. For application-specific use, it's a class to extend so you can substitute your own well-tailored, single-purpose data-entry screens.

As the top part of our DEForm, it lets us get an instant data-entry form, built by examining the header of the DBF file. It lets you open and edit any DBF instantly. It also lets you, for one evil example, put letters into numeric fields, trashing any application that depends on the DBF.

Treat it like you treat Microsoft's Regedit utility: a handy way to read the data and a dangerous way to edit it. (Power isn't good or evil. The way you use power is good or evil.)

Using the DEPanel Class

I didn't write the DEPanel for reuse. I wrote it as an integral part of the DEForm. This doesn't mean that all this machinery is just for the DEForm. DEForms will work with any class that extends DEPanel, which means you can use these classes for application-specific forms.

For application-specific data-entry forms that use the rest of this machinery, create a class that extends this one. Then ignore this class. You'll have a Panel that you can use any way you like.

Understanding the DEPanel Class

The data members include a Vector, fields, that holds DEFields. For now, a DEField is a TextField plus a text String that can be used to the left of the field as a label.

Ignore the other data members. They are anachronisms dating back to the failed masked-entry field days. If the Sun code had been up to the job, we'd have automatically generated masks that would, for example, restrict numeric fields to numeric values.

Those masks would have considerably reduced the evil potential of the DEPanel, without putting any constraint on its more helpful uses. (That implies that some powers are good and other powers are evil, doesn't it? Hmmm. Maybe it's not just the way you use power.) You'll see occasional references to the masks as you look at this code. Ignore them.

Understanding the Public DEPanel Methods

The constructor does some routine chores and then add( )s alternating label and field Components for the DELayout to handle. This is the constructor code:

```
setLayout( new DELayout(5, 5) );

for ( int i = 0 ; i <= last_field ; i++ ) {

    MRTextField tf = ( MRTextField )
        fields.elementAt( i );

    MRLabel l = new MRLabel( tf.getLabel(),
        MRLabel.LEFT );

    add( l );
    add( tf );
    tf.register( this, i );
}
```

The MRTextField's register( ) method lets the field directly communicate with the DEPanel.

The rest of the public methods are either trivial (paramString( ), for one) or vestiges of the masked-entry days that handle keystrokes. Ignore them.

Understanding the Private DEPanel Methods

The private methods also include some that are trivial or old news (get_fm( ), for instance) and others that are masked-entry anachronisms (handle_enter( ), for one). There are only two that are not in these categories.

The first is the min_fld_size( ) method. This is the working code:

```
int longest = 0, tallest = 0;

for ( int i = 0 ; i < fields.size() ; i++ ) {

    Component c =
        ( Component ) fields.elementAt( i );
    Dimension d = c.minimumSize();

    if ( d.width > longest )
        longest = d.width;
    if ( d.height > tallest )
        tallest = d.height;
}
```

Note that this code doesn't depend on the contents of the fields Vector being MRTextField (or derivative) objects. The constructor, however, does make that demand.

The other significant private method is the min_lab_width( ). This is the working part of that method's code:

```
int longest = 0;
FontMetrics fm = get_fm();

for ( int i = 0 ; i < fields.size() ; i++ ) {

    String lab = ( (MRTextField)
        fields.elementAt(i) ).getLabel();
    int wid = fm.stringWidth( lab );

    if ( wid > longest )
        longest = wid ;
}
```

It depends on having an MRTextField, which is necessary since that is a combined TextField and label text.

The Full DEPanel.java Listing

Listing 13-4 is the full DEPanel.java source file.

Listing 13-4:
DEPanel.java

```java
// DEPanel.java -- Data Entry Panel
// Copyright 1997, Martin L. Rinehart

// this code is completely documented in:
// _Java Database Development_, Martin Rinehart,
// Osborne/McGraw-Hill, 1997

/*
     see notes below
*/

import java.awt.*;
import java.util.Vector;

class DEPanel extends Panel {

// ------------------- data members -------------------
// there are no public data members

// protected data members

    protected int field_num;
    protected Vector fields; // DEFields

    protected int last_field;

// static data members
     // there are no public static data members
     // there are no private static data members

     // final static data members

    static final int ENTER = 10;
    static final int TAB = 9;
```

```
// ------------------- public methods -------------------

// constructors

    DEPanel( Vector defv ) {

        fields = defv;
        field_num = 0;
        last_field = fields.size() - 1;

        if ( last_field == -1 )
            return;

        setLayout( new DELayout(5, 5) );

        for ( int i = 0 ; i <= last_field ; i++ ) {

            MRTextField tf = ( MRTextField )
                fields.elementAt( i );

            MRLabel l = new MRLabel( tf.getLabel(),
                MRLabel.LEFT );

            add( l );
            add( tf );
            tf.register( this, i );
        }
    }

// there are no data access methods

// public, class-specific methods

    public void gotMouse( int who ) {

        field_num = who;
    }

// public, non-event overriding methods

    public Dimension minimumSize() {
```

```
        Dimension d = min_fld_size();

        return new Dimension(
            min_lab_width() + d.width,
            d.height * fields.size() );
    }

public String paramString() {

    return ( last_field + 1 ) + " fields, " +
        field_num + " is active -- bounds " +
        bounds().x + "," + bounds().y + "," +
        bounds().width + "," + bounds().height;
    }

public Dimension preferredSize() {

    Dimension d = minimumSize();
    d.width += 30;
    d.height += 10 * ( fields.size() + 1 );

    return d;
    }

// public, event-handling methods

public boolean keyDown( Event e, int k ) {

    if ( (( k == TAB ) && shift_down( e )) ||
        (k == Event.UP) ) {

        handle_shift_tab();
        return true;
    }
    else if ( (k == TAB) ||
        (k == Event.DOWN) ) {

        handle_tab();
        return true;
    }
    else if ( k == ENTER ) {

        if ( field_num == last_field )
```

```
                    return false; // let parent handle it

            handle_tab();
            return true;
        }

        return false;
    }

    public boolean keyUp ( Event e, int k ) {

        if ( (k == TAB) ||
             (k == Event.UP) ||
             (k == Event.DOWN) ||
             (k == ENTER) )
            return true;

        return false;
    }

// ----------------- private methods -------------------

    private FontMetrics get_fm() {

        Font f = getFont();

        if ( f == null )
            f = new Font( "Helvetica", Font.BOLD, 12 );

        return getFontMetrics( f );
    }

    private void handle_enter() {

        new_field( field_num + 1 );
    }

    private void handle_shift_tab() {

        new_field( field_num - 1 );
    }
```

```java
private void handle_tab() {

    new_field( field_num + 1 );
}

private Dimension min_fld_size() {

    int longest = 0, tallest = 0;

    for ( int i = 0 ; i < fields.size() ; i++ ) {

        Component c =
            ( Component ) fields.elementAt( i );
        Dimension d = c.minimumSize();

        if ( d.width > longest )
            longest = d.width;
        if ( d.height > tallest )
            tallest = d.height;
    }
    return new Dimension( longest, tallest );
}

private int min_lab_width() {

    int longest = 0;
    FontMetrics fm = get_fm();

    for ( int i = 0 ; i < fields.size() ; i++ ) {

        String lab = ( (MRTextField)
            fields.elementAt(i) ).getLabel();
        int wid = fm.stringWidth( lab );

        if ( wid > longest )
            longest = wid ;
    }
    return longest;
}

private void new_field( int field_num ) {
```

```
            // wrap start to end
            if ( field_num < 0 )
                field_num = last_field;

            // wrap from end to start
            else if ( field_num > last_field )
                field_num = 0;

              this.field_num = field_num;

            ( (MRTextField) (fields.elementAt( field_num )) ).
                    requestFocus();
        }

        private boolean shift_down( Event e ) {

            return ( e.modifiers & Event.SHIFT_MASK ) ==
                    Event.SHIFT_MASK;
        }

    } // end of DEPanel class

    // there are no private classes in DEPanel.java

    /*
        A DEPanel takes a Vector of DEFields and arranges an
        instant data entry panel. It puts the labels down the
        left and the fields on the right. The labels are
        left-justified near the left margin. The fields are
        left-justified near the longest label.

        The labels are MRLabel objects (an extender of
        Panel, not Label, objects).
    */

    // end of DEPanel.java
```

The DEField and MRTextField Classes

An MRTextField combines a TextField with text to create a default label on a
data-entry form. The DEField was to have been an MRTextField with support for

masked-entry work. I'm covering them together in this section, since the DEField doesn't really exist in this JDB. Its sole function is to discard the mask in the constructor call.

In case you think I'm exaggerating, let's start with Listing 13-5, the full source file:

Listing 13-5:
DEField.java

```
// DEField.java -- Data Entry Field
// location for masked data entry checking

class DEField extends MRTextField {

    DEField( String label, String mask, int wid,
        String init ) {

        super( label, init, wid );
    }

}

// end of DEField.java
```

The MRTextField class isn't quite as trivial, but it comes close. As I've said, the job of the MRTextField is simply to combine the TextField with a String that can be used as a default label for data-entry forms.

The registration process lets the parent panel give each MRTextField identification that the field could use to identify itself to the parent. That is, it explains the panel and whoami variables. This is necessary for masked-entry work. It's an anachronism here.

With that explained, you'll see that the rest of the code here is trivial.

Listing 13-6 is the full MRTextField.java listing.

Listing 13-6:
MRTextField.java

```
// MRTextField.java -- enhanced TextField
// Copyright 1997, Martin L. Rinehart

// this code is completely documented in:
// _Java Database Development_, Martin Rinehart,
// Osborne/McGraw-Hill, 1997

/*
    Combination of a TextField and label text
*/

import java.awt.*;
```

```
class MRTextField extends TextField {

// -------------------- data members --------------------

// there are no public data members

// protected data members:

    protected Panel panel;

    protected String label = "";

    protected MRString string;

    protected int whoami;
    protected int width_field;
    protected int width_string;

// there are no static data members

// -------------------- public methods --------------------

// constructor:

    MRTextField( String lbl, String init, int wid ) {

        super( init, wid );

        label = lbl;
        width_field = wid;
        setString( init );
    }

// data access getXxx() methods:

    public String getLabel() {

        return label;
    }

    public MRString getString() {
```

```
        string = new MRString( super.getText() );
        return string;
    }

// there are no data access isXxx() methods

// data access setXxx() methods:

    public void setLabel( String l ) {

        label = l;
    }

    public void setString( String s ) {

        string = new MRString( s );

        super.setText( s );
    }

    public void setString( MRString s ) {

        string = s;
        super.setText( s.toString() );
    }

// public, class-specific method:

    public void register( DEPanel dep, int fld_no ) {

        panel = dep;
        whoami = fld_no;
    }

// public, non-event overriding method:

    public String paramString() {

        return "MRTextField";
    }

// public, event-handling method:
```

```
        public boolean handleEvent( Event e ) {

            return super.handleEvent( e );
        }

// ------------------ private methods ------------------
// there are no private methods

} // end of MRTextField class

// there are no private classes in MRTextField.java


// end of MRTextField.java
```

Summary

In this chapter we looked at the classes that the DEForm uses.

We started with the DEButtonPanel that holds the buttons at the bottom of the DEForm. It's built with two Panels and a null Label in the default BorderLayout. The component Panels lay out the buttons in GridLayouts. It sounds complicated, but the code itself is short and easy.

Then we looked at the MRLabel class, which uses a Panel and a drawString( ) method in the Panel's paint( ) method. It's a better Label, since the Label doesn't align its text's baseline with the text in a TextField, and since the Label doesn't really respect the X coordinate you supply.

Next we looked at the DELayout LayoutManager. While the buttons could be laid out nicely with the standard LayoutManagers, the labels and fields needed a custom treatment.

With these lower-level pieces explained, we went on to look at the DEPanel class. The DEPanel extends Panel. It takes a Vector of DEFields and add( )s them for handling by the DELayout.

Last, we looked at the DEField and the MRTextField. The DEField is a holdover from the masked-entry field project. Right now it's null. At some point in the future it could hold sophisticated data edit logic. Right now it just covers the MRTextField, which extends TextField, primarily by adding a String for use as a default label used to make an automatic data-entry form.

In Chapter 14 we'll go on to see how the DataBoss lets you combine a ScrollWin with a DEForm for a powerful database view.

Chapter 14

Combining the ScrollWin with the DEForm

In Chapters 12 and 13 you saw how the DEForm puts together a data-entry form from a DBF. In this chapter we'll see how the DEForm is combined with the simultaneous ScrollWin for a powerful database view.

The DEForm doesn't just handle DBFs. It handles anything that is Editable. We'll start with a look at the Editable interface. You'll see that there are lots of things that could be made Editable with very little trouble.

Next we'll look at the DataBoss. It is the coordinator that has the intelligence to keep the right record on view in the DEForm as the user scrolls in the ScrollWin, the intelligence to display the latest data in the ScrollWin as the user edits the data in the DEForm, and more.

The JDB application controls the DBF views with a JDBboss menu. This is a simple application of the MenuPanel and RRectPromptPainter that have become our friends.

Last, we'll look at the versions of DBF and ScrollWin that were created to support this new functionality. While we look at them, I'll discuss the trade-offs between expanding existing classes and creating new, extending classes.

The Editable Interface

Before diving into the DataBoss class, let's look at the Editable interface. The DEForm only requires that the object it edits implement Editable. Our DBF already does this. Many other objects could implement Editable, too.

For example, you could use the Editable and Scrollable interfaces to provide a simple cover for even the most complex JDBC databases. Then these routines could be used for local database development that will be switched to server-based data at a later date.

The Editable Methods

There are six methods needed to make an object Editable. They are

- getLast( )
- getName( )
- getValues( )
- isDeleted( )
- setDeleted( )
- setValues( )

The getLast( ) and getName( ) methods are used the same way they are in the Scrollable interface. Anything that implements Scrollable has these routines.

The isDeleted( ) and setDeleted( ) methods return or set a boolean. They are called with a record number between zero and getLast( ). If the underlying data's delete operation is permanent (after a delete, the record or object just disappears), deleted methods would be coded this way:

```
public boolean isDeleted() { return false; }

public void setDeleted( boolean is_del ) {

    if ( is_del )
        // do a deletion
    else
        // this is an error
}
```

The heart of the interface is the Vector returned or set by getValues( ) and setValues( ). Both the Editable object and the object communicating with it must have a common understanding of the contents of that Vector. But since it's a Vector, this interface politely stays out of the way of any application-specific understanding.

The getValues( ) method also requires an integer record number (if you prefer, you could say "object number") between zero and getLast( ). The setValues( ) method takes an integer from zero through getLast( ) plus 1. If getLast( ) returns 100, setting values for record 101 is an append operation.

Note that it's not necessary for the data store to actually support an append operation if the application doesn't use this special setValues( ) case.

The Full Editable.java Listing

Listing 14-1 is the full Editable.java source file.

Listing 14-1:
Editable.java

```
// Editable.java -- editable data store
// Copyright 1997, Martin L. Rinehart


// this code is completely documented in:
// _Java Database Development_, Martin Rinehart,
// Osborne/McGraw-Hill, 1997


/*
A data store is editable if it can send an editor a Vector
of Strings, each String containing one field's contents,
and it can receive the Vector, (presumably after the editor
makes changes) to update the record.

The records are zero through getLast(). The getValues()
method must get a recno from zero through getLast(). The
setValues() method must get a recno from zero through
```

```
    getLast() + 1. A value of getLast() + 1 indicates an append
    operation.

    Records may be marked deleted. The isDeleted() method
    returns true if this is the case and the setDeleted()
    method (re)sets the deleted status.

    */

    import java.util.Vector;

    interface Editable {

    // Editable has six public methods:

        // what is the number of the last record?
        public int getLast();

         // what is the name of the Editable thing?
         public String getName();

        // return a Vector of Strings, each with a field
        public Vector getValues( int recno );

        // true if the record is flagged as Deleted
        public boolean isDeleted( int recno );

        // set the Deleted flag
        public void setDeleted( int recno, boolean del_status );

        // receive an updated Vector of field Strings
        public void setValues( int recno, Vector values );
```

The DataBoss Class

TOUR

Read the description up to the start of the "Understanding" section. Then decide whether you need to know more.

There's no "Using" section. You'll see how this object is used (it's simple) in Chapter 15, when we cover the JDB mainline.

I first combined a database scroller with an editable record view a decade ago. We were using multiple windows in DOS-based, text-mode applications. The combination worked then and it works today.

The very first time I decided to do this, I had procedural scroller code and procedural data-edit code. Each was written individually for each data table that needed a scroller/editor combination.

When I recoded this using object-oriented programming, I attempted a scroller object and a data-entry object. These objects sent the necessary messages to each other, but the resulting code was very difficult to debug and maintain.

That sort of difficulty usually signals an underlying design flaw. I studied my work and concluded that I was short by one object: a boss.

When the user is manipulating the scroll window, it tells the DEForm what record is currently highlighted. The DEForm responds by showing that record. When the user is manipulating the DEForm, it tells the ScrollWin to adjust its highlight or to refresh its data. Sometimes one is in charge; sometimes the other is in charge.

I was afraid that they'd start arguing. So I created a new object, the DataBoss. Both the scroller and the data-entry form report their activities to the DataBoss. It gives orders to the other object, as needed.

This design has proven sound. The code hasn't been difficult to debug. Changes in one object don't uncover bugs in another object. You'll see that the code is straightforward.

Understanding the DataBoss

Before we begin, let me warn you that a small amount of this code will make a lot more sense after you read Chapter 15. I'll try to steer you around these parts, such as the .DBS file extension, when we get to them.

We'll look at the data first, followed by the public and the private methods.

Understanding the DataBoss' Data

The first data item is the JDB, which is the DataBoss' boss.

```
protected JDB boss;
```

The DataBoss handles most events on its own, but sometimes, such as when the DataBoss' menu is closed, it has to inform the big guy.

The next three data members are objects:

```
protected DBF dbf;
protected DEForm def;

protected JDBboss menu;
```

The JDBboss, like JDBoptions or JDBmenus, is the menu that lets the user open and close data-entry and scroll windows (Scroll, Edit, New, and eXit). We'll look at it in the next section.

The next two data items are the record numbers showing in the data-entry form and the scroll window, respectively:

```
protected int rec_in_def;
protected int rec_in_sw;
```

The next boolean, setting_scroller, is a recursion preventer. It's set true when the scroller is being set in response to navigation triggered by the entry form. (Otherwise, the scroller navigation would order a change in the entry form, which would order a change in the scroller, and so on.)

These two booleans tell the DataBoss whether the respective windows are visible or hidden:

```
protected boolean showing_editor;
protected boolean showing_scroller;
```

The final protected member is the scroll window object:

```
protected ScrollWin sw;
```

Last, there are final static values for the navigation:

```
final static int go_home = -4;
final static int go_prev = -3;
final static int go_next = -2;
final static int go_end  = -1;
```

Understanding the DataBoss' Public Methods

After opening a DBF, the JDB calls the DataBoss, handing it references to itself and the DBF. The constructor starts by storing these values:

```
boss = dad;
dbf = d;
```

After getting the String, file_name, from the DBF, the constructor builds the DataBoss menu (Scroll, Edit, New, and eXit):

```
String file_name = dbf.getName();

menu = new JDBboss( boss, this );
menu.setTitle( ".DBx Controller for " +
    file_name );
menu.show();
```

Next it creates the scroll window and data-entry form. After creating them, it tells them who's boss:

```
sw = new ScrollWin( dbf, "DataBase File: " +
    file_name );

def = new DEForm( dbf, file_name );

sw.setDataBoss( this );
def.setDataBoss( this );
```

Finally, it makes explicit the initializations that Java would do anyway:

```
rec_in_def = 0;
rec_in_sw = 0;

showing_editor = false;
showing_scroller = false;
```

The setRecord( ) method is called by the scroll window whenever it gets a navigation command. It tells the data-entry form to save its data, then set the new record if it's not already set. There are two mysteries that I'll explain here.

First, the scroller isn't terribly bright. If the user clicks on the highlighted row, it will busily redisplay, just as if it had some other row highlighted. That's why it could be calling this routine needlessly.

Second, clicking the Save button on the data-entry form (or calling def.save_click( ), as this method does) will tell the DataBoss that it has changed the data. The DataBoss will order the scroller to update its display. Without the recursion stop, calling save_click( ) would call this routine, which would click the Save button, which...you get the idea.

This is the code:

```
public void setRecord( int recno ) {

    if ( setting_scroller )
        return;

    rec_in_sw = recno;

    if ( showing_editor ) {

        if ( rec_in_def != recno ) {

            def.save_click();
            def.setRecord( recno );
            rec_in_def = recno;
        }
    }
}
```

When you click the Create button, mysterious stuff happens. In Chapter 15, I'll explain the mysteries. If you've read Chapter 15, the create_click( ) method is trivial. If you haven't, it's a mystery. Ignore it for now.

Appending data in the data-entry form would confuse the scroller, which depends on knowing how many records there are in the database. The data_added( ) method tells the scroller to get smart, without getting recursive:

```
public void data_added() {

    setting_scroller = true;
    sw.resetLast();
    setting_scroller = false;
}
```

Similarly, changing the data requires that the scroller refresh its display, without being recursive:

```
public void data_changed() {

    setting_scroller = true;
    sw.repaint();
    setting_scroller = false;
}
```

Clicking the Edit button either shows or hides the data-entry form. The only nontrivial part is that a hidden data-entry form may be on a record other than the one highlighted in the scroller, which requires an update to the data-entry form before it is displayed. See the full listing for the code.

Clicking eXit in the JDBboss menu is the same as clicking the window-closing button. Both trigger a shut_down( ) call, which is all the exit_click( ) method does.

The data-entry form has a simple navigation capability that can be very handy, even when the scroller is displayed. The navigate( ) method is called by the DEForm when it uses this capability. See the full listing for the code.

The scroll_click( ) method has the problems of the edit_click( ), but reversed. When you show it, you have to consult the data-entry form, if it is showing, to highlight the correct record.

There are two shut_down methods. If called with no parameters, the shut_down( ) method calls itself, setting the self-explanatory boolean parameter, called_from_boss, false. A number of user actions will tell the DataBoss to shut down. Under most circumstances, the DataBoss has to tell its boss that the file and related window should be closed. If the JDB has ordered the DataBoss to shut down (the user clicks eXit on the JDB main menu, for example) this isn't wanted.

This is the code:

```
public void shut_down() {

    shut_down( false );
}

public void shut_down( boolean called_from_boss ) {

   if ( showing_editor )
       def.hide();

   if ( showing_scroller )
       sw.hide();

   def.dispose();
   sw.dispose();

   if ( ! called_from_boss ) {

       boss.close_file_file( this );
       boss.close_file_window( this );
   }

   menu.hide();
   menu.dispose();
}
```

Understanding the DataBoss' Private Methods

TOUR

If you haven't read Chapter 15, these methods will be meaningless. The documentation here won't change that.

We're keeping the documentation here so that the whole class is available in this location. But don't waste your time reading it until you understand how the create process works.

The create_dbf( ) method turns the DBS into the header of the same-named DBF. It refuses to overwrite an existing DBF, showing a reasonable message box instead. When the create process succeeds, another message box is shown.

No message appears when the create process fails. You'll see that adding an appropriate message would be simple. Before you do so, however, remember that you, the programmer, are the end user of this code. Remember that this will only fail when your hard disk runs out of space, or in other equally unlikely circumstances. Do you think it's worthwhile?

It's up to you, of course. This is the code:

```java
private void create_dbf( MRString fname ) {

    // convert "foo.dbs" to "FOO.DBF"
        fname.toUpper();
        fname.replace( fname.length()-1, 'F' );

    if ( new File( fname.toString() ).exists() ) {

        MsgBox mb = new MsgBox( fname +
            " already exists. Delete or move it " +
            "before you Create another.",
            "Can Not Overwrite .DBF" );
        mb.show();
        return;
    }

    if ( JDBnew.create_dbf_file(dbf) ) {

        MsgBox mb = new MsgBox( "Database file " +
            fname + " ready for use.",
            ".DBF File Ready" );
        mb.show();
    }
}
```

The create_dbs( ) method (refer to the full listing for the code) prepares the DBS from an existing DBF. Unlike the create_dbf( ) method, it's perfectly happy to overwrite an existing DBS. (Think through the differences. You'll probably agree that this seeming inconsistency is a reasonable treatment. It's not hard to change if you don't like it.)

Unlike the create_dbf( ) method again, create_dbs( ) launches a message box on success and on failure. Think about the causes of failure for the two file types. This will fail on any error in the source DBF, not just on an out-of-disk-space error.

The Full DataBoss.java Listing

This is the full DataBoss.java source file.

Listing 14-2:
DataBoss.java

```
// DataBoss.java -- manages editable, ScrollWin & DEForm
// Copyright 1997, Martin L. Rinehart


// this code is completely documented in:
// _Java Database Development_, Martin Rinehart,
// Osborne/McGraw-Hill, 1997

/*
     see comments at bottom of file
*/
import java.awt.*;
import java.io.File;

class DataBoss extends Object {

// -------------------- data members --------------------

// there are no public data members

// protected data members:

    protected JDB boss;

    protected DBF dbf;
    protected DEForm def;

    protected JDBboss menu;

    protected int rec_in_def;
    protected int rec_in_sw;
```

```
    protected boolean setting_scroller;
    protected boolean showing_editor;
    protected boolean showing_scroller;

   protected ScrollWin sw;

// static data members

    // there are no public static data members
    // there are no private static data members

    // final static data members

    final static int go_home = -4;
    final static int go_prev = -3;
    final static int go_next = -2;
    final static int go_end  = -1;

// -------------------- public methods --------------------

// constructor:

    DataBoss( JDB dad, DBF d ) {

        boss = dad;
        dbf = d;

        String file_name = dbf.getName();

        menu = new JDBboss( boss, this );
        menu.setTitle( ".DBx Controller for " +
            file_name );
        menu.show();

        sw = new ScrollWin( dbf, "DataBase File: " +
            file_name );

        def = new DEForm( dbf, file_name );

        sw.setDataBoss( this );
        def.setDataBoss( this );
```

```
            rec_in_def = 0;
            rec_in_sw = 0;

        showing_editor = false;
        showing_scroller = false;
    }

// there are no data access getXxx() methods
// there are no data access isXxx() methods

// data access setXxx() methods

    public void setRecord( int recno ) {

        if ( setting_scroller )
            return;

        rec_in_sw = recno;

        if ( showing_editor ) {

            if ( rec_in_def != recno ) {
                def.save_click();
                def.setRecord( recno );
                rec_in_def = recno;
            }
        }
    }

    public void setScroller( ScrollWin s ) {

        sw = s;
    }

// public, class-specific methods:

    public void create_click() {

        // called by JDBboss menu

        MRString fn = new MRString( dbf.getFileName() );
```

```
        if ( fn.toUpper().endsWith(".DBF") )
            create_dbs( fn );
        else
            create_dbf( fn );
}

public void data_added() {

    setting_scroller = true;
    sw.resetLast();
    setting_scroller = false;
}

public void data_changed() {

    setting_scroller = true;
    sw.repaint();
    setting_scroller = false;
}

public void edit_click() {

    // called by JDBboss menu
    // also called by DEForm on Exit or
    //          WINDOW_DESTROY

    if ( showing_editor ) {

        def.save_click();
        def.hide();
        showing_editor = false;
    }
    else {

        if ( showing_scroller ) {

            if ( rec_in_def != rec_in_sw ) {

                def.setRecord( rec_in_sw );
                rec_in_def = rec_in_sw;
            }
        }
```

```
            def.show();
            showing_editor = true;
        }
    }

public void exit_click() {

    // called by JDBboss menu
    shut_down();
}

 public void navigate( int where, int new_recno ) {

        // called by DEForm
        // where = go_home, go_prev, go_next or go_end

        rec_in_def = new_recno;

        if ( rec_in_sw != new_recno ) {
            sw.navigate( where );
            rec_in_sw = new_recno;
        }
 }

public void scroll_click() {

    // called by JDBboss menu
      // and by WINDOW_DESTROY event in ScrollWin

    if ( showing_scroller ) {

        sw.hide();
        showing_scroller = false;
    }
    else {

            if ( showing_editor ) {

                if ( rec_in_def != rec_in_sw ) {

                    sw.navigate( rec_in_def );
                    rec_in_sw = rec_in_def;
```

```
                }
            }
        sw.show();
        showing_scroller = true;
        }
    }

    public void shut_down() {

        shut_down( false );
    }

    public void shut_down( boolean called_from_boss ) {

        if ( showing_editor )
            def.hide();

        if ( showing_scroller )
            sw.hide();

        def.dispose();
        sw.dispose();

        if ( ! called_from_boss ) {

            boss.close_file_file( this );
            boss.close_file_window( this );
        }

        menu.hide();
        menu.dispose();
    }

// public, non-event overriding method:

    public String paramString() {

        return "DataBoss";
    }

// there are no public, event-handling methods:
```

```
// ------------------- private methods -------------------

// private methods:

    private void create_dbf( MRString fname ) {

        // convert "foo.dbs" to "FOO.DBF"
            fname.toUpper();
            fname.replace( fname.length()-1, 'F' );

        if ( new File( fname.toString() ).exists() ) {

            MsgBox mb = new MsgBox( fname +
                " already exists. Delete or move it " +
                "before you Create another.",
                "Can Not Overwrite .DBF" );
            mb.show();
            return;
        }

        if ( JDBnew.create_dbf_file(dbf) ) {

            MsgBox mb = new MsgBox( "Database file " +
                fname + " ready for use.",
                ".DBF File Ready" );
            mb.show();
        }
    }

    private void create_dbs( MRString fname ) {

        MsgBox mb;

        // convert "foo.dbf" to "FOO.DBS"
            MRString sname = new MRString( fname );
            sname.toUpper();
            sname.replace( sname.length()-1, 'S' );

        if ( JDBnew.create_stru_file(dbf) ) {

            mb = new MsgBox( "Structure file " +
                fname + " ready for use.",
                "Structure File Ready" );
```

```
                    mb.show();
            }
            else {

                mb = new MsgBox( "Unable to create " +
                     fname + ".", "Structure File Not Ready" );
                mb.show();
            }
        }

} // end of DataBoss class

// there are no private classes in DataBoss.java

/*
    The DataBoss manages the combination of a DBF
    with a ScrollWin and a DEForm. It synchronizes the
    navigation so that the highlighted ScrollWin record
    is the record shown in the DEForm. It ensures that
    data updates in the DEForm are shown in the ScrollWin.
    Via a JDBboss menu it lets the user show and hide the
    ScrollWin and the DEForm. A Create option creates
    a .DBF from a .DBS table description or, if a .DBF is
    open, it will create a .DBS table description.

    Creating a .DBS from a .DBF overwrites an existing
    .DBS of the same name. Creating a .DBF from a .DBS
    creates an empty .DBF. Overwriting an existing .DBF
    is not permitted.
*/

// end of DataBoss.java
```

The JDBboss Menu

The JDBboss class instantiates a menu for each DBF (or, as Chapter 15 explains, DBS) that you open. Its key data member is the String array of prompts:

```
protected String[] prompts = {
    "&Scroll",
    "&Edit",
```

```
"&Create",
"e&Xit"
```

The constructor uses a RRectPromptPainter and MenuPanel, set up with the values you specify via the Options menu:

```
prompt_painter = new RRectPromptPainter(
    men_vals[8], men_vals[9] );
prompt_painter.setHiColor(
    (int) men_vals[6], (int) men_vals[7] );
prompt_painter.setLoColor(
    (int) men_vals[4], (int) men_vals[5] );

menu_panel = new MenuPanel( prompts,
    1/3.0, prompt_painter, this );

  menu_panel.setFollowsCursor( true );
```

The JDBboss' public handleEvent( ) method calls its one private method, menu_click( ). The heart of menu_click( ) is a switch that calls the appropriate DataBoss method this way:

```
switch( i ) {

    case 0:
            databoss.scroll_click();
        break;

    case 1:
        databoss.edit_click();
        break;

    case 2:
        databoss.create_click();
        break;

    case 3:
        databoss.exit_click();
        break;
}
```

Listing 14-3 shows the full JDBboss.java listing.

```java
// JDBboss.java -- JDB menu options menu
// Copyright 1997, Martin L. Rinehart

// this code is completely documented in:
// _Java Database Development_, Martin Rinehart,
// Osborne/McGraw-Hill, 1997

/*
    Menu for the DataBoss -- controls DBF entry form
    and scroll window.
*/

import java.awt.*;

class JDBboss extends Frame {

// -------------------- data members --------------------

// there are no public data members

// protected data members:

    protected JDB boss;

    protected DataBoss databoss;

    protected MenuPanel menu_panel;

    protected RRectPromptPainter prompt_painter;
    protected String[] prompts = {
        "&Scroll",
        "&Edit",
        "&Create",
        "e&Xit"
    };

// there are no static data members

// -------------------- public methods --------------------

// constructor:
```

```
    JDBboss( JDB dad, DataBoss mom ) {

        boss = dad;
        databoss = mom;

        double[] men_vals = boss.getMenuValues(
            JDBlib.data_controller_menu );

        show(); hide(); // workaround position bug

        resize( 400, 150 );

        prompt_painter = new RRectPromptPainter(
            men_vals[8], men_vals[9] );
        prompt_painter.setHiColor(
            (int) men_vals[6], (int) men_vals[7] );
        prompt_painter.setLoColor(
            (int) men_vals[4], (int) men_vals[5] );

        menu_panel = new MenuPanel( prompts,
            1/3.0, prompt_painter, this );

          menu_panel.setFollowsCursor( true );

        setLayout( new CenterLayout(32) );
        add( menu_panel );
        boss.register( menu_panel,
            JDBlib.data_controller_menu );
    }

// there are no data access methods

// public, class-specific method:

    public void shut_down() {

        hide();
    }

// public, non-event overriding method:

    public String paramString() {
```

```
            return "boss: " + boss;
        }

// public, event-handling method:

    public boolean handleEvent( Event e ) {

        if ( e.id == Event.WINDOW_DESTROY ) {
            shut_down();
            return true;
        }

        if ( e.target == menu_panel ) {
            menu_click( e );
            return true;
        }

        return true;
    }

// ------------------ private methods ------------------

// private method:

    private void menu_click( Event e ) {

        if ( e.arg == null ) return;

        int i = ( (Integer) e.arg ).intValue();
        boss.setCurrentMenuGroup( i );

        switch( i ) {

            case 0:
                    databoss.scroll_click();
                break;

            case 1:
                databoss.edit_click();
                break;

            case 2:
```

```
                    databoss.create_click();
                    break;

            case 3:
                    databoss.exit_click();
                    break;
        }

    }

} // end of JDBboss class

// there are no private classes in JDBboss.java

// end of JDBboss.java
```

The New DBF Class

You'll face this question constantly as you work in any object-oriented language: Do I create a new class, inheriting from the old one, or do I add to the existing class?

Our DBF class, for example, is Scrollable, but not Editable. Should we make a new class, perhaps "DBFe," that adds the Editable interface, or should we just add to the DBF class?

Designing Deep or Flat Class Families

If your class tries to do everything, it gets big quickly. Before you know it, it's too big to be useful in web-based applets or applications.

On the other hand, it's easy to overdo the inheritance. For example, we could have "DBF" that just has the basic DBF code; "DBFs" could add the Scrollable interface; "DBFe" could have the Editable interface; and "DBFse" could have both interfaces.

Java's been praised for its relatively flat inheritance structure (relative to something like the Microsoft Foundation Classes). C++ uses deeply nested class structures, some say. This is nonsense. Neither Java nor C++ says anything about how you design class structures. Both support deep and flat designs.

The design decision is up to you. I begin with a basic prejudice in favor of small code, which tells me to extend an existing class, not to fatten one.

One of my other basic prejudices is to favor simplicity, which tells me to add the code to a single class.

I think about the absolute amount of code that a new feature set will add. If it is very small, the simpler approach is to just add it to the existing class. If it's a lot of code, then I'll use an extending class.

I also think about the frequency of use of any new features. If I'll always use the features, they go into a single class. If they're going to be rarely used, they'll go into an extending class.

Of course, the typical case, such as the one I faced with the DBF class, is that the code's not too big, but it's not insignificant, either. And it will be used frequently, but not always.

I've been programming for more than 30 years. I still find that a lot of design choices are finally made by flipping a coin. Heads we extend; tails we keep it simpler but fatter. With the DBF class, my coin came up tails.

Understanding the New DBF Class

Our old DBF implemented the Scrollable interface, so that you could look at a DBF with a ScrollWin. Since the design coin came up tails, I added the Editable interface:

```
class DBF implements Scrollable, Editable {
```

The getLast( ) and getName( ) methods are part of the Scrollable and Editable interfaces, so we've already got the first third of Editable implemented. We need two methods for getting and setting the values, and two to handle the deleted status.

The getValues( ) public method delegates the hard work to a private method:

```
public Vector getValues( int recno ) {

    go( recno );
    read_values();
    return values;
}
```

The setValues( ) method also delegates the real work:

```
public void setValues( int recno, Vector vals ) {

    if ( !writeable ) {
        ( new MsgBox(".DBF is not writeable") ).show();
        return;
    }
    values = vals;
      go( recno );
    write_fields( recno );
}
```

The public isDeleted( ) method uses the existing go( ) method and then returns the comparison of the first byte to the final static DELETED. The setDeleted( ) public also handles the full job. It's not as simple, but it's completely straightforward, as you can see in the full listing.

The private read_values( ) routine uses the fields Vector (Vector of fld_stru objects) to loop through the record buffer, getting one field at a time with the read_field( ) method:

```
fld_stru fs;

int recloc = 1; // point past deleted byte
for ( int i = 0 ; i < num_fields ; i++ ) {

    fs = (fld_stru) fields.elementAt(i);
    read_field( i, fs, recloc );
    recloc += fs.length;
}
```

Except for date values, the read_field( ) method just transfers the appropriate bytes from the record buffer into a String for the values Vector:

```
values.setElementAt
    ( new String(record_buffer, 0, bufloc,
        fs.length), fldno );
```

The date code converts the recorded "YYYYMMDD" date to the more human-readable "MM/DD/YYYY" form. Check the full listing for the ALD.

The write_fields( ) routine is very similar to read_fields( ). It calls write_field( ) looping through all the fields. The write_field( ) is very much like read_field( ), except that the date conversion goes in the opposite direction. Again, check the full listing for the ALD.

The Full DBF Listing

This is the full, revised DBF.java source file.

Listing 14-4:
DBF.java

```
// DBF.java -- DBF (.DBF file) class
// Copyright 1997, Martin L. Rinehart

// this code is completely documented in:
// _Java Database Development_, Martin Rinehart,
// Osborne/McGraw-Hill, 1997
```

```
/*
  Uses a .DBF file as a Java object that stores and
  retrieves records.
*/

import java.awt.*;
import java.io.*;
import java.util.*;

class DBF implements Scrollable, Editable {

// -------------------- data members --------------------

// public data members:

    public String file_name;

    public String message;

    public boolean readable;

    public boolean writeable;

// protected data members:

    protected String access; // "r" or "rw"

    protected int date_last_update;

    protected Vector fields;

    protected int len_header;
    protected int len_record;

    protected int num_recs;
    protected int num_fields;

    protected RandomAccessFile raf;
    protected byte[] record_buffer;
    protected int record_number;

    protected byte type_byte;
```

```java
    protected Vector values;

// static data members
    // there are no public static data members
    // there are no private static data members

    // final static data members:

    final static byte DELETED     = (byte) '*';
    final static byte NOT_DELETED = (byte) ' ';

 // ------------------- public methods -------------------

// constructors:

    DBF( String pathname ) {

        this( pathname, "r" );
    }

    DBF( String pathname, String access ) {

        this.access = access;

        fields = new Vector();
        readable = writeable = false;
        dbf_read( pathname );

        if ( readable ) {

            values = new Vector( num_fields );
            for ( int i = 0 ; i < num_fields ; i++ )
                values.addElement( null );
        }
    }

// data access getXxx() methods:

    public Vector getDEFs() {

        Vector def_vec = new Vector( num_fields );

        for ( int i = 0 ; i < num_fields ; i++ )
```

```
            def_vec.addElement( make_def(i) );

      return def_vec;
  }

  public Vector getFieldVals( int fno ) {

        Vector vals = new Vector();
        fld_stru fs = ( fld_stru ) fields.elementAt( fno );

        MRString m = new MRString( fs.name );
        m.padTo( 10 );

        vals.addElement( m.toString() );

        vals.addElement( new MRString(fs.type).toString() );

        m = new MRString( "" + (int)(fs.length) );
        m.leftPadTo( 5 );
        vals.addElement( m.toString() );

        m = new MRString( (byte)
            ( fs.decimals + ( byte ) '0') );
        m.leftPadTo( 2 );
        vals.addElement( m.toString() );

        return vals;
  }

  public String getFileName() {

        return file_name;
  }

public int getLast() {

    // returns last item #
    return num_recs - 1;
}

  public String getName() {
```

```
            return file_name;
      }

    public int getNumFields() {

            return num_fields;
      }

    public String getString(int index) {

        // a string representing scrollable[index]
        // index is from zero through getLast()

        go( index );
        return new String( record_buffer, 0 );
    }

    public Vector getValues( int recno ) {

        go( recno );
        read_values();
        return values;
    }

// data access isXxx() method:

    public boolean isDeleted( int recno ) {

        go( recno );
        return record_buffer[0] == DELETED;
    }

// data access setXxx() methods:

    public void setDeleted( int recno,
        boolean del_status ) {

        if ( recno != record_number )
            go( recno );

        byte b = del_status ? DELETED : NOT_DELETED;
```

```
            record_buffer[0] = b;

            try {
                raf.seek( file_pos(record_number) );
                raf.write( b );
            }
            catch ( IOException ioe ) {;}
        }

    public void setValues( int recno, Vector vals ) {

        if ( !writeable ) {
            ( new MsgBox(".DBF is not writeable") ).show();
            return;
        }
        values = vals;
          go( recno );
        write_fields( recno );
    }

// public, class-specific methods:

    public void close() {

        try {
            raf.close();
        }
        catch ( IOException ioe ) {
        }
    }

    public void dbf_read( String fn ) {

        try {
            raf = new RandomAccessFile( fn, access );
        }

        catch (IOException ioe) {
            message = "File open error";
            return;
        }

        byte[] buffer = new byte[32];
```

```
    try {
        raf.read( buffer );
    }

    catch (IOException ioe) {
        message = "File read error";
        return;
    }

// ready to read; DBF header is in buffer[]

    file_name = fn;

    date_last_update =
        (1900 + buffer[1]) * 10000 ;
    date_last_update += buffer[2]*100 ;
    date_last_update += buffer[3];

    num_recs = int_from4( buffer, 4 );
    len_header = int_from2( buffer, 8 );
    num_fields = ( (len_header - 1) / 32 ) - 1;
        // num_fields will be reset
        // for FoxPro .DBFs

    len_record = int_from2( buffer, 10 );

    record_buffer = new byte[len_record];
      for ( int i = 0 ; i < len_record ; i++ )
          record_buffer[i] = (byte) ' ';

    for ( int i = 0 ; i < num_fields ; i++ ) {

        try {
            raf.read( buffer );
        }
        catch (IOException ioe) {
            message = "File read error";
            return;
        }

        if ( (buffer[0] == 0xD) ||
            (buffer[11] == 0 ) ) {
```

```
                    num_fields = i;
                    break;
            }

            fld_stru fs = new fld_stru();

            for ( byte b = 0 ; b < 10 ; b++ ) {

                    if ( buffer[b] > 0 )
                        fs.name[b] = buffer[b];
                    else
                        fs.name[b] = (byte) ' ';
                }

            fs.type = buffer[11];
            fs.length = ( byte )
                    unsigned_byte( buffer[16] );
            fs.decimals = buffer[17];

            fields.addElement( fs );
        }

    readable = num_fields > 0;
    if ( access.equals("rw") )
            writeable = readable;
    }
/*
    public String field_string( int i ) {

        fld_stru fs = (fld_stru) fields.elementAt(i);

        return non_null_string( fs.name, 10 ) +
            " " + (char) fs.type +
            " " + fs.length +
            " " + fs.decimals;
    }
*/
    public void go( int recno ) {

        try {
            raf.seek( file_pos(recno) );
            record_number = recno;
```

```
            raf.read( record_buffer );
        }
        catch (IOException ioe) {;}
    }

    public void replace( int recno ) {

        // check for append
        if ( recno == num_recs ) {
            num_recs++;
            rewrite_numrecs();
        }

        // go ahead
        try {
            raf.seek( file_pos(recno) );
            record_number = recno;

            raf.write( record_buffer );
        }
        catch ( IOException ioe) {

            ( new MsgBox("Write failure") ).show();
            System.out.println( "Write failed: " +
                ioe.toString() );
        }
    }

    public boolean useMonospace() {

        return true;
    }

// public, non-event overriding method:

    public String paramString() {

        return file_name + " read: " + readable +
            " write " + writeable;
    }

// there are no public, event-handling methods
```

```
// ------------------ private methods ------------------

// private methods:

    private String get_dec_init( fld_stru fs ) {

        byte[] b = new byte[fs.length];

        int dpos = fs.length - fs.decimals - 1;
        if ( dpos > 0 ) {

            for ( int i = 0 ; i < dpos ; i++ )
                b[i] = (byte) '0';
        }

        if ( dpos > -1 ) b[dpos] = (byte) '.';
        if ( dpos < fs.length - 1 ) {

            for ( int i = dpos ; i < fs.length ; i++ )
                b[i] = (byte) '0';
        }
        return new String( b, 0 );
    }

    private String get_dec_mask( fld_stru fs ) {

        byte b[] = new byte[fs.length];
        int dpos = fs.length - fs.decimals - 1;

        if ( dpos > 0 ) {

            for ( int i = 0 ; i < (dpos - 1) ; i++ )
                b[i] = (byte) '0';

                b[dpos-1] = (byte) '9';
        }
        if ( dpos > -1 )
            b[dpos] = (byte) '.';

        if ( dpos < fs.length - 1 ) {

            for ( int i = dpos+1 ; i < fs.length ; i++ )
```

```java
                b[i] = (byte) '9';
        }
        return new String( b, 0 );
}

private String get_init( fld_stru fs ) {

    switch ( fs.type ) {
        case 'C': {
            return "";
        }

        case 'D': {
            return "12/31/1999";
        }

        case 'N':
        case 'F': {
            if ( fs.decimals == 0 )
                return get_int_init( fs );
            else
                return get_dec_init( fs );

        }

        case 'L':
            return "Y";

        default:
            return "";
    }
}

private String get_int_init( fld_stru fs ) {

    byte[] b = new byte[fs.length];

    for ( int i = 0 ; i < fs.length ; i++ )
        b[i] = (byte) '0';

    return new String( b, 0 );
}
```

```java
    private String get_int_mask( fld_stru fs ) {

        byte b[] = new byte[fs.length];

        for ( int i = 0 ; i < ( fs.length-1 ) ; i++ )
            b[i] = (byte) '0';

          b[fs.length-1] = (byte) '9';

        return new String( b, 0 );
    }

    private String get_mask( fld_stru fs ) {

        switch ( fs.type ) {

            case 'C': {
                return "x";
            }

            case 'D': {
                return "99/99/9999";
            }

            case 'N':
            case 'F': {
                if ( fs.decimals == 0 )
                    return get_int_mask( fs );
                else
                    return get_dec_mask( fs );
            }

            case 'L':
                return "L";

            default:
                return "x";
        }
    }

    private long file_pos( int recno )
        throws IOException {
```

```java
        if ( (recno < 0) || (recno >= num_recs) )
            throw( new IOException("Bad record number") );

        return ( (long) len_header ) +
            ( (long) len_record ) * recno;

    }

    private int int_from2( byte[] b, int start ) {

// reads int from little-endian byte array buffer

        int result;
        result = unsigned_byte( b[start+1] );

        result <<=8;
        result += unsigned_byte( b[start] );

        return result;

    }

    private int int_from4( byte[] b, int start ) {

// reads long from little-endian byte array buffer

        int result;
        result = unsigned_byte( b[start+3] );

        result <<= 8;
        result += unsigned_byte( b[start+2] );

        result <<= 8;
        result += unsigned_byte( b[start+1] );

        result <<=8;
        result += unsigned_byte( b[start] );

        return result;

    }

    private byte[] int_to4( int n ) {
```

```
// makes little-endian 4-byte array from int
        byte[] b = new byte[4];

        b[0] = ( byte )   (n & 0xFF);
        b[1] = ( byte ) ( (n & 0xFF00) >> 8 );
        b[2] = ( byte ) ( (n & 0xFF0000) >> 16 );
        b[3] = ( byte ) ( (n & 0xFF000000) >> 24 );

        return b;
    }

    private DEField make_def( int index ) {

        fld_stru fs = new fld_stru();
        fs = (fld_stru) fields.elementAt( index );

        String label = ( new String( fs.name, 0 ) ).trim();
        label = MRString.toUlower( label );
        String mask = get_mask( fs );

        int width = fs.type == 'D' ? 10 : fs.length;

        String init = get_init( fs );

        DEField def = new DEField(
                label, mask, width, init );

        return def;
    }

    private String non_null_string( byte[] b, int len ) {

// returns string of b[] thru last non-zero byte

        int i = 0;
        while ( i < len && b[i] > 0 ) i++;

        return new String( b, 0, 0, i );
    }

    private void read_field( int fldno,
        fld_stru fs, int bufloc ) {
```

```
        if ( fs.type == 'D' ) {

            // change YYYYMMDD to MM/DD/YYYY
            byte[] d = new byte[10];
            d[0] = record_buffer[bufloc + 4];
            d[1] = record_buffer[bufloc + 5];
            d[2] = (byte) '/';
            d[3] = record_buffer[bufloc + 6];
            d[4] = record_buffer[bufloc + 7];
            d[5] = (byte) '/';
            d[6] = record_buffer[bufloc];
            d[7] = record_buffer[bufloc + 1];
            d[8] = record_buffer[bufloc + 2];
            d[9] = record_buffer[bufloc + 3];

            values.setElementAt
                ( new String(d, 0), fldno );
        }
        else
            values.setElementAt
                ( new String(record_buffer, 0, bufloc,
                    fs.length), fldno );
    }

    private void read_values() {

        fld_stru fs;

        int recloc = 1; // point past deleted byte
        for ( int i = 0 ; i < num_fields ; i++ ) {

            fs = (fld_stru) fields.elementAt(i);
            read_field( i, fs, recloc );
            recloc += fs.length;
        }
    }

    private void rewrite_numrecs() {

        try {
            raf.seek( 4 );
            raf.write( int_to4(num_recs) );
        }
```

```
        catch ( IOException ioe ) {;}
    }

    private String type_string( byte b ) {

        switch( b ) {
            case 'C': return "C";
            case 'D': return "D";
            case 'L': return "L";
            case 'N': return "N";
            case 'F': return "F";
        }
        return "U";
    }

    private int unsigned_byte( byte b ) {

        return ( (int) b ) & 0x000000FF;
    }

    private void write_field( int fldno,
        fld_stru fs, int recloc ) {

        String s = ( String ) ( values.elementAt(fldno) );

        if ( fs.type == 'D' ) {

            // change MM/DD/YYYY to YYYYMMDD
            byte[] d = new byte[10];
            s.getBytes( 0, 10, d, 0 );

            record_buffer[recloc]   = d[6];
            record_buffer[recloc+1] = d[7];
            record_buffer[recloc+2] = d[8];
            record_buffer[recloc+3] = d[9];

            record_buffer[recloc+4] = d[0];
            record_buffer[recloc+5] = d[1];

            record_buffer[recloc+6] = d[3];
            record_buffer[recloc+7] = d[4];
        }
        else
```

```java
            s.getBytes(
                    0,
                    s.length() < fs.length ?
                        s.length() : fs.length,
                    record_buffer,
                    recloc );
    }

    private void write_fields( int recno  ) {

        fld_stru fs;
        int recloc = 1;

        for ( int i = 0 ; i < num_fields ; i++ ) {

            fs = (fld_stru) fields.elementAt(i);
            write_field( i, fs, recloc );
            recloc += fs.length;
        }

        replace( recno );
    }

} // end of DBF class

// private class in DBF.java:

class fld_stru {

    public byte[] name;
    public byte type;
    public byte length;
    public byte decimals;

    fld_stru() {
        name = new byte[10];
    }
}

// end of DBF.java
```

The New ScrollWin Class

The old ScrollWin didn't know that there was such a thing as a DataBoss. To coordinate the scroller and the data-entry form, we've got to have a smarter ScrollWin.

Again, there's the same design issue: Do we create a new, ScrollWin-extending class, or do we simply fatten ScrollWin?

In this case, the ScrollWin would frequently be used without a DataBoss, since it scrolls RAM-based lists, binary files, and everything else in addition to DBF records.

On the other hand, the amount of additional code was very small, so I again opted for the simpler approach.

I added a DataBoss public data member. The constructor explicitly sets this member null. A trivial setDataBoss( ) method is provided for consistency. I didn't bother with a getDataBoss( )—the reference is public, after all.

The handleEvent( ) method adds this code for a WINDOW_DESTROY event:

```
if ( databoss != null ) {

    databoss.scroll_click();
    return true;
```

Similar code calls parent.databoss.scroll_click( ) in the scroll_canvas class' handleEvent( ) method. Finally, the scroll_canvas' paint_line( ) method adds this call when it paints the highlighted line:

```
if ( parent.databoss != null )
    parent.databoss.setRecord( recno );
```

Listing 14-5 shows the full ScrollWin.java source, with these modifications.

Listing 14-5:
ScrollWin.java

```
// ScrollWin.java -- a generic scrolling Window
// Copyright 1997, Martin L. Rinehart

// this code is completely documented in:
// _Java Database Development_, Martin Rinehart,
// Osborne/McGraw-Hill, 1997

/*

    This window will scroll anything that implements
    the Scrollable interface.
```

```
        It will synchronize with a data databoss if an object
        that implements databoss is provided.
*/

import java.awt.*;

class ScrollWin extends Frame {

// -------------------- data members --------------------

// public data members:

    public DataBoss databoss;

    public boolean end_app;

     public boolean refuse_close;

// protected data members:

    protected int client_height;
    protected int client_rows;
    protected int client_width;

    protected int font_height;

    protected int hilite_row;

    protected int last_top_row;
    protected int leading;

    protected int old_height;
    protected int old_width;

    protected int row_height;

    protected Font s_font;
    protected int s_last;
    protected Scrollable scroll_object;

    protected int top_row;
```

```
    protected Scrollbar vscroll;

// private data members:

    private scroll_canvas canvas;

    private boolean font_set = true;

    private boolean initialize;

    private boolean paint_working;

// static data members

    // there are no public static data members
    // there are no private static data members

    // final static data members:

    final static int go_home = -4;
    final static int go_prev = -3;
    final static int go_next = -2;
    final static int go_end  = -1;

// ------------------- public methods -------------------

// constructors:

    ScrollWin( Scrollable s ) {

        super( "Scroll Window" );

        scroll_object = s;
        s_last = s.getLast();

        vscroll = new Scrollbar(); // defaults to vertical
        vscroll.setBackground( Color.lightGray );
        add( "East", vscroll );

        canvas = new scroll_canvas( this );
        add( "Center", canvas );
```

```
        hilite_row = 0;
        initialize = true;

        databoss = null;

          resize( 500, 300 );
    }

    ScrollWin( Scrollable s, String title ) {
        this( s );
        setTitle( title );
    }

// there are no data access getXxx() methods
// there are no data access isXxx() methods

// data access setXxx() methods:

    public void setEndApp( boolean b ) {

        end_app = b;
    }

    public void setRefuseClose( boolean b ) {

        refuse_close = b;
    }

    public void setDataBoss ( DataBoss d ) {

        databoss = d;
    }

// public, class-specific method:

    public void navigate( int where ) {

        switch ( where ) {
            case go_home:
                home();
                break;
```

```
            case go_prev:
                up();
                break;

            case go_next:
                down();
                break;

            case go_end:
                end();
                break;

            default:
                go_to( where );
        }
    }

    public void resetLast() {

        s_last = scroll_object.getLast();
          end();
    }

// public, non-event overriding methods:

    public void paint( Graphics g ) {

        if ( initialize )  {
            calc_row_height( g );
            initialize = false;
        }

        if ( paint_working ) return;
        paint_working = true;

        if ( (size().width != old_width) ||
            (size().height != old_height) ) {

            resize();
        }
        canvas.repaint();
```

```
        paint_working = false;
    }

    public String paramString() {

        return "wid: " + client_width +
            " hgt: " + client_height +
            " rows: " + client_rows;
    }

    public void repaint() {

        super.repaint();
    }

// public, event-handling method:

    public boolean handleEvent( Event e ) {

        if ( e.id == Event.WINDOW_DESTROY ) {

            if ( databoss != null ) {

                databoss.scroll_click();
                return true;
            }

            if ( refuse_close )
                return true;

            else if ( end_app )
                System.exit( 0 );

            else
                hide();

            return true;
        }

        if ( e.id == Event.KEY_ACTION )
            if ( handle_keypress(e) )
                return true;
```

```
                if ( e.id == Event.SCROLL_LINE_UP ) {
                    up();
                    return true;
                }

                if ( e.id == Event.SCROLL_LINE_DOWN ) {
                    down();
                    return true;
                }

                if ( e.id == Event.SCROLL_PAGE_UP ) {
                    pgup();
                    return true;
                }

                if ( e.id == Event.SCROLL_PAGE_DOWN ) {
                    pgdn();
                    return true;
                }

                if ( e.id == Event.SCROLL_ABSOLUTE ) {
                    int v = vscroll.getValue();
                    top_row = v <= last_top_row ?
                        v : last_top_row;
                    repaint();
                    return true;
                }

                return super.handleEvent( e );
        }

// ------------------- private methods -------------------

// private methods:

    private void calc_row_height( Graphics g ) {

        String font_name;
        font_name = scroll_object.useMonospace() ?
            "Courier" : "Helvetica";

        Font f = g.getFont();
```

```
        g.setFont( new Font(font_name,
            /* f.getStyle() */ Font.PLAIN, f.getSize() ) );
        s_font = g.getFont();

        font_height = s_font.getSize();
        leading = ( font_height + 3 ) / 5;
        row_height = font_height + leading;
    }

private void down() {

    if ( hilite_row < client_rows - 1 ) {
        hilite_row++;
        if ( (hilite_row + top_row) > s_last )
            hilite_row--;
        repaint();
        return;
    }

    if ( top_row < last_top_row ) {
        top_row++;
        repaint();
    }
}

private void end() {

    if ( (top_row < last_top_row) ||
         (hilite_row < ( s_last - last_top_row )) ) {
        top_row = last_top_row;
        hilite_row = s_last - last_top_row;
        repaint();
    }
}

private void go_to( int recno ) {

    // if recno is visible, don't move page
    if ( (recno >= top_row) &&
         (( recno - top_row ) <= client_rows) ) {
        hilite_row = recno - top_row;
    }
```

```
            repaint();
    }

    private boolean handle_keypress( Event e ) {

        switch (e.key) {

            case Event.UP:
                up();
                return true;

            case Event.DOWN:
                down();
                return true;

            case Event.PGUP:
                pgup();
                return true;

            case Event.PGDN:
                pgdn();
                return true;

            case Event.HOME:
                home();
                return true;

            case Event.END:
                end();
                return true;
        }
        return false;
    }

    private void home() {

        if ( (top_row > 0) || (hilite_row > 0) ) {
            top_row = 0;
            hilite_row = 0;
            repaint();
        }
    }
```

```
    private void pgdn() {

        if ( top_row < last_top_row ) {
            top_row += client_rows;
            top_row = top_row > last_top_row ?
                last_top_row : top_row;
            repaint();
            return;
        }
        int last_row = s_last - last_top_row;

        if ( hilite_row < last_row ) {
            hilite_row = last_row;
            repaint();
        }
    }

    private void pgup() {

        if ( top_row > 0 ) {
            top_row -= client_rows;
            top_row = top_row < 0 ? 0 : top_row;
            repaint();
            return;
        }

        if ( hilite_row > 0 ) {
            hilite_row = 0;
            repaint();
        }
    }

    private void resize() {

        client_height = size().height - insets().top -
            insets().bottom;

// client area is laid out:
//    text
//  [ leading
//    text ] . . .
//    leading
```

```
        // round to integral # of rows:
        if ( client_height < row_height)
            client_rows = 1;
        else
            client_rows = client_height / row_height;

        client_height = row_height * client_rows;

        resize( size().width, client_height +
            insets().top + insets().bottom );

        old_width = size().width;
        old_height = size().height;

        last_top_row = s_last - client_rows + 1;
        if ( last_top_row < 0 ) last_top_row = 0;

        if ( last_top_row > 0 ) vscroll.show();
        else vscroll.hide();

        client_width = size().width - insets().left -
            insets().right -
            ( vscroll.isVisible() ?
                vscroll.size().width : 0 );
    }

    private void up() {

        if ( hilite_row > 0 ) {
            hilite_row--;
            repaint();
            return;
        }

        if ( top_row > 0 ) {
            top_row--;
            repaint();
        }
    }

} // end of ScrollWin class
```

```java
// private class in ScrollWin.java:

class scroll_canvas extends Canvas {

// there are no public data members

// protected data member:

    protected ScrollWin parent;

// final static data member:

    final static int paint_delay = 1000;

// constructor:

    scroll_canvas( ScrollWin sw ) {
        parent = sw;
    }

// public, non-event overriding method:

    public void paint( Graphics g ) {

        if ( parent.s_last == -1 ) {

            paint_empty_line( g );
            return;
        }

        g.setFont( parent.s_font );
        if ( parent.vscroll.isShowing() ) set_vscroll();

        int max = parent.client_rows + parent.top_row - 1;
        max = max > parent.s_last ?
            parent.s_last : max;

        int rows_showing =
            parent.s_last - parent.top_row + 1;
        boolean filled =
            rows_showing == parent.client_rows;
```

```java
            if ( (!filled) && (parent.hilite_row >
                ( parent.client_rows - 1 )) )
                    if ( parent.client_rows > 0 )
                        parent.hilite_row =
                            parent.client_rows - 1;

        int print_pos = parent.font_height;
        int print_row = 0;
        for ( int i = parent.top_row; i <= max; i++ ) {

            paint_line( g, i, print_pos,
                print_row == parent.hilite_row );

            print_pos += parent.row_height;
            print_row++;
        }
    }

// public, event-handling method:

    public boolean handleEvent( Event e ) {

        if ( e.id == Event.MOUSE_DOWN ) {
            handle_click( e );
            return true;
        }

          if ( (parent.databoss != null) &&
                (e.id == Event.WINDOW_DESTROY) ) {

                parent.databoss.scroll_click();
                return true;
            }
        return super.handleEvent( e );
    }

// private methods:

    private void handle_click( Event e ) {

        parent.hilite_row = what_row( e.y );
```

```
        if ( (parent.top_row + parent.hilite_row) >
            parent.s_last )
            parent.hilite_row = parent.s_last -
                parent.top_row;

        repaint();
    }

    private void paint_empty_line( Graphics g ) {

        g.drawString( "<empty file>", 1,

            parent.font_height );
    }

    private void paint_line( Graphics g, int recno,
        int print_pos, boolean hilite ) {

        if ( hilite ) {

            if ( parent.databoss != null )
                parent.databoss.setRecord( recno );

            g.setColor( Color.black );
            g.fillRect(
                parent.insets().left,
                print_pos + parent.leading -
                    parent.row_height,
                parent.client_width,
                parent.row_height );
            g.setColor( Color.white );
        }
        else {
            g.setColor( Color.black );
        }

        g.drawString( parent.scroll_object.
            getString(recno), 1, print_pos );
    }

    private void set_vscroll() {
```

```
             if ( parent.last_top_row >  0 )
                parent.vscroll.setValues(
                    (parent.s_last * parent.top_row) /
                        parent.last_top_row,
                    parent.client_rows,
                    0,
                    parent.s_last );
        }

    private int what_row( int y ) {

        while ( parent.row_height == 0 )
            Thread.yield();

        return ( y + 1 ) / parent.row_height;
    }

} // end of scroll_canvas

// end of ScrollWin.java
```

Summary

In this chapter we looked at the way a scrolling window and a data-entry form can be made to work together as a team.

Just as the scrolling is done by a ScrollWin that can handle scrolling anything that implements Scrollable, the DEForm can handle editing anything that implements Editable. We began with a look at this interface.

The Editable interface specifies six functions. Two of them, getName( ) and getLast( ), are also part of the Scrollable interface. The isDeleted( ) and setDeleted( ) methods handle the record's (or object's) deleted status. The other two, getValues( ) and setValues( ), read and write the individual fields in a database record—or any other parts of something that implements Editable.

Then we took a look at the DataBoss. Both the scroller and the data-entry form keep the DataBoss posted whenever they change something that the other might want to know about. The DataBoss coordinates the two. It has to dance gracefully around some subtle possibilities for infinite recursion.

We took a very quick look at the JDBboss class. It is the menu that pops up when the user opens a database: Scroll, Edit, Create, and eXit.

We closed with a look at the new DBF and ScrollWin classes. I chose to expand these classes (costing code size) instead of adding extending classes (which would have added complexity). The DBF now implements Editable. The ScrollWin now reports to a DataBoss, if you choose to provide one.

While we were doing this, we kept running into mysteries such as the DBS file type that JDB handles. In Chapter 15, we'll explore the New option and see how JDB not only edits data, but also lets you edit the header information that goes into making a new DBF.

Chapter 15

Creating New DBFs

Y ou've seen the scroller working simultaneously with the data-entry form. In this chapter, we're going to use this data-editing power to edit the header data that specifies the structure of a DBF. The options that have been mysteries until now will become crystal clear.

We'll begin by spending some time using JDB. We'll create a DBS (DataBase Structure) file from an existing DBF. Then we'll edit the structure and use the revised structure data to create a new DBF. We'll also use the New option to create a DBS from scratch. You add field description records to that DBS, and when all the fields are described, click Create to create your DBF.

Then we'll look at the underlying code. The JDBclose menu is similar to the static menus we've used, but it is dynamic. It expands and contracts as you open and close files.

We'll also look at the revised JDB front-end code. Where we stubbed out the functionality with message boxes before, we'll actually be opening and closing files. You'll see how we keep Vectors that track the open files and file windows.

Ready? Load your Chapter 15 JDB, and you'll be able to follow along, trying everything as we go. For those who are reading this during takeoff or landing, we'll have screen shots here.

Using JDB

TOUR

Have you been fiddling with JDB's New and Create options? Got them figured out? Skip this section.

If you haven't, following this discussion is probably a more economical use of your time than muddling through on your own.

Begin by looking at this description of the first fields in a contact file:

```
Name          Type    Length  Decimals
-----------   ----    ------  --------
CNTCT_KEY     N            8         0
LAST_NAME     C           16         0
FULL_NAME     C           40         0
ADDRESS1      C           40         0
ADDRESS2      C           40         0
   . . .
```

It's a data table, isn't it?

Beginning very early in the world of relational theory, the scientists said that the data about the tables in a system was itself data and could be stored in tables in the system.

We call this *meta data*—it's data about the data. For example, column 2 is called "LAST_NAME," its type is "C," its length is 16, and so on.

Implementors realized that storing the meta data in tables means there's less code to write. A tool for editing the data is a tool for editing the meta data.

This is precisely the approach that JDB takes. JDB can edit any DBF. By putting the table description data into a DBF, JDB can edit table descriptions.

The Mysterious .DBS

The .DBS extension is part of my implementation of this idea: it's a DataBase Structure file. Its contents are the data about the fields that you find in the header of a DBF. Its fields are

- Name
- Type

- Length
- Decimals

Each field in the associated DBF becomes a record in the DBS. Let's create one.

Load this chapter's JDB project and execute JDB. Open the ASAMP.DBF file. Figure 15-1 shows me doing this.

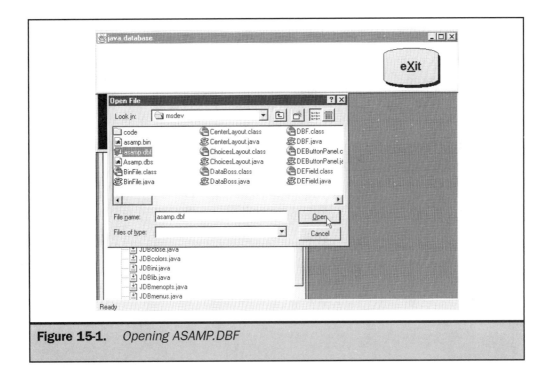

Figure 15-1.   *Opening ASAMP.DBF*

That launches the data controller menu, from which you can select the scroller and/or the data-entry screen. Click the Create button, as you see here:

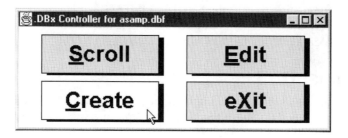

After you click Create, a dialog box appears, as shown here, to let you know your DBS file is available.

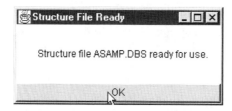

Return to the main menu and choose Open again. This time, in the Open File dialog box, open ASAMP.DBS.

The data controller menu for ASAMP.DBS lets you open a scroller and a data-entry form. In Figure 15-2, you see that I've opened both.

Creating a DBF

When you choose Create on FOO.DBF's data controller menu, FOO.DBS is automatically created. If FOO.DBS exists, it will be replaced with the newly created one. There's no warning dialog box. (Add one if you like. I treat my DBS files as temporary work files—they're completely disposable.)

The reverse process is more finicky. When you click Create on a FOO.DBS' data controller menu, a new, empty FOO.DBF will be created, but only if no FOO.DBF exists. Create gives you an error dialog box if you attempt to overwrite an existing DBF, as shown here:

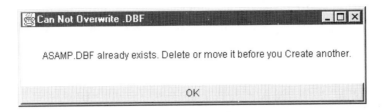

When you create a DBF, it's initially empty. Overwriting an existing DBF has the potential for wiping out a large amount of possibly valuable data.

If you don't want the data in a DBF, simply delete it. If you do want it, rename it.

One of the things JDB does not do for you is to copy data from an existing DBF into a DBF of the same name after you've revised the structure. To expand a field, for example, you'll need to rename the existing DBF, create the DBS, enter the new field size, and create a new, empty DBF. Then you have to write a little utility that reads the old DBF and writes its data into the new one.

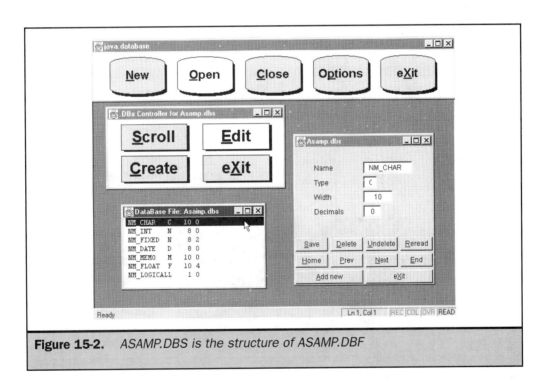

Figure 15-2.   *ASAMP.DBS is the structure of ASAMP.DBF*

Most database products have a structure-revision capability built in, but it's extremely complex. You might add some very simple change capabilities to JDB, such as allowing a field's size to change, or for fields to be added or deleted. The general case gets far more complex.

For example, adding one field and deleting another can result in the same structure as simply renaming a field. How do you distinguish one from the other? How do you handle data that won't fit when a field's size is reduced? Type changes are particularly challenging. Some are reasonable (date to character) and some are not (character to date).

Writing a little utility to copy one DBF's data to another is simple by comparison. (Create two new DBF objects to open your DBF files. Loop from zero to getLast( ), calling getValues( ) for the source, fix up the values as needed, and putValues( ) to the destination. Finishing by calling close( ) is tidy, but not necessary.)

Creating a Phone List Table

Let's create an entirely new database. For this, choose New on the main menu. As you see in Figure 15-3, I'm creating ANEWDBF.

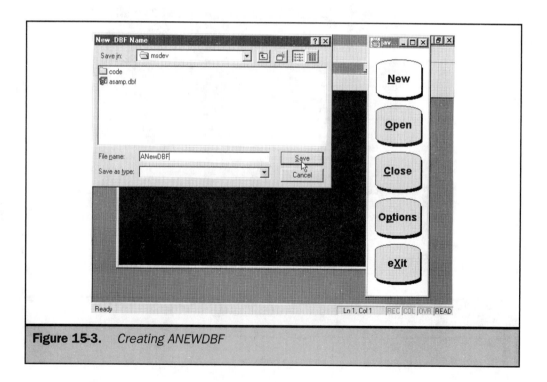

Figure 15-3.   *Creating ANEWDBF*

This will create ANEWDBF.DBS, a new, empty structure file. The dialog box shown here confirms that the DBS is ready to use.

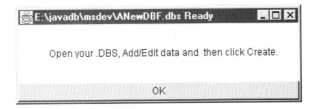

Your next step is to open the new DBS.

I've opened both the scroller and the data-entry window. Click the Add button on the DEForm and enter a field's data. Then click Add again and enter another field, until you have populated the structure with whatever fields you'll want in your own phone list table. Mine's shown in Figure 15-4.

To get your integers to line up correctly, use the END key, backspace once for each digit, and then type the digits.

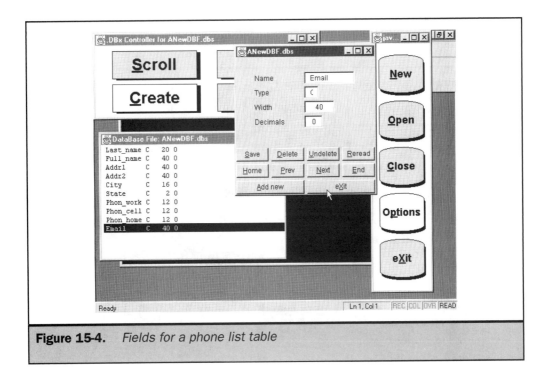

Figure 15-4. *Fields for a phone list table*

This is a bug, sort of, in JDB. If your numbers are not right-justified, you can go into the field, add spaces on the left, and click Save. Nothing happens! JDB's comparison logic strips spaces, which means it can't tell the difference between " 1" and "1 ". Since JDB thinks the data is unchanged, it doesn't save.

To get around this quirk, change the number when you add the correct spaces. Save, then correct the number, and Save again.

Another alternative is to not worry about it. The creation process will read 20 from "twenty " or " twenty".

When your structure data is ready, click Create on the DBS' data controller menu. As Figure 15-5 shows, JDB reports that your new DBF is ready for use.

Now you can open the new DBF and add some data, as Figure 15-6 shows that I've done.

At this point, you can delete the DBS. Its entire contents are saved in the header of the DBF. If you want to get the DBS back at a later date, simply open the DBF and click Create.

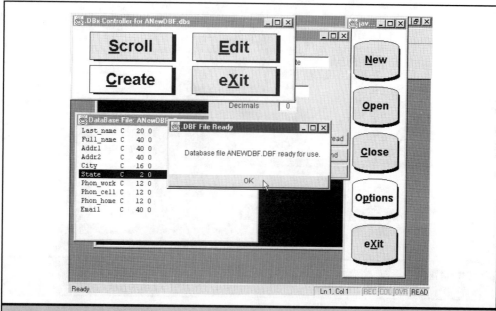

Figure 15-5.   *The phone list DBF is ready*

Figure 15-6.   *Using JDB to enter data*

Create a DBF or two on your own. Use JDB until you're comfortable with the creation process and DBS files begin to feel like old friends. When you come back, we'll look at the code.

The JDBclose Menu Class

This section is highly recommended. Unlike the static menus, JDBclose is dynamic, expanding and contracting as you open and close files.
And the code is very short.

The Close button on the main menu launches the file-closing menu, which you see in Figure 15-7.

Like our other menus, the code for the JDBclose menu is short. Unlike our other menus, JDBclose is dynamic, not static. The Close All and eXit choices are always present. The rest of the choices depend on what files (if any) you have open. Even though a DBF could have three windows (data controller menu, scroll window, and data-entry form), it's just one file for the purposes of the JDBclose menu.

If you'd like to see how dynamic this menu is, start JDB and open two or three files. Then click Close to launch this menu. But don't choose anything on the Close

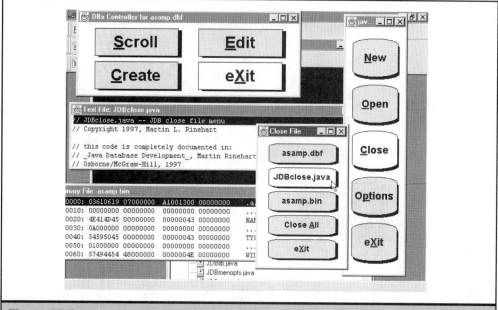

Figure 15-7. *You can close one or all files*

menu. Leave the Close menu in a position where it won't get covered by the next file you open.

Instead of closing anything, open another file while the Close menu is visible. You'll see a new member added to the Close menu, on the fly. (This is also a slick demonstration of the power of ChoicesLayout.)

Let's take a look at the new features in JDBclose.

This is another comment about JDB. It's in the sufficient stupidity group of bugs.

The stupidity is that the Close All choice is presented even when there is only one file open. If you have just FOO.DBF open, for example, you get to Close All or just FOO.DBF. All, of course, is just FOO.DBF. Duh.

If I weren't busy writing this book, I'd leave JDBclose alone, but I'd recode JDB so that if there is just one file open, clicking Close closes that file. What else could Close mean with one file open?

Until I get the time, I'm letting this bug slide. It's harmless, after all. Why don't you try a fix in your copy?

Understanding the JDBclose Method

The data is similar to all the other menus. The two permanent choices initialize the prompt array:

```
protected String[] prompts = {
    "Close &All",
    "e&Xit"
} ;
```

The constructor is identical to the constructors of the static menus. The only new wrinkle is in the private menu_click( ) method. It begins in a common way, exiting if there's no work to do, and picking the prompt number from the Event's arg variable if there is work:

```
private void menu_click( Event e ) {

    if ( e.arg == null ) return;

    int where = (( Integer ) e.arg).intValue();
```

Next it checks for an eXit click. The eXit prompt is at length –1, as this shows:

```
if ( where == menu_panel.prompts.length - 1 )
        shut_down() ;
```

The Close All prompt is at length –2. The boss.close( ) method expects a file number from zero through one less than the number of menus. The special value, –1, tells the boss that Close All was clicked.

Unlike our other operations, which are all quick, Close All can take some serious work. (Open 20 or more files and then click Close All if you want to see for yourself.) This means that the hourglass cursor comes in handy.

That should explain this code:

```
else if ( where == menu_panel.prompts.length - 2 )
{
    int c = getCursorType();
    setCursor( Frame.WAIT_CURSOR );
    boss.close( -1 );
    setCursor( c );
}
```

The last choice is the normal one, where you've clicked a particular file:

```
else
    boss.close( where );
```

The Full JDBclose.java Listing

Listing 15-1 is the full JDBclose.java source file.

Listing 15-1:
JDBclose.java

```
// JDBclose.java -- JDB close file menu
// Copyright 1997, Martin L. Rinehart

// this code is completely documented in:
// _Java Database Development_, Martin Rinehart,
// Osborne/McGraw-Hill, 1997

import java.awt.*;

class JDBclose extends Frame {

// -------------------- data members --------------------

// there are no public data members

// protected data members:

    protected JDB boss ;

    protected boolean is_back ;

    protected MenuPanel menu_panel ;

    protected RRectPromptPainter prompt_painter ;
    protected String[] prompts = {
        "Close &All",
        "e&Xit"
    } ;

// there are no static data members

// -------------------- public methods --------------------
```

```
// constructor:

    JDBclose( JDB dad ) {

        boss = dad ;

        show(); hide(); // workaround position bug

        setTitle( "Close File" );

        prompt_painter = new RRectPromptPainter(
            JDBlib.default_h_round,
            JDBlib.default_v_round ) ;
        prompt_painter.setHiColor( JDBlib.default_hi_back,
            JDBlib.default_hi_fore ) ;
        prompt_painter.setLoColor( JDBlib.default_lo_back,
            JDBlib.default_lo_fore ) ;

        menu_panel = new MenuPanel( prompts,
            1/3.0, prompt_painter, this ) ;
        menu_panel.setFollowsCursor( true );

        setLayout( new CenterLayout(32) ) ;
        add( menu_panel );
        boss.register( menu_panel,
            JDBlib.close_menu );

        resize( 175, 250 );
    }

// there are no data access methods

// public, class-specific method:

    public void shut_down() {

        hide() ;
    }

// public, non-event overriding method:

    public String paramString() {
```

```java
            return "boss: " + boss;
    }

// public, event-handling method:

    public boolean handleEvent( Event e ) {

        if ( e.id == Event.WINDOW_DESTROY ) {
            shut_down() ;
            return true ;
        }

        if ( e.target == menu_panel ) {
            menu_click( e ) ;
            return true ;
        }

        return true ;
    }

// ------------------ private methods ------------------

// private method:

    private void menu_click( Event e ) {

        if ( e.arg == null ) return ;

        int where = (( Integer ) e.arg).intValue();

        if ( where == menu_panel.prompts.length - 1 )
                shut_down() ;
        else if ( where == menu_panel.prompts.length - 2 )
        {
            int c = getCursorType();
            setCursor( Frame.WAIT_CURSOR );
            boss.close( -1 );
            setCursor( c );
        }
        else
            boss.close( where );
```

```
    }

} // end of JDBclose class

// there are no private classes in JDBclose.java

// end of JDBclose.java
```

The New JDB Mainline

TOUR

If you want to dive right into the file handling, skip right to the "Summary" of this chapter and then indulge yourself in Chapter 16. You'll want to come back here when, for example, you want to improve the Close click.

The JDB.java we covered in Chapter 9 has been revised and extended to accommodate the actual file handling. While all the work of creating DBF and DBS files is encapsulated in the JDBnew class that we'll look at in Chapter 16, there are still front-end matters that only JDB can handle.

Obviously, the menu clicks that were stubbed out (New, Open, and Close) have to be implemented. Equally important, and more challenging, is keeping lists of the files and windows opened so that the Close menu, for one example, is properly maintained.

The New Data

In this section I'm going to skip even vitally important items if they're reasonably self-explanatory. I don't think you'll need any help with, for instance, members like this:

```
    protected FileDialog open_file_dialog;
```

These two Vectors, however, are critical:

```
    protected Vector file_wins;
    protected Vector files;
```

When you open a file, two things are opened: the disk file and a display window. When you close a file, you need to close both the file and the window.

The file_wins Vector holds references to the Frames of binary and text files. It holds references to the DataBoss objects for DBF and DBS files. The files Vector holds references to the files, which will be DBF, TxtFile, or BinFile objects.

When we open a file, we'll add to these Vectors. In the following two lines from open_binfile( ), bf is a readable BinFile and sw is the ScrollWin that shows it:

```
files.addElement( bf );
file_wins.addElement( sw );
```

Similar logic handles the other file types. The close process, which we'll cover next, removes elements from these Vectors.

The New Public Close Methods

For ease of reference, we'll discuss the methods in the order they appear in the file. Since the file-closing methods are public, they're going to come ahead of the file-opening methods.

The first is the simple close( ) method.

The close( ) Method

The prompts in the JDBclose menu are listed in the order you opened the files. This is also the order that the object references are held in the files and file_wins Vectors. So a click on the third prompt calls for closing the third file. (The third prompt is Vector element number two, since counting starts at zero.)

The close( ) method is called with either the number of the file to close or a minus one, indicating that Close All was clicked. The close( ) method handles either case, delegating the actual closing work:

```
public void close( int i ) {

    if ( i != -1 )
        close_file( i );
    else
        while ( files.size() > 0 )
            close_file( 0 );
}
```

The close_file( ) Method

The close_file( ) method is the one that close( ) asks to do the work. It just divides the job into closing the file and closing the associated window:

```
public void close_file ( int i ) {

    close_file_file( i );
    close_file_window( i );
}
```

This gets the job done, though I'm not pleased with the name "close_file_file( )." (I must have been having a bad-name day.)

Closing the File

There are two close_file_file( ) methods. One is called with a reference to the actual file to close. The other is called with the location of the file reference in the files Vector. The first just converts its object to a reference for the second:

```
public void close_file_file( Object o ) {

    close_file_file( file_wins.indexOf(o) );
}
```

The work is done by the close_file_file( ) that takes an integer, this way:

```
public void close_file_file( int i ) {

    Object file = files.elementAt( i );
```

The first job is to close the actual file. This is done by calling the appropriate covering class' close( ) method, this way:

```
if ( file instanceof DBF )
    ( (DBF) file ).close();
else if ( file instanceof TxtFile )
        ( (TxtFile) file ).close();
    else
        ( (BinFile) file ).close();
```

The second item is removing the file from the files Vector:

```
files.removeElementAt( i );
```

If you skipped the MenuPanel classes "Understanding" section (back in Chapter 8), you missed the fact that there is a remove( ) method for that class. This is used next to eliminate this file from the JDBclose menu:

```
close_menu.menu_panel.remove( i );
```

The final item is to close the Close menu if there aren't any more open files:

```
if ( files.size() == 0 )
    close_menu.hide();
```

Closing the Window

There are three close_file_window( ) methods. The first one is like the first close_file_file( ) method. It converts an object reference to a Vector location and calls the second form:

```
public void close_file_window( Object o ) {

    close_file_window( file_wins.indexOf(o), true );
}
```

The closing process can be initiated from the DataBoss (via an eXit click on the data controller menu, for example). That's a bit different than a close initiated from the Close menu. So the second close_file_window( ) simply adds a boolean specifying that this call is not from the DataBoss:

```
public void close_file_window( int i ) {

    close_file_window( i, false );
}
```

The real work is done by the third close_file_window( ). Its parameter name makes the meaning of the second argument very clear:

```
public void close_file_window( int i, boolean
    called_from_databoss ) {
```

The contents of the file_wins Vector will be either a ScrollWin (BinFile and TxtFile use ScrollWin) or a DataBoss (for DBF and DBS files). The ScrollWins are hidden and then discarded. The DataBoss is told to shut_down( ). If the original call came from the DataBoss, the hiding and disposing has already been done.

In every case, the final detail is to remove the reference from the file_wins Vector. This is the working part of the routine:

```
if ( ! called_from_databoss ) {

    if ( file_wins.elementAt(i) instanceof
        ScrollWin ) {

        ScrollWin sw = ( ScrollWin )
            file_wins.elementAt( i );
        if ( sw != null ) {

            sw.hide();
            sw.dispose();
        }
    }
    else {

        DataBoss db = ( DataBoss )
            file_wins.elementAt( i );
        db.shut_down( true );
    }
}

file_wins.removeElementAt( i );
```

The New and Revised Private Methods

The most important additions to JDB are a new menu_click( ) method and file-opening logic that actually opens files. We'll start with the menu_click( ) method.

The Revised menu_click( ) Method

Skipping minor details (see the full listing), we see that the menu_click( ) method is a switch, with the elements corresponding to the main menu order: New, Open, Close, Options, and eXit. The New option is the most complex. The code here, however, is the simplest:

```
case 0:
    new JDBnew( this );
    break;
```

Whenever you see the *new* operator used without an assignment, you know you're looking at good old procedural code, with a sprinkle of object flavorings on top. The whole file-creation process is covered in detail in Chapter 16.

The Open code ties with New for simplicity:

```
case 1:
    open_file();
    break;
```

We'll look at open_file( ) later in the next section of this chapter.

The Close code is complicated by the fact that there may be nothing to close. It either launches the close_menu, or it gives you an appropriate message:

```
case 2:
    if ( files.size() == 0 ) {
        mb = new MsgBox(
            "There are no open files.",
            "Nothing to Close" );

        mb.show();
    }
    else {

        close_menu.show();
    }
    break;
```

The final two options, Options and eXit, are the same as you saw in Chapter 9.

File-Opening Methods

The open_binfile( ) and open_txtfile( ) methods are almost the same as the ones you saw when we worked on the first FileViewer application. There are three more items to handle:

- Adding the file to the files Vector
- Adding the file window to the file_wins Vector
- Adding a prompt to the Close menu

Handling these items is straightforward. These are the three statements added to open_binfile( ):

```
files.addElement( bf );
file_wins.addElement( sw );
close_menu.menu_panel.add(
    bf.getFileName(),
    files.size() - 1 );
```

Remember that the Close menu has Close All and eXit as the two last prompts, so you cannot simply add( ) the new prompt at the end. You have to insert it at the proper location.

This extra work is also added to the open_txtfile( ) method.

The open_dbf( ) method is entirely new. It starts by creating a new DBF object based on the response to the FileDialog. Then, if the resulting DBF is readable, it creates a DataBoss, adds the DBF to the files Vector, adds the DataBoss to the file_wins Vector, and adds the new prompt to the Close menu.

```
private boolean open_dbf() {

    DBF dbf = new DBF(
        open_file_dialog.getFile(), "rw" );

    if ( dbf.readable ) {

        DataBoss db = new DataBoss( this, dbf );
        files.addElement( dbf );
        file_wins.addElement( db );

        close_menu.menu_panel.add(
```

```
                    dbf.file_name,
                    files.size() - 1 );
    }

    return dbf.readable;
}
```

Finally, we come to the open_file( ) method that selects one of these file-opening routines. It starts by launching the FileDialog and exiting if the user Cancels out:

```
private void open_file() {

    open_file_dialog.show();

    if ( open_file_dialog.getFile() == null )
        return;
```

Next it uses the file_ext( ) method to pick out the final extension characters:

```
    String ext =
        file_ext( open_file_dialog.getFile() )
        .toUpperCase();
```

The file_ext( ), as its name suggests, picks the extension part from a filename, returning, for one example, "DBF" from "FOO.DBF". Use the full listing if you want to check, for example, for UNIX compatibility.

Next it attempts to open "DBF" and "DBS" extensions as DBFs:

```
    if ( ext.equals("DBF") && open_dbf() )
        return;

    if ( ext.equals("DBS") && open_dbf() )
        return;
```

Finally, it attempts to open a text file or, as a last resort, a binary file, just as our FileViewer did:

```
        if ( open_txtfile() )
            return;

    if ( open_binfile() )
        return;

     // else
     MsgBox mb = new MsgBox(
        "Could not open " +
            open_file_dialog.getFile(),
        "File Not Opened" );
     mb.show();
}
```

The Full JDB.java Listing

Listing 15-2 is the full JDB.java source file.

Listing 15-2:
JDB.java

```
// JDB.java -- Java DataBase mainline
// Copyright 1997, Martin L. Rinehart

import java.awt.*;
import java.util.Vector;

class JDB extends Frame {

// -------------------- data members --------------------

// there are no public data members

// protected data members:

    protected JDBclose close_menu;
    protected int current_menu_class;
    protected int current_menu_group;

    protected Vector file_wins;
    protected Vector files;

    protected JDBini ini_file;
```

```java
    protected String[] main_menu_prompts = {
            "&New",
            "&Open",
            "&Close",
            "O&ptions",
            "e&Xit"
    };

    protected MenuPanel[] menu_list;
    protected MenuPanel menu_panel;
    protected double[][] menu_option_values;

    protected FileDialog open_file_dialog;
    protected JDBoptions option_menu;

    protected RRectPromptPainter prompt_painter;

     // static data members

     // there are no public static data members

     // protected static data member:

    protected final static Color[] color_vals = {

        Color.red, Color.green, Color.blue,
        Color.yellow, Color.cyan, Color.magenta,
        Color.orange, Color.pink, Color.white,
        Color.lightGray, Color.gray, Color.darkGray,
        Color.black
    };

     // final static data member:

    protected static final double[] val_table = {
        1024.0, 16.0, 12.0, 8.0,
           4.0,  3.0,  2.0, 1.5, 1.0 };

// ------------------- public methods -------------------

    public static void main( String[] args ) {
```

```
        ( new JDB() ).show();
    }

// constructors:

    JDB( int i ) {
        // don't call this constructor
        // VCafe will write stuff here
            //{{INIT_CONTROLS
          setLayout(null);
          addNotify();
          resize(insets().left + insets().right + 430,insets().top
            + insets().bottom + 270);
          setTitle("Untitled");
          //}}
          //{{INIT_MENUS
          //}}
    }

    JDB() {

        show(); hide(); // workaround position bug

        resize ( 500, 300 );
        setTitle( "java.database" );

        prompt_painter = new RRectPromptPainter(
            JDBlib.default_h_round,
            JDBlib.default_v_round );
        prompt_painter.setHiColor( JDBlib.default_hi_back,
            JDBlib.default_hi_fore );
        prompt_painter.setLoColor( JDBlib.default_lo_back,
            JDBlib.default_lo_fore );

        menu_panel = new MenuPanel( main_menu_prompts,
            0.667, prompt_painter, this );
        menu_panel.setFollowsCursor( true );

        setLayout( new CenterLayout(32) );

        add( menu_panel );
```

```
            menu_list = new MenuPanel[JDBlib.num_menus];
            menu_list[0] = menu_panel;

            option_menu = new JDBoptions( this );

            open_file_dialog =
                new FileDialog( this, "Open File" );

            files = new Vector();
            file_wins = new Vector();

            close_menu = new JDBclose( this );

            menu_option_values = new double[
                JDBlib.num_menus][10];

            ini_file = new JDBini( this );
            JDBini.read_ini();
    }

// data access getXxx() methods:

    public String getMenuName( int i ) {

        return JDBlib.menu_names[i];
    }

     public MenuPanel getMenuPanel( int i ) {

        return menu_list[i];
    }

    public double[] getMenuValues( int i ) {

        return menu_option_values[i];
    }

// there are no data access isXxx() methods

// data access setXxx() methods:
```

```java
    public void setCurrentMenuClass( int i ) {

        current_menu_class = i;
    }

    public void setCurrentMenuGroup( int i ) {

        current_menu_group = i;
    }

    public void setMenuOption( boolean which, Object o ) {

        // which: true == horizontal for shape
        //                 background for colors

        // o instanceof Integer for shape
        //              Color for colors

        if ( o instanceof Color )
            set_menu_color( which, (Color) o );
        else
            set_menu_shape( which,
                (( Integer ) o).intValue() );
    }

    public void setMenuValues( int men_num, double[] d ) {

        for ( int i = 1 ; i < 11 ; i++ )
            menu_option_values[men_num][i-1] = d[i];
    }

// public, class-specific methods:

    public void close( int i ) {

        if ( i != -1 )
            close_file( i );
        else
            while ( files.size() > 0 )
                close_file( 0 );
    }
```

```
public void close_file ( int i ) {

    close_file_file( i );
    close_file_window( i );
}

public void close_file_file( Object o ) {

    close_file_file( file_wins.indexOf(o) );
}

public void close_file_file( int i ) {

    Object file = files.elementAt( i );

    if ( file instanceof DBF )
        ( (DBF) file ).close();
    else if ( file instanceof TxtFile )
            ( (TxtFile) file ).close();
      else
        ( (BinFile) file ).close();

    files.removeElementAt( i );

    close_menu.menu_panel.remove( i );

    if ( files.size() == 0 )
        close_menu.hide();
}

public void close_file_window( Object o ) {

    close_file_window( file_wins.indexOf(o), true );
}


public void close_file_window( int i ) {

    close_file_window( i, false );
}
```

```
public void close_file_window( int i, boolean
    called_from_databoss ) {

    if ( ! called_from_databoss ) {

        if ( file_wins.elementAt(i) instanceof
            ScrollWin ) {

            ScrollWin sw = ( ScrollWin )
                file_wins.elementAt( i );
            if ( sw != null ) {

                sw.hide();
                sw.dispose();
            }
        }
        else {

            DataBoss db = ( DataBoss )
                file_wins.elementAt( i );
            db.shut_down( true );

        }
    }

    file_wins.removeElementAt( i );
}

public void register( MenuPanel mp, int which_menu ) {

    menu_list[which_menu] = mp;
}

public void setupLoColorMenus() {

    int menu_num = find_target_menu();

    if ( JDBlib.is_zmenu[menu_num] ) {

        Color c = new Color(
            (int) menu_option_values[menu_num][4] );
        int menu_loc = find_color( c );
        menu_list[JDBlib.back_colors_menu].setHilight(
```

```
                    menu_loc );

            c = new  Color (
                (int) menu_option_values[menu_num][5] );
            menu_loc = find_color( c );
            menu_list[JDBlib.fore_colors_menu].setHilight(
                menu_loc );
        }
        else {
            MenuPanel mp =
                menu_list[menu_num];

            PromptPainter pp = mp.painter;

            Color c = pp.getLoBackColor();
            int menu_loc = find_color( c );
            menu_list[JDBlib.back_colors_menu].setHilight(
                menu_loc );

            c = pp.getLoForeColor();
            menu_loc = find_color( c );
            menu_list[JDBlib.fore_colors_menu].setHilight(
                menu_loc );
        }
    }

    public void setupHiColorMenus() {

        int menu_num = find_target_menu();

        if ( JDBlib.is_zmenu[menu_num] ) {

            Color c = new Color(
                (int) menu_option_values[menu_num][6] );
            int menu_loc = find_color( c );
            menu_list[JDBlib.back_colors_menu].setHilight(
                menu_loc );

            c = new  Color (
                (int) menu_option_values[menu_num][7] );
            menu_loc = find_color( c );
            menu_list[JDBlib.fore_colors_menu].setHilight(
```

```
                menu_loc );
        }
    else {

        MenuPanel mp =
            menu_list[menu_num];

        PromptPainter pp = mp.painter;

        Color c = pp.getHiBackColor();
        int menu_loc = find_color( c );
        menu_list[JDBlib.back_colors_menu].setHilight(
            menu_loc );

        c = pp.getHiForeColor();
        menu_loc = find_color( c );
        menu_list[JDBlib.fore_colors_menu].setHilight(
            menu_loc );
        }
    }


public void setupShapeMenus() {

    int menu_num = find_target_menu();

    if ( JDBlib.is_zmenu[menu_num] ) {

        double rad = menu_option_values[menu_num][8];
        int menu_loc = find_shape_index( rad );
        menu_list[JDBlib.horz_shapes_menu].setHilight(
            menu_loc );

        rad = menu_option_values[menu_num][9];
        menu_loc = find_shape_index( rad );
        menu_list[JDBlib.vert_shapes_menu].setHilight(
            menu_loc );
        }
    else {

        MenuPanel mp = menu_list[menu_num];

        RRectPromptPainter rp =
```

```
                              ( RRectPromptPainter ) ( mp.painter );

                double rad = rp.hradius;
                int menu_loc = find_shape_index( rad );
                menu_list[JDBlib.horz_shapes_menu].setHilight(
                    menu_loc );

                rad = rp.vradius;
                menu_loc = find_shape_index( rad );
                menu_list[JDBlib.vert_shapes_menu].setHilight(
                    menu_loc );
            }
        }

// public, non-event overriding method:

    public String paramString() {

        String s = "";

        for ( int i = 0 ; i < main_menu_prompts.length ;
            i++ ) {

            s = s + main_menu_prompts[i];
            if ( i < main_menu_prompts.length - 1 )
                s = s + ", ";
        }

        return s;
    }

// public, event-handling method:

    public boolean handleEvent( Event e ) {

        if ( e.id == Event.WINDOW_DESTROY )
            shut_down();

        if ( e.target == menu_panel ) {
            menu_click( e );
            return true;
        }
```

```java
        return true;
    }

// ------------------ private methods -------------------

// private methods:

    private int find_color( Color c ) {

        for ( int i = 0 ; i < color_vals.length ; i++ )
            if ( c.equals(color_vals[i]) )
                return i;

        return 0;
    }

    private int find_shape_index( double d ) {

        for( int i = 0 ; i < val_table.length ; i++ ) {
            if ( d >= val_table[i] )
                return i;
        }
        return 0;
    }

    private int find_target_menu() {

        return JDBlib.menu_classes[current_menu_class][0];
    }

    private String file_ext( String s ) {

        if ( s == null )
            return "";

        int dot_loc = s.indexOf( '.' );
        if ( dot_loc == -1 )
            return "";

        if ( dot_loc == (s.length( )-1) )
            return "";
```

```
      return s.substring( dot_loc + 1, s.length() );
 }

private void menu_click( Event e ) {

    if ( e.arg == null ) return;

    MsgBox mb;

    switch( (( Integer ) e.arg).intValue() ) {

        case 0:
            new JDBnew( this );
            break;

        case 1:
            open_file();
            break;

        case 2:
            if ( files.size() == 0 ) {
                mb = new MsgBox(
                    "There are no open files.",
                    "Nothing to Close" );

                mb.show();
            }
            else {

                close_menu.show();
            }
            break;

        case 3:
            option_menu.show();
            break;

        case 4:
            shut_down();
    }
}
```

```java
private boolean open_binfile() {

    BinFile bf = new BinFile(
        open_file_dialog.getFile() );

    if ( bf.isReadable() ) {

        ScrollWin sw = new ScrollWin(
            bf, "Binary File: " +
            bf.getFileName() );

        sw.resize( 540, 300 );
         sw.setRefuseClose( true );
        sw.show();

        files.addElement( bf );
        file_wins.addElement( sw );
        close_menu.menu_panel.add(
            bf.getFileName(),
            files.size() - 1 );
        return true;
    }
    return false;
}

private boolean open_dbf() {

    DBF dbf = new DBF(
        open_file_dialog.getFile(), "rw" );

    if ( dbf.readable ) {

        DataBoss db = new DataBoss( this, dbf );
        files.addElement( dbf );
        file_wins.addElement( db );

        close_menu.menu_panel.add(
            dbf.file_name,
            files.size() - 1 );
    }
```

```
            return dbf.readable;
      }

   private void open_file() {

      open_file_dialog.show();

      if ( open_file_dialog.getFile() == null )
         return;

      String ext =
         file_ext( open_file_dialog.getFile() )
         .toUpperCase();

      if ( ext.equals("DBF") && open_dbf() )
         return;

      if ( ext.equals("DBS") && open_dbf() )
         return;

       if ( open_txtfile() )
           return;

      if ( open_binfile() )
         return;

       // else
      MsgBox mb = new MsgBox(
         "Could not open " +
            open_file_dialog.getFile(),
         "File Not Opened" );
      mb.show();
   }

   private boolean open_txtfile() {

      TxtFile tf = new TxtFile(
         open_file_dialog.getFile() );

      if ( tf.isReadable() ) {
```

```
            ScrollWin sw = new ScrollWin(
                tf, "Text File: " +
                tf.getFileName() );

            sw.resize( 540, 300 );
             sw.setRefuseClose( true );

            sw.show();

            files.addElement( tf );
            file_wins.addElement( sw );
            close_menu.menu_panel.add(
                tf.getFileName(),
                files.size() - 1 );
            return true;
        }
      return false;
}

private void set_menu_color(
    boolean is_back, Color c ) {

    int[] mclass = JDBlib.menu_classes[
        current_menu_class];

    for ( int i = 0 ; i < mclass.length ; i++ )
        set_menu_color( mclass[i], is_back, c );
}

private void set_menu_color( int i,
    boolean is_back, Color c ) {

    if ( JDBlib.is_zmenu[i] ) {

        if ( current_menu_group == 0 ) { // normal color
            if ( is_back )
                menu_option_values[i][4] = c.getRGB();
            else
                menu_option_values[i][5] = c.getRGB();
        }
        else {                               // hilight color
```

```
                    if ( is_back )
                        menu_option_values[i][6] = c.getRGB();
                    else
                        menu_option_values[i][7] = c.getRGB();
                }


            }
            else {

                MenuPanel mp = menu_list[i];
                PromptPainter pp = mp.painter;

                if ( current_menu_group == 0 ) { // normal color
                    if ( is_back )
                        pp.setLoBackColor( c );
                    else
                        pp.setLoForeColor( c );
                }
                else {                            // hilight color
                    if ( is_back )
                        pp.setHiBackColor( c );
                    else
                        pp.setHiForeColor( c );
                }

                mp.hide();
                mp.show();
                Thread.yield();
            }
        }

        private void set_menu_shape(
            boolean is_horizontal, int index ) {

            int[] mclass = JDBlib.menu_classes[
                current_menu_class];

            for ( int i = 0 ; i < mclass.length ; i++ )
                set_menu_shape(
                    mclass[i], is_horizontal, index );
        }
```

```java
private void set_menu_shape(
    int i, boolean is_horizontal, int val ) {

    double value = val_table[val];

    if ( JDBlib.is_zmenu[i] ) {

        if ( is_horizontal )
            menu_option_values[i][8] = value;
        else
            menu_option_values[i][9] = value;
    }
    else {

        MenuPanel mp = menu_list[i];
        PromptPainter pp = mp.painter;
        RRectPromptPainter rp =
            ( RRectPromptPainter ) pp;

        if ( is_horizontal )
            rp.setHRadius( value );
        else
            rp.setVRadius( value );

        mp.hide();
        mp.show();
    }
}

private void shut_down() {

    JDBini.write_ini();

      if ( option_menu != null )
          option_menu.shut_down();

    dispose();
    System.exit( 0 );
}

  //{{DECLARE_CONTROLS
  //}}
```

```
        //{{DECLARE_MENUS
        //}}
} // end of JDB class

// there are no private classes in JDB.java

// end of JDB.java
```

Summary

We began by using the Create option on a DBF's data controller menu. This wrote the DBF's meta data (structure information) into another DBF, but I've given these meta data tables the extension .DBS, for DataBase Structure. Editing the DBS lets you revise the database structure. Clicking the Create option on a DBS creates a new, empty DBF. We don't let the DBF-creation process override an existing DBF. To modify the structure of an existing DBF, you have to create a new one and write a utility program to copy the data from the old DBF into the new one. We also used the main menu's New option to create a new, empty DBS. Adding the field-description data to the DBS gets you ready to create a new DBF, just as editing the field-description data did when you started with an existing DBF.

We looked at the code, starting with the JDBclose menu. It is similar to the static menus we've seen earlier, but it is dynamic. As you open and close files, options are added to and deleted from the Close menu.

The adding and deleting menu option code is actually done in JDB, which is significantly larger than it was previously. The main additions are file-opening and -closing code.

You saw that for JDB (as with any database system) opening a file really means opening both the file and a screen window (or two or three windows) so that the user can see the file. There's a fair amount of bookkeeping involved in maintaining Vectors of open files and windows and adjusting the Close menu appropriately.

The one thing that we didn't look at was the bottom-level bit-fiddling code that actually created the DBF and DBS files. This was all encapsulated in the JDBnew class, which is the topic of Chapter 16.

Chapter 16

The JDBnew Class

In Chapter 15 we looked at the entire process by which DBFs' structures could be looked at in DBS files and by which new DBFs could be created from DBS files. Except that we skipped one class: JDBnew.

JDBnew is the one that actually creates the files. If you don't think you're doing real database programming until you're up to your elbows in bits and bytes and file writes, then you'll love this chapter. JDBnew is our topic and juggling bytes into disk files is its job.

We'll begin by looking at the data, which is straightforward. Then we'll go on to the public methods.

Most of the public methods are static. We'll begin with a look at the test mainline and the constructor, which are exceptions to that rule. Remember that we called the constructor without bothering to record the reference it returned, this way:

```
new JDBnew( this );
```

Java is a pure object-oriented language, unlike a mixed procedural and object language, such as C++. Right?

If enough people say a thing, I suppose it must be true. The JDBnew class illustrates perfectly, however, that even pure object systems sometimes need great runs of old-fashioned procedural code. There is, to my knowledge, no difference between the working of procedural code in a library and procedural code in static (classwide) functions. Using a constructor but ignoring the returned reference is another way to call procedural code. Never do this unless you've thought the problem through and decided that it calls for a procedural approach.

After the constructor, we'll go on to the static methods. The two key ones create DBS files from scratch and DBF files from DBS files.

We'll go on to the private methods. As you'd expect, the public methods delegate most of the hard work to private methods, where all the gritty details are hidden.

TOUR

If you think that low-level database programming is something that someone should do for you, study the public methods and ignore the private ones. If the details of this work interest you, enjoy the whole chapter.

JDBnew's Data

We'll start with the data, which is delightfully simple. All the data members are protected. The first is a FileDialog:

```
protected FileDialog file_dialog;
```

The next three are the ones that break apart the file path and name:

```
protected MRString file_ext;
protected MRString file_name;
protected MRString file_path;
```

In UNIX, the use of a filename suffix, separated by a period, is a common way to identify files. FOO.C, for example, would probably be a C source file. That's not a true extension, or identifier of what the operating system understands as a file type, as the extension is in DOS-based systems.

Don't let that variable name throw you. The "file_ext" part may be a true DOS extension, or it might just be a UNIX suffix. The code works either way.

The final data member is the Frame that owns the JDBnew object:

```
protected Frame owner;
```

The Public Methods

There are nonstatic and static methods. We'll look at the nonstatic ones first. Ignoring a trivial paramString( ), there are only two.

The Public, Nonstatic Methods

There are two nontrivial public, nonstatic methods: a mainline (for testing) and the constructor.

The Test Mainline

There is a mainline that I used for testing. You can add a single slash to return this one to the land of the living:

```
/*
    public static void main( String[] args ) {

        new JDBnew( new Frame() );
        System.exit( 0 );
    }
// */
```

The Constructor

Far more important is the constructor. You call it with a reference to the owning Frame, which JDBnew saves:

```
JDBnew( Frame owner ) {

    this.owner = owner;
```

Next JDB creates a Frame to be parent of the FileDialog. The totally modal Windows File Dialog is one of my pet peeves. I find myself looking at one far too often where I see that I should have done something before opening a file. Most of the time, if it weren't modal, I could go fix the problem, then open the file. But it's modal, so you have to Cancel out, fix the problem, and relaunch the file-opening dialog box.

JDB doesn't have this problem. The file dialog box is only modal with respect to its parent window. So I create a new, anonymous, hidden Frame as the FileDialog's parent Frame. That way you can use any part of JDB that you like while the FileDialog is waiting for input.

This is the code:

```
Frame f = new Frame(); // nearly modeless!

file_dialog = new FileDialog( f,
    "New .DBF Name", FileDialog.SAVE );

file_dialog.setFile( "*.DBF" );

file_dialog.show();
```

Next handle the ALD about users changing their minds and not picking a file:

```
if ( file_dialog.getFile() == null )
    return; // user cancelled file dialog
```

If we've got a file, we put the full path and name, extension included, into an MRString:

```
MRString from_fd =
    new MRString( file_dialog.getFile() );
```

Then we work around Windows' bad habit of leaving a default type at the end of the name:

```
if ( from_fd.endsWith(".*.*") )
    from_fd.trimRight( 4 );
```

Next we locate the period, if any:

```
int dot_loc = from_fd.indexOf( '.' );
```

If there isn't a period, the constructor creates the default file extension:

```
if ( dot_loc == -1 ) {

    file_name = from_fd;
    file_ext = new MRString( "dbf" );
}
```

Otherwise, the constructor separates the name into a name part (before the period) and an extension part (after the period):

```
else {

    file_name = from_fd.substring( 0, dot_loc );
    file_ext = from_fd.substring( dot_loc + 1 );
}
```

If you'll be using JDB on UNIX systems and you'll be using multiple embedded periods in the name, you'll have to improve that logic so that you find just the last period. Since it's in an MRString, you'll have an easy job. Just add an indexOfLast( ) method to MRString, and use it here to replace the indexOf( ) method.

At this point there might not be any filename. (Suppose you meant to type "*.xyz" and press ENTER, but you missed the "*" and just typed ".xyz" plus ENTER.) This ALD has to be handled:

```
if ( file_name.length() == 0 ) {

    MsgBox mb = new MsgBox(
        "Cannot continue New process " +
```

```
                    "without a file name.",
                    "Cannot Continue"  );
              mb.show();

              return;
         }
```

At this point we've got valid file_name and file_ext values. Now we get the third party, the file_path, from the FileDialog:

```
         file_path = new MRString(
              file_dialog.getDirectory() );
```

Then the constructor calls the create_stru_file( ) method to actually create the DBS file. Here there's one line of work and a lot of ALD:

```
    boolean wrote_ok;

    String fname = full_stru_name();
    if ( ! exists(fname) ) {

         wrote_ok = create_stru_file( fname );

         if ( ! wrote_ok ) {

              MsgBox mb = new MsgBox(
                   "Error while writing " +
                   full_stru_name() + ".",
                   "File Write Error" );
              return;
         }
    }
```

If the constructor is still running, it's succeeded. Its last job is to report success:

```
    MsgBox mb = new MsgBox(
         "Open your .DBS, Add/Edit data and " +
         " then click Create.",
         full_stru_name() + " Ready");
```

```
        mb.show();
    }
```

That was simple, wasn't it?

OK, maybe it wasn't simple. If we didn't have all the user-interface ALD, it would have been simple. We'll go on now to the public static methods, where we'll begin to escape from UI-based ALD and get on with the database work.

The Public, Static Methods

There are three public static methods: create_dbf_file( ), create_stru_file( ), and exists( ). The first two do the heavy lifting in this class. We'll start with creating a DBF.

The create_dbf_file( ) Method

The structure file is another table, so the DBF class handles it nicely. (The parameter here—DBF dbs—still seems odd, doesn't it?) You create a DBF from a DBS, as the beginning of create_dbf_file( ) shows:

```
public static boolean create_dbf_file( DBF dbs ) {

    // returns true if the .DBF is created

    MRString fname = new MRString( dbs.getFileName() );
    fname.toUpper();

    if ( ! fname.endsWith(".DBS") ) {
        MsgBox mb = new MsgBox(
            "Can only be Created from .DBS.",
            "Cannot Create Database File" );
        mb.show();

        return false;
    }
```

Next we check to see that the data in the DBS is usable. This method depends on privates OK_X and err_in_X—where X is one of name, type, length, or decimals—to do its work. The OK_X( ) does the checking; the err_in_X( ) reports an error if there is one. This is the calling code in create_dbf_file( ):

```
// check the data

int flen;

for ( int i = 0 ; i <= dbs.getLast() ; i++ ) {

    Vector vals = dbs.getValues(i);

    if ( ! ok_name(vals.elementAt( 0 )) ) {

        err_in_name( vals.elementAt(0) );
        return false;
    }

    if ( !ok_type(vals.elementAt( 1 )) ) {

        err_in_type( vals.elementAt(1) );
        return false;
    }

    String s = ( String ) vals.elementAt(2);
    if ( ! ok_length(s) ) {

        err_in_length( s );
        return false;
    }

    flen = new MRString( s ).intValue();

    if ( !ok_decimals(vals.elementAt( 3 ),
        flen) ) {

        err_in_decimals( vals.elementAt(3) );
        return false;
    }
}
```

Here fname is the full path, name, and extension. The handy MRString makes it easy to change ".DBS" to ".DBF":

```
fname.toUpper();
fname.replace( fname.length() - 1, 'F' );
```

You UNIX users may want to change that toUpper( ) call. JDB is not case sensitive, so you'll have to decide how you'll be handling these data files.

Now we're ready to create the DBF file. We begin by creating a new, random-access file:

```
RandomAccessFile dbf = null;
boolean ok = true;
try {

    dbf = new RandomAccessFile(
        fname.toString(), "rw" );
}
catch( IOException ioe ) {

    ok = false;
}
```

Constantly checking for errors as we go, the header, fields, and footer of the DBF's header are written:

```
if ( ok )
    ok = write_dbf_header( dbs, dbf );

if ( ok )
    ok = write_dbf_fields( dbs, dbf );

if ( ok )
    ok = write_dbf_footer( dbf );
```

If nothing failed (it probably didn't), then we close the file:

```
if ( ok ) {

    try {
```

```
                    dbf.close();
            }
            catch ( IOException ioe ) {

                    ok = false;
            }
    }
```

If something went wrong (this code may never get used!), a dialog is launched to give you the bad news and a false is returned.

```
if ( ! ok ) {

        MsgBox mb = new MsgBox( "Could not write " +
                "new .DBF. Possibly due to lack of space.",
                ".DBF Not Created" );
        mb.show();

        return false;
}
```

Otherwise, success is reported to the calling code:

```
        return true;
}
```

This leaves a lot of details pushed into the private methods, of course. We'll cover them in the next section. Here we'll go on to the create_stru_file routine, which uses an existing DBF to create a new DBS.

The create_stru_file( ) Method

Again, the first job is to check that we're being passed a DBF file:

```
public static boolean create_stru_file( DBF dbf ) {

    // returns true if the .DBS is created

    MRString fname = new MRString( dbf.getFileName() );
```

```
fname.toUpper();

if ( ! fname.endsWith(".DBF") ) {

    MsgBox mb = new MsgBox(
        "Can only be Created from .DBF." +
        "New creates an empty .DBS",
        "Cannot Create Structure File" );
    mb.show();

    return false;
}
```

Then the MRString again makes the name change simple:

```
fname.replace( fname.length()-1, 'S' );
```

Next the create_stru_file( ) method is used to do the real work. If it fails, there are more ALDs to handle:

```
boolean ok = create_stru_file( fname.toString() );

if ( !ok ) {

    MsgBox mb = new MsgBox( "Could not create " +
        (fname.toString( )) + " from .DBF",
        ".DBS Not Created" );
    mb.show();

    return false;
}
```

On success, we open the DBF, handle the ALDs, and then initialize the screen fields:

```
DBF strufile = new DBF( fname.toString(), "rw" );

if ( ! dbf.writeable  ) {
```

```
                    MsgBox mb = new MsgBox( "Cannot write to " +
                        fname + ". File is empty.",
                        "Empty .DBF File" );
                    mb.show();
                }

                int nflds = dbf.getNumFields();

                for ( int i = 0 ; i < nflds ; i++ ) {

                    Vector vals = dbf.getFieldVals( i );
                    strufile.setValues( i, vals );
                }

                return true;
            }
```

The exists( ) Method

The last public static method is exists( ), which uses the java.IO package's File class. The File's exists( ) method really does the work:

```
        public static boolean exists( String s ) {

            return new File( s ).exists();
        }
```

The Private Methods

Here we'll get into the details of building DBFs. The structure file is a DBF with four predefined fields: name, type, width, and decimals. The database file is a DBF with the fields defined in the structure file.

Here's a quick refresher on the DBF's format:

- Header
- Records
- Footer

When we create a new DBF or DBS, we'll have an initially empty file, so we'll just write

- Header
- Footer

Since the footer is trivial, we'll treat it as a final part of the header, and then we'll only have the header to write. Looked at this way, the DBF header components are

- bytes header data
- bytes for each field
- bytes for the footer

When we've written these pieces, we've created our DBF or DBS.

The create_stru_file( ) Method

We can create a DBS from a DBF. We build a DBF from a DBS. When your system is functionally recursive, as this is, you have to find some point to seed the process. It has to begin somewhere. The create_stru_file( ) method is where JDB begins. Which also implies that it is absolutely bottom-level code.

The create_stru_file( ) method is the most inelegant, brute-force routine I've written in years. Its two virtues are that it's small (in EXE size, not in source lines) and it works.

It begins by creating and blank-filling a byte array, large enough for the whole file:

```
private static boolean create_stru_file(
    String fname ) {

    byte[] sf = new byte[162]; // 16 * 10 + 2

    for ( int i = 0 ; i < 162 ; i++ )
        sf[i] = 0;
```

Then it pokes the nonzero bytes into the array, beginning with the ID byte at the head of the file:

```
    sf[0] = 3; // DBF w/o memos
```

Next it pushes in a date. Care to guess what day I wrote this code?

```
    sf[1] = 0x61; // 6/25/97
    sf[2] = 6;
    sf[3] = 0x19;
```

Then it sets the little-endian size word:

```
sf[8] = -95; // 0xA1
sf[10] = 0x13;
```

Each of the four fields is entered in the same way. I'll show you the name here. Refer to the full listing for the other three. The first thing to do is to write the name of the field, which is "NAME" for the first one:

```
sf[32] = 0x4E; // NAME
sf[33] = 0x41;
sf[34] = 0x4D;
sf[35] = 0x45;
```

Then the type of the field is written. NAME is character data:

```
sf[43] = 0x43; // field type = C
```

Finally, the width of the field is written as:

```
sf[48] = 10;    // field width
```

After doing all four fields, there's nothing left but the footer:

```
sf[160] = 0x0D; // CR
sf[161] = 0x1A; // Ctrl+Z -- long live CP/M!
```

The final step is to create the file and write the byte array, returning true if successful:

```
try {

    RandomAccessFile raf = new RandomAccessFile(
        fname, "rw" );

    raf.seek( 0 );
    raf.write( sf );
    raf.close();
```

```
                    return true;
            }
            catch ( IOException ioe ) {

                    return false;
            }
        }
```

The Error-Reporting Routines

Next in the file are the err_in_X( ) methods. I originally wrote a general-purpose error-reporting routine. When I was done, I decided that four separate routines would actually be shorter. (Was I just having a bad-code day? Can you do better?)

The err_in_X( ) methods are all similar. They assemble and display an appropriate message. This is the first one:

```
        private static void err_in_decimals( Object o ) {

            String s = ( String ) o;

            MsgBox mb = new MsgBox(
                "Error in decimals: " + s +
                ". Must be integer, less than field length.",
                "Error In Decimals" );
            mb.show();

            return;
        }
```

See the full listing for the other three.

The full_stru_name( ) Method

The full_stru_name( ) method is very simple after you break the full name into path, name, and extension components:

```
        private String full_stru_name() {

            return ( file_path.toString() ) +
```

```
                              ( file_name.toString() ) + ".dbs";
        }
```

The little_end2( ) Method

The little_end2 routine is one of the troubles we get using a little-endian file on machines that are big- and little-endian. It converts an integer into two bytes in a byte array buffer. (Don't worry! Our biggest integer is the maximum field width: 255.)

```
        private static void little_end2( int number,
            byte[] buffer, int bufloc ) {

            int left_byte = number & 0x000000FF;
            buffer[bufloc] = ( byte ) left_byte;

            int right_byte = ( number & (0x0000FF00) ) >> 8;
            buffer[bufloc + 1] = ( byte ) right_byte;
        }
```

The Error-Checking Methods

The error-checking routines are not terribly thorough. If you do an end-user version of JDB, you'll want to make these industrial strength. As written, they catch a lot of the stupid things we programmers might do, but they don't guarantee good data.

This is the decimal-checker:

```
        private static boolean ok_decimals( Object o,
            int length ) {

            MRString m = new MRString( (String) o );
            m.trim();

            if ( !  MRString.isDigits(m) )
                return false;

            return m.intValue() < length ;
        }
```

See the full listing for the other routines. If you add a new valid field type, remember to tell OK_type( ) about your addition. To be thorough, you'll also want to update the error message in err_in_type( ), too.

The Field-Buffer Methods

The set_field_buffer( ) routine takes a record in the DBS file and converts it into the corresponding 32 bytes for the DBF header. The routine that writes the fields in the DBF's header loops over each record in the DBS. It calls this method to fill the 32-byte buffer, and then it writes it out.

The set_field_buffer( ) method calls the write_buffer_clear( ) method. We'll look at them both here.

The set_field_buffer( ) Method

The set_field_buffer( ) method begins by clearing the buffer:

```
private static void set_field_buffer( byte[] buffer,
    int fldno, DBF dbs ) {

    write_buffer_clear( buffer ); // zero fill
```

Then it gets the values from the DBS for fldno, the current record in the DBS:

```
Vector vals = dbs.getValues( fldno );
```

Next it creates MRStrings for the name, type, length, and decimals:

```
MRString name = new MRString( (String)
    vals.elementAt(0) );

MRString type = new MRString( (String)
    vals.elementAt(1) );

MRString length = new MRString( (String)
    vals.elementAt(2) );

MRString decimals = new MRString( (String)
    vals.elementAt(3) );
```

Then it enters the name. Recall that in the DBF header, the name is null-terminated. That's handled by trimming trailing blanks before entering the data:

```
name.trimRight();
for ( int i = 0 ; i < name.length() ; i++ )
    buffer[i] = ( byte ) name.chars[i];
```

The 11th byte, buffer[10], is left null (it terminates a name that takes all ten name characters). The 12th byte gets the type:

```
buffer[11] = ( byte ) type.chars[0];
```

The length is entered, converted from the ASCII characters courtesy of an MRString's intValue( ) method:

```
int flen = length.intValue();
buffer[16] = ( byte ) flen;
```

And last but not least, the number of decimal places, if any, is added:

```
buffer[17] = ( byte ) decimals.intValue();
```

The write_buffer_clear( ) Method

The write_buffer_clear( ) routine is straightforward:

```
private static void write_buffer_clear( byte[] buf ) {

    for ( int i = 0 ; i < buf.length ; i++ )
        buf[i] = 0;
}
```

We should really have a System.arrayFill( ) method. On Intel hardware we can get code that's orders of magnitude more efficient than this. (For 32 bytes it probably doesn't matter, however.)

The DBF-Writing Methods

Now we get to the three write_dbf_X( ) methods, where X is one of header, fields, or footer. You've already seen the set_field_buffer( ), which does the real work for the write_dbf_fields( ) method. The write_dbf_header( ) method has to do its own work, though. The write_dbf_footer( ) method is trivial. We'll start with the hard one.

The write_dbf_header( ) Method

The write_dbf_header( ) method begins by creating and clearing its own buffer:

```
private static boolean write_dbf_header( DBF dbs,
    RandomAccessFile dbf ) {

    byte[] buffer = new byte[32];
    // write_buf_clear( buffer ); // zeros by default
```

As the comment says, this method is content to let the compiler do the initial clear. Since there's no reuse of this buffer, that's the only clearing that's needed.

Next it writes the header ID byte into the buffer:

```
        buffer[0] = 3; // id byte
```

Then it puts in a date. Note that while all DBS files (which are disposable) are created 6/25/97, the actual date is written into the DBF:

```
        Date today = new Date();

        // WARNING: this will fail in 2028!
        buffer[1] = ( byte ) today.getYear(); // year-1900
        buffer[2] = ( byte ) ( today.getMonth() + 1 );
            // Java Jan. = 0
        buffer[3] = ( byte ) today.getDate();
```

The year is stored in a byte as the number of years since 1900. This eliminates the famous Year 2000 problem. But with signed bytes, it means that we can only have years from 1900 through 2027.

Actually, we could go back to 1772—which is 1900 minus 128. Assuming you don't need years before 1900, you could easily work out a scheme to use the year byte as an unsigned value. This extra work would add another 128 years to the useful life of JDB. As the comment points out, my version will only survive for 30 years.

The Year 2028 Problem

If you used the negative values of the year byte, you could add 128 years to the life of JDB. It wouldn't be very hard to move the 2028 problem I've created here to a 2156 problem. Why didn't I do this?

Well, 30 years ago, COBOL was the hot new language, replacing Fortran. It could automatically handle records with repeating subfields. Neat stuff! Of course, there's still some COBOL (and even Fortran) in use, but basically C replaced them both. Then C++ replaced C. Now Java's replacing C++.

Will Java still be used in 2028? I'd guess that the hot language then will be replacing the hot language that replaced whatever hot language replaced Java. You add the extra 128 years. I think 30 is more than enough.

The comments in the source explain the calculation needed to write the file's length into bytes 4 through 7:

```
// num_recs (0) is buffer[4] thru buffer[7]

// 32-byte header + ? 32-byte fields +
// 1 byte (out of 2) footer
// the CP/M EOF mark (^Z) isn't counted
```

Again, the comments explain the number of fields:

```
int num_fields = dbs.getLast() + 1;
        // num_fields is number in the new .DBF,
        // not the number in the .DBS
```

The header here is the whole DBF header, not just the header's header that this routine is writing:

```
int len_header = ( num_fields + 1 ) * 32 + 1;
```

Since there are no fields, the header length *is* the file's length. (The extra "+ 1" is really the final footer byte.) That's written to bytes 8 and 9, since we know it fits easily in a 16-bit short:

```
little_end2( len_header, buffer, 8 );
```

Then the record length is computed and written:

```
// start with deleted flag, then add fields
int len_record = 1;

for ( int i = 0 ; i < num_fields ; i++ ) {

    Vector vals = dbs.getValues( i );
        // vals are: "name", "type", "length" and
        // "decimals"

    MRString slen =
        new MRString( (String) vals.elementAt(2) );

    len_record += slen.intValue();
}

little_end2( len_record, buffer, 10 );
```

Finally, we get to the simple job of actually writing the header into the file:

```
try {

    dbf.seek( 0 );
    dbf.write( buffer );
}
catch ( IOException ioe ) {

    return false;
}

return true;
```

The write_dbf_fields( ) Method

The field-writing routine uses set_field_buffer( ) for the hard work. It just calls this routine in a loop, writing as it goes:

```
private static boolean write_dbf_fields( DBF dbs,
    RandomAccessFile dbf ) {

    byte[] buffer = new byte[32];
```

```
        int num_fields = dbs.getLast() + 1;

        for ( int i = 0 ; i < num_fields ; i++ ) {

            set_field_buffer( buffer, i, dbs );
            try {

                dbf.write( buffer );
            }
            catch ( IOException ioe ) {

                return false;
            }
        }

        return true;
    }
```

The write_dbf_footer( ) Method

The footer is the simplest of all:

```
    private static boolean write_dbf_footer(
        RandomAccessFile dbf ) {

        byte[] fbuf = new byte[2];

        fbuf[0] = 13;
        fbuf[1] = 26; // ^Z, the CP/M eof mark

        try {

            dbf.write( fbuf );
        }
        catch (IOException ioe ) {

            return false;
        }

        return true;
    }
```

The Full JDBnew.java Listing

Listing 16-1 is the full JDBnew.java source file.

Listing 16-1:
JDBnew.java

```java
// JDBnew.java -- create new DBF/.DBS structures
// Copyright 1997, Martin L. Rinehart

// this code is completely documented in:
// _Java Database Development_, Martin Rinehart,
// Osborne/McGraw-Hill, 1997

/*
    Procedure for creating a new .DBF or for editing the
    structure of an existing .DBF.
*/

import java.awt.*;
import java.io.*;
import java.util.Vector;
import java.util.Date;

class JDBnew extends Object {

// -------------------- data members --------------------

// there are no public data members

// protected data members:

    protected FileDialog file_dialog;

    protected MRString file_ext;
    protected MRString file_name;
    protected MRString file_path;

    protected Frame owner;

// there are no static data members

// -------------------- public methods --------------------

    /*
```

```
        public static void main( String[] args ) {

            new JDBnew( new Frame() );
            System.exit( 0 );
        }
// */

// constructor:

    JDBnew( Frame owner ) {

        this.owner = owner;

        Frame f = new Frame(); // nearly modeless!

        file_dialog = new FileDialog( f,
            "New .DBF Name", FileDialog.SAVE );

        file_dialog.setFile( "*.DBF" );

        file_dialog.show();

        if ( file_dialog.getFile() == null )
            return; // user cancelled file dialog

        MRString from_fd =
            new MRString( file_dialog.getFile() );

        if ( from_fd.endsWith(".*.*") )
            from_fd.trimRight( 4 );

        int dot_loc = from_fd.indexOf( '.' );

        if ( dot_loc == -1 ) {

            file_name = from_fd;
            file_ext = new MRString( "dbf" );
        }
        else {

            file_name = from_fd.substring( 0, dot_loc );
            file_ext = from_fd.substring( dot_loc + 1 );
```

```
    }

    if ( file_name.length() == 0 ) {

        MsgBox mb = new MsgBox(
            "Cannot continue New process " +
            "without a file name.",
            "Cannot Continue"  );
        mb.show();

        return;
    }

    file_path = new MRString(
        file_dialog.getDirectory() );

    boolean wrote_ok;

    String fname = full_stru_name();
    if ( ! exists(fname) ) {

        wrote_ok = create_stru_file( fname );

        if ( ! wrote_ok ) {

            MsgBox mb = new MsgBox(
                "Error while writing " +
                full_stru_name() + ".",
                "File Write Error" );
            return;
        }
    }

    MsgBox mb = new MsgBox(
        "Open your .DBS, Add/Edit data and " +
        " then click Create.",
        full_stru_name() + " Ready");

    mb.show();
}
```

```
// there are no data access methods

// there are no public, class-specific methods

// public, non-event overriding method:

    public String paramString() {

        return "Path " + file_path.toString() +
            " Name " + file_name.toString() +
            " Extension " + file_ext.toString();
    }

// there are no public, event-handling methods

// public static methods:

    public static boolean create_dbf_file( DBF dbs ) {

        // returns true if the .DBF is created

        MRString fname = new MRString( dbs.getFileName() );
        fname.toUpper();

        if ( ! fname.endsWith(".DBS") ) {
            MsgBox mb = new MsgBox(
                "Can only be Created from .DBS.",
                "Cannot Create Database File" );
            mb.show();

            return false;
        }

        // check the data

        int flen;

        for ( int i = 0 ; i <= dbs.getLast() ; i++ ) {

            Vector vals = dbs.getValues(i);
```

```
        if ( ! ok_name(vals.elementAt( 0 )) ) {

            err_in_name( vals.elementAt(0) );
            return false;
        }

        if ( !ok_type(vals.elementAt( 1 )) ) {

            err_in_type( vals.elementAt(1) );
            return false;
        }

        String s = ( String ) vals.elementAt(2);
        if ( ! ok_length(s) ) {

            err_in_length( s );
            return false;
        }


        flen = new MRString( s ).intValue();

        if ( !ok_decimals(vals.elementAt( 3 ),
            flen) ) {

            err_in_decimals( vals.elementAt(3) );
            return false;
        }
    }

    fname.toUpper();
    fname.replace( fname.length() - 1, 'F' );

    RandomAccessFile dbf = null;
    boolean ok = true;
    try {

        dbf = new RandomAccessFile(
            fname.toString(), "rw" );
    }
    catch( IOException ioe ) {
```

```
        ok = false;
    }

    if ( ok )
        ok = write_dbf_header( dbs, dbf );

    if ( ok )
        ok = write_dbf_fields( dbs, dbf );

    if ( ok )
        ok = write_dbf_footer( dbf );

    if ( ok ) {

        try {

            dbf.close();
        }
        catch ( IOException ioe ) {

            ok = false;
        }
    }

    if ( ! ok ) {

        MsgBox mb = new MsgBox( "Could not write " +
            "new .DBF. Possibly due to lack of space.",
            ".DBF Not Created" );
        mb.show();

        return false;
    }


    return true;
}
```

```
public static boolean create_stru_file( DBF dbf ) {

    // returns true if the .DBS is created

    MRString fname = new MRString( dbf.getFileName() );
    fname.toUpper();

    if ( ! fname.endsWith(".DBF") ) {

        MsgBox mb = new MsgBox(
            "Can only be Created from .DBF." +
            "New creates an empty .DBS",
            "Cannot Create Structure File" );
        mb.show();

        return false;
    }

    fname.replace( fname.length()-1, 'S' );

    boolean ok = create_stru_file( fname.toString() );

    if ( !ok ) {

        MsgBox mb = new MsgBox( "Could not create " +
            (fname.toString( )) + " from .DBF",
            ".DBS Not Created" );
        mb.show();

        return false;
    }

    DBF strufile = new DBF( fname.toString(), "rw" );

    if ( ! dbf.writeable  ) {

        MsgBox mb = new MsgBox( "Cannot write to " +
            fname + ". File is empty.",
            "Empty .DBF File" );
        mb.show();
```

```
        }

        int nflds = dbf.getNumFields();

        for ( int i = 0 ; i < nflds ; i++ ) {

            Vector vals = dbf.getFieldVals( i );
            strufile.setValues( i, vals );
        }

        return true;
    }

    public static boolean exists( String s ) {

        return new File( s ).exists();
    }

// ------------------ private methods ------------------

// private methods:

    private static boolean create_stru_file(
        String fname ) {

        byte[] sf = new byte[162]; // 16 * 10 + 2

        for ( int i = 0 ; i < 162 ; i++ )
            sf[i] = 0;

        sf[0] = 3; // DBF w/o memos

        sf[1] = 0x61; // 6/25/97
        sf[2] = 6;
        sf[3] = 0x19;

        sf[8] = -95; // 0xA1
        sf[10] = 0x13;

        sf[32] = 0x4E; // NAME
        sf[33] = 0x41;
        sf[34] = 0x4D;
```

```
sf[35] = 0x45;

sf[43] = 0x43; // field type = C
sf[48] = 10;   // field width

sf[64] = 0x54; // TYPE
sf[65] = 0x59;
sf[66] = 0x50;
sf[67] = 0x45;

sf[75] = 0x43; // field type = C
sf[80] = 1;          // field width

sf[96] = 0x57; // WIDTH
sf[97] = 0x49;
sf[98] = 0x44;
sf[99] = 0x54;
sf[100] = 0x48;

sf[107] = 0x4E; // field type = N
sf[112] = 5;     // field width

sf[128] = 0x44; // DECIMALS
sf[129] = 0x45;
sf[130] = 0x43;
sf[131] = 0x49;
sf[132] = 0x4D;
sf[133] = 0x41;
sf[134] = 0x4C;
sf[135] = 0x53;

sf[139] = 0x4E; // field type = N
sf[144] = 2;     // field width

sf[160] = 0x0D; // CR
sf[161] = 0x1A; // Ctrl+Z -- long live CP/M!


try {

    RandomAccessFile raf = new RandomAccessFile(
        fname, "rw" );
```

```
            raf.seek( 0 );
            raf.write( sf );
            raf.close();

            return true;
        }
        catch ( IOException ioe ) {

            return false;
        }
    }

    private static void err_in_decimals( Object o ) {

        String s = ( String ) o;

        MsgBox mb = new MsgBox(
            "Error in decimals: " + s +
            ". Must be integer, less than field length.",
            "Error In Decimals" );
        mb.show();

        return;
    }

    private static void err_in_length( Object o ) {

        String s = ( String ) o;

        MsgBox mb = new MsgBox(
            "Error in length: " + s +
            ". Must be integer, less than 256.",
            "Error In Length" );
        mb.show();

        return;
    }

    private static void err_in_name( Object o ) {
```

```java
        String s = ( String ) o;

        MsgBox mb = new MsgBox(
            "Error in name: " + s +
            ". Must be alphanumeric, w/o blanks.",
            "Error In Name" );
        mb.show();

        return;
    }

    private static void err_in_type( Object o ) {

        String s = ( String ) o;

        MsgBox mb = new MsgBox(
            "Error in type: " + s +
            ". Must be one of C D F L M or N.",
            "Error In Type" );
        mb.show();

        return;
    }

    private String full_stru_name() {

        return ( file_path.toString() ) +
            ( file_name.toString() ) + ".dbs";
    }

    private static void little_end2( int number,
        byte[] buffer, int bufloc ) {

        int left_byte = number & 0x000000FF;
        buffer[bufloc] = ( byte ) left_byte;

        int right_byte = ( number & (0x0000FF00) ) >> 8;
        buffer[bufloc + 1] = ( byte ) right_byte;
    }

    private static boolean ok_decimals( Object o,
        int length ) {
```

```
        MRString m = new MRString( (String) o );
        m.trim();

        if ( !  MRString.isDigits(m) )
            return false;

        return m.intValue() < length ;
}

private static boolean ok_length( Object o ) {

        MRString m = new MRString( (String) o );
        m.trim();

        if ( !MRString.isDigits(m) )
            return false;

        int val = m.intValue();

        return ( val > 0 ) && ( val < 256 );
}

private static boolean ok_name( Object o ) {

        MRString m = new MRString( (String) o );
        m.trimRight();

        return MRString.isVarName( m );
}

private static boolean ok_type( Object o ) {

        String s = (String) o;


        return     s.equals("C") ||
                s.equals("D") ||
                s.equals("F") ||
                s.equals("L") ||
                s.equals("M") ||
                s.equals("N");
```

```
    }

private static void set_field_buffer( byte[] buffer,
    int fldno, DBF dbs ) {

    write_buffer_clear( buffer ); // zero fill

    Vector vals = dbs.getValues( fldno );

    MRString name = new MRString( (String)
        vals.elementAt(0) );

    MRString type = new MRString( (String)
        vals.elementAt(1) );

    MRString length = new MRString( (String)
        vals.elementAt(2) );

    MRString decimals = new MRString( (String)
        vals.elementAt(3) );

    name.trimRight();
    for ( int i = 0 ; i < name.length() ; i++ )
        buffer[i] = ( byte ) name.chars[i];

    buffer[11] = ( byte ) type.chars[0];

    int flen = length.intValue();
    buffer[16] = ( byte ) flen;

    buffer[17] = ( byte ) decimals.intValue();
}

private static void write_buffer_clear( byte[] buf ) {

    for ( int i = 0 ; i < buf.length ; i++ )
        buf[i] = 0;
}

private static boolean write_dbf_header( DBF dbs,
    RandomAccessFile dbf ) {
```

```java
byte[] buffer = new byte[32];
// write_buf_clear( buffer ); // zeros by default

buffer[0] = 3; // id byte

Date today = new Date();

// WARNING: this will fail in 2028!
buffer[1] = ( byte ) today.getYear(); // year-1900
buffer[2] = ( byte ) ( today.getMonth() + 1 );
    // Java Jan. = 0
buffer[3] = ( byte ) today.getDate();

// num_recs (0) is buffer[4] thru buffer[7]

// 32-byte header + ? 32-byte fields +
// 1 byte (out of 2) footer
// the CP/M EOF mark (^Z) isn't counted

int num_fields = dbs.getLast() + 1;
    // num_fields is number in the new .DBF,
    // not the number in the .DBS

int len_header = ( num_fields + 1 ) * 32 + 1;

little_end2( len_header, buffer, 8 );

// start with deleted flag, then add fields
int len_record = 1;

for ( int i = 0 ; i < num_fields ; i++ ) {

    Vector vals = dbs.getValucs( i );
        // vals are: "name", "type", "length" and
        // "decimals"

    MRString slen =
        new MRString( (String) vals.elementAt(2) );

    len_record += slen.intValue();
```

```
        }

        little_end2( len_record, buffer, 10 );

        try {

            dbf.seek( 0 );
            dbf.write( buffer );
        }
        catch ( IOException ioe ) {

            return false;
        }

        return true;
    }

    private static boolean write_dbf_fields( DBF dbs,
        RandomAccessFile dbf ) {

        byte[] buffer = new byte[32];

        int num_fields = dbs.getLast() + 1;

        for ( int i = 0 ; i < num_fields ; i++ ) {

            set_field_buffer( buffer, i, dbs );
            try {

                dbf.write( buffer );
            }
            catch ( IOException ioe ) {

                return false;
            }
        }

        return true;
    }

    private static boolean write_dbf_footer(
```

```
        RandomAccessFile dbf ) {

        byte[] fbuf = new byte[2];

        fbuf[0] = 13;
        fbuf[1] = 26; // ^Z, the CP/M eof mark

        try {

            dbf.write( fbuf );
        }
        catch (IOException ioe ) {

            return false;
        }

        return true;
    }

} // end of JDBnew class

// there are no private classes in JDBnew.java

/*
    This writes an empty structure file. The fields are:
        NAME          C  10
        TYPE          C  1
        LENGTH        N  5
        DECIMALS      N  2

    The records added to this file correspond to the
    fields in a .DBF table file.
*/

// end of JDBnew.java
```

Summary

JDBnew is a library of procedural code, going down to the very lowest level. It's called a "class" because Java insists that we call it a class.

We began by looking at the data it uses. Then we moved on to the code.

There are a test mainline and constructor. These are the only nonstatic public methods. The constructor is the one that JDB calls when you click the New button on the main menu. It actually creates the new, empty DBS file.

The public statics include create_stru_file( ) and create_dbf_file( ), which build DBS and DBF files, respectively. The DBS is built from scratch. The DBF is built from a DBS that describes its fields.

Private methods include a create_stru_file( ) that does the hard work. It creates a byte array, clears it to zeros, and then writes an entire DBF header and footer, using the predefined four fields that make up a DBS file. If you were looking for the very beginning of the JDB system, you found it in the private create_stru_file( ) method.

The rest of the private methods are devoted to building DBFs from DBSes. They include error-checking and -reporting routines. The error checking is adequate for a tool for programmers, such as JDB. You'll have to make it industrial strength before you have an end-user tool.

The other private methods write a DBF header by writing the header's header, the header's fields records, and then the header's footer. Collectively, they translate the DBS' information into a DBF that you can use with JDB or any other program that can handle or import data from a DBF file.

We've now got a complete capability in JDB. Complete, that is, unless you've noticed the Memo field that is in the ASAMP.DBF file. It's through the memo field that we get the effect of variable-length fields in relational tables. That's where Chapter 17 is heading.

Chapter 17

Variable-Length Storage

With JDB, creating and using DBF files for storing data tables is simple. Unfortunately, the world is full of data that doesn't conveniently fit into fixed-length fields in records.

For almost every event table there's someone who wants to make notes. The doctor needs to write a few sentences about the patient's visit. The salesperson wants to add a little text describing the special characteristics of a sale. The professor will jot down ideas for improving the lecture next time.

And those are examples from classic, text-oriented data processing. Today we want to attach photos of each home for the house broker, we add representative audio clips to our music database, and video clips will become commonplace, too. In the age of multimedia data, tables of fixed-length values need help. (You'll find, by the way, that almost every type of data needs accompanying tables, too.)

In RAM, variable-length data is handled by allocating space from the *heap,* the pool of free RAM. A *memory manager* maintains a list of available RAM spaces. When it gets a request for space, it finds space and returns a pointer or reference to the space.

The memory manager also handles lots of bookkeeping, without bothering the application. If the available piece is more than the application wants, it splits it in two, one free and the other used. It keeps lists of the locations of free space so that it can fill additional requests for data.

The memory manager also performs *garbage collection,* collecting multiple small pieces of free space into large, useful pieces. All the bookkeeping is done internally. The calling application simply requests space and either gets the space or gets an appropriate message if the requested space isn't available.

If you were to change the memory manager so that it managed space in a disk file, instead of space in RAM, you would have an elegant way of handling variable-length data. If we had a class to manage the whole process, we'd have an elegant, encapsulated mechanism for permanently storing any type of data.

This is, of course, a description of the class we'll be looking at here: the HeapFile. When you create a HeapFile, you specify some reasonable initial storage amount. (You can be stingy; the HeapFile expands its disk file whenever it runs out of space. Like a good memory manager, it doesn't bother the application about this.)

Whenever you want storage, you tell the HeapFile how much, and it returns a pointer to the allocated space. This space stores your data until you tell the HeapFile that you don't need the space. It returns unused space to its internal free space list.

In this chapter we'll look first at the dBASE memo field, since memo data is one type our DBFs already anticipate. The history of this field type is very instructive, although it is mostly a history of design mistakes and their eventual correction. It will help us steer clear of a lot of our predecessors' errors.

Then we'll go on to using the HeapFile. If you think a class that manages disk space using a circular-first-fit allocation algorithm and that does continuous, on-the-fly garbage collection is a sophisticated challenge, you'll be surprised. It's as simple to use as our DBF objects.

Then we'll dive into the implementation. If you love fiddling with system software, you'll find plenty to like here. If you've got applications to build, you could skip all this, too. Black box classes that do what you want are fine, as long as you have the code and documentation for that evil day when something goes wrong.

Let's begin with the memo field.

The dBASE Memo Field

The original database tool for eight-bit microprocessors running the CP/M operating system that gave us the DBF file format was dBASE II. (Marketing guru Hal Pawluk named the original, version 1.0 program dBASE II. There never was a dBASE I.) It didn't handle variable-length strings.

If your application required handling notes (such as the doctor's notes about the patient's visit), you added enough 256-byte character fields to handle the largest acceptable note. This was horribly wasteful of space. (Most early microcomputers used 8-inch floppy disks, holding 1MB of data. There were no hard disks.)

The memo field was added with dBASE III. This stored a ten-byte pointer into an associated file. The memo file allocated 512-byte pages. Each note was given as many pages as it required.

In data entry, the memo field was not editable. When the cursor was on the memo field, a control-key combination launched a small text editor. Pressing the save-key combination in the editor sent the memo back to disk.

If an edit expanded the memo so that it needed additional pages, the whole memo was written to a larger disk space. The original space was orphaned. Enterprising programmers wrote and sold space-recovery utilities that compressed this orphaned space out of the memo file.

In the 1980s, companies created products that competed with dBASE. The implementation of the memo field was one of the areas for competition. One competitor introduced automatic garbage collection, recovering and reusing space that had been orphaned. Another changed from fixed-length pages to variable-length allocations.

Our HeapFile implements a true, variable-length, garbage-collected storage scheme. We'll skip all the intermediate steps.

Using the HeapFile

Using a HeapFile is very simple. One constructor creates a new file, and a second uses an existing file. A meticulous application will use the close( ) method when it is done with the heap file. As you saw with classes like BinFile and DBF, the whole file I/O process is hidden from the application.

Storage is managed with alloc( ) and free( ) methods that will be very familiar to C programmers. The alloc( ) method throws an exception if, for example, you've run out of disk space. All other details, such as expanding the file when it runs out of space, are hidden from the application.

Finally, read( ) and write( ) move byte arrays from and to allocated storage.

There is one more task, and it's one that the HeapFile can't handle. Your application must remember where it's put things. You have to provide some place on disk to record the pointers that you have used for your data. The DBF's memo field is one such place.

Opening and Closing HeapFiles

The constructors open the underlying files. The two important constructors are

- HeapFile(String pathname, int free_size)
- HeapFile(String pathname, String access)

The first form is used to create a new heap file and prepare it for read/write access. You call it with an initial size, in bytes. Whenever the file runs out of space, it adds 50 percent to its size, so you don't need to allocate much initial space. (Actually, the algorithm's a bit more sophisticated than I've just stated, but the conclusion is valid. Pick some amount of space on the small side of sensible and you'll be OK.)

The second constructor opens an existing heap file for "r" or "rw" access.

It's an error to use the first constructor form on an existing file. It's an error to use the second form if the file you name doesn't exist. As with our other files, the public booleans—readable and writeable—tell you if you've got the access you need.

The close( ) method closes the disk file. You should dispose of the HeapFile object's reference after a close( ), since there's no provision for reopening the file. In most applications it's acceptable to let Java close the disk file when it terminates the application.

Managing HeapFile Storage

You call alloc( ) to allocate a block of storage. Alloc takes an integer parameter that specifies the number of bytes you want. The alloc( ) method returns an integer reference to the block it allocates. You use that reference to read( ), write( ), and eventually free( ) the storage block.

Whenever you alloc( ) space, you need to catch a HeapFileAllocException. This is thrown when the HeapFile can't find enough disk space to satisfy your allocation request. (The HeapFile quietly expands its disk file as needed, without bothering you, as long as there is disk space available.)

This is an example:

```
// create new 20KB heap file:
HeapFile hf = new HeapFile ( "MyHeap.Fil", 20000 );

if ( ! hf.writeable )
    // handle error here!
```

```
try { int myblock = hf.alloc( 1000 ); }
catch ( HeapFileAllocException hfe ) {
    /* handle error here */ }

// here you have your block
    hf.write() and hf.read() as you wish

// optionally
    hf.free( myblock );

// also optional
    hf.close();
```

Let's assume that you didn't free( ) your block of storage. Instead, you wrote the myblock reference value to a disk file. The next run of your application will continue to use the allocated block, this way:

```
// int myblock was read from some file

// reopen heap file for read/write
HeapFile hf = new HeapFile( "MyHeap.Fil", "rw" );

if ( ! hf.writeable ) // handle error here!

// here you still have the block
    hf.read( myblock ) as you wish and/or
    hf.write( myblock ) as needed

// optionally
    hf.free( myblock );

// also optional
    hf.close();
```

Freeing the allocated block is optional. You don't do it if you want the data in that block to be available for a subsequent run of the application.

Calling the close( ) method is optional, but for a different reason. Java closes open files when it terminates your application, so you can skip this if you prefer. It's only necessary if you want to close the disk file before the application terminates. (Closing a file encourages most operating systems to physically write any cached data. But don't count on it.)

Reading and Writing HeapFile Data

The read( ) and write( ) methods are as simple as possible. These are their main forms:

```
public int read( int ptr, byte[] b )
public int write( int ptr, byte[] b )
```

The int ptr is the one returned by a call to alloc( ). The byte array holds or receives the data. The return value is the number of bytes actually read or written. Both routines limit their action to the smaller of the allocated block or the byte array's length. There's no way to read or write outside the allocated block.

Actually, there's no way to read or write outside the allocated block if you use the pointers that alloc( ) hands you. If you want to create your own pointers, then there's no limit to where you can read or write. There's no limit to the damage you can cause. Proceed at your own risk.

Another read form lets you write a limited portion of the array:

```
public int read( int ptr, byte[] b, int nbytes )
```

You use this form when the number of bytes you want to read is smaller than both the array size and the allocated block's size.

Storing HeapFile Pointers

For persistent variable-length data, you need the HeapFile and you need a companion that keeps track of the pointers. The DBF's memo field is one possibility.

Assume that you want to store long text blocks, WAVs, BMPs, or some other variable-length data. Assume that a DBF provides a memo field for this purpose. In your application, open the DBF and open an associated HeapFile. When it's time to store the data, alloc( ) the HeapFile space, write( ) the data, and assign the pointer to the DBF's memo field.

The memo field in a DBF is ten bytes long. This means that you can write the pointer in ASCII characters, which will avoid endian issues. It's not as compact and efficient as a four-byte int, but it makes debugging a simple, WYSIWYG matter.

You must make sure that your data-entry forms do not let the user edit the pointer, of course. (You don't want to give away too many copies of JDB.) Pop up a text editor or play the WAV or whatever when the user gets to the memo field.

If the memo's contents are editable (the doctor's patient notes, for example), you have to check the size before you write back to the HeapFile. If you need more space, free( ) the current block and alloc( ) a larger one.

Understanding the HeapFile

TOUR

Read the following section on HeapFile theory and then quit or keep going. If you're fascinated by this sort of low-level code, by all means keep going. If you're happy to use the HeapFile as a black box, then quit. You'll never need to know the details.

That assumes, of course, that my code is perfect. If that's not true (and it's certainly not the way the smart money is betting), you can come back to this section when you need to fix a bug, or convert all the ints to longs so you can handle terabyte files.

We'll start here with a theory section that explains how this class *should* operate. Then we'll dive into the data and methods that instantiate the theory.

The HeapFile in Theory

The HeapFile begins life by grabbing a large (relatively large, that is) chunk of disk space. Then it parcels it out in small pieces. When it needs more space, it grabs some more disk space and keeps going.

When the consuming application is done with a piece, it returns it. Internally, we handle the bookkeeping to keep track of what's free and what's not. We do garbage collection to combine multiple small free pieces into individual large free pieces.

Now let's dig a little deeper.

Keeping the Books

The bookkeeping is done by maintaining a doubly linked list of free spaces. Initially, this is just one element: the first space we got on disk. As we hand off new pieces, at first we're just carving pieces off the end of the free piece. We adjust the size of the free piece downward as we carve off pieces.

It gets more interesting when the application returns file blocks and when we go to the file for additional space. In either operation, the resulting free space may not be contiguous. That's where the doubly linked list comes in.

When a block is freed, we insert it into the doubly linked list. This is done by scanning the list for the insertion point that keeps the list continuously ordered in ascending sequence. Keeping the list ordered makes the garbage collection simple, as we'll see momentarily. Before we think about garbage collection, let's look at the allocation algorithm.

The Circular-First-Fit Algorithm

With a list of noncontiguous blocks of free space, you have to decide how to allocate the space. This problem has been studied extensively in computer science for

RAM-based applications, such as compilers' and operating systems' space allocation strategies.

There is general agreement that the *best-fit* algorithm is the worst choice. The best fit is the block that is nearest in size to the allocation request. By always picking the best fit, you guarantee that the pieces remaining in the free space list are the smallest possible ones. This quickly leaves you with lots of tiny, mostly useless pieces of space.

Other methods are *first-fit* and *circular-first-fit*. In the former, you begin with the head of the list and select the first block that fits. In the latter, you remember the location of the last allocation and you begin searching for an adequate piece at that location. If you come to the tail of the list, you resume searching at the head of the list, stopping if you come full circle.

Various studies have authoritatively concluded that the first-fit method is superior to the circular-first-fit method. Others have authoritatively reached the opposite conclusion. So take your pick, depending on the application.

In our use, the circular approach is ideal. We'll normally be doing lots of allocations and less frequent freeing. We expand the file in 50-percent chunks when we run out of space. We'll often put the circular pointer at the start of the new space we grabbed, and it will stay there as we allocate from that space. It will only start circling when that space is fully consumed.

Continuous Garbage Collection

There are two types of garbage collection in use. In one type, a system of indirect pointers is used. The application doesn't receive a pointer, it receives a pointer to a pointer. This lets the memory manager shuffle the used blocks around however it chooses. The memory manager tries to organize all the free blocks into a small number (one is ideal) of large blocks of contiguous space.

That lets the memory manager avoid any fragmentation problem, but it means that every reference to the data is done with indirect pointers. The other alternative is to hand direct pointers to the application, but that means that the memory manager can't move an assigned block. This latter approach is fine for our HeapFile.

With direct pointers and fixed-location assigned blocks, garbage collection is limited to joining any contiguous free blocks into a single, larger free block.

We use a combine( ) method that will convert a given block and the next block in the list into a single block if they are contiguous. The free( ) method calls combine( ) with the block being freed, which will combine it (if possible) with the block on the right. Then it calls combine( ) with the freed block's previous list member. This will combine (again, if possible) the previous block with this one.

By attempting to combine a freed block with its next, and then its previous block with the freed block, we always combine free blocks into the smallest possible number of free blocks. There will never be any contiguous free blocks. (They exist only momentarily, during the free( ) process.)

The Block Structures

The assigned and free blocks are structured differently, but both structures are simple. The simplest of all the structures is the overall file structure, which we'll save for last.

The free block is a 12-byte structure followed by any amount of available bytes. It looks like this:

```
The Free Space Structure

|0 1 2 3|4 5 6 7|8 9 0 1|2 . . .
|prev   |next   |size   | . . .
```

The prev, next, and size values are integers. The prev and next pointers specify disk locations relative to the start of the file. The size records the amount of available space. (Add 12 to get the total block size.)

The assigned block is even simpler. It is simply a size integer followed by size bytes of data:

```
HeapFile's View of the Allocated Block

|0 1 2 3|4 . . .
|size   | . . .

Application's View of the Allocated Block

        |0 . . .
        | . . .
```

The pointer returned to the allocation points at the first available byte. The application is unaware of the size integer. Again, the size is the number of available bytes. (Add four to get the full block size.)

The file's structure is this:

```
The HeapFile's File Structure

|0 1 2 3|4 . . .
|c ptr  |data blocks
```

The circular pointer is written into the first four bytes. The remainder is data blocks.

Tricks of the Trade

There is no chain of assigned blocks. It's up to the applications that use the HeapFile to keep track of assigned pointers. The HeapFile's list of free blocks can be used to create a list of used blocks. If there are 10,000 used bytes between adjacent free space list members, you know that they are in use. You will not know whether this is one large piece or dozens of small pieces, however.

This means that the application can do anything it wants with its blocks. This includes subdividing larger blocks into smaller individual blocks. An application could correctly free blocks that are only pieces of a larger allocated block. If it's not immediately obvious how this could work: good. Leave it alone. If you immediately saw how this works, leave it alone anyway.

Internally, the first block is considered sacred. It will never be cut down to a piece that is allocated in whole to fulfill an application's request. This means that we can always count on having a free block starting at the fifth byte. This simplifies the code in many ways. For example, a free( ) call can never free the head block in the list.

We're ready to dive into the code. If you just want to use the HeapFile, load this chapter's project file and begin experimenting with the mainline included in the HeapFile. If you want details, they're all here.

The HeapFile's Data Members

There are public, protected, and final static data members in the HeapFile. The good news is that there are no more than four items in any of these categories.

The HeapFile's Public Data

The public data members are

- String message
- String path_name
- boolean readable
- boolean writeable

The message holds a status message that you can display, for example, after a HeapFileAllocException. The path_name is the one you provide to the constructor. The readable and writeable booleans are the same old friends we've used in all the other classes that cover a disk file. Check them after you open the file to be sure there wasn't any problem.

The HeapFile's Protected Data

The first protected member is the circular pointer used to search for the next block to allocate:

```
    protected int circ_pointer;
```

The second is self-explanatory:

```
    protected long file_length;
```

Finally, there's the file object:

```
    protected RandomAccessFile raf;
```

The HeapFile's Final Static Data

The final static data are all int values. They are

- GIGABYTE = 1024 * 1024 * 1024
- HEAPSIZE = 256
- OVERHEAD = 16 (needed for bookkeeping)
- MINIMUM_BLOCK_SIZE = 8

The constant GIGABYTE could also be written "1073741824", but I don't find that as readable as "1024 * 1024 * 1024".

The tiny HEAPSIZE is the default if your constructor doesn't provide a bigger one. This small value makes it easy to test the file-expansion logic. You'll want to provide something more sensible in the constructor call when you create application-specific HeapFiles.

The HeapFile's Public Methods

The HeapFile includes a mainline for testing, a pair of constructors, and five public, class-specific methods. There are also two convenience methods that supply optional parameter values. We'll begin with a look at the mainline.

The HeapFile Mainline

The mainline begins by creating larger and smaller byte arrays, filled with "A"s and "B"s:

```
            byte[] As = new byte[100];
            byte[] Bs = new byte[100];
```

```
for ( int i = 0 ; i < 100 ; i++ ) {

    As[i] = (byte) 'A';
    Bs[i] = (byte) 'B';
}

byte[] smallAs = new byte[8];
byte[] smallBs = new byte[8];

System.arraycopy( As, 0, smallAs, 0, 8 );
System.arraycopy( Bs, 0, smallBs, 0, 8 );
```

These give you something handy to write to allocated blocks.

Next the constructor is called to create a new HeapFile. It will not open an existing HeapFile. So if the readable value is false, the alternate constructor is called to open an existing HeapFile:

```
HeapFile foo = new HeapFile( "foo.bar", 256 );

if ( !foo.readable )
    foo = new HeapFile( "foo.bar", "rw" );

System.out.println( foo.message );
```

This is a terrible practice, by the way. Opening an existing HeapFile without an associated DBF (or other file) that stores the used space pointers is only useful if you are checking the HeapFile's file-expansion code. Real applications don't do this.

After opening the HeapFile, an array of pointers is established and filled by allocating blocks. Since the actual block size is four bytes larger than the allocated size, I've used 12-byte units to get actual 16-byte blocks. These are atypically small, but they're very convenient for our ScrollWin's look into a BinFile. This code creates the blocks:

```
int[] ptrs = new int[15];

int wrote;
    try {

        int i = 0;
        while ( i < 12 ) {
```

```
                    ptrs[i] = foo.alloc( 12 );
                    foo.write( ptrs[i], As );
                    i++;
          }
```

Next the mainline frees some of the blocks. Since it is freeing contiguous blocks, you'll see individual, larger free blocks if you trace the next and prev pointers in the BinFile view. This is the code:

```
               foo.free( ptrs[0] );
               foo.free( ptrs[1] );
               foo.free( ptrs[2] );

               foo.free( ptrs[6] );
               foo.free( ptrs[7] );
               foo.free( ptrs[8] );
               foo.free( ptrs[9] );

               // foo.free( ptrs[13] );
```

The read( ) method is tested with this code:

```
          int new1 = foo.alloc( 100 );
          foo.write( new1, Bs );

          byte[] msg = new byte[1000];
          int amt_read = foo.read( new1, msg );
          System.out.print( "Read " + amt_read +
               " bytes: " );
          System.out.write( msg, 0, amt_read );
          System.out.println();

          amt_read = foo.read( new1, msg, 25 );
          System.out.print( "Read " + amt_read +
               " bytes: " );
          System.out.write( msg, 0, amt_read );
          System.out.println();

          amt_read = foo.read( ptrs[3], msg );
          System.out.print( "Read " + amt_read +
```

```
                    " bytes: " );
        System.out.write( msg, 0, amt_read );
        System.out.println();
```

If you modify the preceding, putting a larger HeapFile on a floppy and then letting it fill much larger pieces (or start with a nearly full floppy), you'll be able to force the HeapFileAllocException, which is caught here:

```
    }
    catch ( HeapFileAllocException he ) {

        System.out.println( he.getMessage() );
    }
```

Finally, the HeapFile is closed and reopened as a binary file that you can examine in your ScrollWin:

```
        foo.close();

        BinFile bf = new BinFile( "foo.bar" );
        ScrollWin sw = new ScrollWin( bf, "foo.bar" );
        sw.setEndApp( true );
        sw.show();

    }
```

The HeapFile's Constructors

There are two main constructors:

```
    // create a new file:
    HeapFile( String pathname, int free_size )

    // existing file:
    HeapFile( String pathname, String access )
```

In the source file, a third convenience constructor leads off. It just supplies the default access for existing HeapFiles:

```
HeapFile( String pathname ) {

    // open pathname for reading
    this( pathname, "r" );
}
```

The constructor that opens an existing HeapFile is straightforward:

```
HeapFile( String pathname, String access ) {

    // open pathname for "r" or "rw"
    readable = writeable = false;
    path_name = pathname;

    try {

        raf =
            new RandomAccessFile( path_name, access );

        readable = true;
        writeable = access.equals( "rw" );

        read_circ_pointer();

        message = path_name + " opened for \"" +
            access + "\" access";

        return;
    }
    catch ( IOException ioe ) {

        message = "Failed opening " + path_name;
    }

}
```

As its name suggests, the read_circ_pointer( ) method reads the circular list pointer from the file.

The process of creating a new HeapFile is only slightly more complex. It begins by setting up initial values:

```
path_name = pathname;
readable = writeable = false;
```

Then it attempts to open an existing file. If there is a nonnull existing file, this process is cause for quitting:

```
try {
    raf = new RandomAccessFile( path_name, "rw" );

    file_length = raf.length();
    if ( file_length > 0 ) {

        message = path_name + " already exists.";
        raf.close();
        return;
```

If the file opened is null, the constructor writes a byte array of the appropriate length. This will zero-fill the file, since Java zero-fills arrays.

The circ_pointer initially points to the first (and only) block, which begins at the fifth byte. As the notes here indicate, the zero-filling also writes null prev and next pointers:

```
byte[] buf =
    new byte[ free_size + OVERHEAD ];

circ_pointer = 4;
buf[3] = 4; // circ pointer is bytes 0-3

raf.write( buf );

// prev (bytes 4-7) = 0;
// next (bytes 8-11) = 0;
```

A final write adds the size, and then we have some housekeeping details:

```
raf.seek( 12 );
raf.writeInt( free_size );
```

```
            message = path_name + " created.";

            readable = writeable = true;
```

If you check the full listing, you'll see that the code also handles details such as catching IOExceptions.

The HeapFile's Public, Class-Specific Methods

There are five important additional public methods. The close( ) method closes the disk file. The alloc( ) and free( ) methods allocate and free the file's space. Finally, the read( ) and write( ) methods handle the data.

We'll start here with alloc( ). It begins by checking that the size is not too small (or negative):

```
public int alloc( int size )
    throws HeapFileAllocException {

    if ( size < MINIMUM_BLOCK_SIZE )
        throw new HeapFileAllocException(
            "size " + size + " is too small" );
```

Next it asks the private find_block( ) method to pick a block that's large enough. That method does all the work of looking through the existing blocks, trying to find the circular first fit. It expands the file if it can't find existing space. It throws the HeapFileAllocException if it gives up without success:

```
int alloc_from;
try {

    alloc_from = find_block( size );
}
catch ( HeapFileAllocException ae ) {

    throw ae;
}
```

Finally, the circular pointer is set to point to the new block, and the alloc_block( ) method actually allocates the requested space:

```
        if ( alloc_from != circ_pointer )
            reset_circ_pointer( alloc_from );

        return alloc_block( size );
```

The close( ) method calls the RandomAccessFile's close( ). See the full listing for the ALD.

The free( ) method begins with a check for a reasonable size in the block. It gives up if the block's too small (or negative):

```
    public void free( int ptr ) {

        int size = read_size( ptr );

        if ( size < MINIMUM_BLOCK_SIZE )
            return; // probably a bad pointer
```

Next it converts the block from an allocated one into a free block. This means backing up the pointer to point to the real start of the block and then decreasing the size by eight bytes to allow space for the additional free space bookkeeping data:

```
        ptr -= 4; // convert to llist pointer
        size -= 8; // subtract prev & next ptrs
        write_llist_size( ptr, size );
```

Then the new free block is inserted into the linked list, and garbage collection is done by combining it with its next block and then combining (if possible) the previous block with this block:

```
        list_insert( ptr );
        combine( ptr );
        combine( read_llist_prev(ptr) );
```

There are two read methods. The first is a convenience method that adds the optional block size parameter. It defaults to reading the full block this way:

```
    public int read( int ptr, byte[] b ) {
```

```
        // reads full block
        int file_space = read_size( ptr );
        return read( ptr, b, file_space );
    }
```

The full read routine has more work to do. It begins by checking the size of the block. It will read the lesser of the requested size or the block's size. It also checks the array's length. If that is still smaller, it reduces the read size to the array's size. This is the logic:

```
    public int read( int ptr, byte[] b, int nbytes ) {

        // returns # of bytes read
        int file_space = read_size( ptr );
        int read_size = file_space < nbytes ?
            file_space : nbytes;
        if ( read_size > b.length )
            read_size = b.length;
```

Once that's done, the actual read is straightforward:

```
        try {

            raf.seek( ptr );
            raf.read( b, 0, read_size );
        }
        catch( IOException ioe ) {

            message = ioe.getMessage();
            return 0;
        }

        message = "read OK";
        return read_size;
    }
```

The final public method is write( ). It writes the lesser of the length of the array you pass or the space available in the block:

```
public int write( int ptr, byte[] b ) {


    // returns # of bytes written
    int file_space = read_size( ptr );
    int write_size = file_space >= b.length ?
        b.length : file_space;
```

Again, the actual writing is simple:

```
try {

    raf.seek( ptr );
    raf.write( b, 0, write_size );
}
catch ( IOException ioe ) {

    message = ioe.getMessage();
    return 0;
}
message = "write OK";
return write_size;
```

The HeapFile's Private Methods

As happens frequently, those nice, straightforward public methods are supported by private ones that do all the hard work. We'll look at them here in alphabetical order, as they appear in the source.

The Block-Allocation Method

The public alloc( ) method finds an adequately large block and sets the circular pointer to point to it. The alloc_block( ) method does the actual allocation. This is a matter of either chopping off a piece from the end of the block, if at least OVERHEAD bytes will remain free, or returning the entire block.

This code chooses the appropriate process:

```
private int alloc_block( int nbytes ) {

    // size of current block is >= nbytes
```

```
circ_pointer = read_circ_pointer();
int ptr = circ_pointer;

int this_size = read_llist_size( ptr );

int excess = this_size + 8 - nbytes;

if ( excess >= OVERHEAD ) { // carve from block end
```

The Old English verb "cleave," which means cut into two pieces, precisely describes our operation. When there is more than OVERHEAD space in the block, we will cleave the block into an end piece exactly large enough to satisfy the allocation request and a free piece containing the rest of the bytes.

The piece returned contains four bytes where we'll record its size and then the number of bytes requested. The nominal pointer returned points to the fifth byte, where the calling program can actually write its data. The remaining free piece has its size adjusted appropriately. This is the code:

```
int chop_size = nbytes + 4;
int block_end = ptr + 12 + this_size;

int piece_start = block_end - chop_size;

write_llist_size( ptr, this_size - chop_size );

return setup_piece( piece_start,
    chop_size - 4 );
}
```

The alternative to cleaving the current block is to return the entire block. Since the block will be disappearing from the free space list, the first step is to be sure that the circular pointer doesn't point to it:

```
protect_circ_pointer( ptr );
```

Next, the pointers need to be adjusted so that the prev and next blocks point to each other:

```
// point prev <--> next
int prev =
    read_llist_prev( ptr );
int next =
    read_llist_next( ptr );

write_llist_next( prev, next );
write_llist_prev( next, prev );
```

The eight-byte adjustment you've seen earlier comes in again in assigning this block's size. In the free space list, each block has 12 bytes of bookkeeping data (prev, next, and size integers). In an allocated block, only four bytes are needed for the size. The final step in this allocation is to adjust the size and return the new, setup block:

```
this_size += 8;
int where = setup_piece( ptr, this_size );

return where;
```

A word to the wise—you can save a line by writing that code this way:

```
this_size += 8;
return setup_piece( ptr, this_size );
```

If your compiler is reasonably smart, the resulting code will be the same either way. What will not be the same is the way your debugger behaves when you step through the code. The longer form makes debugging simple.

The Garbage-Collection Method

The alloc_block( ) method handles the cleaving process. The reverse process takes two contiguous blocks and combines them into one. The combine( ) method merges one block with its next block, when they are contiguous.

It begins by getting the address of the next block and calling the protect_circ_pointer( ) method, which will advance the circular pointer if it points to the next block. (This ensures that the circular pointer doesn't point to a block that was merged out of existence.) This is that starting code:

```
int next = read_llist_next( ptr );
protect_circ_pointer( next );
```

Next, the size is read for the current block. If the next block starts immediately after this one ends, allowing for 12 overhead bytes, the blocks are contiguous and will get combined:

```
int size = read_llist_size( ptr );

if ( next == (ptr + size + 12) ) { // combine them
```

The combining process begins with computing the new total size and recording it:

```
int new_size = read_llist_size( ptr ) +
    read_llist_size( next ) + 12;
write_llist_size( ptr, new_size );
```

Then it gets the next pointer from the next (about to be eliminated) block:

```
int new_next = read_llist_next( next );
```

This becomes the next pointer for the current block, and the current block becomes the prev pointer for the new next block:

```
        write_llist_next( ptr, new_next );
        write_llist_prev( new_next, ptr );
    }
}
```

The combine( ) method only combines the current block with the next one. The free( ) method calls it twice, the first time combining the freed block with the next block, and then combining the previous block with the newly freed block.

The File-Expansion Method

The find_block( ) method, which we'll cover next, calls expand_file( ) when no existing free block is large enough to satisfy an allocation request. It is called with the number of new bytes required (including bookkeeping space). It attempts to allocate this space if the heap file is less than a gigabyte in size, this way:

```
private void expand_file( int nbytes )
    throws HeapFileAllocException {
```

```
int fsize;
byte[] b;

try {

    fsize = ( int ) raf.length();
    if ( fsize > GIGABYTE )
        throw new HeapFileAllocException(
            "Heap file too large to expand" );

    raf.seek( fsize );

    b = new byte[nbytes];
    raf.write( b );
}
catch ( IOException ioe ) {

    throw new HeapFileAllocException(
        "Space for " + nbytes +
        " bytes not available." );
}
```

The final static GIGABYTE is two to the 30th power, as its name suggests. You could increase it somewhat. Bear in mind that Windows computers are limited to 2Gb per disk, however. I think that even a 1Gb HeapFile is way past anything reasonable for local database work. Files measured in tens of megabytes are candidates for a full-blown DBMS accessed via JDBC.

The above expansion gets the space needed. The target expansion is the greater of 50 percent in total size or 150 percent of the requested space, to allow for additional requests to be met without expanding the file again. This code attempts to grab the extra space:

```
int new_space = fsize / 2;

int other_new_space = ( nbytes * 3 ) / 2;
if ( other_new_space > new_space )
    new_space = other_new_space;

b = new byte[new_space - nbytes];

try {
```

```
        raf.write( b );
    }
    catch ( IOException ioe ) {}

}
```

If the extra space isn't available, no exception is thrown, since the minimum space requirement has been met.

The Block-Finding Methods

The find_block( ) method attempts to find an adequately large block of space. It has two jobs. First, it circles through the existing blocks looking for one that is large enough. If it finds one, it returns a pointer to it.

Its other job begins if it can't find an existing block. It will then expand the file, turn the new space into a new block in the free space list, and return a pointer to the new space.

We'll start with the first job. This is the circling code:

```
    private int find_block( int nbytes )
        throws HeapFileAllocException {

        int start_block = read_circ_pointer();
        int this_block = start_block;

        do {
            . . .
// working code comes here
            . . .
            this_block = read_llist_next( this_block );
            if ( this_block == 0 )
                this_block = 4;
        }
        while ( this_block != start_block );
```

The find_block( ) circle starts with the block the circle pointer designates. The start_block variable records this value. The bottom-tested loop terminates when it gets back to the starting value. The current pointer, this_block, is replaced by the next pointer via the read_llist_next( ) method. At the end (the next pointer equals zero), the process circles back to byte four. (The first four bytes in the file store the circular pointer's value.)

The omitted code checks for adequate space and returns a pointer to the block being checked when it finds space. It computes the amount by which the block's size exceeds the requested size, allowing eight bytes for bookkeeping data.

If the size of this excess space exceeds the final static OVERHEAD, it returns the current block. When the available space exceeds OVERHEAD, the allocating code will split the block into two pieces. The end of the block will be returned to the calling program, and the beginning of the block will be retained in the free space list, with its size appropriately reduced.

If the size of the block is adequate but there are less than OVERHEAD bytes remaining, the whole block is returned to the calling program and the block is dropped from the free space list. The first block (starting at byte four) is never allocated this way, so the list always has at least a head item.

Fortunately, the code that does this is much shorter than this explanation has been. This is the code that lives inside the circle mechanism:

```
int this_size = read_llist_size( this_block );
int excess = this_size + 8 - nbytes;

if ( excess >= OVERHEAD )
    return this_block;

if ( (excess >= 0) && (this_block != 4) )
    return this_block;
```

Most of the time, the preceding code does the job. As it often happens, however, the code that handles the exceptional case is longer than the code that handles the normal case. This code attempts to expand the file:

```
// usually RETURNS above (within do statement)
// Only gets here on failure to find block

int old_length, new_length;
try {

    old_length = ( int ) raf.length();
    expand_file( nbytes + 12 );
    new_length = ( int ) raf.length();
}
catch ( IOException ioe ) {

    throw new HeapFileAllocException(
        "Failed calling raf.length()" );
```

```
        }
        catch ( HeapFileAllocException he ) {

            throw he;

        }
```

The IOException here should never occur. We need to handle the exception, regardless. The expand_file( ) method will throw the HeapFileAllocException when it can't get adequate disk space. (I've tested this with a HeapFile on my A—floppy—drive. Bear in mind that if you test this on your hard disk, you're testing my code, your JVM, and your operating system simultaneously. That prospect scares me.)

If the expansion succeeds, the new space is added into the free space list. This is done by setting it up as an allocated block. Its size is written to its first four bytes, and the nominal pointer is set just past the size. Then free( ) is called.

Calling free( ) with an allocated block takes care of the case when the former end of the file held a free block. The free( ) method will garbage-collect, combining the new space with any free space at the end of the preexpansion file. This is the code:

```
        int new_bytes = new_length - old_length;

        // set up new addition as an allocated block
        int new_block_size = new_bytes - 4;
        int new_ptr = old_length + 4;
        write_size( new_ptr, new_block_size );

        // then link the block into the free space list
        free( new_ptr );

        return find_last_block();

    }
```

The other find method finds the tail block in the free space list. By comparison with find_block( ), it's delightfully simple. This is the code:

```
    private int find_last_block() {

        int ptr = circ_pointer;
        int old_ptr, next_ptr;
```

```
        do {

            next_ptr = read_llist_next( ptr );
            old_ptr = ptr;
            ptr = next_ptr;
        }
        while ( ptr != 0 );

        return old_ptr;
    }
```

The List-Insertion Method

The list_insert( ) method has two jobs. First, it finds the correct location in the list for doing the insertion. Then it does the actual insertion. It finds the correct insertion point by searching from the beginning of the list, following the chain until it comes to a pointer past the block it will be inserting. This is the search code:

```
    private void list_insert( int ptr ) {

        int list_ptr = 4; // begin w/head of list

        int next_item = read_llist_next( list_ptr );

        while ( (next_item > 0) && (next_item < ptr) ) {

            list_ptr = next_item;
            next_item = read_llist_next( list_ptr );
        }
```

There are three cases in list insertion: head, middle, and tail. I've used a permanent head item, which eliminates the first of those cases. This is the code for inserting a new tail item:

```
        if ( next_item == 0 ) { // add new tail item

            // prev = list_ptr; next = 0;
            write_llist_ptrs( ptr, list_ptr, 0 );
            write_llist_next( list_ptr, ptr );
        }
```

Here, ptr is the value of the new block's pointer. The list_ptr value is the item after which the new block is linked. The write_llist_ptrs( ) method writes list_ptr as the prev pointer for the new block, and zero as the next pointer, indicating the end of the list. Then it replaces the old tail's next pointer with a pointer to this block.

The other case is insertion between two existing blocks. That requires updating four pointers: The old block's next becomes a pointer to this block. The inserted block's prev and next point to the old block and its former next. Finally, the former next block's prev pointer is set to the inserted block. This is the code:

```
else { // insert between existing items

    // list_ptr <--> ptr <--> next
    int next = read_llist_next( list_ptr );
    write_llist_next( list_ptr, ptr );
    write_llist_ptrs( ptr, list_ptr, next );
    write_llist_prev( next, ptr );
}

}
```

The Circular-Pointer Methods

The circular pointer needs to be reset if it is pointing to a block that gets deleted during garbage collection, or if it is pointing to a block that gets handed to the application. Both operations call protect_circ_pointer( ). The only complication is that the last block in the list has a zero value for its next pointer. To maintain the circle, this is converted to four. (The first four bytes store the value of the circular pointer.) This is the code:

```
private void protect_circ_pointer( int ptr ) {

    // 2nd of two blocks may be deleted by combine()
    // block may be deleted by alloc()

    // this moves the circ pointer forward if it's
    // pointing to the block that will be deleted

    if ( read_circ_pointer() != ptr )
        return; // no problem!

    int next = read_llist_next( ptr );
    reset_circ_pointer( next == 0 ? 4 : next );
}
```

The read_circ_pointer( ) method picks up the integer value of the first four bytes. Note that all the pointers are handled with readInt( ) and writeInt( ) calls. The individual Java Virtual Machines handle the big-endian/little-endian conversions when they are required. This is the read_circ_pointer( ) code:

```
private int read_circ_pointer() {

    try {

        raf.seek( 0 );
        circ_pointer = raf.readInt();
        return circ_pointer;
    }
    catch ( IOException ioe ) {

        message = "Failed reading circular pointer";
        return -1;
    }
}
```

The Other Read Methods

The first dozen bytes of the available blocks are used to store prev and next pointers, and the size of the block. These are read by the read_llist_next( ), read_llist_prev( ), and read_llist_size( ) methods. This is the read_llist_next code:

```
private int read_llist_next( int pointer ) {

    try {

        raf.seek( pointer + 4 );
        return raf.readInt();
    }
    catch ( IOException ioe ) {

        message = "Failed reading list block next";
        return -1;
    }
}
```

The read_llist_prev( ) and read_llist_size( ) methods are similar except that the seek( ) locations and error messages are modified appropriately.

The read_size( ) method uses the nominal pointer to read the block size stored four bytes before the nominal value:

```
private int read_size( int pointer ) {

    try {

        raf.seek( pointer - 4 );
        return raf.readInt();
    }
    catch ( IOException ioe ) {

        message = "Failed reading block size";
        return -1;
    }
}
```

Other Methods

The circular pointer is recorded in the file's first four bytes, and it's recorded in the circ_pointer int in memory. The reset_circ_pointer( ) method updates both of these:

```
private void reset_circ_pointer( int ptr ) {

    try {

        raf.seek(0);
        raf.writeInt( ptr );
        circ_pointer = ptr;
    }
    catch ( IOException ioe ) {

        message = "Failed writing circular pointer";
    }
}
```

The setup_piece( ) method is passed a real_pointer, which points to the actual block start. It creates the nominal pointer that the application will use, which is four bytes past the real_pointer. It writes the size of the block in the first four bytes this way:

```
private int setup_piece( int real_pointer, int size ) {

    int pointer = real_pointer + 4;
    write_size( pointer, size );

    return pointer;
}
```

The File-Writing Methods

The first four bytes of a free memory block hold the prev pointer. The second four bytes hold the next pointer. The write_llist_next( ) and write_llist_prev( ) methods write these pointers to the file. This is the write_llist_next( ) code:

```
private void write_llist_next( int pointer,
    int new_next ) {

    try {

        raf.seek( pointer + 4 );
        raf.writeInt( new_next );
    }
    catch ( IOException ioe ) {

        message = "Failed writing list block next";
    }
}
```

The write_llist_prev( ) method is almost identical, except that it doesn't add four in the seek( ) and the message is modified appropriately.

When it's possible to write both pointers at once, the write_llist_ptrs( ) method is more efficient. It's straightforward:

```
private void write_llist_ptrs( int pointer,
    int new_prev, int new_next ) {

    try {
```

```
            raf.seek( pointer );
            raf.writeInt( new_prev );
            raf.writeInt( new_next );
        }
        catch ( IOException ioe ) {

            message = "Failed writing list block pointers";
        }
    }
```

The third set of four bytes holds the size of the block. It's written by write_llist_size( ), which is another one like write_llist_next( ), with appropriate modifications to the seek( ) and message.

When a block is handed to the calling program, the prev, next, and size values are lost. It is no longer in the linked list. The four bytes preceding the block, however, are invisible to the calling program, but are used to maintain the block's size. This is written by write_size( ) this way:

```
    private void write_size( int pointer,
        int new_size ) {

        try {

            raf.seek( pointer - 4 );
            raf.writeInt( new_size );
        }
        catch ( IOException ioe ) {

            message = "Failed writing block size";
        }
    }
```

The HeapFile's Private Class

The HeapFileAllocException class does absolutely nothing except provide another name for the underlying Exception class. This is the code:

```
class HeapFileAllocException extends Exception {

    HeapFileAllocException( String msg ) {
```

```
        super( msg );
    }
}
```

You could remove the one working line from this constructor without changing the class. It just reminds me of what I want this class to do.

It's a good practice to provide covering classes, such as this one, for exceptions. If you just throw Exception objects, you'll end up with catch blocks that really don't know what they might be catching. Adding a self-explanatory name to your exception makes the calling code more readable.

The Full HeapFile.java Listing

Listing 17-1 is the full HeapFile.java source file.

Listing 17-1:
HeapFile.java

```java
// HeapFile.java -- garbage-collected heap on disk
// Copyright 1997, Martin L. Rinehart

// this code is completely documented in:
// _Java Database Development_, Martin Rinehart,
// Osborne/McGraw-Hill, 1997

/*
    HeapFile.java uses all ints. Must be recoded with longs
    for HeapFiles 2GB and larger.
*/

import java.io.*;

class HeapFile extends Object {

// -------------------- data members --------------------

// public data members:

    public String message;

    public String path_name;

    public boolean readable;
```

```
    public boolean writeable;

// protected data members:

    protected int circ_pointer;

    protected long file_length;

    protected RandomAccessFile raf;

// static data members
    // there are no public static data members
    // there are no private static data members
    // final static data members

    final static int GIGABYTE = 1024 * 1024 * 1024;

    final static int HEAPSIZE = 256;

    final static int OVERHEAD = 16; // bookkeeping bytes

    final static int MINIMUM_BLOCK_SIZE = 8 ;

// -------------------- public methods --------------------

    //*
        public static void main( String[] args ) {

            byte[] As = new byte[100];
            byte[] Bs = new byte[100];

            for ( int i = 0 ; i < 100 ; i++ ) {

                As[i] = (byte) 'A';
                Bs[i] = (byte) 'B';
            }

            byte[] smallAs = new byte[8];
            byte[] smallBs = new byte[8];

            System.arraycopy( As, 0, smallAs, 0, 8 );
            System.arraycopy( Bs, 0, smallBs, 0, 8 );
```

```
    HeapFile foo = new HeapFile( "foo.bar", 256 );

  if ( !foo.readable )
      foo = new HeapFile( "foo.bar", "rw" );

   System.out.println( foo.message );

int[] ptrs = new int[15];

int wrote;
  try {

      int i = 0;
      while ( i < 12 ) {

          ptrs[i] = foo.alloc( 12 );
          foo.write( ptrs[i], As );
          i++;
      }

    foo.free( ptrs[0] );
    foo.free( ptrs[1] );
    foo.free( ptrs[2] );

    foo.free( ptrs[6] );
    foo.free( ptrs[7] );
    foo.free( ptrs[8] );
    foo.free( ptrs[9] );

    // foo.free( ptrs[13] );

    int new1 = foo.alloc( 100 );
    foo.write( new1, Bs );

    byte[] msg = new byte[1000];
    int amt_read = foo.read( new1, msg );
    System.out.print( "Read " + amt_read +
        " bytes: " );
    System.out.write( msg, 0, amt_read );
    System.out.println();

    amt_read = foo.read( new1, msg, 25 );
```

```
                        System.out.print( "Read " + amt_read +
                            " bytes: " );
                        System.out.write( msg, 0, amt_read );
                        System.out.println();

                        amt_read = foo.read( ptrs[3], msg );
                        System.out.print( "Read " + amt_read +
                            " bytes: " );
                        System.out.write( msg, 0, amt_read );
                        System.out.println();


                        /*
                        int new2 = foo.alloc( 12 );
                        foo.write( new2, Bs );

                        int new3 = foo.alloc( 28 );
                        foo.write( new3, Bs );
                        */
                        // int new4 = foo.alloc( 60 );
                        // foo.write( new4, As );

                    }
                    catch ( HeapFileAllocException he ) {

                        System.out.println( he.getMessage() );
                    }

                     foo.close();

                    BinFile bf = new BinFile( "foo.bar" );
                    ScrollWin sw = new ScrollWin( bf, "foo.bar" );
                    sw.setEndApp( true );
                    sw.show();

                }
            // */

    // constructors:

        HeapFile( String pathname ) {
```

```java
        // open pathname for reading
        this( pathname, "r" );
    }

    HeapFile( String pathname, String access ) {

        // open pathname for "r" or "rw"
        readable = writeable = false;
        path_name = pathname;

        try {

            raf =
                new RandomAccessFile( path_name, access );

            readable = true;
            writeable = access.equals( "rw" );

            read_circ_pointer();

            message = path_name + " opened for \"" +
                access + "\" access";

            return;
        }
        catch ( IOException ioe ) {

            message = "Failed opening " + path_name;
        }

    }

    HeapFile( String pathname, int free_size ) {

        // create pathname with free_size available bytes
        // opened for "rw"

        // does NOT open existing, non-empty file

        path_name = pathname;
        readable = writeable = false;
```

```
            try {
                raf = new RandomAccessFile( path_name, "rw" );

                file_length = raf.length();
                if ( file_length > 0 ) {

                    message = path_name + " already exists.";
                    raf.close();
                    return;
                }
                else {

                    byte[] buf =
                        new byte[ free_size + OVERHEAD ];

                    circ_pointer = 4;
                    buf[3] = 4; // circ pointer is bytes 0-3

                    raf.write( buf );

                    // prev (bytes 4-7) = 0;
                    // next (bytes 8-11) = 0;

                    raf.seek( 12 );
                    raf.writeInt( free_size );

                    message = path_name + " created.";

                    readable = writeable = true;
                }
            }
            catch ( IOException ioe ) {

                    message = path_name + " not created.";
            }
        }

// there are no data access methods

// public, class-specific methods:

    public int alloc( int size )
```

```
            throws HeapFileAllocException {

        if ( size < MINIMUM_BLOCK_SIZE )
            throw new HeapFileAllocException(
                "size " + size + " is too small" );

        int alloc_from;
        try {

            alloc_from = find_block( size );
        }
        catch ( HeapFileAllocException ae ) {

            throw ae;
        }

        if ( alloc_from != circ_pointer )
            reset_circ_pointer( alloc_from );

        return alloc_block( size );
    }

    public void close() {

        try {

            raf.close();
        }
        catch ( IOException ioe ) {

            message = "Failure during close";
        }

        readable = writeable = false;
    }

    public void free( int ptr ) {

        int size = read_size( ptr );

        if ( size < MINIMUM_BLOCK_SIZE )
            return; // probably a bad pointer
```

```
        ptr -= 4; // convert to llist pointer
        size -= 8; // subtract prev & next ptrs
        write_llist_size( ptr, size );

        list_insert( ptr );
        combine( ptr );
        combine( read_llist_prev(ptr) );
    }

    public int read( int ptr, byte[] b ) {

        // reads full block
        int file_space = read_size( ptr );
        return read( ptr, b, file_space );
    }

    public int read( int ptr, byte[] b, int nbytes ) {

        // returns # of bytes read
        int file_space = read_size( ptr );
        int read_size = file_space < nbytes ?
            file_space : nbytes;
        if ( read_size > b.length )
            read_size = b.length;

        try {

            raf.seek( ptr );
            raf.read( b, 0, read_size );
        }
        catch( IOException ioe ) {

            message = ioe.getMessage();
            return 0;
        }

        message = "read OK";
        return read_size;
    }

    public int write( int ptr, byte[] b ) {
```

```
              // returns # of bytes written
              int file_space = read_size( ptr );
              int write_size = file_space >= b.length ?
                  b.length : file_space;

              try {

                  raf.seek( ptr );
                  raf.write( b, 0, write_size );
              }
              catch ( IOException ioe ) {

                  message = ioe.getMessage();
                  return 0;
              }
              message = "write OK";
              return write_size;
          }

// public, non-event overriding method:

      public String paramString() {

          return "RAF: " + raf.toString();
      }

// there are no public, event-handling methods

// ------------------ private methods ------------------

// private methods:

      private int alloc_block( int nbytes ) {

          // size of current block is >= nbytes

          circ_pointer = read_circ_pointer();
          int ptr = circ_pointer;

          int this_size = read_llist_size( ptr );

          int excess = this_size + 8 - nbytes;
```

```
        if ( excess >= OVERHEAD ) { // carve from block end

            int chop_size = nbytes + 4;
            int block_end = ptr + 12 + this_size;

            int piece_start = block_end - chop_size;

            write_llist_size( ptr, this_size - chop_size );

            return setup_piece( piece_start,
                chop_size - 4 );
        }
        else { // return whole block

            protect_circ_pointer( ptr );

            // point prev <--> next
            int prev =
                read_llist_prev( ptr );
            int next =
                read_llist_next( ptr );

            write_llist_next( prev, next );
            write_llist_prev( next, prev );

            this_size += 8;
            int where = setup_piece( ptr, this_size );

            return where;
        }
    }

    private void combine( int ptr ) {

        // combine current block with next block
        // in list, if they are contiguous

        int next = read_llist_next( ptr );
        protect_circ_pointer( next );

        int size = read_llist_size( ptr );
```

```
        if ( next == (ptr + size + 12) ) { // combine them

            int new_size = read_llist_size( ptr ) +
                read_llist_size( next ) + 12;
            write_llist_size( ptr, new_size );

            int new_next = read_llist_next( next );
            write_llist_next( ptr, new_next );
            write_llist_prev( new_next, ptr );
        }
    }

    private void protect_circ_pointer( int ptr ) {

        // 2nd of two blocks may be deleted by combine()
        // block may be deleted by alloc()

        // this moves the circ pointer forward if it's
        // pointing to the block that will be deleted

        if ( read_circ_pointer() != ptr )
            return; // no problem!

        int next = read_llist_next( ptr );
        reset_circ_pointer( next == 0 ? 4 : next );
    }

    private void expand_file( int nbytes )
        throws HeapFileAllocException {

        int fsize;
        byte[] b;

        try {

            fsize = ( int ) raf.length();
            if ( fsize > GIGABYTE )
                throw new HeapFileAllocException(
                    "Heap file too large to expand" );

            raf.seek( fsize );
```

```
            b = new byte[nbytes];
            raf.write( b );
        }
    catch ( IOException ioe ) {

            throw new HeapFileAllocException(
                "Space for " + nbytes +
                " bytes not available." );
        }

        int new_space = fsize / 2;

        int other_new_space = ( nbytes * 3 ) / 2;
        if ( other_new_space > new_space )
            new_space = other_new_space;

        b = new byte[new_space - nbytes];

        try {

            raf.write( b );
        }
    catch ( IOException ioe ) {}

}

private int find_block( int nbytes )
    throws HeapFileAllocException {

    int start_block = read_circ_pointer();
    int this_block = start_block;

    do {

        int this_size = read_llist_size( this_block );
        int excess = this_size + 8 - nbytes;

        if ( excess >= OVERHEAD )
            return this_block;

        if ( (excess >= 0) && (this_block != 4) )
            return this_block;
```

```
            this_block = read_llist_next( this_block );
            if ( this_block == 0 )
                this_block = 4;
        }
        while ( this_block != start_block );

        // usually RETURNS above (within do statement)
        // Only gets here on failure to find block

        int old_length, new_length;
        try {

            old_length = ( int ) raf.length();
            expand_file( nbytes + 12 );
            new_length = ( int ) raf.length();
        }
        catch ( IOException ioe ) {

            throw new HeapFileAllocException(
                "Failed calling raf.length()" );
        }
        catch ( HeapFileAllocException he ) {

            throw he;
        }

        // gets here when file is successfully expanded

        int new_bytes = new_length - old_length;

        // set up new addition as an allocated block
        int new_block_size = new_bytes - 4;
        int new_ptr = old_length + 4;
        write_size( new_ptr, new_block_size );

        // then link the block into the free space list
        free( new_ptr );

        return find_last_block();
    }

private int find_last_block() {
```

```
    int ptr = circ_pointer;
    int old_ptr, next_ptr;

    do {

        next_ptr = read_llist_next( ptr );
        old_ptr = ptr;
        ptr = next_ptr;
    }
    while ( ptr != 0 );

    return old_ptr;
}

private void list_insert( int ptr ) {

    int list_ptr = 4; // begin w/head of list

    int next_item = read_llist_next( list_ptr );

    while ( (next_item > 0) && (next_item < ptr) ) {

        list_ptr = next_item;
        next_item = read_llist_next( list_ptr );
    }

    // note: this list's head item is permanent,
    // so we never insert a new head item

    if ( next_item == 0 ) { // add new tail item

        // prev = list_ptr; next = 0;
        write_llist_ptrs( ptr, list_ptr, 0 );
        write_llist_next( list_ptr, ptr );
    }
    else { // insert between existing items

        // list_ptr <--> ptr <--> next
        int next = read_llist_next( list_ptr );
        write_llist_next( list_ptr, ptr );
        write_llist_ptrs( ptr, list_ptr, next );
        write_llist_prev( next, ptr );
    }
```

```
        }

        private int read_circ_pointer() {

            try {

                raf.seek( 0 );
                circ_pointer = raf.readInt();
                return circ_pointer;
            }
            catch ( IOException ioe ) {

                message = "Failed reading circular pointer";
                return -1;
            }
        }

        private int read_llist_next( int pointer ) {

            try {

                raf.seek( pointer + 4 );
                return raf.readInt();
            }
            catch ( IOException ioe ) {

                message = "Failed reading list block next";
                return -1;
            }
        }

        private int read_llist_prev( int pointer ) {

            try {

                raf.seek( pointer );
                return raf.readInt();
            }
            catch ( IOException ioe ) {

                message = "Failed reading list block prev";
                return -1;
```

```
        }
    }

    private int read_llist_size( int pointer ) {

        try {

            raf.seek( pointer + 8 );
            return raf.readInt();
        }
        catch ( IOException ioe ) {

            message = "Failed reading list block size";
            return -1;
        }
    }

    private int read_size( int pointer ) {

        try {

            raf.seek( pointer - 4 );
            return raf.readInt();
        }
        catch ( IOException ioe ) {

            message = "Failed reading block size";
            return -1;
        }
    }

    private void reset_circ_pointer( int ptr ) {

        try {

            raf.seek(0);
            raf.writeInt( ptr );
            circ_pointer = ptr;
        }
        catch ( IOException ioe ) {

            message = "Failed writing circular pointer";
```

```java
            }
        }

        private int setup_piece( int real_pointer, int size ) {

            int pointer = real_pointer + 4;
            write_size( pointer, size );

            return pointer;
        }

        private void write_llist_next( int pointer,
            int new_next ) {

            try {

                raf.seek( pointer + 4 );
                raf.writeInt( new_next );
            }
            catch ( IOException ioe ) {

                message = "Failed writing list block next";
            }
        }

        private void write_llist_prev( int pointer,
            int new_prev ) {

            try {

                raf.seek( pointer );
                raf.writeInt( new_prev );
            }
            catch ( IOException ioe ) {

                message = "Failed writing list block prev";
            }
        }

        private void write_llist_ptrs( int pointer,
            int new_prev, int new_next ) {
```

```java
        try {

            raf.seek( pointer  );
            raf.writeInt( new_prev );
            raf.writeInt( new_next );
        }
        catch ( IOException ioe ) {

            message = "Failed writing list block pointers";
        }
    }

    private void write_llist_size( int pointer,
        int new_size ) {

        try {

            raf.seek( pointer + 8 );
            raf.writeInt( new_size );
        }
        catch ( IOException ioe ) {

            message = "Failed writing list block size";
        }
    }

    private void write_size( int pointer,
        int new_size ) {

        try {

            raf.seek( pointer - 4 );
            raf.writeInt( new_size );
        }
        catch ( IOException ioe ) {

            message = "Failed writing block size";
        }
    }

} // end of HeapFile class
```

```
// private class in HeapFile.java

class HeapFileAllocException extends Exception {

    HeapFileAllocException( String msg ) {

        super( msg );
    }
}

/*
    HeapFile lets you alloc() and free() space within a
    disk file. When you alloc( nbytes ) a pointer to a
    block of that size is returned. You use it for your
    application, which can read() or write() an array
    of bytes to that block.

    The space is persistent. If the application stores
    its pointers in a file, it can use the space across
    multiple runs.

    When you are done with the space, you free() it. The
    space is returned to the HeapFile's free space list.
    The HeapFile does not clear the space. When security
    requires it, the application should clear its space
    before free()ing it.

    Internally, the HeapFile allocates space using a
    circular-first-fit algorithm. When it cannot find
    a block with enough free space to satisfy an alloc()
    request, it goes to disk for the larger of 50% more
    heap space or 150% of the new request.

    The HeapFile does continuous garbage collection,
    converting every pair of contiguous free space blocks
    into a single, larger block.

    The four bytes that precede the space allocated hold
    an int that specifies the size of the block. An
    application that passes pointers to HeapFile (via
    free(), read() or write() calls) must provide a pointer
    that HeapFile created via an alloc() operation.
```

```
    An application can create sub-blocks within its own
    blocks by writing an int (big-endian, of course) into
    a byte array and passing the number of the first byte
    past the int as a pointer. In most cases it would be
    better to let HeapFile alloc() all space.

    A malicious or badly programmed application can trash
    the HeapFile by passing pointers to space it didn't
    alloc(), or pointers to space that doesn't contain a
    valid int immediately preceding the block.

    The HeapFile does not maintain a used block list. Its
    intent is to handle a large number of allocated blocks
    with minimal overhead (e.g., a million variable-length
    strings in a data file). This means that the client
    application has to be trustworthy.

    The absolute size limit is 2GB - 1, since the code
    uses all int variables. The expand_file() method
    refuses to expand a file larger than 1GB. (Design
    target size is under 10MB.)

    The expand_file() method can be improved to get up to
    the 2GB-1 limit. Passing that limit requires recoding
    this class and the client application. (All pointers
    will have to be longs.)
*/

// end of HeapFile.java
```

Summary

Variable-length data is necessary even in the relational world of classic data processing. Many applications were written that made use of dBASE III's memo fields, which let you attach variable-length memoranda to records.

In addition to classic applications for variable-length data—such as a doctor recording notes about a patient visit—new file types for sound, pictures, or video put heavy demands on our ability to handle variable-length data. The HeapFile is our tool for easily attaching such data to tables.

Our HeapFile uses a disk file as if it were a RAM-based heap store. Your application uses calls to alloc( ) and free( ) space in the disk file. If your application stores the pointers returned by alloc( ), this space is persistent.

Using a HeapFile approach gets us past the early mistakes made with the original dBASE memo fields. We can allocate exactly the space required, not a fixed page length, and we can do continuous garbage collection instead of orphaning space when a variable-length item's size is increased.

Internally, our HeapFile uses a circular-first-fit algorithm to assign space. A best-fit algorithm would create lots of small, useless pieces of space. The circular-first-fit algorithm is better for our application than the plain first-fit algorithm, since we'll often get a large space at the end when we expand the file. The circular-first-fit algorithm will allocate from that space without searching, until it is consumed.

Like the DBF, the HeapFile lets us cover a complex process with a simple-to-use class. If this code were perfect (you don't believe it is, do you?), you could just use it as a black box. The "Understanding" section here completely documents the internals, just in case.

If you've enjoyed this class, you'll be really delighted with Chapter 18, where we dive into the details of b-tree indexes. These indexes will let us maintain tables in several sorted orders simultaneously.

Chapter 18

B-Trees and Other Pyramids

If you enjoyed the HeapFile, you'll love this chapter and the next two. We'll cover the B-trees that form the heart of database search engines.

In some very early work, an attempt was made to keep data tables sorted. This didn't work for two reasons. First, physically sorting a large table (millions of records) is impractical. Second, even if you can sort a table into physical order, you find that most tables need to be searched in multiple orders.

For example, your customer table probably needs to appear in alphabetical order for end user access. But for the sales applications, it needs to be in primary key order. Analytical users will also want the table to be in order by customer category, by location, and by other classifications.

The need to have a file appear sorted in multiple ways simultaneously is met by *file indexes*. These work just as library indexes work. The typical library will have indexes by book title, by author, and by topic. The indexes are sorted. Just as it's simpler to sort file cards than to sort the actual books, it's simpler to sort computer indexes, rather than full tables.

These indexes need to be highly efficient. Finding a single customer by name in half a second might be acceptable, but displaying 20 customer names in a scroll window would be completely unacceptable if it took half a second to find each name.

B-trees are the invention that makes near-instantaneous access to tables possible in as many different orders as the application requires. In this chapter we're going to look at the theory underlying B-trees. In the next two chapters we'll provide a Java implementation that's faster than most C++ B-trees, since we'll make a simple but powerful addition to the classic theory.

Before we start with B-trees, however, we'll look at binary searching and binary trees. You'll see how these provide a basis for rapid file access. Then I'll explain how they can fail. Once you understand how these can work and can fail, you'll understand the problem that B-trees solve. We'll finish by looking at the way B-trees solve the problem.

Binary Searching

TOUR

If you've ever programmed a binary search, skip right ahead to the "Binary Trees" section.

If you're not an old pro at binary searching, let's look at a noncomputerized example. We'll do a binary search for "binary" in the dictionary.

You begin by writing the word "start" on one piece of paper and the word "end" on another. Slip these pieces of paper into the dictionary at the start and end of the definitions.

The Binary Search Algorithm

With "start" and "end" in place, open the dictionary to its center. More precisely, open it halfway between "start" and "end." Then decide which of these three conditions applies:

- The word you seek is on the open pages.
- The word you seek comes before the open pages.
- The word you seek comes after the open pages.

When the first condition applies, you've found the location of your word. Read the definition or check the spelling (or even find out that "binary" came from the Latin *binarius*, meaning two-by-two). Your search is done.

But we know that "binary" isn't in the center of the dictionary. It's much earlier. That's the second of our three possibilities.

For a word that precedes the open pages, you stick the paper that reads "end" into the dictionary where it's open. You know that half the dictionary holds words that come after "binary," so you needn't consider that half again for this search.

Then you repeat the process, opening halfway between the "start" and "end" papers. You check the three possibilities.

If you've found your word, the search is done.

If the word is to the left of the open spot, move the "end" paper to the open spot and again open halfway between "start" and "end."

If the word is to the right of the open spot, move the "start" paper to the open spot and again open halfway between "start" and "end."

Continue until you find the word.

Now you or I would start by opening the dictionary pretty near the start, since we know that we'll find "binary" near the front. If there were thumb tabs, we could even open right to the first letter we want. But forget this. Humans have preexisting knowledge in lots of subject domains that lets us do tricks like this. Your computer has no such knowledge.

The Binary Search Speed

Even without any knowledge of the distribution of the values in a database, binary searches aren't slow. Let's look up "binary" in my favorite dictionary. The dictionary's got about 1,500 pages of definitions. How many times will we move those two pieces of paper before I find "binary"?

I just tried. It took ten moves to find "binary," which is just what theory predicts. When you open your dictionary, you see two facing pages. In 1,500 pages of definitions there are 750 two-page spreads.

If there were two possibilities, you'd need one or two tries to find the right one. (You'd open right to it, or you'd try the other possibility.) If there were four possibilities, you'd only need one more try. The first try narrows the field to one of two two-item possibilities. (Actually, you could get lucky and hit the right answer on your very first try. This makes the average number of tries a bit less than I'm going to suggest here. Don't worry about it.)

If there were eight possibilities, we need one try to get to four, another try to get to two, and one or two more to find the answer. Similarly, if there were 16 possibilities, we'd need one more try than for eight. Thirty-two takes one more try than 16, and so on.

The good news is that if I used a dictionary of 3,000 pages, it would take only one more try than it takes for a 1,500-page dictionary.

A good approximation of the average number of tries in a binary search is N where you have 2^N possibilities. That's ten tries for 1,024 possibilities, for example.

This means that the number of tries required in a binary search is relatively small, even for very large numbers of entries. Ten searches will find the answer in 1,024 possibilities, 20 searches will find the answer in a million possibilities, and 30 will find the answer in a billion possibilities.

Binary Trees

Suppose our dictionary is on disk. We've organized the dictionary as records in a database. The records start with the word entry and then have the pronunciation, derivation, and definition(s). We've got a simple, fixed-length record that ends with a pointer into a HeapFile where we store over-length definitions.

We can use a binary search to quickly find any word. If we have about 256,000 words, we'll need 18 tries to find whatever word we're looking for. Now, can we do better than a binary search?

The answer is emphatically yes. We can do a lot better.

Using an Index File

The first idea is to create a subfile that only contains the words and their record numbers in the main dictionary. Let's store a 20-byte word and a 4-byte integer pointer. Assume that entries in the main dictionary have 300-byte records and that our disks are read in 16K pages.

With the full dictionary, we'll read about 50 words in each disk read (16K divided by 300 bytes per entry). Using the small index into the main dictionary, we'll read over 650 words with each disk read. The actual reduction is 12.5 to 1. Put another way, the index takes about 6MB. The full dictionary takes about 75MB, not counting the HeapFile.

Extracting just the information you need to search is a very useful step. Any file that is extracted this way for searching can be called an *index* file. The use of the index file is the same as the use of a library index. Those little index file cards are a lot handier than the books they represent.

Let's again ask if we can do better than using an index file that holds just the information we need for searching. The answer is still emphatically yes. We can do a lot better.

Using a Binary Tree

Let's not organize the index file alphabetically. Let's find the middle word in the dictionary and put that into our index in the first location. Now take the two words from the middle of the left and right halves, and put them into the second and third positions. Then put the words that divide the quarters into the next four positions, and so on.

This creates a binary tree that looks like this:

```
                    innerve
                  /         \
        denature            railing
        /      \            /      \
   caroler garrote  monument  stowage
      . . .
```

The file will look like this:

```
entry     0: innerve
entries 1-2: denature railing
entries 3-6: caroler garrote monument stowage
. . .
```

What we'll really write into the index file is the words and their locations in the main file. If the main file has 256,000 entries, the binary tree will start like this:

```
      Word          In main
      ----------    -------
0: innerve           128000
1: denature           64000
2: railing           192000
3: caroler            32000
4: garrote            96000
5: monument          160000
6: stowage           224000

. . .
```

The advantage of this approach is that you can do just one disk read and then do several levels of searching. With our 16K disk pages and 24-byte index entries, you can do about eight levels of search by reading a single page. You can do 16 levels of search by reading two pages. Searching 24 levels (which will find one entry in about 16 million) requires reading only three disk pages.

Actually, a real binary tree generally has pointers to the left and right words, in addition to pointers into the dictionary. This is the same data with the additional pointers:

	Word	In main	Lft	Rgt
0:	innerve	128000	1	2
1:	denature	64000	3	4
2:	railing	192000	5	6
3:	caroler	32000	7	8
4:	garrote	96000	9	10
5:	monument	160000	11	12
6:	stowage	224000	13	14

. . .

One more addition is usually added, as well. This is a backward reference to the parent. The whole index entry would look like this:

	Word	In main	Lft	Rgt	Prnt
0:	innerve	128000	1	2	-1
1:	denature	64000	3	4	0
2:	railing	192000	5	6	0
3:	caroler	32000	7	8	1
4:	garrote	96000	9	10	1
5:	monument	160000	11	12	2
6:	stowage	224000	13	14	2

. . .

The special value, –1, indicates that the root, "innerve," has no parent.

We built this binary tree by searching the finished data set. We picked "innerve" because it's the exact middle entry. If your database is static, a perfectly balanced binary tree such as this one is ideal for searching. It will work well for a dictionary.

A balanced binary tree will let you search a database for a value with the minimum number of disk reads. (The first law of computer science should be, "There's always a better way." This structure is the best yet built when the data must be read from disk and when there's no preknowledge about the distribution of values.) With three disk reads needed to find one entry in 24 million, this structure is lightning fast.

Unfortunately, few databases are static. Most indexes have to be maintained as data records are added and deleted.

Building Binary Trees

Before we start building binary trees, let's add one more realistic concept. If you have exactly $2^N - 1$ entries, you will nicely fill a binary tree. That means that 511 entries work perfectly. So do 1,023. Any number in between means that some of our bottom-level nodes won't have both children. At the bottom level, we could see situations like this:

```
 .  .  .
   /           \
Inness      innkeeper
               /
         inning
```

The entries in the tree will look like this:

```
      Word       In main  Lft  Rgt  Prnt
      --------   -------   ---  ---  ----
x:  Inness       128001    -1   -1    x
x:  innkeeper    128002     x   -1    x
x:  inning       128003    -1   -1    x
```

Bearing in mind that we'll fill parent and child pointers with –1 values when there is no value to point to, let's build a binary tree, starting with an empty database. The first word we see is "blossom." Our database starts like this:

```
      Word       In main  Lft  Rgt  Prnt
      --------   -------   ---  ---  ----
0:  blossom         0      -1   -1    -1
```

The next word that arrives is "blot," which we add as the right child of our root, this way:

```
    blossom
          \
         blot
```

The index looks like this:

```
     Word        In main  Lft  Rgt  Prnt
     ---------   -------  ---  ---  ----
0:   blossom           0   -1    1    -1
1:   blot              1   -1   -1     0
```

If the words arrive at random, the tree will grow to the left and to the right. If the first entry was reasonably close to the middle, the resulting tree might be nicely balanced. On the other hand, if the words continue to arrive in order, the tree will grow in only one direction. Let's take in "blotch," "blotchy," and "blotter." Our tree just grows to the right:

```
        blossom
               \
           blot
               \
              blotch
                   \
                 blotchy
                      \
                   blotter
```

Our index now looks like this:

```
     Word        In main  Lft  Rgt  Prnt
     ---------   -------  ---  ---  ----
0:   blossom           0   -1    1    -1
1:   blot              1   -1    2     0
2:   blotch            2   -1    3     1
3:   blotchy           3   -1    4     2
4:   blotter           4   -1   -1     3
```

What we've got really isn't a binary tree at all. It's a linked list. Searching a linked list takes an average of N/2 searches for N items. Instead of reading three 16K disk pages to find one item in 24 million, you'll need to read, on average, 18,000 pages (assuming 24-byte entries). We just went from lightning fast to a long session of staring at the hourglass.

What we need is something like a binary tree that will always keep itself nicely balanced. That is a description of the B-tree.

B-Trees

The B-tree has been with us since Bayer and McCreight invented it in the early '70s. It's now part of every database system, relational or otherwise. At worst, it achieves half the theoretical efficiency of a perfectly balanced binary tree. Half as fast as a perfectly balanced binary tree is very, very fast. It's always nicely balanced. It doesn't matter if it's filled with values that arrive at random or already in sequence.

There is only one problem with the B-tree: it's very confusing. I wrestled with the concepts here for a long time until I discovered what was wrong. It's the name.

B-Trees Are Pyramids, Not Trees

In computers we've become used to the idea that our trees are upside down. This is the slightly silly computer tree:

```
          root
          /    \
      node      node
      /   \         \
  leaf     node      node
           /         /    \
       leaf      leaf    leaf
```

The node at the top is called the *root*. The nodes that don't have children are called *leaves.* They come toward the bottom. If you turn the thing upside down, our trees are something like the trees that Mother Nature grows.

The B-tree pushes the analogy past the breaking point. The leaves grow on the ground. When you get a bunch of leaves in one spot, you sprout a twig. As more leaves grow on the ground, more twigs are pushed up. When enough twigs are pushed up, a branch pops up to hold them together. When enough branches gather, you get the tree's trunk.

Is that ridiculous? No? Well, let me add that the twigs aren't really twigs at all. They're just other leaves. Ditto for the branches and trunk. They're all leaves. But they all start growing on the ground.

Can we put this one away? Searching a B-tree is a lot like searching a balanced binary tree. Otherwise, the name "tree" doesn't apply.

A B-tree is more like a pyramid. If you have some children's blocks, you'll be able to see this analogy. For those of you who don't have wooden blocks, try these print ones:

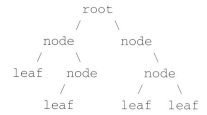

Before we get into the B-tree, we'll play with these blocks. You'll see that we're really working hard on the B-tree algorithms.

We'll start with an algorithm for building a pyramid.

- Rule 1: Put the first block on the left.
- Rule 2: Place all your remaining blocks, one at a time, following rule 3.
- Rule 3: If there are two contiguous blocks with no block on top, center a block on top of them. Otherwise, place your block to the right of the bottom-right block.

I'll follow these rules with our print blocks. This is the place we reach with rule 1:

```
 ---
| A |
 ---
```

Now let's grab the next block and place it according to rule 3:

```
 ---  ---
| A || B |
 ---  ---
```

This is pretty simple, isn't it? Now we've got two contiguous blocks, so the next block is placed like this:

```
    ---
   | C |
 -------
| A || B |
 ---  ---
```

There aren't any contiguous, untopped blocks, so the next block goes like this:

```
    ---
   | C |
 -------  ---
| A || B || D |
 ---  ---  ---
```

Here are the next blocks, added according to our rules:

```
Add E:                  Add F:
                                  ---
                                 | F |
                                 --- ---
       --- ---              --- ---
      | C | E |            | C | E |
      -----------          -----------
     | A | B | D |        | A | B | D |
      --- --- ---          --- --- ---
```

If you have more blocks, your pyramid will keep growing:

```
Add G:                  Add H:                  Add I:
      ---                     ---                     --- ---
     | F |                   | F |                   | F | I |
     --- ---                 --- --- ---             --- --- ---
    | C | E |               | C | E | H |           | C | E | H |
    -----------  ---        -----------  ---        -----------  ---
   | A | B | D | G |       | A | B | D | G |       | A | B | D | G |
    --- --- --- ---         --- --- --- ---         --- --- --- ---
```

You place block K on your own. Why are we playing with blocks? Because they are a good analogy for the B-tree. The B-tree is a pyramid. Each node is like one of our blocks. Let's take a closer look at the B-tree's building blocks.

The B-Tree's Nodes

Each node in a B-tree is a pointer and key value sandwich. You start with a pointer, then add values and pointers alternately. Starting and ending with pointers gives you one more pointer than you have values. The number of pointers is called the node's *order.* This is an order five node:

```
Order five node:

ptr "KeyVal1" ptr "KeyVal2" ptr "KeyVal3" ptr "KeyVal4" ptr
```

I'll define my own term, *size,* which is the size of the node counted in key values, not in pointers. The size of a node is one less than its order.

In each node, the key values are stored in sorted order. Our dictionary might start with a node like this:

```
ptr "denature" ptr "innerve" ptr "railing" ptr
```

The first pointer points to another node that has values less than "denature." The second pointer, between "denature" and "innerve," points to another node for the values that come between those two words.

This is a B-tree of single-letter values:

```
    D H
   / | \
 ABC EFG IJK
```

Its root node has two values. The other nodes have three values each. This could be a B-tree of size three.

A B-tree has at least size/2 value entries in every node, excepting the root node. The root node has at least one entry (unless the tree is empty). No node has more than size values. In each node, the number of pointers is always one more than the number of values.

The values in each node are stored in sequential order. I'll describe them here as stored from left to right, with the lower values on the left. The pointers lead to other nodes whose values fall in the position of the pointer.

Searching the B-Tree

The B-tree is searched by scanning the values in the nodes, beginning in the root node. Each node is scanned in the same way.

To scan a node, you look at the values from left to right. At each value in the node you perform the following procedure, starting with the left-most value:

- ■ If the value you want is the value in the node, your search is done.

- ■ If the value you want is less than the value in the node, you follow the pointer on the left to the next node.

- ■ If the value you want is greater than the value in the node, you move to the next value in the node and repeat this procedure.

- ■ If there is no value to the right, you follow the rightmost pointer to the next node.

If any pointer you would follow is null, your search is unsuccessful and done. The value you sought is not in the B-tree. The last value scanned in an unsuccessful search is the first one larger than the sought value. This is very helpful if you are looking for a place to insert a new value.

Inserting into the B-Tree

The binary tree degenerated into a linked list when we inserted values that arrived in sorted order. The B-tree doesn't have this vice. It's built like a pyramid. Let's go back to our blocks.

Building a B-Tree with Blocks

When you add the first entry to a B-tree, you place the block (key value) on the left. It is the first value in a node that has all null pointers. It looks like this:

```
 ---
| A |
 ---
```

In this example, we'll use a node size of four. You continue to place blocks (values) into the node until it is full. Here, B, C, and D have been inserted:

```
 --- --- --- ---
| A | B | C | D |
 --- --- --- ---
```

At this point, all the pointers are null. Now we want to add one more value. Since the node is full, you split the node into two parts. The left node gets the lower values, and the right node gets the higher values. The median value is pushed upward into a parent node. This is what you get when you add the E block:

```
                 ---
                | C |
                 ---
              /        \
 --- ---            --- ---
| A | B |          | D | E |
 --- ---            --- ---
```

As more values come in, you place them all at ground level. For example, here the F and G blocks have been inserted:

```
                 ---
                | C |
                 ---
              /        \
 --- ---            --- --- --- ---
| A | B |          | D | E | F | G |
 --- ---            --- --- --- ---
```

When a new value arrives for a full node, that node is again split, forcing its median value upward to the parent node. Here's the pyramid after the arrival of the H block:

```
              --- ---
             | C | F |
              --- ---
            /    |    \
   --- ---     --- ---     --- ---
  | A | B |   | D | E |   | G | H |
   --- ---     --- ---     --- ---
```

If we continued building this way, eventually our root node would overflow. Here's where we'd be before Q arrived:

```
      --- --- --- ---
     | C | F | I | L |
      --- --- --- ---
    /   /   /   |    \
   /   /   /    |      --- --- --- ---
  AB  DE  GH   JK     | M | N | O | P |
  --  --  --   --      --- --- --- ---
```

When Q arrives, we begin by splitting the bottom node and pushing up the median value, as always:

```
      --- --- --- ---        ---
     | C | F | I | L | <-| O |
      --- --- --- ---        ---
    /   /   /  /    \ /        \
   /   /   / /   --- ---     --- ---
  AB  DE  GH JK | M | N |   | P | Q |
  --  --  -- --  --- ---     --- ---
```

At the higher level, you are performing a node insertion. The algorithm is the same for every node. If the new value is one too many, you split the node and push the median value upward.

```
                        ---
                       | I |
                        ---
                     /        \
          --- ---              --- ---
         | C | F |            | L | O |
          --- ---              --- ---
        /    |   |          /    |    \
       /     |   |         /   --- ---   --- ---
      AB    DE  GH       JK  | M | N | | P | Q |
      --    --  --       --   --- ---   --- ---
```

The essential difference between most computer trees and the B-tree is that the other computer trees grow like natural trees, pushing out new leaves as needed. The B-tree grows like a pyramid. The split process pushes up the median value, which means the structure is self-balancing.

Look at the preceding example, and picture the arrival of a series of H values, "Ha," "Hb," "Hc," and so on. With a tree, that would sprout a long branch growing below and to the right of "H." (A gardener would grab the pruning shears.) With the pyramid, "Ha" and "Hb" would add to the node that now has "G" and "H." The arrival of "Hc" would push a new median value upward.

The "Ha" would be added to the node that held "C" and "F." This is where we'd be:

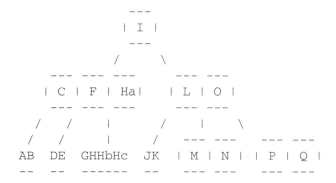

As more "Hx" values ("Hd," "He," and so on) arrived, another "Hx" would be added to the parent node. The "C" and "F" node would eventually overflow, forcing it to split, pushing "Ha" up into the root node, which would then have "Ha" and "I." The top levels would look like this:

```
       Ha,I
      /   |   \
   C,F   Hd,Hg   L,O
```

The pyramid stays nicely balanced because median values are the only ones that migrate upward.

The Insertion Algorithm

Now let's write some rules for building these B-tree pyramids. Assume that we are inserting value V into a B-tree. Ground level is the number of pointers followed from the root to the bottom level.

- Rule 1: If there is no root node, create one and make V its first value. Ground level is zero. Done.

- Rule 2: If there is a root node, search for the ground-level node that V belongs in. This is the insertion node.

- Rule 3: If the insertion node is not full, insert V in sorted order. Done.

- Rule 4: To insert V into a full node, order the values in the node, including V. Leave the lower size/2 values in the existing node. Insert the higher size/2 values into a new node at the same level. The median value is pushed up to the parent level.

- Rule 5: To push the median value to the parent level when there is no parent node (we're splitting the root node), create a new node and insert the value. This new node is now the root node. Increment ground level. Done.

- Rule 6: To push the median value when there is a parent node (we're splitting any node below the root), the median value becomes V and the parent node is the new insertion node. Repeat beginning with rule 3.

Deleting from the B-Tree

In deletions, you want to observe the same principles that keep the B-tree pyramid successful: You always delete at the ground level, and you never leave a node (except the root) with less than size/2 values.

If the deletion is for a value above ground level, you push it downward by replacing the deleted entry with either the immediate predecessor or successor at the next lower level. Suppose you need to delete item F from the root of this B-tree:

```
                      --- ---
                     | F | M |
                      --- ---
                    /    |    \
    --- --- ---      --- ---      --- --- ---
   | A | B | C |    | I | L |    | O | R | U |
    --- --- ---      --- ---      --- --- ---
```

This deletion is simple, assuming a size of four, since the left child node of value F has more than size/2 entries. You simply replace F with its immediate predecessor:

```
                      --- ---
                     | C | M |
                      --- ---
                    /    |    \
    --- ---          --- ---      --- --- ---
   | A | B |        | I | L |    | O | R | U |
    --- ---          --- ---      --- --- ---
```

If the predecessor child node has no extra values, you can do exactly the same thing with the successor child node. If both child nodes have exactly size/2 values, you combine them into a single node and then delete the parent value. If you needed to delete C in the above example, this would be the result:

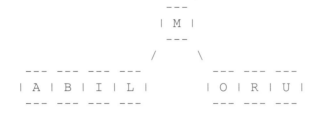

The situation is similar when you need to make a deletion at ground level and your nodes have exactly size/2 entries. In this case, you reverse the process of insertion. Instead of splitting and promoting the median, you combine, dropping the parent median. Consider deleting the B in this example:

```
                    --- ---
                   | C | M |
                    --- ---
                  /    |     \
     --- ---      --- ---     --- --- ---
    | A | B |    | I | L |   | O | R | U |
     --- ---      --- ---     --- --- ---
```

Because AB and its sibling IL both have size/2 values, you drop the C, after the deletion, leaving this result:

```
                      ---
                     | M |
                      ---
                   /        \
   --- --- --- ---          --- --- ---
  | A | C | I | L |        | O | R | U |
   --- --- --- ---          --- --- ---
```

When you have a choice of siblings, if either one has more than size/2 entries, you can rotate to maintain a balanced tree. Suppose that you wanted to delete the L in this example:

```
                    --- ---
                   | C | M |
                    --- ---
                  /    |     \
     --- ---      --- ---     --- --- ---
    | A | B |    | I | L |   | O | R | U |
     --- ---      --- ---     --- --- ---
```

You can delete it by rotating M down into L's location and O up into M's location, to get this result:

It's often possible to do a deletion in more than one way. This is another valid B-tree that holds the same data you just saw:

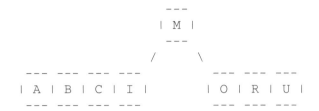

```
                      ---
                     | M |
                      ---
                  /         \
 --- --- --- ---              --- --- ---
| A | B | C | I |            | O | R | U |
 --- --- --- ---              --- --- ---
```

When you have a choice, the only law you must observe is that you leave at least size/2 entries in every node except the root. (When we get to implementation, we'll consider a little lawbreaking.)

Summary

What we need for fast database access are indexes that we can search rapidly. These will work like the library card files that let a library show books by title, author, and topic, regardless of the actual storage of the books.

B-trees are the database equivalent of these card files. They are built to take advantage of the efficiency of binary searching in binary trees, but to eliminate the problems of binary trees.

Binary searching lets you quickly find any item in a sorted list. It takes a little less than N probes to find one item in 2^N possibilities. That's ten probes to search a thousand items; 20 to search a million items, and so on.

If we extract a short key from a longer record, we can significantly reduce the number of disk reads required to find an item. If we organize our key data into binary search order, we can get dramatic results. In one realistic example, we found that we could search a dictionary of 24 million entries with just three 16K disk reads.

The problem with binary trees is that they are only practical if you have a static database (such as a dictionary). If your data tables have insertions and deletions, the binary tree can fail. In the worst case, if the data arrives in sorted (ascending or descending) order, the binary tree degenerates into a linked list. Searching a linked list is horribly slow.

The B-tree structure, invented by Bayer and McCreight in the early '70s, preserves the advantages of binary trees, but eliminates the insertion and deletion problems.

The B-tree is a pyramid of nodes. The nodes hold the key values in sorted order. When you need to insert into a full node, you split the node into two parts. The left part holds the lower half of the values and the right part holds the upper half. The median value is pushed upward to the next level.

The B-tree grows from the ground up. If there is no parent node, when you push up a median value, you create a new parent (root) node. When there is a parent node, the value is inserted into it in sorted order. If the parent node is full, it is split, pushing up its median value.

Each node is a sandwich of pointers and values. At the bottom level, the pointers are null. Above the bottom level, they point to lower-level nodes.

The pointer that precedes the first value points to the node that holds lower values. The pointer between the first and second values points to the node that holds the intervening values, and so on. The rightmost pointer points to values higher than the last value in the node.

The literature speaks of the *order* of a node, which is its maximum number of pointers. I prefer to talk about the *size* of the node, which is the number of key values, or one less than the order.

In Chapter 19 we're going to begin moving from theory to working code. You'll see that I've added an optimization that significantly speeds up B-tree access. Our Java B-trees are going to be competitive with C++ B-trees. You wouldn't have it any other way, would you?

Chapter 19

Building B-Trees

In Chapter 18 you mastered the theory behind B-tree indexing. The index gives you simple, fast access to your file, based on the values of indexed criteria. You can have as many indexes as you like, which lets you keep a single file sorted in multiple ways, simultaneously. And you learned that B-trees preserve most of the speed of binary trees, without showing any vices.

In this chapter we're going to begin the transition from theory to practice. In the first of three main sections we'll discuss a variety of implementation issues, such as how big our index values and nodes will be, and how we can optimize our speed by minimizing index file I/O.

Then we'll look at the traditional linear scan of index nodes and consider substituting a binary search within the node. Before we're done, we'll have B-trees that will be the envy of any programmer who ever considered database internals.

Finally, we'll take a close look at the Btree_node object. The NDX class that will actually encapsulate the B-tree is built from these nodes.

Let's begin with the practical considerations.

Implementing B-Trees

When we look at examples, we often look at nodes with a size of four. During testing I made extensive use of nodes that had six key values. But these aren't real. In this section we're going to consider what sorts of things get indexed and how the indexes can be built taking full account of the realities of practical computer implementations.

We'll start by thinking about the indexes you'll be using in practice.

Typical Indexes

In the next section we'll be looking at real B-trees. However, before you can do any planning, you have to know how long the key values that you'll be indexing are. That's what we'll be looking at here.

Let's begin with the object files that we discussed in Chapter 11. (These are not object-oriented programming objects. They're the real world, kickable objects about which we'll collect information.)

Object File Indexes

First, we'll need to index the object file on some human-readable identifier such as the last names of people, our products' names, or whatever name applies to the particular class of object. The name index will be used by the software that lets the user scroll through the files in index order, as we'll discuss in Chapter 21.

I've used names as long as 40 characters and as short as 16 characters. In practice a last name field for people that is 20 or 24 characters is adequate. A reasonable size for the key does not have to fit the whole name, by the way. I like to scroll the names in one window while the full record is displayed in a separate data-entry window.

We'll also need to index the object files, and all other files, on their primary key. The other files, such as event files, will refer to the objects by their primary key. Just as we humans use the names for lookup, all our application code will use the key for lookup.

The NDX code you'll see in the next chapter uses Strings for key values. You could extend it to handle integers as well. A simpler solution is to have the Indexable object (you'll see that Indexable is the simple interface the NDX requires) pass a fixed-length String version of any numeric values. A ten-character key is adequate for any positive integer. For many object types, six or eight characters will be adequate.

How Long Are My Integers?

You have to decide when you implement the Indexable interface how long your keys will be. The B-tree depends on maintaining an array of fixed-length keys in each node. The shorter the key, the faster the B-tree, so you don't just automatically go for ten characters for an integer key.

I've found a procedure that works reliably in practice. Begin by making a realistic estimate of the maximum number of objects you'll have in a file. If it's customers, how many might there be? (If you're a large chain of department stores, you could have millions of customers. If you're manufacturing airplanes, you'll have sales to a few dozen airlines.)

When you've come up with a realistic estimate, double it. That allows for a generous supply of deleted records. Finally, allow one extra character. (If you think you might have a thousand objects, you'll need 2,000 keys. Use a five-byte string.)

Next consider the analytical work you'll need to support. Do you need sales summaries by region or product code? Any such breakdown that is used commonly in your applications should also get an index. Most of these indexes use very small key values.

If you'll need to aggregate results by country, for example, you could use the two-character, Internet country code. Here in the United States, you might use the two-character postal abbreviation to index objects by state.

Indexing Event Tables

Events (again, refer to Chapter 11 for the definition) don't normally have names. As with object tables, however, you'll need to index them by their keys.

Event tables do have foreign keys for the objects that are involved in the events. Sales tables, for example, almost always have customer keys. You'll normally index an event on its own key and on each foreign key. (Your sales system, for example, will need to refer to the sales for each customer when it's time to prepare a statement.)

You may also want to index events by some portion of their time stamps. For example, you might want an index by month or quarter for preparing financial statements or for doing analysis by these periods.

Indexing Detail Tables

At the bottom level of your data system, you can skip the primary key index. For example, your sales event might have a line-item detail record in a detail table. There will be one detail record for each product involved in the sale. This detail record would hold keys to the sale and to the product.

You don't need to index these detail tables on their own keys. You need to index these details on each of their foreign keys, however.

To continue with the same example, the sales detail table would be indexed by the sale key. This is the index you'll use to find all the details that comprise an individual sale. You'll use that key to prepare invoices. The detail records will also be indexed on their product keys. The product index will let you find out how many widgets are in inventory, for example.

Typical Indexes

Have you noticed something about these indexes? They're almost all short. In working systems, the majority of the indexes are on keys and foreign keys. Those run as short as four bytes (the airplane manufacturer's customer list) to as long as ten bytes.

You'll often meet even shorter indexes, such as the two-byte country and state codes. Occasionally, you'll see longer index values. The names used for human reference to object tables are a common example.

In practice, you'll see indexes from two to 24 bytes long. (One-byte values appear, but only rarely. Longer values also appear, but even more rarely.) In most applications, the average index value size is probably well under ten bytes long.

The actual size of the key becomes important when we start to think about index node sizes.

Node Sizes and Tree Heights

What do you suppose will be the number of disk reads needed to locate an item in your applications? Make a guess. Most of you will change your guess by the time you get to the end of this section.

We're concerned about node sizes and tree heights because those determine the number of disk reads. You want to minimize the number of disk reads, of course, to optimize performance.

What node size minimizes disk reads? It depends on lots of factors. You want to pick the size that will optimize the performance of your system. The best way to do this is experimentally. Test different sizes with actual data in an actual system.

Frankly, I don't bother with that sort of tuning. My NDX object hard-codes the value 16K for the node size. Let me explain why.

Reading Single Nodes

First, the minimum node size to consider is the amount of data your computer actually reads in a single read operation. For PCs with the older, DOS-based file system, that's a function of the size of our hard disks. Typical values run from 4K to 16K. With today's disks, the lower values are becoming rare. Higher values are certainly possible.

Why is the disk page size the minimum node size? You minimize the number of disk reads by maximizing the amount of useful information that is read. The individual node is the organizer that guarantees that the data is relevant to the query.

The first index read brings the root node into RAM. Assuming that your minimum disk read brings in 16K and that your key is eight bytes long, as we'll discuss later in this chapter, this could read about 1,000 key values. Your typical ground-level node will hold about 1,000 key values, which means you can pick an individual key value in a million-record file with exactly two disk reads!

Actually, we'll do better than this in practice. By simply leaving the nodes in RAM, we'll always have the root node available without a disk read. In the preceding example, there's about one chance in 1,000 that our ground-level node is the one we want. Realistically, we'll find a pointer in the root, which is in RAM, and then we'll be using one disk access (reading the ground-level node) to find each key in our million-record file.

If we used a smaller node size, we might get lucky and find that the initial read got the root and the lower-level nodes we needed. Ignoring a small amount of node overhead space, we see that the total number of possible disk pages is a constant, regardless of node size. If our node size is less than the disk's page size, our probability that the current page holds the next node is one divided by the total number of pages. In the example earlier, that's about one in 1,000, which means that the smaller node size will almost never help.

Node sizes that exceed disk page size may be helpful. If your system will have very few indexes, you might experiment with very large node sizes. Bear in mind, however, that using too much RAM may just result in your operating system paging your nodes in and out of RAM. Transferring disk I/O from the application to the operating system won't speed up anything.

Calculating Node Sizes

When we get to our Btree_node class, you'll see that each node gets 32 bytes of overhead. In practice, I ignore this overhead when I consider B-tree calculations. It's the overhead that accompanies each key value that is important.

I don't store pointers in the ground-level nodes. At ground level, each downward pointer is null. If you know which nodes are on the ground (we'll always know), then you can store just the keys. Each key requires the key value and the record number in the source data file. Using integers for the record numbers costs four bytes per key.

Above ground level, the key values alternate with downward pointers. Using integer pointers, that's another four bytes per key value. (There's one more pointer than value, of course. As with the node overhead, I ignore that in calculations.)

Finally, your nodes range from half full to full. A reasonable assumption is that they'll average three-quarters full.

These formulas tell you approximately how many keys you'll have at each level:

```
K = key length, in bytes
N = node length, in bytes

Ground level keys/node:  ( N/(K+4) ) * .75
Upper level keys/node:   ( N/(K+8) ) * .75
Maximum keys in root node: N/(K+8)
```

The following table assumes that you use 16K nodes, that the root node is full, and that the ground-level nodes are three-quarters full.

```
Maximum Records in a Two-Level Index
```

Key Length	Number of Records
4	2,132,800
8	1,000,000
16	480,000

These large values mean that in practice your indexes will almost always have just a root node and ground-level nodes. Your first key lookup will take two disk reads. Subsequent lookups will find the root node in RAM and will find the key you want with a single disk read.

Node Construction

In theory, all your nodes are sandwiches of pointers and key values. Now it's time to think about implementing the theory.

I begin by allocating 32 bytes for overhead. This makes it easy to look at our nodes using our binary file viewer. It wastes 12 bytes, but in a 16K node, that doesn't matter. Even my Scottish grandfather would tolerate that minuscule waste.

What Grandpa MacPherson wouldn't tolerate, however, was storing null pointers at the ground level.

Separating Ground and Upper Nodes

All ground-level pointers are null. This means that if you know a node is at ground level, you don't need the pointers at all. Discarding the pointers saves four bytes per key value. Since typical keys average somewhere between six and ten bytes for the value, that overhead is material.

These are the keys you'll get at ground level in a 16K node:

```
Keys at Ground Level

    Key         With    Without
 Length     Pointers   Pointers  Improvement

      4        1,000      1,500          50%
      8          750      1,000          33%
     16          500        600          20%
```

The saving from eliminating the keys is very important with short keys, and short keys are the majority of all keys. It's a bit more trouble to code, but if I hadn't done it, I'd be having big trouble with Grandpa Mac's ghost. You wouldn't want that, would you?

The Pointer/Value Sandwich

Everything I've read about B-trees talks about the pointer/value arrangement in the B-tree node. It's very convenient to conceptualize the node that way. The pointer between two values points to the node that logically comes between those values.

Nothing I've seen about the nodes actually leaves conceptual space for the associated record numbers. They're just a detail that we programmers will wrestle with when the time comes. Let's do the wrestling.

I've built my nodes from three arrays. There's an array of pointer values. Then there's an array of record numbers. Finally, there's an array of pointers, but only if the node is not a ground-level node.

The sandwich of pointers and values is a good conceptual mechanism, but it would make searching the key values much more difficult, for just one example.

Tree Construction

It's convenient to build a B-tree as an array of node objects. Mine is just called "nodes." You always start searching at the root node. I enter this as the first element in the array, node[0].

The next node in the tree would be node[1]. That's a child of the root. I keep a variable, ground_level, to identify the bottom of the structure. This is what the tree looks like:

```
Btree_node[] nodes;

nodes[0] = root
nodes[1] = first node below root
. . .
nodes[ground_level] = ground-level node
```

Of course, in practice ground_level is normally equal to zero for very small tables or one for all but the largest tables. When we get to the NDX code in Chapter 20, you'll see that I've allowed for ten levels in the tree. This would support astronomically large files. It's useful, however, for testing the tree mechanisms, where you use tiny nodes.

Using this array means that you won't need upward pointers in your nodes. The parent of nodes[1] is nodes[0]; the parent of nodes[n] is nodes[n–1].

Efficient File I/O

Let's think about the file I/O. Specifically, let's think about the minimization of file I/O. I'll distinguish between two very different activities: index construction and operation.

In operation, an index on a table will be updated whenever a record is added, modified, or deleted. This involves lots of disk I/O. Bear in mind that the index includes a header record that stores data such as the total number of index entries. The header page has to be written when a record is added or deleted, which almost doubles the necessary I/O.

While there may be lots of disk I/O during data entry, there's also lots of time for disk I/O. Being in operation implies that there's a user doing some normal user task, such as editing data in a form. A good typist buzzing along at 60 words per minute is only entering seven characters each second—on a 133MHz CPU that gives you about 20 million clock cycles between keystrokes. We can sandwich in all the necessary disk I/O with no visible delays.

Index construction, however, is another matter. This is where every reviewer who ever tested a database comes in. Product A is inferior to Product B because the latter loaded and indexed a million-record table in 23 percent less time than the former. How many times have you looked at those comparisons?

Although those tests generally don't help you pick the faster database product (operation speed is what counts), you wouldn't want our B-trees to be embarrassed when someone tries them, would you?

I set a flag, building_full_file, during a reindex operation. When this flag is set, no nonessential disk activity is performed. An index insertion that would normally write the revised node doesn't write the node.

If building_full_file is true, the only node writes are done when it's necessary to replace a node in the tree. At the end of the full-file operation, the header and the nodes in RAM are written to disk. It's a bit artificial, but it's not really a lot of extra programming.

An important saving comes from looking at the address of nodes in the tree, both in operation and in building the indexes. If the node in RAM is the one that's needed, no disk read is done. In practice, this means that your root node is almost RAM resident. (It gets tossed about a bit when it is filled and gets split.) As we've seen, a RAM-resident root eliminates half of all disk reads in typical files.

Before we go on to the code, let's look at the process of finding a key value. You do this to locate a record, and you do this every time you need to insert a record, too. It's the most common of all index operations.

Linear and Binary Searches

Ever since Bayer and McCreight invented the B-tree, the nodes have been searched linearly, simply scanning for the appropriate value or insertion point. Everything I've ever seen on the subject explains that you use a linear search within the node, which is how I've done it, too.

For this project I asked myself if this *truth* was really true. Using realistic page sizes, you get large nodes. If you adopt my plan of not having null, downward pointers at the ground level, you can get a lot of values in a node. Wouldn't a binary search be worth the additional trouble?

To test, I wrote the class you'll see in Listing 19-1. It includes a random-text generator, which makes it easy to fill arrays with String values. I programmed a linear search first and tested it using the linear search to insert 150 values into a sorted String array.

Running under Visual Cafe's debugger, the first 150 values took 220 milliseconds. I added a zero to the array_size value. 1,500 values took 10,650 milliseconds, which is a very big number, indeed.

Generating Random Strings

This called for some careful testing. I began by modifying the routine to do nothing but create the Strings. For my 1,500-key sample, this meant creating 1,500 String values, each 20 bytes long. I generated each character by asking a Random object for a floating-point value (it's between 0 and 1.0) and then multiplying by 26 and adding the result to 'A'. That operation is repeated 20 times to fill a byte array, and then the String constructor is called.

Stripping the program down to just the necessary loops and the random-String-generation code, and being careful not to run under the debugger, I got an average run time of 174 milliseconds. This includes all the overhead of recording the times, looping over 1,500 items, and so on.

The Art of Testing

Testing is an art, not a science. There's simply too much going on to get repeatable results unless you do something really elemental, like running an assembly language routine in DOS.

Each of the numbers I discuss here is the average of five runs. The actual time for just creating the random String values varied from 160 to 280 milliseconds, for example. The variations were so large that one run with no insertions whatsoever was slower than a run that did insertions using a binary search.

Within limits, you can improve the accuracy of a test by running more trials and by running with larger sizes. Still, if your test results show that two approaches are within 10 percent of each other, I'd ignore the tests and look for other decision criteria—such as code maintainability or executable size.

In this testing, the results are so far apart that the variability of the test data is irrelevant, however.

Faking the Locate( ) Method

To isolate the time that the locate( ) method (the linear or binary search) was taking, I needed to find out how much time the other portions of the code were taking. One potential consumer of large amounts of time was all the data shifting. Physically inserting a String reference into an array means moving data to the right to make room for the insertion. If new values arrive at random, that requires shifting half the entries in the array, on average. This needed examination.

Locate( ) Without Insertion

After I found out how much time it took to generate the random strings, I added a call to an imitation locate( ) routine, which reported that each item came at the end of the list. (Item 2 sorted after item 1, item 3 sorted after item 2, and so on.) This let me fill the array, but necessitated no shifting of data in the array. The program just stored String zero at array[0], String 1 at array[1], and so on.

The average time for this improved version was still 196 milliseconds. Storing the String references in the array (not to mention calling and returning from the locate( ) method) was nearly free.

Locate( ) with Insertion

Next I wanted to see what effect shifting the values in the array (due to insertions) had. I changed my false locate( ) method to report that each item gets inserted in the middle of the existing items. String 100 was reported as belonging at array[50], for example. That requires shifting the rightmost 50 items one slot to the right.

There are a lot of shifts. Shifting half the existing values moves nothing when the array is empty, but it moves 749 items when you insert the 1,500th String. The average number of items shifted is 374.5. Multiplied by 1,500 insertions, that comes to 561,750 individual shifts.

Fortunately, System.arraycopy( ) is written so that you can do the shifts in this unlikely way:

```
// move second 50 items right to make space
// for a new item 50:

System.arraycopy( array, 50, array, 51, 50 );
```

That will move item 50 to slot 51, the former item 51 to slot 52, and so on. The method is smart enough to work from the right end back to item 50, so that you get the result you want.

I've noted earlier that System.arraycopy( ) on an Intel machine leads right into the strength of the CISC architecture. The average time with all the shifting increased to just 210 milliseconds. (On the Intel chip, the array shift can be done with a single instruction: REPZ MOVSD.)

A Real, Linear Locate( )

Then I added back my linear search locate( ) function. It actually finds the correct location for each random string. The average time for inserting 1,500 items ballooned to 910 milliseconds. The vast majority of that time is spent doing String comparisons. The number of comparisons is the same as the number of shifts: 561,750. Each String comparison may require several individual comparisons when the left-hand sides of the compared strings have matching characters.

A binary search can, in theory, cut down that count dramatically.

Changing to a Binary Locate( )

How did the binary search do? At first it made scrambled eggs out of my array. I always program the rather simple close-in operation—moving the left or right bound into the center—backwards. When I got it straightened out, I carefully tested the results for valid sort order, and then I ran a full 1,500 items. It took 240 milliseconds!

The binary searches (1,500 of them, on an average of 750 items) cost a total of only 30 milliseconds. The linear searches cost 700 milliseconds to do the same work. Linear searches were over 20 times slower than binary searches.

Benefits and Costs

The benefit of the binary search is most evident when you subtract the nonlocate time from the total. This gives you just the time spent in the locate( ) routine. Here's the summary:

```
Average Times, in Milliseconds

                     Total   No-Search   Net Search
                     Time      Time         Time
Visual Cafe
    Linear Search     910       210          700
    Binary Search     240       210           30

Visual J++
    Linear Search   1,032       276          756
    Binary Search     386       276          110
```

The No-Search Time column shows the times for the locate( ) method that simply inserts each item into the middle of the existing items. This gives the overhead of the necessary shifting, but does no actual searching.

The advantage of the binary search with either compiler is compelling. In the faster Visual Cafe, it's overwhelming.

Whenever I see results like this, I wonder about the hidden costs, however. How much does the binary search add to the executable size? In this case, it's dirt cheap. These are the results:

```
Executable Size, in Bytes

                     Visual   Visual
                      Cafe      J++
    Binary Search     2,639    2,528
    Linear Search     2,441    2,344
```

In this case, the faster code adds exactly 198 bytes to the executable using Visual Cafe or 184 bytes using Visual J++. Either is a small price for the speed advantage.

The other costs are small, too. For example, the binary search routine is not as readable and maintainable as the linear search. But you could just discard it if you wanted a better one. It's not an hour's job to code a new one.

If there's a moral in this story, it's that lots of expert agreement sometimes happens when experts follow each other without double-checking. B repeats what A said. C, finding that A and B agree, repeats the misinformation. Pretty soon it's accepted wisdom.

When you think you see a better way, go for it. Most of the time I find that the experts are right and that my "improvement" was just foolish. But discovering that you're wrong is informative and harmless. Sometimes, however—such as in this case—you'll discover that the experts don't know all there is to know.

The Test Program

TOUR

Are you convinced that the binary search is dirt cheap but incredibly valuable? I am. If you are too, skip right ahead to "Understanding the Btree_node Class" section.

Are you from Missouri? Do you refuse to believe anything until you can see it for yourself? This section includes my test code and instructions that let you use it for your own tests.

The BSearch project on your disk will let you do your own testing. It's crude in that it depends on you to select a locate( ) method by commenting out all but one of several choices. Then you rebuild and run the test.

That sounds like more trouble than it is in practice, however. This is the relevant section of the code:

```
/* no locate, no shift

private static int locate( String s ) {

    return array_filled;
} // */

/* no locate, average shift

private static int locate( String s ) {

    return array_filled / 2 ;
} // */
```

```
/* BSearch locate

private static int locate( String s ) {
. . .
    code omitted: see full listing
. . .

} // */

//* linear locate

private static int locate( String s ) {

    int comp;

    for ( int i = 0 ; i < array_filled ; i++ ) {

        comp = s.compareTo( array[i] );
        if ( comp < 0 )
            return i;
    }

    return array_filled;
} // */
```

I've used my comment trick here. You uncomment a routine by adding a single slash to its preceding comment line. You comment it out by deleting that slash. In the preceding sample, the linear locate code is uncommented.

In the rfill( ) method, you can also experiment with insertion versus no insertion, if you want. You could uncomment the line that increments the array_filled variable and comment out the call to insert( ). This will give you insertion-free timings. This is the rfill( ) method:

```
private static void rfill( int length ) {

    while ( array_filled < array.length ) {

        String new_string = rstring( length );
        // array_filled++;
        insert( new_string );
    }
}
```

Listing 19-1 shows the full test program. If you don't load the chapter's work from disk, you'll need a copy of the MsgBox class to run these tests. Or, you can replace the call to MsgBox with a System.out.println( ) call.

Listing 19-1:
BSearch
compares
linear and
binary
searches

```
// BSearch.java -- Binary Search
// Copyright 1997, Martin L. Rinehart

// this code is completely documented in:
// _Java Database Development_, Martin Rinehart,
// Osborne/McGraw-Hill, 1997

/*
  Use to compare linear and binary search on String arrays
*/

import java.awt.*;
import java.util.Random;
import java.io.*;

class BSearch extends Object {

// -------------------- data members --------------------

// there are no public data members

// protected static data members:

    protected static String[] array;
    protected static int array_size = 1500;
    protected static int array_filled = 0;

    protected static Random random = new Random( 1 );

// there are no other data members

// -------------------- public methods --------------------

    public static void main( String[] args ) {

        array = new String[array_size];
        long start_time = System.currentTimeMillis();

        rfill( 20 );
```

```java
            long end_time = System.currentTimeMillis();

            System.out.println( " It took " +
                ( end_time - start_time ) + " millis." );

            for ( int i = 0 ;
                i < ( array_size < 10 ? array_size : 10 ) ;
                i++ )
                System.out.println( array[i] );

            MsgBox mb = new MsgBox( "Done" );
            mb.show();

            while ( mb.isVisible() ) ;

            System.exit( 0 );
        }

// there are no other public methods

// ------------------ private methods ------------------
// private methods:

    private static void rfill( int length ) {

        while ( array_filled < array.length ) {

            String new_string = rstring( length );
            // array_filled++;
            insert( new_string );
        }
    }

    private static void insert( String s ) {

        int where = locate( s );

        if ( where < array_filled )
            System.arraycopy( array, where,
                array, where+1, array_filled - where );

        array[ where ] = s;
```

```
        array_filled++;
    }

    /* no locate, no shift

    private static int locate( String s ) {

        return array_filled;
    } // */

    /* no locate, average shift

    private static int locate( String s ) {

        return array_filled / 2 ;
    } // */

    /* BSearch locate

    private static int locate( String s ) {

        int left, right, center, comp;

        if ( array_filled == 0 )
            return 0;

        left = 0;
        right = array_filled - 1;

        while ( (right - left) > 1 ) {

            center = ( left + right ) >> 1;
            comp = s.compareTo( array[center] );

            if ( comp == 0 )
                return center + 1;

            if ( comp < 0 )
                right = center;
            else
                left = center;
        }
```

```
        comp = s.compareTo( array[left] );
            if ( comp < 0 )
                return left;
            if ( comp == 0 )
                return right;

        comp = s.compareTo( array[right] );
            if ( comp < 0 )
                return right;
            // comp == 0 or > 0
                return right + 1;

    } // */

    //* linear locate

    private static int locate( String s ) {

        int comp;

        for ( int i = 0 ; i < array_filled ; i++ ) {

            comp = s.compareTo( array[i] );
            if ( comp < 0 )
                return i;
        }

        return array_filled;
    } // */

    private static String rstring( int len ) {

        byte[] b = new byte[len];

        for ( int i = 0 ; i < len ; i++ )
            b[i] = rletter();

        return new String( b, 0 );
    }

    private static byte rletter() {
```

```
          return (byte) ( 'A' +
              (int) ( 26 * random.nextFloat() ));
      }

} // end of BSearch class

// there are no private classes in BSearch.java

// end of BSearch.java
```

Understanding the Btree_node Class

 There is no "Using the Btree_node Class" section, because it's the NDX class (next chapter) that uses these objects. If you're content with the theory you've got and intend to just use these B-trees, treating the NDX class as a black box, skip right forward to the summary.

TOUR

If you're going to dive into "Understanding the NDX Class" in the next chapter, this class is a necessary prerequisite. And it's relatively short and simple.

The Btree_node is the basic building block that the NDX class (see Chapter 20) uses to build its B-trees. We'll run through the data and methods here in the same order they appear in the source.

The Btree_node's Data Members

The first data member is address:

```
    protected int address;
```

This is the disk address (relative to the beginning of the file) of this node's on-disk copy. Next is a self-explanatory boolean:

```
    protected boolean is_upper_node;
```

The keys are all the same length. These variables are the ones that handle the keys:

```
protected int key_length;
protected String[] keys;
```

The next group of data members, with their comments, is self-explanatory:

```
protected int node_length;  // in bytes
protected int node_size;    // max # of keys
protected int number_of_keys;
```

It's unlikely that the necessary data will precisely fill a node. The pad_size is the number of bytes between the last data value and the end of the node. The String, padding, is pad_size long. It's written to push the node to its boundary on disk:

```
protected int pad_size;
protected String padding;
```

The NDX object that uses these nodes is not, technically, a parent of these nodes. It's accorded that respect, regardless:

```
protected NDX parent;
```

This array holds the pointers that are conceptually sandwiched in between the key values:

```
protected int[] pointers;
```

Last but not least, this array holds the actual record numbers that go along with each key's value:

```
protected int[] record_numbers;
```

The Btree_node's Public Methods

In this section we'll look at the constructors first, and then we'll look at the other public methods.

The Btree_node's Constructors

There are two constructors used by this class. The first builds a new B-tree node. The second simply reads an existing node from disk. The latter is called far more often than the former. The former has a lot more work to do. It begins by carefully storing all the data that it is passed:

```
Btree_node( int address, int key_length,
        int node_length, NDX parent, boolean is_upper )
        throws IndexException {

    this.address = address;
    this.key_length = key_length;
    this.node_length = node_length;
    this.parent = parent;
    is_upper_node = is_upper;
```

Then it calls the one private method to perform the service it promises:

```
compute_node_size();
```

Next it creates and blank-fills a byte array, as long as a single key value:

```
byte[] b = new byte[key_length];
for ( int i = 0 ; i < key_length ; i++ )
    b[i] = (byte) ' ';
```

This array is used in the next section. The job here is to fill the keys and record_numbers arrays with initial values:

```
keys = new String[node_size];
record_numbers = new int[node_size];

String blank_key = new String( b, 0 );
for ( int i = 0 ; i < node_size ; i++ ) {

    keys[i] = blank_key;
    record_numbers[i] = -1;
}
```

For nodes above ground level, the same service needs to be provided for the pointers array. Note that this array is one longer than the two we just saw:

```
if ( is_upper_node ) {

    pointers = new int[node_size+1];
    for ( int i = 0 ; i <= node_size ; i++ )
        pointers[i] = -1;
}
```

When the node is on disk, as is usually the case, the job is much simpler. This is the entire second constructor:

```
Btree_node( int address, NDX parent )
    throws IndexException {

    read_node( address );
    this.parent = parent;
}
```

The Btree_node's Other Public Methods

The other interesting public methods are add_key( ) and find( ). Vital, but certainly less interesting, are the read_node( ) and write_node( ) methods that actually do the disk I/O. We'll begin with adding a key.

THE ADD_KEY( ) METHOD   Adding a key is done by add_key( ). It begins with a comment that the rest of the code has to respect:

```
public void add_key( String key, int recno,
        int rptr, int where ) {

    // calling code must call find() and check for
    // available space
```

Remember that when the node is full, inserting a new key is a matter of splitting the node into two nodes and pushing up the median value to a higher level. This multinode process is handled by the NDX object. These methods provide the services that an individual node can perform on its own.

That said, the process is straightforward. If the new entry is not being added at the end, it moves the existing keys and record numbers over one slot, beginning at the site of the insertion:

```
if ( where < number_of_keys ) {

    System.arraycopy( keys, where, keys, where+1,
        number_of_keys - where );
    System.arraycopy( record_numbers, where,
        record_numbers, where+1,
        number_of_keys - where );
}
```

The same service is provided for the pointers in nonground nodes. This code has to remember that the pointers array is one longer than the other arrays:

```
if ( is_upper_node ) {

    if ( where < number_of_keys )
        System.arraycopy( pointers, where+1,
            pointers, where+2,
            number_of_keys - where );

    pointers[where+1] = rptr;
}
```

Finally, add_key( ) inserts the new data and increments its count of keys:

```
    keys[where] = key;
    record_numbers[where] = recno;
    number_of_keys++;
}
```

THE FIND( ) METHOD   This method performs a binary search to locate a target key value in the keys array. It begins with declarations and presetting the parent's boolean, found, to false:

```
public int find( String s ) {

    int left, right, center, comp;

    parent.found = false;
```

A quick exit is taken if the array is empty:

```
if ( number_of_keys == 0 )
    return 0;
```

For a nonempty array, we begin by setting pointers to the left and right (lower and higher) ends of the array:

```
left = 0;
right = number_of_keys - 1;
```

Remember our search for "binary" in the dictionary? We moved "start" and "end" papers and then looked in the center between these papers. This heart of the find( ) method does exactly that.

The binary search is done in this loop that closes the left and right pointers in toward each other until they touch:

```
while ( (right - left) > 1 ) {

    center = ( left + right ) >> 1;
    comp = s.compareTo( keys[center] );

    if ( comp == 0 ){

        parent.found = true;
        return center + 1;
    }

    if ( comp < 0 )
        right = center;
    else
        left = center;

}
```

When the pointers touch, you can't continue dividing by two. Adding left and right and dividing by two will just produce the left value again when right equals left plus one. So we have to decide about the two remaining possible values.

The target is compared with the left value first:

```
comp = s.compareTo( keys[left] );
```

If the comparison is negative, the target comes before the left value:

```
if ( comp < 0 )
    return left;
```

If the comparison returns zero, we've found the target:

```
if ( comp == 0 ) {

    parent.found = true;
    return right;

}
```

If the comparison was positive, we've got a target greater than the left value. In this case, we do essentially the same thing, this time with the right value:

```
comp = s.compareTo( keys[right] );
    if ( comp < 0 )
        return right;

    // comp == 0 or > 0
        parent.found = ( comp == 0 );
        return right + 1;
}
```

THE FILE I/O PUBLIC METHODS   These methods are called by the NDX object to actually read and write nodes. The first read_node( ) accepts an address. It sets this as the node's address and then calls the full read_node( ) method:

```
public void read_node( int addr )
    throws IndexException {
```

```
        address = addr;
        read_node();
    }
```

The full read node seeks for this address and then starts reading. The code begins this way:

```
public void read_node() throws IndexException {

    try {

        parent.raf.seek( address );
        key_length = parent.raf.readInt();
        node_length = parent.raf.readInt();
```

There are lots more items to be read. I'll not bore you with them here, but there are two more points to make. First, the NDX file (its full listing is in Chapter 20) ends with comments that show the layout of the whole file, including these nodes, on disk.

Second, the boolean is_upper_node is read and written as an integer (0 for false, 1 for true). This is a convenience for programmers who look at the binary dump of these files. (Otherwise, Java would write the boolean as a single byte, making the node a nuisance to decipher.)

The Btree_node's Private Method

There is only one private method. As its name promises, it computes the size of the node. (Recall that I define size as the number of keys the node holds, which is one less than its order, the number of pointers it holds.)

The job here is to divide the available space into spaces for the key values, the keys' associated record numbers, and if it's not a ground-level node, the pointers array. Overhead has to be taken into consideration.

The calculation is not terribly complex, but any error here trashes the whole B-tree system. I relied on extensive comments, which you can read here in lieu of my writing an explanation of each line. I will comment, however, on that little "&=" trick after you've looked at the code.

```
private void compute_node_size() {

    int extra = is_upper_node ? 8 : 4;

    // total array space:
        node_size = ( node_length - OVERHEAD );

    // one less space for final upper pointer:
        node_size -= is_upper_node ? 4 : 0;

    // max # of keys (add 'extra' for record #s
    // and upper node pointers):
        node_size /= ( key_length + extra );

    // make it a multiple of two:
        node_size &= 0xFFFFFFFE;

    pad_size = node_length - OVERHEAD -
        node_size * ( key_length + extra );

    // remember the extra pointer
        pad_size -= is_upper_node ? 4 : 0;

    padding = new String( new byte[pad_size], 0 );
}
```

This line rounds the positive integer down to the next lower multiple of two:

```
    // make it a multiple of two:
        node_size &= 0xFFFFFFFE;
```

You experienced bit fiddlers recognize that hex value as all ones except for the last bit, which is zero. The "and" operation simply assures that the least-significant bit is reset (zero). I like simple, direct solutions. I dislike tricky, obscure code.

This is simple, direct, tricky, and obscure code. I let it pass here because other solutions take a lot more code. I wouldn't accept this without the comment that explains precisely what it does. (Pop quiz: does that line round negative numbers toward or away from zero? If you answered immediately, you need to get out more.)

Btree_node.java's Full Listing

Listing 19-2 shows the full Btree_node.java file.

Listing 19-2:
Btree_node
.java

```
// Btree_node.java -- ground and upper B-tree nodes
// Copyright 1997, Martin L. Rinehart

// this code is completely documented in:
// _Java Database Development_, Martin Rinehart,
// Osborne/McGraw-Hill, 1997

import java.io.*;

class Btree_node extends Object {

// -------------------- data members --------------------

// there are no public data members

// protected data members:

    protected int address;

    protected boolean is_upper_node;

    protected int key_length;
    protected String[] keys;

    protected int node_length;  // in bytes
    protected int node_size;    // max # of keys
    protected int number_of_keys;

    protected int pad_size;
    protected String padding;
    protected NDX parent;
    protected int[] pointers;

    protected int[] record_numbers;
```

```java
// static data member:

    final static int OVERHEAD = 32;

// ------------------- public methods -------------------

// constructors:

    Btree_node( int address, int key_length,
            int node_length, NDX parent, boolean is_upper )
            throws IndexException {

        this.address = address;
        this.key_length = key_length;
        this.node_length = node_length;
        this.parent = parent;
        is_upper_node = is_upper;

        compute_node_size();

        byte[] b = new byte[key_length];
        for ( int i = 0 ; i < key_length ; i++ )
            b[i] = (byte) ' ';

        keys = new String[node_size];
        record_numbers = new int[node_size];

        String blank_key = new String( b, 0 );
        for ( int i = 0 ; i < node_size ; i++ ) {

            keys[i] = blank_key;
            record_numbers[i] = -1;
        }

        if ( is_upper_node ) {

            pointers = new int[node_size+1];
            for ( int i = 0 ; i <= node_size ; i++ )
                pointers[i] = -1;
        }
    }
```

```
    Btree_node( int address, NDX parent )
        throws IndexException {

        read_node( address );
        this.parent = parent;
    }

// there are no data access methods

// public, class-specific methods:

    public void add_key( String key, int recno,
            int rptr, int where ) {

        // calling code must call find() and check for
        // available space

        if ( where < number_of_keys ) {

            System.arraycopy( keys, where, keys, where+1,
                number_of_keys - where );
            System.arraycopy( record_numbers, where,
                record_numbers, where+1,
                number_of_keys - where );
        }
        if ( is_upper_node ) {

            if ( where < number_of_keys )
                System.arraycopy( pointers, where+1,
                    pointers, where+2,
                    number_of_keys - where );

            pointers[where+1] = rptr;
        }

        keys[where] = key;
        record_numbers[where] = recno;
        number_of_keys++;
    }

    public int find( String s ) {
```

```
int left, right, center, comp;

parent.found = false;

if ( number_of_keys == 0 )
    return 0;

left = 0;
right = number_of_keys - 1;

while ( (right - left) > 1 ) {

    center = ( left + right ) >> 1;
    comp = s.compareTo( keys[center] );

    if ( comp == 0 ){

        parent.found = true;
        return center + 1;
    }

    if ( comp < 0 )
        right = center;
    else
        left = center;
}

comp = s.compareTo( keys[left] );
    if ( comp < 0 )
        return left;
    if ( comp == 0 ) {

        parent.found = true;
        return right;
    }

comp = s.compareTo( keys[right] );
    if ( comp < 0 )
        return right;

    // comp == 0 or > 0
        parent.found = ( comp == 0 );
```

```
                    return right + 1;
        }

    public void read_node( int addr )
        throws IndexException {

        address = addr;
        read_node();
    }

    public void read_node() throws IndexException {

        try {

            parent.raf.seek( address );
            key_length = parent.raf.readInt();
            node_length = parent.raf.readInt();
            node_size = parent.raf.readInt();
            number_of_keys = parent.raf.readInt();
            is_upper_node = parent.raf.readInt() == 1;
            parent.raf.readInt();
            parent.raf.readInt();
            parent.raf.readInt();

            keys = new String[node_size];
            record_numbers = new int[node_size];
            pointers = new int[node_size+1];

            int i;
            byte[] b = new byte[key_length];
            for ( i = 0 ; i < node_size ; i++ ) {

                parent.raf.read( b );
                keys[i] = new String( b, 0 );
            }

            for ( i = 0 ; i < node_size ; i++ )
                record_numbers[i] = parent.raf.readInt();

            if ( is_upper_node )
                for ( i = 0 ; i <= node_size ; i++ )
                    pointers[i] = parent.raf.readInt();
```

```
        }
    catch ( IOException ioe ) {

        throw new IndexException( ioe.getMessage() +
            " (while reading index node)" );
    }
}

public void write_node() throws IndexException {

    if ( address == -1 )
        address = parent.file_length;

    try {

        parent.raf.seek( address );
        parent.raf.writeInt( key_length );
        parent.raf.writeInt( node_length );
        parent.raf.writeInt( node_size );
        parent.raf.writeInt( number_of_keys );
        parent.raf.writeInt(
            is_upper_node ? 1 : 0 );
        parent.raf.writeInt( 0 );
        parent.raf.writeInt( 0 );
        parent.raf.writeInt( 0 );

        int i;
        for ( i = 0 ; i < node_size ; i++ )
            parent.raf.writeBytes( keys[i] );

        for ( i = 0 ; i < node_size ; i++ )
            parent.raf.writeInt( record_numbers[i] );

        if ( is_upper_node )
            for ( i = 0 ; i <= node_size ; i++ )
                parent.raf.writeInt( pointers[i] );

        parent.raf.writeBytes( padding );
    }
    catch ( IOException ioe ) {

        throw new IndexException( ioe.getMessage() +
```

```
                        " (while writing index node)" );
            }
      }

// public, non-event overriding method:

    public String paramString() {

        return "Btree_node";
    }

// there are no public, event-handling methods

// ------------------ private methods ------------------
// private method:

    private void compute_node_size() {

        int extra = is_upper_node ? 8 : 4;

        // total array space:
            node_size = ( node_length - OVERHEAD );

        // one less space for final upper pointer:
            node_size -= is_upper_node ? 4 : 0;

        // max # of keys (add 'extra' for record #s
        // and upper node pointers):
            node_size /= ( key_length + extra );

        // make it a multiple of two:
            node_size &= 0xFFFFFFFE;

        pad_size = node_length - OVERHEAD -
            node_size * ( key_length + extra );

        // remember the extra pointer
            pad_size -= is_upper_node ? 4 : 0;

        padding = new String( new byte[pad_size], 0 );
    }
```

```
} // end of Btree_node class

// there are no private classes in Btree_node.java

/*
    See notes at end of NDX.java
*/

// end of Btree_node.java
```

Summary

We began by looking at some of the items we'll typically index. These included names of objects such as people and products. Importantly, most indexes will be on primary and foreign keys. These indexes will be for values four to ten bytes long. Other small values, such as two-byte country codes, will get indexed, too. An eight-byte index value will be typical.

The length of the key value is important in determining the actual node size and B-tree height. Considering the actual overhead that goes with the key value (pointers and record numbers), we calculated some typical index heights. With an eight-byte key value, you can index a million-record file with just a two-level index. Making the first (root) node RAM resident, you will typically need just a single disk read to look up any key.

Our nodes will not actually be built as sandwiches of pointers and values, as we conceptualized them. We'll put pointers and values, along with record numbers, into separate arrays. For the ground-level nodes (the vast majority of all nodes) we won't bother with pointers, since they're all null. The savings are material.

We'll keep the node tree as a simple array. The root will be nodes[0]. We won't need backward pointers in the nodes since nodes[n–1] is the parent of nodes[n].

In normal operation, we'll write all nodes as they get new values. For full-file operations, such as reindexing, we'll only write nodes to disk when they will be overwritten in the nodes array. At the end of full-file operations, we'll write RAM-based nodes and the file header page to disk.

For this project, I checked the conventional wisdom that says you should use a simple linear search to locate items within a node. I compared this with a binary search. In testing I found that the binary search was eight to 20 times faster than the linear one. It added less than 200 bytes to the executable.

Finally, we took a detailed look at the Btree_node class. It handles operations, such as adding a key and doing the binary search, that can be done within a single node.

Multinode operations, such as splitting a node and promoting the median value, are the job of the NDX class, which encapsulates our B-trees. That is the subject of Chapter 20.

Chapter 20

The Indexable Interface and NDX Class

W e started with the theory of B-trees in Chapter 18. In the last chapter we switched from theory to implementation concerns and actually looked at the code for the node objects. In this chapter we're going to look at the B-tree, which I've wrapped in the NDX class.

The extension .NDX was the one that Wayne Ratliff used for the original dBASE index files. I'm recycling it here, using it for the name of the NDX objects that encapsulate files and logic for our indexes.

If you really love diving into database internals, you'll be really happy here. If you just want to use the NDX as a black box, you'll also be happy here. (You black boxers can skip most of this chapter!)

We'll begin with a look at the mainline class I've created to test NDX objects. It builds the index and then launches the index file (a BinFile) in a scroll window so you can look at the internals. It's dead simple.

Then we'll look at the Indexable interface that you need to implement to use an NDX. If you like simple interfaces that aren't any trouble to implement, you'll be happy.

Before getting to the NDX, I'll show you the fakeNDX that I used to test the NDX object. If you want to do your own testing, you'll find this very flexible.

The NDX discussion will begin with a rather short section on "Using the NDX Class." If you don't care about the database internals, you'll be able to stop after this section and begin using your own NDX objects. If you like internals, or are just curious, we'll continue with a discussion of "Understanding the NDX Class." It's not trivial.

Finally, I'll note some minor changes to the BinFile as it's used in this project's chapters. Now let's take a look at the NDX-using mainline.

A Mainline NDX User

You've seen it before. Once all the hard work is done, using the functionality becomes a piece of cake. Given an Indexable foo (we'll get to that interface in the next section), these lines create a B-tree and then pop the B-tree file into a ScrollWin:

```
NDX bar = new NDX( filename, access, foo, 0 );

ScrollWin sw = new ScrollWin( bar, filename );
sw.setEndApp( true );
sw.resize( 520, 400 );
sw.show();
```

The NDX constructor opens an existing index file, or if the index file doesn't exist (or if it doesn't appear current), it will create the B-tree index from scratch. In other words, it's just about no work to use the NDX class. Listing 20-1 shows the full source file, with the all the ALD in place:

Listing 20-1:
A mainline
for testing
the NDX

```
// NDXtest.java -- file index test routine
// Copyright 1997, Martin L. Rinehart

class NDXtest {

    public static void main( String[] args ) {

        String filename = "test.ND0";
        String access = "rw";

        fakeNDX foo = new fakeNDX();
        try {

            NDX bar = new NDX( filename, access, foo, 0 );


            ScrollWin sw = new ScrollWin( bar, filename );
            sw.setEndApp( true );
            sw.resize( 520, 400 );
            sw.show();
        }
        catch ( IndexException ie ) {

            MsgBox mb = new MsgBox( ie.getMessage() );
            mb.show();

            while ( mb.isVisible() );
        }
    }
}

// end of NDXtest.java
```

Your NDX is now ready to insert and delete keys. In Chapter 21 we'll begin to use it, scrolling a file in index (not physical) order. The rest of this chapter explains the magic.

Indexable

TOUR

To effectively use these B-tree indexes, you'll need to create Indexable objects. This section is a necessity, but it won't take long.

To be Indexable, an object has to tell you how many elements it has, how many indexes it supports, and for each element and index, it has to report a key value. Let's take these in order.

Your old friend getLast( ) is part of the Indexable interface. If you want a DBF, for example, to be Indexable, you're a third done with no work. This function is already implemented:

```
public int getLast(); // last record or object number
```

If the DBF (or object file, or whatever) is for an object class such as customers, chances are you'll need indexes on name, primary key, and possibly on other items. This function needs to be implemented. A single return statement will probably do the trick:

```
public int getNumberOfIndexes();
```

Finally, there's a bit of actual work to be done to build this routine:

```
public String getKeyValue( int record_num, int index_num );
```

In our DBF example, you would go( ) to record_num. Then a switch might return a name for index_num zero, a String version of the primary key for index_num one, and so on. These Strings need to be fixed length (don't forget to blank-pad the numbers), but otherwise there's not much to do to create an Indexable DBF or other class.

Listing 20-2 shows the full Indexable.java source file:

Listing 20-2:
The simple
indexable
interface

```
// Indexable.java -- the Indexable interface
// Copyright 1997, Martin L. Rinehart

// this code is completely documented in:
// _Java Database Development_, Martin Rinehart,
// Osborne/McGraw-Hill, 1997

interface Indexable {

    public int getLast(); // last record or object number

    public int getNumberOfIndexes();

    public String getKeyValue( int record_num, int index_num );
}

// end of Indexable.java
```

The fakeNDX Class

If you'll be using the NDX as a pure black box, you can skip this class. If you'll want to run your own tests before you put it into service, this class will come in very handy.

I've made extensive use of a fakeNDX object to test the NDX class. I knew that testing by creating different files with lots of different values wouldn't be as useful as testing specific results. For this I wanted a data generator that was easy to control. The fakeNDX returns values from a testdata array that begins this way:

```
final static String[] testdata = {
    "Allen ", //  0
    "Ann   ",
    "Barney",
    "Bill  ",
    "Bob   ",
    "Bobbie", //  5
    "Charly",
    "Chip  ",
```

By using a node size that allowed eight key values per node at the ground level, I would run this data to test insertion at the end of the node. Then I would move "Allen " into the middle, to test insertion at the front. Putting "Chip " in the middle let me test insertion at the end.

I also added the random-name generator from the BSearch class. Calling rstring(6) gets a six-byte String of random characters. You'll see that fakeNDX begins returning random strings when your getLast( ) value exceeds the size of the testdata array.

This is the implementation of the full Indexable interface:

```
public int getLast() { return 20; }

public int getNumberOfIndexes() { return 1; }

public String getKeyValue( int record_num,
        int index_num ) {

    if ( record_num < testdata.length )
        return testdata[record_num];
    else
        return rstring( 6 );
}
```

The getKeyValue( ) method here is artificially simplified by its ignoring the index number parameter. A real getKeyValue( ) will probably include a switch on index_num.

Listing 20-3 shows the full fakeNDX.java source file.

Listing 20-3:
An expandable
data source

```
// fakeNDX.java -- fake indexable file
// Copyright 1997, Martin L. Rinehart

import java.util.Random;

class fakeNDX implements Indexable {

final static String[] testdata = {
    "Allen ", //  0
    "Ann   ",
    "Barney",
    "Bill  ",
    "Bob   ",
    "Bobbie", //  5
    "Charly",
```

```
"Chip   ",
"Chuck ",
"Dave   ",
"Dexter", // 10
"Donny ",
"Doris ",
"Evan   ",
"Fanny ",
"Felix ", // 15
"Fran   ",
"Frank ",
"Grace ",
"Harry ",
"Iris   ", // 20
"Jane   ",
"Jean   ",
"Joan   ",
"Judy   ",
"Karen ", // 25
"Larry ",
"Lou    ",
"Louis ",
"Louise",
"Martin", // 30
"Mary   ",
"Melvin",
"Mike   ",
"Nancy ",
"Oscar ",
"Paul   ",
"Peter ",
"Quincy",
"Ralph ",
"Roger ",
"Sam    ",
"Sandra",
"Sue    ",
"SueAnn",
"Suzy   ",
"Tammy ",
"Tim    ",
"Tom    ",
```

```
        "Ursula",
        "Violet",
        "Wendy ",
        "Xavier",
        "Yvonne",
        "Zelda "
};

static Random random = new Random( 1 );

    public int getLast() { return 20; }

    public int getNumberOfIndexes() { return 1; }

    public String getKeyValue( int record_num,
            int index_num ) {

        if ( record_num < testdata.length )
            return testdata[record_num];
        else
            return rstring( 6 );
    }

    private String rstring( int len ) {

        byte[] b = new byte[len];

        for ( int i = 0 ; i < len ; i++ )
            b[i] = rletter();

        return new String( b, 0 );
    }

    private byte rletter() {

        return (byte) ( 'A' +
            (int) ( 26 * random.nextFloat() ));
    }
}

// end of fakeNDX.java
```

Note that I've supplied my Random object with a specific seed. This means that it will always generate the same list of names. If you want more random results, remove the parameter in the Random constructor.

The NDX Class

TOUR

If you're willing to let the NDX be a black box, just read the "Using" section. The "Understanding" section is for those of you who want to know everything.

Here we'll have a short discussion on "Using the NDX Class." It's simple. Then we'll dive into "Understanding the NDX Class." That, as you probably guessed, is not so simple.

Using the NDX Class

To use the NDX class, you start with an Indexable object. If you were creating a customer list, for example, you could extend the DBF class with these methods:

```
public int getNumberOfIndexes()  {

    return 3;
}

public String getKeyValue( int record_num,
    int index_num ) {

    go( record_num );

    switch ( index_num ) {
        case 0:
            return . . . // fixed-length name
            break;
        case 1:
            return . . . // whatever
        case . . .
    }
}
```

Note that there's no getLast( ) here. If you start with a DBF, it's already got a getLast( ). Also, you'll need to declare that your class implements Indexable. If you forget, your compiler will remind you, of course.

With the Indexable ready you're ready for the NDX. You turn over a reference to the Indexable and a name for the B-tree's disk file for each index. To continue our example, that would look like this:

```
// my_dbf is a DBF extended to be Indexable

    NDX ndx0 = new NDX( "my_dbf.ND0", "rw", my_dbf, 0 );
    NDX ndx1 = new NDX( "my_dbf.ND1", "rw", my_dbf, 1 );
    . . .
```

The first time these constructors are called, the index files will be created. Subsequently they'll be opened for reuse.

Now you're ready to use the indexes. If ndx0 is on last names, for example, this will find the first "Smith":

```
    int found_rec = ndx0.find( "Smith" );
```

In practice, you'll be looking for some value the user has entered; not a hard-coded search key. If you do hard-code a key, be sure that its length matches the index key values' length. Values you retrieve from a table are fixed-length to begin with, so this normally isn't a problem.

The other relevant public functions of the NDX are

- delete(int recno)
- insert(String key, int recno)
- reindex( )

Your data editor should call delete( ) when you delete a record and insert( ) when you add a record. When an existing record is modified, you should delete( ) the original value and insert( ) the new value.

The reindex( ) rebuilds the entire index. This isn't normally necessary. You'll find it helpful in batch-processing routines that rebuild everything overnight or on the weekend. Internally, the NDX uses reindex( ) when it creates a new file or when it finds that its existing file has a different number of keys than the Indexable has records.

In Chapter 21 we'll add additional public functions to support index-based scrolling. The ones here support a minimal B-tree.

That's the interface. Beneath the surface you can picture the filing and searching as done by magic. Or perhaps by an army of very, very fast clerks. Or, just possibly, by the Java code we'll look at next.

Understanding the NDX Class

Again, we'll look at the data members first, then the public and private methods.

The NDX Class' Data Members

As we noted in Chapter 19, when we're reindexing the whole file, we'll suppress noncritical disk writes. This flag is the one we'll look at before disk writes:

```
protected boolean building_full_file;
```

The next three values are filled in by every search. The integer, find_key, is the location in the node of either the key that matches, if there is a match, or the first key greater than the value sought, if there's no match. The find_level is the location of the node containing the match in the nodes array. The boolean, found, is set true when we find an exact match. These data members are declared here:

```
protected int find_key;
protected int find_level;
protected boolean found;
```

If the full index is contained in the root node, ground_level is zero. A typical index has the root at level zero and ground_level will be one. Ground level seldom exceeds two, even in very large files. This is its declaration:

```
protected int ground_level;
```

The next variable is a convenience that remembers the number of keys in half a node:

```
protected int half_size;
```

These variables remember the information passed when the constructor is called:

```
protected int index_num;
protected Indexable indexable;
```

Knowing the length of the fixed-length keys is vital:

```
    protected int key_length;
```

The next group includes the nodes array that holds the working part of the tree, and key data that's updated continuously:

```
    protected Btree_node[] nodes; // 0 is root
    protected int number_of_keys;
    protected int number_of_pages;
```

The page_size is needed, for example, whenever a new node is created:

```
    protected int page_size;
```

This member's name explains its job:

```
    protected int root_node_address;
```

An insertion operation requires a find operation, then an add operation. The find starts at level zero and works down to ground level. The add operation starts at ground level and works its way back up, until it encounters a node that doesn't need to be split to accommodate the new key. This member keeps track of our location in the tree during both procedures:

```
    protected int working_level;
```

Lastly, there are two final static members. The first sets the maximum depth of the tree to something you'll never encounter unless you're testing with very small page sizes. The second has two values, appropriately noted, for testing and for use in regular operation.

```
// final static data member:

    final static int MAX_LEVELS = 10;

    final static int PAGE_SIZE = 128; // testing
    // final static int PAGE_SIZE = 16 * 1024; // running
```

I've left the testing value active, since the project files for this chapter are geared toward NDX testing. Be sure to switch to the real value before you go into operation, or you'll have a very slow B-tree system.

The NDX Class' Public Methods

The first public method is the sole constructor. It starts by calling the BinFile's constructor (NDX extends BinFile), and giving up immediately if there was any trouble:

```
NDX( String path_name, String access,
     Indexable i, int index_num )
     throws IndexException {

     super( path_name, access );

     if ( access.equals("rw") ) {

         if ( !writeable ) return;
     }
     else // access == "r"
         if ( !readable ) return;
```

Next it stores the parameter values and takes care of some bookkeeping:

```
indexable = i;
this.index_num = index_num;

number_of_keys = 0;
page_size = PAGE_SIZE;
file_length = page_size;
number_of_pages = 1;
```

The bookkeeping values will be overwritten when it reads the header, if there is an existing file. The initial values here only survive for a new file.

Next it gets a sample key to find the length of its keys:

```
String key = indexable.getKeyValue( 0, index_num );
key_length = key.length();
```

It's definitely depending on the Indexable to provide fixed-length keys. There's no checking here.

The class starts with an uninitialized state for ground_level, and it creates a tiny array to hold the tree of nodes:

```
ground_level = -1;
nodes = new Btree_node[MAX_LEVELS];
```

The Indexable has a getLast( ) method, but so does the underlying BinFile. That's the one that's called here. It returns minus one for a new file. If the file is new, we write our header and reindex( ) to build a new B-tree:

```
if ( getLast() < 0 ) {

    write_header();
    file_length = page_size;

    reindex();
}
```

For an existing file, the constructor calls read_header( ), which, as the comment notes, also reads the root node. It checks that the number of keys in the index matches the current size of the Indexable. If this check fails, it also reindexes, rebuilding the entire B-tree. This is the end of the constructor:

```
else {

    read_header(); // also reads root node

    if ( number_of_keys != (indexable.getLast()+1) )
        reindex();
}
}
```

In Chapter 21 we'll take a closer look at the delete( ) process. When you come to the five private split( ) methods, bear in mind that a full delete( ) will require an equally extensive combine( ) process. There are a number of simpler alternatives, of which this is the smallest:

```
public void delete( int recno )
    throws IndexException {

    reindex();
}
```

The public find( ) method relies on private_find( ) to do the real work. Its job is to return the record number corresponding to the key value. This returns negative one if it doesn't find the value you specify:

```
public int find( String key )
    throws IndexException {

    private_find( key, true );

    if ( found )
        return nodes[find_level].
            record_numbers[find_key];
    else
        return -1;
}
```

The public portion of insert( ) does even less than find( ). It adds a third parameter—we'll work with it when we get to the privates—to a call to the private find( ):

```
public void insert( String key, int recno )
    throws IndexException {

    insert( key, recno, -1 );
}
```

Reindexing is conceptually simple. You start with an empty index and then get and insert every key value and associated record number, one at a time. Like the other publics, this leaves the real work for the private routines:

```
public void reindex() throws IndexException {

    building_full_file = true;
    ground_level = 0;

    int last = indexable.getLast();

    for ( int i = 0 ; i <= last; i++ ) {

        String key =
            indexable.getKeyValue( i, index_num );
        insert( key, i, -1 );
    }

    write_nodes();
    building_full_file = false;
}
```

Note that reindex( ) sets the boolean building_full_file true before it begins and turns it false again when it's done its job.

The NDX Class' Private Methods

There's some hard work lurking here. But our first methods will be simple ones. By the time you get to splitting nodes, you'll be nicely warmed up. We'll start with one of the simplest.

THE ADD_NODE( ) METHOD   The interesting thing about the add_node( ) method is that it doesn't really add a node. It returns the location at which the next node should be written. An original add_node( ) actually wrote an empty node. I found out that this was a waste, since this one's called when an existing node is being split, for example. The new node will get written when the key(s) has been added, so there's no sense in doing a disk write at this point.

As this code shows, if we're not building the full file, adding a node updates the header data, so it calls for rewriting the header:

```
private int add_node() {

    int where = file_length;
    file_length += page_size;
    number_of_pages++;
```

```
        if ( ! building_full_file )
            write_header();

        return where;
    }
```

THE INSERT( ) METHOD   The insert( ) method has two very different jobs. Rarely, it will be called to add the very first node in the file. Commonly, it will be called to insert into an existing B-tree. The overall structure looks like this:

```
    private void insert( String key, int recno, int rptr )
        throws IndexException {

        if ( number_of_keys == 0 ) {

            . . . add the first node

        }
        else {

            . . . do a real insert

        }
    }
```

Now let's look at the two processes, beginning with adding the first node. This starts by adding a node and recording the address:

```
        int where = add_node();
        root_node_address = where;
```

Then it inserts a new node object into the nodes array and records the starting ground_level value:

```
        nodes[0] = new Btree_node(
            where, key_length,
            page_size, this, false );

        ground_level = 0;
```

Finally, it adds the key, writes the node, and records the initial number of keys:

```
nodes[0].add_key( key, recno, -1, 0 );
nodes[0].write_node();

number_of_keys = 1;
```

That was fairly simple, wasn't it? The job is even simpler when we don't need to create the initial tree. (At least it's simpler in this routine, which delegates all the heavy lifting to supporting methods.) We start by finding the key:

```
private_find( key, false );
```

The second parameter in the private_find( ) call tells the search not to stop when it finds the key value. If there were ten "Smith"s in the file, for example, this search would continue until it's just past the last one. That lets us insert the new "Smith" at the end of the list, which is important in many database operations. (Index by country, then index by last name. Your "Smith"s will be neatly grouped by country if the indexing preserves the initial order for matching values.)

The search also stops at ground level, which is where you always begin the insertion. This code initializes working_level and creates a convenient reference to the ground-level node:

```
working_level = ground_level;
Btree_node node = nodes[working_level];
```

Then you add the key, if the node isn't full, or you split the node if it's full. (Splitting a node is a nontrivial process. In fact, it's just plain complicated. But not here.) This is the code:

```
if ( node.number_of_keys < node.node_size )
    node.add_key( key, recno, rptr, find_key );
else
    split_a_node( key, recno, rptr );
```

Then we complete the job by updating the count and, perhaps, rewriting the data in RAM:

```
            number_of_keys++;

            if ( ! building_full_file )
                write_nodes();
```

THE PRIVATE_FIND( ) METHOD   The private_find( ) is the hardest-working routine in the whole class. Its job is made a lot easier by the fact that it's the node itself that does the binary search within the node. (See Chapter 19.)

The basic job is some setup and then a loop that works down to the ground level. (It will bail out of the loop when that's permitted.) This is the overall structure:

```
private void private_find( String key,
    boolean stop_when_found ) throws IndexException {

    found = false;
    working_level = 0;
    Btree_node node = nodes[0];

    while ( working_level < ground_level ) {

        . . . heavy lifting happens here

    }

    // reached ground level
    find_level = ground_level;
    find_key = node.find( key );
}
```

The boolean stop_when_found is set true by the public find( ). That wants to actually find the first "Smith", for example. It's set false when we're looking for a place to insert the next "Smith".

Now let's look at what happens inside the loop. We start by calling the find( ) method of the node. That's the one that does the binary search. It will stop at a match, or at the first key value past the one we're seeking:

```
        find_key = nodes[working_level].find( key );
```

Next there's this messy bit of code that does a bailout when it's found an exact match, but only if it's allowed to do so. There's a possible match if the find_key value is less than the number of keys. (When it equals the number of keys, it's pointing just past the last one.) If that hurdle is passed, we check stop_when_found to see if bailout is allowed. If it's allowed, we check to see if the key value equals the value we're seeking. If that final hurdle is passed, we're done and can return. This is the code:

```
if ( find_key < node.number_of_keys )
    if ( stop_when_found &&
        node.keys[find_key].equals(key) ) {

        find_level = working_level;
        found = true;
        return;
    }
```

Of course, with all those hurdles, we'll seldom stop there. When stop_when_found is false, we're seeking the right ground_level node. This code use the pointer in the current level to drop down to the next node:

```
int next_address = node.pointers[find_key];

working_level++;
Btree_node next = nodes[working_level];
```

Don't confuse that node in RAM with the ones on disk. Now that we know which node we want, the next job is to see if it's the next entry in the nodes array. If it's not in the array, we write the node that's in the array and read the new one:

```
if ( next.address != next_address ) {

    next.write_node();
    next.read_node( next_address );
}
```

Finally, we set up our node reference:

```
node = next;
```

If you got all that, let's go on. If you didn't, you can go back to the top of the loop and process the next node. Don't do that more than once or twice though. Realistically, ground_level will probably never pass two.

THE READ_HEADER( ) METHOD   The read_header is a lot of ALD, such as this:

```
number_of_keys = raf.readInt();
file_length = raf.readInt();
number_of_pages = raf.readInt();
```

Refer to the full listing for the ALD in the code. The comment at the end of the full listing details the file structure, including the header structure.

THE SPLIT_A_NODE( ) METHOD   There are five methods, beginning with split_a_node( ), that handle the process of splitting nodes and pushing up values. They are

- split_a_node( )
- split_insert_left( )
- split_insert_middle( )
- split_insert_right( )
- split_push_up( )

The split_a_node( ) routine creates the sibling node. Then it calls one of the split_insert( ) methods to do the shifting of values, record numbers, and pointers. The split_insert( ) methods call the push_up( ) method with the median values that get passed to the next level. Finally (I bet you knew this was coming), the split_push_up( ) method will again call split_a_node( ) if the next level up has a full node.

TOUR

Our job here is to carefully shift half the data into the new sibling node and then push up the median values. If you pay close attention to split_a_node( ) and split_insert_left( ), you'll be able to skim over split_insert_middle( ) and split_insert_right( ).

You will, that is, unless you find a bug. This code is all perfect, isn't it? (If you're sure that it's perfect, let me talk to you about buying this beautiful old iron bridge I own in New York City.)

The split_a_node( ) routine is the simple one of these five. It begins by creating a handy reference to the current node, and then creating an empty sibling node, appropriately initialized with the next disk address. We've already seen the routines that do all this work:

```
private void split_a_node( String key, int recno,
    int rptr ) throws IndexException {

Btree_node node = nodes[working_level];

int where = add_node();

Btree_node sibling = new Btree_node(
    where, node.key_length, node.node_length,
    node.parent, node.is_upper_node );
```

Next it calls the appropriate split_insert( ) method. If the inserted value is the middle value that gets pushed up, for instance, the split_insert_middle( ) routine does the work. This is the decision code:

```
int mid = node.node_size / 2 ;

if ( find_key < mid )
    split_insert_left(
        node, sibling, key, recno, rptr );
else if ( find_key == mid )
    split_insert_middle(
        node, sibling, key, recno, rptr );
else
    split_insert_right(
        node, sibling, key, recno, rptr );
```

THE SPLIT_INSERT_LEFT( ) METHOD   Code's simple when it delegates all the real work, isn't it? Unfortunately, there's no way to avoid rolling up your sleeves and doing the actual work at some point. The split_insert( ) routines are the ones that actually push the data around.

The split_insert_left( ) method is called when the new value gets inserted to the left of the median value. This means that it's quite simple to write the upper half of the key values and record numbers into the new, right sibling node. That's the first part of the job:

```
private void split_insert_left(
    Btree_node left, Btree_node right, String key,
    int recno, int rptr ) throws IndexException {
```

```
int mid = left.node_size / 2;
System.arraycopy( left.keys, mid,
    right.keys, 0, mid );
System.arraycopy( left.record_numbers, mid,
    right.record_numbers, 0, mid );
```

Of course, we can't ever forget that the upper nodes also have pointers to move. When we do these moves, the leftmost pointer never leaves the left node. All operations in keys 0 through N become operations in pointers 1 through N+1. (Yes, my wastebasket was overflowing with hand-drawn splits before I became convinced that this was true.)

Bearing that in mind, this is the code that moves the higher half of the pointers into the right sibling:

```
if ( left.is_upper_node )
    System.arraycopy( left.pointers, mid,
        right.pointers, 0, mid+1 );
```

Next we carefully save the values that will get pushed up. They are the ones just left of the midpoint:

```
String push_key = left.keys[mid-1];
int push_recno = left.record_numbers[mid-1];
```

You wouldn't forget those upper-level pointers, would you? All this code is needed just to save one pointer:

```
int push_ptr;
if ( left.is_upper_node )
    push_ptr = left.pointers[mid];
else
    push_ptr = -1;
```

Now we're ready to do the insertion in the left node. This means moving the appropriate keys, record numbers, and if necessary, pointers, to the right to make room for the insertion. You have to approach bits like this with an accountant's attitude. You've got to correctly move exactly the values you want. This is the code:

```
if ( find_key < mid-1 ) {

    System.arraycopy( left.keys, find_key,
        left.keys, find_key+1, mid-find_key );
    System.arraycopy(
        left.record_numbers, find_key,
        left.record_numbers, find_key + 1,
        mid - find_key );
    if( left.is_upper_node )
        System.arraycopy( left.pointers, find_key+1,
            left.pointers, find_key+2,
            mid - find_key - 1 );
}
```

Finally, we're ready to drop the new values into the nice hole we've made in the left node. That's easy:

```
left.keys[find_key] = key;
left.record_numbers[find_key] = recno;
if ( left.is_upper_node )
    left.pointers[find_key+1] = rptr;
```

Did I say finally? We're not quite done. You have to adjust the accounting data:

```
left.number_of_keys = mid;
right.number_of_keys = mid;
```

I leave the right node in the RAM-resident tree. This is optimal for insertions where the data arrives presorted. It's a good choice half the time when the data arrives at random. It's always wrong if the data is arriving in reverse-sorted order, but that's rare and unavoidable.

```
nodes[working_level] = right;
```

Of course, we have to push the median values up to the next level. At any rate, somebody has to do this:

```
        split_push_up( push_key, push_recno, push_ptr,
            left, right );
```

Finally (really finally, this time!), we write the left node to disk since we're about to lose the RAM-based copy. The right node gets written as well if we're not building the full file:

```
        // right sibling remains in list
            left.write_node();
            if ( ! building_full_file )
                right.write_node();
```

THE SPLIT_INSERT_MIDDLE( ) METHOD   When the value you're inserting happens to be the median value that gets pushed up to the next level, the split process is much simpler. You have none of the aggravations involved with inserting the new data into the left or right sibling nodes.

We start by finding the midpoint:

```
    private void split_insert_middle(
        Btree_node left, Btree_node right, String key,
        int recno, int rptr ) throws IndexException{

        int mid = left.node_size / 2;
```

Then we copy exactly half the keys, record_numbers, and if necessary, pointers into the right node:

```
        System.arraycopy( left.keys, mid, right.keys, 0,
            mid );
        System.arraycopy( left.record_numbers, mid,
            right.record_numbers, 0, mid );
        if ( left.is_upper_node )
            System.arraycopy( left.pointers, mid+1,
                right.pointers, 1, mid );
```

Then the bookkeeping data is updated:

```
        left.number_of_keys = mid;
        right.number_of_keys = mid;
```

Next that mystery rptr is used. When the split is above ground level, the pointer to the right of the key is pushed up along with the key. That comes to rest as the new leftmost pointer in the right sibling:

```
    if ( left.is_upper_node )
        right.pointers[0] = rptr;
```

Finally (really, finally), you perform the same actions as we saw in split_insert_left( ). The right node is saved in RAM, the push-up process is done, and the data is saved:

```
    nodes[find_level] = right;

    split_push_up( key, recno, right.address,
        left, right );

    // right sibling remains in list
        left.write_node();
        if ( ! building_full_file )
            right.write_node();
```

THE SPLIT_INSERT_RIGHT( ) METHOD   The split_insert_right( ) method is similar to split_insert_left( ), but it's by no means the mirror image. The left insert method involved moving half the data into the right node and then sliding some of the data in the left node.

In this routine, we shift the data that comes before the insertion from the left node into the right node. Then we stick in the new values. Then we shift any remaining data from left to right. From there on, the process will get familiar.

We start by finding the midpoint and the data that will eventually be pushed up:

```
    private void split_insert_right(
        Btree_node left, Btree_node right, String key,
        int recno, int rptr ) throws IndexException {

        int mid = left.node_size / 2;

        String push_key = left.keys[mid];
```

```
int push_recno = left.record_numbers[mid];
int push_ptr;
if ( left.is_upper_node )
    push_ptr = left.pointers[mid+1];
else
    push_ptr = -1;
```

Then we shift the data that becomes the left side of the right node (the data that precedes the insertion point in the right node). This is the code:

```
if ( (find_key - mid) > 1 ) {

    System.arraycopy( left.keys, mid+1,
        right.keys, 0, find_key - mid - 1 );
    System.arraycopy( left.record_numbers, mid+1,
        right.record_numbers, 0,
        find_key - mid - 1 );
}
if ( left.is_upper_node )
    System.arraycopy( left.pointers, mid+1,
        right.pointers, 0, find_key - mid );
```

Building the right node from left to right, we're up to dropping in the new, inserted values:

```
int where = find_key - mid - 1; // loc in right
right.keys[where] = key;
right.record_numbers[where] = recno;
if( left.is_upper_node )
    right.pointers[where+1] = rptr;
```

Lastly, if we haven't reached the end of the data, we add any remaining data into the right node:

```
if ( where < mid ) {

    System.arraycopy( left.keys, find_key,
        right.keys, where+1, mid - where - 1 );
    System.arraycopy(
```

```
                    left.record_numbers, find_key,
                    right.record_numbers, where+1,
                    mid - where - 1 );
                if ( left.is_upper_node )
                    System.arraycopy( left.pointers, find_key,
                        right.pointers, where+2,
                        mid - where - 1 );
            }
```

The remainder of the routine should look familiar by now:

```
            left.number_of_keys = mid;
            right.number_of_keys = mid;

            nodes[find_level] = right;

            split_push_up( push_key, push_recno, push_ptr,
                left, right );

            // right sibling remains in list
                left.write_node();
                if ( ! building_full_file )
                    right.write_node();
        }
```

THE SPLIT_PUSH_UP( ) METHOD   Ready to push that median data up to the next level? That job completes the whole split process. It's not as full of accounting-type work as the split_insert( ) methods were. But it's really two separate processes.

If we're splitting the root node, we create a new root and stack it on top of the existing nodes. Otherwise we push the data up into some upper-level node that already exists. This is the overall structure:

```
        private void split_push_up( String key, int recno,
            int rptr, Btree_node left, Btree_node right )
            throws IndexException {

            if ( working_level == 0 ) {

                . . . stack new root on top
            }
```

```
      else {

          . . . push into existing node

      }
  }
```

You'll see that the processes are very different. We'll start with the creation of a new root node. The first job is to increment ground_level and to shove all the existing nodes down one slot in the array:

```
// build new root node
ground_level++;
System.arraycopy( nodes, 0, nodes, 1,
    ground_level );
```

Next we create a new node, which becomes nodes[0]. We'll also record some vital bookkeeping data:

```
int where = add_node();

Btree_node node = new Btree_node( where,
    key_length, page_size, this, true );
nodes[0] = node;
root_node_address = where;
```

Then we do a pseudosearch for the place to insert the data we're pushing up. It's quick:

```
find_key = find_level = 0;
```

With that done, add_key( ) has everything it needs, so we use it to write the new data:

```
node.add_key( key, recno, -1, 0 );
```

At this point, we're ready to write the new addresses. Note that this is where the new leftmost pointer is created. It will never move.

```
node.pointers[0] = left.address;
node.pointers[1] = right.address;
```

Adding into an existing node is actually simpler, even though we have to allow for the case where the parent node is already full (so we'll need to split the parent node).

When we created a new root, we didn't worry about the working_level. It was zero when we started and was zero when we were done. In this case, however, we're going to move up a level:

```
working_level--;
```

Then we create a handy reference to the node that was the parent. We'll do a new find in the former parent node:

```
Btree_node node = nodes[working_level];

find_key = node.find( key );
```

Finally (this is the final "finally" in the whole split process!), we add the new data if it fits, or split this node if it's already full:

```
if ( node.number_of_keys < node.node_size ) {

    node.add_key( key, recno,
        right.address, find_key );
}
else {
    split_a_node( key, recno, right.address );
}
```

THE WRITE_HEADER( ) METHOD   The write_header( ) method is the reverse of read_header( ). It's full of ALD like these:

```
raf.writeInt( number_of_keys );
raf.writeInt( file_length );
raf.writeInt( number_of_pages );
```

As with read_header( ), see the full listing for the rest of the ALD. See the comments at the bottom of the full listing for the file structure details.

THE WRITE_NODES( ) METHOD   If you've digested the complexities of the split process, you're ready for a short vacation. This is it. The write_nodes( ) process rewrites the header and all the RAM-resident nodes this way:

```java
private void write_nodes() throws IndexException {

    write_header();

    for ( int i = 0 ; i <= ground_level ; i++ )
        nodes[i].write_node();
}
```

Simple enough?

One more thing. There is a private class, IndexException, at the end of NDX.java. It's a trivial class that just provides a new exception name. It's near the end of the full listing.

The Full NDX.java Listing

Listing 20-4 shows the full NDX.java source file.

Listing 20-4:
NDX objects
implement
B-trees

```java
// NDX.java -- create and maintain B-tree index files
// Copyright 1997, Martin L. Rinehart

// this code is completely documented in:
// _Java Database Development_, Martin Rinehart,
// Osborne/McGraw-Hill, 1997

import java.io.*;

class NDX extends BinFile {
// -------------------- data members --------------------

// there are no public data members

// protected data members:

    protected boolean building_full_file;
```

```
        protected int find_key;
        protected int find_level;
        protected boolean found;

        protected int ground_level;

        protected int half_size;

        protected int index_num;
        protected Indexable indexable;

        protected int key_length;

        protected Btree_node[] nodes; // 0 is root
        protected int number_of_keys;
        protected int number_of_pages;

        protected int page_size;

        protected int root_node_address;

        protected int working_level;

// final static data member:

        final static int MAX_LEVELS = 10;

        final static int PAGE_SIZE = 128; // testing
        // final static int PAGE_SIZE = 16 * 1024; // running

// -------------------- public methods --------------------

// constructor:

        NDX( String path_name, String access,
            Indexable i, int index_num )
            throws IndexException {

            super( path_name, access );

            if ( access.equals("rw") ) {
```

```
                        if ( !writeable ) return;
                }
                else // access == "r"
                    if ( !readable ) return;

                indexable = i;
                this.index_num = index_num;

                number_of_keys = 0;
                page_size = PAGE_SIZE;
                file_length = page_size;
                number_of_pages = 1;

                String key = indexable.getKeyValue( 0, index_num );
                key_length = key.length();

                ground_level = -1;
                nodes = new Btree_node[MAX_LEVELS];

                if ( getLast() < 0 ) {

                    write_header();
                    file_length = page_size;

                    reindex();
                }
                else {

                    read_header(); // also reads root node

                    if ( number_of_keys != (indexable.getLast()+1) )
                        reindex();
                }
            }

// there are no data access methods

// public, class-specific methods:

    public void delete( int recno )
        throws IndexException {
```

```
            reindex();
    }

    public int find( String key )
        throws IndexException {

        private_find( key, true );

        if ( found )
            return nodes[find_level].
                record_numbers[find_key];
        else
            return -1;
    }

    public void insert( String key, int recno )
        throws IndexException {

        insert( key, recno, -1 );
    }

    public void reindex() throws IndexException {


        building_full_file = true;
        ground_level = 0;

        int last = indexable.getLast();

        for ( int i = 0 ; i <= last; i++ ) {

            String key =
                indexable.getKeyValue( i, index_num );
            insert( key, i, -1 );
        }

        write_nodes();
        building_full_file = false;
    }

// public, non-event overriding method:

    public String paramString() {
```

```
                return "NDX";
        }

// there are no public, event-handling methods

// ------------------ private methods ------------------

// private methods:

    private int add_node() {

        int where = file_length;
        file_length += page_size;
        number_of_pages++;

        if ( ! building_full_file )
            write_header();

        return where;
    }

    private void insert( String key, int recno, int rptr )
        throws IndexException {

        System.out.println( "Inserting: " + key );

        if ( number_of_keys == 0 ) {

            int where = add_node();
            root_node_address = where;

            nodes[0] = new Btree_node(
                where, key_length,
                page_size, this, false );

            ground_level = 0;

            nodes[0].add_key( key, recno, -1, 0 );
            nodes[0].write_node();

            number_of_keys = 1;
```

```
        }
        else {

            private_find( key, false );

            working_level = ground_level;
            Btree_node node = nodes[working_level];

            if ( node.number_of_keys < node.node_size )
                node.add_key( key, recno, rptr, find_key );
            else
                split_a_node( key, recno, rptr );

            number_of_keys++;

            if ( ! building_full_file )
                write_nodes();
        }
    }

    private void private_find( String key,
        boolean stop_when_found ) throws IndexException {

        found = false;
        working_level = 0;
        Btree_node node = nodes[0];

        while ( working_level < ground_level ) {

            find_key = nodes[working_level].find( key );
            if ( find_key < node.number_of_keys )
                if ( stop_when_found &&
                    node.keys[find_key].equals(key) ) {

                    find_level = working_level;
                    found = true;
                    return;
                }

            int next_address = node.pointers[find_key];

            working_level++;
```

```
        Btree_node next = nodes[working_level];

        if ( next.address != next_address ) {

            next.write_node();
            next.read_node( next_address );
        }
        node = next;
    }

    // reached ground level
    find_level = ground_level;
    find_key = node.find( key );
}

private void read_header() throws IndexException {

    try {

        raf.seek( 0 );

        number_of_keys = raf.readInt();
        file_length = raf.readInt();
        number_of_pages = raf.readInt();
        page_size = raf.readInt();
        key_length = raf.readInt();
        ground_level = raf.readInt();

        root_node_address = raf.readInt();
        nodes[0] = new Btree_node( root_node_address,
            key_length, page_size, this,
            ground_level != 0 );
        nodes[0].read_node();
    }
    catch ( IOException ioe ) {

        writeable = readable = false;
        message = ioe.getMessage() +
            " (reading header block)";
        return;
    }
}
```

```java
private void split_a_node( String key, int recno,
    int rptr ) throws IndexException {

    Btree_node node = nodes[working_level];

    int where = add_node();

    Btree_node sibling = new Btree_node(
        where, node.key_length, node.node_length,
        node.parent, node.is_upper_node );

    int mid = node.node_size / 2 ;

    if ( find_key < mid )
        split_insert_left(
            node, sibling, key, recno, rptr );
    else if ( find_key == mid )
        split_insert_middle(
            node, sibling, key, recno, rptr );
    else
        split_insert_right(
            node, sibling, key, recno, rptr );
}

private void split_insert_left(
    Btree_node left, Btree_node right, String key,
    int recno, int rptr ) throws IndexException {

    int mid = left.node_size / 2;
    System.arraycopy( left.keys, mid,
        right.keys, 0, mid );
    System.arraycopy( left.record_numbers, mid,
        right.record_numbers, 0, mid );

    if ( left.is_upper_node )
        System.arraycopy( left.pointers, mid,
            right.pointers, 0, mid+1 );

    String push_key = left.keys[mid-1];
    int push_recno = left.record_numbers[mid-1];
    int push_ptr;
    if ( left.is_upper_node )
```

```
            push_ptr = left.pointers[mid];
        else
            push_ptr = -1;

        if ( find_key < mid-1 ) {

            System.arraycopy( left.keys, find_key,
                left.keys, find_key+1, mid-find_key );
            System.arraycopy(
                left.record_numbers, find_key,
                left.record_numbers, find_key + 1,
                mid - find_key );
            if( left.is_upper_node )
                System.arraycopy( left.pointers, find_key+1,
                    left.pointers, find_key+2,
                    mid - find_key - 1 );
        }
        left.keys[find_key] = key;
        left.record_numbers[find_key] = recno;
        if ( left.is_upper_node )
            left.pointers[find_key+1] = rptr;

        left.number_of_keys = mid;
        right.number_of_keys = mid;

        nodes[working_level] = right;

        split_push_up( push_key, push_recno, push_ptr,
            left, right );

        // right sibling remains in list
            left.write_node();
            if ( ! building_full_file )
                right.write_node();
    }

private void split_insert_middle(
    Btree_node left, Btree_node right, String key,
    int recno, int rptr ) throws IndexException{

    int mid = left.node_size / 2;
```

```
          System.arraycopy( left.keys, mid, right.keys, 0,
              mid );
          System.arraycopy( left.record_numbers, mid,
              right.record_numbers, 0, mid );
          if ( left.is_upper_node )
              System.arraycopy( left.pointers, mid+1,
                  right.pointers, 1, mid );

          left.number_of_keys = mid;
          right.number_of_keys = mid;
          if ( left.is_upper_node )
              right.pointers[0] = rptr;

          nodes[find_level] = right;

          split_push_up( key, recno, right.address,
              left, right );

          // right sibling remains in list
              left.write_node();
              if ( ! building_full_file )
                  right.write_node();
      }

  private void split_insert_right(
      Btree_node left, Btree_node right, String key,
      int recno, int rptr ) throws IndexException {

      int mid = left.node_size / 2;

      String push_key = left.keys[mid];
      int push_recno = left.record_numbers[mid];
      int push_ptr;
      if ( left.is_upper_node )
          push_ptr = left.pointers[mid+1];
      else
          push_ptr = -1;

      if ( (find_key - mid) > 1 ) {

          System.arraycopy( left.keys, mid+1,
              right.keys, 0, find_key - mid - 1 );
```

```
        System.arraycopy( left.record_numbers, mid+1,
            right.record_numbers, 0,
            find_key - mid - 1 );
    }
    if ( left.is_upper_node )
        System.arraycopy( left.pointers, mid+1,
            right.pointers, 0, find_key - mid );

    int where = find_key - mid - 1; // loc in right
    right.keys[where] = key;
    right.record_numbers[where] = recno;
    if( left.is_upper_node )
        right.pointers[where+1] = rptr;

    if ( where < mid ) {

        System.arraycopy( left.keys, find_key,
            right.keys, where+1, mid - where - 1 );
        System.arraycopy(
            left.record_numbers, find_key,
            right.record_numbers, where+1,
            mid - where - 1 );
        if ( left.is_upper_node )
            System.arraycopy( left.pointers, find_key,
                right.pointers, where+2,
                mid - where - 1 );
    }

    left.number_of_keys = mid;
    right.number_of_keys = mid;

    nodes[find_level] = right;

    split_push_up( push_key, push_recno, push_ptr,
        left, right );

    // right sibling remains in list
        left.write_node();
        if ( ! building_full_file )
            right.write_node();
}
```

```
private void split_push_up( String key, int recno,
    int rptr, Btree_node left, Btree_node right )
    throws IndexException {

    if ( working_level == 0 ) {

        // build new root node
        ground_level++;
        System.arraycopy( nodes, 0, nodes, 1,
            ground_level );

        int where = add_node();

        Btree_node node = new Btree_node( where,
            key_length, page_size, this, true );
        nodes[0] = node;
        root_node_address = where;

        find_key = find_level = 0;
        node.add_key( key, recno, -1, 0 );

        node.pointers[0] = left.address;
        node.pointers[1] = right.address;
    }
    else {

        working_level--;
        Btree_node node = nodes[working_level];

        find_key = node.find( key );
        if ( node.number_of_keys < node.node_size ) {

            node.add_key( key, recno,
                right.address, find_key );
        }
        else {
            split_a_node( key, recno, right.address );
        }
    }
}

private void write_header() {
```

```
        try {

            raf.seek( 0 );
            raf.writeInt( number_of_keys );
            raf.writeInt( file_length );
            raf.writeInt( number_of_pages );
            raf.writeInt( page_size );
            raf.writeInt( key_length );
            raf.writeInt( ground_level );
            raf.writeInt( root_node_address );

            raf.writeInt( 0 ); // spare

            for ( int i = 0 ;
                i < ( (page_size - 32) >> 2) ; i++ )
                raf.writeInt( -1 ); // record numbers
        }
        catch ( IOException ioe ) {

            writeable = readable = false;
            message = ioe.getMessage() +
                " (writing header block)";
        }
    }

    private void write_nodes() throws IndexException {

        write_header();

        for ( int i = 0 ; i <= ground_level ; i++ )
            nodes[i].write_node();
    }

} // end of NDX class

// private class in NDX.java:

class IndexException extends Exception {

    IndexException( String s ) {

        super( s );
```

```
        }
    }

    /* File header page:

     0- 3 number of keys
     4- 7 file_length
     8-11 number of pages
    12-15 page size
    16-19 key length
    20-23 ground level
    24-27 root node address
    28-31 spare

    32-(page_size - 1) record numbers

    ground node page:

                L1 = key length * node size + 31
                L2 = L1 + 1
                L3 = L1 + 4*node size
                L4 = L3 + 1
                L5 = L3 + 8*(node size + 1)

         0- 3 key length
         4- 7 node length     // page size
         8-11 node size        // max # of keys
        12-15 number of keys
        16-19 is_upper_node
        20-31 spare
        32-L1 keys
        L2-L3 record numbers

    upper node page, as above, plus:

        L4-L5 pointers

    */

    // end of NDX.java
```

The New BinFile Class

The BinFile class that we used in Chapter 3 records its size values in public variables when you open it. If you expand or contract the file, you have to update these variables. This got to be a nuisance.

This version of the BinFile actually goes to disk for the current size when you call getLast( ). The old last_row data member has become a last_row( ) method. See the getLast( ) public method and the last_row( ) private method for the details.

Listing 20-5 shows the revised BinFile.java source file.

Listing 20-5:
A more
dynamic
BinFile

```java
// BinFile.java -- Binary File class
// Copyright 1997, Martin L. Rinehart

// this code is completely documented in:
// _Java Database Development_, Martin Rinehart,
// Osborne/McGraw-Hill, 1997

/*
    handle any file as a binary, random access file
*/

import java.io.*;

class BinFile implements Scrollable {

// -------------------- data members --------------------

// there are no public data members

// protected data members:

    protected int bytes_read;

    protected int file_length;
    protected String path_name;
    protected int file_rows;

    protected byte[] inbuf;
    protected int last_row;

    protected String message;

    protected byte[] outbuf;
```

```
    protected RandomAccessFile raf;
    protected boolean readable;

     protected boolean writeable;

// static data members

    // there are no public static data members
    // there are no private static data members

    // final static data member:

    final static int len_outbuf = 82;

// ------------------- public methods -------------------

// constructors:

    BinFile( String pathname ) {
        this( pathname, "r" ); // default to read-only
    }

    BinFile( String pathname, String access ) {

        path_name = pathname;
        readable = writeable = false;

        if ( access.equals("r") || access.equals("rw") ) {

            if ( bin_open(access) ) {

                message = "OK";
                readable = true;
                writeable = access.equals("rw");

                inbuf = new byte[16];
                outbuf = new byte[len_outbuf];
            }
            else {
                message = "Could not open " + path_name;
            }
```

```
        }
        else {

            message = "Access '" + access + "' not valid";
        }
    }

// data access getXxx() methods:

    public String getFileName() {

        return path_name;
    }

    public int getLast() {

        // returns last item #
        return readable ? last_row() : -1;
    }

    public String getMessage() {

        return message;
    }

    public String getString( int index ) {

        // a string representing scrollable[index]
        // index is from zero through getLast()

        int file_loc = index << 4; // 16 bytes at a time
        try {
            raf.seek( file_loc );
            bytes_read = raf.read( inbuf );
        }
        catch (IOException ioe) {
            bytes_read = 0;
            message = "File read error";
        }

        prepare_outbuf( index );
```

```
            return new String(outbuf, 0);
        }

// data access isXxx() methods:

    public boolean isReadable() {

        return readable;
    }

    public boolean isWriteable() {

        return writeable;
    }

// there are no data access setXxx() methods

// public, class-specific methods:

    public void close() {

        if ( raf != null ) {
            try { raf.close(); }
            catch( IOException ioe ) {}
        }
    }

    public boolean useMonospace() {

        return true;
    }

// public, non-event overriding method:

    public String paramString() {

        return path_name + " read: " + readable
        + " write: " + writeable;
    }

// there are no public, event-handling methods
```

```
// ----------------- private methods -------------------

// private methods:

    private boolean bin_open(String access) {

    // returns true on success

        try {
            raf = new RandomAccessFile( path_name, access );
            try {
                file_length = (int) raf.length();
                file_rows = (file_length+15) >> 4;
                if ( file_rows > 0x80000000L )
                    return false;

                // note: rows are 0 thru last_row
                last_row = ( (int) file_rows ) - 1;
                return true;
            }
            catch ( IOException ioe ) {
                return false;
            }
        }
        catch ( IOException ioe ) {
            return false;
        }
    }

    private int last_row() {

        try {
            file_length = (int) raf.length();
            file_rows = (file_length+15) >> 4;
        }
        catch ( IOException ioe ) {
            return -1;
        }
        return file_rows - 1;
    }

    private void prep_asc() {
```

```
        int outloc = 50;

        for ( byte i = 0; i < bytes_read; i++ ) {
            outbuf[outloc] = FDlib.byte2asc( inbuf[i] );
            outloc++;

            if ( (i==3) || (i==11) ) {
                outbuf[outloc++] = (byte) ' ';
            }
            else if ( i == 7 ) {
                outbuf[outloc++] = (byte) ' ';
                outbuf[outloc++] = (byte) ' ';
            }
        }
    }

    private void prep_hex() {

        int outloc = 10;

        for ( byte i = 0; i < bytes_read; i++ ) {
            FDlib.byte2hex( inbuf[i], outbuf, outloc );
            outloc += 2;

            if ( (i == 3) || (i == 11) ) {
                outbuf[outloc++] = (byte) ' ';
            }
            else if ( i == 7 ) {
                outbuf[outloc++] = (byte) ' ';
                outbuf[outloc++] = (byte) ' ';
            }
        }
    }

     private void prep_loc(int loc) {

        FDlib.int2hex( (loc<<4), outbuf, 0 );
        outbuf[8] = (byte) ':';
        outbuf[9] = (byte) ' ';
    }

    private void prepare_outbuf(int loc) {
```

```
// outbuf gets location, then hex, then ascii

        for ( int i = 0; i < len_outbuf; i++ )
            outbuf[i] = (byte) ' ';

        prep_loc(loc);
        prep_hex();
        prep_asc();
    }

} // end of BinFile class

// there are no private classes in BinFile.java

// end of BinFile.java
```

Summary

This chapter covered the NDX class, which encapsulates a B-tree index file. We started with a look at a sample mainline which showed that simply calling the NDX constructor with an Indexable object was all you needed to do to build the B-tree.

To make an object Indexable, you implement a three-function interface. The first, getLast( ), is already implemented if you extend the DBF class. The second, getNumberOfIndexes( ), simply returns the appropriate integer. The last method, getKeyValue( ), returns a fixed-length String for each index.

I've included here a fakeNDX class that simulates a data table, providing test data. You can use this to do your own NDX testing.

The NDX class itself is simple to use. For those who don't want to just use the NDX as a black box, we took an in-depth look at its internals.

In Chapter 21 we'll be extending the NDX to implement index-based scrolling.

Chapter 21

Index-Based Scrolling

W e've got a Btree-based NDX class that makes it dead simple to create and maintain indexes for our database tables. In this chapter, we're going to put these indexes to use with a basic addition to the NDX class. We'll define and implement the ScrollableX class, which provides for scrolling a table (or anything that implements ScrollableX) in index order.

Before we get started, let me explain where we're going.

Picture a contact-list application. You enter contacts as you meet people, but you want the list to appear sorted by last name, so that it's easy to find people. Or maybe you're going to visit New England, and you want to see the same list in ZIP code order (low numbers are in the East). Or you want to see a list of all your contacts at one company, which is another sort order.

What's required is a scrolling capability that's based on displaying a window full of records in the order they appear in an index, not in the physical order of the data source.

In this chapter we're going to look at how this type of scrolling can be accomplished. Then we'll take a quick look at a class that provides random names, which we'll use for testing.

From there we'll go to a mainline that shows how really trivial it is to use these tools. It's only a bit more trouble to create an index-based scrolling window than it is to create a physical-order scrolling window.

To be more exact, all the hard work is encapsulated in a new class, ScrollWinX. We'll look first at the interface it requires, ScrollableX, and then at the ScrollWinX class itself.

You'll see that this work required enhancements to the NDX class, too, but we'll postpone looking at that class until Chapter 22.

Let's get started.

Abandoning Physical Order

The first good news is that you'll be an indexed scrollmeister if you stick with this chapter until you get to the section "Understanding the ScrollWinX Class." You'll be able to use this scroll window just as easily as you use the regular scroll window. The other good news is that it won't take too long to get there.

When you lose the physical order, as you do when you use an index, you have to work strictly with relative order. There are only two locations in an index that are easy to find: first and last. All other indexed items are found by relative movement.

Our *physical* scroller starts by requesting item 0. Then it asks for item 1, item 2, and so on, until it fills its window.

In contrast, an *indexed* scroller asks for the first item. Then it asks for the next item, and then the next, and it keeps asking for the next item until it fills its window.

This maps nicely to our basic navigation commands. The simplest navigation scrolls the window by a single line (moves forward or backward one record). The page-up and page-down movements of the window require moving forward or backward by a window's worth of records. The home command requires starting at the initial record. The end command requires starting at the last record and backing up by enough records to fill the window.

The only tricky bit is ensuring that we stop forward movement in time to keep a window full of data. I do this by reading the last full page of data and recording the record numbers in an array. Then I check each forward-movement command to see if it returns a record that is a member of this array. If it does, it's simple to back up a little, to be sure the window stays full.

The only difficulty in the code is the actual work of climbing around in the B-tree, getting the next or previous index value. In this chapter, we'll just assume that our NDX is smart enough to do that. The NDX.java in this chapter's project files on disk has the necessary smarts. We'll look at it in detail in the next chapter.

One problem with relative movement is that you can't make as much use of the vertical elevator. There's no way to find a numeric location in the file. That means that dragging the elevator car can't work. The elevator is still useful as an alternative to the keyboard for movement by line and page.

Now let's get on to the code.

The Indexable RandNames Class

You'll recognize RandNames as another incarnation of what I had called fakeNDX. It begins with a list of names, almost in alphabetical order. You set a final static int, filesize, to any value you like. If filesize exceeds the size of the name list, it starts generating random names. Refer to Listing 21-1 for the details.

Listing 21-1:
RandNames
implements
indexable

```
// RandNames.java -- fake indexable file
// Copyright 1997, Martin L. Rinehart

import java.util.Random;

class RandNames implements Indexable {

final static String[] testvals = {
    "Allen ", //  0
    "Barney",
    "Ann   ",
    "Al    ",
    "Bob   ",
    "Bobbie", //  5
    "Charly",
    "Chip  ",
```

```
"Chuck ",
"Dave  ",
"Dexter", // 10
"Donny ",
"Doris ",
"Evan  ",
"Fanny ",
"Felix ", // 15
"Fran  ",
"Frank ",
"Grace ",
"Harry ",
"Iris  ", // 20
"Jane  ",
"Jean  ",
"Joan  ",
"Judy  ",
"Karen ", // 25
"Larry ",
"Lou   ",
"Louis ",
"Louise",
"Martin", // 30
"Mary  ",
"Melvin",
"Mike  ",
"Nancy ",
"Oscar ", // 35
"Paul  ",
"Peter ",
"Quincy",
"Ralph ",
"Roger ", // 40
"Sam   ",
"Sandra",
"Sue   ",
"SueAnn",
"Suzy  ",
"Tammy ",
"Tim   ",
"Tom   ",
"Ursula",
"Violet",
```

```
        "Wendy ",
        "Xavier",
        "Yvonne",
        "Zelda "
};

static Random random = new Random( 1 );
final static int filesize = 7;

    String[] testdata;

    RandNames() {

        testdata = new String[filesize];
        boolean vals_are_short
            = testvals.length < filesize;

        System.arraycopy( testvals, 0, testdata, 0,
            vals_are_short ? testvals.length : filesize );

        if ( vals_are_short )
            for ( int i = testvals.length ;
                i < filesize ; i++ )
                testdata[i] = rstring( 6 );
    }

    public int getLast() { return filesize - 1; }

    public int getNumberOfIndexes() { return 1; }

    public String getKeyValue( int record_num,
            int index_num ) {

        return testdata[record_num];
    }

    private String rstring( int len ) {

        byte[] b = new byte[len];

        for ( int i = 0 ; i < len ; i++ )
            b[i] = rletter();
```

```
            return new String( b, 0 );
    }

    private byte rletter() {

            return (byte) ( 'A' +
                (int) ( 26 * random.nextFloat() ));
    }
}

// end of RandNames.java
```

The ScrollNDX Mainline

To scroll on an index, you need to start with something that is Indexable. You give the Indexable to the NDX. Our NDX has been extended to implement ScrollableX, the index-based scrolling interface. You give the ScrollableX to a ScrollWinX.

Then, as always, you make little adjustments to the ScrollWinX and show( ) it. Listing 21-2 shows the full mainline from this chapter's project files.

Listing 21-2:
Index-based
scrolling
mainline

```
// ScrollNDX.java -- demonstrates index-based scrolling
// Copyright 1997, Martin L. Rinehart

// this code is completely documented in:
// _Java Database Development_, Martin Rinehart,
// Osborne/McGraw-Hill, 1997

class ScrollNDX {

    public static void main( String[] args ) {

            String fn = "RNames.nd0";
            Indexable idx = new RandNames();

            NDX ndx = null;
            try { ndx = new NDX( fn, "rw", idx, 1 ); }
            catch ( IndexException ie ) {}

            ScrollWinX swx = new ScrollWinX( ndx, fn );
            swx.setEndApp( true );
```

```
        swx.resize( 520, 100 );
        swx.show();
    }

} // end of ScrollNDX

// end of ScrollNDX.java
```

ScrollableX

The ScrollableX interface is similar to the Scrollable interface, except that it adds two methods, find( ) and move( ), and the go( ) method is defined very differently. These are the methods:

- public String find (String key)
- public String getString( )
- public void go(int where)

- public int move(int distance)
- public boolean useMonospace( )

You'll normally add a find( ) capability to your programs that handle larger files. For example, you may want to type "Smi" in some text field and have the scroller display the names starting with "Smi".

The move( ) method is also new. It's the basic navigation tool that the scroller uses. Displaying a page full of names is done by a succession of move(1) calls, interspersed with getString( ) calls to get something to display.

The go( ) method looks familiar, but it's very different. The go(0) call goes to the first record, in index order. I use go(–1) to go to the last record, in index order. The interface specifies that any nonzero argument is interpreted as a call for the last record.

Numbered Index-Based Records

Why can't you go( ) to a particular record by its number? In a list of names, for example, go(0) gets the first name, go(1) gets the second name, and so on. It's unambiguous and genuinely useful. You would use it, for example, to respond to the user dragging the elevator car.

Xbase programmers (Clipper, dBASE, and FoxPro) have asked for this capability for years. The vendors, who normally listen closely to their customers, have not provided the capability.

From this you can conclude that the capability has proven out of reach. With our interface, you could go(0) and then move(i) to get to a numbered record, but think about what would happen with a million-record file.

I think that it's possible to have a numbered B-tree. The tricky part is maintaining the numbers as you insert and delete keys. If you're up for a real challenge, this problem is still open.

Listing 21-3 shows the full ScrollableX interface definition.

Listing 21-3:
An interface
for index-
based
scrolling

```
// ScrollableX.java -- Index-based scrolling interface
// Copyright 1997, Martin L. Rinehart

// this code is completely documented in:
// _Java Database Development_, Martin Rinehart,
// Osborne/McGraw-Hill, 1997

interface ScrollableX {

// ScrollableX has five public methods:

    // Search for a key and return the key or the
    // first higher key value if the key is not found.
    // Sets the current record.
    public String find ( String key );

    // return a displayable String for the current record
    public String getString();

    // go to a record (in index order)
    // go( 0 ) -> goto first record
    // go ( non-zero ) -> goto last record
    public void go( int where );

    // Move, in index order, relative to the current
    // record. Return the record # of the new current
    // record. Use move(0) for the record # of the current
    // record.
    public int move( int distance );

    // true if the output requires a monospaced font
    public boolean useMonospace();
}

// end of ScrollableX.java
```

The ScrollWinX Class

The ScrollWinX is just like a ScrollWin, except that it implements ScrollableX, for index-based scrolling instead of Scrollable, which was for physical-order scrolling. In this section we'll take a look at how you use this class, and, for those who want to improve on my work, we'll look under the hood at how it all functions.

Using the ScrollWinX Class

Using the ScrollWinX is just like using the ScrollWin, except that the object you pass it implements ScrollableX, not Scrollable. Our NDX class implements ScrollableX, as you'll see in Chapter 22.

As a quick review, there are two constructors:

- ScrollWinX(ScrollableX s)
- ScrollWinX(ScrollableX s, String title)

The first form creates a scrolling window with the rather unimaginative title "Scroll Window." The latter form lets you supply an imaginative title. (Or, as you'll see in my code, it lets you supply an unimaginative, but different, title.)

You setEndApp(true) if you want a click on the close button to trigger a System.exit( ). Otherwise, the close button just triggers a hide( ).

You setRefuseClose(true) if you want a click on the close button to be ignored. You don't set both setEndApp( ) and setRefuseClose( ) to true.

A call to resize( ) is generally a good idea. The width should be long enough for the getString( ) value plus the insets, plus space for the vertical elevator.

TOUR

You are now a scrollmeister! If you're ready to prove it, take this test: modify the DBF class to implement ScrollableX. You can scroll it in physical order with a ScrollWinX when you do this.

Don't type a line of code until you're confident that you can have your DBF implementing ScrollableX in just ten or 20 minutes. If you think it will take longer, study the interface carefully. Study the interface until you know how to implement it in five minutes. Allow the remaining time for debugging.

Read the "Understanding" section when you're ready to improve my code, fix a bug, or use a DataBoss.

Understanding the ScrollWinX Class

Let's start with a word of warning. This class maintains, but doesn't implement, the DataBoss capabilities of the ScrollWin. When you're ready to use a DataBoss with the ScrollWinX, you'll have to improve this code.

This section will be very brief. If you're ready to dive into this code, you might want to go back to Chapter 2 to look at the basic ScrollWin again. Here we'll just look at the new features.

The data is basically the same as for Scrollable except for handling the problem of stopping scrolling when you come to the end of the list. Here, the integer array, last_record_numbers, handles the problem. In Scrollable, this problem was solved with integers s_last and last_top_row.

The public methods are all substantially unchanged or identical to the ScrollWin methods. The constructor, for example, is only changed in accepting a ScrollableX object, rather than a Scrollable object. There is a lot of new code in the private methods, however.

The first private method is new. The adjust( ) method is called whenever you move toward the end of the file. Its job is to back up so that the window stays full if you have gone too far. To understand the code, begin by remembering that the ScrollableX move( ) method returns the current record number if you move(0).

The navigation (line down, page down, or end) is done as if there were no end-of-file problem, leaving the file positioned at some record (possibly the very last one). The adjust( ) method looks for the record number in a list of the record numbers corresponding to the records shown when the last record in the ScrollableX is showing in the last line of the window.

If it finds the record in this list, it backs up enough lines to show the last line at the bottom of the window (assuming there are enough lines to fill the window). All of this is more complicated to explain than to do. This is the code:

```
private void adjust() {

    int where = scroll_object.move( 0 );
    int adj = in_lasts( where );

    scroll_object.move( -adj );
}
```

All the navigation methods are changed. They used to go( ), but now they move( ). (Except home( ) and end( ), which use the new go( ) to find the first and last record.) Many of the navigation methods become simpler.

The down( ) method, for example, still moves the hilite bar down if it's possible. We've initialized a variable, max_rows, to hold the count of the number of rows on screen. The screen holds client_rows; max_rows equals client_rows except when there aren't enough records to fill the screen.

As before, adjusting the hilite row is a nuisance. There may, for example, be enough records to fill the screen, but the user has just tugged the screen's lower border down, stretching it below the end row of the table. You can see in the code that this is a lot of ALD. On the other hand, actually scrolling the data is trivial: you move(1) and then adjust( ). This is the code:

```
private void down() {

    if ( hilite_row < client_rows - 1 ) {
        hilite_row++;
        if ( hilite_row > (max_rows-1) )
            hilite_row--;
        repaint();
        return;
    }

    scroll_object.move( 1 );
    adjust();
    repaint();

}
```

I've changed my mind about what the home and end keys mean. In this implementation, "end" means move the hilite bar to the bottom of the screen if it's not at the bottom. If the hilite bar is already at the bottom, then it moves the file to the end. The code is simple:

```
private void end() {

    if ( hilite_row >= max_rows - 1 ) {

        scroll_object.go( -1 );
        adjust();
    }
    hilite_row = max_rows - 1;
    repaint();
}
```

The home key works the same way, moving the hilite bar when it's not at the top, going to the top of the file otherwise. This is the code:

```
private void home() {

    if ( hilite_row == 0 )
        scroll_object.go( 0 );
```

```
        hilite_row = 0;
        repaint();
    }
```

The adjust( ) method asks in_lasts( ) for the location of the current record in the vector of record numbers that corresponds to the file being positioned with its last record showing in the last line of the window. A simple scan does the trick:

```
private int in_lasts( int recno ) {

    for ( int i = 0 ; i < max_rows ; i++ ) {

        if ( last_record_numbers[i] == recno )
            return i;
    }
    return -1;
}
```

The page-down and page-up routines are also new. The nonobvious part is that they move the hilite bar to the top or bottom of the screen when your file is already at the top or bottom and can't be moved. This is the code:

```
private void pgdn() {

    int rec = scroll_object.move( 0 );

    scroll_object.move( client_rows - 1 );
    adjust();

    int new_rec = scroll_object.move( 0 );
    if ( rec == new_rec )
        hilite_row = max_rows - 1;

    repaint();
}

private void pgup() {

    int rec = scroll_object.move( 0 );
    int new_rec = scroll_object.move( -client_rows );
```

```
        if ( rec == new_rec )
            hilite_row = 0;

        repaint();
    }
```

The set_lasts( ) method depends on the fact that move( ) doesn't actually move after it reaches the end of the file. Assume that move(1) reaches the last record. The next call to move(1) won't go any farther, so it stays at the same record. At the end of the file, move(0) and move(1) return the same record number.

This wouldn't be important except for the special case. In the typical case, you go(–1) to the end of the file. Then you back up one less than client_rows to get to the record showing in the top line of the window. You record this record's number in last_record_numbers[0] and loop to the end, recording the rest of the numbers.

The special case is that there may not be enough records to fill the window. In this case, you'll come to a premature end. The variable max_rows is set to some value less than client_rows when this happens.

This is one of those routines where the ALD dominate. Here's the code:

```
    private void set_lasts() {

        last_record_numbers = new int[client_rows];

        scroll_object.go( -1 );
        scroll_object.move( -(client_rows - 1) );
        int rec = scroll_object.move( 0 );
        max_rows = client_rows;

        for ( int i = 0 ; i < client_rows ; i++ ) {

            last_record_numbers[i] = rec;
            rec = scroll_object.move( 1 );
            if ( rec == last_record_numbers[i] ) {

                max_rows = i+1;
                break;
            }
        }
        scroll_object.go( 0 );
    }
```

If all those ALD get on your nerves, the up( ) routine will soothe and calm you. Try this one:

```
private void up() {

    if ( hilite_row > 0 )
        hilite_row--;
    else
        scroll_object.move( -1 );

    repaint();
}
```

The private class, scroll_canvas, is mostly the same as before. Its paint( ) method is modified to use move( ) instead of go( ). This is somewhat complicated by mystery code that I'll explain here.

The painting is done by successive calls to move( ). After paint( ) finishes the painting, it uses one more call to move( ) to back up to the position of the file before painting. The tricky part is that if the file's last row isn't reached, the final move( ) will move to the line just past the last visible line. If the last row is showing in the window, the final move(1) will really have been a move(0). In the latter case, the backward move needs to go one less record than you'd otherwise move.

Again, you can check for the end condition by looking at the record number before and after you move( ). If the record number doesn't change, you didn't really move( ). With that said, this code should make sense:

```
int old_rec;
int rec = parent.scroll_object.move( 0 );
int move_less = 0;

for ( int i = 0 ; i < parent.max_rows ; i++ ) {

    String s = parent.scroll_object.getString();
    paint_line( g, s, print_pos,
        i == parent.hilite_row );

    print_pos += parent.row_height;

    old_rec = rec;
    rec = parent.scroll_object.move( 1 );
    if ( rec == old_rec ) {
```

```
                move_less++;
                break;
            }
        }
        parent.scroll_object.move(
            -(parent.max_rows - move_less) );
    }
```

I've modified the paint_empty_line( ) method to say "<no data>" when that's the case. (The original said "<empty file>.") I've also fixed a tiny bug in the original's paint_line( ). The black box for the highlight row doesn't get to the far left in the original. That's fixed. See the full listing for the code.

The vertical elevator is set to show a tiny car in its center, since index-based scrolling doesn't have the data needed to handle this as we did for physical scrolling. (You can improve on my work here.) This is my code:

```
    private void set_vscroll() {

        if ( parent.max_rows == parent.client_rows )
            parent.vscroll.setValues( 50, 1, 0, 100 );
    }
```

After I finish this book, I'm going to think about those numbered indexes. If I can't solve that problem, I'll revisit the elevator this way: I'll use go(0) and move(i) to do exact numeric positioning in small files. For large files I'll leave it as it is now, but if the file isn't too large, we'll have the same behavior we had for numeric scrolling. A little testing should tell me how big a "large" file is, for this purpose. You might want to do something similar.

The Full ScrollWinX.java Listing

Listing 21-4 shows the full ScrollWinX.java source file.

Listing 21-4:
The index-based scroll window

```
// ScrollWinX.java -- Scrolling Window, for Indexables
// Copyright 1997, Martin L. Rinehart

// this code is completely documented in:
// _Java Database Development_, Martin Rinehart,
// Osborne/McGraw-Hill, 1997

/*
```

```
        This window will scroll anything that implements
        the ScrollableX interface.

        It will synchronize with a data databoss if an object
        that implements databoss is provided.
*/

import java.awt.*;

class ScrollWinX extends Frame {

// -------------------- data members --------------------

// public data members:

    public DataBoss databoss;

    public boolean end_app;

    public boolean refuse_close;

// protected data members:

    protected int client_height;
    protected int client_rows;
    protected int client_width;

    protected int font_height;

    protected int hilite_row;

    protected int[] last_record_numbers;
    protected int leading;

    protected int max_rows;

    protected int old_height;
    protected int old_width;

    protected int row_height;

    protected Font s_font;
```

```
    protected ScrollableX scroll_object;

    protected int top_row;

    protected Scrollbar vscroll;

// private data members:

    private scroll_canvas canvas;

    private boolean font_set = true;

    private boolean initialize;

    private boolean paint_working;

// static data members

    // there are no public static data members
    // there are no private static data members

    // final static data members:

    final static int go_home = -4;
    final static int go_prev = -3;
    final static int go_next = -2;
    final static int go_end  = -1;

// ------------------- public methods -------------------

// constructors:

    ScrollWinX( ScrollableX s ) {

        super( "Scroll Window" );

        scroll_object = s;

        vscroll = new Scrollbar(); // defaults to vertical
        vscroll.setBackground( Color.lightGray );
        add( "East", vscroll );

        canvas = new scroll_canvas( this );
```

```
        add( "Center", canvas );

        hilite_row = 0;
        initialize = true;

        databoss = null;

          resize( 500, 300 );
    }

    ScrollWinX( ScrollableX s, String title ) {

        this( s );
        setTitle( title );
    }

// there are no data access getXxx() methods
// there are no data access isXxx() methods

// data access setXxx() methods:

    public void setEndApp( boolean b ) {

        end_app = b;
    }

    public void setRefuseClose( boolean b ) {

        refuse_close = b;
    }

    public void setDataBoss ( DataBoss d ) {

        databoss = d;
    }

// public, class-specific method:

    public void goLast() {

        scroll_object.go( -1 );
    }
```

```java
    public void navigate( int where ) {

        switch ( where ) {
            case go_home:
                home();
                break;

            case go_prev:
                up();
                break;

            case go_next:
                down();
                break;

            case go_end:
                end();
                break;
        }
    }

    public void resetLast() {

        set_lasts();
          end();
    }

// public, non-event overriding methods:

    public void paint( Graphics g ) {

        if ( initialize ) {
            calc_row_height( g );
            initialize = false;
        }

        if ( paint_working ) return;
        paint_working = true;

        if ( (size().width != old_width) ||
            (size().height != old_height) ) {
```

```
                resize();
        }
        canvas.repaint();
        paint_working = false;
    }

    public String paramString() {

        return "wid: " + client_width +
            " hgt: " + client_height +
            " rows: " + client_rows;
    }

// public, event-handling method:

    public boolean handleEvent( Event e ) {

        if ( e.id == Event.WINDOW_DESTROY ) {

            if ( databoss != null ) {

                databoss.scroll_click();
                return true;
            }

            if ( refuse_close )
                return true;

            else if ( end_app )
                System.exit( 0 );

            else
                hide();

            return true;
        }

        if ( e.id == Event.KEY_ACTION )
            if ( handle_keypress(e) )
                return true;
```

```
        if ( e.id == Event.SCROLL_LINE_UP ) {
            up();
            return true;
        }

        if ( e.id == Event.SCROLL_LINE_DOWN ) {
            down();
            return true;
        }

        if ( e.id == Event.SCROLL_PAGE_UP ) {
            pgup();
            return true;
        }

        if ( e.id == Event.SCROLL_PAGE_DOWN ) {
            pgdn();
            return true;
        }

        if ( e.id == Event.SCROLL_ABSOLUTE ) {

            repaint();
            return true;
        }

        return super.handleEvent( e );
    }

// ------------------- private methods -------------------

// private methods:

    private void adjust() {

        int where = scroll_object.move( 0 );
        int adj = in_lasts( where );

        scroll_object.move( -adj );
    }
```

```java
private void calc_row_height( Graphics g ) {

    String font_name;
    font_name = scroll_object.useMonospace() ?
        "Courier" : "Helvetica";

    Font f = g.getFont();
    g.setFont( new Font(font_name,
        /* f.getStyle() */ Font.PLAIN, f.getSize() ) );
    s_font = g.getFont();

    font_height = s_font.getSize();
    leading = ( font_height + 3 ) / 5;
    row_height = font_height + leading;
}

private void down() {

    if ( hilite_row < client_rows - 1 ) {
        hilite_row++;
        if ( hilite_row > (max_rows-1) )
            hilite_row--;
        repaint();
        return;
    }

    scroll_object.move( 1 );
    adjust();
    repaint();


}

private void end() {

    if ( hilite_row >= max_rows - 1 ) {

        scroll_object.go( -1 );
        adjust();
    }
    hilite_row = max_rows - 1;
```

```
        repaint();
    }

    private boolean handle_keypress( Event e ) {

        switch (e.key) {

            case Event.UP:
                up();
                return true;

            case Event.DOWN:
                down();
                return true;

            case Event.PGUP:
                pgup();
                return true;

            case Event.PGDN:
                pgdn();
                return true;

            case Event.HOME:
                home();
                return true;

            case Event.END:
                end();
                return true;
        }
        return false;
    }

    private void home() {

        if ( hilite_row == 0 )
            scroll_object.go( 0 );

        hilite_row = 0;
        repaint();
    }
```

```
    private int in_lasts( int recno ) {

        for ( int i = 0 ; i < max_rows ; i++ ) {

            if ( last_record_numbers[i] == recno )
                return i;
        }
        return -1;
    }

    private void pgdn() {

        int rec = scroll_object.move( 0 );

        scroll_object.move( client_rows - 1 );
        adjust();

        int new_rec = scroll_object.move( 0 );
        if ( rec == new_rec )
            hilite_row = max_rows - 1;

        repaint();
    }

    private void pgup() {

        int rec = scroll_object.move( 0 );
        int new_rec = scroll_object.move( -client_rows );

        if ( rec == new_rec )
            hilite_row = 0;

        repaint();
    }

    private void resize() {

        client_height = size().height - insets().top -
            insets().bottom;

// client area is laid out:
//    text
```

```
//   [ leading
//     text ] . . .
//     leading

        // round to integral # of rows:
        if ( client_height < row_height)
            client_rows = 1;
        else
            client_rows = client_height / row_height;

        if ( hilite_row >= client_rows )
            hilite_row = client_rows - 1;

        client_height = row_height * client_rows;

        resize( size().width, client_height +
            insets().top + insets().bottom );

        old_width = size().width;
        old_height = size().height;

        set_lasts();

        if ( max_rows == client_rows )
            vscroll.show();
        else
            vscroll.hide();

        client_width = size().width - insets().left -
            insets().right -
            ( vscroll.isVisible() ?
                vscroll.size().width : 0 );
    }

    private void set_lasts() {

        last_record_numbers = new int[client_rows];

        scroll_object.go( -1 );
        scroll_object.move( -(client_rows - 1) );
        int rec = scroll_object.move( 0 );
        max_rows = client_rows;
```

```
        for ( int i = 0 ; i < client_rows ; i++ ) {

            last_record_numbers[i] = rec;
            rec = scroll_object.move( 1 );
            if ( rec == last_record_numbers[i] ) {

                max_rows = i+1;
                break;
            }
        }
        scroll_object.go( 0 );
    }

    private void up() {

        if ( hilite_row > 0 )
            hilite_row--;
        else
            scroll_object.move( -1 );

        repaint();
    }

} // end of ScrollWinX class

// private class in ScrollWinX.java:

class scroll_canvas extends Canvas {

// there are no public data members

// protected data member:

    protected ScrollWinX parent;

// constructor:

    scroll_canvas( ScrollWinX sw ) {
        parent = sw;
    }

// public, non-event overriding method:
```

```java
public void paint( Graphics g ) {

    if ( parent.max_rows == -1 ) {

        paint_empty_line( g );
        return;
    }

    g.setFont( parent.s_font );
    if ( parent.vscroll.isShowing() ) set_vscroll();

    boolean filled =
        parent.max_rows == parent.client_rows;

    if ( (!filled) && (parent.hilite_row >
        ( parent.max_rows - 1 )) )
            if ( parent.client_rows > 0 )
                parent.hilite_row =
                    parent.max_rows - 1;

    int print_pos = parent.font_height;

    int old_rec;
    int rec = parent.scroll_object.move( 0 );
    int move_less = 0;

    for ( int i = 0 ; i < parent.max_rows ; i++ ) {

        String s = parent.scroll_object.getString();
        paint_line( g, s, print_pos,
            i == parent.hilite_row );

        print_pos += parent.row_height;

        old_rec = rec;
        rec = parent.scroll_object.move( 1 );
        if ( rec == old_rec ) {

            move_less++;
            break;
        }
```

```
        }
        parent.scroll_object.move(
            -(parent.max_rows - move_less) );
    }

// public, event-handling method:

    public boolean handleEvent( Event e ) {

        if ( e.id == Event.MOUSE_DOWN ) {
            handle_click( e );
            return true;
        }

          if ( (parent.databoss != null) &&
                (e.id == Event.WINDOW_DESTROY) ) {

                parent.databoss.scroll_click();
                return true;
            }
        return super.handleEvent( e );
    }

// private methods:

    private void handle_click( Event e ) {

        parent.hilite_row = what_row( e.y );

        if ( parent.hilite_row > parent.max_rows )
            parent.hilite_row = parent.max_rows;

        repaint();
    }

    private void paint_empty_line( Graphics g ) {

        g.drawString( "<no data>", 1,

                parent.font_height );
    }
```

```
    private void paint_line( Graphics g, String s,
        int print_pos, boolean hilite ) {

        if ( hilite ) {

/*          if ( parent.databoss != null )
                parent.databoss.setRecord( recno ); */

            g.setColor( Color.black );
            g.fillRect(
                0,
                print_pos + parent.leading -
                    parent.row_height,
                parent.client_width,
                parent.row_height );
            g.setColor( Color.white );
        }
        else {
            g.setColor( Color.black );
        }

        g.drawString( s, 1, print_pos );
    }

    private void set_vscroll() {

        if ( parent.max_rows == parent.client_rows )
            parent.vscroll.setValues( 50, 1, 0, 100 );
    }

    private int what_row( int y ) {

        while ( parent.row_height == 0 )
            Thread.yield();

        return ( y + 1 ) / parent.row_height;
    }

} // end of scroll_canvas

class DataBoss  {
```

```
        void scroll_click() {}
        void setRecord( int i ) {}
}

// end of ScrollWinX.java
```

Summary

Database systems normally require their tables to be indexed on multiple criteria. A person file might be indexed on last name, name of employer, country or state, and so on. Our systems will normally want to scroll through the data based on one of the index orders. For this, we need a different sort of scrolling window.

The difference is that scrolling by index can't be done by absolute position. With a B-tree index, your positioning can only be absolute for the first and last records (or for a record you find by key). Other positioning is done by moving relative to the current position.

For driving the test projects, I've supplied a RandNames class. It starts with a list of about 50 real names and then generates random names. The first 50 names are almost in alphabetical order, which makes it very useful, for example, for inserting out-of-order names precisely where they will force splits in the B-tree nodes. It also lets you change the size of your test "file" without the trouble of actually changing a file.

We looked at ScrollNDX, the mainline program that creates our index-based scroller. It's one step longer than a physical-order scroll. You create the Indexable and pass it to the NDX constructor. It's the NDX, which now implements ScrollableX, that is passed to the ScrollWinX. The rest is the same, and it's still very simple.

We took a deeper look at using the ScrollWinX in the next section. The minimum constructor takes an object that is ScrollableX. If you're not in too big a hurry, you can add another parameter to supply a title for the scroll window. Calls to setEndApp( ) or setRefuseClose( ) adjust behavior when the user clicks the close button. A resize( ) is usually needed, also, before you show( ) the scroll window.

For those who want to improve my code, such as by adding a DataBoss or by improving the vertical scroll bar, we went on to look at the new code. Scrolling by relative positions is mostly simpler than scrolling by absolute positions.

We didn't look at the NDX class, which is one of the main subjects of our next, final chapter. In Chapter 22 we're going to take a look at objects, fast. It's both a fast look at objects, and a long look at making our databases fast.

Chapter 22

Object Databases, Very Fast

With the addition of indexes and the ability to scroll through our data in index order, we've got the basic tools needed to handle relational data. What you may not have noticed is that we've also got the tools we need to store objects. If you did any high-volume testing, you saw that what we don't yet have are high-speed indexes, in spite of the performance gains that intranode binary searching promised. In this chapter we're going to take a brief look at storing objects, and then we're going to focus on making our object stores go very, very fast.

We'll begin with a look at object storage. You'll see that tables with attached variable-length storage work perfectly for objects. The DBF and the HeapFile combine to handle objects gracefully. The NDX, combined with the ScrollWinX, lets us handle objects in the variety of orders that real systems require.

But as written, the NDX B-trees aren't fast enough for serious use. The first thing I did to speed up my objects was to get control over the disk I/O, courtesy of the BinFileXO (Binary File, eXtended for Objects). When you use stream I/O, you have no idea how many actual disk reads and writes you're triggering. The BinFileXO class uses stream I/O (and Java's convenient methods, like readInt( ) and writeInt( ) for integers) in RAM buffers. It uses fast, random file I/O to actually read and write the buffers. You get total control over the disk I/O.

As convenient as the BinFileXO class is, there's a major additional speed improvement available from simply eliminating the bulk of the stream I/O. I converted the Btree_node to providing function-only access to its data. This makes the B-trees start to come alive, as we'll see when we take another look at the Btree_node class.

My final speed improvement was to add a disk-buffering scheme that drastically cuts the total number of disk reads and writes. We'll take another look at NDX, which now extends BinFileXO. You'll see the new file-buffering machinery and the implementation of the ScrollableX interface, which we discussed in Chapter 21.

Let's begin with our fast look at objects and tables.

Tables Are Object Tools

Our tables work very well for storing most of the data members in objects. First, we'll look at storing data members as the same as storing objects. Then we'll consider some problems, such as when you use objects as data members in other objects, and when you have arrays for data members. Finally, I'll add some thoughts on when to use normalized design and when to use the HeapFile to eliminate tables.

Storing Data Is Storing Objects

Objects combine data and code, according to everything I've read about objects. That's the theory, at least. When a theory departs too far from reality, however, you'd better scrap the theory.

In languages like C++ and Java, classes supply the code. Objects don't have code. Objects have data. The code is stored in .class files, managed cooperatively by the Java Virtual Machine and the underlying operating system. (For simplicity, from now on we'll just credit this joint work to the JVM.)

The objects are instantiated in RAM. They aren't stored on disk at all. They're transitory. To make an object *persistent* (to have its life span exceed the life of a single run of the application), you need to store its data members before the application terminates. If the next run of the application reloads the data members from their disk storage, you'll have reinstantiated the same object. The code will again be available, courtesy of the JVM.

Did I say "reinstantiated the same object"? That's not true, of course. You'll have a brand-new object that happens to have the same data members as the former object. But if you have the same data members, acted on by the same methods, there'll be no way to tell the difference between the new object and the old one. For all practical purposes, we'll be using one object that appears to live from one run to the next.

DBFs Store Data Members

Do you want to convert DBF storage to OBF (object base files) storage? Just change all occurrences of "DBF" to "OBF" and you're done. There's no need to change anything else.

Just as the class provides the template for the object, the DBF's header provides the template (field definitions) for the record. If you prefer pure object storage, let me rephrase that: the OBF's header provides the template (data member definitions) for the object.

You have to handle the mapping of Java data types to DBF storage. The simplest method is to write numbers into the DBF's fixed-point, ASCII representations. Write two functions: toValues( ) and fromValues( ). These convert the object's data members to and from fixed-length Strings that correspond to the field definitions (oops!—to the data member definitions) of the DBF.

You can add any data types to the DBF that are more convenient, of course. But don't even think about writing binary numbers until you've finished this chapter.

The one data type that appears to be difficult at first is the object data member. When you begin to store objects, there's a tendency to forget the principles of database design. Resist it!

A separate object class gets a separate table. If your Big object has a member of type Embed, create one table for Big objects and another for Embed objects. Remember to have a primary key as the first field in each table. After you store Embed in its table, store the primary key of Embed as a data item in the Big table. You can call it a "persistent object reference," if you like. Old-timers (like me) will probably just call it a "foreign key." It means the same.

Of course, that brings us to arrays. Anything that's variable in length can be handled by attaching a HeapFile. You store the data in the HeapFile, and you store the HeapFile pointer in the data table. But that's not always a good idea.

Use, Don't Abuse, HeapFile Storage

In relational database design, the data isn't in first-normal form if there are repeating fields. The sale record, for example, cannot embed zero or more detail records. The detail records are put in a table of their own.

With objects, there's no need for a separate table. Courtesy of the HeapFile, you can store the array data *in situ* in the object table. (Well, at least it will seem like it's *in situ*. It will really be in the HeapFile.)

That's normally a bad idea, however. For example, the sale detail records have a product key (oops!—make that a "product persistent object reference"), the number of items ordered, and other data. The sale detail records are very handy for inquiries into the number of widgets you have sold.

You could put the sale detail array directly into the object record. (May I speak of it that way, though it's really in an attached HeapFile entry?) Having that array in the object record makes it easier to generate an invoice. It makes it easier, for another example, to find all the widgets you sold to Fred.

But it makes it considerably more difficult to just count the total widgets that you've sold. Clean, normalized design pays off here.

Let's think about another example. Your history detail tables could be embedded in the records for whatever objects need the histories. Your product record, for example, could contain product price history arrays.

The history detail table in a normalized design will have a foreign key identifying the associated product, an effective date, and the price. The fact that the only foreign key is the key of the associated product suggests that this data won't be accessed from other dimensions, so it might be included in the product object's record.

On the other hand, you might find that you'll want to add a memo-type field that lets you add descriptive information about the price change. If the data is normalized (with a separate history table), this is simple. If the array is embedded in the object, then you're getting HeapFile data that, among other things, has pointers to other HeapFile data. Does that sound like simple, elegant software?

Nine times out of ten, I use the normalized design. On the occasions that I don't normalize, about nine times out of ten I regret it later.

If you switch from relational to object storage by switching your jargon, you'll do well. Don't let the added flexibility of objects talk you into changing the principles of good database design. Keep the design the same. Just change the jargon.

That's our brief tour of object storage. Now we're ready to start talking about fast object storage.

BinFileXO

You did notice, didn't you, that the NDX is a true object store? After a header record, the NDX holds Btree_node objects. They're neatly cross-referenced internally by a nonstandard but invaluable system that achieves the B-tree's aims. Still, they're objects, and we're storing them on disk.

When I tested my original NDXes on medium-sized data sets, they ground to a halt pretty quickly. I was storing objects, but not very efficiently. It didn't take too long to figure out what the problem was.

Disk I/O by the Block

Our code calls nice methods like

```
node.read()
node.write()
```

At an outside level, these calls look like they trigger actual disk I/O. One reads a node and the other writes the node, right?

The problem is that they only have the appearance of doing a single read or write. There's no way to know how many reads and writes you're getting. Internally, the write( ) method has lines like this:

```
writeInt( this_int );
writeInt( that_int );
writeBytes( some_String );
```

What does that translate into in terms of disk writes? Will that all happen in one buffered write? Or do those three lines trigger three disk writes? (Or worse, are we actually doing a disk write for every byte?) You don't know. If you drop your whole JVM into a heavy-duty debugger and trace down to the bottom, you'll know exactly how one version of one JVM implementation works. You won't know how the next upgrade will work.

On the other hand, if you write your own file I/O, you'll know exactly how it works. This is just what I did.

I wanted to preserve the convenience of stream I/O calls, but use RandomAccessFile byte array reads and writes. (I'm assuming here that the latter reads and writes full arrays, with minor adjustments allowing for the native file system's buffering. This seems to be true in practice.)

Using the BinFileXO

For this purpose, the BinFileXO was created. It has calls like

- readInt( )
- readBytes( )

- writeInt( )
- writeBytes( )

These work like standard stream I/O. But they work in RAM, on byte arrays. When you want the buffers to go to or from disk, you use these calls:

- readPage( )
- writePage( )

These read or write the entire byte array, using the RandomAccessFile to do the I/O. They also reinitialize the associated buffer pointers so that you'll start reading from or writing to the start of the new buffer.

The only constraint is that you need to pick a fixed page size. For some applications, such as our NDX, this is no problem.

To create a BinFile, you have three choices:

- BinFileXO(String pathname)
- BinFileXO(String pathname, String access)
- BinFileXO(String pathname, String access, int size)

The default access is "r", as always. The default page size is 16K.

There are separate buffers for input and output. You read the input buffer this way:

```
readPage( int address );
```

The address should be a multiple of the page size. It doesn't have to be, but using anything else is strictly for the brave and foolish.

Reading a page sets the input pointer to the start of the buffer. You read from the buffer with these methods:

- int i = readInt( );
- String s readBytes(int length);

Each read advances the input pointer to point to the next byte past the data read.

Why are there just two read methods? There is a defined interface in the java.io package, DataInput. It specifies a read method for each Java native data type. The BinFileXO doesn't implement the DataInput interface, obviously. There are two reasons.

First, implementing the full interface would change this from a small class to a large one. I like small. Second, as you'll see when we get to the "Understanding" section, implementing another Java data type is dead simple. You'd copy readInt( ), edit its name and types, and you'd be in business with a new type. We leave all the real work to java.io's DataInputStream class. The DataInputStream implements DataInput, so all the methods you need are there. It's just a matter of calling them.

The output is the mirror image. You write into the output buffer with:

- writeInt(int i)
- writeBytes(String s)

Each write advances the output pointer to the byte just past the write.

When you want the buffer to be written to disk, you call

writePage(address)

Again, the address should be a multiple of the page size. The actual write will write the whole buffer, which is a byte array exactly as long as the page size.

BinFileXO extends BinFile, so you can also call BinFile methods. (See Chapter 4 for BinFile documentation.)

Does that sound straightforward?

Understanding the BinFileXO Class

TOUR

This time I'm inviting everyone to come along for the whole ride. The BinFileXO is about an order of magnitude faster than straight stream I/O, and it's just as simple to use.

But you won't find it useful if you can't pop in the additional Java data types that you find necessary for your application. You'll see how this is done when you look at the public methods.

After you've seen how to do it, the tour will be over. There aren't any private methods.

Before we get started, let me give you the overview. The BinFileXO is built on separate byte arrays to buffer input and output. These are used to create ByteArrayInputStream and ByteArrayOutputStream objects. Those objects, in turn, are used to create DataInputStreams and DataOutputStreams that actually support the stream I/O.

Does this sound a bit complex? Actually, I've already made a serious misstatement in the interest of keeping things simple. You'll see the actual truth when we start working with the DataInputStream and DataOutputStream objects. As we do the work, I'll explain the principles. It's another one of those things that's easier to do than to explain.

Let's begin at the beginning, with these two lines:

```
import java.io.*;

class BinFileXO extends BinFile {
```

We need to import the full java.io package (not java.awt, for once). We're extending our BinFile, which will hide all the ALD of actually working with the file.

The protected data members are these:

```
protected ByteArrayInputStream bytes_is;
protected ByteArrayOutputStream bytes_os;

protected byte[] buffer_in;
protected byte[] buffer_out;
protected int buffer_size;

protected DataInputStream data_is;
protected DataOutputStream data_os;
```

I'll explain each of these as we come to it. The other data member is the constant 16K, the default buffer size:

```
final static int BUFSIZE = 16 * 1024;
```

The full listing shows a mainline, commented out, that you can use for testing. There are three constructors. The first two simply add the default values "r" and BUFSIZE if you don't provide explicit overrides. We'll begin with the real constructor, which begins by exiting if the extended BinFile didn't succeed in opening the underlying file, this way:

```
BinFileXO( String pathname, String access, int size ) {

    super( pathname, access );

    if ( access.equals("rw") &&
        (! writeable) )
            return;

    if ( !readable )
        return;
```

Next it stores your page size and creates buffers:

```
buffer_size = size;

buffer_in = new byte[buffer_size];
buffer_out = new byte[buffer_size];
```

The ByteArrayInputStream lets you pass it a buffer. It uses this buffer internally. The ByteArrayOutputStream must have been written by a different programmer. It takes a size and creates its own buffer. (Our buffer_out array will be useful later.) Our ByteArray variables are initialized this way:

```
bytes_is = new ByteArrayInputStream( buffer_in );
bytes_os =
    new ByteArrayOutputStream( buffer_size );
```

Finally, we use the ByteArray objects to create the DataInputStream and the DataOutputStream that implement DataInput and DataOutput, respectively. This part is easy:

```
data_is = new DataInputStream( bytes_is );
data_os = new DataOutputStream( bytes_os );
```

The last step is to point to the start of both buffers, which is done this way:

```
reset();
```

Next we'll look at the public, class-specific methods. When we're done with these, we're done with the class.

The first is readBytes( ), which illustrates an important point. BinFileXO assumes that you'll read and write your own buffers correctly. It ignores the possibility of an IOException being thrown. (Remember, this is the RAM-based read. The constructor has already found the necessary buffer space.)

The readBytes( ) method creates a byte array of the appropriate length, reads into it from the DataInputStream, and then uses it to create a String. This is the code:

```
public String readBytes( int len ) {

    byte[] b = new byte[len];
```

```
    try { data_is.read( b ); }
    catch ( IOException ioe ) {}

    return new String( b, 0 );
}
```

Did that one look simple? Reading an integer is even simpler. I'd omit it altogether, but for one very important fact. Look at the code first:

```
public int readInt() {

    int i = 0;

    try { i = data_is.readInt(); }
    catch ( IOException ioe ) {}

    return i;
}
```

The important fact is that if you want to read almost any of the other Java data types, you copy this routine and then change "Int" to "Float," "Double," "Char," or whatever. Change the type of i and you're done. If you're feeling particularly diligent, you might change i to some letter appropriate to the type you're handling. We're talking about a minute's worth of work, all told.

There are two ReadPage methods. One is the simple one I pointed out in the "Using" section. The other lets you read directly into your own buffer, which is how Btree_node pages are read. Both throw IOException. (This is real disk I/O. You can't ignore the possibility of exceptions here.) This is the code:

```
public void readPage( int loc, byte[] buffer )
    throws IOException {

    raf.seek( loc );
    raf.read( buffer );
}

public void readPage( int loc ) throws IOException {

    raf.seek( loc );
    raf.read( buffer_in );
```

```
            bytes_is.reset();
    }
```

The reset( ) method resets the DataInputStream and the ByteArrayOutputStream. Resetting the latter has the effect of resetting the DataOutputStream. This is the method:

```
    public void reset() {

        try {

            data_is.reset();
            bytes_os.reset();
        }
        catch ( IOException ioe ) {}
    }
```

Are you beginning to agree that DataInputStream and DataOutputStream were written by separate programmers? They didn't even seem to talk to each other.

The seek( ) routine discards the IOException that the underlying RandomAccessFile method can throw. It's simple:

```
    public void seek( int loc ) {

        try { raf.seek( loc ); }
        catch ( IOException ioe ) {}
    }
```

Stream writing is even easier than stream reading. This is the String write:

```
    public void writeBytes( String s ) {

        try { data_os.writeBytes(s); }
        catch ( IOException ioe ) {}
    }
```

Integers are just as simple. Again, this is the one you'll have to edit to handle additional primitive types. Think you're up to it?

```
public void writeInt( int i ) {

    try { data_os.writeInt(i); }
    catch ( IOException ioe ) {}
}
```

Now, do you remember that data output buffer? We'll use it here. The DataOutputStream programmer didn't think that we'd like to access the internal byte array directly, which annoys me. The ByteArrayOutputStream will hand out a byte array, if you ask it to, however. This does that job:

```
public void writePage( int loc ) throws IOException {

    raf.seek( loc );

    byte[] b = bytes_os.toByteArray();
```

I copy that array into buffer_out, being careful not to go past buffer_size. (The DataOutputStream will expand the buffer indefinitely as you write more data.) This does the copy:

```
System.arraycopy( b, 0, buffer_out, 0,
    b.length < buffer_size ?
        b.length : buffer_size );
```

Finally, we write the output buffer to the RandomAccessFile and reset the ByteArrayOutputStream:

```
raf.write( buffer_out );

bytes_os.reset();
```

The final method is a writePage( ) that lets you write your own buffer. You'll see how the Btree_node class uses this to advantage. It's simple:

```
public void writePage( int loc, byte[] buffer )
    throws IOException {
```

```
        raf.seek( loc );
        raf.write( buffer );
    }
```

The Full BinFileXO Listing

Listing 22-1 shows the full BinFileXO.java source file.

Listing 22-1:
RAM-based
streams with
buffered I/O

```
// BinFileXO.java -- Binary File, eXtended for Objects
// Copyright 1997, Martin L. Rinehart

// this code is completely documented in:
// _Java Database Development_, Martin Rinehart,
// Osborne/McGraw-Hill, 1997

/*
    Does stream I/O within pages; reads/writes
    whole pages to random underlying file.
*/

import java.io.*;

class BinFileXO extends BinFile {

// -------------------- data members --------------------

// there are no public data members

// protected data members:

    protected ByteArrayInputStream bytes_is;
    protected ByteArrayOutputStream bytes_os;

    protected byte[] buffer_in;
    protected byte[] buffer_out;
    protected int buffer_size;

    protected DataInputStream data_is;
    protected DataOutputStream data_os;
```

```
// static data members
    // there are no public static data members
    // there are no private static data members
    // final static data member:

    final static int BUFSIZE = 16 * 1024;

// ------------------- public methods --------------------

    /*
        public static void main( String[] args ) {

            BinFileXO xo = new BinFileXO(
                "test.dat", "rw", 16 );

            for ( int i = 0 ; i < 10 ; i++ ) {

                xo.writeInt( i );
                xo.writeBytes( "A B C D " );
                xo.writeInt( i << 4 );

                try { xo.writePage( i * 16 ); }
                catch ( IOException ioe ) {}
            }

            for ( int i = 0 ; i < 10 ; i++ ) {

                try { xo.readPage( i * 16 ); }
                catch ( IOException ioe ) {}

                int i1 = xo.readInt();
                String s = xo.readBytes( 8 );
                int i2 = xo.readInt();
                System.out.println( i + ": " +
                    i1 + " " + s + " " + i2 );
            }

            ScrollWin sw = new ScrollWin( xo, "test.dat" );
            sw.resize( 520, 300 );
            sw.setEndApp( true );
            sw.show();
        }
```

```
    // */

// constructors:

    BinFileXO( String pathname ) {

        this( pathname, "r", BUFSIZE );
    }

    BinFileXO( String pathname, String access ) {

        this( pathname, access, BUFSIZE );
    }

    BinFileXO( String pathname, String access, int size ) {

        super( pathname, access );

        if ( access.equals("rw") &&
            (! writeable) )
                return;

        if ( !readable )
            return;

        buffer_size = size;

        buffer_in = new byte[buffer_size];
        buffer_out = new byte[buffer_size];

        bytes_is = new ByteArrayInputStream( buffer_in );
        bytes_os =
            new ByteArrayOutputStream( buffer_size );

        data_is = new DataInputStream( bytes_is );
        data_os = new DataOutputStream( bytes_os );

        reset();
    }

// there are no data access methods
```

```java
// public, class-specific methods:

    public String readBytes( int len ) {

        byte[] b = new byte[len];

        try { data_is.read( b ); }
        catch ( IOException ioe ) {}

        return new String( b, 0 );
    }

    public int readInt() {

        int i = 0;

        try { i = data_is.readInt(); }
        catch ( IOException ioe ) {}

        return i;
    }

    public void readPage( int loc, byte[] buffer )
        throws IOException {

        raf.seek( loc );
        raf.read( buffer );
    }

    public void readPage( int loc ) throws IOException {

        raf.seek( loc );
        raf.read( buffer_in );
        bytes_is.reset();
    }

    public void reset() {

        try {

            data_is.reset();
            bytes_os.reset();
```

```
        }
        catch ( IOException ioe ) {}
    }

    public void seek( int loc ) {

        try { raf.seek( loc ); }
        catch ( IOException ioe ) {}
    }

    public void writeBytes( String s ) {

        try { data_os.writeBytes(s); }
        catch ( IOException ioe ) {}
    }

    public void writeInt( int i ) {

        try { data_os.writeInt(i); }
        catch ( IOException ioe ) {}
    }

    public void writePage( int loc ) throws IOException {

        raf.seek( loc );

        byte[] b = bytes_os.toByteArray();
        System.arraycopy( b, 0, buffer_out, 0,
            b.length < buffer_size ?
                b.length : buffer_size );
        raf.write( buffer_out );

        bytes_os.reset();
    }

    public void writePage( int loc, byte[] buffer )
        throws IOException {

        raf.seek( loc );
        raf.write( buffer );
    }
```

```
// public, non-event overriding method:

    public String paramString() {

        return "BinFileXO";
    }

// there are no public, event-handling methods

// ------------------ private methods ------------------
// there are no private methods

} // end of BinFileXO class

// there are no private classes in BinFileXO.java

// end of BinFileXO.java
```

Btree_node

After I had written BinFileXO, I converted the NDX and Btree_node classes to using it. The performance improved by about an order of magnitude. It still wasn't close to acceptable, however. It took almost 59 seconds to reindex a 2K record table using an 8K index page.

So I timed the different activities, putting in lots of calls to System.currentTimeMillis( ) to record the amount of time spent on the various functions. Guess what? The most expensive process was the stream I/O, even though it was strictly in RAM. In the above example, disk writes took 1,240 milliseconds, while the stream I/O took 27,490 milliseconds.

It seemed that Java was continuing the grand C++ tradition of abysmal stream I/O performance. To check, I wrote my own routine for converting an integer to and from a big-endian, four-byte array. Then I timed 100,000 iterations of converting to and from the array, both with my code and with stream I/O.

The result was ridiculous. My pure Java was five times faster than Sun's work. They should have been working in C++ and assembler to implement the JVM. The Intel chip has a special instruction that makes endian conversions blaze. It seems Sun was working in Java, and not in very good Java, at that. (Sun's work is still mostly great.)

Then I began to think about the process. Unless some higher-level routine calls for a record number, the NDX will go through life without needing any access to the array of record numbers. It writes to this array when it inserts the value and then ignores it. At the upper level, most of the pointers aren't needed most of the time. Why was I putting these values into arrays?

The answer, of course, was that I put them into arrays because arrays are handy structures. They're convenient. But since I had it all working, it seemed like using function access to read the byte array could save lots of conversions. Using my own conversion would save some of the remaining time.

So I converted from array access to function access. It worked beautifully. The disk I/O times weren't changed, but the stream I/O time went to near zero. The NDX was getting to the point where it was capable of real work on real data tables.

Understanding the Btree_node Class

TOUR

This "Understanding" section will be brief, and it will show you how to save about an order of magnitude in your own I/O if you use stream techniques. If you never read or write to streams, however, you can skip this section.

Again, there's no "Using" section here because the NDX class is the only user. This section will quickly hit the changes from the version of this class that we covered in Chapter 19.

The data members are the same, except that the arrays for keys, pointers, and record numbers have been deleted. The constructors are unchanged. The public getXxxx methods are new. The first two are straightforward:

```
public String getKey( int key_num ) {

    return new String( data_buffer, 0,
        loc_key(key_num), key_length );
}

public int getLeftPointer() {

    if ( is_upper_node )
        return getPointer( 0 );
    else
        return -1;
}
```

The getKey( ) method is used to replace the old array access with function access. The same is true of pointers and record numbers, as these examples show:

```
old:   node.keys[i]            new: node.getKeys( i )
       node.pointers[0]             node.getPointers( 0 )
```

The getLeftPointer( ) and getRightPointer( ) methods make the code that navigates in the B-tree much more readable, as you'll see in the NDX class.

The other getXxxx( ) methods rely on loc_xxx( ) private methods to translate a number into a location in the data buffer. This is representative:

```
public int getPointer( int ptr_num ) {

    return bytes2int( data_buffer, loc_ptr(ptr_num) );
}
```

Data is assigned via equivalent set( ) methods. This one is typical:

```
public void setPointer( int ptr_num, int ptr ) {

    fillBytes( data_buffer, loc_ptr(ptr_num), ptr );
}
```

Except that array accesses have been replaced by calls to these get( ) and set( ) methods, the other public methods are unchanged. See the full listing for the details.

When we split nodes, we used System.arraycopy( ) to move keys, pointers, and record numbers from one node to another. These have been replaced by calls to move( ) methods that move the bytes from one node's data buffer to another node's buffer. This one is representative:

```
public void move_pointers( int from,
    Btree_node dst_node, int to, int len ) {

    System.arraycopy( data_buffer, loc_ptr(from),
        dst_node.data_buffer, loc_ptr(to), len * 4 );
}
```

We also used System.arraycopy( ) to shift data items within a single node. These have been replaced by the shift( ) methods, which operate directly on the data buffer. This is typical:

```
public void shift_keys( int from, int to, int len ) {

    System.arraycopy( data_buffer, loc_key(from),
        data_buffer, loc_key(to), len*key_length );
}
```

The write_node( ) method is dramatically different. It uses fillBytes( ) to write integers into Java-approved, big-endian byte buffers. Then it uses the BinFileXO's writePage( ) service to write its own buffer. This is the code:

```
public void write_node() throws IndexException {

    if ( address == -1 )
        address = parent.file_length;

    fillBytes( data_buffer,  0, key_length );
    fillBytes( data_buffer,  4, node_length );
    fillBytes( data_buffer,  8, node_size );
    fillBytes( data_buffer, 12, number_of_keys );
    fillBytes( data_buffer, 16,
        is_upper_node ? 1 : 0 );

    try {

        parent.writePage( address, data_buffer );
    }
    catch ( IOException ioe ) {

        throw new IndexException( ioe.getMessage() +
            " (while writing index node)" );
    }
}
```

Many private methods are unchanged or substantially similar. The first change I'll note is that compute_node_size( ) records key_start, pointer_start, and record_number_start as it lays out the node. These ints record the starting location for their respective values in the data buffer. These are used in the three loc( ) methods, of which loc_key( ) is typical:

```
private int loc_key( int num ) {

    return key_start + ( num * key_length );
}
```

Finally, static methods have been added that actually do the big-endian conversion. The first reads an integer from the data buffer:

```
private static int bytes2int( byte[] b, int start ) {

    int i3 = ( (0x000000FF & b[start  ]) << 24 );
    int i2 = ( (0x000000FF & b[start+1]) << 16 );
    int i1 = ( (0x000000FF & b[start+2]) <<  8 );
    int i0 = (   0x000000FF & b[start+3]        );

    return i0 + i1 + i2 + i3;
}
```

I timed several versions of this method. The one you see here (did you notice the funny reverse order of those variable names?) was fastest. I quit doing these tests when I remembered that I was testing just one particular compiler, not Java.

The companion method, fillBytes( ), writes an integer into the buffer. This is the code:

```
static void fillBytes( byte[] b, int start,
    int value ) {

    b[start]   = (byte) ( value >>> 24 );
    b[start+1] = (byte) ( value >>> 16 );
    b[start+2] = (byte) ( value >>>  8 );
    b[start+3] = (byte) ( value        );
}
```

You did remember that the ">>>" operator does a logical shift (inserts zeros on the left, regardless of sign) didn't you?

The Full Btree_node.java Listing

Listing 22-2 is the full Btree_node.java source file.

Listing 22-2:
Btree_nodes
without
stream I/O

```
// Btree_node.java -- B-tree nodes
// Copyright 1997, Martin L. Rinehart

// this code is completely documented in:
// _Java Database Development_, Martin Rinehart,
// Osborne/McGraw-Hill, 1997

import java.io.*;

class Btree_node extends Object {

// -------------------- data members --------------------

// there are no public data members

// protected data members

    protected int address;

    protected byte[] data_buffer;

    protected boolean is_upper_node;

    protected int key_length;
    protected int key_start;

    protected int node_length;  // in bytes
    protected int node_size;     // max # of keys
    protected int number_of_keys;

    protected int pad_size;
    protected String padding;
    protected NDX parent;
    protected int pointer_start;

    protected int record_number_start;

// static data member:

    final static int OVERHEAD = 32;
```

```java
// ------------------- public methods -------------------

// constructors:

    Btree_node( int address, int key_length,
            int node_length, NDX parent, boolean is_upper )
            throws IndexException {

        this.address = address;
        this.key_length = key_length;
        this.node_length = node_length;
        this.parent = parent;
        is_upper_node = is_upper;

        compute_node_size();

        data_buffer = new byte[parent.page_size];

        byte[] b = new byte[key_length];
        for ( int i = 0 ; i < key_length ; i++ )
            b[i] = (byte) ' ';

        String blank_key = new String( b, 0 );
        for ( int i = 0 ; i < node_size ; i++ ) {

            setKey( i, blank_key );
            setRecordNumber( i, -1 );
        }

        if ( is_upper_node )
            for ( int i = 0 ; i <= node_size ; i++ )
                setPointer( i, -1 );
    }

    Btree_node( int address, NDX parent )
        throws IndexException {

        this.parent = parent;
        this.address = address;
        data_buffer = new byte[parent.page_size];
        read_node();
        compute_node_size();
```

```
    }

// data access methods:

// data access getXxxx() methods:

    public String getKey( int key_num ) {

        return new String( data_buffer, 0,
            loc_key(key_num), key_length );
    }

    public int getLeftPointer() {

        if ( is_upper_node )
            return getPointer( 0 );
        else
            return -1;
    }

    public int getPointer( int ptr_num ) {

        return bytes2int( data_buffer, loc_ptr(ptr_num) );
    }

    public int getRecordNumber( int rec_num ) {

        return bytes2int( data_buffer, loc_rec(rec_num) );
    }

    public int getRightPointer() {

        if ( is_upper_node )
            return getPointer( number_of_keys );
        else
            return -1;
    }

// data access setXxxx() methods:

    public void setKey( int key_num, String key ) {
```

```
            key.getBytes( 0, key.length(), data_buffer,
                loc_key(key_num) );
        }

    public void setPointer( int ptr_num, int ptr ) {

            fillBytes( data_buffer, loc_ptr(ptr_num), ptr );
        }

    public void setRecordNumber( int rec_num, int recno ) {

            fillBytes( data_buffer, loc_rec(rec_num), recno );
//          record_numbers[rec_num] = recno;
        }

// public, class-specific methods:

    public void add_key( String key, int recno,
            int rptr, int where ) {

        // calling code must call find() and check for
        // available space

        if ( where < number_of_keys ) {

            shift_keys( where, where+1 );
            shift_record_numbers( where, where+1 );
        }
        if ( is_upper_node ) {

            if ( where < number_of_keys )
                shift_pointers( where+1, where+2 );

            setPointer( where+1, rptr );
        }

        setKey( where, key );
        setRecordNumber( where, recno );
        number_of_keys++;
        }

    public int find( int ptr ) {
```

```
    if ( ! is_upper_node )
        return -1;

    for ( int i = 0 ; i <= number_of_keys ; i++ ) {

        int p = getPointer( i );
        if ( p == ptr )
            return i;
    }

    return -1;
}

public int find( String s ) {

    int left, right, center, comp;

    parent.found = false;

    if ( number_of_keys == 0 )
        return 0;

    left = 0;
    right = number_of_keys - 1;

    while ( (right - left) > 1 ) {

        center = ( left + right ) >> 1;
        comp = s.compareTo( getKey(center) );

        if ( comp == 0 ){

            parent.found = true;
            return center + 1;
        }

        if ( comp < 0 )
            right = center;
        else
            left = center;
    }
```

```
        comp = s.compareTo( getKey(left) );
            if ( comp < 0 )
                return left;
            if ( comp == 0 ) {

                parent.found = true;
                return right;
            }

        comp - s.compareTo( getKey(right) );
            if ( comp < 0 )
                return right;

            // comp == 0 or > 0
                parent.found = ( comp == 0 );
                return right + 1;
    }

public void move_keys( int from,
    Btree_node dst_node, int to, int len ) {

    System.arraycopy( data_buffer, loc_key(from),
        dst_node.data_buffer, loc_key(to),
        len * key_length );
    }

public void move_pointers( int from,
    Btree_node dst_node, int to, int len ) {

    System.arraycopy( data_buffer, loc_ptr(from),
        dst_node.data_buffer, loc_ptr(to), len * 4 );
    }

public void move_record_numbers( int from,
    Btree_node dst_node, int to, int len ) {

    System.arraycopy( data_buffer, loc_rec(from),
        dst_node.data_buffer, loc_rec(to), len*4 );
    }

public void read_node() throws IndexException {
```

```
    try { parent.readPage( address, data_buffer ); }
    catch ( IOException ioe ) {

        throw new IndexException( ioe.getMessage() +
            " (while reading index node)" );
    }

    key_length = bytes2int( data_buffer, 0 );
    node_length = bytes2int( data_buffer, 4 );
    node_size = bytes2int( data_buffer, 8 );
    number_of_keys = bytes2int( data_buffer, 12 );
    is_upper_node = bytes2int( data_buffer, 16 ) == 1;
}

public void shift_keys( int from, int to, int len ) {

    System.arraycopy( data_buffer, loc_key(from),
        data_buffer, loc_key(to), len*key_length );
}

public void shift_pointers( int from, int to,
    int len ) {

    System.arraycopy( data_buffer, loc_ptr(from),
        data_buffer, loc_ptr(to), len*4 );
}

public void shift_record_numbers( int from, int to,
    int len ) {

    System.arraycopy( data_buffer, loc_rec(from),
        data_buffer, loc_rec(to), len*4 );
}

public void write_node() throws IndexException {

    if ( address == -1 )
        address = parent.file_length;

    fillBytes( data_buffer,  0, key_length );
    fillBytes( data_buffer,  4, node_length );
    fillBytes( data_buffer,  8, node_size );
```

```
        fillBytes( data_buffer, 12, number_of_keys );
        fillBytes( data_buffer, 16,
            is_upper_node ? 1 : 0 );

        try {

            parent.writePage( address, data_buffer );
        }
        catch ( IOException ioe ) {

            throw new IndexException( ioe.getMessage() +
                " (while writing index node)" );
        }
    }

// public, non-event overriding method:

    public String paramString() {

        return "Btree_node";
    }

// there are no public, event-handling methods

// ------------------- private methods -------------------
// private methods:

    private void compute_node_size() {

        int extra = is_upper_node ? 8 : 4;

        // total array space:
            node_size = ( node_length - OVERHEAD );

        // one less space for final upper pointer:
            node_size -= is_upper_node ? 4 : 0;

        // max # of keys (add 'extra' for record #s
        // and upper node pointers):
            node_size /= ( key_length + extra );

        // make it a multiple of two:
```

```
            node_size &= 0xFFFFFFFE;

        pad_size = node_length - OVERHEAD -
            node_size * ( key_length + extra );

        // remember the extra pointer
            pad_size -= is_upper_node ? 4 : 0;

        key_start = OVERHEAD;
        record_number_start = key_start +
            key_length * node_size;
        if ( is_upper_node )
            pointer_start = record_number_start +
                4 * node_size;

        padding = new String( new byte[pad_size], 0 );
    }

    private int loc_key( int num ) {

        return key_start + ( num * key_length );
    }

    private int loc_ptr( int num ) {

        return pointer_start + ( num * 4 );
    }

    private int loc_rec( int num ) {

        return record_number_start + ( num * 4 );
    }

    private void shift_keys( int from, int to ) {

        shift_keys( from, to, number_of_keys - from );
    }

    private void shift_pointers( int from, int to ) {

        shift_pointers( from , to,
            number_of_keys + 1 - from );
```

```
    }

    private void shift_record_numbers( int from, int to ) {

        shift_record_numbers( from, to,
            number_of_keys - from );
    }

// static methods:

    private static int bytes2int( byte[] b, int start ) {

        int i3 = ( (0x000000FF & b[start  ]) << 24 );
        int i2 = ( (0x000000FF & b[start+1]) << 16 );
        int i1 = ( (0x000000FF & b[start+2]) <<  8 );
        int i0 = (   0x000000FF & b[start+3]         );

        return i0 + i1 + i2 + i3;
    }

    static void fillBytes( byte[] b, int start,
        int value ) {

        b[start]   = (byte) ( value >>> 24 );
        b[start+1] = (byte) ( value >>> 16 );
        b[start+2] = (byte) ( value >>>  8 );
        b[start+3] = (byte) ( value         );
    }

} // end of Btree_node class

// there are no private classes in Btree_node.java

/*
    See notes at end of NDX.java
*/

// end of Btree_node.java
```

Understanding the NDX Class

TOUR

Even if you're going to use the NDX as a black box and don't care about its internals, stay on the bus for now. I'll be explaining timing and tuning and other topics that are widely relevant. We'll have a later point where you black-box users can leave the tour.

The interface to the NDX class is still the same. See Chapter 20 for the section "Using the NDX Class." What has changed, however, is the speed of this class. As I mentioned, entirely eliminating the stream I/O from the Btree_node class increased speed dramatically, but I still wasn't happy.

For example, the test case I mentioned earlier that ran in 59 seconds dropped to 3,790 milliseconds. For the first time I was able to test 10K record indexing. My time to reindex 10K records dropped to just under 35 seconds.

How did that compare with commercial database products? The almost unchallenged database speed king is Microsoft's FoxPro. (Borland's Database Engine, which underlies dBASE and Paradox, is the next best.) FoxPro handles my 10K record reindexing in about a second.

Realistically, a commercial product like FoxPro will have its indexing written in assembler, or in C with a heavy dose of inline assembler. There will be top programmers whose full-time job is to make the engine faster. I didn't expect to beat FoxPro.

But I did set a goal. That was to get to within an order of magnitude of FoxPro. I continued to run tests and study the timings. One fact became apparent: my NDX was doing a lot of disk I/O. If I could do a better job of buffering the I/O, I might be able to speed up the process significantly.

The Disk-Buffering Strategy

One problem you face with any buffering strategy is that you never know when the operating system's paging mechanism is going to start putting your RAM into a disk file. If you're too greedy about grabbing RAM, your system can slow down, not speed up.

I decided that a megabyte of RAM was a reasonable amount to use. This is 64 16K pages. This doesn't appear to cause a paging problem.

Another problem you face in devising a buffering strategy is that the mechanism—deciding what gets saved in RAM and what goes to disk—can easily cost more time than the buffering saves. You need a neat solution that's as simple as possible.

I decided on the ultimate in simplicity. I'd simply buffer the first 64 pages. With 20-byte keys, that would completely buffer an index on a file with about 40,000 records. Since this software is not designed to compete with Oracle's databases, that seemed like a good size to be able to handle. I'd rather go at top speed on the smaller files than look for a solution that scaled nicely up into the higher ranges. Million-record databases are important, but I'll let Oracle and its competitors worry about them.

So my buffering mechanism became very simple. If the page's address put it in the first 64 disk pages, it stayed in a vector of page references. During full-file operations, such as reindexing, the pages weren't written to disk until the operation was complete. The read operation became a matter of looking at the array first. If it held a null pointer, the page was read from disk. Otherwise, it would just return the pointer.

I didn't hard-code the 64-page buffer number. I use a variable. The large buffer here is only used when you are doing a job such as reindexing. For regular operation, I buffer just four pages. Real systems are built with multiple tables, and each table can have multiple indexes. One megabyte of buffer works well. Lots of megabytes of buffers wouldn't work at all.

We'll look at the details in a minute. First, I'll bet you want to know how well it worked. When I got the bugs out, I did my first test. I reindexed 10,000 records in 4,680 milliseconds! I was a very happy camper. Coming in at around one-fifth the speed of FoxPro was better than I had hoped.

Actually, when I removed all the timing code except for simply recording the time at the start and end of the whole reindexing operation, my time dropped down to 3,470 milliseconds.

I'm quite convinced that additional work on the NDX class could find significantly more speed. I don't see any reason to think that the existing code is optimal. It is, however, getting to the point where the timing mechanisms themselves can seriously affect the results, so additional tuning will get tricky.

Can FoxPro be beaten with a Java program? I think so. FoxPro must still be doing a sequential scan within the index node, or something else that's inefficient. (If you meet any of the FoxPro programmers, don't let them get their hands on Chapter 19. We'll never catch 'em if they take that binary search stuff to heart!)

Understanding the NDX Class' Code

TOUR

Here's where we'll say good-bye to the black-box users of the NDX class. You folks can meet us at the "Summary," where we'll wrap up this book.

As with the Btree_node, there's a lot that's been changed and a lot that's remained the same. Globally, every access to the Btree_node data arrays was converted to function access, this way:

```
old:     node.keys[i]
new:     node.getKey( i )
```

Here we'll concentrate on the two important additions to NDX. First, it now implements ScrollableX. The business of moving to the next or previous key in the B-tree is not as simple as you might like it to be.

Then we'll look at the data buffering. You'll see that this wasn't as complex as you might have feared it would be.

Implementing ScrollableX

The basic assumption of ScrollableX is that the index is some sort of ordered list with a pointer to a current spot. We know it's a bit more complex than this. The major addition to the data is a pair of pointers. These locate the current spot:

```
int current_key_loc;
int current_level;
```

The current_key_loc is the location of the current key relative to the start of the node. (The first key in the node is number zero.) The current_level is the location in the nodes array. Level 0 is the root.

Next you need public methods that implement the interface. As usual, they delegate the hard work to private methods. This is find( ):

```
public String find( String key ) {

    try { private_find( key, true ); }
    catch ( IndexException ie ) {}

    if ( found ) {

        current_level = find_level;
        current_key_loc = find_key;

        return getString();
    }
    else
        return "";
}
```

My getString( ) method returns the key. You'll want most systems to override this with something a bit more sophisticated. This is the simple version:

```
public String getString() {

    return nodes[current_level].
        getKey( current_key_loc );
}
```

The go( ) method depends on two private methods with self-explanatory names:

```
public void go( int where ) {

    if ( where == 0 )
        move_to_far_left();
    else
        move_to_far_right();
}
```

The move( ) process is not simple. However, the public routine avoids the complexities by just calling move_forward( ) or move_backward( ) an appropriate number of times. This is the method:

```
public int move( int distance ) {

    if ( distance != 0 ) {

        if ( distance > 0 )
            for ( int i = 0 ; i < distance ; i++ )
                move_forward();

        else
            for ( int i = 0 ; i > distance ; i-- )
                move_backward();
    }
    return nodes[current_level].
        getRecordNumber( current_key_loc );
}
```

The private move( ) methods depend on two boolean methods, at_far_left( ) and at_far_right( ). The at_far_left( ) method returns true in the special case where you are at the leftmost key in the leftmost, ground-level node. It begins with an immediate return if the current key isn't the leftmost in the node or if you're not at ground level:

```
private boolean at_far_left() {

    if ( (current_key_loc > 0 ) ||
        (current_level < ground_level) )
        return false;
```

Then it marches upward, using a new find( ) method of the Btree_node. This find( ) method does a scan of the pointers in a node to find a given address. It depends on the fact that a lower-level node only gets into the nodes array by following a pointer in a higher-level node. This means that you will always be able to find, for example, the address of nodes[2] by scanning the pointers in nodes[1]. The algorithm is to march up the tree from ground level to root. At each node, you exit with a false value if the address isn't found at pointer zero. This is the code:

```
    int level = ground_level;

    while ( level > 0 ) {

        int was_at = nodes[level].address;
        level--;

        if ( nodes[level].find( was_at ) > 0 )
            return false;
    }
    return true;
}
```

The at_far_right( ) method is almost identical, except that its test is for the current_key being the rightmost pointer.

Now we'll look at the move_backward( ) process. You can refer to the full listing for the move_forward( ) code—it's the mirror image of moving backward, of course.

Think about the problem for a minute. If you're in a ground node, moving backward means decrementing the current_key value (if it's not already at zero). When you are at the leftmost key at ground level, you back up to the key to the left of your pointer (return to picturing the node as a sandwich of pointers and keys), except when your pointer is the leftmost pointer in the parent. If your pointer is the leftmost, you recursively back up to the next level until you reach the root.

When you're not at ground level, backing up means following the pointer to the left of the current key downward. If it points to a nonground node, you pick the rightmost pointer and keep going down, until you come to the ground. The rightmost key at ground level is the key you want.

Picture a second-level node with three keys and with four pointers to four ground-level nodes. The lowest key in the whole structure is the leftmost key in the leftmost ground-level node. The highest key is the rightmost key in the rightmost ground-level node. If you add another level, the same statements still apply. The rightmost key of any substructure is always the rightmost key of the rightmost ground-level node in the structure. When you back up, you are always backing up to the rightmost key when you enter a substructure. So following a downward pointer is done by finding the rightmost key in the substructure that the pointer identifies.

After several tries, I finally got this code to be no more complex than the underlying concepts. The move_backward( ) method starts by doing nothing at all if you're already at the first key:

```
private void move_backward() {

    if ( at_far_left() )
        return;
```

Next, if you're above ground level, it goes to the rightmost key in the substructure pointed to by the pointer on the left:

```
    if ( current_level < ground_level )
        move_to_right_ground();
```

At ground level, it decrements the current key or finds the next parent key to its immediate left:

```
    else {

        if ( current_key_loc > 0 )
            current_key_loc--;
        else
            move_to_left_parent();
    }
}
```

To continue in alphabetic order, we'll change subjects momentarily. The move_to_far_left( ) method is the one that go(0) calls. It brings up our next subject, data buffering, by calling io_set_tree( ) instead of directly reading new pages into the nodes array. This is the code:

```
private void move_to_far_left() {

    current_level = 0;

    while ( current_level < ground_level ) {

        int addr =
            nodes[current_level].getLeftPointer();
        current_level++;

        try { io_set_tree( current_level, addr ); }
        catch ( IndexException ie ) {}

    }
    current_key_loc = 0;
}
```

There is a move_to_far_right( ) that does the mirror image job. It uses getRightPointer( ) where the one above uses getLeftPointer( ). Now let's get back to the move_backward( ) process.

The first of the supporting cast is move_to_left_parent( ). It uses a loop that stops at the root, if it doesn't otherwise end. Inside the loop it begins by noting your current node's address and finding it in the parent node's pointer list:

```
am_at = nodes[current_level].address;

current_level--;
current_key_loc =
    nodes[current_level].find( am_at ) - 1;
```

Subtracting one gets you to the left pointer. If the location is not zero, we've found the left parent. If not, the loop keeps going until it reaches the root:

```
if ( current_key_loc >= 0 )
    return;
```

The process of moving to the rightmost, ground-level key is similar, but the loop goes from the current level down to ground level. Again, it depends on io_set_tree( ) to read pages into the nodes array. This is the code:

```
private void move_to_right_ground() {

    int loc = nodes[current_level].
        getPointer( current_key_loc );

    while ( current_level < ground_level ) {

        current_level++;
        try { io_set_tree( current_level, loc ); }
        catch ( IndexException ie ) {}
        loc = nodes[current_level].getRightPointer();
    }
    current_key_loc =
        nodes[ground_level].number_of_keys - 1;
}
```

Implementing Buffered-Disk I/O

The buffered-disk I/O is, fortunately, much easier than climbing around the B-tree. As you've seen, the methods that need a new node don't go to disk. Instead, they go to io_set_tree( ), requesting a particular page at a given level in the nodes array.

The lowest level of the io_( ) methods, where the disk may actually get read or written, is occupied by io_get_node( ) and io_put_node( ). This is the basic process in io_get_node( ):

```
int page_number = address / page_size;

if ( in_RAM(page_number) )
    b = node_store[page_number];

else {

    b = new Btree_node(address, this );

    if ( page_number < number_of_stored_nodes )
        node_store[page_number] = b;
}
return b;
}
```

The node_store array keeps pointers to the nodes. The in_RAM( ) method returns true if the page number is not outside the range of the array and the value in the array is not null. When the page is in RAM, all that's required is to return the stored object reference. Otherwise, a new node is constructed and read from disk. If its page number is not out of range, a reference to it is added to the node_store array.

The full io_get_node( ) routine is about twice as long as the code shown here. The rest of the code is the ALD concerned with creating a node that extends the length of the index. See the full listing for these details. It's the same as you saw in Chapter 20, except that the object reference is added to the node_store, if it's in range.

The io_put_node( ) process is called after updating a node. Skipping the ALD, the basic job is this:

```
int page_num = ( nodes[level].address ) / page_size;
if ( building_full_file && (in_RAM( page_num )) )
    return;

nodes[level].write_node();
```

If the building_full_file flag is set and the page is in RAM, this routine doesn't bother with the disk write.

The io_set_tree( ) method has two forms. It can be called with a node object, or with a disk address. The version that handles the node object is trivial:

```
private void io_set_tree( int level, Btree_node b )
    throws IndexException {

    io_put_node( level );
    nodes[level] = b;
}
```

The alternate version would be trivial except that it can be called when the node-splitting process is pushing up a new root node. That's handled this way:

```
if ( level == 0 ) { // root node

    ground_level++;

    if ( nodes[0] != null )
        System.arraycopy(nodes, 0, nodes, 1,
            ground_level );
}
```

With those ALD dispensed with, the rest of the job takes just two statements:

```
io_put_node( level );
nodes[level] =
    io_get_node( address, level < ground_level );
```

The last of the disk I/O routines is io_write_nodes( ), which replaces the old write_nodes( ) method. The one point to remember is that the B-tree does not use nodes in sequence, so the node_store may intermix nodes that have been read with others that have never gotten off the disk. This is the code:

```
private void io_write_nodes() throws IndexException {

    if ( building_full_file )
        return;

    for ( int i = 0 ;
        i < number_of_stored_nodes ; i++ ) {

        if ( node_store[i] != null )
            node_store[i].write_node();
    }
}
```

One final note on the code before the listing. The header page is still read and written by use of stream I/O. The read_header( ) and write_header( ) routines are good examples of how simple it is to use the BinFileXO class that NDX extends.

The Full NDX Class Listing

Listing 22-3 shows the full NDX.java source file.

Listing 22-3:
The final
NDX source

```
// NDX.java -- create and maintain B-tree index files
// Copyright 1997, Martin L. Rinehart

// this code is completely documented in:
// _Java Database Development_, Martin Rinehart,
// Osborne/McGraw-Hill, 1997

import java.io.*;
```

```
class NDX extends BinFileXO implements ScrollableX {
// -------------------- data members --------------------

// there are no public data members

// protected data members:

    protected boolean building_full_file;

    protected int current_key_loc;
    protected int current_level;

    protected int find_key;
    protected int find_level;
    protected boolean found;

    protected int ground_level;

    protected int half_size;

    protected int index_num;
    protected Indexable indexable;

    protected int key_length;

    protected Btree_node[] node_store;
    protected Btree_node[] nodes; // 0 is root
    protected int number_of_keys;
    protected int number_of_pages;
    protected int number_of_stored_nodes;

    protected int page_size;

    protected int root_node_address;

    protected int working_level;

// final static data member:

    final static int MAX_LEVELS = 10;
    final static int MAX_STORED_NODES = 64; // 1MB
    final static int MIN_STORED_NODES = 4;  // 64KB
```

```
        final static int PAGE_SIZE = 128; // testing
        // final static int PAGE_SIZE = 16 * 1024; // running

// ------------------- public methods --------------------

// constructor:

    NDX( String path_name, String access,
        Indexable i, int index_num )
        throws IndexException {

        super( path_name, access, PAGE_SIZE );

        if ( access.equals("rw") ) {

            if ( !writeable ) return;
        }
        else // access == "r"
            if ( !readable ) return;

        indexable = i;
        this.index_num = index_num;

        number_of_keys = 0;
        page_size = PAGE_SIZE;
        file_length = page_size;
        number_of_pages = 1;

        String key = indexable.getKeyValue( 0, index_num );
        key_length = key.length();

        ground_level = -1;
        node_store = new Btree_node[MAX_STORED_NODES];
        nodes = new Btree_node[MAX_LEVELS];

        number_of_stored_nodes = MIN_STORED_NODES;

        if ( getLast() < 0 ) {

            write_header();
            file_length = page_size;
```

```
                reindex();
        }
        else {

            read_header(); // also reads root node

            if ( number_of_keys !=
                 (indexable.getLast()+1) ) {

                page_size = PAGE_SIZE;
                 file_length = page_size;
                number_of_keys = 0;
                number_of_pages = 1;
                key_length = key.length();
                ground_level = -1;
                write_header();

                reindex();
            }
        }
    }

// there are no data access methods

// public, class-specific methods:

    public void delete( int recno )
        throws IndexException {

        reindex();
    }

    public String find( String key ) {

        try { private_find( key, true ); }
        catch ( IndexException ie ) {}

        if ( found ) {

            current_level = find_level;
            current_key_loc = find_key;
```

```
            return getString();
    }
    else
        return "";
}

public String getString() {

    return nodes[current_level].
        getKey( current_key_loc );
}

public void go( int where ) {

    if ( where == 0 )
        move_to_far_left();
    else
        move_to_far_right();
}

public void insert( String key, int recno )
    throws IndexException {

    insert( key, recno, -1 );
}

public int move( int distance ) {

    if ( distance != 0 ) {

        if ( distance > 0 )
            for ( int i = 0 ; i < distance ; i++ )
                move_forward();

        else
            for ( int i = 0 ; i > distance ; i-- )
                move_backward();
    }
    return nodes[current_level].
        getRecordNumber( current_key_loc );
}
```

```
    public void reindex() throws IndexException {

        building_full_file = true;
        number_of_stored_nodes = MAX_STORED_NODES;
        ground_level = -1;

        int last = indexable.getLast();

        for ( int i = 0 ; i <= last; i++ ) {

            String key =
                indexable.getKeyValue( i, index_num );
            insert( key, i, -1 );
        }

        building_full_file = false;
        write_header();
        io_write_nodes();
        number_of_stored_nodes = MIN_STORED_NODES;
    }

    public boolean useMonospace() { return true; }

// public, non-event overriding method:

    public String paramString() {

        return "NDX";
    }

// there are no public, event-handling methods

// ------------------ private methods ------------------

// private methods:

    private int add_node() {

        int where = file_length;
        file_length += page_size;
        number_of_pages++;
```

```
        if ( ! building_full_file )
            write_header();

    return where;
}

private boolean at_far_left() {

    if ( (current_key_loc > 0 ) ||
        (current_level < ground_level) )
        return false;

    int level = ground_level;

    while ( level > 0 ) {

        int was_at = nodes[level].address;
        level--;

        if ( nodes[level].find( was_at ) > 0 )
            return false;
    }
    return true;
}

private boolean at_far_right() {

    if ( (current_key_loc < ( nodes[current_level].
            number_of_keys - 1 )) ||
        (current_level < ground_level) )
        return false;

    int level = ground_level;

    while ( level > 0 ) {

        int was_at = nodes[level].address;
        level--;

        if ( nodes[level].find( was_at ) <
            nodes[level].number_of_keys )
            return false;
```

```
        }
    return true;
}

private boolean in_RAM( int page_num ) {

    if ( page_num >= number_of_stored_nodes )
        return false;

    return ( node_store[page_num] != null );
}

private void insert( String key, int recno, int rptr )
    throws IndexException {

    if ( number_of_keys == 0 ) {

        io_set_tree( 0, -1 );
        root_node_address = nodes[0].address;
        ground_level = 0;

        nodes[0].add_key( key, recno, -1, 0 );
        io_put_node( 0 );

        number_of_keys = 1;

    }
    else {

        private_find( key, false );

        working_level = ground_level;
        Btree_node node = nodes[working_level];

        if ( node.number_of_keys < node.node_size ) {

            node.add_key( key, recno, rptr, find_key );
            io_put_node( working_level );
        }
        else {

            split_a_node( key, recno, rptr );
```

```
                if ( ! building_full_file )
                    io_write_nodes();
            }
            number_of_keys++;
        }
    }

    private Btree_node io_get_node( int address,
        boolean is_upper )
        throws IndexException {

        Btree_node b;
        if ( address == -1 ) {

            int where = add_node();

            b = new Btree_node( where, key_length,
                page_size, this, is_upper );

            int page_number = where / page_size;
            if ( page_number < number_of_stored_nodes )
                node_store[page_number] = b;

            return b;
        }

        int page_number = address / page_size;

        if ( in_RAM(page_number) )
            b = node_store[page_number];

        else {

            b = new Btree_node(address, this );

            if ( page_number < number_of_stored_nodes )
                node_store[page_number] = b;
        }
        return b;
    }

    private void io_put_node( int level )
```

```
        throws IndexException {

    if ( nodes[level] == null )
        return;

    int page_num = ( nodes[level].address ) / page_size;
    if ( building_full_file && (in_RAM( page_num )) )
        return;

    nodes[level].write_node();
}

private void io_set_tree( int level, Btree_node b )
    throws IndexException {

    io_put_node( level );
    nodes[level] = b;
}

private void io_set_tree( int level, int address )
    throws IndexException {

    Btree_node b;

    if ( level == 0 ) { // root node

        ground_level++;

        if ( nodes[0] != null )
            System.arraycopy(nodes, 0, nodes, 1,
                ground_level );
    }
    io_put_node( level );
    nodes[level] =
        io_get_node( address, level < ground_level );
}

private void io_write_nodes() throws IndexException {

    if ( building_full_file )
        return;
```

```
        for ( int i = 0 ;
            i < number_of_stored_nodes ; i++ ) {

            if ( node_store[i] != null )
                node_store[i].write_node();
        }
    }

    private void move_backward() {

        if ( at_far_left() )
            return;

        if ( current_level < ground_level )
            move_to_right_ground();

        else {

            if ( current_key_loc > 0 )
                current_key_loc--;
            else
                move_to_left_parent();
        }
    }

    private void move_forward() {

        if ( at_far_right() )
            return;

        if ( current_level < ground_level )
            move_to_left_ground();

        else {

            if ( current_key_loc <
                (nodes[ground_level].number_of_keys - 1) )
                current_key_loc++;
            else
                move_to_right_parent();
        }
    }
```

```
private void move_to_far_left() {

    current_level = 0;

    while ( current_level < ground_level ) {

        int addr =
            nodes[current_level].getLeftPointer();
        current_level++;

        try { io_set_tree( current_level, addr ); }
        catch ( IndexException ie ) {}

    }
    current_key_loc = 0;
}

private void move_to_far_right() {

    current_level = 0;

    while ( current_level < ground_level ) {

        int addr =
            nodes[current_level].getRightPointer();
        current_level++;

        try { io_set_tree( current_level, addr ); }
        catch ( IndexException ie ) {}

    }
    current_key_loc =
        nodes[ground_level].number_of_keys - 1;
}

private void move_to_left_ground() {

    int loc = nodes[current_level].
        getPointer( ++current_key_loc );

    while ( current_level < ground_level ) {
```

```
            current_level++;
            try { io_set_tree( current_level, loc ); }
            catch ( IndexException ie ) {}
            loc = nodes[current_level].getLeftPointer();
        }
        current_key_loc = 0;
    }

    private void move_to_left_parent() {

        int am_at;

        while ( current_level > 0 ) {

            am_at = nodes[current_level].address;

            current_level--;
            current_key_loc =
                nodes[current_level].find( am_at ) - 1;

            if ( current_key_loc >= 0 )
                return;

            am_at = nodes[current_level].address;
        }
        current_key_loc = 0;
    }

    private void move_to_right_ground() {

        int loc = nodes[current_level].
            getPointer( current_key_loc );

        while ( current_level < ground_level ) {

            current_level++;
            try { io_set_tree( current_level, loc ); }
            catch ( IndexException ie ) {}
            loc = nodes[current_level].getRightPointer();
        }
        current_key_loc =
            nodes[ground_level].number_of_keys - 1;
```

```
    }

    private void move_to_right_parent() {

        int am_at;

        while ( current_level > 0 ) {

            am_at = nodes[current_level].address;

            current_level--;
            current_key_loc =
                nodes[current_level].find( am_at );

            if ( current_key_loc <
                nodes[current_level].number_of_keys )
                return;
        }
        current_key_loc--;
    }

    private void private_find( String key,
        boolean stop_when_found ) throws IndexException {

        found = false;
        working_level = 0;
        Btree_node node = nodes[0];

        while ( working_level < ground_level ) {

            find_key = nodes[working_level].find( key );
            if ( find_key < node.number_of_keys )
                if ( stop_when_found &&
                    node.getKey(find_key).equals(key) ) {

                    find_level = working_level;
                    found = true;
                    return;
                }

            int next_address = node.getPointer( find_key );
```

```
            working_level++;

            io_set_tree( working_level, next_address );
            node = nodes[working_level];
        }

        // reached ground level
        find_level = ground_level;
        find_key = node.find( key );
    }

    private void read_header() throws IndexException {

        try { readPage( 0 ); }
        catch ( IOException ioe ) {

            writeable = readable = false;
            message = ioe.getMessage() +
                " (reading header block)";
            return;
        }

        number_of_keys = readInt();
        file_length = readInt();
        number_of_pages = readInt();
        page_size = readInt();
        key_length = readInt();
        ground_level = readInt();

        root_node_address = readInt();

        ground_level--;
        io_set_tree( 0, root_node_address );
    }

    private void split_a_node( String key, int recno,
        int rptr ) throws IndexException {

        Btree_node node = nodes[working_level];

        Btree_node sibling = io_get_node( -1,
```

```
        working_level < ground_level );

    int mid = node.node_size / 2 ;

    if ( find_key < mid )
        split_insert_left(
            node, sibling, key, recno, rptr );
    else if ( find_key == mid )
        split_insert_middle(
            node, sibling, key, recno, rptr );
    else
        split_insert_right(
            node, sibling, key, recno, rptr );
}

private void split_insert_left(
    Btree_node left, Btree_node right, String key,
    int recno, int rptr ) throws IndexException {

    int mid = left.node_size / 2;
    left.move_keys( mid, right, 0, mid );
    left.move_record_numbers( mid, right, 0, mid );

    if ( left.is_upper_node )
        left.move_pointers( mid, right, 0, mid+1 );

    String push_key = left.getKey( mid-1 );
    int push_recno = left.getRecordNumber( mid-1 );
    int push_ptr;
    if ( left.is_upper_node )
        push_ptr = left.getPointer( mid );
    else
        push_ptr = -1;

    if ( find_key < mid-1 ) {

        left.shift_keys( find_key, find_key+1,
            mid - find_key );
        left.shift_record_numbers( find_key,
            find_key + 1, mid - find_key );
        if( left.is_upper_node )
            left.shift_record_numbers( find_key+1,
```

```
                    find_key+2, mid - find_key - 1 );
        }
        left.setKey( find_key, key );
        left.setRecordNumber( find_key, recno );
        if ( left.is_upper_node )
            left.setPointer( find_key+1, rptr );

        left.number_of_keys = mid;
        right.number_of_keys = mid;

        int above_ground = ground_level - working_level;

        split_push_up( push_key, push_recno, push_ptr,
            left, right );

        io_set_tree( ground_level + above_ground, right );
    }

    private void split_insert_middle(
        Btree_node left, Btree_node right, String key,
        int recno, int rptr ) throws IndexException{

        int mid = left.node_size / 2;

        left.move_keys( mid, right, 0, mid );
        left.move_record_numbers( mid, right, 0, mid );
        if ( left.is_upper_node )
            left.move_pointers( mid+1, right, 1, mid );

        left.number_of_keys = mid;
        right.number_of_keys = mid;
        if ( left.is_upper_node )
            right.setPointer( 0, rptr );

        int above_ground = ground_level - working_level;

        split_push_up( key, recno, right.address,
            left, right );

        io_set_tree( ground_level + above_ground, right );
    }
```

```
private void split_insert_right(
    Btree_node left, Btree_node right, String key,
    int recno, int rptr ) throws IndexException {

    int mid = left.node_size / 2;

    String push_key = left.getKey( mid );
    int push_recno = left.getRecordNumber( mid );
    int push_ptr;
    if ( left.is_upper_node )
        push_ptr = left.getPointer( mid+1 );
    else
        push_ptr = -1;

    if ( (find_key - mid) > 1 ) {

        left.move_keys( mid+1, right, 0,
            find_key - mid - 1 );
        left.move_record_numbers( mid+1, right, 0,
            find_key - mid - 1 );
    }
    if ( left.is_upper_node )
        left.move_pointers( mid+1, right, 0,
            find_key - mid );

    int where = find_key - mid - 1; // loc in right
    right.setKey( where, key );
    right.setRecordNumber( where, recno );
    if( left.is_upper_node )
        right.setPointer( where+1, rptr );

    if ( where < mid ) {

        left.move_keys( find_key, right, where+1,
            mid - where - 1 );
        left.move_record_numbers( find_key, right,
            where+1, mid - where - 1 );
        if ( left.is_upper_node )
            left.move_pointers( find_key + 1, right,
                where+2, mid - where - 1 );
    }
```

```java
        left.number_of_keys = mid;
        right.number_of_keys = mid;

        int above_ground = ground_level - working_level;

        split_push_up( push_key, push_recno, push_ptr,
            left, right );

        io_set_tree( ground_level + above_ground, right );
}

private void split_push_up( String key, int recno,
    int rptr, Btree_node left, Btree_node right )
    throws IndexException {

    if ( working_level == 0 ) {

        // build new root node
        io_set_tree( 0, -1 );
        Btree_node node = nodes[0];

        root_node_address = node.address;

        find_key = find_level = 0;
        node.add_key( key, recno, -1, 0 );

        node.setPointer( 0, left.address );
        node.setPointer( 1, right.address );
    }
    else {

        working_level--;
        Btree_node node = nodes[working_level];

        find_key = node.find( key );
        if ( node.number_of_keys < node.node_size ) {

            node.add_key( key, recno,
                right.address, find_key );
            io_put_node( working_level );
        }
        else {
```

```
                    split_a_node( key, recno, right.address );
            }
        }
    }

    private void write_header() {

        writeInt( number_of_keys );
        writeInt( file_length );
        writeInt( number_of_pages );
        writeInt( page_size );
        writeInt( key_length );
        writeInt( ground_level );
        writeInt( root_node_address );

        int pad_words = page_size - 7;
        for ( int i = 0 ; i < pad_words ; i++ )
            writeInt( -1 );

        try { writePage( 0 ); }
        catch ( IOException ioe ) {

            writeable = readable = false;
            message = ioe.getMessage() +
                " (writing header block)";
        }
    }

} // end of NDX class

// private class in NDX.java:

class IndexException extends Exception {

    IndexException( String s ) {

        super( s );
    }
}
```

```
/* File header page:

  0- 3 number of keys
  4- 7 file_length
  8-11 number of pages
12-15 page size
16-19 key length
20-23 ground level
24-27 root node address
28-31 spare

32-(page_size - 1) record numbers

ground node page:

            L1 = key length * node size + 31
            L2 = L1 + 1
            L3 = L1 + 4*node size
            L4 = L3 + 1
            L5 = L3 + 8*(node size + 1)

     0- 3 key length
     4- 7 node length      // page size
     8-11 node size        // max # of keys
    12-15 number of keys
    16-19 is_upper_node
    20-31 spare
    32-L1 keys
    L2-L3 record numbers

upper node page, as above, plus:

    L4-L5 pointers

*/


// end of NDX.java
```

Summary

In this final chapter, we began with a fast look at using our existing tables to store objects. Since we only need to store data members to make our objects persistent, tables are well-suited to the task. If you like, you can swap jargon sets and you'll be working with an object store, not a relational one.

Using normalized designs is still a good idea. Objects that embed other objects as data members can be handled if you store the embedded objects in a separate object table. The primary key in that table (or, if you prefer, the object identifier) is stored as a foreign key in the embedding object (or as a persistent object reference, if you prefer). Arrays can be handled in the HeapFile, but standard normalization is usually a better approach.

After this fast look at object stores, we took a look at making our objects fast. Using stream I/O, my index trees were too slow for serious use. So I created the BinFileXO (Binary File, eXtended for Objects) class. That class lets you use stream I/O calls to read and write in RAM-based byte arrays. Calls to readPage( ) and writePage( ) actually do the disk I/O, using fast, random file access. This made an order of magnitude improvement in the indexing process.

After implementing the BinFileXO class, the B-tree indexes started to be capable of serious, if slow, work. Further timings showed me that most of the time was being spent in the stream I/O, even though it was in RAM. To eliminate this, I got rid of the data arrays and left all data in the byte-array buffers, accessing it through function calls. This made another big improvement.

I was still about 35 times slower than FoxPro, the indexing speed king, however. My goal was to come to within an order of magnitude of FoxPro's speed. I added a disk-buffering scheme that will be very efficient for small to moderate data stores. It stores the first 64 pages (B-tree nodes) in RAM during reindexing. By going to disk just once for each node, my NDX class became only 3.5 times slower than FoxPro on a 10K record file, well within my order of magnitude target.

And that, sorry to say, wraps up the NDX class and this book. There's lots more to say and do on this topic, but I'm already well past the time and space budgets my publisher has provided. And your database toolkit has what it needs for you to put together serious applications.

Back in the first chapter, we started with the overview of the book, and with a look at the template-based structure of my classes. By now, you'll be able to look at any of my classes and know how it's organized. In fact, you'll know even without looking.

In the second chapter we went on to create a general-purpose scroll window, which we used extensively through the rest of the book. In the second-to-last chapter, we created another scroller that worked with indexed data.

The next chapters built a FileViewer that handled text files, binary files, and DBF data tables. Then we created a front end for our JDB application. We had some fun customizing the application, and we used an INI file as a database for the application's customized parameters.

In Chapter 11, we took a break from code and looked at the database design process. I showed you the method that I use, which is both simpler than classic normalization techniques and yields designs that are provably superior to all but the best designs created with standard techniques.

The JDB application itself kept us busy for the next five chapters. When we were done, it could open any DBF, and create an instant data-entry form that let you edit the data. It also coordinated the form with the scroll window, giving you two simultaneous views of the data in the table.

We also used JDB to create and edit database structure files. These in turn can create DBFs. Alternately, DBF files can be used to create database structure files.

Then we went on to handling variable-length data, such as text and multimedia types, via the HeapFile. This class uses a disk file to create storage that works like a heap in RAM, but, being on disk, is permanent. By storing pointers into the HeapFile in your data tables, you can attach variable-length data to a fixed-length table.

Our final topic was B-tree indexing. We studied its theory first and then went on to implement the NDX class and its related Btree_node class. After the penultimate chapter on index-based scrolling, we came to the finish here by tackling speed issues. The result was that our pure Java indexes will now run at speeds that are respectable, even compared with the best commercial database work.

Now that you've got the tools, it's time to put them to work. I expect you'll be building some great applications. I hope you've enjoyed this tour.

Index

SYMBOLS
; (semicolon), JDB.INI, 396
_ (underscore), JDB.INI, 397

A

abstract keys, second-normal form, 428
add( ), MenuPanel, 283
add_key( ), Btree_node class, 738-739
addLayoutComponent( ), CenterLayout, 238
add_node( ), NDX class, 768-769
adjust( ), ScrollWinX class, 814-815, 816
algorithms
    B-tree insertion, 712
    binary search, 699
    ChoicesLayout, 256-257
aligning labels and TextFields, DEForm (data-entry form), 442
alloc( ), HeapFile, 645-648, 659-660, 662-664
alloc_block( ), HeapFile, 662-664

alphabetic character function, MRString class, 147
array method, TxtFile class, 59-60
arraycopy( ). *See* System.arraycopy( )
arrays
    BinFileXO class, 841, 843
    JDB.java, 341-342
    MRString class, 128
ASAMP.DBF, DBF format, 178, *179*
ASAMP.DBS, DBF class, *567*
ASCII
    converting bytes to (FDlib class), 113
    dumps (BinFile class), 102-103
Ashton-Tate, history of DBF format, 177
aspect ratios, ChoicesLayout, 255-256
assign( ), JDB.INI, 397
assign_menu( ), JDB.INI, 397-398
at_far_left( ), ScrollableX interface, 870-871
at_far_right( ), ScrollableX interface, 871

B

B-trees, 705-715, 717-752
    See also binary trees; Btree_node class
    benefits and costs, 728-729
    building, 717-752
    building with blocks, 709-712
    costs and benefits, 728-729
    deleting from, 712-715
    detail table indexes, 720
    event table indexes, 719-720
    file I/O, 724-725
    implementing, 718-725
    index files, 718-720
    insert( ), 730
    inserting into, 708-712
    insertion algorithm, 712
    integer length, 719
    linear and binary searches, 725-735
    locate( ), 726-728
    node construction, 722-723
    node order, 707
    node separation, 723
    node sizing, 720-722
    nodes, 705, 707-708, 720-723
    object file indexes, 718-719
    pointer/value sandwiches, 723
    as pyramids, 705-707
    random string generation, 725-726
    reading single nodes, 721
    rfill( ), 730
    searching method, 708, 725-735
    self-balancing, 711
    separating ground and upper nodes, 723
    sizing nodes, 720-722
    summary, 751-752
    test program, 729-735
    testing as art, 726
    tree construction, 723-724
bestFit( ), MRString class, 173
binary files, 91-121
    BinFile class, 93-111
    FDlib class, 111-115
    FileViewer class, 115-120
    overview, 92
    summary, 120-121
binary trees, 697-716
    See also Btree_node class
    B-trees, 705-715, 717-752

    building, 703-704, 709-712
    index files and, 698, 700-701
    overview, 701-703
    searching overview, 698-700
    summary, 715-716
BinFile class, 93-111
    ASCII dumps, 102-103
    close( ), 95
    code listings, 105-111, 797-803
    constructors, 94-95
    data access methods, 95
    data members, 96, 105-106, 797-798
    DEBUG, 101-102
    dumps, 102-104
    file I/O, 96-101
    getFileName( ), 95
    getLast( ), 95, 101
    getMessage( ), 95
    getString( ), 95, 101-102
    hex dumps, 103-104
    isReadable( ), 95
    isWriteable( ), 95
    location preparation, 104
    methods, 101-105
    NDX class extension, 797-803
    output buffers, 104-105
    private methods, 101-102, 109-111, 801-803
    public methods, 95-96, 101, 106-109, 798-800
    RandomAccessFile( ), 93-94
    RandomAccessFile class, 97-101
    read( ), 99-100
    TxtFile class as extension of, 60
BinFileXO class, 838-852
    arrays, 841, 843
    buffers, 843
    ByteArrayInputStream, 843
    ByteArrayOutputStream, 843, 846
    code listing, 847-852
    creating BinFiles, 840
    data members, 842, 847-848
    DataInputStream, 843, 845
    DataOutputStream, 843, 845, 846
    file I/O, 839
    importing java.io, 842
    mainline test, 842
    overview, 838-841
    public methods, 848-852
    read methods, 840-841

readBytes( ), 843-844
readInt( ), 844
readPage( ), 844-845
reset( ), 845
seek( ), 845
String write, 845
write methods, 839, 841
writeBytes( ), 845
writeInt( ), 846
writePage( ), 846-847
blinker, data-entry form, 443-445
block allocation, HeapFile, 662-664
block finding, HeapFile, 667-670
block structures, HeapFile, 651-652,
  654-655
boolean data members, ScrollWin class, 30
boolean endsWith( ), MRString class,
  131-132, 139-140
boolean functions, MRString class, 147-148
Boyce-Codd normal form, 429-431
    See also normalization
    superkeys, 430
    tuples, 430-431
Btree_node class, 735-751, 852-866
    See also B-trees; binary trees
    add_key( ), 738-739
    code listing, 744-751, 856-866
    compute_node_size( ), 743-744
    constructors, 737-738
    data members, 735-736, 744-745, 857
    file I/O public methods, 741-742
    fillBytes( ), 855, 856
    find( ), 739-741
    getKey( ), 853-854
    getLeftPointer( ), 853, 854
    getRightPointer( ), 854
    loc( ) methods, 855-856
    object databases, 852-866
    overview, 852-853
    private methods, 742-744, 750-751,
      854, 864-866
    public methods, 736-742, 745-750,
      853, 858-864
    read_node( ), 741-742
    set( ), 854
    shift( ), 854-855
    static methods, 856
    System.arraycopy( ), 854-855
    write_node( ), 855
    writePage( ), 855

buffered-disk I/O, implementing, 874-878
buffering strategy, NDX class and object
  databases, 867-868
buffers, BinFileXO class, 843
button_click( ), DEForm (data-entry form),
  451-452
ByteArrayInputStream, BinFileXO class,
  843
ByteArrayOutputStream, BinFileXO class,
  843, 846
bytes
    converting to ASCII (FDlib class), 113
    converting to hexadecimals (FDlib
      class), 112
    MRString class and, 127, 128

C

calc_layout( ), ChoicesLayout, 260
calculate_cols_rows( ), ChoicesLayout, 262
candidate keys, second-normal form, 428
CenterLayout, 232-248
    addLayoutComponent( ), 238
    code listings, 233, 235-237, 242-248
    data members, 242-243
    layoutContainer( ), 238-240
    minimumLayoutSize( ), 240-241
    origin of, 232-233
    overview, 233-234, 237-238
    preferredLayoutSize( ), 241-242
    public methods, 235-236, 243-248
    removeLayoutComponent( ), 242
char lastChar( ), MRString class, 133
characteristic histories
    database design, 426
    detail tables, 423-424
characteristics
    database design, 417, 425, 426
    detail tables and, 420-424
charAt( ), MRString class, 130-131
ChoicesLayout, 248-271
    algorithms, 256-257
    calc_layout( ), 260
    calculate_cols_rows( ), 262
    code listings, 251-253, 264-271
    constructors, 250-251
    data members, 264-265
    defining layouts, 253-254
    enumerating layouts, 254-255
    layoutContainer( ), 257-259

mathematical theory, 253-257
methods, 257-264
other_dimension( ), 263
overview, 248-250
private methods, 259-264, 268-271
public methods, 251-252, 257-259,
  265-268
second_is_better( ), 260, 263
target aspect ratios, 255-256
circ_pointer, HeapFile, 658
circular-first-fit algorithm, HeapFile,
  649-650
circular-pointer methods, HeapFile,
  671-672
class-specific public methods
HeapFile, 659-662
JDB.java, 345-346, 355
classes
database design, 416
structure, 7
template.java, 12-15
close( )
BinFile class, 95
DBF class, 198, 202-203, 578
HeapFile, 646, 647, 656
close_file( ), DBF class, 578-579
close_file_file( ), DBF class, 579-580
close_file_window( ), DBF class, 580-581
color
JDBcolors.java, 371-375
JDB.java, 341, 347, 349
RRectPromptPainter (MenuPanel),
  309
combine( ), HeapFile, 650, 664-665
compilers, JDB.INI and, 393-395
compute_node_size( ), Btree_node class,
  743-744
concat( ), MRString class, 131, 137-139
constructors
BinFile class, 94-95
Btree_node class, 737-738
ChoicesLayout, 250-251
DBF class, 196, 199-200
DEForm (data-entry form), 448
DEPanel layout, 492
HeapFile, 646, 656-659, 679-681
JDBClose menu class, 573
JDB.INI, 386
JDB.java, 342-344, 352
JDBnew class, 606-609

JDBopts.java, 364
MenuPanel, 282-283
method structure, 9-10
MRString class, 126-130
MsgBox class, 188
NDX class, 765
PointerList class, 78
ScrollWin class, 29, 31-32, 52
ScrollWinX class, 813
TxtFile class, 61, 63-65
conversions (FDlib class)
bytes to ASCII, 113
bytes to hexadecimals, 112
integers to hexadecimals, 111-112
nibbles to hex digits, 113
copy( ), MRString class, 131
Create button, DBF class, 566
create_dbf( ), DataBoss class, 514-515
create_dbf_file( ), JDBnew class, 609-612
create_stru_file( ), JDBnew class, 612-614,
  615-617
current values, redundant data, 433

D

data access methods
BinFile class, 95
DBF class, 197-198, 200-202
JDB.java, 344, 353-355
method structure, 10
PointerList class, 78
ScrollWin class, 32
TxtFile class, 61-62, 65
data members
B-tree test program, 731
BinFile class, 96, 105-106, 797-798
BinFileXO class, 842, 847-848
Btree_node class, 735-736, 744-745,
  857
CenterLayout, 242-243
ChoicesLayout, 264-265
DataBoss class, 515-516
DBF class, 198-199, 214-215, 530-531
DEForm (data-entry form), 446-447,
  454-455
DELayout LayoutManager, 485
DEPanel layout, 494
HeapFile, 652-653, 676-677
JDBboss menu, 524
JDBClose menu class, 574

JDBcolors.java, 371-372
JDB.INI, 386, 403
JDB.java, 340-342, 351, 585-586
JDBmenopts.java, 367
JDBnew class, 625
JDBopts.java, 363
JDBshapes.java, 376
MenuPanel, 289-290
MenuSample, 278
MRLabel, 476-477
MRString class, 155
MRTextField, 501
NDX class, 763-765, 783-784, 877-878
PointerList class, 79, 82-83
PromptPainter (MenuPanel), 316
PromptPanel (MenuPanel), 304-305
RRectPromptPainter (MenuPanel),
    307, 311
ScrollWin class, 30-31, 42-43, 52,
    547-548
ScrollWinX class, 820-821
TxtFile class, 62-63, 71
data structure overview, 7-8
data-entry form, 435-469
    blinker, 443-445
    DEForm, 441-442, 445-469
    dialog box suppression, 441
    expanded, *440*
    grid views, 440
    JDBboss menu, *438*
    JDB.java, 436-443
    Open button, 436, *437*, *438*
    opening DBFs, 437-441
    record views, 440
    scrolling, 438-439
    summary, 469
    version warning, 443-445
data_added( ), DataBoss class, 512
databases. *See* DBF class; DBF format;
    designing object and relational
    databases; JDB front-end code; object
    databases
DataBoss class, 508-522
    code listing, 515-522
    create_dbf( ), 514-515
    data members, 515-516
    data overview, 509-510
    data_added( ), 512
    private methods, 514-515, 521-522
    public methods, 510-513, 516-520

ScrollWin class, 30, 41
setRecord( ), 511-512
shut_down( ), 513
DataInputStream, BinFileXO class, 843, 845
DataOutputStream, BinFileXO class, 843,
    845, 846
dBASE memo fields, HeapFile, 645
DBF class, 195-230, 527-545, 563-602
    See also DBF format
    ASAMP.DBS, *567*
    close( ), 198, 202-203, 578
    close_file( ), 578-579
    close_file_file( ), 579-580
    close_file_window( ), 580-581
    code listings, 214-230, 529-545
    constructors, 196, 199-200
    Create button, 566
    creating, 566-568
    data access methods, 197-198,
        200-202
    data members, 198-199, 214-215,
        530-531
    dbf_read( ), 203-204
    DBS extensions, 565-568
    field_string( ), 206
    file_pos( ), 208
    fld_stru private class, 213
    FOO.DBS, 566
    FoxPro format, 204-205
    get_dec_mask( ), 208
    getFieldVals( ), 200
    get_init( ), 208
    get_int_init( ), 208
    get_mask( ), 208
    getString( ), 195-196
    getValues( ), 201, 528-529
    go( ), 198, 206
    inheritance, 527-528
    int_from4( ), 209-210
    int_to4( ), 210
    isDeleted( ), 201
    JDBClose menu class, 571-577
    JDB.java, 564-571, 577-602
    meta data, 565
    MRString class, 200-201
    overview, 195-198, 528-529
    Phone List tables, 568-571
    private methods, 208-213, 222-230,
        538-545
    public data members, 196

public methods, 196-198, 199-208, 215-222, 531-537
read_field( ), 210, 529
read_values( ), 210-211, 529
record_buffer, 204
replace( ), 198, 207-208, 211-212
setDeleted( ), 201-202
setValues( ), 202, 528-529
summary, 230, 602
type_string( ), 212
unsigned_byte( ), 209, 212
write_fields( ), 202, 212-213
DBF format, 175-195
  See also DBF class
  ASAMP.DBF, 178, *179*
  field records, 181
  FileViewer, 182-187
  footers, 182
  getXxx( ), 197
  header structure, 180-181
  history of, 177-178
  isXxx( ), 197
  MsgBox class, 187-195
  overview, 176
  record structure, 181-182
  setXxx( ), 197-198
  structure, 178-182
  tablewide data header, 180-181
DBF storage, object databases, 837
DBF-writing methods, JDBnew class, 620-624
dbf_read( ), DBF class, 203-204
DBS extensions, DBF class, 565-568
DEBUG, BinFile class, 101-102
DEButtonPanel, 472-475
  public methods, 474-475
decimal digit functions, MRString class, 147-148
DEField, 499-503
DEForm (data-entry form), 441-442, 445-469
  aligning labels and TextFields, 442
  button_click( ), 451-452
  code listing, 453-469
  components of, 471-473
  constructors, 448
  data members, 446-447, 454-455
  DataBoss, 508-522
  DBF class, 527-545, 563-602
  DEButtonPanel, 472-475

  DEField, 499-503
  DELayout LayoutManager, 480-491
  delete_click( ), 452
  DEPanel layout, 442
  Editable interface, 506-508
  JDBboss menu, 522-527
  labels, 442
  methods, 447-453
  MRLabel, 475-480
  MRTextField, 499-503
  new_values( ), 452-453
  overview, 445-446
  private methods, 451-453, 462-469
  public methods, 447-451, 455-462
  reread_click( ), 453
  save_click( ), 449-450
  ScrollWin class, 546-560
  setRecord( ), 449
  summary, 469
DELayout LayoutManager, 480-491
  code listing, 484-491
  data members, 485
  DEPanel, 491-499
  private methods, 483-484, 489-491
  public methods, 481-483, 486-489
delete( )
  MRString class, 131, 139
  NDX class, 762
delete_char_at( ), MenuLib, 302
delete_click( ), DEForm (data-entry form), 452
DEPanel layout, 491-499
  code listing, 494-499
  constructors, 492
  data members, 494
  DEForm (data-entry form), 442
  min_fld_size( ), 493
  min_lab_width( ), 493
  private methods, 493-494, 497-499
  public methods, 492-493, 495-497
designing object and relational databases, 413-434
  characteristic histories, 423-424, 426
  characteristics, 417, 425, 426
  classes, 416
  detail tables, 419-424
  events, 415-416, 425
  foreign keys, 417
  ID values, 422
  keys, 417, 422

method summary, 424-427
normalization, 427-431
objects, 415, 425
paper-based forms and, 417-418
primary keys, 417
processes, 416
redundant data, 432-433
relationships, 418-419, 425
repeating characteristics, 420-423, 426
rules, 426-427
sequential keys, 422
summary, 433-434
detail tables, 419-424
B-tree indexes, 720
characteristic histories, 423-424
repeating characteristics, 420-423
dialog box suppression, data-entry form, 441
disk-buffering strategy, NDX class and object databases, 867-868
divide_into_lines( ), TxtFile class, 66
domain-key normal form, normalization, 431
down( )
ScrollWin class, 35
ScrollWinX class, 814
drawPrompt( )
MenuLib, 301-302
RRectPromptPainter (MenuPanel), 308
dumps, BinFile class, 102-104

E

Editable interface, 506-508
code listing, 507-508
methods, 506-507
editing JDB.INI, 383-384
editors, searching for methods with, 12
end( )
ScrollWin class, 36
ScrollWinX class, 815
end_of_row( ), MenuPanel, 285
endsWith( ), MRString class, 131-132, 139-140
eolIsSignificant( ), JDB.INI, 397
error-checking methods, JDBnew class, 618-619
error_in_X( ), JDBnew class, 617

event table indexes, B-trees, 719-720
event-handling public methods, JDB.java, 346-347, 358
event-related public methods, MenuPanel, 284-285
events
database design, 415-416, 425
defined, 415
MenuPanel, 277-278
unreliable Visual Cafe keyboard, 445
Exception class, HeapFile, 675-676
exception handling, HeapFile, 669
exists( ), JDBnew class, 614
expand_file( ), HeapFile, 665-667

F

fakeNDX class, 757-761
code listing, 758-760
getKeyValue( ), 758
getLast( ), 758
RandNames class, 807-810
Random objects, 761
testdata array, 757
FDlib class, 111-115
code listing, 114-115
converting bytes to ASCII, 113
converting bytes to hexadecimals, 112
converting integers to hexadecimals, 111-112
converting nibbles to hex digits, 113
methods, 111-113
public methods, 114-115
field records, DBF format, 181
field-buffer methods, JDBnew class, 619-620
field_string( ), DBF class, 206
file expansion, HeapFile, 665-667
file I/O
B-tree, 724-725
BinFile class, 96-101
BinFileXO class, 839
Btree_node class, 741-742
file locking, TxtFile class and, 61
file reading, JDB.INI, 393-402
file structure, 6-15
class structure, 7
data structure, 7-8
exceptions, 15

method structure, 9-11
template.java, 12-15
file writing, JDB.INI, 387-393
file-opening methods, JDB.java, 583-585
file-writing methods, HeapFile, 674-675
FileDialog( )
    FileViewer class, 183
    TextViewer class, 85-86
file_ext( ), JDB.java, 584
FileInputStream, JDB.INI, 396
FileOutputStream, JDB.INI, 387, 393
file_pos( ), DBF class, 208
FileViewer class, 115-120, 182-187
    See also TextViewer class
    code listings, 118-120, 185-187
    DBF format, 182-187
    FileDialog( ), 183
    main( ), 117
    MsgBox, 184
    project exercise, 120
    public methods, 119-120
    ScrollWin, 117-118, 184-185
fillBytes( ), Btree_node class, 855, 856
find( )
    Btree_node class, 739-741
    NDX class, 767
    ScrollableX interface, 811-812, 869,
      871
find_block( ), HeapFile, 667-670
find_last_block( ), HeapFile, 669-670
first-fit algorithm, HeapFile, 649-650
fits( ), RRectPromptPainter (MenuPanel),
    310
fld_stru private class, DBF class, 213
FOO.DBS, DBF class, 566
footers
    DBF format, 182
    JDB.INI, 389
foreign keys, database design, 417
forms
    data-entry, 435-469
    normalization, 427-431
fos.write( ), JDB.INI, 389-390
FoxPro format, DBF class, 204-205
frames, JDBnew class, 606-609
free( ), HeapFile, 647, 650, 655, 660, 669
front-end code. *See* JDB front-end code
full_stru_name( ), JDBnew class, 617-618

G

garbage collection, HeapFile, 650, 664-665
get_dec_mask( ), DBF class, 208
getFieldVals( ), DBF class, 200
getFileName( ), BinFile class, 95
get_init( ), DBF class, 208
get_int_init( ), DBF class, 208
getKey( ), Btree_node class, 853-854
getKeyValue( ), fakeNDX class, 758
getLast( )
    BinFile class, 95, 101
    fakeNDX class, 758
    NDX class, 756, 766
    scrolling, 23
    TxtFile class, 61, 65
getLeftPointer( ), Btree_node class, 853,
    854
get_mask( ), DBF class, 208
getMessage( ), BinFile class, 95
getRightPointer( ), Btree_node class, 854
get_speed_letter( ), MenuPanel, 287-288
getString( )
    BinFile class, 95, 101-102
    DBF class, 195-196
    ImScrollable class, 25
    ScrollableX interface, 870
    scrolling, 23, 24
    TxtFile class, 61, 65
get_tok( ), JDB.INI, 399-402
getValues( ), DBF class, 201, 528-529
go( )
    DBF class, 198, 206
    numbered index-based records, 811
    ScrollableX interface, 811-812, 870
good_width( ), MsgBox class, 190-191
go_to( ), ScrollWin class, 36
grid views, data-entry form, 440

H

handle_click( ), ScrollWin class, 40
handleEvent( )
    JDB.java, 346-347
    MsgBox class, 191
    ScrollWin class, 33-34, 40, 546
handle_keypress( ), ScrollWin class, 36
header structure, DBF format, 180-181
headers, JDB.INI, 388
HeapFile, 643-696

alloc( ), 645-648, 659-660
alloc_block( ), 662-664
block finding, 667-670
block structures, 651-652, 654-655
bookkeeping, 649
circ_pointer, 658
circular-first-fit algorithm, 649-650
circular-pointer methods, 671-672
class-specific public methods,
    659-662
close( ), 646, 647, 656
code listing, 676-695
combine( ), 650, 664-665
constructors, 646, 656-659, 679-681
data members, 652-653, 676-677
dBASE memo fields, 645
Exception class, 675-676
exception handling, 669
expand_file( ), 665-667
file expansion, 665-667
file-writing methods, 674-675
find_block( ), 667-670
find_last_block( ), 669-670
first-fit algorithm, 649-650
free( ), 647, 650, 655, 660, 669
garbage collection, 650, 664-665
list_insert( ), 670-671
mainline test, 653-656
managing storage, 646-647
opening and closing, 646, 654, 657
overview, 644-646
private class, 675-676
private methods, 662-675, 684-695
protect_circ_pointer( ), 671
public methods, 653-662, 677-684
read( ), 648, 655-656, 660-661
read_circ_pointer( ), 657, 672
read_llist_...( ), 672
read_size( ), 673
reset_circ_pointer( ), 673
setup_piece( ), 673-674
sizing, 666
storing pointers, 648
summary, 695-696
theory of, 649-652
write( ), 648, 661-662
write_llist_...( ), 674-675
write_size( ), 675
HeapFile storage, object databases, 838
hex digits, converting nibbles to, 113

hex dumps, BinFile class, 103-104
hexadecimals
    converting bytes to (FDlib class), 112
    converting integers to (FDlib class),
        111-112
hide( ), JDBmenus.java, 334, 335
home( ), ScrollWinX class, 815-816

I/O. *See* buffered-disk I/O; file I/O
ID values, database design, 422
importing java.io, BinFileXO class, 842
ImScrollable class, 24-27
index files
    B-trees and, 718-720
    binary trees and, 698, 700-701
index-based records, numbered and go( ),
    811
indexable RandNames class, scrolling,
    807-810
Indexable.java, NDX class, 756-757
indexing overview, scrolling, 806-807
inheritance, DBF class, 527-528
INI files and portability, JDB front-end
    code, 326
initialization data. *See* JDB.INI
in_lasts( ), ScrollWinX class, 816
insert( )
    B-tree test program, 730
    MRString class, 132, 140-141
    NDX class, 762, 767, 769-771
instantiating objects, object databases, 837
int indexOf( ), MRString class, 132
int intValue( ), MRString class, 132, 141
int lastNonblankLoc( ), MRString class, 133
int length( ), MRString class, 133-134
int nextWord( ), MRString class, 134, 143
int prevWord( ), MRString class, 134-135,
    144-145
integer length, B-trees, 719
integers
    converting to hexadecimals (FDlib
        class), 111-112
    MRString class and, 128
interfaces, scrolling and, 18-24
int_from4( ), DBF class, 209-210
int_to4( ), DBF class, 210
io_get_node( ), buffered-disk I/O, 874-875

io_put_node( ), buffered-disk I/O, 874, 875, 876
io_set_tree( ), buffered-disk I/O, 875
io_write_nodes( ), buffered-disk I/O, 876
isDeleted( ), DBF class, 201
isReadable( ), BinFile class, 95
isWriteable( ), BinFile class, 95
isXxx( ), DBF format, 197

J

Java
    databases. *See* DBF class; DBF format; designing object and relational databases; JDB front-end code; object databases
    file structure. *See* file structure
java.io
    importing, 842
    JDB.INI and, 385-386
JDB front-end code, 323-379
    INI files and portability, 326
    JDBcolors.java, 371-375
    JDB.java, 339-362
    JDBlib.java, 330-333
    JDBmenopts.java, 366-371
    JDBmenus.java, 333-339
    JDBopts.java, 363-366
    JDBshapes.java, 376-379
    main menus, *325*
    menus, 325-330
    overview, 324-330
    shape menus, 328, *329*
    summary, 379
JDBboss menu, 522-527
    code listing, 524-527
    data members, 524
    data-entry form, *438*
    menu_click( ), 514
    private methods, 526-527
    public methods, 524-526
JDBClose menu class, 571-577
    code listing, 574-577
    constructors, 573
    data members, 574
    methods, 573-574
    private methods, 576-577
    public methods, 574-576
JDBcolors.java, 371-375
    data members, 371-372

    private methods, 374-375
    public methods, 372-374
JDB.INI, 381-412
    ; (semicolon), 396
    _ (underscore), 397
    assign( ), 397
    assign_menu( ), 397-398
    code listing, 402-411
    compilers and, 393-395
    constructors, 386
    data members, 386, 403
    editing, 383-384
    elements of, 385-386
    eolIsSignificant( ), 397
    file reading, 393-402
    file writing, 387-393
    FileInputStream, 396
    FileOutputStream, 387, 393
    footers, 389
    fos.write( ), 389-390
    get_tok( ), 399-402
    headers, 388
    java.io and, 385-386
    menus, 388-392
    overview, 382-385
    parsers, 394-395
    private methods, 406-411
    private read-related methods, 397-402
    private write-related methods, 389-393
    programmers overview, 384-385
    public methods, 387-389, 395-397, 403-406
    reading files, 393-402
    read_ini( ), 395-397
    skip_to_EOL( ), 402
    StreamTokenizer, 395-396
    structure of, 393
    summary, 411-412
    tokenizers, 394-397
    users overview, 383-384
    wordChars( ), 397
    write( ), 389-393
    write_ini( ), 387-389
    write_menu( ), 388-389, 390
    write_rect( ), 390, 392-393
    writing files, 387-393
    zmenu code, 391
JDB.java, 339-362

code listings, 350-362, 585-602
color, 341, 347, 349
constructors, 342-344, 352
data access methods, 353-355
data members, 340-342, 351, 585-586
data-entry form, 436-443
DBF class, 564-571, 577-602
file-opening methods, 583-585
file_ext( ), 584
handleEvent( ), 346-347
Menu Options menu, 343
menu_click( ), 582
MenuPanel, 341, 342-343
open_binfile( ), 583
open_file( ), 584
private methods, 347-350, 358-362,
  581-585, 595-602
PromptPainter, 349
public class-specific methods,
  345-346, 355
public data access methods, 344
public event-handling methods,
  346-347, 358
public methods, 342-347, 586-595
RRectPromptPainter, 349
setupLoColorMenus( ), 345-346
shape menus, 346
shut_down( ), 350
static arrays, 341-342
JDBmenopts.java, 366-371
  data members, 367
  private methods, 369-371
  public methods, 367-369
JDBmenus.java, 333-339
  code listing, 336-339
  hide( ), 334, 335
  overview, 333-336
  show( ), 334
  shut_down( ), 335
JDBnew class, 603-641
  code listing, 625-640
  constructors, 606-609
  create_dbf_file( ), 609-612
  create_stru_file( ), 612-614, 615-617
  data members, 625
  data overview, 604-605
  DBF-writing methods, 620-624
  error-checking methods, 618-619
  error_in_X( ), 617
  exists( ), 614

field-buffer methods, 619-620
frames, 606-609
full_stru_name( ), 617-618
little_end2( ), 617
mainline test, 605
private methods, 614-624, 632-640
public methods, 605-614, 625-632
set_field_buffer( ), 619-620
summary, 640-641
write_buffer_clear( ), 620
write_dbf_fields( ), 623-624
write_dbf_footer( ), 624
write_dbf_header( ), 621-623
year 2028 problem, 622
JDBopts.java, 363-366
  constructors, 364
  data members, 363
  private methods, 365-366
  public methods, 364-365
JDBshapes.java, 376-379
  data members, 376
  private methods, 378-379
  public methods, 377-378

K

keyboard events
  Visual Cafe, 275, 445
  Visual J++, 275
keyDown( ), MenuPanel, 284
keys
  abstract, 428
  candidate, 428
  foreign, 417
  primary, 417
  sequential, 422
  super-, 430

L

labels, aligning DEForm (data-entry
  form), 442
Lashlee, Hal, history of DBF format, 177
layoutContainer( )
  CenterLayout, 238-240
  ChoicesLayout, 257-259
LayoutManagers, 231-271
  CenterLayout, 232-248
  ChoicesLayout, 248-271
  DELayout, 480-491

summary, 271
left( ), MRString class, 133
leftPadTo( ), MRString class, 133, 142
linear and binary searches, B-trees, 725-735
list_insert( ), HeapFile, 670-671
little_end2( ), JDBnew class, 617
loc( ), Btree_node class, 855-856
locate( ), B-trees, 726-728
Long, Jeb, history of DBF format, 177
lowercase alphabetics, MRString class, 148

M

main( )
    FileViewer class, 117
    method structure, 9
mainline tests
    BinFileXO class, 842
    HeapFile, 653-656
    JDBnew class, 605
    NDX class, 754-756
    ScrollNDX, 810-811
memo fields (dBASE), HeapFile and, 645
memory, variable length storage. *See*
    HeapFile
Menu Options menu, JDB.java, 343
menu_click( )
    JDBboss menu, 514
    JDB.java, 582
MenuLib, 301-304
    delete_char_at( ), 302
    drawPrompt( ), 301-302
    private methods, 303-304
    public methods, 302-303
    removeAmpersand( ), 302
MenuPanel, 273-321
    add( ), 283
    code listing, 288-301
    constructors, 282-283
    creating menus, 276-277
    data members, 289-290
    end_of_row( ), 285
    event-related public methods,
        284-285
    get_speed_letter( ), 287-288
    JDB.java, 341, 342-343
    keyboard events, 275
    keyDown( ), 284
    menu events, 277-278
    MenuLib, 301-304

MenuSample.java code listing,
    278-281
    methods, 283-288
    mouseDown( ), 284
    mouseUp( ), 285
    nonevent public methods, 283-284
    overview, 274-276, 281-282
    paint( ), 284
    post_Event( ), 285
    private methods, 285-288, 294-301
    programmer's view of, 276-281
    PromptPainter, 315-320
    PromptPanel, 283, 304-306
    public methods, 283-285, 290-294
    remove( ), 284
    reset_hilite( ), 286
    reset_menu( ), 286-287
    resize( ), 284
    RRectPromptPainter, 306-315
    sample menu, 274
    set_longest_prompt( ), 287
    summary, 320-321
    user's view of, 274-276
menus
    JDB front-end code, 325-330
    JDBClose menu class, 571-577
    JDB.INI, 388-392
    JDBmenus.java, 333-339
MenuSample, 278-281
    data members, 278
    public methods, 278-280
meta data, DBF class, 565
method structure, 9-11
    constructors, 9-10
    data access public methods, 10
    main( ), 9
    private methods, 11
    public methods, 10
methods
    See also private methods; public
        methods
    BinFile class, 101-105
    ChoicesLayout, 257-264
    DEForm (data-entry form), 447-453
    Editable interface, 506-507
    FDlib class, 111-113
    JDBClose menu class, 573-574
    ScrollWin class, 32-38
    searching for, 12
    structure, 9-11

TxtFile class, 63-70
min_fld_size( ), DEPanel layout, 493
minimumLayoutSize( ), CenterLayout,
    240-241
min_lab_width( ), DEPanel layout, 493
mouseDown( ), MenuPanel, 284
mouseUp( ), MenuPanel, 285
move( )
    MsgBox class, 190
    ScrollableX interface, 811-812, 870
    ScrollWinX class, 814-815, 817, 818
move_backward( ), ScrollableX interface,
    871-872
move_to_far_left( ), ScrollableX interface,
    872-873
move_to_far_right( ), ScrollableX
    interface, 873
move_to_right_ground( ), ScrollableX
    interface, 874
MRLabel, 475-480
    data members, 476-477
    private methods, 480
    public methods, 477-480
MRString class, 123-173
    advantages of, 124-125
    alphabetic character function, 147
    array of bytes and, 128
    bestFit( ), 173
    boolean endsWith( ), 131-132,
        139-140
    boolean functions, 147-148
    bytes and, 127
    char lastChar( ), 133
    charAt( ), 130-131
    Chars and, 128
    code listing, 152-172
    concat( ), 131, 137-139
    constructors, 126-130
    copy( ), 131
    data members, 155
    DBF class, 200-201
    decimal digit functions, 147-148
    delete( ), 131, 139
    disadvantages of, 125
    insert( ), 132, 140-141
    int indexOf( ), 132
    int intValue( ), 132, 141
    int lastNonblankLoc( ), 133
    int length( ), 133-134
    int nextWord( ), 134, 143

int prevWord( ), 134-135, 144-145
integers and, 128
left( ), 133
leftPadTo( ), 133, 142
lowercase alphabetics, 148
padTo( ), 134, 143-144
private methods, 149-152, 170-172
project exercises, 172-173
public methods, 130-146, 155-170
replace( ), 135
resolution and, 151
right( ), 135
static functions, 149
static methods, 147-149
strings and, 128-129
substring( ), 135
summary, 173-174
System.arraycopy( ), 137
testing with, 152
toLower( ), 135-136
toUpper( ), 136
trim( ), 136
trimLeft( ), 136, 145-146
trimRight( ), 136-137
uppercase alphabetics, 148
variable names function, 148
whitespace function, 148
MRTextField, 499-503
    code listing, 500-503
    data members, 501
    public methods, 501-503
MsgBox class, 187-195
    code listing, 191-195
    constructors, 188
    FileViewer class, 184
    good_width( ), 190-191
    handleEvent( ), 191
    move( ), 190
    OK button, 191
    overview, 188-189
    private methods, 190-191, 194
    public data and methods, 189-190,
        192-193
    reshape( ), 190
    show( ), 188

N

navigate( ), ScrollWin class, 32
NDX class, 753-803, 867-898

add_node( ), 768-769
BinFile class, 797-803
buffering strategy, 867-868
code listings, 783-796, 876-896
constructors, 765
data members, 763-765, 783-784,
    877-878
delete( ), 762
disk-buffering strategy, 867-868
fakeNDX class, 757-761
find( ), 767
getLast( ), 756, 766
implementing buffered-disk I/O,
    874-878
implementing ScrollableX, 869-874
Indexable.java, 756-757
insert( ), 762, 767, 769-771
mainline test, 754-756
object databases, 867-898
overview, 761-762
private methods, 768-783, 787-796,
    881-895
private_find( ), 767, 770, 771-773
public methods, 765-768, 784-787,
    878-881
read_header( ), 766, 773
reindex( ), 762, 766, 768
ScrollableX interface, 811-812
split_a_node( ), 773-774
split_insert_left( ), 774-777
split_insert_middle( ), 777-778
split_insert_right( ), 778-780
split_push_up( ), 780-782
summary, 803
write_header( ), 782-783
write_nodes( ), 783
new_values( ), DEForm (data-entry form),
    452-453
nibbles
    converting to hex digits, 113
    defined, 112
nodes
    B-tree, 705, 707-708, 720-723
    Btree_node class, 735-751
normalization, 427-431
    attributes and, 427-428
    Boyce-Codd normal form, 429-431
    domain-key normal form, 431
    first-normal form, 427
    fourth-normal form, 431
second-normal form, 427-428
third-normal form, 429

O

OBF storage, object databases, 837
object databases, 835-898
    BinFileXO class, 838-852
    Btree_node class, 852-866
    DBF storage, 837
    designing. See designing object and
        relational databases
    HeapFile storage, 838
    instantiating objects, 837
    NDX class, 867-896
    OBF storage, 837
    overview, 836-838
    persistence, 837
    summary, 897-898
    tables, 836-838
object file indexes, B-trees, 718-719
objects
    database design, 415, 425
    defined, 415
    instantiating, 837
OK button, MsgBox class, 191
Open button, data-entry form, 436, 437,
    438
open_binfile( ), JDB.java, 583
open_file( ), JDB.java, 584
opening DBFs, data-entry form, 437-441
order of nodes, B-trees, 707
other_dimension( ), ChoicesLayout, 263
output buffers, BinFile class, 104-105

P

padTo( ), MRString class, 134, 143-144
paint( )
    MenuPanel, 284
    ScrollWin class, 33
    ScrollWinX class, 818
painting
    PromptPainter (MenuPanel), 315-320
    RRectPromptPainter (MenuPanel),
        306-315
paint_line( ), ScrollWin class, 40
paper-based forms, database design,
    417-418
parsers, JDB.INI and, 394-395

Pawluk, Hal, history of DBF format, 177
persistence, object databases, 837
pgdn( ), ScrollWinX class, 816
pgup( ), ScrollWinX class, 816-817
Phone List tables, DBF class, 568-571
pointer/value sandwiches, B-trees, 723
PointerList class, 77-85
    code listing, 82-85
    constructors, 78
    data access methods, 78
    data members, 79, 82-83
    listing, 82-85
    public members, 79-81
    public methods, 78-79, 83-85
    System.arraycopy( ), 81
    TxtFile class and, 60
pointers, storing HeapFile, 648
post_Event( ), MenuPanel, 285
preferredLayoutSize( ), CenterLayout,
  241-242
primary keys, database design, 417
private methods
    B-tree test program, 732-735
    BinFile class, 101-102, 109-111,
      801-803
    Btree_node class, 742-744, 750-751,
      854
    ChoicesLayout, 259-264, 268-271
    DataBoss class, 514-515, 521-522
    DBF class, 208-213, 222-230, 538-545
    DEForm (data-entry form), 451-453,
      462-469
    DELayout LayoutManager, 483-484,
      489-491
    DEPanel layout, 493-494, 497-499
    HeapFile, 662-675, 684-695
    JDBboss menu, 526-527
    JDBClose menu class, 576-577
    JDB.INI, 389-393, 397-402, 406-411
    JDB.java, 347-350, 358-362, 581-585,
      595-602
    JDBmenopts.java, 369-371
    JDBnew class, 614-624, 632-640
    JDBopts.java, 365-366
    JDBshapes.java, 378-379
    MenuLib, 303-304
    MenuPanel, 285-288, 294-301
    method structure, 11
    MRString class, 149-152, 170-172
    MsgBox class, 190-191, 194

NDX class, 768-783, 787-796, 881-895
RRectPromptPainter (MenuPanel),
  310, 315
ScrollWin class, 34-38, 47-52, 54-55,
  552-560
ScrollWinX class, 825-834
TxtFile class, 66-70, 74-77
private_find( ), NDX class, 767, 770,
  771-773
processes
    database design, 416
    defined, 416
PromptPainter (MenuPanel), 315-320
    data members, 316
    JDB.java, 349
    public methods, 317-319
PromptPanel (MenuPanel), 283, 304-306
    data members, 304-305
    public methods, 305
protect_circ_pointer( ), HeapFile, 671
public functions, ScrollWin class, 30
public methods
    B-tree test program, 731-732
    BinFile class, 95-96, 101, 106-109,
      798-800
    BinFileXO class, 848-852
    Btree_node class, 736-742, 745-750,
      853, 858-864
    CenterLayout, 235-236, 243-248
    ChoicesLayout, 251-252, 257-259,
      265-268
    DataBoss class, 510-513, 516-520
    DBF class, 196-198, 199-208, 215-222,
      531-537
    DEButtonPanel, 474-475
    DEForm (data-entry form), 447-451,
      455-462
    DELayout LayoutManager, 481-483,
      486-489
    DEPanel layout, 492-493, 495-497
    FDlib class, 114-115
    FileViewer class, 119-120
    HeapFile, 653-662, 677-684
    JDBboss menu, 524-526
    JDBClose menu class, 574-576
    JDBcolors.java, 372-374
    JDB.INI, 387-389, 395-397, 403-406
    JDB.java, 342-347, 586-595
    JDBmenopts.java, 367-369
    JDBnew class, 605-614, 625-632

JDBopts.java, 364-365
JDBshapes.java, 377-378
MenuLib, 302-303
MenuPanel, 283-285, 290-294
MenuSample, 278-280
method structure, 10
MRLabel, 477-480
MRString class, 130-146, 155-170
MRTextField, 501-503
MsgBox class, 189-190, 192-193
NDX class, 765-768, 784-787, 878-881
PointerList class, 78-79, 83-85
PromptPainter (MenuPanel), 317-319
PromptPanel (MenuPanel), 305
RRectPromptPainter (MenuPanel),
   307-310, 312-315
ScrollWin class, 32-34, 43-47, 52-54,
   548-552
ScrollWinX class, 821-825
template.java, 13-14
TextViewer class, 89
TxtFile class, 71-74
pyramids, B-trees as, 705-707

R

RAM, variable length storage. *See*
  HeapFile
RandNames class
   See also fakeNDX class
   scrolling, 807-810
Random objects, fakeNDX class, 761
random string generation, B-trees, 725-726
RandomAccessFile( )
   BinFile class, 93-94, 97-101
   seeking past existing end of, 207
ratios, ChoicesLayout, 255-256
Ratliff, Wayne, history of DBF format, 177
read( )
   BinFile class, 99-100
   BinFileXO class, 840-841
   HeapFile, 648, 655-656, 660-661
readBytes( ), BinFileXO class, 843-844
read_circ_pointer( ), HeapFile, 657, 672
read_field( ), DBF class, 210, 529
read_header( ), NDX class, 766, 773
reading files, JDB.INI, 393-402
read_ini( ), JDB.INI, 395-397
readInt( ), BinFileXO class, 844
read_llist_...( ), HeapFile, 672

read_node( ), Btree_node class, 741-742
readPage( ), BinFileXO class, 844-845
read_size( ), HeapFile, 673
read_values( ), DBF class, 210-211, 529
record structure, DBF format, 181-182
record views, data-entry form, 440
record_buffer, DBF class, 204
redundant data
   current values, 433
   totals, 432-433
reindex( ), NDX class, 762, 766, 768
relational databases, designing. *See*
  designing object and relational
  databases
relationships, database design, 418-419,
  425
remove( ), MenuPanel, 284
removeAmpersand( ), MenuLib, 302
removeLayoutComponent( ),
  CenterLayout, 242
repeating characteristics
   database design, 426
   detail tables, 420-423
replace( )
   DBF class, 198, 207-208, 211-212
   MRString class, 135
reread_click( ), DEForm (data-entry form),
  453
reset( ), BinFileXO class, 845
reset_circ_pointer( ), HeapFile, 673
reset_hilite( ), MenuPanel, 286
resetLast( ), ScrollWin class, 33
reset_menu( ), MenuPanel, 286-287
reshape( ), MsgBox class, 190
resize( )
   MenuPanel, 284
   ScrollWin class, 33
resolution, Visual Cafe and Visual J++, 151
rfill( ), B-tree test program, 730
right( ), MRString class, 135
rounding, RRectPromptPainter
  (MenuPanel), 306-315
RRectPromptPainter (MenuPanel), 306-315
   code listing, 311-315
   color, 309
   data members, 307, 311
   drawPrompt( ), 308
   fits( ), 310
   JDB.java, 349
   private methods, 310, 315

public methods, 307-310, 312-315

S

save_click( ), DEForm (data-entry form), 449-450
ScrollableX interface, 869-874
    at_far_left( ), 870-871
    at_far_right( ), 871
    find( ), 811-812, 869, 871
    getString( ), 870
    go( ), 811-812, 870
    implementing, 869-874
    move( ), 811-812, 870
    move_backward( ), 871-872
    move_to_far_left( ), 872-873
    move_to_far_right( ), 873
    move_to_right_ground( ), 874
    scrolling, 811-812
scroll_canvas class, ScrollWin class, 38-40
scrolling, 17-56, 805-834
    data-entry form, 438-439
    getLast( ), 23
    getString( ), 23, 24, 25
    ImScrollable class, 24-27
    indexable RandNames class, 807-810
    indexing overview, 806-807
    interfaces and, 18-24
    problem of, 20-21
    Scrollable object, 23
    ScrollNDX mainline test, 810-811
    ScrollWin class, 27-55
    ScrollWinX class, 812-834
    squirrel analogy, 21-22
    strings and, 23
    summary, 56, 560-561
ScrollNDX, mainline test, 810-811
ScrollWin class, 27-55, 546-560
    See also ScrollWinX class
    boolean data members, 30
    code listings, 41-55, 546-560
    constructors, 29, 31-32, 52
    data access methods, 32
    data members, 30-31, 42-43, 52, 547-548
    DataBoss class and, 30, 41, 508-522, 546-560
    DEForm (data-entry form) and, 546-560
    down( ), 35

end( ), 36
FileViewer class, 117-118, 184-185
go_to( ), 36
handle_click( ), 40
handleEvent( ), 33-34, 40, 546
handle_keypress( ), 36
methods, 32-38
navigate( ), 32
overview, 27-28
paint( ), 33
paint_line( ), 40
private classes, 38-41
private data members, 31
private methods, 34-38, 47-52, 54-55, 552-560
protected data members, 30-31
public data members, 30
public functions, 30
public methods, 32-34, 43-47, 52-54, 548-552
resetLast( ), 33
resize( ), 33
scroll_canvas class, 38-40
static data members, 31
termination, 29
text files and, 28-29
ScrollWinX class, 812-834
    See also ScrollWin class
    adjust( ), 814-815, 816
    code listing, 819-834
    constructors, 813
    data members, 820-821
    down( ), 814
    end( ), 815
    home( ), 815-816
    in_lasts( ), 816
    move( ), 814-815, 817, 818
    overview, 812-819
    paint( ), 818
    pgdn( ), 816
    pgup( ), 816-817
    private methods, 825-834
    public methods, 821-825
    set_lasts( ), 817
    set_vscroll( ), 819
    up( ), 818
searching
    B-tree, 708
    binary tree, 697-716
    for methods, 12

second_is_better( ), ChoicesLayout, 260, 263

seek( ), BinFileXO class, 845

sequential keys, database design, 422

set( ), Btree_node class, 854

setDeleted( ), DBF class, 201-202

set_field_buffer( ), JDBnew class, 619-620

set_lasts( ), ScrollWinX class, 817

set_longest_prompt( ), MenuPanel, 287

setRecord( )
    DataBoss class, 511-512
    DEForm (data-entry form), 449

setupLoColorMenus( ), JDB.java, 345-346

setup_piece( ), HeapFile, 673-674

setValues( ), DBF class, 202, 528-529

set_vscroll( ), ScrollWinX class, 819

setXxx( ), DBF format, 197-198

shape menus
    JDB front-end code, 328, *329*
    JDB.java, 346

shapes, JDBshapes.java, 376-379

shift( ), Btree_node class, 854-855

show( )
    JDBmenus.java, 334
    MsgBox class, 188

shut_down( )
    DataBoss class, 513
    JDB.java, 350
    JDBmenus.java, 335

sizing
    B-tree nodes, 720-722
    compute_node_size( ), 743-744
    HeapFile, 666

skip_to_EOL( ), JDB.INI, 402

split_a_node( ), NDX class, 773-774

split_insert_left( ), NDX class, 774-777

split_insert_middle( ), NDX class, 777-778

split_insert_right( ), NDX class, 778-780

split_push_up( ), NDX class, 780-782

squirrel analogy, scrollable interface, 21-22

static arrays, JDB.java, 341-342

static data members
    ScrollWin class, 31
    TxtFile class, 62-63

static functions, MRString class, 149

static methods
    Btree_node class, 856
    MRString class, 147-149

storage, variable length. *See* HeapFile

storing pointers, HeapFile, 648

StreamTokenizer, JDB.INI, 395-396

String class. *See* MRString class

String getString( ), TxtFile class, 61

String write, BinFileXO class, 845

strings
    MRString class and, 128-129
    scrolling and, 23

substring( ), MRString class, 135

superkeys, Boyce-Codd normal form, 430

System.arraycopy( )
    Btree_node class, 854-855
    MRString class, 137
    PointerList class, 81

T

tables, object database, 836-838

tablewide data headers, DBF format, 180-181

target aspect ratios, ChoicesLayout, 255-256

Tate, George, history of DBF format, 177

template.java, 12-15
    public methods, 13-14

termination, ScrollWin class, 29

testdata array, fakeNDX class, 757

test_for_text( ), TxtFile class, 69-70

tests, mainline. *See* mainline tests

text editors, searching for methods, 12

text files, 57-90
    PointerList class, 77-85
    ScrollWin class and, 28-29
    summary, 90
    TextViewer class, 85-90
    TextViewer code, 58
    TxtFile class, 59-77

TextFields, aligning, 442

TextViewer class, 85-90
    See also FileViewer class
    code listing, 58, 88-90
    FileDialog( ), 85-86
    public methods, 89
    Visual Cafe and, 87

tokenizers
    get_tok( ), 399-402
    JDB.INI and compilers, 394-397

toLower( ), MRString class, 135-136

totals, redundant data, 432-433

toUpper( ), MRString class, 136

Tour guides, overview, 6

trees, binary. *See* B-trees; binary trees;
   Btree_node class
trim( ), MRString class, 136
trimLeft( ), MRString class, 136, 145-146
trimRight( ), MRString class, 136-137
tuples, Boyce-Codd normal form, 430-431
TxtFile class, 59-77
       array method, 59-60
       as BinFile class extension, 60
       code listing, 70-77
       constructors, 61, 63-65
       data access methods, 61-62, 65
       data members, 62-63, 71
       divide_into_lines( ), 66
       file locking and, 61
       getLast( ), 61, 65
       getString( ), 61, 65
       listing, 70-77
       methods, 63-70
       PointerLists, 60
       private methods, 66-70, 74-77
       protected data members, 62
       public methods, 71-74
       static data members, 62-63
       test_for_text( ), 69-70
type_string( ), DBF class, 212

U

unsigned_byte( ), DBF class, 209, 212
up( ), ScrollWinX class, 818
uppercase alphabetics, MRString class, 148

V

value/pointer sandwiches, B-trees, 723
variable length storage. *See* HeapFile
variable names function, MRString class,
   148
versions warning, data-entry form, 443-445
Visual Cafe
       keyboard events, 275, 445
       resolution, 151
       TextViewer class and, 87
       unreliable keyboard events, 445

Visual J++
       keyboard events, 275
       resolution, 151

W

whitespace function, MRString class, 148
windows
       close_file_window( ), 580-581
       scrolling. *See* scrolling
wordChars( ), JDB.INI, 397
write( )
       BinFileXO class, 839, 841
       HeapFile, 648, 661-662
       JDB.INI, 389-393
write_buffer_clear( ), JDBnew class, 620
writeBytes( ), BinFileXO class, 845
write_dbf_fields( ), JDBnew class, 623-624
write_dbf_footer( ), JDBnew class, 624
write_dbf_header( ), JDBnew class, 621-623
write_fields( ), DBF class, 202, 212-213
write_header( ), NDX class, 782-783
write_ini( ), JDB.INI, 387-389
writeInt( ), BinFileXO class, 846
write_llist_...( ), HeapFile, 674-675
write_menu( ), JDB.INI, 388-389, 390
write_nodes( )
       Btree_node class, 855
       NDX class, 783
writePage( )
       BinFileXO class, 846-847
       Btree_node class, 855
write_rect( ), JDB.INI, 390, 392-393
write_size( ), HeapFile, 675
writing files, JDB.INI, 387-393

Y

year 2028 problem, JDBnew class, 622

Z

zmenu code, JDB.INI, 391

About the CD

The CD has three main directories:

- MSDEV for Microsoft Developer Studio (Visual J++) users
- VCAFE for Symantec Visual Cafe users
- OTHER for all other Java users

Each directory has subdirectories such as \MSDEV\CHP02, for Chapter 2, \MSDEV\CHP03, for Chapter 3, and so on.

Make a working (sub)directory where you will experiment with this code. You can leave the disk code on CD or copy the relevant portion (MSDEV, VCAFE, or OTHER) into a directory on your hard disk. When you begin a chapter, clean out your working directory and copy the entire contents of \xxxxx\CHPnn into your working directory, and copy the entire contents of \xxxxx\CHPnn into your working directory.

Visual J++ and Visual Cafe users will find the project and .class files are already created. Open a project, press CTRL-F5 and you are running. JDK and other Java IDE users will find all the Java files ready, but you will need to compile them and run the mainline class, in the JDK, or build a project in your favorite IDE.

These are JDK 1.0 files. Most of them run without modification under 1.1, although you will find small differences. For example, the HeapFileException private class in NDX.java needs to be placed in a HeapFileException.java file.

If we find and fix bugs, we will have the latest versions of the .java source files available at **www.osborne.com**.

WARNING: BEFORE OPENING THE DISC PACKAGE, CAREFULLY READ THE TERMS AND CONDITIONS OF THE FOLLOWING COPYRIGHT STATEMENT AND LIMITED CD-ROM WARRANTY.

Copyright Statement

This software is protected by both United States copyright law and international copyright treaty provision. Except as noted in the contents of the CD-ROM, you must treat this software just like a book. However, you may copy it into a computer to be used, and you may make archival copies of the software for the sole purpose of backing up the software and protecting your investment from loss. By saying, "just like a book," The McGraw-Hill Companies, Inc. ("Osborne/McGraw-Hill") means, for example, that this software may be used by any number of people and may be freely moved from one computer location to another, so long as there is no possibility of its being used at one location or on one computer while it is being used at another. Just as a book cannot be read by two different people in two different places at the same time, neither can the software be used by two different people in two different places at the same time.

Limited Warranty

Osborne/McGraw-Hill warrants the physical compact disc enclosed herein to be free of defects in materials and workmanship for a period of sixty days from the purchase date. If the CD included in your book has defects in materials or workmanship, please call McGraw-Hill at 1-800-217-0059, 9am to 5pm, Monday through Friday, Eastern Standard Time, and McGraw-Hill will replace the defective disc. The entire and exclusive liability and remedy for breach of this Limited Warranty shall be limited to replacement of the defective disc, and shall not include or extend to any claim for or right to cover any other damages, including but not limited to, loss of profit, data, or use of the software, or special incidental, or consequential damages or other similar claims, even if Osborne/McGraw-Hill has been specifically advised of the possibility of such damages. In no event will Osborne/McGraw-Hill's liability for any damages to you or any other person ever exceed the lower of the suggested list price or actual price paid for the license to use the software, regardless of any form of the claim.

OSBORNE/McGRAW-HILL SPECIFICALLY DISCLAIMS ALL OTHER WARRANTIES, EXPRESS OR IMPLIED, INCLUDING, BUT NOT LIMITED TO, ANY IMPLIED WARRANTY OF MERCHANTABILITY OR FITNESS FOR A PARTICULAR PURPOSE. Specifically, Osborne/McGraw-Hill makes no representation or warranty that the software is fit for any particular purpose, and any implied warranty of merchantability is limited to the sixty-day duration of the Limited Warranty covering the physical disc only (and not the software), and is otherwise expressly and specifically disclaimed. This limited warranty gives you specific legal rights; you may have others which may vary from state to state. Some states do not allow the exclusion of incidental or consequential damages, or the limitation on how long an implied warranty lasts, so some of the above may not apply to you. This agreement constitutes the entire agreement between the parties relating to use of the Product. The terms of any purchase order shall have no effect on the terms of this Agreement. Failure of Osborne/McGraw-Hill to insist at any time on strict compliance with this Agreement shall not constitute a waiver of any rights under this Agreement. This Agreement shall be construed and governed in accordance with the laws of New York. If any provision of this Agreement is held to be contrary to law, that provision will be enforced to the maximum extent permissible, and the remaining provisions will remain in force and effect.

NO TECHNICAL SUPPORT IS PROVIDED WITH THIS CD-ROM.